The oriental, the ancient and the primitive

In *The Oriental, the Ancient and the Primitive* one of the world's foremost anthropologists looks in depth at kinship practice in Asia and the Near East, and continues the comparative survey of pre-industrial family formation undertaken in *The Development of the Family and Marriage in Europe* (1983) and elsewhere.

Professor Goody's findings cause him to question many traditional assumptions about the 'primitive' east, and he suggests that, in contrast to pre-colonial Africa, kinship practice in Asia has much in common with that prevailing in parts of pre-industrial Europe. Goody examines the transmission of productive and other property in relation both to the prevailing political economy and to family and ideological structures, and then explores the distribution of mechanisms and strategies of continuity across cultures. He concludes that notions of western 'uniqueness' are often misplaced, and that much previous work on Asian kinship has been unwittingly distorted by the application of concepts and approaches derived from other, inappropriate, social formations, simple or post-industrial.

JACK GOODY is a Fellow of St John's College, Cambridge.

Literacy
Literacy in Traditional Societies (edited, 1968)
The Domestication of the Savage Mind (1977)
The Logic of Writing and the Organization of Society (1986)
The Interface between the Written and the Oral (1987)

Family
Production and Reproduction: A Comparative Study of the Domestic Domain (1977)
The Development of the Family and Marriage in Europe (1983)
The Oriental, the Ancient and the Primitive: Systems of Marriage and the Family in the Pre-industrial Societies of Eurasia (1989)

Culture
Cooking, Cuisine and Class: A Study in Comparative Sociology (1982)

The State
Technology, Tradition and the State in Africa (1971)

The oriental, the ancient and the primitive

Systems of marriage and the family in the pre-industrial societies of Eurasia

JACK GOODY

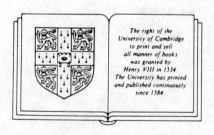

The right of the
University of Cambridge
to print and sell
all manner of books
was granted by
Henry VIII in 1534.
The University has printed
and published continuously
since 1584.

CAMBRIDGE UNIVERSITY PRESS

Cambridge
New York   Port Chester
Melbourne   Sydney

Published by the Press Syndicate of the University of Cambridge
The Pitt Building, Trumpington Street, Cambridge CB2 1RP
32 East 57th Street, New York, NY 10022, USA
10 Stamford Road, Oakleigh, Melbourne 3166, Australia

© Cambridge University Press 1990

First published 1990

Printed in Great Britain by
Redwood Burn Limited, Trowbridge, Wiltshire

British Library cataloguing in publication data
Goody, Jack
The oriental, the ancient and the primitive:
systems of marriage and the family in the pre-
industrial societies of Eurasia. – (Studies in
literacy, family, culture and the state)
1. Marriage & kinship
I. Title   II. Series
306.8′1

Library of Congress cataloguing in publication data
Goody, Jack.
The oriental, the ancient, and the primitive: systems of marriage
and the family in the pre-industrial societies of Eurasia/Jack
Goody.
p.   cm. – (Studies in literacy, family, culture and the
state)
Bibliography.
Includes index.
ISBN 0–521–36574–0. – ISBN 0–521–36761–1 (pbk.)
1. Marriage customs and rites – Asia.   2. Marriage customs and
rites – Europe.   3. Asia – Social life and customs.   4. Europe – Social
life and customs.   I. Title.   II. Series.
GT2772.A2G66 1989
392′.5′095 – dc20   89–7283 CIP

ISBN 0 521 36574 0 hard covers
ISBN 0 521 36761 1 paperback

Contents

v

Illustrations

Figures

Maps

Tables

Preface

If we disagree with others we are not unquestionably wise, and they are not unquestionably foolish.

Article X of Prince Umayado's Injunctions

This book is not a work of scholarship in the usual sense. I am not an expert in the societies which I discuss; I have read a little about them but what I know is derived mainly from field studies that others have made, the results of intensive research which exhaust neither the spatial nor the historical dimensions. Part of my original interest stemmed from an attempt to understand why the particular groups I first studied in Africa differ in certain definite ways from pre-industrial Europe. Reading the accounts presented by my colleagues of the domestic domain in the major civilisations of Asia to extend the contrast to that vast region I was led to wonder whether there too, certain general differences might not be related, among other factors but in some significant way, to differences in the productive systems.

The development of the analysis of social organisation in Africa meant that many conceptual clarifications have been made in the study of family, kinship and marriage. Models based on those societies have often been adopted in the examination of Asian societies. While these models were sometimes more appropriate than those of European historians and sociologists, they created problems for the analysis of Asian domestic systems, which tended to be seen as more 'primitive' than they really were and therefore as more of an obstacle in the onward march of 'modernisation' than was actually the case, thus reinforcing the ethnocentric notions of Marx and Weber about the place of oriental societies in world history.

In concentrating upon a particular set of societies, I have of course omitted many others, including important states in East and South-east Asia. Of these Japan is the most obvious but to consider that fascinating society, influenced as it is by China in its technology, its literature and its religion, that is both by Confucianism and by Buddhism, would have taken us further afield with little compensating benefit. More important than the geographic omissions, I have neglected many topics that could reasonably be seen as falling within the rubric of family, kinship and marriage. This selectivity derives from a particular theoretical framework, or rather a particular set of interests and hypotheses, concerning the status of women in hierarchical societies. By hierarchical in this context I mean first of all those societies in which individuals and strata are differentiated with regard to rights in land as the basic means of production and as a central focus of prestige and status.

In my account of the family, marriage and kinship in Asia, I have tried to summarise and develop a break in the paradigm, or rather in several paradigms which were accepted in the past, not only by many anthropologists but also by orientalists, historians, scholars of all kinds, and which were also embedded in the folk wisdom of the West. In talking of breaking a paradigm, I am not thinking in terms of Kuhn's scientific revolutions, despite the terminology, nor yet in terms of the contribution of any individual, but of the process of reformulating knowledge, of building up on what has gone before rather than setting it completely aside. The reluctance to recognise the cumulative aspects of scholarship has done much to retard the social sciences, because it has led, or at least allowed, each generation to search for a new approach for its own sake. The result is a conception of a discipline in which one dominant ideological trend followed another in a series of periodic stages; just as Romanticism displaced Classicism, so Structuralism pushed aside Functionalism and Functionalism replaced Evolutionism.

My feeling then and now was that such discussions did not constitute the fundamental priority for anthropology, much less for the comparative study of human society in general. Indeed they were positively distracting since they diverted attention from the work that needed doing on another level of generalisation, utilising what Merton (1959) referred to as theories of the middle range but which might well constitute the upper limit of fruitful hypotheses in the social sciences.

In the search for such hypotheses European scholars have engaged in what has been in many ways a valuable exercise, namely the attempt to compare their material with the evidence from other societies, notably from India following the discovery of the close relationships among the body of 'Indo-European' languages. It made sense to explore further comparisons at the level of social institutions, and the researches of many individuals, of Maine, Fustel de Coulanges and, in this century, Dumézil, Benveniste and Westrup (to choose only a few) drew on this connection as a source of theoretical insight. At the time I began thinking about these matters, these approaches still had a dominant influence in the study of family, marriage and kinship in the ancient and oriental worlds. Since then different perspectives have taken shape. One important trend has been the attempt to link up with demographic studies and with family history, in which some of the major areas of discussion have been defined by historians and sociologists of later Europe.

This trend has again produced a number of advances in our knowledge, partly by serving to modify the framework of enquiry adopted by the Indo-Europeanists. But in the longer term we have to face the problem of wider comparison if we are to provide a satisfactory evaluation of our own material, let alone improve the state of the art.[1] I have tried to offer some pointers as to how this might be done in the light of the analytic field studies from various parts of the world that have been one of the major contributions of social anthropology, taking comparison beyond the linguistic framework (anthropologists are not too impressed with the overlap between language, race and 'culture') and looking more closely at some of the similarities that seem to relate to modes of production, modes of communication and other features that underlie the major civilisations of the Eurasian continent.

That immediately raises important sociological and historical problems about the earlier categorisation and periodisation of those major systems, for as far as the family was concerned, the gap between we, the West, and they, the East, was of course seen by nineteenth-century scholars as part of a broader set of differences. While my enquiry touches upon this question, I do not explicitly pursue the problem of categorisation in this volume; perhaps later.

Many would consider a comparative examination of Asian practices in the field of marriage and the family as foolhardy if not a foolish undertaking in itself, even for an expert. My excuse is first that I was drawn to such a consideration by my interest both in Africa and Europe, which led me to attempt to specify general similarities and differences. Secondly, the investigation is selective, both in terms of the features I examine and the societies I choose, the features being dictated by theoretical concerns with transfers within and between families, the societies by the need to concentrate on the major systems rather than peripheral tribal groups. But thirdly, I have been emboldened to continue because it was possible for me to consult many friends from many countries over time, sometimes through books, sometimes personally. While the general notions are mine, I have drawn heavily over the years on my association at Cambridge with Meyer Fortes, Edmund Leach, S. J. Tambiah, Nur Yalman and especially Esther Goody (who carried out most of the fieldwork in India and is co-author of chapter 6), as well as upon discussions with M. N. Srinivas, André Beteille, Kathleen Gough, Keith Hopkins, Moses Finley, John Crook, Arthur Wolf, Rubie Watson, Ziba Mir-Hosseini, Vanessa Maher, Martha Mundy, Paul Sant

Cassia, Gene Hammel, David Sabean and many others. Some have shown me unpublished material, among them Jerry Dennerline, Pat Ebrey, Hill Gates, Susan Greenhalgh, Susan Mann, Susan Naquin, Helen Siu and Janice Stockard for China, Nancy Levine for Tibet, Martha Mundy for Arab societies and John Crook for Rome. I am grateful to all of these, to many colleagues in France, as well as to the following individuals for reading chapters: Arthur Wolf (2–4), Anna Grimshaw (5), André Beteille (6–9), Declan Quigley (6–9), Keith Hopkins (10, 13 and 14), Harvey Goldberg (11 and 12), Martha Mundy (12), Sheila Murnaghan (13), John Crook (14), Paul Sant Cassia (15), Maria Couroucli (15) and Ernest Gellner.

For helping to process the manuscript over a long period of years I have to thank my many assistants including Wunderly Rich Stauder, Sarah Cattermole, Carolyn Wyndham, Antonia Lovelace, Sarah Horell, Janet Reynolds, Andrew Sargent, Hamish Park, Bill Young and Dafna Capobianco. I count myself fortunate in the very high quality of help I have received. For assistance with computing facilities, I am grateful to Janet Hall, with the publication of this volume to Richard Fisher of Cambridge University Press, and for the series to Michael Black and Patricia Williams. Part of the material presented here was given as a course of lectures to the Collège de France in Spring 1985 as the result of an invitation from Françoise Heritier-Augé. Very preliminary versions were delivered to undergraduates at Cambridge in earlier years. A variety of other academic institutions have offered me the facilities I needed to continue the study: the Smuts Fund and the William Wyse Fund of the University of Cambridge and Trinity College respectively, the Wenner-Gren Foundation, the Leverhulme Foundation, the Ecole des Hautes Etudes en Sciences Sociales of Paris, the National Museum of Ethnology of Osaka (Minpaku), Japan, the Whitney Humanities Center, Yale, and above all to the continuing facilities offered to me by St John's College and the University of Cambridge. Each of these bodies I thank for the support they have provided.

I have long been indebted to Asha and Suhrid Sarabhai and to the Sarabhai and Khilnani families more generally for their friendship which has provided Esther Goody and myself with the opportunity to try and understand, albeit superficially, some aspects of Indian life. That opportunity has enabled us to get to know the Sharmas of Nandol, East Africa and Leicester. I had the good fortune to spend a short time in Taiwan with Arthur Wolf and the personnel of the Academia Sinica; a three-month visit to Japan under the auspices of Takeo Funabiki and Shigehu Tanabe enabled me to learn more about East Asia at first hand, while I owe much to the efforts of Helen Siu and other friends from Hong Kong who helped me to understand something of the culture and history of South China. I have spent some two years in the Near East but only three months in an academic capacity. My knowledge of the area has been mediated by my friendship, since undergraduate days, with Emrys Peters, as well as with Arabists of various nationalities, and especially with my former students, Vanessa Maher, Martha Mundy and Paul Sant Cassia. Modern Europe, except for the eastern Mediterranean, remains in the background of the present volume, but my understanding has clearly been influenced over the years by my friends, Peter Laslett, Tony Wrigley, and other members of the Cambridge Group, Alan Macfarlane, Martine Segalen and our neighbours in the Lot.

When I started this enterprise many years ago, I made use of what were then considered to be representative field studies. There were few synthetic works on marriage, the family and kinship for these major societies. Lévi-Strauss' masterly volume (1949), translated as *The Elementary Structures of Kinship*, covered part of the field in a very stimulating manner. Since then some general studies of aspects of particular civilisations have appeared and I thank those authors whom I have plundered mercilessly (but usually with acknowledgements). On China there has been the book by A. Wolf and C.-S. Huang, *Marriage and Adoption in China 1845–1945* (1980), and the general review by H. D. R. Baker, *Chinese Family and Kinship* (1979), as well as much specialist material emanating from interdisciplinary groups in the United States, a very encouraging development and one in which I have been honoured to be asked to participate in a minor way. On India we are better endowed, with general works by Kapadia (1955), Shah (1974) and others, but apart from monographs I have made most use of Irawati Karve's *Kinship Organization in India* (1953) and D. G. Mandelbaum's *Society in India* (1970); however the social history of the family in the sub-continent has been little explored in the critical way that has begun to happen with China and Europe. My sources on other societies, in which I have been interested in particular topics, have been more restricted; for Tibet largely Carrasco (1959), Ekvall (1968) and Levine (1988), for ancient Egypt, Hopkins (1980) and Pestmann (1961), for the Arabs and ancient Israel, a variety of works but especially Peters (1990), Maher (1974) and Mundy (1979; 1982; 1988), for Greece, Finley (1955) and Lacey (1968), for Rome, Crook (1967a), Dixon, Saller and others. In none of these areas have I hoped or intended to be comprehensive.

One fact that encouraged me to continue with a seemingly unending task was the invitation from the editors to contribute an introduction to the *Histoire de la famille* (1986). I had long had in mind the need for a summing up of one of the few areas of enquiry where social anthropology had made any major substantive as distinct from an inspirational contribution to the comparative study of human cultures and societies, that is, in the study of kinship, family and marriage. While this encyclopaedia took a different form from the one I had envisaged, it nevertheless provided a unique and valuable summary of the work that had been accomplished by a variety of scholars on various regions of the world, and this in turn was a useful check on my own more sporadic reading and more directed analysis.

Nevertheless this present study could never have pretended to be complete, nor was that the intention. New works come out more quickly than I can read the reviews; many of the old I have wrongfully neglected, even when they were written in the few languages I understand. But my aim has been the clarification of the analysis of some aspects of marriage and the family in the major societies of Eurasia and at the same time to point to specific similarities, at least at the domestic level, setting these in the context of a wider theoretical analysis and debate. This effort can be viewed as part of a wider scheme to redraw the lines of comparison in order to see earlier Europe in the same general frame of reference as earlier Asia, not only in terms of domestic groups, but also of proto-industrialisation, politics, religion, modes of communication and culture, that is 'high culture', more generally. Other writers have stressed similarities at the level of the tributary mode of production. My own understanding calls attention to a wider range of similarities at the domestic level which relate not so much to the modes of extracting surplus as to the productive processes themselves, though clearly these are not independent.

Transcription to Roman script

The transcription of Chinese script into Roman presents difficulties to the non-specialist since the Pinyin version, introduced on the mainland, provides a rival system to the earlier Wade–Giles method and to French variants. In addition, some of the words occurring in field studies are of local origin and may have no counterpart in a written form. Since I am not writing a specialist monograph for sinologists, I have not aimed at an overall rationalisation but have used the words as they appear in the works of the authors I cite and then tried, where possible to give the alternative transcription (p. = Pinyin). With the names of dynasties I have used the new forms; place names have generally been left as they are in current English usage but I have put the alternatives in brackets where I could identify them. Family names I have left alone. It is enough for most of us to individualise the older forms of Chinese names without complicating the issue by introducing new nomenclatures for Mencius or Mao.

Since they use an alphabetic script, Indian languages present fewer problems, except for the diacriticals. Some Indian scholars suggested leaving them out; I have included them where I could. The transcription of Arabic is more in flux than that of Indian languages and here again there is a problem of which European language the writer uses. I have simply followed my advisers.

Summary

The geographical scope of this book is straightforward but the thematic content is complex, more so than I had originally intended, especially as the review of Asian systems of kinship has led me to deal with the way a number of other topics are related to the main arguments. Fears that these central paths may be difficult to follow in the thickets of ethnographic data and their attempted explanations, in the development and qualifications of the various themes pursued over such a wide area, suggest that the reader may welcome a short summary. And it will make his journey easier if he bears in mind that, first, I am dealing with the ideas scholars have had about kinship in particular societies from a historical perspective and I am considering the systems themselves from a comparative standpoint; and secondly, that in speaking of Asian and European in contrast to African systems, the primary referent is not geographical but the very broad type of socio–economic organisation.

The enquiry pursues three interconnected topics which will be elaborated in the first chapter, namely, the primitivisation of the East (and of the historic past) and the need for a partial reconceptualisation of these systems of marriage and kinship in the light of the type of domestic production as well as of the nature of the religion and the mode of communication; secondly, the analysis of the way that the transmission of productive and other property is related to the political economy on the one hand and to the family on the other, as well as to the ideological structures; thirdly, the cross-cultural distribution of mechanisms and strategies of management and devolution, which leads to a modification of the extreme, Kiplingesque, version of the East–West divide, with its implications of what we and others could and can do to bring about the coming of the modern world.

In treating the first of these topics I have tried to demonstrate the similarities between certain features of the kinship systems of the major Asian societies and those of pre-industrial, Mediterranean Europe, with a view of taking them out of the category of primitive or even of Oriental societies as this has been understood in much historical, sociological and anthropological discussion. My alternative point of contrast has been with Africa where the type of agricultural production, the nature of technical and knowledge systems, and the oral mode of communication make for significant differences not only at the level of the political economy (the concepts of neither 'feudal' nor 'oriental' society being appropriate), but also at the level of family and marriage.

I have discussed this theme at two main levels. Following up an earlier account I have pointed out the way in which the existence of restricted land and of other productive resources in Asia poses different problems of access, management and devolution than one finds with the less populous societies of pre-colonial Africa, with their extensive, shifting agriculture. I have isolated a series of mechanisms and strategies of continuity and heirship which are found widely, though in different combinations, throughout Eurasia, and which help to organise the domestic economy and domestic life more generally.

The first of these to be examined is the nature of marriage transactions, which are seen as basically different from African bridewealth, even where described as 'brideprice' and held to involve the total incorporation of a wife in the family or lineage of her husband. Such notions are relics of nineteenth-century discussions which presumed a general shift from brideprice (or purchase) to dowry, and for the analysis of African systems of marriage have long been set aside in favour of 'bridewealth'. It is even more essential to set them aside for the more complex social systems of Europe and Asia, because of a number of additional reasons. While the sale of sexual, genetricial and other human services is a feature of many of these societies, the use of this term for bridal transactions in parts of Asia and earlier Europe (in contrast to the 'dowry' of more recent times and of the upper groups), and the notion that the standard marriage arrangement involved the sale of women (or men, for that matter) seem particularly inappropriate when in most cases the bulk of such payments are handed over to the bride, or serve as a gage or dower in the case of divorce. In other words such transactions are part of the process whereby women become endowed with property by other males and females, part of the broad pattern of devolution down the generations which is linked not only to the nature of the political economy but to the hierarchical position of a particular individual or group within it.

I have tried to investigate the nature and distribution of these hierarchical differences, which are not only of interest in themselves but are relevant to my thesis in two ways. Such differences emerge from the particular sort of stratification that characterises Eurasian societies, based as they are on complex agriculture in which the strata relate very differently to the system of production, in type of activity, in size of holding and in kind of access, that is, as owner, tenant or labourer. And they are manifest in both the economic and kinship aspects of the domestic domain where their very existence says something about the nature of family systems in 'advanced Oriental society'. But equally important are some striking similarities in the distribution of these differences among the various societies we are examining, suggesting that we are dealing not simply with features marking particular ideologies or cultures but structural factors which cross-cut socio–cultural boundaries in significant ways. Moreover the similarities occur not only across the boundaries of those 'oriental' societies, but across those of the Near East and Mediterranean as well.

The direction of such an argument leads to a revision of aspects of the thesis of the Uniqueness of the West in relation to the rise of capitalism, not only at the level of the family but of the domestic and indeed the macro-economy. That is not a question pursued at great length. But the analysis requires us to modify the way scholars effectively, though not always deliberately, primitivise the kinship systems of the major Asian societies, either by the employment of concepts and approaches developed in simpler communities or by starting with questions derived from the study of post-industrial cultures.

1

The nature of the enterprise

This study has arisen out of two interests. First, in the past, accounts of the major oriental and Mediterranean societies have often presented a picture of the position of women, and of domestic life more generally, which seemed to disregard the fact that at marriage they were endowed rather than purchased. Secondly, this approach has led to an opposition between East and West which encouraged ethnocentric notions, sociological and popular, about differences in family and marriage which various authors have tried to relate to the process of modernisation. Some have seen Marx's Asiatic mode of production as characterised by an Asiatic mode of reproduction. In the eyes of others, the more appropriate comparison was with Africa or even Australia. My account tries to reconsider these views by looking at the domestic relations of those societies in terms of certain substantive hypotheses and general theories, as a result of which I try to place them in a context that is in many respects less exotic than these approaches suggest.

The role of the family in the development of 'capitalism', 'industrialisation', 'modernisation', is a common theme of the social sciences and forms the backcloth to the global sociological theses such as those of Max Weber, of many Western historians committed, consciously or unconsciously, to a strong view of the uniqueness of the West, of anthropologists contrasting family and kinship, complex and simple exchange, of demographers interested in and concerned about the demographic transition, the value of children and domestic strategies. It is the general argument of this book that for pre-industrial times, the differences in the Asian and the European structures and organisation of marriage and the family fell within a specific range of variation that is generally consistent with their roughly similar forms of productive activity based on Bronze Age developments.

That is the general framework. But the analysis depends upon looking again at a number of more particular issues in the study of the domestic domain of Asian societies, which is aimed at making them more 'understandable' in European terms, and Europe more comprehensible in Asian

1

ones; in other words it is aimed at modifying notions of uniqueness in respect of modes of reproduction, just as elsewhere I have tried to do with modes of production and modes of communication. While I have no intention of neglecting the important differences in forms of family, in means of livelihood, in types of script, and so on, it is difficult to see these as crippling to further development, at least to the development of a high degree of mercantile and proto-industrial activity. My concerns will be principally with discussions of the family, marriage and the farm (or other enterprise) at lower levels of generality, but in the end they bear upon this central question.

That is the general perspective. But I begin this chapter by presenting the more specific hypotheses which I have developed in earlier works, then turn to some of the more general considerations involved to see how these relate to the study of marriage and marital transfers; for we need to clear up the problems in some earlier models before we develop others.

The substantive hypothesis concerns the analysis of the distribution of what I have earlier called the woman's property complex which is linked to the practice of diverging devolution whereby parental property is transmitted to women as well as to men. In a previous volume, *Production and Reproduction* (1976), I drew some general contrasts between the systems of marriage and the family in Africa and Asia, differences that I saw as related to their systems of production. This contrast represented dominant trends which might of course be overridden under particular circumstances: I was attempting to deal with these relations statistically, but in a largely verbal rather than numerical way. Briefly the argument ran like this. The advanced agriculture that arose in the Bronze Age, and which replaced shifting cultivation by plough or irrigation farming, permitted the growth of more complex societies, the 'civilisations' of the European prehistorian (as well as in Chinese usage) that meant new crafts, new occupations and new hierarchies. The individuals and groups in those hierarchies tried to preserve or improve the status of their daughters as well as of their sons. For in the reproduction of the system of stratification, downward as well as upward movement was always possible within if not between groups. This fact had important implications for marriage, namely, the tendency for like to marry like in isogamous unions, for the distribution of property to women in diverging devolution, namely, by the direct or indirect endowment at marriage or by inheritance at death, as well as for the adoption of other mechanisms by which property and status were passed on. One example of these mechanisms is the presence of the type of union where an inheriting daughter could attract a husband for his labour on the farm or for his capacity to produce an heir. But there were also a number of other practices, notions and sentiments, all of which existed in relation to a marked socio-economic hierarchy and were therefore likely to vary according to one's position within it.

In looking earlier at the distribution of these features, one obvious area in which the tendency to endogamy (or, better, in-marriage since we are rarely talking of an obligation but rather a tendency) had been modified was in Europe after the Roman period. From that time marriage between close kin was prohibited, although not of course 'class' endogamy in a more general sense, as·Marc Bloch insisted when he spoke of circles of marriage. So, too, was adoption, concubinage and the levirate which many other Eurasian societies had used as 'strategies of heirship' – or perhaps better, 'strategies of continuity' since maintenance in life as well as at death was involved. In a subsequent volume entitled *The Development of the Family and Marriage in Europe* (1983) I tried to offer some explanation of certain 'pecularities' of the Western situation in relation to the 'ideology' and practice of the Christian Church. Those I interpreted as partly shaped in accordance with the demands of an ecclesiastical organisation which commanded a dominant position following the break-up of the Roman Empire, shaped perhaps 'casually', perhaps by 'elective affinity', perhaps intentionally, more likely by implicit selection.

In this third part of the enterprise, I return to the concomitants of diverging devolution, and specifically to the relationship between a woman's role as daughter, whose status is a matter of continuing concern to her natal family, and her role as a wife who in many cases marries away even if not out, that is, within the same group or grouping. In my view the implications of this dual position have been neglected by many recent anthropological theorists of the 'other cultures', at least in Asia, partly because their models are often derived from a 'simpler' set of societies (simpler not only from an economic standpoint), and partly because of the tendency to dichotomise the human universe into 'primitive' and 'advanced', placing Asia firmly in the former category and Europe in the latter. This is part of a wider failure properly to evaluate the place of the East in human history. In this volume I want to try and point out how I think the position of women in the natal family, the conjugal family and the wider kin group, especially the lineage, has often been misrepresented or partially represented in these societies (especially in terms of brideprice, incorporation and similar notions) and in what direction these ideas should be modified. I am particularly concerned to point out some general trends, some common institutions, found in these Asian societies which relate to their own socio-economic situation and which at the same time provide a link with pre-industrial (and indeed proto-industrial or non-industrial) Europe and the Mediterranean. Not common in the sense that everybody possesses all of them all the time. But all are in a significant sense 'available' for inclusion in the cultural repertoire, although those adopted at any particular time, place and strata will depend upon a variety of political, religious, ecological and other factors.

So I am trying to carry out two related tasks. Firstly, I am looking at the position of women in relation to their natal and conjugal families, especially with regard to the continuation of their ties with the former and their possible incorporation in the latter. Secondly, I am trying to point to various related aspects of marriage and domestic organisation in different cultures which represent variations drawn from a wider set of possibilities distributed throughout the major societies of Asia and the Mediterranean, and which have to be seen against the background of some broad differences with African societies.

I want to develop the argument by examining accounts of societies or communities from a particular point of view, starting with the negative rather than the positive side, that is, by calling attention to the problem with accounts of the way in which wives are said to be incorporated in their husbands' families or lineages. One of the main facts that impressed me, and which led me to query the adequacy of these notions, was that in those very examples chosen by comparative sociologists as the extreme cases of the incorporation of women, namely, China and Rome, daughters in the upper strata were often endowed with property, whether at marriage, directly or indirectly, or later on as an inheritance. To take a dowry as one's entire 'portion' or 'lot', as we say in English, may appear to be cutting oneself off from one's natal family and to be attaching oneself to that of one's husband with whom one establishes, sooner or later, some kind of a conjugal estate. As with those, usually younger, sons in parts of Europe or Japan who took their endowment and had no longer any legal claim on their family wealth, this was often the case in dowry systems. But of course relationships with natal kin continued to be important in many other spheres of social life. Even if they left for long periods the prodigal son or daughter was welcomed back; and more usually they lived in the vicinity if not the neighbourhood and continued to interact with their kin.

A related institution that seemed to me critical was that of the marrying-in son-in-law.[1] This practice was virtually unknown in Black Africa, except in a more generalised form in some matrilineal societies and again as bride-service, a preliminary to bride-removal, in some others. But it is a recurrent feature of the major agricultural societies of Europe and Asia where it is usually associated with a daughter acting as heiress in the absence of sons. Filiacentric unions (often called uxorilocal, although I prefer to reserve this latter term for the situation where this represents the major form of post-marital residence) are often practised more widely for other reasons in dominantly virilocal societies, as has been shown for southern China and for Finland (Wolf 1985a; Abrahams 1986) where they are also used to augment labour on the farm even when younger brothers are around. But wherever it appears, the institution of the in-coming son-in-law marrying a brotherless daughter is highly significant, first, because this union represents one of several alternative strategies of heirship, which, like strategies of management, and especially the management of labour disposal and dispersal, are also mechanisms of continuity; secondly because it results from a preference for passing property and other rights between members of the elementary family, daughters if there are no sons, rather than seeking heirs among more distant males in the collateral line. Looking at the same question at the level of succession to office rather than inheritance of property, England owes the earlier and present Queen Elizabeth (and the latter's marrying-in husband) to this practice. The Dutch royal family have provided an even more striking example in recent years. Inevitably the presence of this practice must modify the notion of an agnatic lineage or dynasty holding continuing rights to office or property, such as we find in Africa, since under a set of recurring circumstances these rights are transmitted through the women of the elementary family rather than to cousins or more distant males, not to heiresses alone but in a smaller measure to all other women in the form of dowry or inheritance. In other words, the system places more emphasis on maintaining the position, the status, the style of life, of one's own daughters, than of members of the lineage in a wider sense. By 'style of life' I mean not only those features pertaining to a particular class or strata, but also those reflecting the standard of living of a particular family.

It is these lower level concerns that tend to bring the kinship systems of Europe and Asia together, even though some have 'lineages' and some do not. That is to say, in all the major Asian societies we find 'domestic groups' of limited but varying size to which are linked an estate, that is, a conjugal fund, a family farm or larger 'joint undivided family' of the Indian type; sometimes as in the Chinese case these groups operate within a charitable corporation of the lineage type, sometimes as in North India within a wider unilineal descent group, and elsewhere within a bilateral range of kin. The particular kin-group context is important in various ways. But in each case the position at the domestic level contrasts with that associated with the so-called 'corporate' kin groups of Africa, where the estate, usually of the more open kind appropriate to shifting cultivation, is not subject to the same kind of internal economic stratification nor yet to the pressures for maintaining the status of daughters at the expense of lineage interests. Such differences were concealed by earlier, undifferentiated notions of lineage, clan or descent group, which were intrinsic to much nineteenth-century (and later) theorising about kinship and marriage, and which saw them as self-contained boxes, as exclusive compartments of social organisation, the presence of which defined social systems as being patrilineal or matrilineal. These notions needed considerable modification in the Eurasian context, since they failed to take account of the allocation of rights to daughters (and hence to wives and mothers) as well as to sons (and hence to husbands and fathers), rights whose exercise could lead not only to internal fission but to a measure of exclusion (or to the appearance of exclusion) from the 'lineage' itself. The potential claims of women and their physical movement at marriage pose problems both for the families they leave behind and for those they join when they enter into a virilocal marriage. Their rights are often limited, but the very fact that women inherit as 'heiresses' clearly provides some kind of handle, model or incentive for claiming a 'share' even when they have brothers; this we see clearly in Hebrew and other texts. The continuity of the family estate depended primarily on males, indeed sometimes on one se-lected son, a situation that could lead to a conflict in the attempts to meet the claims of those who are left and of those who leave. While the continuity of the lineage or 'extended family' might be patrilineal or agnatic in this loose sense, its particular status depended upon its departing daughters as well as its resident sons.

In drawing attention to similarities I do not wish to set aside or under-estimate cultural or subcultural differences in kinship patterns of the kind that, among others, A. Wolf has recently discussed for China (1985a) or Karve (1953) for India. Some of these differences may be linked to specific social and ecological factors while others seem to be virtually 'free vari-ations' within the repertoire of the overall system (though we need to be careful lest such a suggestion lead to a loose analysis and to unfortunate reifications). Nor do I wish to ignore the fact that kinship and marriage have changed significantly over time in relation to political, religious or economic factors, as for example when individuals and families in China placed property in charitable trusts to maintain ancestral halls, temples and schools, possibly in order to counteract the potentially democratising influ-ence of the newly introduced examination system, thus creating 'lineages' (that is, corporation lineages) in a special sense (Beattie 1979:118, 128; Baker 1979:136ff.). Any systematic consideration of such changes over space and time, even a review of the very broad kind I gave in my account of pre-industrial Europe (1983), is well beyond the scope of this essay and the capacity of this author.

In the first two sections I shall mostly be content to concentrate, though not exclusively, on ethnographic and other accounts from the first part of this century, which rarely provide the range of temporal, hierarchical or geographic variation that one needs. Nevertheless, aside from trying to lay out the features associated with diverging devolution and the particular practices adopted by specific societies or subgroups, I have attempted to indicate the ways in which these institutions tend to differ as between higher and lower groups, terms which I use in a highly general way to indicate relative status based on various, locally defined criterion, but always with some implications of access to property. This raises further analytical questions, for while I am concerned with internal differences, mainly hierarchical ones, I am also interested in the general similarities in kinship between societies, for example, in the tendency for widow remarriage to be prohibited among higher groups and permitted among lower ones. Such facts pose important problems for explanation. Once they have been established, one can no longer be entirely satisfied with a purely 'cultural' account, that is, with one framed in terms of the parameters of any particular culture. Nor yet can one be content with an analysis wholly phrased in terms of the structure or functioning of particular societies since the feature displays a wider distribution than its connection with Hinduism or Confucianism might suggest. We have to look at factors operating at a more inclusive level than the study of particular societies, especially ethnographic accounts of village life, might suggest.

In doing this I am following up certain aspects of the analysis upon which Tambiah and I were engaged in an earlier publication. While the substantive subject matter was 'bridewealth and dowry', the underlying problems were wider in scope. Tambiah remarked upon some general similarities (as well as differences) between India and China, calling attention to the necessity of reviewing explanations made in terms of 'Indian cultural values' in view of these 'structural similarities' (1973:71). The specific phraseology is irrelevant; I was interested in similar problems which are not so much cross-cultural as transcultural. Neither of us would wish to deny the validity of exploring a variety of explanations and levels of explanation, those given by the actors, those presented in terms of the actor's concepts, those related to a particular cultural or social formation. All these various types have been accorded much attention by anthropologists, especially by those who have undertaken intensive fieldwork. Neither of us would underestimate the value, indeed the necessity, of exploring all these understandings, especially as a preliminary to more inclusive, comparative explanations. But at the same time we recognise that certain problems, topics and situations are illuminated by the realisation that rather similar forms of belief and practice have a wider distribution which needs accounting for in terms perhaps of modes of communication or production, and which at the same time alters the observer's appreciation of any particular cultural context, irrespective of whether or not it alters that of the actors.

Theorising

Let me now turn to some of the broader implications for approaches to comparative sociology, for what one might call the theorising rather than the theory. This book represents an attempt to understand aspects of marriage and the family in the major societies of Asia, the Near East (West Asia) and the adjacent Eastern Mediterranean, taking into account the modes of livelihood and the levels of stratification; political, religious and ideological factors also play their part but these I do not consider in any great detail. In any case the enquiry tries to get away from the influential tendency to see 'kinship systems' as things in themselves. For I have recently argued (1985) that while this approach, which has been advocated by such important scholars as Fortes, Lévi-Strauss and Dumont, has led to many gains, the restricted paradigm has also brought about some distinct losses, in particular the failure to provide a link with the studies of scholars in other related fields, especially those in history, demography and sociology. As in much of social theory, such approaches need to be treated as complementary rather than as either contradictory or belonging to separate spheres.

The comparative study of what Morgan called systems of consanguinity and affinity, what we would now call family, kinship and marriage, has undergone many changes of emphasis and direction over the years. In recent times there has been the stress on marriage as a system of exchange (the exchange of women, above all), and there has also been the long-term enquiry into systems of descent and filiation. These particular interests have been broadly associated with two so-called theories of kinship, that of the alliance 'school' associated with the name of Lévi-Strauss and that of the descent school associated with the name of Radcliffe-Brown. In fact the genealogies of these approaches extend back much further, well into the nineteenth century, where we find forms of marriage, and especially since Frazer, of cross-cousin marriage, looked upon as systems of exchange, as well as numerous discussions on the place of clans and lineages (that is, descent groups) in the organisation and development of human societies.

The emergence of various versions of functional and structural anthropology, associated with the development of field studies, was accompanied by a shift away from, even a setting aside of, the chronological or diachronic perspective. Nevertheless it was impossible to eliminate that dimension altogether from the agenda. For example, the terms elementary and complex employed by Lévi-Strauss do not have a purely morphological reference, just as the comparison between direct and generalised exchange has a distinct temporal direction about it. Equally with descent and filiation, where the move from unilineal to bilateral systems is generally assumed to have had an 'evolutionary' character (e.g. Goode 1963), even if the bilateral reckoning of kin was a characteristic of the Eskimo as well as of Europeans. One thesis implicit in this study is that notions of alliance or descent, as conceived in these discussions, often provide less than adequate categories, models or tools for considering the wider issues, partly because their treatment has been overly formal and underly relational. Too formal, and yet also perhaps insufficiently so. That is to say, the notions have been too gross and require further discriminations to be made, especially when we look at the institutions they purport to describe in relation to other facets of the type of society in which they are found, let alone to those of a particular social formation itself. Cross-cousin marriage or patrilineal descent groups can take very different forms in terms both of meaning (or signification) and of function (or process), depending not only on the particular culture but also on more general factors such as the broad type of livelihood of the people concerned. Some writers, not only ones under Marxist influence, have tried to establish relations between the economy and the lineality of descent groups (including their absence in 'bilateral' systems). We need to look beyond 'lineality' to the structure, organisation and role of kin groups if we are to understand the differences as well as the similarities at this level between, say, China and Africa. Furthermore, for this and for the wider purposes of understanding the overall development of kinship in human societies, we have to examine carefully those aspects of the mode of reproduction that are most closely associated with the type of livelihood, with the mode of production, as well as those religious and political factors which can be of dominating significance in these spheres.

The difficulty arises partly from the idea that kinship and marriage are 'dominant' in pre-industrial societies, a proposition which must be examined with some care even in the simplest. For the concept of kinship as a sub-system of the total social system is of analytic rather than substantive significance when we are dealing with what has sometimes been called the domestic mode of production but is better seen as household production that takes place within various modes or systems of production in the more usual sense. That is to say, it is difficult to point to a specific kinship domain that is not also an economic, political and religious one. There is no institutional distinction as there is, to some degree at least, with the Church in Europe. Where production takes place largely within the household, a wide range of activities are closely interlocked, not simply at the level of some abstract kinship model. For example, marriage, which involves the re-ordering of sexual and other rights over women and men, is the means by which conjugal families are established and households reshaped. Not only is this significant for reproduction but it is of great importance for production too. Hence decisions about marriage will be influenced by the nature of the productive process, by the position of the partners with regard to these activities as well as by the existing constitution of domestic groups.

Consequently the situation is already more complex than some theorising suggests. One serious constraint upon any analysis is that social scientists have worked too long with a dichotomous frame in which 'primitive' or simple kinship systems are seen as utterly distinct from more 'advanced' or complex ones. Elementary structures, pre-industrial systems, corporate kin groups, kinship as infrastructure, too much of this discussion presumes a dichotomy between we and they which is not only theoretically wrong and empirically misleading, but spells the death of social anthropology in a very practical sense. As a field of study, we are digging our own graves if we continue to frame our enquiry in terms of carrying out participant observation on the disappearing world of the primitive. But even in a comparative historical enquiry, similar questions are raised. The framework is especially problematic when we find that China and India are only too often included in the elementary category and medieval Europe in the complex. The ethnocentric bias is only too obvious, but why is it also theoretically wrong? Such a categorisation depends on looking at institutions of kinship out of their total social context. But we cannot radically separate marriage and the family from production, as Lévi-Strauss tends to do, nor from property, as Fortes tended to do. Even from the standpoint of exchange alone, it seems questionable to compare cross-cousin marriage in China or India, except at a very formal level, with the Australian systems practised by hunters and gatherers. For one reason the items of exchange had such very different meanings in the different productive systems, not only from the actor's point of view (that goes perhaps without saying) but also from the observer's. To operate at a level of abstraction that treats cross-cousin marriage or the lineage as 'things in themselves' is to adopt an approach in anthropology equivalent to a linguistics that confined itself to phonetics.

It is not only a matter of the separation of modes of marriage from modes of production, but more generally of the nature of anthropological formalism and abstraction; what was chosen as the centre of analytical concern. It seems curious today to think that Murdock and others referred to Europe as having an Eskimo system (even an Eskimo social organisation). They referred of course to a certain type of terminology for close kin, and there was much to be said for the effort earlier anthropologists put into laying out the distribution of certain widespread features of kinship systems, including what Malinowski flippantly dismissed as kinship algebra, and then classifying them in various ways, by types of marriage, types of kin group, types of terminology. These were important activities in which there is still a long way to go.

At this moment in time it was also important to criticise the premature attempts of nineteenth-century evolutionists to spell out long-term developments in patterns of marriage and other institutions, and to concentrate instead upon the synchronic perspective in field studies. Both these activities are important, the formalistic classification and the field enquiry; in botany and zoology the Linnaean classification, the laboratory examination and the behavioural observations all have their place. But particular field studies must also be situated, and few would argue about this in any other field of study, in a developmental frame, a frame that is at once ontogenetic and phylogenetic, that is, historical, even evolutionary, as well as developmental in the socio-cultural sense. That means seeing institutions like the lineage, concubinage or polyandry in the context of specific socio-economic formations, which are themselves representative of types of social system.

The nature of the categorisation of social systems one uses depends to some extent on the nature of the problem one has in mind, but the choice may carry deep epistemological significance. Many anthropologists have tended to regard their generalisations, their concepts, their procedures, as applying to 'elementary' structures – to use the phrase incorporated in the title of Lévi-Strauss' book – which are seen to range from Australian aborigines to the inhabitants of China and India. A similar kind of distinction between simple and complex, traditional and modern, is an implicit part of the analyses of many European social scientists, and it is a usage into which it is very easy to fall. But the results can be dangerous. The problem has been recently raised in an account of Weber's sociological theories where the author remarks that comparative sociology 'has suffered the consequences of a strong anthropological bias' towards tribal societies and against the large-scale historical states that made up Weber's subject matter (Collins 1986:5). Such a bias tends to oppose modern family structures to tribal ones, leaving out the enormously important 'intermediary' category of agrarian states. That is the very gap this book tries to fill although I see its origin as connected not with anthropology as such but with a more general predisposition to categorise societies in binary terms, as elementary and advanced, industrial and pre-industrial. The result is a tendency to primitivise the Oriental civilisations. Weber largely avoided this trap. At the same time he tended to draw too sharp a line between the West and the East in relation to the family and other matters largely because of the nature of his enquiry into the origins of 'rational' capitalism, which he saw as associated with other general, pre-existing, features of society that were unique to the West.

There are of course many times when a line needs to be drawn between industrial and pre-industrial societies. But too often that line gets confused with one between the West and the Rest. If the *pre-industrial* West is seen to hold the seeds to later developments in its socio-economic system, then there is a temptation to place a wide range of its institutions, including the family, in a different category from those of societies of the East which did not achieve industrialisation at that same time, even though the fact that since then some of them have done so in extra measure should give pause for thought. This search for earlier differences in family life that might bear upon the advent of capitalism (or modernisation or the demographic transition) has tended seriously to distort the analysis of systems of marriage and the family. What has to be proven is often assumed in advance and lines are drawn in ways that presume expected conclusions. But there are more important dividing lines for many other purposes, often lines of a fairly traditional kind, that bear upon the differences and similarities in family structures.

For this particular enquiry one important category comprises those societies that have undergone the process that prehistorians describe as 'civilisation'. In the past the highly ethnocentric culture of western sociologists[2] has often seen this development as specifically European, linked with a certain type of rationality, bureaucracy and authority that was considered to be peculiarly characteristic of that continent. In trying to look at common aspects of these processes in the Old World, I have deliberately tried to modify some of the general assumptions of those European writers who believe the Uniqueness of the West extended to its familial, political and religious institutions in ways that were functionally relevant to the growth of capitalism. The evidence seems weak enough in itself but before making any judgement at all we need to clear away the kinds of ethnocentric assumptions and conceptual devices that have given it the wrong kind of support.

It is one thing to reject the radical discontinuity represented by the primitive–advanced, traditional–modern, and similar dichotomies that at times have almost seemed to define anthropology as a discipline. At the other extreme lies the all-too-easy insistence on the distinctiveness of all cultural or social formations that relativists espouse, or the untheoretical, unproblematic continuity that many historians and economists accept, at least implicitly. I refer not to their attachment to the continuity of events, which is rarely at issue, but the continuity of social systems, which raises theoretical questions. Is there not some framework more complex, more intellectually satisfying, than simple dualism or yet simpler monism, both of which are of course understandable, even acceptable, in some contexts, both 'folk' and 'analytic', but quite unacceptable as the basis of general theoretical approaches? If we are to construct an understanding of social and cultural relations, then we must begin with the observation or abstraction of some regularities as well as with some categorisation of social systems. However even those schema that go beyond the binary rarely stray far from the simple framework adopted by our nineteenth-century predecessors, that is: capitalist/industrial, feudal, ancient, and then primitive. Still today these formalised folk-categories are often the broad classificatory tools, implicitly of many historians and explicitly of classical Marxist theory. Another categorisation, equally crude, is based upon modes of livelihood; it is the one that forms the basis of much anthropological and archaeological discussion, from the beginning down to today, and which was partially incorporated in Marx's thought as the result of reading Morgan's *Ancient Society*. This is the hunting and gathering, pastoral, agricultural, industrial classification. Turning to the field of kinship, to understand the range of marriage systems, not simply in one society but more widely, we need some overall scheme that enables us to take into account both the differences and the similarities, some broad, some subtle, in modes of livelihood. We should consider, for example, the differences in meaning that cattle have in societies with hoe agriculture on the one hand and with plough farming on the other, for their workload bears upon the role of livestock in marriage transactions. This particular distinction in economics is critical in my own discussions of family and marriage, but it is by no means the only relevant variable. What is important is to elaborate the folk and analytic categories in ways that illumine the processes and distribution of social action.

Transfers, sale and incorporation

On this question of transactions some general comments on categories and concepts are needed as a guide to the studies that follow. One of the points I have tried to make has to do with the concept of brideprice and bridewealth in the analysis of Asian societies. The first of these terms has long been in use and comes to us in a direct line from those European commentators of the nineteenth century who thought that in the stage of society before women were endowed, they were sold, for a price, a brideprice. The term 'bridewealth' was later adopted by students of African societies who found the European concepts of sale inadequate, indeed definitely misleading, for any satisfactory account of marriage in that continent. In descriptions of marriage in the major Asian and ancient Mediterranean societies many writers have retained the use of brideprice, others have half-heartedly adopted bridewealth, while a third contingent have written of the flow of 'gifts' or 'goods' without further specifying the recipient or the nature of the transactions.

Bridewealth in Africa seems to me (as to others) a very different transaction from that found in these major Asian societies, at least in the major zones of settled agriculture, so that there appears to be little point in stretching the term to cover that whole range of prestations (Goody 1973).

This reluctance is not merely a matter of nominalism, of naming a transaction, but relates to ideas about the position of women, the nature of marriage, the type of clan and lineage, indeed about the general kind of society we are examining, whether we are dealing with arrangements for marriage and the family, for clan and for kin, for women and for men, that are nearer to the western pole or nearer to that of so-called simple or primitive societies.

The application of the notion of brideprice to the major Asian societies raises even greater difficulties, for the term is problematic for another reason. Some societies use the same word for marriage transactions as they do for some 'commercial' operations, words that can be satisfactorily translated as sale, purchase, barter. However, words do not necessarily signify nor create identity. In the course of a church marriage in contemporary English society, the father is said to 'give away' his daughter. One may contend that such a usage is a survival of a past state of affairs, although this line of argument (as many structural–functional anthropologists have insisted) has its dangers. But even in the past, even when the father had a hand in arranging the marriage, he 'gave away' his daughter only in a very special sense, not as one gives a gift at Christmas.

One further problem concerns the givers and receivers. We can define transactions between members of the groom's and the bride's kin by the direction of the flow of objects, that is, bridewealth or brideprice going one way, dowry the other. This is how many anthropological paradigms treat the question, and it is a model which has dominated much recent discussion about marriage. However there are similar but more extensive problems with such a simplistic approach to those Bourdieu discerned in the analysis of the gift. He objected that Mauss' discussion of the gift as exchange was overly abstract and externalised in that it overlooked significant factors such as time; yet among the Kabyles, as for many other peoples, the timing of the return gift is of the essence of the transaction. The difficulty arises from an over-simplification, an over-formalisation, that excludes dimensions important to the actor and the observer alike. The same is true of a paradigm of marriage transactions of the following kind, in which I choose the example of bridewealth or brideprice:

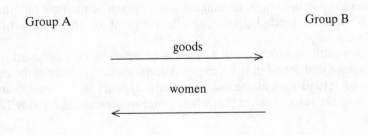

Group A   Group B

goods ⟶

women ⟵

Many authorities have pointed out that, except in some limiting cases, such transactions take place in rights over women (and men), not in women 'as objects'. For the rights transferred in systems of marriage are variable, not constant; this variation may sometimes be related to the quantum of goods (as perhaps in the larger transfers found in patrilineal than matrilineal societies in Africa) but other factors are clearly involved. Secondly, the originators and recipients, immediate and ultimate, of the transaction are concealed under the algebraic headings A and B, which stand for anyone. A transaction in which the goods from the groom's kin are received and retained by the father is very different from one that he passes on to the bride herself (even in advance); while the latter has often been called 'brideprice' in accounts of Asian societies, in many cases it represents an indirect endowment of the bride which may well co-exist with direct forms of dowry or inheritance. In other words the transaction may be linked to the process of devolution between the generations of the same family as well as to that of exchange between different ones. Finally, as with the gift the matter of timing is of the greatest importance since the lateral movement of goods between individuals and groups may be phased over a shorter or longer period, and may be related to the gradual transfer of increased rights, or, more probably, to the demonstration that the marriage is likely to endure and to be fertile.

The same is true of lineal transfers between the generations since the question of the quantity, the quality and the timing of the devolution of property to heirs (whether males or females, whether staying or leaving) is critical to the organisation of the family estate and to its personal relationships. In the case of a transfer directly from the parents to the bride, it matters a great deal for the estates of her natal and conjugal families whether she receives her portion at marriage, by inheritance or indeed whether she postpones her claim altogether, or at least until her son reaches adulthood. At no point will everything be transferred, neither in the society as a whole (which varies for example by strata) nor for individuals (who vary within those strata). But in some societies certain points of transfer will prevail over the others. Where individually provided education is critical and marriage less so, adolescence is likely to constitute an important point. Where productive action occurs outside the house, parents are more likely to provide for themselves in old age and only to hand on their property at death. In their review of dowry in complex societies, Harrell and Dickey remark that I 'fail to distinguish the situations in which families in complex societies practise inheritance through dowry from those in which both sons and daughters inherit only on the death or retirement of their parents' (1985: 100). In my first very broad consideration of the situation (1976), I concentrated on the

concomitants of devolution; the variables in which I was interested appeared
to be linked more generally to the diverging transmission of property to
women rather than dowry alone. But of course in other contexts it becomes
necessary to make further discriminations. Another factor of importance in
the case of marital prestations, is the extent to which the wife's possessions
are then merged with those of her husband, its timing and the degree of
control that he exercises during the marriage and that she exercises as a
widow. Each of these features constitutes an aspect of diverging devolution,
so important in Eurasia, whereby transfers are made to daughters as well as
sons. But each variant has somewhat different implications for social
interaction.

The plan

Let me now turn to the question of execution. My aim is to examine the role
of women in family, marriage and kinship systems with a view to throwing
light on some of these discussions. The critical issue is what happens to
women at marriage. I began with the Chinese material with a view to
offering a critique of the comparison between aspects of kinship in China
and other parts of the world, especially the nature of cross-cousin marriage,
there and in Australia, and the nature of the lineage system, there and in
Africa. The comparison is an implicit contrast. From the nineteenth century
onwards, many writers have taken China to represent the extreme case of
patrilineal descent (although at times the focus of the analysis was its
patriarchal family), where women were exchanged at marriage in the form
envisaged by Lévi-Strauss and others as part of the elementary structures of
simpler societies. For many writers too, there we encountered the prototypical form of the gens that supposedly characterised early European and
Asian societies and that was later identified with the lineages found in North
Africa (Durkheim 1893), and subsequently in the southern parts of that
continent by Evans-Pritchard and others. However, certain features of
Chinese domestic life seemed to run contrary to this model which in any case
appeared to lump together societies with very different social systems, very
different levels of complexity.

But it was not only the specific position of China that was important but its
relevance for broader theoretical discussions of women and marriage. If for
the 'extreme' case of China it could be shown that a woman and her children
retained rights in her natal kin, then the theoretical case against the notion
that 'normal' marriage involved the total incorporation of wives or the
exchange of women (as distinct from rights over women) was weakened. For
in that case women, except slaves, were not mere chattels to be defined

solely in terms of male perspectives and phallocratic interests, dominant as these might be in many contexts of social action.

The desire to examine the most extreme case arose partly from 'political' considerations, from which 'feminist' concerns, sparked off by Engels as well as by non-academic interests, were not absent. The position that women held in the major Eurasian societies seemed in some ways 'stronger', at least for holders of property, than in African societies, partly because some wealth, at times even land, was allocated to them in the form of a dowry at marriage or as an inheritance at the death of parents.

China led to Tibet, interesting for certain resemblances to early Europe, but with a system of polyandrous marriage that made little sense in the perspective of Chinese lineages, yet became more comparable, more understandable, when attention was directed to the domestic domain. South of Tibet lies the subcontinent of India, where like China, the analysis of kinship has generally concentrated on the differences with Europe and often with its resemblance to 'elementary systems'. There for a short time I joined Esther Goody in a village in Gujarat. Similar institutions were found, again distributed differently in the hierarchy, as well as regionally between North and South.

Since I am trying to discern some general tendencies in Eurasian societies, I then turn from South India to West Asia, first to ancient Egypt and ancient Israel. The accessibility of material on family life in ancient times made it possible to trace similar institutions in much earlier societies, although significantly these societies already practised 'advanced' forms of agriculture. Moving to a more recent period in that area, I then briefly examine the nature of marriage transactions among the Arabs under Islam, again pointing to some continuities and varieties on similar themes that lead to a re-valuation of classical accounts of earlier times, especially those that dwell upon the notions of brideprice and the sale of women in normal marriages. A critical part of my enquiry is an attempt to link the study of Asia with that of Greece and Rome, hence bringing together the traditions of East and West. Here I need to say a few words about the relation of this discussion to earlier attempts to link the family institutions of Asia with those of ancient Greece and Rome. The background of these early enquiries lay partly in William Jones' discovery, at the end of the eighteenth century, of the affinity between Indian and European languages, an enquiry that was stimulated by the conquest of India by the European powers. Given its genesis, it is not surprising that this discovery encouraged a 'racial' or 'ethnic' bias which sought to see Indo-European institutions as characteristically different from those of Semitic or other Asiatic peoples. While this assumption was not absolutely intrinsic to the 'comparative sociology' of legal historians such as Maine or Vinogradoff, Sanskritic and Hindu practices were seen as much closer to the patterns of historical Europe than those of the Far East. And the tendency continues to influence the perceptions of many scholars, including such notable figures as Dumézil and Benveniste, the scope of whose research has a linguistic definition.

In a great number of discussions, by jurists, historians and anthropologists, early Rome emerged as another society, comparable to China, in which married women were seen as incorporated in their husband's lineage. I deliberately chose to start my enquiry not with Rome but from the other end of the Eurasian landmass, and with China rather than India. For the same reason I include some consideration of Semitic and other speakers of Afro-Asiatic languages, such as ancient Egyptian, since I wanted to locate the comparative enquiry at the level of the political economy and socio-cultural organisation rather than race, language or even 'culture' in one sense (that is, particular cultural constellations). Important as these are, they are not always the primary contexts for considering those aspects of family structure in which I was interested.

Europe clearly underwent some radical changes in its system of marriage and the family since the classical period, largely under the influence, I have argued (1983), of the Christian Church. This becomes clear by contrasting its institutions with the nature of marriage transactions and the structural position of women as daughters and wives in the ancient world, in Greece and especially in Rome, societies which, like the Chinese and the Arab, have been taken by many authors as extreme examples of 'patriliny'. But in the penultimate chapter on Greece and the Eastern Mediterranean in more recent centuries, I try to bring out the continuities in that region over time, at least at the level of the problems facing holders and heirs, and the givers and receivers of rights over men, women and their property in marriage. In this way I hope to bring out the link between Asia and pre-industrial Europe on the one hand and to indicate the influence of Christendom on the other.

In the course of this study, I discuss a number of specific topics looked at by historians, demographers and sociologists as well as others beloved of anthropologists – incest, hypergamy, infanticide, polyandry and so on. I do this mainly in terms of their relation to my general theme and in the context of particular societies. At the same time I try to see these practices and societies not as exotic or primitive but as lying in the same range as, and therefore comparable to, the institutions of the West. With these general points in mind, let me turn then to the first section on China.

I

China

2

The incorporation of women: marriage transactions and the continuity of the 'house'

Earlier work on China by anthropologists placed a great deal of emphasis on the clan, the lineage and extended family, together with forms of preferential marriage. Part of this concern was initially derived from nineteenth-century preoccupations about evolutionary trends and from comparative analysis that used elementary concepts on a global scale. The outcomes were then applied as if the institutions they referred to operated similarly in Africa and in Australia as in China. Lévi-Strauss (1949) included China, as he did Burma, in his formidable analysis of the elementary systems of kinship, while Freedman, whose two studies of the Chinese lineage (1958; 1966) were pathbreaking in a variety of ways, drew deliberate comparisons with African systems, adapting the insights developed there to the complex state society of China. Like African lineages, those of the East (in China and India) were exogamous, whereas no such prohibition existed in the Near East and Mediterranean, even where such lineages were to be found (in Islam, ancient Israel and possibly the classical world). Up to a limited point the results were profitable. But they would have been yet greater had these authors also looked more closely at the structure of domestic groups. By this phrase I mean that constellation of productive and reproductive groupings that centre around the *domus*, that is the 'house' as an association of people, property and custom, which is not confined to those living together at one particular moment but comprises a number of partly overlapping units, the family (the conjugal unit), the household (the consumption unit), the enterprise, often focusing on the farm (the production unit), and the dwelling group. Had they given more weight to these low-level groupings, they would not only have found similarities of another kind but important differences as well. At the same time they might have been led to make links with two other kinds of intellectual interest in kinship and marriage, namely, that of the demographers on the one hand and that of the historians and sociologists of the family on the other. Anthropology might have become less restricted to a limited range of topics, more capable of dealing with the complex situ-

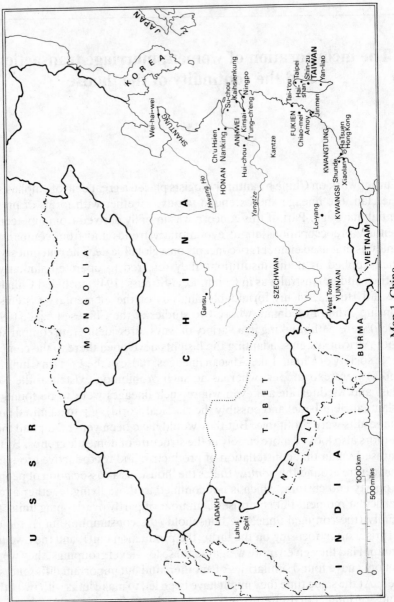

Map 1 China

ations that occur not only in the so-called advanced societies but in most of the world now faced with problems arising out of what is known as 'the demographic transition', that is, the transition from high fertility and high mortality to a lowering, first of mortality, then gradually of fertility. For it is the transitional situation between the two that produces the very high levels of population growth that have had such a profound influence on the social and ecological systems of the entire world.

One particular example of the operation of the restricted paradigm (certainly not manifest in Freedman's work) was the tendency to identify kinship systems with kinship terms. At the beginning of the second of Lévi-Strauss' five chapters (the first presents a criticism of Granet) on 'the Chinese System' of generalised exchange, he writes: 'In this analysis of the Chinese kinship system, we shall follow in the main the work of Han-Yi Fêng and we shall keep to his transcription of the terms' (1969 [1949]:325). This study by Fêng (1937) is also entitled 'The Chinese Kinship System' although it is virtually confined to an analysis of one set of terms alone. The same tendency was apparent in much earlier work on the kinship systems of native North American Indians and Australians, and the topic has received similar attention in studies carried out in South Asia. Most recently a magisterial work on Dravidian kinship by T. R. Trautmann begins: 'The Dravidian system of kinship presents, in the elegant logic of its rule of cross cousin marriage and the terminology in which that logic plays itself out, an anti-world to minds accustomed to think in Indo-European languages' (1981:1).

These statements do not simply represent a shorthand usage – for 'kinship' read 'kinship terms'; they embody assumptions about the role of terminology in the field of kinship which dominate the subsequent analyses, although in very different ways. Attempting a historical reconstruction which has some affinities with the parallel undertakings of L. H. Morgan (1870) and W. H. R. Rivers (1914), Lévi-Strauss compares China with the Miwok of North America largely on the basis of terms for kin relationship and concludes his own study of China with words that reflect the earlier tendency to derive structure from terminology:

We are thus brought to the hypothesis of the coexistence, in ancient China, of two kinship systems: the first, practised by the peasants, and based on a real or functional division into exogamous moieties, the exchange of sisters, and marriage between bilateral cross-cousins; the other, of feudal inspiration, and based on cycles of alliance between patrilineages (distributed or not into exogamous moieties), and marriage with the matrilateral cross-cousin and niece. That is, a system of restricted exchange and a system of generalized exchange. (1969:369–70)

The thesis has a close affinity with that developed in a work on 'sororal polygamy' in 'feudal' China by the sinologist, Marcel Granet, who was much influenced by the Durkheimian school of sociology in Paris. Part of his thesis, based on nineteenth-century anthropological discussion, ran as follows: 'il y a des raisons de croire qu'à l'origine une Communauté ne comprenait que deux groupes familiaux échangeant entre eux leurs filles: cette hypothèse est la seule qui rende compte de la nomenclature de parenté chinoise . . .' (1920:45). Variations upon this thesis, including the notion of an earlier matriliny preceding patriliny, continue to be suggested by Chinese and foreign scholars alike (e.g. Cartier 1986a:446–8). Needless to say, there are other possible hypotheses, but what is remarkable is the dependence that is placed upon deductions from kinship terms alone. The same dependence on this limited body of evidence appears in Wilkinson's study *The Family in Classical China* (1926). The author was British Crown advocate at Shanghai and presumably had access to actual cases, then and in the recent past. Instead of consulting these records or of observing current practice, he returns to his undergraduate studies of Maine, to which are added McLellan, Morgan (two other lawyers) and Frazer, and proceeds to delve into the 'classical' sources, once again basing his study primarily on 'terms of relationships', and on concepts like 'mother-right' and 'marriage-by-capture'. In the cases of both Granet and Wilkinson, Chinese systems of kinship are compared with those of simple hunters and agriculturalists, which the bulk of the Chinese had ceased to be for at least four thousand years, well before their European counterparts. Indeed it was only because of their long literary tradition that such studies could even be contemplated.

When Lévi-Strauss is talking about China and Trautmann about the Dravidian system, they are not of course discussing information that has been derived from the ethnographer's notebook. Lévi-Strauss is engaged in reconstructing ancient China and Trautmann ancient India, South India. In their different ways both are dealing with specific kinds of evidence to do with kinship terms and with marriage prohibitions, notions about the latter being sometimes derived from assumptions about the former and sometimes from normative statements. This kind of evidence requires a historical treatment such as Trautmann provides and other authors signally fail to do; but even in his case there is a tendency to identify terms with the wider system of family, marriage and kinship, on which historical evidence is so much more difficult to obtain.

My own focus of interest, theoretical and empirical, lies elsewhere. I want to look at some ethnographic studies which can provide a more comprehensive basis for analysing the pre-Revolutionary system, although they obviously require supplementation from other sources. Secondly I want to extend the facets of social life under consideration to take into account a wider range, especially as some, such as cousin marriage, that form the basis of earlier enquiries are certainly not the only ones relevant to the study of kinship and indeed they may be of relatively little significance in the particular societies under review. For example, if we look at the important work of Wolf and Huang, *Marriage and Adoption in China, 1845–1945* (1980), which is based not only on observation but on a very extensive analysis of demographic and historical records, we find no discussion of cross-cousin marriage at all and very little on lineages. One possibility is that this discrepancy results from the changes that have taken place in recent times. A second course is to cast doubt upon earlier reconstructions of the Granet, Lévi-Strauss type as well as the material on which they were based. Another possibility is that we are looking at regional variations. A fourth suggests that the discrepancy may be due to the particular foci of interest of the commentators or observers, leading us to modify the emphasis of certain of the basic ethnographic reports. For example, some of the theoretical aspects of Freedman's two major studies, *Lineage Organization in Southeastern China* (1958) and *Chinese Lineage and Society* (1966), were influenced by the relative strength of lineage ties in south-east China, the area around Hong Kong and adjacent to Taiwan, whereas in North China such ties were in certain ways less strong (Baker 1979:137).[1] More importantly they were influenced on the theoretical side by earlier studies of African lineages which in this context were both a source of strength and of weakness. A weakness from the standpoint of my general argument which is that in many ways Europe provides a more satisfactory basis of comparison for the domestic level of Asian kinship than Africa, let alone the native inhabitants of Australia or North America.

Freedman's first study of lineage organisation in China was based largely on secondary material, his earlier fieldwork having been undertaken primarily in Singapore. He perceived the strength of lineage ties as being indicated by the position of women who were regarded, even in major marriages, as incorporated in their husband's lineage in a way that cut them off from their natal kin. All of this was in accordance with a strongly patrilineal, Confucian model whereby women were seen as chattels transferred from one group to another.

The question of the incorporation of a woman in the husband's 'family' (whether lineage, kin or other group) is directly relevant to notions of 'the exchange of women in marriage' and to theoretical attempts to elucidate problems such as the differences in the cross-cultural incidence of divorce; some writers, for example, Gluckman, Leach, Fallers and I. M. Lewis, have seen full incorporation as meaning that divorce is impossible. It is the concept of incorporation I want first to examine in the context of traditional China because this society, together with early Rome, has been assumed by many writers (such as the anthropologists, Radcliffe-Brown and Fortes) to represent the extreme instance of patriliny, marked by the incorporation of a woman in the husband's kin group and the exclusion from her natal one.

First a general point. To speak of the exchange or transfer of *women*, except as a shorthand, overlooks the fact that such exchanges are rarely complete. The rights transferred, or brought into being, at marriage patently vary in different societies and in different forms of union, and these variations are obviously crucial to any discussion of the transfer of property at marriage, an issue that is raised by any consideration of dowry or bride-wealth. But are there any societies in which the transfer and hence the alienation in major marriages is ever complete in this way? Of course that is so in slave unions, possibly in some other cases, but here I am dealing primarily with the culturally dominant form. If no incorporation occurred with such marriages in China, then less 'extreme' instances must be open to yet more questioning.

A common view of traditional Chinese society is of one that places a strong emphasis on agnatic descent through males, while the females, their feet since Song times swaddled in early infancy so that work in the fields was virtually impossible (Levy 1966), are regarded as the pawns of men. The woman, it is often pointed out, does not inherit property; it is the man who has the obligation of supporting his parents in their old age and of perpetu-ating the worship of the ancestors, 'the continuity', as Hsu (1949) has called it, 'of incense and fire'. That at least was one very widespread view, ex-pressed for example in the early work of A. H. Smith, *Village Life in China* (1899), which although subtitled 'a study in sociology' is very much the product of a Protestant missionary. On the other hand, even writers with a similar background have taken a different view, and in a more anecdotal volume on *Home Life in China* (1914), I. T. Headland, a Professor at Peking University, presents a more positive picture of the role of Chinese women, even before the Revolution of 1911. A woman's property rights were stressed, her achievements emphasised. The situation was by no means unitary, either in interpretation or in fact.

Diversity and unity

Part of the difference between the two accounts is a matter of hierarchy; while Smith's observations were made largely at the village level, Head-land's experience lay among the upper strata of the urban bourgeoisie. At about the same time, two Chinese scholars themselves contributed to the discussion in a volume in the sociology series of the London School of Economics on *Village and Town Life* (Leong and Tao 1915), which while it condemned practices such as footbinding, saw women as firmly linked both to their natal and to their conjugal families, especially after the recent modifications in mourning roles. Longer-term structural reasons also led them to dispute the general view held of the Chinese family in the West. And a later picture drawn by a Chinese sociologist, Lin Yueh-hwa (1947), again stressed the contrast between these two views. In his introduction to that study Firth remarks: 'As against the common view of the Chinese woman as a suppressed being, subordinate to her menfolk and her mother-in-law in ways which render her almost a chattel, we are given here examples of a woman who has money of her own, investing in business; of sisters-in-law fighting beyond the control of their husbands' uncle; of a man being nagged by his own wife for defending his daughter-in-law; of a daughter-in-law . . . chasing her husband round the room with a knife . . .' (1947:xiii–xiv).

Of course, the situation with regard to women varied considerably in different parts of pre-Revolutionary China, both regionally and hierarchically. Nevertheless, to obtain an idea of the nature of marriage transactions I turn to specific accounts of particular regions undertaken by Chinese scholars. Before looking at these there are two further preliminary remarks that need to be made. My examples are in the first instance taken from the rural areas. But China was also a country of great cities at a time when much of Europe had little but small towns; and there existed a strong divide between town and country, between the 'mercantile' and the 'feudal', as well as an extensive hierarchical differentiation from an early period. Traditionally the Chinese saw their society as divided not only into a rural hierarchy based largely though by no means exclusively on agriculture but into scholars, artisans and merchants, plus a group of *declassé* consisting of criminals and those carrying out despised tasks (Fried 1953:211). Because of their differing relations to material and cultural resources, differences in the nature of the central relationships can be expected. This kind of differentiation is typical of the 'civilised', urbanised, societies of Eurasia where it is important to maintain and advance the position in the hierarchy of married daughters as well as of sons. These are societies that depend upon an elaborate agriculture, together with its concomitant artisanal activity and rural manufacturers, which produce the surplus required to sustain urban life with its more specialist activities and its mercantile exchanges. In these activities China was well advanced. Already in the classical age of the Han, slaves could own and deal in currency; both in town and country, money was used in the pursuit of subsistence and of profit (Fried 1953:220). The entrance of money and considerations of the profit and the loss into marriage transactions is not a function of the contact with industrial capitalism, as some have supposed; its roots go back to the Bronze Age societies of the early historical period and it is particularly associated with the gradual development of commerce, crafts, manufacture and 'proto-industrialisation', what others have called the 'petty capitalist mode of production' and seen as articulated with the feudal (Gates 1987a), or characterised as 'tributary' (E.

Wolf 1982), the area where Chinese historians have sought 'the sprouts of capitalism'.

So if we turn to the study of villages and concentrate on the agricultural sector, we must not forget the complexities, hierarchical, occupational and regional, of Chinese society as a whole, for this is at the root of our concern about making comparisons that are more appropriate to the material than those with societies with very different modes of production and communication. At the same time, despite the hierarchical, occupational and regional differences, a number of factors are common to marriage in China. In a recent paper (1985a), A. Wolf sees these as: (i) virilocal marriage (the major marriage model); (ii) male inheritance of the estate; (iii) similar 'affinal' ties, as illustrated in the role of the mother's brother; (iv) agnatic lineages. In the subsequent discussion, my own selection of common features lies at a more specific level. Some of these are related to the general type of socio-economic system, but others derive from the dominance of literate Han society and culture, both on the level of ritual and of law.

Throughout China, for example, the marriage ceremony displayed many similarities in the ceremonies as well as in the provision of gifts. So too the content of marital, affinal and kin relations, especially as expressed in mourning behaviour, in duties towards one's parents, and in the socio-cultural repertoire of mechanisms for continuing the direct line of descent, that is, adoption, concubinage and so forth. In the case of this repertoire, the incidence and character of practices differ in different areas but they fall within a range of interlinking possibilities; indeed I argue that it represents a 'selection' from a set of mechanisms found among a much larger set of societies, namely the major societies of Eurasia. But in some other respects similarities in social practice across this vast country can also be linked to the system of cultural transmission. At the local level the cultural penetration of standard texts was more in evidence than the political presence of the state. Common instruction was given in the wide network of local schools, often maintained for their members by lineage trusts (*yizhuang*), although other establishments were more openly available to the community as a whole. Of course not every child attended, although the need to keep farm or shop accounts was often a stimulus to send one son to be taught to read and write, quite apart from the reverence given to the academic profession and the opportunities it offered for individual and lineage advancement. At times the written word even played a part in the education of a minority of women, some of whom achieved literary fame during the later Han (25–220) and the Tang (626–907), yet earlier than the women authors of Heian Japan or troubadour Europe (Cartier 1986a:461; Bogin 1976).

The curriculum of schools was highly standardised because the students read precisely the same classics throughout the land; according to one nineteenth-century observer, 'there is probably no country in the world where there is so much uniformity in the standards of instruction, and in all its details, as in China' (A. H. Smith 1899:70). Instruction began with the Trimetrical Classic, composed some nine and a half centuries ago, which was learned by heart, the object of education being 'to pump the wisdom of the ancients into the minds of the moderns' (p. 91). At later stages of instruction many Confucian precepts got passed on in the same way. But national legislation too embodied norms of kinship behaviour which, while they were not always followed to the letter, played an important regulatory role. Thus the rules of mourning grades, less complicated than much practice (Baker 1979:113), were listed at length and became part of the reference system of families everywhere (Hoang 1915), even though significant differences existed. Again, the particular corporate form taken by many Chinese lineages may well have resulted from national legislation dating from the fourteenth century (Twitchett 1959). In these various ways divergence and diversity were held in check by political and educational pressures towards unity.

A Yangtze village

The first of the ethnographic studies I want to look at is Fei Hsiao-tung's classic account of a village in the Yangtze (p. Yangzi) Valley in his book *Peasant Life in China* (1939). Two aspects of this analysis may appear to support the idea of the incorporation of women. The first is what he calls 'adoptive marriage', the second, widow inheritance and disposal. Adoptive marriage was known here as *siaosiv*, the *sim-pua* of Taiwan, and referred to the little daughter-in-law, the 'fostered' infant brought into a household to marry a son or a hoped-for son. While there was no formal adoption, the degree of incorporation was considerable, not least at the psychological level where it depended on the early transfer of the child. On the other hand the transaction does not represent a 'sale' of the daughter in the usual sense of the word but rather a simplified and less expensive form of marriage.[2] For the gifts which the husband's family had to produce in an ordinary marriage were considerable; Fei estimates they amounted to 500 dollars, that is, the family income for a whole year. Moreover adult women were scarce since the cost of their upkeep as children, he claims, led to female infanticide. Certainly the deliberate infanticide or neglect of girl children was a feature of Chinese society, though this practice may have been related to the fact that daughters had claims upon resources at marriage as well as to the expense of feeding them. Indeed the relationship between infanticide and high dowries was noted by a Song official (Ebrey forthcoming:157), as was the alternative of postponing a woman's marriage. Such views lay behind the argument for sumptuary laws, which were instituted in the eleventh century.

According to Fei, it was especially among poor families (those prone to infanticide) and especially in times of economic depression that the forms of 'major' marriage gave ground to a union with the *siaosiv* (*xiaoxifur*, the 'foster daughter-in-law' marriage that A. Wolf for Taiwan calls 'minor' marriage to the *sim-pua* or adopted daughter-in-law). By this transaction the parents of a young son acquired an infant wife by paying reduced marriage payments, amounting to above 100 dollars; the boy's parents became the foster-parents of the girl and the future mother-in-law might even suckle her future daughter-in-law.

Of the married women in the village 17 per cent had been *siaosiv*; and of the unmarried girls 39 per cent were in this status, which was virtually one of incorporation; some of them did not even know their own parents. But this form of marriage was definitely of lower prestige than 'major marriages'; its disadvantages were openly recognised and Fei links its high frequency with the economic depression that existed at the time of his study, though the data from Taiwan discussed in chapter 4 show that in a somewhat different form it could be very widespread, since in the south-east it was certainly not linked only to 'crisis' situations.[3] Indeed A. Wolf notes that these marriages occurred among rich as well as poor families and there was a less radical separation as the children might continue to visit their parents, even if their emotional attachments were to their new households (1985c). Moreover famines, times of distress, seemed to diminish rather than increase the number of minor marriages, since parents then tended to retain a daughter who was more likely to be an only child. Even though there was a virtually complete transfer of rights over the girl, there was no 'sale' as such, a token payment of one yen being made at the marriage. Nor was the notion of sale prevalent in the major marriages where a direct dowry was paid. But payments were also made by the groom's family. While the verb might sometimes be used when 'brideprice' was transferred, the notion of sale or price is analytically inappropriate. But in a society that was so dominated by markets as China, the idiom of the market place was utilised for many other transactions (Skinner 1964), as in 'the sale of wives' in nineteenth-century England which was a way of publicly arranging a divorce (Menefee 1981): usage of the term may reflect its wider semantic field, covering a wider gamut of transactions, including some idea of compensation for the disposal of a daughter. Certainly in major marriages there appears nothing demeaning for the participants in such transactions and, according to A. Wolf (p.c.), a recent survey showed that old women in the South wanted to recount what had been given as 'brideprice' just as in the North they remembered every item in their dowry, a regional difference to which I will return.

But there was another aspect of major marriage which might give rise to the impression that a wife was incorporated into her husband's lineage. I refer here to the practice whereby the parents could marry off their son's widow; in this way a poor man might be taken into the house to breed sons to the dead man's name (*wannipon, huang ni bang*, or 'yellow muddy leg'), as in the system of widow-concubinage found among the Nuer of the southern Sudan (Evans-Pritchard 1951). Such a man not only took over the deceased's house but his name as well. Indeed as in other cases of marrying-in males, the institution represents an acquisition of conjugal rights over males roughly parallel to that over females in major marriages. Elsewhere, in upper groups, 'control' over the widow, which appears to be stronger in the North than in the South, took the form of forbidding any remarriage, but here it was a means whereby she was able to provide continuity for the estate of her conjugal family by bringing in a second husband from a poorer family.

The fate of the widow is one to which I will return in the next chapter. But any account of her role must take into consideration the fact that where there were no sons, she was the one capable of continuing her husband's line; to do so implied not so much his ownership of her as her rights in the control of the couple's property, as an account from early this century makes clear. 'In the ownership of property her rights are included in those of her husband, and a man cannot sell property without the consent of his wife. In case her husband is dead and she has no son, she succeeds to the property, or may sell it for her support, if she is poor' (Headland 1914:98). We can speak here of a conjugal fund in which each had rights of a different kind.

Despite a woman's lifetime commitment to her conjugal family, there were some circumstances in which as a widow in an upper family she might succeed in returning to her natal kin, and possibly in getting remarried from there (Lin 1947:133). But whatever the nature of this commitment, her kin continued to play a role in her affairs as well as in those of her offspring. While she had no obligation to support her parents (indeed, this duty was the obverse of her brother's right of inheritance), she might offer them periodic gifts and occasional financial help (Fei 1939:32). Her parents in turn continued to influence the course of her life, for the bond with their offspring was never entirely severed. The importance of the mother's role was emphasised at the birth of a child, for her behaviour was seen as influencing its personality. But at this time her own parents also 'share the tension' (p. 35) and shortly before the child was delivered, they offered their daughter a special kind of medicinal soup. During this critical period a mother moved in with her daughter for several days and performed various household tasks on her behalf.

After the first thirty days, during which an infant was believed to acquire a social personality, the *menyu (man yue*, child-reaching-full-month) or naming ceremony took place. As in many other societies, the young child was regarded as especially vulnerable to attack by evil forces; it was therefore given a false name (a name of abuse, says Fei) as a disguise (Baker 1979:29). When the child was shaved in confirmation of its change of status, this important ceremony was performed by its maternal uncle, the wife's brother, thus emphasising not only the indissolubility of the sibling bond but the importance of what Fortes has called complementary filiation, that is the relationship with non-agnatic relatives in a broadly patrilineal system. 'In actual life, interest is taken in a child by relatives both on the father's and mother's side' (Fei 1939:44), but the relation with the mother's brother is often especially strong.

The child keeps close contact with his relatives on his mother's side. His maternal grandmother comes to assist his mother in childbirth. The child will visit his maternal relatives many times a year. His maternal uncle has special obligations towards him. He . . . selects a name for the child; he escorts him when presenting him for the first time to his schoolmaster. He will present a valuable gift, ornament, or cash, when his sister's son gets married. On the child's side his maternal uncle is a protector against harsh treatment by his father. He can run to his maternal uncle in case of need. His maternal uncle will act as mediator in conflict between father and son. When property is divided among brothers, the maternal uncle is the formal judge. When the maternal uncle dies, his sister's children will mourn for him. (Fei 1939:86–7)

In economic affairs it was advisable for an adult man to maintain ties with his maternal family. In Taiwan, since the families tended to come from different villages, his *ch'in ch'i (qin qi)* might be free when he needed help with harvesting; they would come without expecting to be paid, but with the idea that sometime in future they too might need the same kind of aid (Gallin 1966:177).[4]

The question of the continuing ties of a woman with her natal group must not be confused with her position as wife; the two issues are related but not identical. Many commentators have spoken of the lowly status of a new bride in Chinese society. Fei writes of the discipline to which she was submitted in contrast to the relative freedom she enjoyed in her natal home; although she had to prepare all the meals, at table she took the lowest place and might not even be present. Her lowly position might drive her to flee to her mother for a spell, but a Chinese proverb ran 'Spilled water cannot be gathered up', so that no one outside her conjugal home could really help her. At bottom, it was said, she accepted this position as just, supported as it was by religious or sanctified beliefs (1939:46).

However correct this stereotype may be, her subordinate position was more the result of her status as a new bride than as a wife. If she succeeded in pleasing her mother-in-law, which she might do when she passed the silk-worm test of breeding and raising the worms, her lot was easier, for such activity was important to the social and economic position of the whole household. When she became a mother, her status improved still more.

Finally she herself became the dominant mother-in-law ruling her son's bride with the same rod of iron that had been applied to her.

While Chinese women, at least those from groups where their feet were bound, did not generally work in the fields, they were responsible for producing, spinning and weaving silk, not only for households but also for the market and to pay taxes. During the Tang period some areas paid their entire tax in silk cloth and considerable expansion occurred under the Song dynasty which gave rise to some workshop production (Gates 1987b; Li 1981). So it is wrong to see Chinese women as concerned only with reproduction and hence always ready to be handed over to another agnatic group who could make use of their procreative powers. They did produce in an important artisanal sector, but this fact is sometimes obscured in studies carried out after the introduction, first of cotton, then of mechanised manufacture in the second half of the nineteenth century, which changed the position in radical ways.

Nevertheless, control over a woman's sexual activity was strong. Premarital intercourse and adultery were condemned but, according to Fei, the expenses of marriage were such that a wife was not divorced for the latter reason alone. Indeed divorce was rare. A wife was unable to repudiate her husband as he could her, but she could run away. If she was treated too severely she might threaten to commit suicide; when this happened, her spirit was thought to revenge itself on her husband. In such a situation her own parents and brothers would seek redress on her behalf, 'sometimes even destroying part of her husband's house' (Fei 1939:49). Such a possibility clearly served as check upon the actions of both husband and mother-in-law, the relationship with the latter being especially full of tension.

Though of low status in some respects and at some periods of their lives, Yangtze women were high in others. They could hold property, which in rare instances included land, and this was transmitted to them *inter vivos*, usually at marriage, from the joint estate of their parents. Moreover most of the other marriage prestations coming from the groom's group were given to the bride for her dowry which, though it eventually came to form part of a joint fund, remained initially under her custody. The indirect element of the dowry was not 'compensation', not an 'economic transaction' (p. 43); it was considered as the 'private property of the woman and shared with her husband and children' (p. 61).[5] It was she who kept the keys to the boxes and cupboards in the marital room, thus emphasising the position of the new conjugal pair as a potentially discrete property-holding unit, which would eventually break away from the husband's family of orientation. When this split occurred the wife was often seen as the cause.[6] For the separation might create some friction because it meant dividing up the estate. If trouble arose, it was the husband's maternal uncle who stepped in and acted as mediator, again emphasising the continuing role played by such kin throughout a person's life (Lin 1947:123; Wolf 1985a).

A Yunnan village

The second study I want to consider is that of West Town in Yunnan, southwest China, based on fieldwork carried out between 1941 and 1943 by Francis L. K. Hsu and reported in his book *Under the Ancestors' Shadow* (1949). As in many other parts of the South, the inhabitants originally belonged to one of the 'minorities', that is, to the non-Han peoples who had been influenced by the Han cultural and political expansion that had occurred over many centuries but who maintained or developed certain practices of their own. Despite the Han influences, they still remain representative of 'minority' cultures in many ways. Unlike those in southeast China, the villages consisted of members of not one but several clans, possession of the same clan name being as elsewhere partly but not entirely a bar to marriage.

Marriage in West Town involved a long process of adjustment to change by all parties, beginning with a betrothal which might take place as early as six years of age. Early betrothal was especially characteristic of marriages that were 'given' by the kinship system, that is, of marriages between cross-cousins, particularly those to the mother's brother's daughter.[7] Exchange marriages, that is, a sister for a sister, were disapproved. Other unions required arrangements of a different kind, in which the role of the go-between was of great importance. Once the match had been organised by human hands, it had to have supernatural confirmation, which was obtained by recourse to a diviner; however since there was no limit to the numbers of specialists that could be consulted on this occasion, such confirmation was not in the end difficult to come by.

At the betrothal a small amount of money was sent to the bride together with the names of the betrothed written on a folder of red paper.[8] In addition there were certain presents, of sugar, tobacco, wine, sweetmeats and, say, 1,000 dollars (then worth about 15 American dollars). The major part of these gifts was used by the girl's family to provide a banquet, but they marked the beginning of a series of prestations to the bride's kin, two specifically of money and more in kind. In 1943, the average money gift was 10,000 dollars, plus 30,000 or more just before the wedding.[9]

In some cases the amount of money which passed in the period up to the marriage was subject to bargaining between the parties. The transfers from the groom's family did not constitute 'bridewealth' in the sense in which the word has been used in Africa, and certainly not a brideprice, although this is the name by which it is usually known. Once again, in major marriages, the image of sale was inappropriate because 'the money given by the boy's family is given supposedly to make up the girl's dowry' (p. 87). In other words the prestations received from the husband were used to establish a fund for the wife which she took with her into marriage. Part of the money might be retained by her parents but the bulk went with the bride. Unlike bridewealth proper, the prestations did not form part of a revolving fund used to supply sons with brides. Hsu's diagram (figure 1) illustrating the set of transactions involved in marriage, might suggest that, in return for gifts, the woman was incorporated in her husband's kin group.

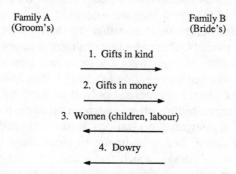

Figure 1 Marriage transactions in West Town

That would be an error of understanding since the objects were immediately returned, at least physically, to the group from which they originated. Hsu himself noted that 'In a patrilocal [virilocal] marriage most of the gifts come back to the man's family in the form of dowry'. A woman's endowment therefore included what I call an indirect dowry, that is, gifts 1 and 2 in figure 1, together with the direct dowry contributed by her natal family which it is at times difficult to distinguish. While a woman's dowry accompanied her to her new home and hence in that sense went back to the man's family, it would have been a largely redundant transaction unless the property was now seen as vested in the wife or in the couple itself. Even in the case of the portion of the prestation from the groom's family claimed by the bride's parents, the 'bridewealth' character was minimal, for what remained in their hands was largely consumed in banquets. So the economic advantage of the marriage transfers to the wife's family was negligible; yet that family had lost a pair of valuable hands (in the house rather than the fields), while the man's family had gained a pair, 'together with some part of the money it paid out and the possibility of getting working hands (children)' (1949:101).

A vivid illustration of the nature of marriage transactions at this period comes from the fictionalised account that Lin Yueh-hwa presents of his village in Fukien in the South. Here half the indirect dowry was sent by the groom's family at betrothal and half when the date of the wedding was fixed, the latter consisting largely of silks and other cloth to be used by the bride for her dresses. At the particular wedding described in the book twenty labourers were sent to carry the trousseau of the bride back to her new home. Included in one of the dressing cases was 'the dowry money which the groom's family had paid', wrapped in red paper (1947:40).

The wealth contributed to the bride and groom established their conjugal fund. 'All the gifts they received this day became their private property because for the first time now they were deemed capable of owning private possessions, where before their marriage all their goods and money had belonged to their parents. Their wedding was thus an important day in which trousseau, furniture and money were laid down as a foundation for a family of their own' (p. 47). Such a common fund was not necessarily set up when the marriage took place but emerged only after partition had taken place and the son had separated his property from that of his parents.

This analysis of marriage prestations is strengthened by Chung-min Chen's study of dowry and inheritance in rural areas in contemporary southwestern Taiwan (1985), which was mainly settled by families from Fukien. The dowry is there defined as those valuables transferred from the bride's natal family to the new conjugal unit, partly for joint use (e.g. domestic appliances) but mainly under the bride's control. It includes, quite specifically, what the parents provide, what the parents-in-law give and what she herself accumulates. Chen describes the sources of a woman's dowry as:

1 her family funds;
2 the 'brideprice' from the groom's family, the amount of which is linked to her own family's contribution (that is, the bride's parents do not demand a larger brideprice than they are prepared to provide out of family funds);
3 her personal savings; all unmarried women are now thought to be working for their dowry, but in fact the notion of a self-acquired dowry already existed in the Song period when one observer in the South noted that poor girls of fourteen and fifteen worked to earn their own dowry. (Ebrey forthcoming:27)

Moreover, dowry is seen as an aspect of the wider process of devolution; the daughters receive a portion at marriage (largely in movables), the sons at division, mostly consisting of patrimonial property. While her share is smaller, a woman ceases to have the same obligations to her parents that is carried by the sons on whose 'filial piety' they depend in their old age and which is offset by a preferential share of the family property.

Some endowment of sons as well as daughters takes place at marriage. Among the Hakka in the same region of Taiwan, it is at marriage 'that he exercises his first major claim on *jia (chia)* wealth, expressed as the *jia*'s endowment of the wedding ceremonies. These establish for him and his bride precisely the domestic semi-autonomy which has in it the potential for partition at some future time' (Cohen 1976:71–2). The division of the estate may occur when one of the sons is young, but even then he cannot assume control until marriage confirms him as jurally adult.

In discussing the gifts made before the wedding, Chen notes that when the kin of the groom visit the bride's family, clothing, jewellery and a small portion of the 'brideprice' is handed over, while the bride's family provides the groom with a new suit. 'A portion of the brideprice will go into the preparation of the dowry when the wedding takes place' (1985:118). In other words, the gifts do not stay with the bride's family at all, so there appears even less reason to call it 'brideprice' or even bridewealth than to refer to the suit of clothes as 'groomprice' or even 'groomwealth'.

At the 'second rite of engagement' the remainder of the 'brideprice' is handed over, and on the wedding day the bride is accompanied to the groom's house with her dowry publicly displayed. This endowment consists of items for her personal use, her trousseau together with her jewellery. 'In addition to the bride's trousseau, one can also find bedroom furnishings, living room furniture and some major appliances such as a refrigerator, television set, stereo console, sewing machine, bicycle and/or motorcycle' (p. 119). If the couple are to set up an independent hearth, kitchenware and cooking utensils are provided. Clearly these items are for the conjugal household rather than for the bride (or groom) individually, helping to set up a new property-owning unit and bringing about a change in the structure of domestic groups. One item that is not made public at this time is the 'private money' given to the bride and which remains under her sole control. Often she does not even tell her husband how much she has or whether she has anything at all.

The character and distribution of these wedding gifts emerges very clearly in Cohen's observations which were based on nineteen weddings in the Hakka village of Yen-Liao. On all these different occasions, he states, the 'bride and groom are the ultimate recipients of most wealth circulating within the wedding framework' (1976:164). The first and most important transaction takes place at the betrothal and passes from the groom's to the bride's family; in the 1960s a 'standard' amount was as high as NT$12,000, that is about US$400. Cohen observes that this 'fee is in no way a form of "brideprice", for its effect is to *partially* subsidize the wedding expenses later borne by the family of the bride; in most cases the dowry brought by the bride costs more than the betrothal money her family receives' (1976:165).[10]

What a bride brings with her at marriage, ostentatiously conveyed through the streets in a specially hired truck, makes up the largest of the wedding transactions. Like the betrothal gifts it consists of allocations to different parties, not to the bride alone. Part goes to the groom's family 'as a whole' and consists of household items such as a radio (or, since 1965, a television set), tables and chairs, an electric fan, a fluorescent lamp and may include farming equipment such as a rice-threshing machine. Part is for the room that has been allocated, decorated and furnished for the new couple by the groom's family, but the items may also include a bicycle or motorcycle (or even a car in the case of a wedding I myself attended in Shin-zu on 6 January 1986) and other items. These latter gifts, like the specific allocation of a new room (*xin-fang*) where the bed is set up and which becomes the couple's social space, constitutes an acknowledgement of their status as 'a property-owning unit' within the larger domestic group or kinship estate. From now on the husband is in a position to demand his 'share' of that estate but the bride too is established as an individual who can hold and dispose of her own wealth (p. 164). Like the groom she is the recipient of personal gifts of jewellery and clothes. But she receives the largest cash gift as 'dowry' from her natal family although she is given more money during other parts of the wedding ceremony, including some directly from her new in-laws, thus confirming her right to her own funds.

As elsewhere the exact amount of her *se-koi* or 'private money' (known in Mandarin as 'private room money') is often kept secret from her husband.[11] In a complex agnatic group, a wife is the only one to have her own individual cash, since her husband's earnings belong to the large family estate. Not only can this money be invested in productive enterprise such as the raising of pigs, but it can also be augmented by the proceeds of her labour outside the day-time hours she is expected to contribute to the household, just as her dowry could earlier be augmented by her own employment. For example, she is allocated a small plot where she grows the vegetables needed when it is her turn to prepare the meals; any surplus she is free to sell and keep the proceeds. In this respect her independence not only provides a focus for fission, but also, like any personal fund, for conflicts of interest over the allocation of time and labour to individual and common activities.

The private money is not always kept by the bride herself. She may ask a father or brother to manage it or request her husband to make specific investments on her behalf. Some may be placed with rotating grain associations, some loaned to individuals (who are usually close relatives), the interest on which is used to pay the biannual dues to the associations (Cohen 1976:180; Fei 1939:267–74). She may employ the income for personal expenditure, for helping her children or for further investment, even in land.[12] She may be pressed by her husband to allow his father to utilise the funds, pressure which is always bitterly resented. But it is not always resisted and as in Europe her dowry sometimes formed the initial capital for a business venture. In richer families she may also be given some of the husband's 'spending money' to add to her peculium. Such transfers indicate that in a broad sense both members of the conjugal group, the *fo* (that is, the Mandarin *fang*), have some rights in the 'private money' (Cohen 1976:183). However one widow who remarried, left her daughter behind but took her private money together with the contents of the 'new room'; in another case a widower held all the property in trust for the children of the marriage.[13] If a widower remarries, this may give rise to the problem of 'the second bed', *le deuxième lit*, that is, of the division of property between the children of two marriages. Partly for this reason, unions with widowers are not favoured by families with eligible daughters, so the brides of widowers tend to be of poorer circumstances, receiving the standard gifts but producing little by way of dowry or 'private money' themselves. Those are attributes of wealthier spouses.

The problems of the 'second bed' in eighteenth-century China are brilliantly laid out by Wang Hui-tsu (Mann forthcoming:336ff). Their recognition was quite explicit and their reduction to writing characteristically led to the expression of a critical attitude towards the imbalance in the treatment of men and women when a marriage ended by death. The Book of Rites declared that 'a match once made should never be broken'. In commenting upon this passage Yu argues in his essay, 'On chaste widows', that when one's spouse dies, one does not remarry. And that while the notion had been applied only to widows, it should be extended to widowers as well. A general 'principle' is thus elicited, or rather invented, from particular contexts. Moreover, the tendency to equal treatment, at least in writing, did not stop there. Of the eighteenth century, Mann observes how the classics stress not only obedience but the 'principle of equality or complementarity between husband and wife' which related to equality of rank and at times 'egalitarian' tendencies of a broader kind (Mann forthcoming:323 ff.). Wedding rituals express the bride's responsibilities and authority as well as her duties, recognising that she will one day take her mother-in-law's place in the family. 'The wedding is not [a case] for congratulations; it is [a case of] generations succeeding each other' (from the *Po Hu T'ung*).

Since this is the first reference to an important sub-theme of this account, let me emphasise one of the effects that writing has on the study and actuality of kinship. Indigenous commentators on the topic may bring out what they perceive as logical contradictions of this kind. Their writings may in turn influence the written code, which feeds back again on the total behavioural situation. But it is not simply a matter of establishing a new, agreed, set of norms. Complexity is built into a situation in ways that make the written historical record difficult to understand, even when one has access to written accounts of actual disputes. For example, Chinese law only recognised slavery for debt in a strictly limited way. But there was a clear contradiction between code and custom. 'Bien que de nombreux articles des Codes impliquent l'illégalité du statut servile, le rapport de servitude est néanmoins considéré comme un état de fait' (Cartier 1988:23). Such internal contradictions carry the potentiality of future changes.

Returning to marriage in West Town, we have seen that this was a gradual process, at least for a woman's first marriage. The emphasis on the difference between first and subsequent marriages is linked to the value placed on virginity, found in China as well as in India and the Near East. One facet of this emphasis relates to the control over property involved in marriage, hence to the wish to limit the partners to those of equal or better status; for a woman, pre-marital sex could lead to a bad marriage or to illegitimate children.[14] But here as elsewhere, a more general factor was present; for the first marriage is the one that detaches a woman socially and physically from her natal family and makes her into a potential mother. At the same time the emphasis on virginity was linked to the binding character of the betrothal; until recently in Western Europe betrothal involved many of the obligations of marriage as we see in the suits for breach of promise and in one of the central themes of Manzoni's famous novel, *I Promessi Sposi* (1822); as in medieval England, the betrothal effectively constituted marriage. And in West Town too until recently, a betrothal had been binding for both sexes. 'Men, of course, could resort to concubinage, but they had to take the first betrothed as the wife without exception' (Fei 1939:91).[15]

On the day before the girl was taken to her husband's house, her property was carried to her new home in a public parade that passed through the centre of town. The average set of possessions displayed on these occasions included two leather chests, three tables with drawers and cabinets, two red lacquered stools, and so on. The bride herself was borne aloft in a red sedan chair specially decorated with fertility symbols, dressed up as the Empress herself. She went as royalty, not as a chattel or a slave. The bridegroom, on the other hand, rode in a blue chair, with his father's sister in another. As in many other societies the bride was expected to show reluctance on leaving her own home and even to shed tears, whether she went willingly or not. When her party arrived at the groom's house, they were taken to the domestic shrines where they knelt and kowtowed, that is, paid their respects. On the day after the wedding the married sister of the bridegroom paid a visit to the temple of the local patron god on behalf of the newlyweds.

Two points about the wedding ceremony for a major marriage are especially relevant to the problems we are considering, first, the role of the father's sister in the sedan chair and, secondly, the role of the groom's sister after the marriage. The parts the sisters played indicate beyond doubt the continuing relationship of a married woman with her natal kin, members of which remain formal participants in critical performances; she is never cut off by incorporation in her husband's lineage.

The continuing role of a woman's family after her wedding, both for her and her descendants, is made equally clear in more recent accounts of wedding ceremonies in the village of Yen-liao in Taiwan. The day before the ceremony the groom makes a series of offerings in the ancestral halls of his mother's father and his paternal grandmother's father, emphasising the continuing ties of an individual to his matrilateral lineages and their ancestors (Cohen 1976:153).[16] This ceremony of kin ngoe-tsu ('honoring the matrilateral ancestors') is followed by a gift of pork to the bride's family (a-p'o-niouc, the maternal grandmother's pork) which is at once handed on to the appropriate agnatic group – or to its various branches if it has already divided. These offerings 'provide yet another context for the expression of ties of cognatic kinship' (p. 156), celebrating in the course of the marriage of a son and daughter all their four grandparents and their ancestors.[17] A further indication of these continuing relationships, if indeed one is needed, is the visit a bride makes to her home the day after the wedding. Accompanied by the groom, she brings offerings for the ancestral hall. Following this ceremony, the bride returns to cook her first meal for her new family. Twice more in the next few weeks she will return on less formal occasions when her natal family will 'host members and relatives of her new one' (p. 164). There is no evidence of any abrupt transfer of a woman, even between households, although she becomes more closely identified with her affinal home when she becomes the mother of children and provides for the continuity of family and lineage.

One reason a daughter has to leave and relinquish her position in her natal household is so that her brother can marry. Not only for reasons of exchange, as anthropologists usually claim, but for reasons of compatibility. Sisters cannot be accommodated in the house even as spinsters for they would not get on with their brothers' wives. The categorical separation represented an attempt to avoid tensions (Stockard 1988), for joint households do not adjust well to in-living spinsters It was this cohabitation that was seen as a cause of discord among the Jewish commentators of medieval Egypt (Goitein 1978: 173); indeed the right of a new wife to escape from just this situation was often included in the written marriage contracts. Laterally expanded households are therefore hardly consistent with high rates of spinsterhood, although in lineally extended ones the possibility remains since all fall under the authority of the father. But in general large households of this kind are dependent on the early marriage of daughters not only for demography and exchange but also for interpersonal reasons.

Demography and exchange tend to ignore the human agents or to treat them as objects. But even women of the royal clan were not simply elements in a system of women for women exchanges (Chaffee forthcoming:212) if this phrase is to be interpreted in the usual anthropological way, though political considerations were undoubtedly important. While parts of their marriage gifts which came from the government itself (the cash at least) rather than the parents might be sent to the husband's family as a kind of groomprice (or was it under the husband's control rather than in their possession?), much clearly remained with her. In any case imperial clans-women often entered marriage with 'considerable resources of their own' (p. 221), not only of wealth but also of titles as well as of honour. In other words, the devolution of property to 'branches of Heaven' was diverging, whether it came from parents or from the state. Part of the property transmitted was vested in daughters; hence women could be dishonoured by making an improper marriage, that is, to a non-elite family, although complaints arose about powerful merchants and great traders paying large sums to marry palace kin; that is, they provided an indirect dowry commensurate with the status of their bride. But some took a negative attitude towards such marriages with a royal clanswoman since they were worried about the potential power she wielded.

The continuity of the 'house'

There was another form of marriage in West Town in which a daughter's continuing relationship to her kin was crucial and in which the ties with her affines were often very weak. This union occurred in households that were without male progeny and was a method of providing the continuity of a specific line. The importance of 'continuing the incense smoke' at the ancestral shrines was a well-known feature of Chinese society whose individualised system of the cult of ancestors insists upon worship by direct descendants rather than by lineage collaterals. Direct continuity was necessary, at least for those who could afford it and who had something to pass on to future generations. But continuity is also a question of support for the living in their old age and of keeping up the farm or other enterprise as a going concern, that is, of management as well as heirship. So this aspect of the problem of continuity is not so much a matter for the larger kin group (which organises the transmission of common 'corporate' property and other cultural features) but for a particular line of inheritance, a 'family' line, a descent line rather than a descent group. Without specific descendants the dead will remain 'hungry ghosts', with no one to offer them succour. 'The discomfort of an heirless person extends beyond his or her worldly existence. After death, his spirit will suffer the fate of a vagabond, crushed by poverty and misery, and will be entirely dependent upon charity' (Hsu 1949:77).

The magnitude of the problem of heirlessness was considerable. The model embodied in most kinship charts and genealogies shows a proliferation (or at least a continuity) of children to each couple. The picture presented by such figures is far removed from the actual situation of real life. In his discussion of the 'family cycle' in India, Collver notes that 'despite the high rate of reproduction, 22 per cent of all parents reach the end of the reproductive period without a living son. About 30 per cent have only one son living and less than half experience the security of having two or more sons.' He argues that this insecurity means that 'the degree of independence enjoyed by the nuclear family in America would be out of the question in rural India'ˢ(1963:96). And in societies marked by such high fertility and high mortality, the other side of the coin is that the incidence of widowhood and orphanhood is much enhanced since death is more likely at all ages, not only in childhood. One function of extended kinship ties is to cater for just this fact.

Infertility apart (and sometimes this can reach high proportions as in Central Africa), the problem of male continuity (a son available to succeed his father at his death) is raised in nearly 40 per cent of the total number of households (Goody and Harrison 1973), because Collver's figures relate not to the survival of children at the death of the parents but at the end of the mother's reproductive period. Several standard 'solutions' are possible within the Chinese cultural repertoire, namely, polycoity (for example, concubinage), adoption or a filiacentric union (if there is a daughter). These 'solutions' are not limited to China but recur in other Eurasian societies, standing in a broad contrast to Africa.

While these three methods of providing continuity were all present in China, they varied both in importance and in detail in different communities. In West Town a man could make an additional union with a concubine (Baker 1979:35ff.). Of the cases of concubinage reported by Hsu, five out of eleven occurred where the first wife had had no children; moreover all these second partners came from afar (1949:252) so that there was no relationship between the families concerned. In these instances there was virtual incorporation, rather than cross-cutting affinity or continuing siblinghood. As R. Watson remarks, 'The language of gifts and reciprocity was used for wives; the idiom of the market place was used for concubines and maids' (forthcoming:375).

Secondly, there was adoption. A man without children could adopt either a stranger or a near agnate such as a brother's son, but in West Town the latter course was not favoured. This local form of adoption differed considerably from that advocated by Confucian teaching and practised in much of China in which only agnates could be adopted (McMullen 1975), or were at least given preference (Smith 1899). Elsewhere it is mainly the poorer groups that allow adoption outside the clan (Leong and Tao 1915:14), although Imperial Edicts, following Confucian doctrine, insisted that adoption should be inside. But local custom depended upon particular clan rules which in turn represented the result of a struggle between Han orthodoxy and regional practice, including the practices of minorities representing the pre-Han population. In Taiwan for example more adopted outside than in.

Adoption rarely took place unless there was property to pass on.[18] If a couple died childless and were the owners of property, Confucian norms dictated that a 'spare' son of a relative might be adopted as heir and as possessor of the spirit tablet of his adoptive father. In North China, the British magistrate Johnston remarked of occupied Weihaiwei at the beginning of this century that the mere fact of childlessness did not necessarily lead a man to adopt a son; 'it is childlessness combined with the ownership of property that induces him to do so' (1910:284). The last of a line would not usually bother to adopt purely for the sake of ancestor worship.

The fact is that the possession of property – especially landed property – is regarded in practice as an inseparable condition of the continuation of the ancestral rites. This theory is often expressed in the formula mei-yu ch'an-yeh mei-yu shên-chu – 'no ancestral property, no ancestral tablets'. If the spirits of the deceased ancestors have been so regardless of the interests of their descendants that they have allowed the family property to pass into the hands of strangers, it is thought that they have only themselves to blame if for them the smoke of incense no longer curls heavenward from the domestic altars. (p. 285)

The same point has been made by Ahern in her study of ancestor worship in Taiwan (1981). But some have argued that even adoption does not necessarily imply a man's total incorporation into the ancestral lineage of his new household; the adopted son, it is said, may worship the dead man as a benefactor rather than an ancestor, a benefactor who has treated him 'as a son' and is therefore to be treated 'as a father'. Not everyone's tablet is necessarily worshipped as an ancestor. In filiacentric unions a man may be the custodian of two tablets, that of his own father and that of his wife's. Clearly he does not completely give up one status in acquiring another. But neither does he approach both tablets in quite the same way, as a son which implies a unique bond.

The decision to adopt and the choice of an heir did not lie in the hands of the property-holder alone, for, as elsewhere, a childless old man was often 'the object of most tender solicitude on the part of brothers and cousins with large families' (Johnston 1910:285). They would urge upon him the necessity to adopt from among their number and if his choice did not meet with general approval, then it would not be properly attested by the relatives and might be treated as null and void. 'Adoption, no less than the sale of land, is an affair not of the individual but of the family' (p. 286).

Johnston reproduced a document from Weihaiwei sealing a family division and mentioning three sons, the second of whom had been '"adopted out" to another branch of the family' (p. 151); in this case the division lay between the other two branches alone, the departing son being recognised but excluded. In the case of an only son, his death sometimes required a 'dead marriage' with a deceased girl arranged by 'ghostly go-betweens'. Following this union, a son, 'probably a young nephew', would then be adopted to inherit the man's share of the family property and to carry on the ancestral rites (pp. 203–5). In one instance of a similar kind a widow sold her jewellery to assist her husband's younger brother in getting married. When a boy was born, she declared her husband was no longer childless and then committed suicide. She had fulfilled her duty by enabling the brother to make a marriage, a kind of 'ghost marriage', that would possibly provide an heir for the dead as well as for the living. If there were two sons of such a union, one would become heir of the deceased; if there was only one, he would be heir to both (p. 231).

Johnston's material on Weihaiwei refers to the opening years of the century, Hsu's to the 1940s, but the practice is still very much alive in Taiwan. Cohen (1976) describes four procedures for male adoption in the Hakka village of Yen-liao. The first was kidnapping from enemy groups, the second straightforward purchase, the third the adoption of agnates (*kuo-fang* (*quo-fang*) 'to pass from one patrilineal segment to another'),[19] and lastly what he calls 'affinal adoption', that is, the adoption of the child into its mother's home, or matrilateral adoption;[20] in this latter case a girl may marry out on the explicit understanding that a son will be returned.

In those cases where there were only daughters, the third possible mechanism of continuity, which was much more popular in West Town, consisted of an alternative form of marriage that involved recruitment to the family and lineage through the woman rather than through the man; the husband came to live with his wife rather than vice versa. This institution of the 'calling in son-in-law', which we have already encountered in the Yangtze valley, may sometimes be linked to a system of complex agnatic lineages; the offspring are recruited to the mother's patronymic group by a secondary form of recruitment, namely matrifilial, forming an attached lineage. But its importance in Eurasia lies mainly in the domestic domain, as a strategy of heirship or management, and it is also found in the cognatic societies of Europe where lineages are absent but where some form of direct transmission is preferred and where it is also used as a mode of recruiting labour on the farm, particularly in pastoral communities which are especially subject to problems of viability, that is, of striking a balance between labour and livestock (Pehrson 1957; Stenning 1958). And it may also be practised for other purposes, as in Japan to recruit a future leader of an *iemoto* or professional group. In Japan and in parts of Taiwan, as in other parts of Europe and Asia, such marriages are found in the absence of lineages. They occur where males would normally dictate the locus of a marriage, where the continuity of the productive enterprise depends upon men rather than women, but where it is a woman who, in the absence of brothers, is the recipient or at least the agent for the transmission of parental property.

This form of marriage, found throughout North Asia (at least as second marriages), is sometimes discussed in relation to a model of a strict patriarchal (or patrilineal) system with which it clearly does not fit. The institution is therefore perceived as an anomaly, even as a survival 'propre au régime du matriarcat' (Schram 1932:117) or of a matrilineal system. In fact it exists in its own right as part of 'the women's property complex', that is, in those societies where women (especially as heiresses but also in other circumstances) can be used to attract a husband with the prospect of an inheritance or other benefits. It is just within the bounds of possibility that the propensity to enter into such marriages could be related to the earlier existence of matrilineal systems in the area. The 'cultural historical' hypothesis does not directly conflict with a structural one but it is clear that firm and detailed evidence about particular cases is needed to support any assumption of a developmental kind, given the widespread connection of these mechanisms of continuity with the system of direct lineal inheritance and male continuity. There was little or no fraternal transmission of property (even when this system was used for succession to office) and hence no inheritance by a brother's son unless that individual were to be adopted. When there were sons, they should receive equal shares, though a special portion might be put aside for the eldest in view of his extra responsibilities in both earthly and supernatural affairs.

These unions with in-coming males ran counter to the dominant pattern of post-marital residence (since they were uxorilocal instead of virilocal) as well as to the dominant system of filiation (since the children were linked maternally instead of paternally). As I have remarked, in West Town *ju chei (ru zhui)* marriages were very much more common than in many parts of China, being estimated to account for more than 30 per cent of all unions; similar figures are given by Barclay (1954) and Wolf and Huang (1980) for Taiwan. Hsu claims there was little status difference between the two forms, perhaps an indication of 'minority' values, whereas in other parts of China the husband and wife in such a union were often unable to raise their voices in community affairs.[21] But even in West Town, 'only a poor fellow' would marry in such a way, though it was sometimes the avenue to riches. Indeed such marriages, which were usually arranged in youth, were described by one informant as 'selling one's family name' (1949:99–100). In any case they were secondary from an analytic standpoint in that they took place within a framework of patronymic groups, of agnatic ancestor worship, of dominantly virilocal residence, and in quite specific circumstances, where there were no available male siblings.

Filiacentric marriage occurred not only in farming families but when a shop assistant married the boss' daughter, and especially in cases where the two families had known each other for a long time. But as in any other marriage, diviners and go-betweens were employed even though the gifts transacted were only two in number, consisting of sugar lumps and tobacco which circulated in the opposite direction to the affinal prestations in an ordinary union, that is, from the family of the bride to that of the groom. In the course of the wedding ceremony it was the groom not the bride who was introduced to the family shrine. No money passed hands but a feast was prepared and the boy took on the name of his father-in-law, although significantly he also retained a reference to his parental clan.

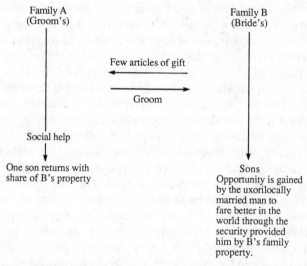

Figure 2 Transactions in a filiacentric marriage, West Town

Hsu wrote of the husband as obtaining 'full membership' of his wife's clan, but here again the transfer of rights, which took the opposite direction to that of an ordinary marriage (since it was mainly rights over a man that were acquired), was no more complete than in the case of a woman. If the husband begat more than one son, one of them had to return to his natal home with part of the property he had helped to accumulate, property which some might regard as delayed groomwealth or even groomprice. In this way a poor family could increase its wealth by means of a marriage that was of mutual advantage to both parties. It is the contractual element that stands out in many Taiwanese examples of such unions where everything is negotiable rather than following a fixed pattern. There is a contract but effectively no ritual, no wedding ceremony as such but only a simple marriage, with most wives being already pregnant when the marriage was registered.

Another form of this union occurred when a widow arranged for her daughter to get married at home in order to provide herself with companionship in old age, since widow remarriage itself was frowned upon. While such remarriages were used extensively in Africa as a mechanism of continuity, especially in the shape of the levirate, they were rarely employed in China. When they did occur, the prestations involved went to the family of the first husband, not to the woman's natal home. The widow's parents themselves might try to stop her entering into such a shameful union, though they could usually be pacified with a share of the payments that were made.

The attitude to the remarriage of women points to the very close social identification of those who entered upon a conjugal union, although it was the identification of one woman with a man rather than vice versa. To marry a woman whose husband was still alive was considered wrong and this stress on a woman's perpetual monogamy was one aspect of the high degree of individualisation of marital unions. A counterpart of the Hindu *sati* was found in the formal suicide of childless widows in Fujian (Fukien), Southeast China in the sixteenth, seventeenth and eighteenth centuries, which constituted a 'demonstration of devotion to the husband and concern for chastity' that 'excited awe and admiration' (Naquin and Rawski 1987:173). The ban on remarriage, of which this was an extreme manifestation, was connected with monogamy (or with very limited polygyny) in other ways. Widespread polygyny as found today in Africa, works mainly because of the longer span of married life experienced by women as compared to men; not only can both widows and widowers remarry, but there is a high differential age of marriage (DMA) between men and women. For example according to the post-enumeration study of 1960 in Ghana, the average age of marriage for women was 17–18 and for men 24–25, a seven-year gap. When we talk of a late age of marriage in Europe, we refer to a late age of marriage for both sexes but with a further delay of two years or so for men. In Africa it is the greater differential that allows a high rate of polygyny (and vice versa) since it means that the married life of women is considerably longer than that of men.

In China on the other hand, while women and men generally married early, polygyny and the remarriage of widows was rare, at least in upper groups. One reason behind what can be seen as this individualisation, permanence and unrepeatability of the conjugal relationships of women, and to a lesser extent of men, was the fact that each marriage involved a re-arrangement of property, an allocation of wealth to the wife (and daughter) or to the husband in the case of filiacentric marriage. For in high status, virilocal, unions, that is, in major marriages, a woman not only received some endowment, indirectly as well as directly, but acquired the right to be maintained from the estate at her husband's death, without having to undertake a leviratic marriage to his brother or to another close agnate. The dowry carried with it an implied dower, a promise of perpetual support as well as a commitment to perpetual monogamy.

West Town is situated on the margins of Han culture, and some of the features it displays are more characteristic of the less sinicised areas than they are of the centres of Han domination, the former tending to be in the South and Southwest, the latter in the North. The extensive resort to filiacentric unions is associated with those areas in which the Han made contact with non-Han peoples whose institutions often appear to have been markedly matrilineal (Wolf 1985a). Nevertheless, the repertoire of practices in which we are interested were certainly found in other parts of China, although in different forms. In Shantung (Shandong) such unions were only entered into as second marriages, so that perhaps greater use was made of adoption as a means of continuing the line.

In this opening chapter on the pre-Revolutionary Chinese family I have looked at the content and meaning of marriage transactions as well as at the alternative forms of continuing a family that are reported in ethnographic sources. I have tried to emphasise that in major marriage at least, and usually in other forms, there was never complete incorporation. In the first place a wife continued to rely on her natal kin if her marriage ran into severe difficulties. They in turn did not cede all their rights and duties. Secondly, a woman's position was not negligible even with regard to property, although she did not often receive landed property from males.[22] In China, as elsewhere, land is never just another good, commodity or item of exchange or transfer; it possesses different qualities and is subject to different rules from movables (Cartier 1988:26). The unwillingness to transfer land to women is clearly related to its role in production and as providing a territorial base for the males in a system of dominantly virilocal marriage and especially in the framework of a patrilineage organisation. Thirdly, her kin retained an interest in the children of her marriage and vice versa. If full incorporation had taken place, involving alienation of the bride from her natal kin, as is the case with slave marriages and to a somewhat lesser extent with the more radical form of the minor union described by A. Wolf for Taiwan, a man would have neither mother's brother nor yet sister's son. Fourthly, a woman could continue her natal line by means of a 'small' union; this is the *ju chei* marriage of West Town, the filiacentric (or uxorilocal) marriage within a generally virilocal system.[23] A similar kind of marriage in the Yangtze village of Kaihsienkung was called *lendiugoxofen*, meaning 'to attach two flowery flags on the ancestral shrines of both Chia ["houses"]' (Fei 1939:71).[24] If a man had no sons, then the parents of his daughter's betrothed might be asked if they would allow one child of that union to take her father's name and become his heir. In both these forms of marriage (and Wolf and Huang give examples of a variety of other such arrangements) the male and female members of a family line acquire rights in men as well as in women. In this perspective it is necessary to be careful about the interpretation of the comment, reported from the overseas Chinese in Singapore but widespread among males elsewhere, that women are 'goods on which one loses'. They were certainly not chattels to be 'sold' at marriage. For the so-called 'bride-price' had in fact little or nothing to do with sale, not yet with bridewealth as found in Africa. It went largely to the wife.[25] Most of the marriage presta-tions from the groom's family formed part of the bride's dowry which also included gifts to the bride from her parents (Fei 1939:43). In a major marriage, at least among those who held property, women too were prop-erty holders; the girl received both a direct and an indirect dowry, the former involving, among other things, the pre-mortem devolution of property.[26] Moreover on entering into a marriage she acquired a right to claim mainten-ance for her entire life: continued residence in the husband's home could be looked upon as a right as much as a duty which could provide a widow with a great deal of power and authority (Baker 1979:22), a power that is exempli-fied by the role of Dowager Empress on the political level. The acquisition of those rights involves the abandonment of others. In a book whose strong criticisms of Chinese marriage show an absence of sympathy, the missionary Smith remarked that the wife could hardly return to her natal home as there is 'no provision for her support' (1899:289), this being a matter for the family whose children she has born and raised.

There is one further point to remember about marriage in traditional Chinese society; it was basically monogamous in the sense that a man contracted a full marital union with only one fertile wife. He might enter into secondary unions with other women whom we may call concubines, remem-bering that the status was a legal one but always inferior to that of a wife; indeed the law prescribed ninety strokes for those who raised the concubine to the position of wife (Baker 1979:36), while a proverb prudently coun-selled husbands: 'if your wife is against it, do not take a concubine', for otherwise the relationship would be one of 'sipping vinegar' (Smith 1899:300).

A man's preferred heir was a son by his first wife and inheritance was lineal rather than lateral; the brother's children became heirs only if they were adopted. But the inheritance line was even narrower than this suggests because joint resources were confined not simply within the family but within the offspring of one couple; that is to say, the property that a woman brought and over which she acquired some rights went to her children alone, not to those of any other sexual partner. The core groupings of the kinship system were thus very small. Even as work groups, 'grand families' (extended families) split up into elementary or expanded families. While siblings might live together in the same house, they rarely appeared to work together; unless he was an only son, a man set up on his own soon after marriage (Fei 1939:66ff.) At this stage the farming group was split, even when co-residence continued and even when the estate had not been formally divided by a partition contract. In many African societies such fission often occurs between groups of maternally related brothers (e.g. Fortes 1949; Goody 1958); in China it was usually individuals on their own.

To return to the opening discussion, if the treatment of the widow is taken as indicating incorporation (as Gluckman, Leach and others have suggested), then its use as a variable in explaining differences in rates of divorce appears to involve a measure of circularity. In any case the idea of an act or process that breaks off relations with one's existing family, an idea that is explicit in some versions of exchangist interpretations of marriage (where women are exchanged, even sold, as objects, for objects), is a feature of some forms of adoption, of slavery (though kinship here is not usually a central issue), possibly of types of minor marriage in the South, but it was not a feature of 'major marriages' in China as a whole. Not only did the wife herself become a holder of rights at marriage (in property as in other ways), but as a daughter she maintained relations with her natal kin as well as gradually acquiring authority in her conjugal family, as a mother, as a mother-in-law and especially as a widow. Her position was neither simple nor static, but changed during her lifetime.

3

The lineage and the conjugal fund

This chapter aims to deal with two main topics, one analytical, the other substantive. First, I want to look at how the analyses of marriage presented in the field studies of Fei and Hsu, which were carried out before the lineage became such a dominating concept in anthropology, should modify our view of the 'exchange of women' between lineages in Chinese society and how such lineages themselves differ substantially from the African model, at least in the South, in ways that are related to the workings of domestic groups.

The second, related, topic is how to reconcile or oppose the notions of the lineage in China with that of the conjugal fund, actual or potential, established at marriage, a fund whose existence is critical in the break-up not of the lineage itself, which has its own corporate estates, but of the residential, cooperative and property-owning groups that operate at the domestic level. In other words I want to examine the articulation of the agnatic lineage with the bilateral family, especially at the level of domestic groups.

Patriliny, widowhood and divorce

I have pointed to the difficulties that arise if we try to view Chinese or any other kinship institutions purely within the framework of patrilineal (or alternatively matrilineal) ties alone. For we then run into problems not only at the general level of the cognatic bonds generated in the elementary family (giving rise to what Fortes called 'complementary filiation') but also more specifically. For in Asia, in contrast to Africa, daughters as well as sons often receive a parental endowment which makes the retention of property within the lineage difficult if not impossible, as does the priority in inheritance given to brotherless daughters in preference to more distant male members of the lineage.

Such practices are sometimes seen as inconsistent with the 'patrilineal' nature of Chinese society and therefore as remnants from the past when

52

stricter, unilineal, rules obtained. I have earlier referred to Schram's view of the practice of the appointed daughter which he sees as harking back to a 'régime du matriarcat'. Such formulations have an old-fashioned, nineteenth-century ring about them, but both for southern China and for southern India, hypotheses that link contemporary institutions to earlier matrilineal systems continue to be put forward. Given the long-term persistence of certain aspects of kinship, historical explanations of this general kind must always remain a possibility. They are not contradictory to structural ones. On the other hand they need to be historical and not pseudo-historical. In the absence of documentary testimony, we need to look very carefully to see whether the presence of these institutions is not capable of more adequate explanations based on assumptions that are less open to question and more easy to test.

The analytic problems to which such ideas give rise are illustrated in another section of Father Schram's account of marriage among the T'ou-jen Manchus of Gansu to the north of China. Of this group he writes 'Le bru est incorporé dans la famille de son mari ... La famille de la mari l'ayant achetée, elle est devenue sa propriété, sa famille d'origine n'a plus de droits sur elle' (1932:82). So it is with surprise that the author notes the long and frequent visits that the bride makes back to her natal home, together with her husband and children. In any case the absurdity of the notion of this marriage as a sale comes out clearly from a glance at the accompanying prestations which pass in both directions, largely to the bride but also to the groom. In rich families the parental gifts to the bride may even include some land which the husband has to cultivate and give the produce to his wife (pp. 47–8). As among the Mongols and in Taiwan, it is land over which the wife's family retains the ultimate rights.

The same kind of assumption lies behind other uses of the terms brideprice and incorporation, and they have been promoted, in some measure, by applications of the analysis of lineage systems to Chinese society, or rather from a failure to appreciate that different notions of 'belonging' (for example, notions of 'descent' or 'filiation') may operate at different levels of social organisation and in different contexts. That is to say, their relevance is contextual within a particular society. But it is also very different between societies. The presence of a genealogical structure of a unilineal kind signifies little in itself. So that an attempt to reduce our understanding to a common set of 'principles' or to an underlying 'structure' may inhibit rather than advance the analytic process.

Let me turn to the first main theme of this chapter. Both in the introduction and in the previous chapter, I have criticised the idea of certain scholars that 'normal' marriage involves the full incorporation of the wife into the family or lineage of the husband. The idea was given a more adequate theoretical formulation in the first of two volumes by Maurice Freedman on lineage organisation in China (1958). The work was seminal in many respects. But it sometimes relied on a concept of the lineage as an all-encompassing, box-like structure between which individuals, especially women at marriage, were moved 'bodily' from one to the other, a view which was equally consistent with certain kinds of descentist and alliance approaches to the enquiry into the nature of kin groups and marriage.

Freedman's view of the importance of the lineage at the domestic level in southeast China and the related notion of 'incorporation' rested on three main features, the giving of brideprice, the fate of the widow and the absence of divorce. The previous chapter has attempted to re-examine the appropriateness of the notions of brideprice and sale to Chinese marriage and found them wanting. Although I referred mainly to earlier examples of the employment of the ideas of incorporation, brideprice and sale by scholars of China, similar usages still continue. For example, Baker speaks of the price paid for a bride (1979:127) and while he puts brideprice in parenthesis and argues that the girl was 'not sold completely away from the control and care of her natal family', he does suggest that the 'bride-price might be seen as the purchase of the girl's reproductive labour and ritual services rather than as outright purchase of her person' (pp. 127–8). The formula is more acceptable. But given the usual destination of the 'brideprice', even this qualified use of the concept seems out of place. So too, I would argue, with the notion of incorporation in relation to widowhood and divorce.

In his study of lineage organisation in southeast China (1958), Freedman uses the fate of the widow as a measure of her absorption into the husband's kin group. According to the ideals of gentry behaviour a widow did not remarry. If she did choose to take another husband or had one provided for her (as seems sometimes to have been the case among poorer families), certain rights over her continued to lie with her original affines. None of them could marry her because of a law of the land against the levirate (though this was found among the Manchu) and the inheritance of widows (though this practice was found, as in India, among 'lower' groups). Widow remarriage was therefore subject to incest prohibitions among affines; this fact, Freedman argues, shows the extent to which the woman had been incorporated in the husband's group, that is, had been turned into a permanent sister. But we have seen that precisely the same argument concerning incorporation was put forward by Gluckman and others for the levirate, the obligation to marry (not to forgo) widows within the group and to breed children to the dead man's name, the very opposite of what we find in China; that is to say, the strength of the lineage is seen as lying in the fact that a woman is made a permanent wife rather than a permanent sister. The argument works equally well both ways. On the other hand, its weakness becomes clear when we examine the ethnographic situation in more detail. Van der Valk (1956) speaks of the 'outright buying' of wives in Fukien (Fujien) where the husband could subsequently 'sell' her. But under the Qing code rights of disposal in remarriage reverted to her natal kin if there were no competent survivors in her husband's family. Code reflected existing custom rather than innovative law. In many parts of Fukien, it was the natal family that in fact arranged a second marriage and received the customary gifts. Freedman concludes that 'the evidence from Fukien . . . is not all of one piece, but generally it seems to indicate that the passage of brideprice gave those who paid it very wide and continuous control over women' (1958:31–2).

A degree of control over the widow certainly existed, especially in the North, and some bereaved women had to stay and marry outsiders (rather than affines) to produce an heir. But where either this directed remarriage or the inheritance of widows existed, as in the Yangtze village studied by Fei, it must be seen in the context of those other institutions that ensure the perpetuation of a specific line rather than as an index of the incorporation or even the enslavement of women. For women were essential to the continuity of the family in a variety of ways, not only as mothers of their husband's children (real or fictive) in their conjugal family but sometimes in their own natal groups. The first alternative, as reproducer for the husband's family, did not negate all ties with the natal one though marriage entailed the radical transfer (not the sale) of procreative rights that Baker points out. Freedman recognises this general point when he speaks of the incomplete alienation of women. In the Yangtze case, a wife retained her own surname, mourned for her own parents, and most importantly, provided a link between families and lineages which was of much greater effectiveness than if she had been the subject of a simple exchange. Widow remarriage of the type described for the Yangtze village was an exception to the general practice, at least at the higher levels where widows normally stayed in the house of their late husband. This course of action was not always easy for a young woman when no partition of the property had taken place, as we see from Lin's account of the fate of the widow Huilan. She wept, screamed and threatened suicide until she was allowed to return to her parent's home from whence she remarried, even though her father-in-law was convinced her departure would bring disgrace upon his house (1947:92, 101, 133).

For older women the situation was different, both from the customary and from the legal points of view. If a widow had no adult sons, she succeeded to her husband's share of the patrimony. According to Waltner, this control was not 'true inheritance but rather the result of the concept that a married couple formed one legal unit' (1981:132). The woman represented 'the joint legal personality of the couple', although she could neither sell that property nor take it with her into a new marriage. But while the widow's control was restricted, it nevertheless grew out of her participation in the conjugal fund established apart, if not completely separately, from that of her in-laws. Before partition her dowry remained under her control; afterwards it was merged with that of her husband. If she had no sons, the control she exercised as a widow could be very extensive, unless she left to remarry; normally in upper groups she could only remarry if she brought the husband into her affinal home (Waltner 1981). For she had given up claims on her natal family in return for perpetual maintenance out of her own and her husband's property. If the 'true inheritance', which is said to have been absent, implies complete control by a single individual, then that is a very rare feature of pre-industrial societies, or indeed of any societies at all. Familial and community constraints are attached to all property, and it is a fiction of Western jurisprudence that claims otherwise.

The lineage's control over a widow seems to have been stronger in the North, where it could even take over half her property. Since little resort was made to filiacentric unions, women had a smaller role to play as holders of property and the lineages may have had a greater measure of a certain kind of solidarity (A. Wolf 1985a). Whereas in the South, the existence of property-holding corporations meant that a stronger distinction was drawn between conjugal family and lineage.

In the South, as we have seen, Freedman sees the ban on the inheritance of widows and the rarity of divorce as indices of the incorporation of a bride, 'the completeness with which she was received'; she passes from being a jural minor as a daughter to becoming a jural minor as a wife, even though later on as a widow she might 'control the affairs of a large household' (1966:56).[1] The evidence suggests that women's control was fundamental, especially as a mother and widow. Moreover their independence was sometimes greater than this account would suggest, for women might reject widowhood or even marriage itself, and break away from their affinal ties. Yang's description of Nanching (Nanjing) shows one adult woman in six living in an 'old maid house' (1945), and while such refuges were not widespread in the country at large, in certain areas of the South they were not uncommon. These houses represented a neutral home for spinsters or for married women who had been alienated first from their natal homes by marriage and then from their conjugal ones by widowhood or separation. Indeed if a woman went back to her natal home, she might seek to die in an 'old maid house' because her spirit could return to such a place which had its own tablets, altars and sacrifices for the dead women (Freedman 1966:56).[2]

In pre-Revolutionary China women were often spoken of as having roles that were defined purely by marriage. But other reports point to the existence of various kinds of 'sisterhood' in the Shunde county of Kwangtung

(Guandong), under such names as 'All-pure', 'Never-to-be-married'. The members of these groups swore to avoid marriage which they believed to be 'miserable and unholy' (Smith 1899:287). Smith saw their very existence as an index of the terrible fate awaiting the Chinese bride but we also need to take into account the more positively motivated sisterhoods of Buddhist nuns who gave up the possibility of marrying for religious reasons, just as prostitutes, whose presence was pervasive in urban circles (Hershatter forthcoming; R. Watson forthcoming), did not marry, or married late, for occupational ones. But there are similar Vegetarian Halls of a sectarian kind in contemporary Hong Kong, belonging to 'The Way of Former Heaven Sect', which are particularly popular with unattached women, especially working and retired domestic servants. As in Nanking such halls are organised on the basis of pseudo-kinship, practise 'ancestor' worship and provide tablets for the residents when they die (Topley and Hayes 1968). These institutions were already established in Kwangtung during the mid nineteenth century, especially where silk manufacture had given women workers considerable economic independence; numbers of women 'either refused to marry or, having married, refused to live with their husbands . . . Typically they organised themselves into sisterhoods', took an oath never to wed and went through quasi-marriage rituals (Topley 1975:67).

A recent study by Stockard (1988) of the Kwangtung (Canton) delta has thrown more light on these related institutions of 'sisterhood'. Among the silkworkers of that area a form of delayed transfer marriage, of major marriage, existed among all social classes, the 'bridedaughters' visiting their husbands at major festivals but remaining to work with their natal families for three to six years until they joined their husbands at the time they were about to give birth. In the same area are found not only the type of sisterhood reported by Smith, but Girls' Houses (*neuihjai nguk*) to which unmarried girls went to live or to take their evening meals. The members were sometimes silkworkers who had turned delayed transfer marriage into permanent separation, buying themselves out of a residential union with their husbands by providing girls formerly sold or pawned as domestic servants or *mui tsai* to be secondary brides in a 'compensation marriage'. Such secondary brides are paid for out of the earnings of these non-resident wives, who retain the right to have their husband's lineage hall act as 'host' for their ancestral tablet when they die. On joining a sisterhood a first wife might also buy a concubine who would go and live with her husband and bear children on her behalf. And it is people from this same area who are recruited into the contemporary sisterhoods in Hong Kong described by Topley. Spinsterhood is closely related to the opportunities for social and economic independence that wage-labour and delayed marriage provide, in addition to certain gains that may accrue to her natal family. Delayed marriage also exists among agricultural communities in the region where women stay on under favourable economic conditions to help their parents and to save for their own future, savings which remain firmly under their own control and do not form part of the official dowry. Nor is the institution coincidental in time or space with the introduction and distribution of silk filiatures since records show that it had a long history in Kwangtung (Siu, 1989a), a region that saw the Han from the North coming into contact with the local non-Han peoples of the Pearl River Delta. The delayed marriage bears some resemblances to the widespread institution of betrothal in Eurasia, which was itself seen as having the same binding force as marriage, and sometimes as even permitting intercourse itself. In India, a bride only joined her husband after 'marriage', which was indeed very early. In medieval Jewish practice, the betrothal was in effect a marriage (by money, by writ and by intercourse), but co-residence was again delayed; bride and groom had the status of man and wife even if they did not live together, a situation that brought about some serious legal disputes (Friedman 1980:193–4).

Leaving aside the special forms of union and non-union, what emerges is hardly the permanent incorporation of a Chinese woman in her affinal lineage, certainly not if that implies a total separation through marriage from her natal one. Some women remain or become independent, but even those who get married are not entirely swallowed up in their conjugal homes. For as Yang (1945) reports, a woman's brothers do not give up all obligations towards her. Not only does she continue to visit her natal home (though she has to ask permission and goes less and less frequently as the marriage endures), but if she is maltreated as a wife she is protected by her original lineage (Freedman 1966:57); indeed in Amoy her agnatic kin may even intervene at her funeral, forcing the widower to provide better clothes and ornaments for their dead kinswoman. In North Taiwan the lid of a coffin cannot be closed until the family come to see how she has died and whether suicide or homicide are involved. Moreover, these relatives include her maternal as well as her paternal kin. On the day of the funeral her mother's brother attends and her children, grandchildren and son's wives kneel down while he lectures them about their treatment of her, threatening to beat them if necessary. When he goes to pay his respects to their ancestral tablets, the children crawl under the table before him, expressing in this manner their lowly position. They act in this way even when the woman had made a hypergamous marriage and the maternal uncle is addressing his 'betters' (Ahern 1973, 1981; Wolf 1970). But in general, the richer the family, the more concerned they are about their daughter's status.

Thus in certain respects the women of southeastern China seem less cut off from their natal kin, less absorbed into their husband's families, than the male-dominating, patrilineal model of Freedman's first volume (1958) would suggest. Even divorce and separation do not seem all that uncommon in some parts. Data from Taiwan for the year 1906 show that 14.4 per cent of all marriages ended in divorce within five years. Barclay (1954) suggests that this figure may be the result partly of a secondary sex ratio that favoured women (119 males for every 100 women) in the age range 15–49, partly of the possible inclusion of separations which the Japanese authorities may have failed to distinguish, but partly too of the extent of uxorilocal marriages, of which there were a high proportion (21.8 per cent), since these may be less stable as the in-coming man is under a situation of strain (Freedman 1966:61–2). A more recent, age-specific analysis of the data carried out by A. Wolf (1985c) shows divorce to be most frequent in the case of minor marriages, followed by filiacentric unions and major marriages. In the first case the difficulties appear to be intragenerational, resulting from an aversion between those husbands and wives who have been brought up together, and which are more manifest when the mother-in-law is absent; whereas in the two latter the conflicts are intergenerational, related to the man's inferior position in one instance (divorce tending to take place within the first three years) and to a woman's in the other. Or to put the difference in Wolf's words, the problem was sentiment in the one case and property in the others.

Freedman suggests that this high rate of divorce or separation in Taiwan may be associated with the weaker control exercised by the families of marriage and the stronger support offered by the natal ones (1966:62), an argument which we have elsewhere found somewhat circular. He goes on to speculate that where lineages were more organised or of higher status, they may have been less willing to let wives go. But, as Fallers (1957) has pointed out (and as Freedman himself suggests in the context of funerals), 'strong' lineages may well be less inclined to lose all control of their daughters, authority over whom would then be divided. On the other hand, if parental control is weakened, as it was under the Japanese occupation of Taiwan and by the growth of alternative economic opportunities, the result may be easier (but not necessarily more frequent) divorce, fewer arranged marriages and among the Hokkien, less footbinding.

As far as membership of groups is concerned, we are not dealing with exclusive alternatives. It is not so much a question of an individual belonging either to one unit or to another, but of the women of upper families being of more concern to both. This indeed is one way of interpreting Freedman's conclusion that 'a family of high social status probably showed a greater concern to prevent a divorce both because of its need to aim at the ideals of society in order to maintain its standing and because of the breach that would be entailed in its carefully worked out system of marriage alliances'

(1966:63). These reasons would be equally applicable to the bride's kin as to the groom's; as a more valuable object, a woman of high status continues to be of value to both – not just to one. For a crucial fact about upper families is that the women enter into marriage with status and property that represents their position in their natal home and which continues so to do in their conjugal one. As a result, they are supplied with a sufficient dowry to make a satisfactory marriage which once again reflects back upon their kin. Hence divorce is likely to be more difficult in families of high standing. In Hai-shan (Taiwan) the effects of hierarchical variations in the rates of divorce were relatively weak but then the upper groups consisted of rich peasants rather than the gentry, the scholars and the urban bourgeoisie.

The structure and organisation of lineages

I will return to the importance of the conjugal fund, especially in higher groups, its relation to the lineage funds, its role in the fission of the husband's extended family, as well as its relation to other differences of a hierarchical kind. But first let me review the nature of the lineages that are under discussion, with a view to comparing and contrasting them with those of Africa which have frequently served as an analytic model.

It has sometimes been suggested that in China lineages were common in the South and less so in the North (e.g. Baker 1979:67). Others have seen lineages as distributed much more widely in the country, but not everywhere of the same structure. Hazelton (1986) distinguishes three main types, the corporation lineages of Kwangtung with important common property (Freedman 1958, 1966; Baker 1968; Potter 1970), the less well-endowed groups of the lower Yangtze in which there was little common property, often only enough for ritual purposes (see also Zurndorfer 1981, Ebrey 1983, Beattie 1979 and Dennerline 1986) and the 'unincorporated' descent groups of North China (Naquin 1986; Rawski 1986). One of the features of these intermediary lineages was the prominent role played by 'the bureaucratic and literate elite as leaders, organisers, promoters, and controllers of large localized descent groups' (Hymes 1986:131) which is seen as having its roots in the 'official kinship' patterns of Southern Song and even the Yuan.

As the result of a recent field survey, Wolf (1985a) also finds evidence for the existence of lineages throughout the country, and using the Guttman scale procedure divides them into three types, similar but not identical to Hazelton's (table 1). These three types are referred to for convenience as: (1) holding corporate property (corporation lineages); (2) holding hall and grave sites and; (3) having a genealogy (unincorporated). Type 1 is represented in studies of the Liu, Man and Liao lineages of the New Territories by Potter (1968), J. Watson (1975) and Baker (1968) respectively. Type 2 is also

Table 1. *Organisational features and types of Chinese lineage*

Organisational features	Type of lineage		
	I	II	III
1 Segmentary structure	X		
2 Large membership	X		
3 Substantial corporate property	X		
4 Occupation of one or more single surname villages	X	X	
5 Ancestral hall	X	X	
6 Common grave site	X	X	
7 Joint worship of ancestors	X	X	X
8 Possession of a corporate symbol such as a genealogy, scroll or tablet	X	X	X
9 Social solidarity	X	X	X

Source: After A. P. Wolf 1985a

found in the southeast, in the Liu, Ch'en and Li lineages of northern Taiwan studied by Ahern (1973), while Type 3 appeared in the *tzu* (*zu*) of the village of Kaihsienkung in southern Kiangsu (Central China) studied by Fei.

Some of the features of these lineages are relatively 'new'. 'The widespread keeping of written genealogies did not begin until some 900 years ago in the Song dynasty, and was associated with Confucian trends and the growth of literati culture. Such halls apparently did not become common until the 16th century during the Ming dynasty' (Baker 1979:175); their establishment depended upon being able to produce an ancestor who had passed the highest metropolitan examination (*jin shi*), although later on these degrees could be purchased. Ancestral halls are important not simply as centres for worshipping the ancestors; they were used for meetings, feasts, as guest-houses and, most importantly, for schools. The activities associated with them were usually paid for out of a lineage trust, what Wolf refers to as 'substantial corporate property' and which like others he sees as linked with large lineages and with a segmentary structure, in other words, with the 'stronger' lineages found in the south.

This corporate property of the lineage consisted not of the aggregated holdings of its members but of land that had been specifically bequeathed to the corporation as a distinct legal body for special purposes. These purposes included the support of ancestral halls and associated rites and ceremonies, as well as the upkeep of schools which were intrinsic to the maintenance and improvement of lineage wealth and status by the production of scholars, some of whom might eventually occupy important positions in the bureaucracy and would bring benefits to all its members. The way the trusts were founded and the way they operated will shortly become clearer by looking at particular cases from the recent and the historic past. But the extent of these corporate holdings which produced the lineage income, needs stressing. An observer in the thirties claimed that one-third of the cultivated land in Kwangtung was owned in this way (Chen Han-seng 1936:35,37). For such corporations benefited not only from the original bequests but also from additional, supplementary trusts founded by 'segments' of the original lineage, so that 'long-established lineages inevitably took more and more land into trust as the generations went by' until the Liao lineage studied by Baker held 50 per cent of all its lands in trust (1979:36). And it was from the control over these trusts that the lineages derived their power, since the income enabled them to finance the entire gamut of social activities, education, welfare, public works such as irrigation, ancestral ceremonies, community defence and public relations. So it is not surprising to hear that in South China 'land reform cut away at lineage power at a stroke by removing the land base. Almost immediately lineages collapsed' (Baker 1979:204).

While the actual existence of lineages in China was not dependent upon the presence of a trust, their corporate financial strength was. And the trust in turn depended upon the special conception, legitimised by the state, of a charitable foundation, a foundation whose property was inalienable, which would benefit a defined group of people and which would, above all, be free of taxes. These charitable estates (*yizhuang*) were first devised by the statesman Fan Chung-yen (Fan Zhongyan) at Soochow (Suzhou) around 1049 to provide permanent maintenance and education for all the branches of his family. The move may have represented an attempt by the new Song bureaucracy to strengthen its own foundations against the power of the state, now that the old aristocracy, dependent upon inherited wealth, had disappeared (Beattie 1979:9; Twitchett 1959; J. Watson 1982; Twitchett 1982). In T'ung-ch'eng (Tongcheng) in Anhwei (Anhui) province, some hundred miles up the river Yangtze from Nanking (Nanjing), the Chang (Zhang) made great efforts in the seventeenth century at organising themselves along these lines at a time when the elite were threatened not only with violent revolt but with tax changes that could be mitigated by building up corporate wealth of this kind (Beattie 1979:128–9). Even more explicitly than in Europe of the same period, religious foundations were used to protect property against depredation by the state or under other conditions of uncertainty; in China protection was more explicitly the case, since the beneficiaries were one's descendants, but the gift was mediated by the ancestors in an act of religious charity.

It was in the following century that the lineage in the New Territories studied by R. Watson (1985) made a similar trust. Earlier, in the fourteenth century, the area had been settled by 'clansmen' belonging to a patronymic group, let us call it a clan, named Teng (Deng). Nearly four centuries later the majority of the local Teng constituted themselves into a 'unilineal descent group' or lineage, an event connected with the emergence of wealthy families of merchants for whom the wider group offered some support for their privileged position. A number of kinsfolk undertook the formal funding of a corporation, a procedure that sometimes needed royal approval. The members all contributed to the building of a temple and to the assignation of lands to maintain the structure as well as to benefit the descendants of the founders. Thus the corporation, Yu King T'ang, was established in 1751 as a legal entity with its own property, demonstrated descent, written genealogies and a ritual unity which centred around the building of a 'new hall' under the leadership of one individual supported by forty-eight named contributors. Money left over from the construction fund was used to buy land which was set aside to finance community projects and the worship of lineage ancestors; such charitable endeavours included support for a school at which the lineage's children could be educated.

Such estates were not so much a manifestation of the unity of the kin group but rather created a different kind of charitable dependence. According to a sixteenth-century writer, the development of charitable estates represents a falling away from earlier lineage solidarity. 'Charity land exists because there are men of means, whereas under the rules of the *tsung* . . . everything, no matter how valuable, was shared' (quoted by Dennerline 1986:187). Looking at a late nineteenth-century example, Dennerline argues that benefits accrued to the poor, especially to poor scholars. 'They provided insurance for poor scholars' families and lent prestige and power to their gentry managers, buttressing the status of the scholar-gentry class and authenticating its values' (1986:206).

At the same time the landlords both contributed to and benefited from lineage ties. Their peasant agnates were a ready source of tenants and fighting men. But the rich derived most from the schools. It was they who managed the trust funds of the lineage which could be used for business purposes. Their relations of marriage and kinship differed significantly. It was largely in the sphere of religion that all men were equal (before the ancestors and the gods), providing the kind of egalitarian cloak to an essentially unequal world to which Marx later drew people's attention in striking phrases. Thus the 'strength' of corporation lineages was very different from the solidarity perceived in their different ways by Ibn Khaldun and Confucius, and existing to a much greater extent in Africa, and even among the Bedouin and other pastoralists, as well perhaps as in northern China.

In addition to the charitable estates of the lineage, there were also 'community charitable estates', designed to aid families to perform funerals and help orphaned girls to marry, but these were 'clearly directed at the elite' as the income could also be used to enable scholars to devote themselves to study (Walton 1984:55).

However neither in the past nor in the present were lineages in China restricted to the presence of trusts. In a political context their role emerges well prior to the emergence of these bodies. When the Emperor Hsiao-wan moved his court to the traditional Chinese capital of Lo-yang in AD 494, he issued a number of edicts attempting to get his T'o-pa tribesmen to conform to the patterns of their Chinese subjects, in dress, language, names and so forth. He also laid down guidelines by which elite T'o-pa families were to be incorporated within the Chinese ranking system, and which at the same time provided a method of ensuring their control (Dien 1976:62,86). The edict of AD 495 began by referring to the conquerors: 'the descendants of the Tai people have so far lacked (the concept of) lineages or collateral descent lines (*hsing tsu*), and so the heirs of someone possessing merit and excellence have in a muddled way received no specific consideration' (p. 65). In order to change this situation he established eight lineages with their own surnames, members of which had held high office in the past and who could hold those same offices in the future.

The results were interesting, especially in comparison with the 'classical' African lineage and its processes of segmentation on which many of its operations were based and which were so clearly analysed by Evans-Pritchard (1940). I have already mentioned the 'segments' of corporation lineages established by subsequent trusts. Here the process is very different and the 'segmentation' of the lineage is unlike any such process in a group formed 'on a religious, economic, or other basis; it is a segmentation produced by political fiat, and it occurs at the point when the first lineage member holds an office that qualifies his segment to be recognized as such' (Dien 1976:75). Branches that cannot meet the criteria are excluded and 'genteel' status lapsed if five generations passed with no reinforcement of office holding, producing the likelihood of conflict between 'the more traditional and the bureaucratic' or 'genteel' type of segmentation. In the latter case eligibility to high office was eliminated unless it was reinforced, in a rather similar way to dynastic segments in other parts of the world (Goody 1966).

The role of the state in stimulating the formation of lineages runs contrary to many hypotheses based on African examples where the strength of lineages is often opposed to that of the state. In China even the charitable trusts were dependent on the state in a general sense, since they often had to have royal approval. Once established they were not merely instruments of state power but operated in autonomous ways. The Chang lineage in Anhwei seems to have been developed to stave off the risks to its members from both popular revolt and state power (Beattie 1979). Peasant revolts had a long history in Imperial China, forming a dynamic element in its development (Chesneaux 1973:7). Their importance was particularly great on the Southeast coast which had 'long been officially characterised as a very unruly region' (Naquin and Rawski 1987:171). The activities of pirates right along the coast and the existence of protection rackets further fragmented society (p. 184). So it is not altogether surprising to find such lineages in the South of China rather than the North. While they were connected with the intensive rice farming which required cooperative labour and which produced the surplus necessary to establish and maintain a trust, they were mainly found in the new areas of settlement, where land was available and where central control was weaker; hence the importance of the lineage in political affairs in the South where even in the nineteenth century it operated as a self-help organisation along the lines found among non-centralised peoples in Africa, in the mountainous regions of Europe and among nomadic pastoralists (Baker 1979:66–7,152ff.). It also served for attack as well as defence, enabling incoming groups to take over as well as defend land from the autochthonous populations.

So the South and Southeast of China may have given rise to stronger lineages because of the weak control exercised by the central government in the North, whose armies were stationed only in the more vulnerable zones. But it is also the case that the central government ruled through the lineages, exercising a degree of control not so much by means of its local military forces as by its ability to block the promotion of their members in the examination system and by its possession of the central land records on which the existence of the lineage trusts themselves depended. Special statutes provided for the confiscation and redistribution of ancestral trust lands (Baker 1979:158) so that what was given by providing the legal framework for trusts and the permission to create them, could also be taken away. Thus the lineage served both as protection from and as an instrument of the power of the state; and both these aspects of the political system tended to emphasise the role of men rather than of women.

But economic factors too were important in the presence of 'corporation lineages' since their founding required funding of a specific kind. The strengthened position of the lineage in Fukien in Southeast China is related by Ng to mercantile activity, which in turn was linked to local shortages of land; the sea became the paddy-fields. In the rural areas, 'fierce competition for scarce resources . . . required corporate effort and protection'. In overseas activity the turbulent years of the sixteenth and seventeenth centuries privileged large lineages who were able 'to organise voyages and provide manpower and capital. The great profits from trade, in turn, consolidated lineage power; although they became less important for merchants with the return of peace, money continued to be sent back to home villages to support their family and to keep the traditional institutions working' (1983:215–16), a practice that has continued in villages in Quemoy (Kingmen or Jinmen) and the New Territories down to the present day.

The lineage and the domestic group

Before returning to the general comparison of lineage systems, I want to give one further example of the founding and operation of an early lineage since it brings us face to face with the problem of integrating the analysis of the lineage with that of the kind of conjugal and domestic groups we encountered in the previous chapter. This example of the formation of a charitable estate in connection with a lineage is provided by the history of Lou Yi who had been appointed a prefect of his district in 1117. In order properly to establish his descendants he wanted to endow a charitable estate, along the lines of the Fan of the Northern Song (Twitchett 1959). However his financial position deteriorated in the chaos surrounding the fall of the Northern Song and 'his household was forced to take up residence with his wife's family' (Walton 1984:45). One of his sons, Qu, was in penurious circumstances and also became a dependent son-in-law to his wife's family (figure 3). So too did Qu's son, Qiang, who married his mother's brother's daughter, thus continuing the tradition for three generations. However Qu's brother, Shou, did become an official and succeeded in establishing a charitable estate for his lineage which he called 'Daylight

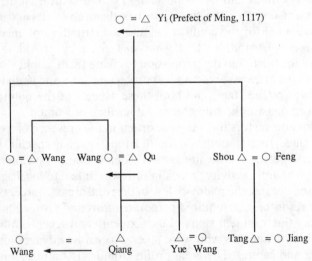

Figure 3 A selective genealogy of the Lou
← marrying-in

Brocade Charitable Estate'. The purpose of creating joint property has sometimes been seen as an attempt to prevent land from being divided by inheritance but it had more obvious benefits, apart from bestowing prestige and the opportunity to worship, in that it employed the advantages gained by degree-taking and office-holding in order to found schools and so increase the possibilities of future success in examinations that would help maintain the status of the whole group (p. 46).

The benefits were limited to the descendants of the sons of Yi and they were later to be supplemented by additional bequests. Shou's brother, Qu, was too poor; his widowed daughter-in-law, Jiang, was likewise unsuccessful in her desire to contribute, but his nephew Yue (Qu's son) did make additions of this kind. However 'even the brother and nephew of the founder did not derive sufficient support from the estate to enable them to remain independent. It was instead their wives' families who provided critical support for Qu and other Lou households and marriage ties that proved far more useful to the Lou than lineage institutions' (p. 49). The estate endured, but later on part was sold, income misappropriated and appeals had to be made to officials to prevent its complete dispersal.

Given this evidence, Walton concludes in a manner that reflects our earlier concern with lineage analysis, namely that 'the tendency to focus on agnatic relations in Chinese society is at least misleading' (p. 55). Men resided with their wives' families, maternal uncles acted like fathers (p. 59), wives contributed to the charitable estates of their husbands' lineage and carried out sacrifices to their dead paternal ancestors (p. 57). While some close marriages took place, wider political ties created or reinforced different kinds of alliance. Widows played independent roles, refusing to remarry under pressure. Wives participated in marriage preparations and took responsibility in the absence of a father. 'Women were key participants, not simply pawns, in the institution of marriage in Song China' and were important in supporting individual households (p. 66). Nor did this role change in the later period. Writing of the Yangtze delta in the nineteenth century, Dennerline observes that charitable estates might be established by women, with land or money they had acquired as daughters (dowry) or as widows (dower), using property which, even if it 'technically belonged to the men' (Dennerline 1986:192), was effectively theirs for use and disposal, at least for approved family ends, since 'benevolence' begins with the proper treatment of kin. As a corollary, such foundations supported widows and orphans, providing women with some security in their marriage arrangements, ensuring that as widows they would not be forced to remarry or to work (p. 194); if the husband was without an heir, a son could be adopted.

Walton rightly concludes that these facts should modify the tendency of students of Chinese society to assume 'an absolute break between a married woman and her natal family' (p. 66). The relevant fact in the history of the Lou lineage is 'the separation of the individual households in virtually every sense except that of consciousness, ritual and otherwise, of the descent from a common ancestor'. Hence the relatively rapid disintegration of the charitable estate and the fact that the household of the brother of its founder depended upon his affinal kin rather than upon his agnates.

Some important points emerge from the history of the Lou, but we need to recall that we are speaking of elite groups. First, in three successive generations, descendants of Yi took up residence with their wives' families, in each case wealthier than the more scholarly, impoverished Lou. From the standpoint of riches, the women married down. But they assisted their husbands, and affines may even have helped found the lineage's charitable estate. Secondly, there was no overall status difference between wife-giving and wife-taking lineages (Walton 1984:51). Thirdly, individual households have distinct identities, pursuing their own policies in some contexts as well as cooperating for mutual benefit in others. Fourthly, women are never simply the pawns of others but themselves players in the game, especially as heiresses.

The Lou was by no means an isolated case but represents a general phenomenon. Ebrey (forthcoming: 155) gives examples of Song epitaphs where upper wives use their dowry, which might include land, to help their husband's family. Indeed a wife might purchase land to help her affines, but it is clear that 'women guarded their dowries with vigilance and never lost sight of the difference between their own property and the larger family's', although this view was opposed by many Confucians (p. 15). China exhibits the classic disagreements and conflicts over the nature of women's property in an affinal context that we find in India, for example, and which is aggravated by the ideology and organisation not so much of agnatic lineages in themselves but of estates controlled by groups of male agnates, whether in lineage corporations or at the level of Joint Undivided Families.

To take the lineage as the starting point may lead to underemphasising the nature of interaction in the domestic domain; but it may also result in misinterpreting what goes on there. Take the treatment of marriage as it affects women. The view that women are handed over ('exchanged', traded, sold) between lineages leads to confusion in the interpretation of marital assigns, to a neglect of the continuing role of matrilateral kin in family ceremonials and to a failure to give proper weight to a number of practices that involve strategies of heirship and management, that is, mechanisms of continuity. From another point of view, the problem is not so much one of taking the lineage as the starting point but of taking a certain type of lineage as the model; as a result it becomes more difficult to analyse the articulation of the domestic domain with the more inclusive levels of the kinship structure, a task we will embark upon in the last two sections. But first to consider briefly some different types of lineage formation.

Lineages and corporations in comparative perspective

I do not intend to examine in any great depth the variety of forms the lineage takes in Africa and elsewhere, but I need to point to some critical features of these various systems in order to advance the present analysis. In Africa the lineage was of greater importance, especially in its segmentary form, in the organisation of relatively egalitarian societies, that is, in societies that lack the centralised political institutions of chiefship. While lineages are also basic to the operation of many states, such as that of the Asante, they then lose some of the political functions to the central authority.

So close is this association between lineage and 'acephalous' polities seen to be that some scholars of West Africa have developed the notion of a lineage mode of production, distinct from the cynegetic mode of hunters and gatherers, proposed by Meillassoux (1964), and from the so-called African mode of production in centralised states outlined by Coquery-Vidrovitch (1969). It is true that some authors have claimed that a kind of stratification already exists in the lineage mode based upon a generational difference between elders and juniors (*ainés* and *cadets*), while others (e.g. Rey 1971) have emphasised the hierarchy based upon the difference between men and women. But class stratification in the more usual sense, or even estates in the way that I have used the term (Goody 1971), is absent.

The mode of production associated with African lineages could be more accurately described than by drawing attention to one type of organisation of its kin groups, for other types are equally consistent with this form of livelihood. What is most characteristic is its dependence upon agriculture of an extensive, shifting kind, in which rights to land are 'individualised' only over what is actually being farmed or occupied at any one time, not to the general pool, though the difference is subject to pressure on resources. Looked at globally, land is rarely a scarce good (although particular types or areas may be) and it is never sold. Where lineages exist, cultivated land is inherited by individuals or by sibling groups within them, in general by close kin as in Asia. On the other hand more distant kin have the right to utilise unfarmed land and, depending upon the segment to which they belong (the genealogical distance from ego, which is also the social distance), they may also engage in a range of joint activities, including defence and attack. In other words they belong to one body politic. But the first factor to be clear about is the nature of land holding. The African situation is characterised by Fortes in the following way. 'In Southern Ghana stretches of land on which cocoa is grown are corporately owned by matrilineally organized descent groups. But these descent groups do not engage corporately in the actual production and marketing of the cocoa crop. This is undertaken by conjugal families working parcels of land allocated by the descent group' (1978:16). As in New Guinea legal control over productive resources is more likely to be vested in a minor branch, a segment of the lineage than in a lineage as a whole, while actual production is a function of the domestic family, a fact that he rightly sees as running against the notion of a 'lineage mode of production'. The corporateness of the lineage has therefore little to do with the joint holding of property rights; although some writers such as Gluckman (1965), Freedman (1966) and myself (1962) have seen transmission of rights in productive property as being critical to the definition, Fortes and Smith (1974) have given precedence to the notion of 'the presumed perpetuity of the corporation as a single juristic personality as the definitive criterion' (1978:17). While Fortes uses Freedman's work to point to the 'striking similarities' between Chinese (Fukien) and African (Tallensi and LoDagaa) lineage organisations and social structure more generally, we must insist that the 'stronger' lineages of Southern China were not only 'strikingly' different in the nature of their corporate arrangements regarding productive property but that they existed within a much more developed social system. It was not the fundamental relevance of the notion so much as a premature generalisation of concepts that tended to overlook the differences and hence to bring China closer to Africa than to Europe. The difficulty comes down to one of dealing in principles (Fortes 1978:26) rather than in variables. Undoubtedly some of the 'basic building blocks' are similar, especially in the non-corporation lineages of China, but the context differs in significant ways, and so too do the resultant kin groups.

The term 'corporate group' has been used of such lineages and their holdings, following Maine's application of the Roman concept to India (1861) and to what he more generally saw as Ancient Law. But the phrase was subsequently extended to almost any boundary-maintaining kinship unit the members of which thought of themselves as having one legal or jural personality, one body (*corpus*) in a sense that was both metaphorical and literal at the same time. Partly in order to make some analytic distinctions that this broad use seemed to obscure, partly because the usage had gotten too far away from established legal terminology, I tried to restrict my use of the term 'corporate' to those groups, kin groups in fact, within which property, in the shape of either land or wealth, immovables or movables, was transmitted. As a member of such a lineage one's claim was not limited only to land that one's father (or mother's brother in a matrilineal system) had actually worked, but to part of the uncultivated land that was held to belong to the lineage or clan; this was 'MacDonald land' in a somewhat different sense, a joint resource that each could directly exploit if the need was there. So there were two analytically distinct notions of 'group' or 'corporate' property. On the one hand, there was the aggregated land cultivated by members of the group in distinct parcels, rights to the use of which were transmitted within the subgroup (the farming group), possibly between specified individuals; on the other hand, there was the land not at present under cultivation but which each member had the right to exploit in the same way because it was jointly owned.

In addition there was the 'common' land which might be reserved by a community for purposes other than as a pool of agricultural land. The difference has partly to do with the nature of the activities for which it is set aside. Hunting, fishing, the gathering of wild foods or firewood, herding, grazing, these do not require the attachment of one individual or a small group to a limited set of resources in the same way; that is, they do not require a system for the tenure of land in the usual sense of providing for subdivision. Nevertheless communities and even kin groups lay claim to specific areas for a variety of purposes, not only on land but also on water where they may exercise common rights in sea tenure (Ruddle and Akimichi 1984). On such common land the longer-term rights that individuals or small groups need for cultivation are normally excluded. Sometimes they exist in a limited way. Under difficult conditions people may be allowed to farm such land but only on a temporary basis. In this it differs from the second type of situation described above (joint as distinct from common, the latter being indivisible) where individuals had full rights of access to their 'corporate' property. Contrast the common land in medieval Europe which was largely pasture and woodland, and could in principle only be used by a person in such a way as not to diminish the rights of others. That is to say, he could not overcharge or take more than his fair share of the wood. Nor could be plough the land without permission of the landlord or of his fellow-common-ers, or both. It is true that when there was pressure on the land, younger sons might go and plough these other, untitled, areas, but to be legal they had to obtain consent.[3] And the right was in theory temporary. In practice, and over the long term, population pressure, as well as political and economic leverage, might lead to a change in status, by enclosure for example, just as under socialist and some strongly centralised regimes the reverse process may aggregate individual plots into joint or common ownership. The use of common rights for individual purposes (and vice versa) on the boundaries of the system often leads to internal conflict as well as longer term changes.

The difference between cultivated land under 'individual' claimants but possibly with reversionary rights vested in kin, and 'common land' owned by the community is relevant in many parts of Europe today as in the past, especially in mountainous areas. In Crete there is a distinction between the *ager* and the *saltus*, the cultivated and the wild, which is linked to the nature of the productive activities undertaken there. The *ager* is farmed and subject to 'private' proprietorship, the *saltus* is used for pasture and subject to communal rights. But it is not only a matter of different types of rights being associated with different forms of production, since individuals or families can exploit the common lands for cultivation, providing they renew the rights each year (Saulnier-Thiercelin 1985:53). That is, the common lands act as a kind of reserve, a safety-valve, a fact which in the longer run may change the balance between the two, a balance that is yet more likely to be altered by the actions of powerful landlords and others interested in new methods of exploitation.

There is yet a further type of relation of a group (in this case a kin group) to property and it is one that characterises Chinese lineages of Wolf's type 1, those that are not merely 'corporate groups' as discussed above but 'corporations' which are endowed with property and the members of which are the trustees. They could never be coparceners of the extensive lands owned by the lineage. Even in Kwangtung and Fukien the majority of individuals did not belong to such corporations, nevertheless their lives were affected by the existence of large areas of land, up to a third or more in places, that lay permanently outside the market (at least for sale, not for rent).

I have employed the term 'corporation' here in a wider sense than it is used in Anglo-American law where it customarily refers to business corporations; these in turn differ from partnerships in which the enterprise is owned by the partners themselves. Given that Chinese lineage corporations also acted in a business capacity, investing in land, which it leased, operating as pawnbroker and moneylender, even participating in maritime trade (Collins 1986:267; Ng 1983:29; Gates 1987a; Faure 1986; Siu 1989), it is worth looking in further depth at the Western institution for comparative purposes. The business corporation is an association of assets, chartered under the law, that are owned by individual or 'institutional' shareholders; shares change hands, the corporation maintains its identity over time. If it is a limited corporation, then the shareholders have only restricted responsibilities for the debts of the corporation.

It is sometimes suggested that this form of limited liability was a European development of the early Middle Ages, the principle of which was phrased in fifteenth-century English law as 'Si quid universitati debitus, singulis non debetur, nec quod debet universitas, singuli debent' (If something is owed to the group, it is not owed to the individuals, nor do the individuals owe what the group owes), and one that was first applied to towns, universities and ecclesiastical orders. Nevertheless the formal 'incorporation' of business enterprises began in England only during the Elizabethan era when the first joint-stock companies ('one body corporate') were formed under the auspices of the state but using private capital, for the purpose of undertaking overseas trade.

Historically this seems a highly ethnocentric, indeed anglocentric, account of cultural developments since forms of limited investment certainly occurred in earlier Mediterranean trade (Goldthwaite 1987:14; Melis 1974) and in yet earlier mercantile enterprises in the ancient Near East. But my immediate point is to emphasise the analytic link between such business corporations and the kinds of corporation found in China from the medieval period, that is, from the Song dynasty (960–1279), which were intended as charitable foundations for lineage members.

The term 'foundation' is used in a specialised sense for a charitable institution. That again is often seen as a specifically English achievement arising out of the medieval 'use' by which, before the sixteenth century, holders of freehold land got round the absence of a will of freeholds by transferring the landed property to a third party who then undertook to transfer it to a stated beneficiary. The critical feature of this practice was the separation of the trustees' right to administer from the beneficiary's right to enjoy. However, it might be thought that for comparative purposes the ongoing lineage of the earlier East provides a better model than the more evanescent family structures of the later West.

Charitable foundations are a special subcategory of trusts designed for socially approved purposes. Another variety found in Anglo-American law is the family trust whereby a settler may make provision for the successive members of his family, either in their lifetime (e.g. by a marriage settlement) or by will, the intention being to promote family security for close relatives, at the same time as avoiding or reducing the payment of tax.

As a concrete example of the nature of charitable foundations, I take a personal instance. I am a member of a college at Cambridge that has been endowed with lands and other property for religious and educational purposes and which enjoys special privileges, regarding tax for example, enabling it to carry out these purposes. As a member of the College the land does not belong to me in any usual sense of the word, nor yet to the members collectively; it belongs to the foundation, to the corporation. When I lived in a house on college land, I payed a ground rent like anybody else, the proceeds of which went to carry out the purposes of the charitable foundation. Those Chinese lineages that possessed trusts operated in a similar fashion, for these were founded for specific purposes of a religious or charitable kind. Indeed it has been suggested that they were even based on the model of bequests to Buddhist foundations. Be that as it may, the aims are religious, such as maintaining the ancestral hall, but also charitable. When the religious duties have been performed, there may be a dividend which is distributed among the members, as happened until recently in many Cambridge colleges. The lineage charity is directed within the kin group, as with the family *waqf* of Islam, rather than towards the members of a religious persuasion or to the community at large. However members of the kin group had no direct access to the endowed lands; they could become tenants, in which case they paid a rent to the foundation, that is, to the lineage as a body distinct from its members, and the proceeds went to carry out the purposes ot the foundation. As with a College, it operates as a commercial body under its appointed managers, perhaps engaging in business ventures in order to maintain and augment its funds.

The role of the lineage is clearly explained in Baker's general account of Chinese kinship, based on his study of the Liao of the New Territories of Hong Kong (1968). Here he observes that ascribed lineage headship remains important in the ritual sphere but that, since lineage and community are identical, real power within the corporation rests with the men of wealth, position, education or political ability who are the managers of the trust. In fact their role would depend on the size and genealogical spread of the lineage. It was the duty of the managers of the trust to keep the records in a chest and to account to the lineage annually for their stewardship. The posts rotated. In the smaller lineages, consisting of close relatives, the elders of each segment would take turns (*lun chang*, rotation estates) and the segment in charge would enjoy the benefits of the excess income for that year. In the larger trusts the managers were professionals who were charged with distributing that income annually among all the members. These wealthy men would be elected to the office of supervisor of the chest (*jian shang*) and as executives (*zhi shi*).

What were the specific functions of the management of a larger trust?

Its first responsibility was to organize the ceremonies of worship of the founding ancestor, and to ensure that the funds to pay for these were forthcoming. Accordingly, economic matters claimed much of its attention. Fields had to be rented out or placed in the care of lineage segments, rent or income had to be collected, lineage property maintained, and the surplus income put by or spent to the best advantage. Where an entire area was under lineage ownership, it was often worth-while for the lineage to invest in irrigation systems (dams, channels, bridges, wells) which would benefit all the land in the area, regardless of whether it was trust land or private land. Money could be invested in other ways too. Lineages often set up schools for their sons, paying for the education, and sometimes even providing rewards in cash or kind for members who were successful enough at their studies to pass the stringent Civil Service examinations. Widows were sometimes cared for at lineage expense; temples and shrines were built and maintained; non-ancestral religious ceremonies on special occasions such as drought and flood were paid for; caretakers for lineage property were employed; feasts were given; halls for ancestor worship were built; and so on.

Lineage investment, therefore, was complex and valuable, and the lineage leadership had to protect that investment. So it organised its own Watch system, which patrolled the lineage-controlled area and gave warning of and some protection against thieves, bandits, flood, fire and civil commotion. (1979:58–9)

Some of these extensive functions are very similar to those carried out by charitable corporations of a religious kind found in other societies, but in addition functions accrue because of the fact that the corporation was also the basis of a local community and a kin group at the same time.

A corporation of this kind holds a fund, an endowment, which at one level is modelled on the endowment of individuals. Just as one can give or leave property to persons, to a daughter as dowry, to a son by inheritance, so too one can leave property to an abstract body, a trust, either attached to an existing group, such as a kin group, or to a specially constituted one. It differs from a share-holding corporation, since individuals cannot withdraw any part of the assets. Share-holding corporations of this kind were found in connection with much early commerce, and in a stricter sense appear in the business corporation, the joint stock company. Economic historians of Europe have linked early mercantile enterprise of the twelfth century to the development of an institution known as the *commenda*, a corporation for overseas trading consisting of shareholders who could be either family or not (and either risk-holders or not). But share-holding partnerships, like the limited liability mentioned before, have a long history in the medieval Near East (Goitein 1978:40) and in Ancient Mesopotamia, in the mercantile activity of Ur around 1500 BC and yet earlier in the well-known (highly monetised, highly commoditised) trade from Assur to the Anatolian colonies in the nineteenth century BC. Similar kinds of partnership existed in China (Gardella 1982).

A characteristic of all these 'corporate' organisations is their reliance on some system of accounting, preferably bookkeeping, for both share-holding and endowed corporations have to be accountable to the membership or to the state (especially if they are relieved of taxes), and possibly to both. That means annual or periodic statements of accounts and the kind of procedure we find developing in Christian churches (Dyer 1980), in Buddhist monasteries (Gunawardana 1979) and in similar bodies elsewhere, which embody supernatural as well as natural checks. That is to say, corruption, fiddling the trust funds, is subject to religious as well as to secular sanctions. An account of a local Ma Tsu temple in Taiwan tells how it lost even some of its supernatural efficacy (*ling*) or reputation (*ling-ch'i, ling qi*) because a manager had transferred land from the temple's endowment to his own name (Sangren 1985:32).[4]

Like the very establishment of formal trusts, such accounting requires the use of writing or similar recording procedures (the abacus computes but does not record). Otherwise the fund may not only be mismanaged but may disappear altogether into various pockets; and without records there is nothing to show the trustees. Endowed corporations, foundations, are therefore features of complex societies, of civilisations with writing, not of societies without. It is not simply that certain aspects of the notion of a corporation become more explicit with writing, but also that new forms of organisation become possible, partly because their constitution, their endowments, their accounts and their distributions can be given a permanent form, partly too because a 'body' becomes more distinct from its members in quite a different way by having a written 'charter' which exists 'out there', separate from each and all. Neither such a distinction nor that embodied in the notion of 'capital' is a function of double-entry bookkeeping, as Sombart and less unequivocally Weber supposed; indeed the notion of the king's two bodies is present in much simpler societies but it becomes more distinct with the appearance of writing which led not to accounting *per se* but to the development of record keeping of various kinds (Gardella 1982; Goody 1986).

In one way the Chinese lineage offered an alternative to the charitable provisions of the Church in Europe. Instead of depending in emergencies and for essential social services on the bounty of the Church, funded by gifts from the past generations, one was dependent upon the lineage trust in a similar manner. Of course the establishment of both types of fund involved some degree of alienation, but in the second type the benefits were limited to the descendants. Unlike alienations to the Church, family or lineage trusts reinforced, indeed restructured, the ties of kinship. Their benefits came from ancestors rather than simply from past generations as in the case of the Church (though the latter were mediated by God, since they were gifts to God) and the ancestors had to be thanked in appropriate ways. But only one's own ancestors were approached; 'offerings presented to a strange soul are regarded as a theft from the holy ones' (de Groot 1892–1910:i,51, quoted Baker 1979:76). The dead without descendants were the special responsibility of the Buddhist church on the seventh lunar month in the course of ceremonies that concentrated upon addressing the world of 'hungry ghosts', the vengeful, unprotected dead, and on having them placed under the firm control of the Rulers of Hell.

Given the nature of these endowed lineages, it is not surprising to find them among the rich rather than the poor. Indeed in Hakka communities in southern Taiwan, the tenants have no lineages at all, for these are confined to the landlords (Cohen 1985). The same is true of late medieval Europe. What were known as lineages or *lignages* were not endowed in the Chinese sense, if only because endowments were largely directed outwards to the

Church rather than inwards to the kin groups. Family property consisted of family lands, so that the *lignages* were not formally constituted corporations in the same way, but groups of kin linked together by claims to status and estate in aristocratic and mercantile families. These groups existed within a society that was largely cognatic (bilateral) in its kinship organisation and had long abandoned, if it had ever possessed, unilineal lineages of any other kind; and the *lignages* consisted of 'descent lines' rather than the much more extensive kind of group found in China, or in a different form in Africa, although in Italy branch lines were sometimes held together over the longer term by joint interests, including claims to property and status (Kent 1977; Herlihy and Klapisch-Zuber 1978; Goody 1983).

Not all lineages in China are 'funded corporations' of this kind. In other genealogically defined groups of Wolf's type 2 and 3, the property held in common might be limited to the ancestral hall and grave site (type 2) or simply to the genealogy (or other 'corporate symbol') itself; there was no common land to rent out, no common fund to lend or invest. All are characterised, as Wolf notes, by 'social solidarity' in some form or other, but the nature of that solidarity, or rather the nature of their association, differs considerably. The corporateness is not of the formal legal kind associated with Western educational, religious and charitable foundations but relates to the more generalised notion put into circulation by Maine and closer to the *solidarité* of Emile Durkheim and the *asabiyyá* of Ibn Khaldun (Issawi 1950:10).

These lineages resemble many Indian examples in that their solidarity may relate to marriage rules, ties of neighbourhood or to other features. Only in a limited way does it relate to land, or to the means of production, largely because of the nature of the productive system. That is to say, members of the one lineage (and this is true of all three types in China) may be highly differentiated regarding the amount of land they possess. Solidarity did not mean equality, as it mainly did in tribal Africa and sometimes in the pastoral societies of the Mediterranean and Near East. At the level of land holding, the egalitarian nature of the lineage under shifting cultivation is largely a function of the practice of that form of agriculture, which places limits on the individual differences that can emerge (Goody 1971). This is not the case with pastoral societies which often have to accommodate varying holdings of livestock by different family groups, so that there is some tendency for stratification to develop within, producing complex lineages that are internally differentiated not only by basic resources but even by styles of life. Nevertheless that inequality is more precarious, encouraging a kind of continuing dependence; the rich may continue to help the poor of their clan, caste or sect, an obligation for specific charity. Moreover, redistributive mechanisms may be brought into play to restrict this development, as with the large bridewealth transactions among the Nuer of the southern Sudan. The existence of these mechanisms relates to the nature of pastoral activity itself, for as we have noted in the reference to the mountainous regions of Europe, this is often carried out on agriculturally marginal land and like hunting, requires a different type of access, communal access, than does farming itself.

The same considerations apply to lineages in societies like India and China where relatively individualised rights over land, inherited between close kin, may lead to the differentiation of one household from the next. In some exceptional situations mechanisms exist whereby the land belonging to a kin group or community is returned to a common pool after a certain number of years and then redistributed to eligible members. Institutions of this kind were found in the Russian *mir* (Male 1971), in parts of India (Gough 1981) but above all in West Asia (Atran 1986); in each case they seem to have reflected the wishes of landlords to equalise the holdings of their 'tenants' rather than the spontaneous desire of the tenantry to redistribute the land on more egalitarian principles.

In China and India, while property, including land, is inherited within the lineage (which constituted my minimal definition of the corporate group), there is no effective practice of the joint ownership of the means of production beyond the minimal segment, the 'house', because rights are more individualised, attached to specific parcels of land and allocated to specific productive units. The system of farming does not require a pool of land on which to move, as is the case with extensive, shifting agriculture; fallow, where practised, is internal to the farm.

In this section I have tried to place Chinese and other lineages in a comparative setting. There are many more distinctions to make of a morphological (e.g. genealogical) kind but perhaps too much attention has been paid to these and not enough to what lineage organisation is about, specifically in relation to the productive system and to political affairs.

One of the major problems has been that comparative analysis has begun, almost inevitably, by taking a term from medieval Anglo–French law, lineage/*lignage*, and then developing the concept as a term of art for very different social contexts. In order to advance either comparative or case analysis we need to refine the concepts. There can be no perfect correlations between ways of organising kin and other aspects of the social system; once in being such institutions tend to persist over time, at least morphologically. But in order to establish any relationships, statistical or other, we need to begin by distinguishing between the kind of grouping found in certain strata in late medieval Europe and that found in early twentieth-century Africa. For this purpose I made a crude distinction between *lignage* and lineage (1983). Even at this elementary level we need to make further distinctions, especially in dealing with China and India. The critical aspects are, first, the role of the 'strongest' Chinese lineages as charitable foundations, constituting different forms of corporate group to those described for Africa; secondly, the hierarchical differences in internal organisation; and thirdly, the difference in the relations of people to the land, depending upon the type of productive system. It is this last factor that particularly affects relationships at the level of domestic groups which we have found to be problematic in many earlier accounts.

The conjugal fund and family fission

In the two final sections of this chapter I want to examine the way the conjugal fund is involved in the fission of domestic groups and to see how this operates in relation to the wider lineage. Let me sum up the relevant features of the pre-Revolutionary system of marriage and property, as they emerge from the village studies we looked at earlier. In a major marriage, a woman receives a dowry, either directly from her parents or indirectly from the groom's family, possibly from both sources; it is misleading to call this latter brideprice or to confuse an indirect dowry with bridewealth proper (even if some may be retained by the father in poor families). After marriage the dowry forms part of a conjugal fund over which the wife continues to exercise some rights and often a degree of control.

There are various corollaries to this system. The direct dowry, however small or large, may be a woman's lot, her portion, her pre-mortem inheritance; it is a devolution of property from the conjugal fund established by, or on behalf of, her parents. The idea that she is now separated from them is in part a reflection of the devolution that has taken place; but it is a mistake to confuse that process with the complete alienation of a daughter and her total incorporation in another kin group, especially as the marriage spells the beginning of the fission of the domestic group she has joined and does not cut her off in any final way from her natal family. However it is true that as a mother and above all as a widow she becomes increasingly part, not so much of her husband's lineage or kin group but of a new domestic group of which she may eventually become the effective head.

This interpretation suggests a modification of Freedman's contention that 'the threat which every woman posed to the family that received her in marriage' resulted from the completeness with which she was received (1966:56). Elsewhere he wrote, 'as the result of a marriage system in which women were bodily and jurally transferred to the families which acquired them as brides, when a married woman fought, she fought for herself, for her children and for her husband' (p. 46).[5]

Two points concerning this reading of Chinese marriage require a comment. First, in all virilocal marriages the woman is necessarily 'bodily transferred' to her husband's domestic group. But in China the effects of diverging devolution (the most obvious of which is the heiress making a filiacentric union) give a different shape to the overall pattern of residence than one would expect from this model of extreme 'patriliny'. Freedman (1966) himself makes this point in a note discussing Wolf's work in Taiwan. Out of a population of 843, only about 30 per cent of the women leaving or entering the village on marriage during the period 1870–1960 did so in the 'standard' Chinese form, which excludes minor marriages, where future brides enter the family as quasi-daughters, as well as filiacentric ones, where men go to live with their wives. Barclay (1954) states that in 1910 20.4 per cent of all registered marriages in Taiwan were 'matrilocal'. It is clear, Freedman concludes, 'that the little daughters-in-law and the married-in sons-in-law, play a very important part in the family life of southeastern China as a whole' (1966:48).

Secondly, the division between brothers arises, in some measure at least, from the fact that a wife does not arrive empty-handed. Not surprisingly it is a woman who provides the most explicit comment on this aspect of domestic life. Liu Wang Hui-chen remarks, 'A son may claim that a certain piece of property, having come to him from his wife's dowry or entirely from his personal career, should not be regarded as a part of the common property. Other sons would retort that whatever he earns himself is not entirely his own fortune, as his personal fortune begins with the initial help of the family' (1959:69).

The role of the wife as a focus for fission is particularly marked in China, since as sons inherit equally, their wives are more readily perceived as the element that disrupt their continuing equality. On the other hand in Korea and Japan there is no equality to begin with, the eldest son being the main heir, with the other sons expected to establish new residences if they marry (M. Wolf 1972; de Vos 1984:11). Residential fission may take place at marriage but women are less likely to be perceived as the causes in the same way. Primogeniture is said to have existed in China in Han times but over the past two thousand years property has been more or less equally divided among the male heirs. The virtues of sharing with close and distant kin have been extolled since Song times (Ping-ti Ho 1954:167). The contribution to the welfare of descendants by means of charitable estates was linked to this ideology of the clan.

A dependant's *peculium*, the personally accumulated or allocated property, provides one source of discord; another is the dowry brought by the wife. Freedman notes the hierarchical differences that obtain. In a poor family a woman is 'equipped with small items of personal property (her trousseau), some or all of which may have been paid for out of the brideprice received for her' (1966:55); the 'brideprice' (or indirect dowry), that is, the prestations passed from the kin of the groom to the bride, clearly have a very different function than is the case in most African societies, even when this goes through her kin. In rich families a daughter is directly endowed; she 'can expect to be sent off with a substantial dowry in the form of jewellery and cash, in addition to the bedroom furnishings, that form a standard part of a bride's trousseau' (p. 55). Even the peasantry were clearly differentiated in the amounts they could spend on the wedding (although many accoutrements like the sedan chair could be hired by the hour, according to Smith, 1899) as well as in the sums that would be given as direct dowry by the bride's parents or as indirect dowry by the groom's. The enormous dowries given by rich Taiwanese in the 1930s might include not only land but sufficient supplies of basic commodities to last the whole lifetime of their daughter together with money for her funeral, 'to demonstrate that their daughter would never burden her husband's family' (Sa 1985:292).

In stating that this dowry represents 'a considerable economic sacrifice' for the men, Freedman goes on to note that they make it 'not because the girl has any specific economic claims on them (she is not a member of the property-owning unit) but because their own status is at stake; a bride-giving family must, in order to assert its status against the family to which it has lost a woman, send her off in the grandest manner they can afford' (1966:55). The status component is of course of fundamental importance; but there are alternative ways of asserting one's position, for example, by demanding higher 'brideprice' payments, thus benefiting the wife-givers in terms of wealth as well as of prestige (indeed the two are usually closely interrelated). The interesting point about Chinese marriage (as compared with African) is the way in which a family chose to 'assert its status'. It did so in a way that gives a woman a claim on her family property; though the sanctions behind such a claim may not necessarily be legal in character, custom carried even greater weight.[6] Moreover the 'family property' on which she has a claim does not simply derive from the agnatic lineage; it comes from the cross-cutting conjugal fund established as the result of the marriage of her parents.

The creation of a conjugal fund is a factor potentially capable of leading to the independence not only of the wife but also of the husband. Both Fei and Hsu insist upon the wife's role in separating her husband from his parents. This is not only a matter of intra-familial tensions leading to fission. Mother and daughter-in-law are bound to be under some strain wherever the form of post-marital residence brings them into close contact, although the nature and intensity of this tension may vary with the age at which marriage takes place; the earlier the marriage, the more of a training role the mother-in-law has to assume (Smith 1899:277) but the closer the two may become in the end. Nevertheless, in many African societies sons contrive to work with

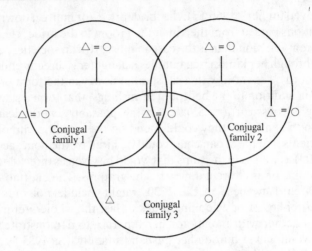

Figure 4 Conjugal funds and economic fission

fathers, daughters-in-law with mothers-in-law, as long as they are alive. But
there it is rarely if ever that a conjugal fund is established at marriage to
produce a divergent set of property interests. In China on the other hand a
splitting of the property interests of parents and children often occurs soon
after marriage (Fei 1939:66ff.).

A conjugal fund may divide not only the generations but the sibling group
as well. While one son, usually the eldest, continues to work with the parents
(and hence even in China may be preferred in his access to the property, at
least while they are alive)[7] the others separate off not as a whole, or even in
small groups, but as individuals. For it is as individuals that they are differentiated by the conjugal funds which have been established.

We can usefully contrast the situation existing in Africa, and for this
purpose I use my own material from the LoDagaa of northern Ghana. In my
account of the developmental cycle of the two subgroups I call the LoWiili
and the LoDagaa (1958), I pointed out that LoWiili sons, who inherit land
and movables from their fathers, farm with him until his death. On the other
hand the LoDagaba who inherit land from their fathers but movable property from their maternal uncles or other uterine kin, tend to split off while
the father is still alive, for if they stayed on, any surplus that they may help
him to produce might be inherited by outside heirs.[8] When the split in the
unit of production takes place (whether before or after the father's death),
small groups of brothers of the same maternal origin tend to stick together.
In China the split operates more atomistically and centres upon the wives of
brothers rather than upon mothers. In richer families the wives bring their

own property and establish a conjugal fund that differentiates members of the sibling group one from another, as well as children from their parents. In poor families the lateral split does not occur in the same way (or has already occurred) since as in Japan and Korea there is in effect only one son who remains on the farm in each generation, a fact that is clearly related to the distribution of the basic productive resource, the farmland, which, under conditions of complex agriculture, is a limited resource. However in taking over the farm the son has to compensate his brothers in an egalitarian way, which is not the case in Japan where unequal division is the rule. Throughout Chinese society it is the mother's brother who supervises the process of division, arranging for the drawing of lots by the children. Even the land set aside to look after elderly parents goes back into the pool and is not retained by the 'inheriting' son.

In richer families, too, a father may be eased out during his lifetime – 'he was never absolutely immune to the gradual wearing down of his authority by his ambitious and pushful sons' (Freedman 1966:153). In this respect, Freedman claims, the Chinese differ from the Tallensi who only become full adults when they cease to have a father. And he sees this difference as related to the attitude towards dead 'fathers', the ancestors. 'A Chinese ancestor', he writes, 'rarely applies negative sanctions to his descendants. As long as he receives the sacrifices due to him (which need consist of nothing more elaborate than simple food, drink and incense), he will normally be content to preside as the benign protector of his offspring . . .' (p. 151). I tried to show in an extended account of the LoDagaa (1962) that a man tended to sacrifice to the ancestors from whom he ultimately derived property, particularly the movable property which was offered in the rituals, patrilineal ancestors in the LoWiili case, matrilineal (or duplicating) ancestors in the LoDagaba. Freedman sees the relatively benign character of Chinese ancestors as connected with the process of easing out the father during his lifetime and the fact that 'if Chinese hate any among their kin, they hate their brothers' (p. 151), especially since, as there is no primogeniture, the property has to be divided among them.

The argument is certainly appealing, though I should add that the contrast is perhaps not as stark as it might seem; among the LoDagaa too, sacrifice is largely a matter of giving the ancestors their due – the trouble is that we are always in debt to them, having received their all; and on the other hand Chinese ancestors, if neglected, do become 'hungry ghosts' and pose a threat to the living. But I have also suggested that in Africa funeral ceremonies too may be more elaborate in those societies where rights and duties are handed over at death and less so in those where a man divests himself of his property (as in some pastoral societies like the Fulani) while he is yet alive. The same argument would tend to support Freedman's analysis of the Chinese, though the extent of intergenerational tension and of premature retirement needs to be carefully considered, relative to the African situation.

However this may be, the point to which I return is that in Eurasia we are dealing with an economic and social system that differs from Africa in certain major respects. For here we find a relatively complex agriculture with scarce productive resources, although their uneven distribution is partly mitigated by alternative possibilities of employment, even as hired hands, in a differentiated economy, with the poor often working for the rich, or else leaving the village altogether. The development of Fukien commercial and seafaring activities in the period 1683–1735 was partly dependent on 'push' factors, rural poverty leading to large-scale emigration, as a result of the unfavourable man–land ratio, the social oppression imposed by the landlords and the people's 'eagerness to undertake extra-village activities' (Ng 1983:4). As a result Amoy became a melting pot. In the early Ch'ing, 'domestic population movements were even larger in scope than those overseas. To work as hired labourers in district towns or prefectural cities had become an alternative life particularly for unemployed peasants' (p. 38). Some were employed in crafts, some in the prosperous loom houses, and some as shop assistants (which offered the 'greatest opportunities').

This differentiation, both within and without the village, meant a hierarchy of labour and resources, as a result of which property was attached to women in order to preserve or advance their status (and that of their families of orientation and procreation), creating conjugal funds that cross-cut lineage ties but which at times excluded productive property. These arrangements affected relations between siblings, between parents and children, between brothers and sisters, between husbands and wives. Siblings were divided by the separate interest in joint resources which were sometimes split at marriage to create a conjugal fund (or at least to provide a dowry). If the resources were not divided among the brothers, then in poorer families the younger might remain on the estate unmarried or quit to take up another occupation. The split between siblings was also one between parents and children, since the parents were often eased out when the children married. The split between brothers and sisters, too, was linked to their divergent interests in property, the women often receiving their 'lot' when they joined their husbands. Of course these splits did not involve what I've elsewhere called definitive fission, but simply a distancing in relative terms. At the same time, husbands and wives were brought closer together, among other things by their property interests; marriage established a conjugal fund that distinguished their holdings from their family or lineage estates. Among shopkeepers and small businessmen, the dowry could be used to promote the enterprise, although a woman's contribution might consist not only of her endowment but her skills as well. In South Taiwanese fishing villages, the dowry might help to purchase a better boat or otherwise assist directly in production. The major constellations of the relationships, both for males and for females, was different from Africa, both at the lineage and the domestic levels of kinship, since their roles and identities were linked to property, and property in turn to systems of production.[9]

I have used the phrase 'conjugal' fund to designate a situation that arises where a woman brings property of a significant kind or quality into her marriage and where this is 'married' in some way with that of her husband. Such a fund may take several forms which are related not only to the nature of 'ownership' but of control. Under English Common Law, as it developed from the twelfth century onwards, a woman's property was merged at marriage with that of her husband's and it was he who managed the joint estate. Lawyers speak of this as a qualified unity of property, qualified because while a man could dispose of his wife's chattels, he could not sell her freehold land without her consent. But, in terms of rights and duties, a woman also acquired a perpetual interest in the fund to which she had contributed, since she had a 'dower right' to a life interest in one third of his freehold, a right which was only extinguished in 1833.

Another form that the endowment of women may take is the virtual separation of the property of husband and wife. It was to counter the excessive power that English Common Law gave to the husband over his wife's patrimony that eighteenth-century lawyers, appealing to equity, worked out a system of marriage settlements to protect the property of the daughters of their rich clients. Under these settlements a family trust was established on behalf of the wife which kept her property from coming under her husband's control. It was the doctrine of separation which was embodied in the Married Women's Property Act of 1882 and is the basis of current English law.

The third main possibility is the 'community of property' characteristic of Roman-Dutch law. Under this system husband and wife are coparceners in the conjugal fund established at their marriage.

All three situations characterise Eurasia rather than Africa. The boundaries between these forms of diverging devolution are important for social relationships in other contexts; but here we are concerned primarily with the general concomitants of the transmission of property from men and women to their sons and daughters (or daughters-in-law). In the Chinese case Freedman notes that after a time a woman's personal property may become merged with that of her husband, if relations between them are good. So 'the husband may grow to acquire such rights over his wife's property as will lead to the emergence of an individual smaller family estate within the larger estate of the family as a whole. From this flows trouble while the family is intact; and when the time comes for partition the husband will lay claim to have the conjugal estate removed from the total pool which is to be divided up among the brothers' (1966:55). Formally, it would seem, the properties of the two spouses are detached from those of their natal families, the woman's at marriage, the husband's at partition, and it is at this time that the independent but associated funds become effectively united into a common conjugal fund.

Partition, the conjugal group and the lineage

The process by which the domestic group divided over time was always a complex one involving various levels of activity, with people ceasing to cook together, to live together or to work together, but the process of partition itself was a question of formally dividing the property belonging to the group.

There is of course much more to 'joint family' living than rights in property. But such rights are basically what Chinese partition contracts are about, just as they occupy the continual attention of the commentators on Hindu laws. Other matters are resolved less formally, orally, but for the partition of property written documents are normally required, which specify how the estate will be divided among the beneficiaries. This process is described in Johnston's account of Weihaiwei at the beginning of this century. When division took place, whether within the father's lifetime or not, a deed (*fên-chia*, 'Division of the Family') had to be drawn up by mutual agreement. If it was done during the father's lifetime, provision had to be made for the senior generation; he would either retain land for himself (Nourish-old-age land) or else stipulate that he would be supported by all of his sons in turn or should receive from them a fixed proportion of the produce of their several shares (1910:149–50). His widow would continue to control this land and, if division had not taken place, she was regarded as possessing a life-interest in her husband's lands which any division document had to recognise. However if she entered into a second marriage, she had to relinquish all rights to the property associated with her first husband.

The ties that continued to exist between those who have separated were manifest in the existence of what was known in medieval Anglo–French law as the *retrait lignager*. Under the fiction of legal theory all land was owned by the Emperor, but in practice, Johnston declared, it was 'privately owned' just as in England (1910:142). But a man could only sell land with the agreement of those falling within certain mourning categories, all of whom had to be given the chance of purchase at a fair price. For this reason resort was often had to mortgage, which might turn into out-and-out sale if the right of redemption (which also applied to land sold) was not exercised after a definite number of years. More distant kin, but not the whole lineage, still retained certain reversionary rights.

It was not necessary for partition to have taken place for the domestic groups (I use the term deliberately in order to encompass co-activities of various kinds) to undergo a considerable measure of fission, including the pursuit of different occupations or economic activities, although these were by definition linked at least at the level of 'accounting'. Such was the case with the shop-keeping partnership established by the brothers-in-law, Dunglin and Fêngchow, before it split into its various components (Lin 1947); income was pooled and one economic activity might provide capital for another.

Contrary to much sociological and economic theorising, such 'undivided families' are critical in the dynamic economy of present-day Taiwan, where some 90 per cent of businesses are 'family firms'. For, while there has been some decrease in the size of the household, 'the size and structural complexity of the family (*chia*)' has increased (Greenhalgh 1985:7; 1990). One reason has been the delay in 'family division' among, for example, 'dispersed agricultural families'. In the data gathered by B. and R. Gallin (1982) the result was an increase in 'family size' from 6.2 to 7.3 persons as well as in family complexity, with joint families rising from 11.8 to 14.3 per cent of the total.

'Family size' refers to the number of persons belonging to the group that in India would be called a Hindu Undivided Family (or more generally a Joint Undivided Family), which comprises the descendants who still retain joint rights in a particular estate. But joint rights do not imply joint activity in the usual senses of the word, or even joint residence; of course, even in rural areas the economic activities of the household have long been diversified, and individuals from the same house worked away in towns or on the farms of other people. Such a wider unit may continue to hold together for ideological reasons ('it is bad to divide the inheritance'), because of the failure of the heirs to agree among themselves, or through the peripheralisation of the joint estate, as when migrants to the town depend upon the income they have themselves generated in a rapidly growing economy rather than upon the farm itself. But there are also more positive reasons for the retention, indeed increase of 'family ties' under rapidly changing economic conditions. The increase in 'family solidarity' in Taiwan could represent a similar kind of first-generation phenomena to that which occurred in nineteenth-century England (Anderson 1971) where, for the purposes of residence, urban migrants exploited wider ties of kinship than would have been the case in the country, examples of which are found in migrant communities elsewhere;[10] it could also represent a type of the more long-standing cooperation in mixed agricultural and commercial activities that was long characteristic of some Chinese lineages and which is shown by the return investment of migrants not simply in individual houses but in whole villages (J. Watson 1975). However, it is clear that in contemporary Taiwan the family estate plays a much more positive role which is connected with later division and hence the increased size and complexity of the property-holding group. In the village of Yen-liao situated in a tobacco-growing area in southwestern Taiwan (Cohen 1976), it was the better-off that belonged to the larger domestic groups. Such kin groups were more differentiated economically than others, at the same time as permitting the most intensive use of labour for the cash crops. Some members of the group might run small firms or be engaged in administration but they acted together economically and socially in specific ways, even when they were living apart.

While economic achievement is related to the support, economic and otherwise, that the 'house' or property-owning unit can give to its members, that group is differentiated in a way that leads to future fission, usually into conjugally based sub-groups. In most cases the critical factor in keeping the group together is the absence of any division of the parental property. As in nineteenth-century Weihaiwei, division may sometimes take place before the death of the father, more usually afterwards, often much later. But whenever it occurs, it has to take a precise written form in which shares are allocated among the male members, while provision is made for the dowry of unmarried daughters and for the 'dower' of widows. Such an agreement also lays down the retirement arrangements for the senior generation if they are handing over their control of resources.

The original couple and their descendants may well have separated residentially before this retirement, especially now that some members of the property-holding group may reside in the country and others in the town. Whether or not partition has occurred, the old have to be taken care of. One 'solution' adopted in Taiwan, which has its counterparts in other parts of the world, is that of 'rotating meals' by which old people, generally as widows or widowers, are transferred between the households of their children (Hsieh 1982; 1985). This is less usual in societies where unigeniture obtains (normally in a preferential rather than an absolute form), because inheritance of the estate goes with the provision of 'bed and board' for the parents, so that a kind of 'stem household' (or even houseful) is a permanent feature of the community.[11] The elderly are 'provided for', but whether they share the same hearth or house is another question.

In societies where the degree of dispersal of the sibling group is minimal (as in many 'traditional' agricultural societies), the problem of rotation hardly arises; those who stay provide direct support for the old. If a couple have daughters alone, then they may adopt a son or import a son-in-law. In medieval England, where adoption was not a possible option, the rotational system could be operated among the daughters, as suggested by the case of King Lear. After the partition of his lands, his daughters should have taken care of him in turn, but they displayed their ingratitude by reneging on this obligation. He finished his days staying with the one daughter who refused to make a public display of gratitude, after suffering intensely at the hands of those who did. Ingratitude is a danger in any partition and hence an added reason for the parents to delay, but as Cohen (1976) suggests, postponement may also offer positive advantages to the sons who can make use of the joint funds to diversify and expand their activities to the benefit of their own conjugal families, their attachment to which will eventually lead to formal division.

The process by which division occurs might be seen as reflecting the tension between the elementary family and the agnatic lineage. But this tension, that centres upon the presence of joint rights to residence, property, labour, produce, food or even sex, exists not only within lineages, although there division displays special features, but also where these are absent, that is, within bilateral groupings. For it reflects more widely the process of founding a new conjugal family out of the two natal families of the partners and the fission to which the estate is necessarily subject. Incoming wives act as foci of differentiation, at least when they become mothers and serve to define maternally centred units within the agnatic group in the manner analysed by Firth, Fortes, Gluckman and others. What is particular about dowry systems is that women already act in this way as wives, because they bring with them an endowment which, whether kept distinct or merged with the husband's, serves as an independent focus for the conjugal pair. The problems that dowry raised for the nature of descent groups was explicitly recognised by Song Neo-Confucians and motivated not only what Ebrey calls their descent line rhetoric but also the strengthening of the descent groups themselves (forthcoming: 175). Here as elsewhere Chinese commentators show an acute appreciation of the tensions that exist within a system such as theirs, an awareness that is difficult to find in other Eurasian societies except in the more implicit form of legal commentaries and literary works.

If their whole entitlement devolved on them at marriage, by choice or by custom, then daughters no longer entertain any effective claims, at least on the family estate. By definition they do not 'inherit'; the marriage transactions have defined the limit of their interest. A partial exception is when daughters are needed to ensure the continuity of the direct line by a filiacentric union. Where a women continue to have a substantial claim on their parents after marriage, they 'inherit' as well as take a dowry. In other words, the allocation of their 'share' remains incomplete until the final partition takes place.

It seems more likely that such a delay will occur when women are entitled to land, since inheritance (as against the dowry) postpones the timing of the division of the basic productive resources. The early claim on movables is less disruptive. But if a woman's marital endowment includes land, whether at marriage or later, then we are less likely to find joint undivided families, at least those continuing after the father's death, since the basic estate (basic from both the standpoint of territory and of production) will already have been subject to some significant dispersal at an earlier point in the cycle. One is less likely to find either this kind of agnatic, male-dominated group (the JUF) or more inclusive lineages, since the trend will be towards the bilateral forms of social organisation.

That trend will become clearer when we look at Sri Lanka in a later chapter. Because, to revert to the opening injunction on the need to elaborate the simple view of much exchange theory, it is not only the timing of transactions that is important (whether at marriage, inheritance, etc.), nor yet the nature and control of the fund (whether it is common or joint, etc.) but the extent and content of the woman's 'share'. In Sri Lanka as in parts of Europe, a bride brought land into the marriage and hence at the very outset the couple were potentially capable of establishing their own independent productive unit based on resources coming from the two families of orientation. The same was even more true of some dowry systems in Europe where the parents virtually handed over control of the enterprise to the new couple, implying the early retirement and late marriage found in County Clare, Ireland (Arensberg and Kimball 1940), and in eighteenth-century Provence (Collomp 1983). Where all the property was handed over at marriage and the parents 'retired' on an annuity, a mortgage or a small property, then the 'house' was dissolved and reconstituted at an earlier phase in the next development cycle. On the other hand, inheritance postponed the transfer (to one child) or the partition (among several) but at whatever time it occurred, the transfer gave rise to radical results.

Where land was kept largely in male hands, as in China and India (less so in Japan), the basic means of production were obviously excluded from the conjugal fund and formed instead part of an agnatic estate from which women benefit as attached members, but one over which they rarely exercise any rights or control, except possibly as widowed mothers and as heiresses under restricted conditions. Under these circumstances, the establishment of the conjugal fund is less threatening, since the incoming spouse is bringing (at least in the first place) movables such as jewellery, furniture, money. Of course its establishment may promote separation, especially among those families where land is of little importance, since the raising of the dowry in cash or other valuables makes demands on the estates. But where land is significant, important and exclusively in male hands, the 'joint agnatic family' continues to be a major focus of interests beyond those of the conjugal family, even when the sons are farming and living separately, at least until the property has been formally divided.

Until that division happens, the position of a woman in the upper groups may be in some ways less favourable than in the lower ones in certain respects, although the aristocratic life-style was at times very different, such women in the Tang period being remarkably independent. Of the more recent past and of more ordinary people, a Japanese commentator on China noted:

Although the status of the female is generally lower than the male's, the housewife's status is rather high, and her opinion influences the family head. Among the poorer farmers in particular, female status is high since the female family members are important not only as agricultural laborers but also as part-time laborers, making osier-baskets and embroidering articles. (Fukutake 1967:86)

The same point is brought out by Baker:

Among the poor, where a wife was expected to work hard for the family, it was likely that she would be in a stronger position as an individual than among the rich, where she contributed no labour to the family and where she was easily replaced by concubines or (more rarely) through divorce. (1979:24–5)

Her ability to contribute to the upkeep of herself, her parents or her husband has some bearing not only upon the postponement of marriage but upon alternative roles for women. If land is included in the woman's endowment, it tends (as in Ireland) to force an allocation to the husband in the interests of 'matching'.[12] If there is no allocation of land to either, then the husband continues to hold rights of a substantial kind in the productive resources of his natal 'house', which consists of the males, the unmarried daughters (those who have not yet been endowed) and the wives, whose position as attached members is ambiguous. Only when the joint family splits, that is, when partition of the property takes place, does the conjugal fund become a conjugal estate in the full sense. That is to say, the exclusion of women from the inheritance of land creates an interest group defined largely by agnatic ties between males, a kind of agnatic lineage. Largely but not entirely; because, as we have seen, if a man has no sons, then he may create an agnatic link (a legal fiction in Maine's sense) either by the adoption of a son or, if he has a daughter, by keeping her in the house (both in the physical and social sense), taking a marrying-in son-in-law and getting a grandchild by that means.

These different procedures do not altogether represent alternative 'cultural' choices, for they may well be found in the same society, depending upon class or upon other contingencies. But they often tend to cluster in ways that are related to property-holding and to the related system of stratification. So having tried to place the apparent contradictions in the theoretical approaches to the Chinese family in the context of the nature of marriage transactions and of the 'mechanisms of continuity', in the next chapter I will return to the question of hierarchical and regional differentiation.

4

Differentiation, hierarchical and regional

In this chapter I want to look at the question of marriage and social differentiation principally at the village level, especially as it relates to transactions and strategies. Not only is this essential for understanding China itself, it is just as important for comprehending a whole set of very general differences in marriage, inheritance, kinship and descent between Eurasia and Africa which I have discussed elsewhere (Goody 1971, 1976). For in the latter case economic differentiation at the village level was minimal, at least in terms of land, whereas in the former we are invariably dealing with a kulak situation, that is, with a distinction between richer and poorer peasants. I then look at regional and local variation, pointing to some features that differ markedly in the North and South of China and others that vary within a specific locality. For the latter purpose I use the recent material from Taiwan which has provided a comprehensive set of detailed analyses oriented towards theoretical problems.

Mobility in the village

It would be wrong to think of the Chinese peasant as fixed permanently at a particular point in a system of stratification that depended largely upon his holding of land. In fact there was much mobility up and down. The point is made right at the outset in Hsu's study of West Town where he remarks that from an early age his father's comments made him aware of 'the rise and fall of families' (1949:3). He goes on to refer to Yang's account of a North China village where he describes the 'cycle' from riches to poverty, based upon the ownership of land. 'No family in our village has been able to hold the same amount of land for as long as three or four generations' (Yang 1945:132), basically because of the tendency of those who come later to spend more but earn less as they rise in the peasant hierarchy. One reason is that land had long been alienable. Already in the Song (960–1279), indeed earlier in the Han, it was possible to sell, mortgage, let or gift land; inequality was inevitable despite early attempts to redistribute land, for instance by the Wei in 485 to 780 (Cartier 1986a:462, 468).[1] There were also the long-term ups and downs of history, which sometimes meant dispossession by incoming dynasties, but at a lower level we have the continual rise and fall of 'houses'.

A yet more dramatic example of a similar process, this time of farmers who became merchants, is provided by Lin. In the winter of 1934 he returned to his native village in the southern province of Fukien.

> I was extremely surprised . . . by the difference in the development of two households with which I had been closely associated since my childhood. The heads of these . . . were brothers-in-law. Twenty-five years ago they were business partners and equally prosperous. Their newly-built houses, standing within earshot of each other, had long been the subject of chattering praises by the travellers who passed along the trading road that ran between the two big residences. Now their situation was totally different. (1947:ix)

Lin's fictionalised account charts the rise of these two families, the increase of the Hwang fortunes and the decline of the Chang whose house became deserted, 'the widow lost in loneliness and poverty'. But even within the successful family there were a number of radical changes of fortune, depending partly on business itself but more often on factors to do with the intervention of early death or illness, the numbers and sex of children and the personality and upbringing of the individuals themselves.

The detailed mechanics of this dynamic movement from poverty to riches and down again emerge clearly from his account of these merchant families, whose activities and numbers were great and long-established, especially in the South. In the past trade was carried out on official and unofficial levels, that is, by private merchants, both on an inter-regional and a foreign basis. An Office of Overseas Trade was set up in Ningpo (Ningbo) during the Northern Song, at the end of the tenth century (Mann 1972:53). The constant refrain of the thirteenth-century traveller, Marco Polo, was 'There are merchants here of wealth and consequence' (for example, 1958:211, 212); in Kinsai (Hang-chow or Hangzhou) merchants from India and elsewhere stored their wares and merchandise in large stone buildings, near to the ten principal market places.[2]

Advanced mercantile activity went back to the distant past, at least to the Shang dynasty (c. 1766–1122 BC). It is true that some scholars showed little esteem for merchants, but this was true for many civilisations including seventeenth-century New England, eighteenth-century England and nineteenth-century France (Chan 1977:17). In any case that sentiment does not appear to have substantially restricted trade over the long run. Even government decrees had little effect and during the Qing there were 'a number of established gentry clans which had a tradition of dividing gentry and mercantile functions among their members over many generations' (p. 21).

Village studies tell us something of shopkeepers but little of merchants.[3] Yet the degree of urbanisation, the extent of craft and proto-industrial production, the volume of trade, largely within but also outside the confines of the state, meant a flourishing town-culture and mercantile bourgeoisie in many parts of China from early times. Mobility was intrinsic to such activities. Farmers became shop-keepers, shop-keepers merchants, merchants gentry,[4] and their fortunes fluctuated with the state of the market.[5] Not only the market; individual fortunes were used to swell the funds of lineage or guild, and they were open to depredation by the state on the one hand and by peasant revolts (Chesneaux 1973) on the other. Stability was rarely long enduring.

One of the means of mobility into the merchant class was through apprenticeship. Quoting from the work of Hamilton (1977) on the Swatow opium guild, Ng remarks:

Even a family business, which was the norm in the Chinese commercial world, would often employ non-kin members, 'who took the positions with the expectation that within a few years they would be independent craftsmen or merchants themselves' . . . Many of the merchants first came to the business world from families without any business background. But the same system provided opportunities for them to join the commercial circle and rise from rags to riches. (1983:180)

For farming stock the situation was not dissimilar and is summarised in the study by Fei and Chang of a village in Yunnan. A lazy man, a man who takes to smoking opium, may have to sell his land to maintain his family. Equally large families automatically impoverish themselves as their estate has to be divided, land to the sons, some movables to the daughters. 'Owing to this division', they write, 'wealthy houses cannot be perpetuated' (1948:117). A poor family, with perhaps one son, may be able to save money and buy more land; the authors' landlord was one of the wealthy men of the village precisely because his father died early, leaving only one child. But his close agnate had almost descended to the poor 'laboring class' (p. 117). Despite corporate arrangements, lineages consisted of families of radically different economic status. Writing of the Tses (Xie) of the New Territories in the Qing period, Faure notes that, although it possessed some sizeable trusts, 'some members of the lineage did not own houses, and the majority of these did not own any cultivated land . . . some of those who owned houses likewise had no cultivated land, or very little of it. They could have rented land from the trusts, from other members of the lineage (but few would have had much land to rent out), or from people in nearby villages. They might have accepted other occupations and have left the village' (1986:56–7).

While such short-term mobility was common throughout China at the level of the peasantry and the merchants, this was not quite so true of the gentry on the one hand, nor yet of the landless on the other. The question of mobility within the gentry has been the subject of much discussion. Certainly the acquisition of degrees, leading to official positions, was a means to wealth and therefore to land; the key to such advancement was achievement rather than ascription, although rich men might purchase degrees and access to education was itself partly a matter of position in the hierarchy, of membership of a well-endowed lineage corporation. When in Song times the bureaucracy was recruited largely through the examination system, one response of the gentry seems to have been to establish some family property held jointly and in perpetuity as an inalienable trust. These charitable estates were first devised around 1049 'in order to provide permanent maintenance and education for all branches of the family' (Beattie 1979:9). Wealthy lineages with corporate estates had their own schools, supported by lands that were managed by the elders but rented out even to lineage members. And attendance at the schools was often limited to the same group, giving the better-off the opportunity to reproduce themselves. Beattie's analysis of the local elite of a county in Anhwei during the Ming and Qing dynasties tends to confirm Fei's contention (1946) that even after the abolition of the examination system, gentry and peasantry constituted two distinct classes, with the former a 'leisure class' comprising some 20 per cent of the population and maintaining its position economically by land ownership and political office. Of course these groups did not constitute a two-class system of the exploiters and the exploited; they were neither exhaustive of the society nor were they themselves undifferentiated into rich and poor. Again clanship and its obligations tied rich and poor together after a certain fashion, all drawing benefit from the existence of trust funds. Nevertheless these categories did form the broad conceptual basis for perceiving the Chinese countryside.

On the other hand, those positions were not maintained automatically, even in the 'leisure class', if only because leisure itself is a commodity that requires expenditure and its enjoyment tends to cut one off from the productive sources of wealth. Moreover the system of equal inheritance among sons meant that individual families (and in an expanding population the class generally) would find it difficult to maintain themselves on a set of fixed assets if they had many male children, unless one could compensate for the division by arranging an equal number of marriages to heiresses. In some cases the family's status and income could be maintained out of the benefits deriving from official service, but the attainment of such a position required hard work, 'more and more a question of preparing one's sons to achieve success in the examinations, which depended to a certain extent upon the family's possessing sufficient resources to underwrite a lengthy education' (Twitchett 1959:130).

It is worth insisting that while trust funds provided benefits for all, lineages often displayed a considerable level of internal economic differentiation (class). R. Watson writes of the Teng lineage of Ha Tsuen, Hong Kong, as being stratified until recently into two distinct classes, peasants (tenant farmers and labourers) and landlord merchants (1981). The analysis of lineage, especially that with an African background, has tended to downplay the element of stratification. Nevertheless this tendency is quite comprehensible because the existence of large descent groups tended to obscure the nature of their 'class' divisions from the participants, both the rich and the poor, who each for their own reasons chose to call attention to the cross-cutting ties.

Hierarchy and marriage

Leaving mobility aside, let us turn to the question of hierarchical differentiation itself. We have already come across references to differences at the domestic level. Widows were less likely to remarry in upper groups (p. 39). Divorce was less frequent (p. 59). Upper families were more concerned about their daughters' status (p. 60); their lineages were more likely to be of type 1, providing greater benefits for their members, for example, in schooling (p. 76). There were differences in dowry, the poor leaning towards the indirect, the rich towards the direct (p. 81). Joint undivided families tended to be richer than the members of stem households (p. 88).[6] Among the poor, women are relatively more important (p. 91); men are more likely to enter into filiacentric unions (p. 46), and girls in the North to reside as prospective daughters-in-law at an early age (according to Fei, though this is not so in Taiwan) (p. 30). The situation is summarised in table 2. But it has to be remembered that we are dealing in trends which in many cases require statistical support and which occur in a system of stratification that is much more complex than either a High–Low division or High–Low (Richer–Poorer) continuum would suggest, and we are dealing in features that are only roughly described by the column headings. For example, it is not only the size of households or even housefuls that differentiates higher and lower groups, but rather the existence of 'houses', of undivided property groups ('joint undivided families', JUFs or unpartitioned families) in the strata that holds more property. The problem of family size in China is complex but it appears that fertility was greater among the richer than the poor (A. Wolf and Hanley 1985:7), that coresident households were larger, and that the incidence of 'grand families' varied considerably between town and country (A. Wolf and Hanley 1985:9; A. Wolf 1985c). In most of these instances, as I discuss later, class factors were cross-cut not only by general regional differences but by specific local variation, not only between towns and countryside but between villages.

Table 2. *High and low trends in China*

	High	Low
1 Lineages	More type 1	More types 2 & 3
2 Marriage transactions	More direct dowry	More indirect dowry
3 Divorce	Rare	More frequent
4 Widow remarriage	Rare	More frequent
5 Inheritance	Equal division among sons	Single son compensates the rest
6 'Households'	Joint	Stem
7 Partition	Later	Earlier
8 Position of women	More concern over daughter's status	Women are relatively freer and 'more important'
9 Position of men	Less likely to enter into filiacentric union	More likely

First I want to stress the difference in the developmental cycles of the domestic groups, which affects the size of households. In his second study of the Chinese lineage in southeast China, Freedman notes that rich and poor families displayed different patterns, as was the case throughout China (1966:43). Relative wealth and status have an important influence upon the forms of marriage and the position of women. These differences of wealth were generated by the more complex productive base that existed in the major Eurasian societies, as compared to Africa.

'A poor family might in the extreme be unable to raise a son to marriageable age and ensure that he stay home to recreate the domestic unit. The chances are that at most one son would marry and continue the family in the same house' (Freedman 1958:27ff.; 1966:44). The poor, if they marry at all, do so late – one bride in each generation; they lived in stem rather than joint households. A rich family, on the other hand, 'produced several sons and retained them, perhaps adding to their number by adoption. The sons remained in an undivided family as long as the parental generation survived. And since these sons married young and the seniors might live long, a joint family of four generations could appear' (1966:45).

The joint or grand families of the rich, where the potential shares were on average high, divided their property when the father died or became senile – sometimes before; when this happened each brother was entitled to his share.[7] But jealousy over the property began at an earlier stage and at the domestic level it was said that the wives, whose quarrelsomeness was well-known, worked upon their husbands to separate.

Fried puts the hierarchical differences even more strongly in his study of the village of Ch'u Hsien, near Nanking, on the Yangtze plain. 'Peasants, tenants, petty merchants and petty artisans do not display joint family organizations . . . The harsh life of a peasant does not generally lead to a condition which finds a married son, his wife and children, sharing the family land with a strong and capable set of parents' (1953:70–1). In the merchant community there was more cohesion even among the heirs who often worked together as partners in the inherited enterprise (p. 52). Joint families existed not only among the better-off landowners but also among officials and merchants, as in the case of the Mo-mo and Chang families of Ch'u Hsien. The former were merchants, the latter landowners, officials and scholars, the nominal head of which was a young graduate of twenty eight but 'the power in the household was wielded by his mother, a capable woman of about fifty' (p. 86).

This difference in household structure is related to the difference in resources; it is the better-off who have enough property effectively to practise equal division among their sons, and who can postpone that division until later in the developmental cycle. It is they, the middle and upper-class peasants, who frequently draw up documents of partition. In the relatively prosperous situation that existed in Taiwan in the earlier part of the twentieth century, 'grand families' were to be found on a considerable scale in some regions (Wolf 1985b) and their numbers appear to be increasing in some rural areas at the present time. Nevertheless it was more generally true that 'petty farmers, who often lack enough land to divide, allow one son to cultivate; he must then pay rent to his brothers engaged in other occupations for the use of the land' of theirs which he farms (Fukutake 1967:86).

However the difference between large and smaller households is not only a matter of the earlier dispersal of sons in the latter case, nor yet of greater mortality. There is also evidence of lower fertility among poorer groups.[8] In Taiwan during the Japanese occupation, landless families who paid no tax produced fewer children than their neighbours who did, a situation Wolf attributes to lower coital frequencies (1985b:182–3,185) although other forms of positive control have been reported for mainland China.[9]

The question of the level of fertility in pre-Revolutionary China has been much debated by demographers, anthropologists and historians (A. Wolf 1985b; Coale 1985). Was the relatively low but steady level of population growth due to negative or positive checks? Both the pressure created by the difficult conditions for raising children and the pressure to control family size according to available resources (that is, pressure eventuating in both negative and positive checks) would be likely to bear most heavily on the poorer sections of the community. But positive pressures may not require positive checks on conception if the negative ones are strong enough to maintain slow growth. Or if any recourse is made to post-natal methods of adjustment such as infanticide or the disposal of children *between* rather than *within* families.[10]

Our early ethnographic sources provide some evidence of hierarchical differences of this kind, even in the village. It is suggested that the fostering of a future bride as a result of life crises occurs more frequently among the poor rather than among the rich; it is on the poor too that falls the greater burden of controlling family size in accordance with their limited resources, not only by abstention from sexual intercourse (Smith 1899; Croll 1985:11) but through the deliberate infanticide of girls (Fei 1939:52; Smith 1899:299), the sale of children of both sexes (Baker 1979:6ff.), as well as by arranging early marriages for girls and filiacentric unions for boys. But though boys were involved, it was primarily through girls that numbers were controlled. If many were to leave their homes in early marriage, then others might be dispensed with yet sooner; as they did not attract bridewealth, they were not normally needed in any marriage transactions, even, in many cases, to create affinal ties.

The choice of the form and timing of marriage, indeed marriage strategies generally, differed according to class but also according to sex. While upper females sometimes married later, upper males tended to marry earlier and to have a greater recourse to concubines in order to provide them with additional sons. In her analysis of households in urban Taiwan early this century, Sa shows that males in the high-status groups, defined by such criteria as the possession of concubines and bondservants, tended to marry earlier than lower groups, among whom marriages are delayed by poverty (1985:298); 92 per cent were married by twenty five, only 67 per cent of the lower group; while 26 per cent of high-status husbands married women older than themselves, only 7 per cent did so in the low-status category. Minor marriages and filiacentric unions were fewer in upper groups, since their members could afford the expense of a full marriage and could be more certain of producing sons by the use of concubines. Of course producing heirs was only one aspect of concubinage; there was always an element of conspicuous expenditure on the services of women. At the beginning of the sixteenth century a Ming scholar describes the people of Hui-chou (Hui-zhou) as 'extremely miserly as to food and clothing . . . but with regard to concubines, prostitutes and lawsuits, they squander gold like dust' (quoted Ping-ti Ho 1954:144).

Fei reports big houses 'in which a large number of kin live together, but this is found only in the gentry' (1946:2). Such households are distinguished not only by size but by sentiment. In the houses of landowners, especially absentee ones, there is neither the early independence nor the partition that occurs among the peasants, since the family depends upon common financial resources combined with 'the retention of political power for protection' (p. 4). Some multiple households in the town he studied even had their own courts; in them 'patriarchy' was pronounced, of the kind depicted in fictional form in *The Dream of the Red Chamber*.

Substantial differences in household size and structure according to strata mean corresponding differences in behaviour, feelings and attitudes between close kin. If brothers and their wives do not live together, there will be less cause for tension, at least on a day-to-day basis, but equally fewer matters of common concern. If property is handed over earlier, there will tend to be less conflict between father and son; or, rather, the son will tend to become the dominant partner while the father, as in *King Lear*, may be thrust aside.

There is a parallel effect on the conjugal and sibling relationships. 'In a family of low status and simple structure . . .', writes Freedman (1962:328–9), 'each brother stood close to his wife, so that while a wife might be made miserable by poverty and hard work, at the lower levels of society she had great strength as an individual'.[11] In higher status groups the solidarity of brothers is greater, strengthened by their mutual opposition to the powerful father who controls their social life. As we will see, much the same type of differentiation exists in India, although Mandelbaum does not find the same unity deriving from opposition to the father (1970:93)

Differences in affinal relations of a specific kind are addressed in R. Watson's account of the Hong Kong village of Ha Tsuen, where she stresses the role of women as intermediaries between their natal and affinal kin. Peasant men on the other hand had little contact with their affines, whereas village women maintain those ties and appear to be much more extrovert than their husbands (1981:609). In the landowning groups, on the other hand, men had wider networks, including affinal ones. They married their friends, whereas the poor married strangers with whose families they had little to do.

I have earlier been dealing mainly with the affinal relations of the bride, but R. Watson notes the contrast between the lack of emphasis male peasants place on affinity as compared with the situation reported for Taiwan (Gallin 1960; Pasternak 1972). The difference she sees as related to the strength and nature of the descent groups. In Ha Tsuen, peasants were 'encapsulated by the landlord-dominated world of the descent group' (p. 612); for they were mostly tenants or labourers and depended upon the richer members of the lineage for land or work. In 1905 36 per cent of the land was owned by the lineage landlords, and 49 per cent by the lineage's ancestral estate managed by the same landlords. All the relations of production and of kinship of the tenants were concentrated within the lineage, with their wives perceived as outsiders whose male kin were of little importance.

The existence of these differences between richer and poorer, combined with a certain degree of mobility between these varying conditions, means that in every lineage, in every kin group, some members will be better off, some worse. In the case of the village of Ch'u Hsien in central China described by Fried (1953), some agnates were buying land while others were selling theirs off. In other words even within the one lineage, different patterns of marriage and family obtained.

At the same time, the lineage itself played a supportive role largely because of its access to corporate funds. The revenues from these funds were destined in the first place for temple maintenance, while part went into the pockets of the comptroller, but 'the most important social function of the surplus from clan lands is to provide a fund for the education of young clan members' (1953:94).

The very fact that lineages of type 1 and their segments were defined in terms of access to trusts meant that they were differentiated not only internally by family holdings but externally in relation to charitable resources (Beattie 1979:128). Hence clans and lineages, according to Fei, were more effective among the gentry, where the fund was of critical significance. Describing his own clan Fei writes: 'When the need for protecting our joint interest in landholding disappeared, our clan faded away' (1946:5). For a clan to be effective 'it must possess some common property – invariably land', usually contributed by a member who had been a government official for the ostensible purpose of keeping up the ancestors' tombs and making regular sacrifices. But in fact this property was the means by which the hierarchical position of the clan was maintained since it financed the education of young members, enabling them to enter the ranks of scholars and to get access to high official positions where they were able to protect the interests of their kinsfolk and to contribute to their needs.

Were these differences in structure and sentiment simply contingent or were there also differences in pattern or even in norm? Cohen suggests the need to modify the notion that there were two patterns of family organisation, one for the gentry, one for the peasants, based on either economic or normative differences, claiming that there was only one set of rules (1976:231) and a basic uniformity of practice. When it is profitable to stay together, he argues, then peasant households, and even Hong Kong boat people, will do so. Since the poorer groups find less reason to keep together, a better distinction, he suggests, is between those who have estates and those who do not.

Cohen's formulation is not inconsistent with the general argument developed here, that some of these similarities and differences are transcultural and relate to 'system variables'. But clearly this is true only within limits. Just as regional factors play a positive part in selecting, developing and interpreting basic mechanisms, so too certain forms of behaviour may be felt to be more consistent with a particular 'station' in life, so that a peasant rising or falling in his rural environment may deliberately adapt his behaviour as well as have it adapted for him by changing circumstance. The two processes are not incompatible, especially within a local peasantry whose members are constantly interacting with one another. There are deliberate shifts of normative behaviour as well as passive adaptations.

For the gentry, however, the importance of the norms of the sub-culture seems to have been greater, and these norms differed, even though they were broadly consistent with the system demands in a wider sense. For example, while there was one set of written norms which dominated judicial proceedings throughout the country and for every class, they exercised less pull on members of lower groups whose practices were not simply deviations from that pattern but related to past customs and to present choices. Certain aspects of the Confucian family ethic are similar to Hindu norms – the ban on divorce and widow remarriage, both of which characterised the 'high' rather than the 'low'. Yet women in elite households were not only acting contingently in accordance with the pressures of a system in which it was more difficult to dissolve highly endowed marriages, nor yet with the implicit norms of their 'class' alone; they were also influenced by their specific training in a particular version of those norms embodied in the writings of Confucius. For in medieval China, as much later (Smith 1899; Headland 1914), they were encouraged to read the moral guidebooks for women such as that written in Han times by Ban Zhao, sister of a historian, as well as the Biographies of Exemplary Women, in order that they could understand womanhood (Waltner 1981:130). But the text books did not inculcate a blind conformity, for not only the contents of writing but the practice itself opened up possibilities of changing the situation of women. The first instructional handbook for women, written by Ben Zhao (or Pen Chao), emphasises the reciprocity in the relationship of husband and wife. But it goes on to say that if women are fully to play their part, they must be educated, that is, able to read and write. The 'Rites' states that it is the rule to start teaching children to read at the age of eight so that cultural training can begin at fifteen. And that training should be for girls as well as for boys (Swann 1932:84–5; Mann forthcoming:330).

One can see how pressure to conform would fall especially strongly on young widows who could acquire merit by not remarrying. While direct contact with this morality was limited to the small proportion of literate women, those who had not mastered the characters provided a much wider audience for moral tales based upon this dominant written ideology. Nevertheless there was a distinct difference in the acceptance of the norm among the high (literate) element and the low (illiterate), 'literate' referring here to proximity to the written word. Such differences were not only a matter of the difficulty the poor had in following those norms, important as this factor

Table 3. *Additional hierarchical variables in China*

	High	Low
1 Mechanisms of Continuity	More adoption	More entry of men into filiacentric unions
2 Type of marriage	Major plus	More minor (in North)
3 Acquisitions and losses	More concubines More bondservants	More sale of children, especially female More female infanticide
4 Age of marriage	Later for females Earlier for males	Earlier for females Later for males
5 Mortality	Lower	Higher
6 Fertility	Higher	Lower (less sex)
7 Relationships	Closer ties between brothers Intergenerational tension	Closer conjugal ties More independence
8 Range of marriage	Greater	Lesser
9 Affinity	More stress	Less stress
10 Normative system	Closer to Confucian norms	Closer to local 'custom'

was; lower groups might take a more positive view of their own practices, especially if these related to earlier cultural values that placed them in opposition to the incoming Han. We are dealing here with an aspect of internal difference which also relates to regional variations and is not only a question of the degree of commitment to the national ideology. Moreover the dominant group may effectively exclude the lower from participation in some practices, as is suggested by the statement of the author, Yü Cheng-hsieh (1775–1840), that 'the rites do not descend to the common people, nor do punishments reach up to the gentlemen' (Mann forthcoming:328).

Before looking further at these regional differences we should now add a second set of features to those listed in table 2, and these are summarised in table 3.

Regional differences

It would be impossible to consider this question without the work of Arthur Wolf (1985a; Wolf and Huang 1980) and the American social historians (especially Ebrey, Mann, Naquin and Rawski), on which I am greatly dependent for this brief discussion. The reason for embarking upon the subject at all is first because the nature of variation, 'internal' and 'external' in relation to any particular system boundary (and these limits are not set just by naming a people, society or culture), is important in trying to discern general attributes; secondly, the varying stress placed on, say, 'uxorilocal-'marriage in different parts of China may raise questions of a functional or structural kind relating to 'concomitant variations', as well as different questions concerning the historical and cultural background of the groups involved or even the quasi-autonomous emergence of variant forms within the general constraints of the particular society and type of social system; and thirdly, it is a problem I want to discuss in greater detail for India.

One of the most striking variations of this kind we have already mentioned, namely, the greater importance given to lineages, at least corporation lineages of type 1, in the South as compared with the North (p. 65), which has been attributed to economic as well as to political and historical differences. Economically, the South was the major rice-growing region, therefore richer and more able to create and maintain trusts. It was the area of later settlement by the Han where land was more readily available, though it had to be acquired and defended. Some of the single-lineage villages seem to have been the result of this initial colonisation, their exclusiveness being maintained by the expulsion of non-clan members (Cartier 1986a). Politically the region lay further from the centre, and hence had to depend to a greater extent upon local forms of social control, including self-help.

A further regional difference regarding marriage transactions was asserted by the missionary Smith at the end of the nineteenth century:

In the South of China ... the transfer of money at the engagement of a daughter, from the parents of the boy to those of the girl, assumes for all practical purposes the aspect of a purchase, which pure and simple, it often is. But in other parts of China we never hear of such a transaction, but only of a dowry from the bride's family, much in the manner of Western lands at times. (1899:270)

Leaving aside the question of his ability to understand marriage payments different from his own, he does recognise that in the North, the customary transactions warrant comparison with Europe, an observation that is supported by A. Wolf (1985a). While there seems to be a general agreement among Sinologists that direct dowry receives a greater stress in the North and indirect in the South, this is by no means a stark contrast, since both types of transfers occur in both areas and in most marriages. The difference seems to be that in the North even peasants might give a substantial dowry.[12] It is clear from the accounts of Taiwan that there too village people may do the same. But in general class differences in the nature of marriage prestations appear to be greater in the South, where land (which is unlikely to be an element in indirect endowments, only in the direct dowry) is less frequently a component.

If this difference is substantive, what is the reason? There is one possible argument which would associate 'stronger' corporation lineages with a greater emphasis on indirect dowry, that is, gifts from the groom's family that go to (or otherwise subsidise) the bride. In the first place, the existence of trusts removes significant quantities of land from the market, indeed from any form of transfer, operating like mortmain in Europe. Such land is simply unavailable for individual endowments. Rights in the land under trusteeship have to be rented, which involves exchanges of money, goods or services. But even on its own, indirect dowry preserves the shape of the lineage property since if given at marriage, most of it returns with the bride. Or it may be delayed so that it merges with the dower provided at the death of the husband. On the other hand, it is the richer families that generally stress the direct endowment of their daughters and these were presumably to be found in greater numbers in the more prosperous South; even if a significant proportion of landed property could not be transferred (except in the form of rights to rent lineage land), that did not affect the better off to the same extent, especially if their wealth had other, or additional, bases.

A related topic has to do with the link between lineages and the nature of affinal ties. I have called attention to R. Watson's analysis of class differences in affinity and marriage transactions in a Hong Kong lineage (1981). Naquin and Rawski (1987) see some evidence of stronger affinal ties in the North, especially in the greater ritualisation (Naquin 1988:21) associated with the absence of 'strong competitive lineages' of the South. Writing of the high incidence of minor marriages in southeast China, Naquin and Rawski (1987:172) remark upon their consequences in minimising affinal ties as well as in eliminating 'brideprice' and in helping to create satisfactory relations between mother and daughter-in-law. Such marriages occurred in an area dominated by 'strong corporate lineages' which tended to 'suppress class conflict'. On the other hand, class differences did exist, as R. Watson (1981) insists for Hong Kong, and were to be found in affinal relations between males within the body of these self-same corporation lineages.

Other regional differences have to do with forms of marriage and with 'mechanisms of continuity', what I have elsewhere called 'strategies of heirship' but which affect continuity in a wider sense, for example, in the use of uxorilocal marriage (or filiacentric unions) whereby a man moves in and provides labour for the father-in-law. This form of union is widespread in Eurasia especially where a man has daughters and no sons. However in some cases the percentage is higher than one would expect from the statistical distribution of families with only daughters. In Chiao-mei in southern Fukien, A. Wolf (1985a) found that 26.4 per cent of all first marriages were filiacentric, possibly due to the departure of young men on labour migration to Southeast Asia. The figure is much higher than that from the Taiwanese community of Hai-shan where roughly 10.8 per cent of men's marriages in the period 1886–1915 (Wolf and Huang 1980) were filiacentric. On the other hand it is lower than that for the village of Chung-she on the same island where such marriages averaged 30 per cent in the period before 1935. According to Barclay 21.8 per cent of all Taiwanese marriages registered in 1906 involved the husband moving into the house of the bride, a figure that dropped with the passage of time until it was 6.3 per cent in 1943 (table 69, Barclay 1954:229).

In most of the South a family without sons would call in a son-in-law to marry a daughter, or even an adopted daughter where there were no 'natural' ones. The higher figures in some parts relate to the greater migration of males or to the need for male help when the sons were too young to work but had elder sisters. However, in other areas of China, especially the North, such marriages were hardly practised at all. Indeed A. Wolf has recently concluded that even in southeast China the evidence for such marriages comes from communities in which Han immigrants have merged with autochthones to produce sinicised communities who adapted earlier practices. Among the Han a man might be called in to marry a widow, but not an unmarried daughter (1985b). For the Chinese generally, even in the South, looked down upon these marriages which were hedged around by complex contracts. 'By common agreement, male adoption was a better way to solve the problem of family continuity if one could find a son to adopt' (Pasternak 1985:324). In that part of Taiwan it was thought that the poorer families would bring in a son-in-law, the richer an adopted son, a difference that Watson (1975) connects with 'stronger' lineages although (depending upon one's definition of strength) neither observation seems to coincide with North–South differences.

The other marriage that was particularly common in Taiwan was 'minor marriage', the passage of a prospective bride into the home of her future husband at an early age by a less expensive form of wedding. Unlike the filiacentric case, marriages of this general type seem to have been distributed throughout China, reaching the highest proportions in parts of Taiwan and Fukien. During the period 1886–1905 in Hai-shan, 40 per cent of first marriages of males were of this kind; a survey in southwestern Fukien in 1943 revealed 51 per cent of households raising prospective brides. But, while such marriages were widespread, Wolf sees the practice in the North as differing from that in the South. In the former such unions arose as a result of crises; a girl might be orphaned or the parents unable to feed her as the result of a famine. She was separated from her natal family, given away or even sold, disposed of in marriage rather than in slavery or by infanticide; whereas in the South it was a marriage between two families, distributed throughout the population and seen as having some positive advantages.

The incidence of major marriage is obviously negatively correlated with that of the filiacentric (uxorilocal) and minor forms. The relative scarcity of the latter in the Han areas of the North obviously means a greater proportion of major marriage. Minor marriages have been variously linked to poverty or prudence (the wish to save money on marriage expenses or on the raising of a daughter who would have to be endowed), to the avoidance of mother-in-law conflict, to the pre-emption of a bride when these are in short supply and to the desire to control marital fertility (Coale 1985). But like filiacentric unions, they ran counter to the Confucian norms of high Han culture. One general aspect of filiacentric unions was to provide substitute male 'heirs' or workers where there were none, especially in those communities where the binding of feet made women little adapted to farm work. Labour requirements could be satisfied in other ways, but what about heirship? The alternative strategy was the adoption of males which seems to have been more prevalent in the North, where that other Confucian norm of major marriage was the general practice.[13]

The problem of explaining these North–South differences has been raised in discussing corporation lineages. Trusts, it was suggested, were more likely to be found in the newer, richer, rice-growing areas of the South, where central control is generally thought to have been less strong, for the distances were great, obstacles many, the 'aborigines' resistant and the lineages more independent.[14] Political, ideological and economic factors were all involved. At first sight the greater percentage of filiacentric unions would seem to fit uneasily with the 'stronger' lineages, while the minor marriages might fit equally well with both the weak and strong hypotheses, depending upon whether one considered it was 'strong' to control one's own daughters or 'strong' to control those of other people. As we have seen, the theoretical background of the discussion of the position of women in relation to the strength of lineages is based on African materials, and failed to take account of the differences in lineage structure; in any case the argument was inconclusive because the idea of strength was ambiguously formulated.

If on the other hand we return to the point that the South is the more recent area of expansion (although it had long been included in the Han dominions), we need to consider Wolf's suggestion that these 'aberrant' forms of marriage are to be found in the areas where the Han came to dominate a non-Han population with different patterns of behaviour. The expansion was partly a matter of conquest and partly of the mass migration of kin groups (or the founders of kin groups). The newcomers established themselves in the richer areas of the South, among people some of whom practised intensive agriculture, others shifting cultivation, but less advanced than the Han were to bring from the North and which enabled them gradually to expand into areas in South China occupied by Austronesian speakers (Fukien) and other minorities. Only in the Ming did they reach Taiwan (Bellwood 1979).

Some of the populations with whom the immigrants often intermarried were apparently organised on a matrilineal basis. Looked at more specifically in terms of the dominant culture, it could also be suggested that in these areas further removed from the original centres of Han ideological production, away from the first home of Confucian learning and of court influence, there was less commitment to follow the norms handed down by the sage, more willingness to adjust to contingent factors, to the practices of the autochthones and to the demands of farming, as well as a greater acceptance of change and variation.

In table 4 I try to summarise the broad North–South differences reported for China. It is striking to compare this listing with that of the hierarchical variations given in tables 2 and 3. If we look at items 2, 3 and 4 in the first and items 1, 2 and 9 in the second hierarchical table, we find that these accord with those listed as items 2 to 7 in the regional table. Only the difference in the type of lineage (1) runs in the counter direction. What is it that tends to make upper groups generally more like the North and lower groups more like the South? The practices prevalent in the North and among upper groups are closer to Confucian norms, that is, closer to those of the original core of Han culture, Confucian and neo-Confucianism, and of the more recent centres in the South, and closer to the norms contained in the written (Confucian) works which formed the basis of schooling for those who were privileged to attend. This distribution is understandable since the North is

Table 4. *Regional variations in China*

	North	South
1 Lineages	Type 1 & 2	Type 3 (Trusts)
2 Marriage transactions	Direct dowry	(+) Indirect dowry
3 Divorce	Rare	More frequent
4 Widow remarriage	Rare	More frequent remarriage of widows and divorcées
5 Mechanisms of continuity	More adoption (agnatic) Uxorilocal marriage only to widows	Adoption (+ non-agnatic). Filiacentric unions
6 Type of marriages	Major (plus early marriage in crisis)	Minor (*sim-pua*) plus major
7 Affinity	Stronger	Weaker
8 Length of settlement	Older (more Han)	Newer (less Han)
9 Women's labour	Less important	More important (especially in Hakka minorities)

the original home of Han society, but of course the great cities, and even the smaller towns, any centres of literate culture were also centres of Han culture and of Confucian learning, whether in the South or in the North. And it was of course the upper groups in the South, like the Brahmins in India, who were more likely to follow the patterns of the North whereas the lower groups were attached to local ways of doing things. Part of the convergence was, I have argued, due to similar socio-economic conditions, part due to the advent of immigrants and the power and prestige of the colonisers. But a major part was due to the influence of the state and Confucian ideology mediated by the educational system. For in China, as in Japan, whose earlier codes were much influenced by the Tang (618–907), the state played an important but variable role in the organisation of both family and farm, often in the direction of attempting to homogenise custom, to stabilise 'houses' and to reinforce male authorities, partly because of its interest in tax, corvée and military service. However it is also true that the North not only contained the original core areas, but was also more open to invasion from the outside by nomads, some of whom in turn were influenced by Islam. Among these nomads,[15] the role of the lineage was strong and may sometimes even have served as a model in China itself. But with the exception of the forms of marriage, it was rather the 'lower' customs of the South that were more in line with the norms of Islam and of other nomadic peoples (for example, the levirate), so that any influence may well have led to the strengthening of existing practices in opposition to those of the outsiders.

Like simple class oppositions, the notion of general differences in the kinship practices of North and South China is a crude dichotomy, more so perhaps than in the case of India which I examine in chapter 8. Those who analyse the data in terms of macro-regions (for example Naquin and Rawski 1987, developing Skinner) can operate at a more particularist, less crude level, especially in terms of centre and periphery, since the expansion of the Han led to many new centres of learning and orthodoxy. Nevertheless the expansion did take place from North to South, and has left its mark on the degree of assimilation of local populations at a variety of levels. Moreover the basic geographical division is one used not only by many observers but also by the actors themselves. So I continue to employ it in a broad heuristic way to try and account for some of the data.

Changes over time

In this account of Chinese kinship and marriage I have dealt briefly with hierarchical and regional variations in the pre-Revolutionary period. The question of earlier changes would take me even further outside my competences, although I have referred to the historical events leading to the creation of corporation and other lineages. Nevertheless it is worth commenting that the broad lines of marriage ritual, prescribed in the *Book of Rites*, did persist over a long period and provided some common focus for marriage ceremonies and arrangements throughout China.

The epithet 'traditional' is sometimes used in our discussion, but never with the implication of static. For any system, however loosely defined, that allows for hierarchical and regional differences must also be dynamic, whether that dynamism comes from external forces, is internally generated, or derives from different adaptations to pre-existing circumstances.

The long-term changes in the patterns of kinship have recently been studied by Ebrey and turn principally on the question of endowment. In her analysis of marriage transactions in the Tang and Song, Ebrey (forthcoming:172) discerns a major shift of emphasis from what I have called indirect dowry (her 'betrothal gifts') to direct dowry, the bulk of the expense of marriage now coming from the bride's family rather than from the groom's, although in both cases the greater part went to the conjugal pair, sometimes to the wife alone. She sees this change as connected with the expansion of the economy that took place over the same period, accompanied by the growth of cities, a decrease in state control over the distribution of land, the shift from aristocratic to examination-based government, the decline of Buddhism and the rise of Neo-Confucianism, the movement in the centre of Chinese culture to the South and the development of local lineages.

More specifically she suggests the change may be connected with three factors. First, the greater commercialisation and freer forms of land tenure would give more people the opportunity to offer dowry (p. 171). Secondly, the elite may have used dowries for advancement in the political domain, a sort of political hypergamy. Thirdly, and not inconsistent with the others, is the possibility that changes in the economy encouraged a shift toward diverging devolution, above all in the elite, but gradually filtering downwards.

In the fluid situation introduced by increasing wealth and the expansion of the scholar–gentry, the elite employed dowry, Ebrey argues, as a means of 'buying' marriage connections. High dowry can, of course, be used to advance the position of daughters and to increase the husband's access to wealth. On the other hand a man could equally well advance his connections by offering high betrothal gifts in order to attract the daughter of a potentially important man. R. Watson (1981) shows how the rich and powerful members of a Hong Kong lineage used dowry to establish affinal ties while peasant males (though not peasant women) avoided their affines. But both in the Song period and in contemporary Hong Kong, upper groups tend to have more far-flung ties of marriage, a fairly general feature of the rich as against the poor. It is clear that direct dowry is highest where affinity is strongest. In principle these ties could be established and maintained by gifts of either kind, as Ebrey appreciates, although in the one case it is the men that are 'climbing' and in the other women (although women also rise through their menfolk and vice versa). It is not clear that dowry can be said to make a better 'bribe' in both cases. Given the frequency with which this shift is reported in Eurasia, we have to look for general rather than specific explanations, even if the timing of the transactions requires a more particular accounting in each case.

If there was an actual change at this period (rather than just a shift of emphasis in the written contracts or the legal records), then it was almost certainly encouraged by the increased circulation of wealth, which would be logically consistent with trends elsewhere. But whatever change occurred was a matter of emphasis rather than of category, of degree rather than of kind, for both types of transactions were certainly present in Chinese society long before that time and both are found down to today. During the Song, wealthy men paid a large indirect dowry to marry a woman of the royal clan. Such women inevitably married hypogamously and under the Qing, the husband could not even enter the presence of his in-laws without express permission (Rawski 1988:26); he derived his title from his wife's status and may even have lived in a house provided by the Imperial Household. The status and residence of the wife determined that of the husband who had to contribute a large sum (described as a *chuang-lien* or dowry), not as a purchase price but in order to establish his claim to marry such a prized woman. However, while either direct or indirect dowry may be used to advance the status of a spouse of either sex, the normal form of marriage is neither hypogamous nor hypergamous but isogamous, bringing together two families of 'roughly comparable social status' (Naquin 1988:4).

The shift of emphasis in dowry occurred around the tenth century; the extension of corporation lineages took place some two centuries later. Ebrey suggests that the insistence on patriliny, in this particular form, may have been partly a response to the spread of diverging devolution. In turn, 'descent line rhetoric and the growth of descent groups can also be given some credit for curbing the trend toward dowry' (forthcoming:175), which sometimes took the form of sumptuary legislation. However, in recent times, the evidence from areas with 'strong' lineages shows that it is the rich who give dowries, not the poor. For the rich, an emphasis on descent is quite consistent with the giving of dowry, while its absence among the poor may have something to do with their dependence as tenants on lineage lands.

The inter-relations between dowry and corporation lineages are undoubtedly complex and may be partly related to a common variable in the economic domain. But it is true that in Islam, in India, and to some extent in ancient Israel problems arose with the inflation of property allocated to women, which frequently gave rise to sumptuary legislation. At the same time this allocation appears to have led to efforts by agnatic groups to retain for themselves what they have in principle given away, in some cases by means of charitable family trusts which benefit the descendants of males rather than females. This is not to resolve a contradiction that continues to exist, especially in lineage societies, but it provides, as Ebrey notes, a dynamic element in the system.

Local variation in Taiwan

Variation was not only a class and regional matter but a local one as well. A full realisation of its extent has been one result of the intensive study of the immigrant Chinese population in Taiwan, which has been made possible not only by the easy and continuous access for fieldworkers but by the existence of detailed records of the population kept by the Japanese colonial regime during the occupation which began in 1895. For that reason the final section of this chapter is devoted to discussing two such studies, by Barclay (1954) and by Wolf and Huang (1980), both of which present data that raise problems for the initial version of the lineage model that dominated earlier anthropology and document the extent of the deviation of Taiwan from the Confucian model. But the second of these accounts also brings up two other matters, first, the extent of local variation within Taiwan (which requires various kinds of explanation) and secondly, the consequences for inter-personal relations of the three different forms of marriage practised there and which represent another axis of differentiation of family life.

In Taiwan and in other colonial regimes, systematic records of people and property were made in order to facilitate social control, to act as a record of booty or to provide a base for future taxation. From 1905 the Japanese police insisted that all households should register their members so they could keep track of people's whereabouts; there were registers of land title and land tax; in addition census data and government statistics existed and it was these latter records (rather than the more detailed registers) that were used by the demographer, Barclay, whose work clearly showed the divergence between Confucian ideals of the big patriarchal family into which women were incorporated in the course of a major marriage on the one hand and the actuality of life in South China on the other.

Far from having enormous households of the kind depicted, say, in *The Dream of the Red Chamber*, which can be paralleled by aristocratic and gentry households elsewhere, the average was not much greater than is found in other parts of Europe and Asia. For what he calls 'ordinary' as distinct from quasi-households, the figures were as follows:

1905	5.19
1915	5.31
1920	5.30
1930	6.64

The households of 'other nationalities', mainland merchants and Japanese colonists, were smaller, under 4.00.[16] These figures fit well with a restudy of the extensive survey of farm families carried out by Buck on mainland China in the 1930s which gives a revised average 'family size' of 5.2 (Buck 1937; Taeuber 1970). This figure is close to the 5.5 household size given for the Tang (c. AD 780); here the core group was an elementary family, although if there was more than one surviving son, they would remain undivided after the death or retirement of the father (Cartier 1986a:464–5). To get an idea of the comparable size of households elsewhere, a figure of 4.8 is given for the period from 1574 to 1821 in England (Laslett 1972:146) and an estimated 4.9 for Japan between the seventeenth century and 1955 (Nakane 1972). Considering that the high status model of the Chinese household is often viewed, internally and externally, as a 'grand' or 'extended' household in opposition to the stem variety of the Japanese, and the 'nuclear' (or stem) variety of western Europe, the differences in size are very much less than this typology might suggest. The comparison of 'family size' however is a complex one, as it is not always clear whether one is dealing with residential, production, consumption or property-holding units, especially in societies like India and China where the latter often continue to exist until a formal division takes place. The long-term nature of this process of separation emphasises the need to consider the time element, that is, the developmental aspect, in the context of labour requirements, heirship and the control of family, face and fortune, not simply the composition or size of any one of these groups at any one point in time. Eurasian societies do not radically diverge in this respect and it is therefore not surprising to find that recent work on East–West differences in family and marriage has tended to shift its focus from the size to the composition of the households (Hajnal 1965, 1982; Goody forthcoming b).

When we look at the composition of Taiwanese households broken down by sex, there are two other factors that stand out. First, there was a predominance of males in the secondary sex ratio, 119 to 100; secondly, a significant proportion of heads of household were female, 12 per cent in 1920 and 1930 (table 46, Barclay 1954:182). At the same time the number of 'non-family' members, however defined, was low.

The picture becomes yet more interesting when we look at these figures in relation to marriage. On the one hand Chinese society offered few alternatives to the married role; the proportion of ever-marrieds is high; in 1905, it was 95.3 per cent for men of 35 and over, and 99.7 per cent for women; and it did not change to any significant extent over the period in question, though the pressure to marry seemed to grow stronger for men under thirty and weaker for women.

At the same time, Barclay argues, the marriage market was influenced by the sex ratio, that is, by the availability of women which in turn was dependent upon the differential treatment of male and female children (table 60, p. 218). This imbalance in the sex ratio resulted both from infanticide and from neglect, deliberate or not. The killing of girls has been a characteristic feature of some of the major Asian societies, being associated at one end of the spectrum with wealthy groups who did not want to disburse dowry for 'excessive' daughters, and at the other end with those poor peasant families who were unable to feed all their children. In China, deliberate female infanticide was mainly of the latter kind; 'under pressure of poverty many families apparently eliminated certain unwanted offspring, either through exposure or deliberate neglect' (p. 135). In India upper groups such as the Rajputs were involved, largely because of the dowry situation. Interestingly in ancient Rome both rich and poor exposed their unwanted infants, the second to get rid of extra workers to feed, the first 'to preserve their fortunes for an elder son' (Thomas 1986:197). Wolf shows that in Taiwan under Japanese rule young children of Hokkien landlords could be given away as 'little daughters-in-law' (*sim-pua*) even to poorer families, not under crisis conditions but under normal ones. Obviously there is no undifferentiated concern for daughters as daughters. It is one of the paradoxes of female endowment systems; daughters are a burden partly because they do have claims, claims on family wealth and honour. Female infanticide and discriminatory care occur in those very societies where women are in some senses treated more equally regarding property (than in Africa for example). But significantly, the giving away or destruction of daughters happens with infants or young children. When they have established their identity as women or girls the position is different; they can then be married and endowed. But the situation is always more problematic than with the 'elementary' forms of marriage, since women (or rights in women) are exchanged neither for goods nor for other women; as they have little exchange value in this sense, their number may be diminished with impunity, indeed with advantages for those who remain.

Missionaries had long reported infanticide on mainland China (Smith 1899) as well as in Taiwan, where the Japanese tried to put a stop to a custom which they had earlier practised themselves, just one among a wider array of positive checks on fertility. There is good evidence that during the Toku-gawa period Japanese families used a range of strategies to arrive at a family composition that enabled them to raise, or at least to maintain, existing standards of living (Hanley 1972, 1977; T. Smith 1977). Japanese families achieved the 'optimum' size by controlling fertility within marriage through abortion and infanticide, as well as by adoption, that is, giving away children in excess of those the family could afford and bringing in children if couples failed to produce the desired number and sex (Hanley 1977:167–8; T. Smith 1977:64–9). These practices were not desperate acts carried out under adverse economic conditions, as Fei (1939), for example, suggests for China, but were deliberately aimed at achieving the right composition (T. Smith 1977:14). On the other hand, in China there is little evidence of the control of fertility by abortion. Like infanticide, this was contrary to Budd-hist teaching. Nevertheless poorer families seem to have adjusted their holdings of children after birth by the infanticide of girls, by the sale and adoption of both sexes, and in the South by early marriage of girls.

Apart from deliberate infanticide, the neglect of children produced a further distortion of the sex ratio: 'the chances of surviving through infancy and childhood had been extremely poor for girls before 1895' (Barclay 1954:212), though this handicap gradually disappeared in later years. As a result in 1905 there were more than twenty 'surplus' males for every hundred females in the age group fifteen to nineteen. The age-specific data on Taiwan suggest that the transfer of children outside the house into a situation where they were less well cared for may have been one of the causes for this imbalance. On the other hand this differential child mortality, higher for females, also occurred in Japan where minor marriages, though not un-known, were rare. In India we find the same disparity; the danger to the female sex came very early in infancy, disappearing in childhood but found again at about fourteen when it continued till fifty-five, suggesting a connec-tion with the very early age of marriage, substantially earlier than China, since girls were supposed to join their husbands soon after puberty (Miller 1981).

By contrast the figures for the USA and Europe show more male deaths than female at all ages. While the infanticide, exposure or abandonment of children widely found in Europe until recently was apparently as frequent, it was not sex-specific. It originated from a different social situation, that of late marriage. Where marriage takes place before, at or soon after puberty, there is little question of pre-marital births, especially where the very possibility of pre-marital sex is inhibited by careful guardianship; infanticide or abandonment is a question of family strategy, the disposal of children of married couples. But with late marriage, especially where the control of sexuality is difficult or absent (as in the case of living-in servants), the disposal of a child is not a question of its sex but of the single status, the employment position (which often excluded marriage) or the personal relationships of the mother.

'Infanticide' has not ceased to be an active factor in Chinese life. Even in 1953 there was a clear masculine bias in the cohorts, the overall ratio being 107.7 males to 100 females. This rate of masculinity might possibly have been due to a bias in the registration of births, but recent material on one-child families suggest that in rural areas the practice is still alive.

The imbalanced sex ratio arose partly from the fact that daughters were costly to raise and costly to marry off. On the other hand they were clearly desirable as brides. The lack of balance in the overall marital exchange can be circumvented by delaying the marriage age of the favoured sex and advancing that of the disfavoured. Later marriage for men, earlier for women. Nevertheless where virtually everybody was expected to get married, there was clearly some pressure to find a bride at an early stage, by the kind of pre-emptive betrothal found in many regions of the world. As we have seen, in parts of southern China the twin problems of the search for a bride and the disposal of a daughter found a resolution in the *sim-pua* (or elsewhere *siaosiv*), the 'adopted' or 'fostered' daughter-in-law; this 'minor marriage' relieved the girl's family of the costs of her upbringing and both sets of parents of the costs of a major wedding; so it provided a constructive alternative to female infanticide.

While the early arrival of a prospective bride into the house of her future husband was more or less in line with Confucian ideals, the other form of marriage that we have discussed, the filiacentric union, ran quite counter to that ideology. In addition two other aspects of Taiwanese marriage did not meet up with Confucian norms, namely, the existence of widow remarriage and divorce. In upper groups and in the written norms, widow remarriage was strongly disapproved of. The idea of loyalty to one husband and the strength of the particular conjugal bond was so strong that, as in India, widows committed suicide on hearing of their husband's death, which was conceived as a highly meritorious act (Johnston 1910:226ff.). Other widows lived on, and on application to the Ministry of Rites, their virtue was celebrated by special insignia, by formulaic biographies in the county gazetteer and occasionally by the erection of a stone arch in their honour. Freedman argued that this attitude followed from a woman's incorporation into the lineage of the husband. It is the case that some wealthy families lived up to this ideal. But despite the public acclaim given to the virtuous widow, those in the lower ranks of society did remarry; the families of their dead husbands could not afford to support them 'for the mere joy of contemplating their fidelity' (Johnston 1910:217). Remarriage of this kind was quite frequent in many parts and in his study of household registers in North

Taiwan, Wolf found that 50 per cent of widows took another husband. Of the remaining 50 per cent, he argues, most were concerned not with chastity but with preserving the independence granted by the death of their husbands. Those who remarried might become the wives of poorer men who missed out on the first round. There were even some advantages for a man in such a union, since marriage to a widow was cheaper to arrange.[17] However, if she already had children, it was more complicated and the new husband had in some cases to move in with the family of the wife's first husband (Barclay 1954:218), as elsewhere in China.

Some marriages were ended by divorce rather than death. Again there is a discrepancy between ideal and actual. When divorce took place it is said to have occurred at the whim of the husband; the wife had to return to her kin in disgrace, never more to be sought in marriage. But as Barclay notes, there was one mitigating factor which characterises most societies with diverging devolution. 'The harshness of this procedure is tempered, mercifully, by prospective loss of the dowry to the husband's family' as well as by a number of other considerations (p. 220). When we look at the records of divorce cases kept by the Japanese (which probably included separations), the figures for 1906 are high (22.3 per cent of registered marriages of each year ended within five years) but they also show a progressive decline to 3.0 per cent in 1929.[18]

A large proportion of those who got divorced must have remarried. The turnover in divorced and widowed spouses 'is remarkably high' (table 65, p. 223). But it was the women who had a better chance of remarrying than the men. With this high turnover there was a surprisingly low proportion of marriages in which men and women were both marrying for the first time, 58.5 per cent in 1906 but rising to 86.4 per cent in 1943 (table 66, p. 225); a larger proportion of men had to accept second-time brides as their first wives. By 1940 marriage had become longer lasting for both sexes, a change that may have reflected a broadening of the marriage choice.

These three different forms of marriage are the focus of the study by Wolf and Huang of Taiwan, entitled *Marriage and Adoption in China, 1845–1945* (1980), which illustrates the shift of emphasis that has occurred in studies of Chinese kinship. A critical feature of this work was its basis not only in historical documents but in intensive fieldwork in the region of Hai-shan. The past is reconstructed in quite a different manner from that undertaken by earlier anthropological writers, being based not only on life histories and documents but also on the very detailed records of the period of the Japanese occupation. This different approach (and the different availability of data) led to other interests and other conclusions. In the first place they showed that while 50 per cent of marriages were contracted 'normally' according to the 'major' pattern, 40 per cent were 'minor' marriages in which families raised their son's wives and another 10 per cent were filiacentric ones. This latter figure is lower than Barclay's for the earlier period but it represents the first marriages of men, whereas those for women are constantly higher, constituting 17.8 per cent in the period 1891–95, and dropping to 10.6 per cent between 1916 and 1920. The reason for this discrepancy was that the inhabitants of the districts in Wolf and Huang's sample were richer than their neighbours; some of the marrying-in husbands were the sons of poor upland farmers eking out a precarious living on the slopes of the central mountain range (p. 126). For men in Hai-shan itself a filiacentric union was less clearly desirable than for an heiress, and this attitude was reflected in the ages of marriage, which are higher for marrying-in men; such a choice often represented their last chance of a bride. But the bride's family were in a greater hurry to marry off their daughter and to secure the services of a son-in-law. The authors recount the interesting case of a man whose father had died a few years previously, following which the brothers divided the estate:

Since then he has been forced to hire laborers to help with transplanting and harvesting. This is expensive and cuts into meagre profits. Worse yet, he cannot even consider renting more land, the only hope he has of enlarging the family's income. So he watches anxiously as his eldest daughter matures and arranges her marriage as soon as she is old enough to attract the man he needs. (1980:136)

Bringing in a son-in-law in this fashion is the functional equivalent of adopting a son, just as 'adopting' or fostering a future daughter-in-law in minor marriage corresponds to the later acquisition of a bride in a major marriage. But in Hai-shan the percentage of marrying-in sons-in-law to 100 marrying-in daughters-in-law was 16.2. While there were only 5.5 per cent of adopted sons to every 100 natural sons, there were 114 'adopted' daughters (that is, young girls entering the house as prospective brides) for every 100 daughters (p. 131). The adoption of males plugs a demographic gap; the acquisition of a future daughter-in-law is a way of pre-empting a bride for one's son, and training her to boot.

The adoption of males took two main forms depending on whether it occurred within the clan or outside. In Hai-shan an adopted agnate was called 'crossing-*pang*-child' (where *pang* meant a line) and no payment was normally involved. 'In many areas of China custom strictly prohibited adopting a male child from a non-agnate' (1980:108) – or only when none other was available; that was Confucian doctrine. The adoptee assumed the rights and duties of a son *vis-à-vis* his adoptive parents but he did not terminate his relationship with the natural family.

The second type of adoption involved 'strangers', even sisters' sons. Such a man was known as a 'boll-worm', the term referring to a wasp trapping a green caterpillar in her nest. This category of non-agnatic adoption became a commercial transaction and entailed a complete break with the natal family, removing all status ambiguity. The adoptees often came from afar, brought by special merchants, and the child was usually spoken of as *khit-e*, purchased.

Both categories wore full mourning at the deaths of their adopted parents. But ideally the boll-worm did not attend the funeral of his own natural parents, or if he did he wore a white armband with a patch of red, the same mourning dress used by a friend. The dress of the 'crossing-*pang*-child', on the other hand, depended on whether or not he had inherited a share of the property of his natural father.

A third form of male adoption was posthumous. If a man died without an heir, a brother might assign a son to his name. The practice works in a similar way to the levirate or ghost marriage among the Nuer of the southern Sudan (Evans-Pritchard 1951), except that it is a transaction in children instead of a transaction in wives. Such adopted children did of course inherit. Wolf and Huang tell how one man took them to the box of his ancestral altar and extracted a contract he had made assigning one of his sons to a dead brother. He was amazed to find that the box contained two contracts, his own and one written by his younger living brother who had followed his lead. This was 'the only way', someone else explained, 'he could prevent the older man's sons claiming two-thirds of the family estate' (1980:112).

The authors argue that in those parts of China where they see lineages as being strongest, the adoption of outsiders was forbidden; there you had to adopt within the clan. As I have argued, the assessment of the comparative strength of lineages raises the question of the criteria to be used and there is little agreement among scholars about this. Nevertheless in the South, where lineages were of the corporation type, all adoption seems to have been less common, greater use being made of other mechanisms of continuity. If you had no sons and wished your daughter to make a filiacentric union in order to secure continuity, you could not marry her to someone within the clan because of the rule of exogamy. The contrast lies with the Mediterranean and the Near East where clans were not exogamous. In ancient Greece clansmen were the preferred spouse of the epiclerate, the brotherless heiress. Father's brother's daughter marriage was associated not so much with the 'strength' of the lineage as with keeping property and other goods within the group. In China this had to be achieved by other means. Whether exo-adoption like exo-gamy is a measure of lineage strength or weakness is impossible to judge and it seems better to use some less global concept. Adopting outside the clan, like marrying inside, clearly represents a greater willingness to conform to Confucian norms, which was to be expected in the North.

Wolf and Huang refer to the prospective brides bought into the households from outside as 'adopted', but the earlier usage of fostered daughter or daughter-in-law is perhaps preferable, especially as they see objections to Freedman's use of the term. Such prospective brides (*sim-pua*) differed radically from purchased servant-girls (*ca-bo-kan*) who did not have the right to marry. However a distinction is also made between those *sim-pua* who are 'matched' (betrothed) and those who are 'unmatched', depending upon whether a prospective spouse existed at the time they entered the household; certain of these later married there while others did not. Some girls were even taken 'unmatched' for therapeutic purposes, it being felt that the parents might give birth to a natural child, even a son, as a result of this act. Subsequently, as we have seen, Wolf has made a further distinction between this southern practice and the northern one whereby orphans, but not members of parental families, are raised by prospective parents-in-law, that is to say, as the result of a crisis. Rather than 'adoption' (turning someone into a kinsman), the institution of the *sim-pua* involves fostering and represents a form of early marriage or engagement, the pre-emption of a spouse in a system where marriage was virtually universal and where girls were sometimes scarce.

Early marriage for men and women is seen as having some advantages. A common Chinese saying runs, 'Plant seedlings early and you will harvest a rice crop early; have a daughter-in-law early and you will enjoy happiness (grandchildren) early' (Croll 1984:55). Happiness is not so much a question of increasing the overall numbers of the workforce as of obtaining help in the fields at the right time, when the grandparents have retired from active farming, that is, of providing for the continuity of the labour force. The most valued and efficient way of doing so is through the birth of male children, especially in those communities where women were deliberately incapacitated for farm work through foot-binding. Hence families were keen to pre-empt a bride for their sons at an early stage, and at the same time, especially in poorer families, they may be willing to allow their daughters to be brought up by others who are anxious to provide for earlier continuity. In such marriages little changes hands except the infant girl; gifts are minimal. In contrast those families who raised their own daughters to marriageable age might have some justification in calling for betrothal gifts since they have raised another family's 'reproducer'. Nevertheless, whatever the link between such gifts and later marriage, they did not constitute 'brideprice' in any meaningful sense, especially as in the past 'the bride's family frequently returned the betrothal gift to the groom's household in the form of a dowry which also constituted a potential source of independence' (Croll 1985:115). Today such gifts seem more likely to be retained but that is a new development under changing circumstances.

It goes without saying that early unions of this or of any kind are marriages of arrangement rather than choice; or to put it in a less ethnocentric way, the choice is the parents' rather than the couples'.[19] There is unlikely to be any allocation of funds to the daughters, either directly or indirectly. But the advantage to the groom's family is that steps are taken to establish continuity at a time when alternatives can be considered if this course does not work. Moreover when the generations follow closely, they can relieve one another of the heavier burdens at an earlier age. That may be more important for males than for females, although male generations are characteristically longer because of their later age of marriage. In any case there is nothing so sad in a farming community as seeing an old couple struggle on without any help in tasks for which they no longer have the strength.

While minor marriages for women were completed at an earlier age than major ones, some two years after sexual maturity, they mostly followed the same general ceremonial form as 'major' weddings; for culturally that was the dominant form, many people even denying the existence of other types except among the very poor whose customs were perceived as warped by poverty and ignorance. I have already called attention to some features of these ceremonies in 'major marriages', but a further example from Taiwan will help bring out some further points. The main rituals involved a procession from the house of the bride to that of the groom and included the display of the property being transferred. Such a display was only mounted by those who could afford such things, although some would hire appropriate items for the occasion. So that when a tenant farmer or farm labourer arranged a marriage for his son 'the elaborate ritual described in textbooks was reduced to a modest bridal procession and a small feast' (Wolf and Huang 1980:72).

At the same time this public ritual emphasised the transfer of rights over the bride: her removal from the custody of her father's line, her introduction to the household of her husband, and then, in the case of the major marriage, the reintroduction to her natal family in a new status. 'The first stage . . . was a ceremony known as *sang-tia:*, which occurred after the hard negotiations over brideprice and dowry were completed' (1980:73). Seated in front of the ancestral altar of the bride's father, the groom's mother placed a brass and a gold ring on the middle finger of the girl's left hand. From this day on the girl's tablet has to be placed in her husband's house; if she died before the wedding day and the husband married again, his children were taught to regard the soul enshrined there as that of a mother.

The second phase is the procession on the wedding day when the bride, wearing a head-dress modelled on that of the Imperial Consort, is conducted across the threshold of her new house by the go-between.[20] During the first few days she carried out various tests, being offered, for example, a cleaver with soil and soot on the handle. Later she was taken on a ceremonial visit to her own home where she was treated as a guest. Nor was this her last visit, for she continued to go back at intervals and her ties were constantly renewed. 'The woman who failed to return home on New Year's Day for three years in succession threatened her natal family and could not return at all unless she took special ritual precautions to protect her brother's good fortune.'

While Wolf and Huang describe this process as one of incorporation into the family of the groom, we have seen that there are problems with this concept since a wife obviously retains many links with her natal family. Moreover in Hai-shan as elsewhere the woman herself is set up at marriage with endowments both from her husband's family and from her own, that is, both by indirect dowry ('brideprice') and by direct dowry. The groom's family gave the bride's 'a sizeable sum of money . . . "engagement money", which is explained as serving "to thank the woman's family for raising her"' The problem with this explanation, comment the authors, is that after receiving it, the bride is sent off with a dowry consisting of gold jewellery, furniture, clothing and, in the case of an exceptionally wealthy family, land. That is why people complain that raising a daughter is like raising a thief because she takes away with her not only the groom's gifts but those from her own family; she is endowed from two sources.

It will be recalled that Freedman claimed the men of the bride's family made this sacrifice not because she had any specific economic claims ('she is not a member of the property-owning group') but because their own status was at stake – hence the open display of dowry. But, suggest Wolf and Huang, this contention would apply only to the rich. Why would a poor farmer be willing to sacrifice so much? Because, they were told, the woman's family must send something so that the bride is treated well in her new home. For, as we have seen, even after handing over the dowry her natal family will make representations if she is maltreated (however broadly this may be defined) and at the end of her days they will appear at her funeral to confirm that she did not die of foul play.

In Freedman's interpretation the family's status is at stake, in keeping with his lineage orientation; in the other account the family are seen as ensuring their daughter makes a satisfactory marriage. It is difficult to see why both factors could not be present simultaneously, nor yet why status should be opposed to property. Status is never purely an economic matter, but on the other hand it can rarely be altogether unconnected. Moreover, considerations of status apply to the life a daughter leads as a wife, not only to the wedding itself. Marriage and the dowry did not serve to cut the girl off altogether but to establish her in her own degree, whether high or low. Once established, she was entitled to the continuing support of the family into which she had married; if her husband died, 'his brother had either to support the widow or allow her to claim her husband's share of the family estate'. In the latter case she was dowered as well as dowried, and had claims neither for property nor usually for maintenance from her natal family. But that group was still concerned with her position, which reflected upon theirs, and they offered her support in difficult circumstances. For the process of handing over a daughter as a wife is also a matter of seeing her properly looked after. In richer families she was sometimes supplied with clothes and other needs 'for her lifetime'; included in this was the furniture that accompanied her, occasionally servants too, and even food for the first few weeks of marriage. In North Taiwan they might also send burial clothes and a bedpan – 'we send everything'.

The accounts of marriage transactions that I have given in chapter 2 and above are those of observers of weddings in the villages of pre-Revolutionary China and of contemporary Taiwan. It should be recalled that important elements of the ritual were found throughout the country, in the different classes, and over a long period. One of the reasons for this relative homogeneity was the fact that marriage had been the subject of written works by scholars in the Warring States period (481–221 BC), and after.[21] They included 'the six rites' in three ancient texts, the *Book of Rites*, the *Book of Etiquette and Ceremonial* and the *Baihu tong*. These six rites (the Chinese literati had a passion for numerical classification) were sending the presents, asking for the girl's name, sending news of favourable divination, sending the evidence, asking the time of the wedding ceremony and meeting in person. In addition to the six rites, variously modified in different areas according to local 'custom' and generative invention, were the three covenants that characterised marriage among the more urban, more literate elements of society, consisting of the contract of marriage, the receipt of the betrothal money and the deed for the delivery of the bride. In addition written lists were also kept of all the wedding gifts.

In Hong Kong around the time of the Second World War, marriage was preceded by a matching of the written birthdates, as well as a matching of family and individual backgrounds.[22] After the presentation of engagement tokens and betrothal gifts, of which a register was kept, there was the ceremony of the delivery of the dowry. 'All items of the dowry were listed on an inventory or a dowry register which was also sent to the boy's house for checking . . .' (Anon 1986:25). Among wealthy families the dowry might include a servant girl to look after the new bride, since this was not only an opportunity for a family to flaunt its position but also 'to demonstrate its concern for the daughter'. So when daughters in upper families had established themselves as persons, they became representative members of their families, and were endowed out of parental property. In other words dowry was a well-established feature of marriage among the bourgeoisie of South China, as it had long been in the rest of the country.

Song records also include written contracts of marriage as well as the 'agreement' or 'detailed cards' which were exchanged between the families, laying out what the groom would present, which might include fields and productive property or *ts'ai-ch'an*, and what she would bring, which again might comprise 'fields, houses, businesses, hills, or gardens' (Ebrey forth-coming:150). Marriage provided one of the great occasions for the use of writing and documents, the paper and forms being available in the stationery stores in the larger towns; possession of a written document did provide some assurance in case of broken engagements or other disagreements (Naquin 1988).

Despite the importance of direct dowry in wealthy groups, the legal validity of a marriage did not depend upon that endowment; as was the case in Islam, that role was played by the indirect dowry (what Ebrey calls the 'betrothal gifts', the endowment provided by the groom) which was essen-tial. According to the *Li Chi*, 'Without receipt of the betrothal gifts there is no contract and no affinity' (see Legge 1885:i, 78; Ebrey forthcoming:3). Nevertheless a Han bride was also equipped by her family in a manner that reflected their wealth; in contemporary India, too, Prasad, found a consis-tent relationship between the size of family income and that of the direct dowry, although clearly other factors such as the status of the husband and the attractiveness of the bride played their part. Dowry is rarely if ever a fixed share, although in one region of early modern France it could form part of a fixed proportion which was made up by inheritance.

The support for a married woman could take a variety of forms and might in places include land. An interesting example comes from Xiaolan in the Pearl River Delta, where the area of cultivable land was constantly being expanded by complex dyking techniques. Land was sometimes given as part of dowry, the contract being framed in red and carried as part of the wedding procession. In other cases the wife was allocated land for her lifetime, to be managed by her husband but reverting to her natal family at her death. In the third instance along this continuum, the bride's father kept the land but provided his married daughter with the income derived from it, which she used as her personal allowance; this latter provision formed part of a partition contract (of 1887) where the wife continued to receive support from the estate even after her father died, as a kind of inheritance (Siu, personal communication).

What proportion of the woman's dowry came directly from the parents and what came from the parents-in-law varied according to the class. But as elsewhere in Eurasia the notion of match might include the matching of property, not necessarily for the bride but for the couple. In China the allocation of wealth to the bride was in effect a way of endowing the couple, since the son had no property of his own until partition took place.

It is sometimes suggested that this process cannot be regarded as devolution because it did not provide for equal shares between siblings. Few systems do. The size of an endowment depended upon the making of a match as well as upon a certain element of competition (with specific partners) and display (against the world). At times the result, as elsewhere in Eurasia, was sumptuary legislation against excessive gift-giving at marriage, whereas in Africa it is against excessive expenditure at death. This has been a long-standing problem; sumptuary rules were already used to regulate the size of betrothal gifts under the northern dynasties (AD 386–581), indicating a higher level of gifts than those listed in the classics (Ebrey forthcoming:140). The girl's family should not make a profit out of such gifts but had to use all to provide an endowment, which was hers rather than her husband's.

One aspect of these transactions is undoubtedly display, as is stressed by Harrell and Dickey (1985) who offer the fact in explanation of dowry. Display is partly a matter of emphasising *differences* in status (although it may also represent simply *changes* of status) and is linked to differences in economic and other facets of stratification. But this aspect of marriage prestations is usually more important among the rich than the poor. If we look at merchant families in towns, the contrast with peasants is considerable, even though the latter may have adopted some of the features of the national, written, rituals, especially those connected with pomp and circumstance. But not all upper groups behave in this way; in some societies weddings are quiet, at least about major property transfers. And it should be added that in China less fuss is often made about the transfer of rights in land, the basic productive resource of peasants and landlords alike, than of lacquered chests and flashy cooking pots. Display is an element of much transfer, not all; but neither does it contradict the wider notion of a direct dowry as devolution. Nor do I see the idea of compensation as necessarily setting aside that of indirect dowry; only in a few cases the element of reward is clearly present, and then hardly in the sense proposed by Divale and Harris (1976) and Harris (1979), that is, as compensation for taking a 'non-productive' female member, a thesis that neglects the role of reproducers as well as the fact that in most agricultural societies work is largely carried out by 'couples', heterosexual ones. The transaction that has been more often interpreted as compensation is 'brideprice' or gifts to the bride's family, but these appear to be rather marginal and are usually susceptible to other explanations. Neither display nor compensation seem the dominant aspects of such transactions, at least from a comparative point of view.

Minor marriages displayed the same three ceremonial phases as the major variety except that there was a pause of one to fifteen years between the second and third phases. 'Dressed in a miniature version of the traditional red wedding gown, the infant bride, seldom more than a year, was carried over the threshold of her husband's home.' Though 'married', she did not yet have a husband. She could for example marry her dead fiancé's brother, which would have been impossible if she was his widow. A girl raised as a *sim-pua* did not enter into a conjugal relation until some time after puberty when she and her fiancé were presented to his ancestors. At times even the worship of the ancestors was omitted. 'My father just told us it was time for us to sleep together', remarked one woman.

This type of early betrothal differed from European examples since, as an infant, the girl was physically transferred to her husband's house where she became a kind of foster-child, assimilated to the status of daughter. As a consequence the family relationships were quite different in quality from those in a major marriage, as noted by Fei Hsiao-t'ung in his account of family life in Kaihsienkung, the Yangtze village in southern Kiangsu (Jiangsu) where 39 per cent of marriages were of this kind. Of ordinary marriages he wrote: 'It comes to be taken more or less for granted that the mother-in-law is a potential enemy of the daughter-in-law. Friction between them is taken as usual and harmony as worth special praise' (1939:48). Further on he describes how an infant girl moves into the home of her future husband. 'The parents of the boy will take a girl as foster-child at a very early age, the future mother-in-law even feeding her at her breast, and will take care of her up to marriage' (p. 53). Under these circumstances the relations between mother-in-law and daughter-in-law were 'greatly modified', the latter often becoming 'very closely attached ... just like a real daughter', 'especially in the frequent cases where there is no real daughter. Even those who are badly treated by the future mother-in-law' looked upon her as a guardian. In the context of his argument about the difficulties such marriages present for their partners, Wolf (1985c) has pointed out that the pressure for early marriage comes largely from mothers (or potential mothers) of sons who are looking for daughters-in-law with whom they can get along, not one who is going to split the family apart with her emphasis on the conjugal rather than the filial side of domestic life. In this way minor marriage demonstrates the domination of the mother rather than the father over both the 'daughter' and the son; their subordination is not a matter of gender alone. In Taiwan there was always a greater demand than supply for such brides, giving rise to the same pre-emptive phenomenon that is sometimes found in Africa (e.g. Goody 1956), namely, the contracted betrothal of a son to a potential bride while she is still in her mother's womb (*zhifu*), or what Cartier calls 'désignation du ventre' (1986a:468; 1986b:213).

I have discussed the question of incorporation largely in terms of an individual's membership of a lineage but there is also the question of the degree to which a woman or man identifies with the household in which they reside, a kind of psychological incorporation. Freedman regards the former as a feature of all Chinese marriage; Wolf treats both in relation to minor marriages. In this latter case the importance of the quasi-total transfer from the standpoint of sexual relations is clear; nevertheless it is the contradictions between the transfer into the status of a quasi-daughter and the need to shift to that of a proper wife which creates the problem for this form of marriage and which often results in its dissolution. Even in extreme cases women are not 'incorporated' that simply or that unconditionally. The early attachment to the foster mother makes for easier affinal relations (divorce is more frequent when she is absent), but at the same time the quasi-sibling relation makes the shift to a conjugal one more difficult.

It was the high incidence of minor marriages in Taiwan that attracted Wolf's theoretical attention. Earlier scholars had tended to neglect these 'deviant' types of marriage, emphasising instead the Confucian ideal of an adult son acquiring a young but nevertheless adult bride by virilocal marriage. But while minor marriages were very common, they were disliked by many young people 'because marrying a "brother" or "sister" was embarassing' and 'uninteresting' (Wolf and Huang 1980:vii). Certainly they decreased radically in number during the 1930s as the young became less dependent on parental ties under the Japanese occupation. And objections to early and arranged marriage formed part of the rallying-cry of young reformers against 'familism' both in China and in India. Long before 1911, reform movements in China had attempted to modernise, that is, to Westernise, the family by changing the status of women which took the form of doing away with the binding of feet, and of promoting 'equality' between spouses, of consensus for the marriage ('freedom to love' rather than 'forced marriage'), as well as a later age of marriage, education for women, monogamy, divorce and the abolition of all marriage payments.

Was there a general reluctance on the part of the boy and girl to engage in these marriages and did such unions present any general difficulties in their outcome? If so, was this related to Westermarck's notion that the explanation of incest taboos lay in the fact that intimate and prolonged association in childhood destroyed sexual attraction (Wolf and Huang 1980:143ff.)? Some of the participants certainly displayed aversion to a marriage which, while encouraged by parents, was the subject of teasing by peers. The same kind of reluctance is found in the Israeli kibbutz where members of the immediate peer group rarely marry. In Hai-shan, on the other hand, they married very frequently – that was the purpose of their being raised together by the senior generation. But, argues Wolf, such a marriage presents difficulties both for the husband and wife, a proposition he tests with regard to rates of adultery, fertility and divorce.

Adultery is not uncommon, for the Chinese peasant is not so prudish, nor are the sexes kept so far apart, as is often thought. While a woman was condemned for adultery, a man could seek sexual satisfaction where he wanted, providing he avoided the wives and daughters of neighbours. Prostitution was well established, especially in the towns, and a wealthy man (for wealth was an important determinant of extra-marital sex) might even set such a girl up as a mistress.[23] Some women worked as prostitutes and later married, and a brotherless daughter might sometimes be sent to a brothel in order to find a husband or to get herself pregnant but also because it was one way she could make a substantial contribution to family income. Note that premarital pregnancy increased enormously over the period of the Japanese occupation and was much higher in the case of filiacentric unions, those which involved just such brotherless women who married at a later age than others. There is no doubt that there was a commercial aspect to sex and marriage in nineteenth-century Taiwan as in the rest of China. Tibetan woman too, earned money through prostitution, as did certain castes in Indian and the poor in Europe. Nevertheless women were rarely sold as such, if only because brothels did not wish to take on permanent responsibility; it was rather a transaction in their sexual services, resembling the wage-labour of young men (and women) who go to work elsewhere and are expected to send back remittances.

While it has been argued by Gronewald that prostitution was merely one form of a traffic in women that included wives and concubines, Mann's concept (1983) of a dual structure regulating female sexuality in late Imperial China, seems preferable, where marriage and reproduction stand opposed to prostitution and procurement (Hershatter forthcoming). Better still would be a grid of roles or institutions set against their respective rights and activities, of the kind Finley proposed for degrees of free and servile status. Such a grid, constructed either from the perspective of a particular culture or from an analytic standpoint, permits a greater degree of subtlety and flexibility in the analysis of sexual partnerships than a crude reduction to market activities favoured by some economists and anthropologists alike.

Adultery is less easy to assess than the resort to commercial sex but Wolf's figures suggest that 16.5 per cent of women entering into major marriages during the years 1881 to 1935 (n=315) were reported to be involved in extra-marital affairs, whereas the proportion rose to 37.7 per cent in the case of minor marriages (n=236). The difference is striking and Wolf sees it as linked to the degree of satisfaction experienced by the partners to the marriage.

Fertility also showed some strong differences in the various forms of union; in minor marriages age-specific marital fertility was 26 per cent to 30 per cent below the rate for major and filiacentric unions. However, lower fertility may be caused by more than aversion to one's partner, for fostered daughters-in-law are more likely to die than girls raised as daughters by their own parents. Hence, even when they survived, poorer health may have meant fewer children. However Wolf shows that *sim-pua* who did not marry their foster-brothers bore almost as many children as women who were raised as daughters, a fact that provides support for the aversion hypothesis.

While on the mainland divorce was unacceptable and rare, in Hai-shan it was equally unacceptable but somewhat more common. The unacceptability of the act was illustrated by the fact that when a bill of divorce had been signed, it was partly burned to dispel any baneful influences and the left-over ink thrown away, preferably in some isolated spot far from human habitation (Wolf and Huang 1980:178). Despite this negative attitude, approximately 12 per cent of first marriages ended in divorce in the period between 1901 and 1940. The rate varied with the type of marriage, with the figures for major marriages being the lowest at 5.9 per cent (n=1651). Since 'strong' lineages were absent in Hai-shan, the question of their relation to conjugality, raised in arguments based on divorce in Africa, are hardly relevant, although it should be noted that in neighbouring areas where lineages were more important, divorce was less frequent in major marriages but more so in filiacentric ones. Whether or not lineages were strong, weak, or existed at all, in making a major marriage a woman gave up many rights in her parental family and, while she could return there for a period in the case of divorce, she then had either to engage in prostitution or enter into another marriage. Divorce was an unattractive solution to marital problems, both for the families and for the partners, especially for the wife.

When women have alternative possibilities of employment, marriage is often easier to dissolve. Topley's work on the Kwantung silk industry (1975) showed the women workers to have had considerable independence. In West Africa market women are equally independent as far as marriage is concerned. Even in some traditional societies women regularly return to their kin in terminal separation at the time of menopause (E. Goody 1973), producing what appear as high rates of 'divorce'. But in fact there is an alternative to marriage for at least part of a woman's adult life, namely, to live with her kin rather than her affines. Such a possibility was less available in China, except under special conditions.

In Taiwan men on the other hand do have alternatives open to them; for this reason among others, filiacentric unions are often more prone to divorce than others, the figure being 16.9 per cent (n=148) as compared with the 2.3 per cent in major marriages (Wolf and Huang 1980:184–5). According to the theory that the 'incorporation' of the spouse makes for difficult divorce, a somewhat circular proposition at best, minor marriages should be very stable. In fact the rates approach those for filiacentric unions, being 15.5 per cent (n=1,117) as against 16.1 per cent (n=411).[24] The reason for this higher rate, they argue, lies in the aversion of the partners to each other, which is the counterpart of the attachment of the bride to the foster-mother who is also the mother-in-law. Divorce is more frequent the earlier the age the girl joins the household. This early attachment is desired by the mother-in-law and produces a closer relation between them so that divorce is less likely while she is present. But it has a negative effect on the duration of the conjugal tie.

Barclay's study uses aggregate data derived from the whole island of Taiwan, while Wolf and Huang are dealing with the records of a particular locality. The distinction is important since the rates of these various forms of marriage, like other aspects of social action, can vary considerably in nearby communities. Even within the Chinese population of Taiwan, differences in the patterns of marriage, the incidence of divorce, the mechanisms of recruitment and the structure of domestic groups cover a considerable range, despite the appearance and the reality of a high degree of cultural unity and despite the fact that the main Han occupation of the island only dates from the seventeenth century, although it began in the twelfth. Some of these differences are due to the diverse backgrounds of the migrants, in particular whether they are Hakka or Hokkien, and to the customs and predispositions they brought with them. In some cases the institutional options available to the migrants may have persisted over a long period of time. But within the range of possibilities, some become more prominent because of particular contingent factors. Such seems to have been the case in Chung-she, a small Hokkien-speaking village in central Taiwan. While the Hakka village of Yen-liao in southwestern Taiwan studied by Cohen had few cases of minor or filiacentric marriage in the period 1866–1906 (1976:33ff.), the Hokkien village of Chung-she had many more but they were differently distributed than in the Hokkien area in the North of the island where Wolf worked; in the centre the percentages for the first marriages of males was 8.0 for minor marriages and 33.3 for filiacentric ones, while in the north it was 40.5 and 10.9 per cent respectively (Pasternak 1985:314). Pasternak suggests that the difference did not relate to ethnic background as such since both are Hokkien nor yet to a 'free' shift of preference over time, but to different conditions for agriculture. Chung-she had poor clay soils, the cultivation of which required much water and heavy labour. The farms were dependent on rainfall and because they produced only one crop a year, they had to be larger than those watered by canal irrigation. Since the flow of water was not controlled by man, the uncertain timing of the rains made it difficult to arrange for the exchange of labour, so that it was essential to maintain a sufficient supply of males within the unit of production in order to carry out the work of the farm. As a result an elderly farmer was not in a position to wait for his young son to grow up; if he had an older daughter he would bring in a son-in-law, not only as an heir but also to work, perhaps temporarily, on his farm. Hence the large percentage of in-coming male workers. Richer families might hire them, poorer families had to marry them, and it was they who had the highest number of in-coming sons-in-law. In this way production and reproduction were always closely intertwined, especially among those who had less room to manoeuvre. What is especially interesting is the fact that under these conditions, the three forms of marriage had different demographic implications than in the North. Pasternak was even able to provide some kind of test for his thesis since when a dam was built and irrigation introduced, the incidence of such in-coming marriages fell to more 'normal' levels.

In China we are dealing with a range of linked institutional forms that social action may take. Some of these, such as adoption, are distributed throughout China but in greatly differing proportions; some practices are available in one region but not in another. Other differences occur between 'ethnic' groups, such as the absence and presence of foot-binding among the Hakka and the Hokkien respectively, suggesting a long-standing or strongly held institution, linked to other socio-cultural practices such as the work of Hakka women in the fields, even ploughing, and their early employment in the tea industry. Contingent factors were also at work. For the same employment opportunities induced some Hokkien women to abandon foot-binding, although later on it was Japanese pressure that led to change; however they still avoided work in the fields. While the value of Hakka girls seems to have made parents generally more reluctant to send them out on minor marriages or to bring in men as working husbands, there was in fact a great difference in the incidence of minor marriages among Hakka living in the North and South of the island. In the South there were relatively few, in the North less than among the Hokkien but still a substantial number which Wolf (1985c) sees as indicating the demand of both Hakka and Hokkien mothers for early introduction into their households of young, prospective brides. The difference among the Hakka seems to be related not so much to the kind of contingent factors suggested by Pasternak as to emergent North–South differences in which the interaction of neighbouring groups tends to produce similar though not identical forms of behaviour, indicating a certain degree of autonomy with regard to changing conditions in general. On the other hand the situation in Chung-she also points to differences between village communities which seem firmly linked to specific ecological and economic variables.

Differences between town and country, which belong to this latter variety, are brought out by comparing Sa's analysis of Taipei households with Wolf's study of the rural area of Hai-shan, situated a few miles away. In 1906 'grand families' accounted for 23.3 per cent of all families in the rural area, whereas among the urban proletariat the figure was 3.7 per cent, among the merchants and shop-keepers 9.3 per cent but in high-status groups it reached 42.0 per cent. 'Grand families' include fraternal expanded families ('frèreches') and those extended families where the father is living with more than one son ('grand' in Sa's terms); in addition 19.2 per cent of the upper households were 'stem' (with one resident child) and only 38.6 per cent elementary compared with 25.4 and 70.1 per cent respectively in the lower groups (Sa 1985; Wolf and Hanley 1985). These differences seem linked to the command of productive resources; nevertheless the town and the adjacent countryside had much in common that served to differentiate the North from the South of the island.

Clearly not all differences and similarities are susceptible to the same type of explanation. Some have to be seen as relatively 'free variation', the result of the search for new solutions to the old problems, of innovations of a less directed kind and even of 'cultural drift'. Some may see such changes as being variations on a common 'theme', but the latter notion is often too vague and at the same time too restrictive to fit either facts or theory. I have tried to deal empirically with this level of variation when analysing the performances of the LoDagaa funeral rituals (1962) as well as more recently the versions of a long recitation, the Bagre, gathered over some twenty-five years (Goody 1987a). Some are clearly intentional, as when new words or new rites are introduced into myth or ceremony; others are less explicable changes, cultural mutations. Both may be generative in various ways that have been more systematically discussed in Barth's study of the Ok of New Guinea (1987). When social interaction is more closely related to the productive system at the domestic level the constraints are greater, the interlocking of words and deeds tighter, than in dealing with myth and ritual. But however constraining the rest of the socio-cultural system, there has always to be room for individual innovation and deviation, and hence, in the longer run, for changes at the group or societal level. A number of the variations found in Taiwan and more widely in China are of this free-floating kind, although it is always possible to assign them to this category out of ignorance of the links with other factors.

Despite these various levels of variation, institutional, contingent and the free-floating, common factors did exist, specifically at the ideological level where Confucian teaching gave a higher valuation to the practices of the upper groups, thereby helping to maintain existing practices which were sometimes thrust upon, sometimes adopted by, with or without the agreement of the power holders, subordinate groups who often found it more difficult to conform.

The fact that choices and institutions existed in a social hierarchy, dominated ideologically by Confucianism, meant that there was a hierarchy of valuation, that is to say, the practices of lower groups tended to be seen as low, which in itself could provide an impetus for change under favourable conditions, those that loosened the bonds of individuals and groups to the dominant social order. For example, in Taiwan the percentages of filia-centric and minor marriages began to fall under the Japanese occupation, as social bonds were loosened, as conditions improved generally and as groups and individuals rose in the hierarchy. But the very existence of alternatives, even among neighbouring communities, classes or ethnic groups, is a potential generator of change in less directed ways, offering the possibility of adopting a 'functional equivalent' when a particular practice is felt to become less appropriate, not only because of changing external circumstances but because of the kind of internal 'contradictions' or difficulties that characterise many human institutions.

I am speaking here primarily of conscious models of alternative forms of social action, since without the intentionality of the human agent, the recognition of difficulties, the acknowledgement of alternatives, the making of the value judgements and the subsequent choice between possibilities, none of these processes are the relevant ones to consider. But a further range of possibilities needs to be taken into account. These are the alternatives that are theoretically available within the system, that is, the practices used by broadly similar societies for purposes that are similar in the relevant aspects. For example, in China an heiress cannot marry a near agnate, such as a father's brother's daughter's son, in order to maintain the property within the 'grand family', the joint undivided family. The immediate reason is that when patrilineal clans are exogamous, other strategies have to be used. Nevertheless close marriage remains a possible solution for preventing the dispersal of property in a system of which diverging devolution is an intrinsic feature, and such marriages are practised both in the Near East and in a different form in South India. It represents a direction that might have been taken, indeed might be taken, other things being equal.

Such system potentialities are transcultural and tend to be associated with a particular system of production, of destruction or communication. The practices of importance to this present study are those that are linked in varying degrees of strength to the other variables in the 'woman's property complex'. That will emerge more clearly when we extend our regard from China westwards. But in these opening chapters I began by looking critically at ways of viewing Chinese marriage and kinship which seemed to overlook important aspects of domestic life, in particular the relationship of the domestic group with the productive system. A relatively advanced agriculture allowed not only for the extraction of a large surplus by the few but for considerable differentiation among the many, a differentiation based largely on rights in land. In addition there was a considerable development of towns, manufacture and trade, which produced further differentiation in rural as well as in urban areas. The establishment and maintenance of that differentiation, I argued, meant attempting to preserve or augment the status of daughters as well as of sons, even though in the majority of cases they departed from the household at marriage. To this end property had to be transferred to them, as dowry, either directly from their parents or brothers or indirectly from the resources of the groom's family.

As a result, domestic institutions differed in some broad but fundamental respects from those in Africa where in the absence of male heirs (or of enough male labour) close collateral males of the same lineage filled the gap. In China, on the contrary, this did not happen despite the stress placed upon the patrilineage, upon patriarchal authority, upon the homoparental (father to son) transmission of land and usually upon male labour in the fields. If a couple had no sons, the daughter might remain in the house and bring in a husband. Continuity and to some extent control passed through her. Where no children at all existed, a girl might be deliberately adopted in order to continue the line by bringing in a husband in the same way. Alternatively a male would be adopted, often an agnatic kinsman, for he did not succeed automatically, by right of lineage membership or by closeness of kinship.

All these institutions to which I have referred are multi-functional. Incoming sons-in-law may provide labour as well as heirs; adoptions may be used to augment the numbers of sons. Concubines, often taken to provide heirs in a barren marriage, may be acquired for other, more immediate gratification. But one important aspect of these institutions is related to the 'woman's property complex', as indeed is the tendency to monogamous marriage, to low rates of divorce and to the ban on the remarriage of widows, at least in the upper groups. For just as economically based stratification is an important aspect of the social system, so too is the differentiation of practice that I have crudely labelled high and low.

The existence of this range of differentiation must lead us to modify earlier anthropological discussions of the Chinese family in two main ways. First it leads to a rejection of the appropriateness of the model of 'primitive', or alternatively African, marriage on which these were often based; secondly, it allows for a degree of internal variation and external similarity that must make us wary of any overly holistic, cultural approach. We need to modify both the model and the approach, to look for more specific differences as well as for more general similarities. By turning westwards to examine other major Asian societies, we can try to see how these general considerations work out in different socio-cultural contexts. But before looking at India, I want first to turn to the region of Tibet that lies between the two, and displays a set of practices that emphasise the links as well as the differences with western Europe. It has become customary to point to the similarities in family systems and in demographic variables between Japan and the West, partly because of the way that industrial capitalism has developed in them both. But an analysis of the situation in Tibet places the argument in a somewhat different perspective, since features of the family chosen as critical in western Europe turn up again and again in this isolated land. This suggests that we may be wrong to see the possible relation between economic change and family variables in terms of any specific comparison to do with single-heir inheritance, 'stem-families' or smaller households, which mark both Japan and England. Instead we need to look at more general features of Eurasian societies, at the links between productive processes and domestic groups under pre-industrial conditions. In this perspective, at the level of family variables the pre-requisites for the rise of capitalism become very broad and the aspects of the uniqueness of the West, unique neither with regard to Japan or Tibet, become bereft both of reality and of analytic significance.

5

Land, polyandry and celibacy in Tibet

China and India have often been contrasted with Japan and the West in respect of their early marriage and their commitments to the model of the 'grand family' (that is, household, houseful or 'house', depending upon context). On the other hand in all three Asian societies marriage was virtually universal, with Japan controlling the growth of its population not only by the age of marriage but also by other, positive, means.

While there is a difference at the level of the model between large family households in China and the single-heir households of Japan, one has to remember that the actual difference in average household size was not great, that the Confucian ethic was a strong feature of Japanese as well as of Chinese education and that many similar practices were found in the repertoires of both countries. In any case in Japan 'grand families' such as that of the Makioka (Tanizaki 1957) existed not as households but in a dispersed state, although the relation between brothers was very different, more egalitarian in one case, more hierarchical in the other.

The case of Tibet, albeit representing a great difference in scale from its two neighbours, to one of whom it is attached politically, illustrates another variation on the same set of themes, since we find households that are at once large (*frèreches*) and stem at the same time, effectively limiting reproduction to the children of one spouse. Regarding the features to which attention was drawn in China, we find the heiress, the incoming son-in-law, occasional polygyny, rarely adoption but a late age of marriage for males (especially among the rich) and a considerable proportion of celibates, men in monasteries, women as spinsters or divorcées; most men marry but brothers do so polyandrously with the express purpose of keeping the 'house' in line with resources. Late marriage for men, celibacy, control of growth, these are features which have been held to be characteristic of the European (that is, the western European) pattern. So too we encounter that other accompanying feature, living-in servants of a life-cycle kind. Even some of the more specific characteristics of the western pattern, spelt out by

Laslett (1983), are there; 'neolocality' and the nuclear household were present, mainly among lower groups, but among the rich too close kin might be dispersed in nearby dwellings.

Situated between China and India, the culture of Tibet owes much to both; from China it acquired political overlordship and from India it accepted Buddhism. It is inhabited by nomads on the plateau, by agriculturalists and by monastic estates on the plains. In the towns were merchants, traders, priests and administrators. Economically its agriculture clearly derived from the West Asian patterns of farming and animal husbandry, though the highland environment led to a specialisation of plants and animals. The plough was widely used, the control of water essential (Goldstein 1978); agriculture was intensive and produced sufficient surplus to maintain artisans and an elaborate monastic and ecclesiastical organisation, for the hierarchy was strong, consisting of priests, aristocrats, commoners and impure outcasts in despised occupations. As in West Asia (and in contrast to East) women had a considerable part to play in farming, so the sexes were highly interdependent in terms of the productive system.

Some of the most detailed data on family and farm comes from Tibetans living outside the country, in the Indian region of Ladakh, Spiti and Lahul, as well as in Nepal. In the mountainous areas of Ladakh resources are restricted, partly because the narrow valley bottoms leave little room for extending the farms. As in Egypt, there is a sharp divide between the barren and the fertile.

In Lahul, the Tibetan woman bore much of the burden of farming; they 'do the manuring, beat the clods of earth in the wake of the plowmen, make ridges in the fields to make irrigation easier, and weed. With occasional help from the men they water the fields and reap, thresh, winnow, and transport the crops' (Carrrasco 1959:35). A similar division of labour is reported from Ladakh, while in Spiti women did all the agricultural work with the exception of ploughing. Part of the reason for the extent of their participation was that the men engaged in trade and had to carry out the labour services inherent in the tenure of land (p. 35), both activities that were intrinsic to the socio-economic system. As a result, husband(s) and wife established a joint unit of production in a very real sense.

The relation between land holding, marriage and the family was close. 'In Tibet', writes Carrasco, 'where land is the most important means of production, the land system reveals the foundation of the social structure' (p. 4). In both Ladakh and Spiti, family property was handed over from one generation to the next at marriage, a transfer obviously related to the late age of marriage of the eldest son as well as to the nature of the union. For those who did not own land did not marry. Some of them become menservants, sometimes permanently, living in the houses of the richer landowners. 'They eat from their master's table, are servants of all work and do not marry, though they often keep company with some unmarried women of the house or neighbourhood.'[1]

In Tibetan custom, when the elder son married, he moved into the big house (*khang-chen*) while the parents retired to a smaller one that had its own fields; in this way they practised a kind of 'neolocality' within the estate or at least a separation of marital dwellings, which also occurred in some European communities, the *Alternteil* of Germany as compared with the West Room of County Clare, a distinction that clearly affects the census returns as to size of dwelling groups (housefuls), and possibly of households (consumption groups) as well, but not the 'house' or property-owning group (JUF or joint undivided family).[2] From another standpoint such households were not always nuclear in the usual sense of the word, since a wife might be shared by the male siblings, an alternative to not marrying aimed at keeping the population in line with resources, family with farm, even more radically than in the models constructed for western Europe in the early modern period. Under the practice of adelphic polyandry, the brothers take a wife and live with their sons and unmarried daughters; when the parents are dead, the small house reverts to the eldest son. Meanwhile the latter has taken over not only the property but also the responsibility as tax-payer and as a supplier of labour for the state. This demand for labour places an obvious strain on simple domestic groups, making the complex forms more viable.[3]

It is important to add here that land is put aside not only for dependent relatives but also for the family monks; they enter the monastery with an endowment. But while land is allocated within the family in this fashion, for the purpose of support, an attempt is made to keep the holding intact over the generations so that there is minimal fragmentation. Polyandry and monasticsm are linked to this system of production and inheritance, although the relation is complex (Carrasco 1959:35).[4] Spare men either share the brother's lot or go into a monastery. That lot includes access to the brother's wife and to the paternity of her children, an alternative to the never-married males of European society who as bachelors had to find their sex in less orthodox ways.

Polyandry and partition

In Ladakh polyandry was widespread:

The eldest son inherits the whole of the family property and it is he who is entitled to marry a wife. The marriage is arranged in his name only and he pays the brideprice [which I would characterise as indirect dowry as it is destined for the wife] to the father or nearest male relative of the bride. If he has only two brothers they both become the *de facto* husbands of his wife. If he has more than two brothers some of them become monks or leave the paternal house, since not more than two brothers can share the wife of their eldest brother. (1959:35–6)

In fact, among the Tibetan Nyinba of Nepal, Levine (1988) points out that all the brothers are not only husbands but fathers, since children are allocated to each of them.

As elsewhere in the Himalayan region (Berreman 1975; Goldstein 1978), polyandry excludes neither monogamy nor yet polygyny which may be practised by the same individual or household at different points in the developmental cycle, depending upon the holding of children, the financial position, as well as on other personal factors.[5] For polygyny is given preference over adoption as a way of ensuring continuity. If the wife is childless, or if a man is rich enough, he may marry a second wife, and even a third if she turns out to be childless; if there are still no children, he has to call in an 'additional husband' from the same family, and if this does not work, only then does he resort to adoption. Such an adopted son is preferred over any offspring a man may subsequently have.

From one standpoint, the situation where brothers share a wife and only take an added one if they have no heir or if financial circumstances permit, represents a more extreme form of monogamy. The African evidence suggests that unions with a single wife are more fertile than polygynous ones but not of course from the standpoint of any particular male for whom two offer more hope than one. From either standpoint polyandry was the most economical form of marriage and was directly connected, by the actors themselves, with the ownership of the means of production and with the fission of domestic groups. In his account of Lahul, Punjab wrote (as an Indian): 'When asked to defend this repulsive custom of polyandry, they say that their holdings are too small to divide, and that experience shows them that it is impossible for two sisters-in-law with separate husbands and families, to live together, whereas two or more brothers with a common wife can agree.'[6] This appears to have been the case in the early eighteenth century, judging by Jesuit observers, just as it is in more recent times. 'The Tibetans' own explanation of their preference for polyandry is highly materialistic', writes Goldstein. 'They choose fraternal polyandry to preserve the productive resources of their corporate family unit intact across generations' (1978:326). Thus it is a matter partly of family limitation but also of the relations between the incoming wives of brothers. As in China and India such women are held to be the cause of the split between brothers. Of course, as elsewhere, the relation between mother-in-law and daughter-in-law is as critical as that between sisters-in-law. It is significant that among the Nyinba, who like some other inhabitants of Nepal permit cross-cousin marriage, fission is more easily avoidable when marriage is with the mother's close kin; equally wives get on better in polygynous marriages when they are sisters.[7] But while women quarrel more, a wife has an interest in maintaining a polyandrous union, otherwise she will have to deal with a co-wife and her children will have to share their patrimony. The fact that the actors themselves view polyandry in relation to partition is brought out very clearly in the account of the Nyinba. They portray the first settlers as marrying monogamously but now practise polyandry (49 per cent of marriages in 1983). This shift represents not so much history as contemporary resource management. 'People say that polyandry prevents the dispersion of household wealth and the fragmentation of land and that it avoids the proliferation of households, thus restricting village growth' (Levine 1988:32). On the other hand, men who marry monogamously divide up the patrimony and thus dissipate their wealth in the creation of separate households. Since the composition of the household is linked so closely to fixed resources, its structure will vary with its holdings. 'Small household' (*khang-chung*) serfs, who were formally slaves and are now freedmen, exchanged their labour for land or wages and could support only small households. There was little to keep brothers together and avoid partition; so they tended to live monogamously and in small households (nuclear families) (Goldstein 1971a and b; Levine 1988:100). Formerly slaves married uxorilocally, and many still do, with the women looking after the children from the great households (*trongba*).

The delayed or postponed division of the estate is not simply a question of preventing subdivision; it also ensures there is enough labour available and has the demographic effect of preventing proliferation. Although both actors and observers stress that the effort to avoid partition has a strong economic and status element, other factors are at work, including the position of the household as a political and taxation unit, and the maintenance of a particular standard of life, since in Tibet, in contrast to Pahari, polyandry was characteristic of the rich rather than the poor (Berreman 1975; Goldstein 1978). It is also the case that polyandrous marriage has an important normative aspect, connected with the solidarity of brothers; the unity of the sibling group as well as the maintenance of property and prestige is ensured by the marriage of several brothers to one woman. However not every 'house' continues indefinitely without partition, despite the mechanism which the Tibetans alone have at their disposal (for many societies share the same ideal of undivided 'houses'). Marriage, retirement, death, none of these entails fission; that comes about with the existence of sexually exclusive couples, wives held not jointly but separately.

But there was rarely any splitting of the inheritance; the younger sons usually either stayed in a polyandrous marriage or else went into the monastery. Indeed in Spiti, where there was no polyandry among the regular landholders, all the younger brothers became *lamas* (in Nyinba the opposite was true, little celibacy, widespread polyandry). But if the eldest died sonless (or with a son under age), the younger brother might leave the monastery and inherit his brother's widow. This can hardly be considered a form of the levirate, since brothers already had access to the common wife, but it played a similar part in attempting to produce sons not so much for the dead brother but for the siblings jointly.

Even so, no sons might be born. If there was a daughter, the same resort to a filiacentric union could be made that we found in many parts of China; 'a bridegroom is chosen for the eldest single daughter. He is usually a younger son who will not inherit land, and he is adopted into her family, comes to live with her, and takes her name. In this case the woman inherits the paternal property and becomes the head of the household' (Carrasco 1959:36). He himself is known in Ladakh as *mag-pa* in contrast to the *bag-pa*, a husband in a virilocal marriage. As with the 'added man' in non-fraternal polyandry, he is at a disadvantage in his new house since he has no rights of inheritance. He is brought in not only to provide heirs but also, among the Nyinba, as a 'strategy of management', for his labour, because of the multiple calls made upon the males in a household. Equally, female labour may be in short supply. In order to redress any such imbalance, a daughter's marriage may be delayed, or that of a young son's advanced by marrying him to an older woman; alternatively, an older, infertile woman may be added to an existing union.

Because younger brothers rarely marry a wife of their own, which would lead to separation, then or later, they have the right to take part in deciding what strategy of heirship should be adopted; if a man should try to marry his daughter in this way, a younger brother who had entered a monastery could object, saying that he would leave the monastery and beget a son. 'A son-in-law can only be adopted with his consent'. The younger brother might cohabit with his brother's wife in order to try and produce a male heir. On the other hand, if she is old, he may put his elder brother in the small house and take a wife himself. If he does not want to leave the monastery, an illegitimate descendant of the family who is living on the property may succeed in establishing a claim. Such a claim does not necessarily prevent the filiacentric union from taking place, but a kinsman who objects to an in-coming son-in-law (the husband of an heiress) or a younger brother who objects to the adoption of a child by his childless elder brother, may receive land in compensation (Carrasco 1959:37).

This situation of joint sibling responsibility has repercussions on divorce. 'In Ladakh an elder brother who insists on divorcing his wife, against the wish of his younger brothers, has to give his wife and brothers some land on which they can live together' (p. 37). While one can readily understand that one man, even the senior husband, cannot unilaterally get rid of the common wife without making some provisions for his younger siblings, this endowment of divorced women also occurs in Spiti, where there is no polyandry; 'a man divorcing his wife against her wish must give her a field or two as maintenance' (p. 37).

This endowment of a divorced wife is linked to her original endowment at marriage by means of a dowry. In central Tibet, 'a father retires after his son's marriage, his most able son succeeds, while the others share his wife and land or else become monks. If there are no sons, a daughter succeeds and a young man is adopted as her husband.' 'Except in such cases, daughters inherit no land, but are only given a share of the movable property when they marry . . . In some cases land can be given as dowry' (p. 47).[8] Here again a divorced woman also received a plot of land for her support and that of her daughters.

Nyinba women do not, according to Levine, bring the same large dowries that are found in northern India. On the other hand, she speaks of the life-long use of dowry land, of dowry slaves (in the old days), of livestock (by wealthy women) and of dowry property that is stored separately until there is an assurance the marriage will last. Women are entitled to dowries, or, if they do not get married, to life-long maintenance. The two are complementary, so that if a daughter receives her dowry and then returns to her natal home, she does so on a sufferance; under present Nepali law, if she does not marry she is a coparcener with rights equal to her brothers. In Tibetan the word for dowry (gēla, shal ba) means a share of an estate, which includes jewellery, clothes, sometimes a maid-servant, bovines or the use of land that reverts to her family on her death (Goldstein 1978:336), as was often the case in China.

We find once again a society in which a woman is entitled to property (1) as a brotherless heiress; (2) in dowry; (3) at the dissolution of her marriage by death or divorce. In this last eventuality she receives it not from her natal family but from the conjugal fund established at her marriage as the result of the contribution of her dowry. Some of the features that appear in other societies with diverging devolution are found here in Tibet; others have specific parallels in western Europe. There is the late age of marriage for the male heir, who becomes householder and husband at the same time, shedding the aged in the fashion of some European households and establishing a real stem family, that is, a family in which the brothers are not normally permitted to reproduce separately unless they leave to marry heiresses. This case obviously carries different implications from that in which the brothers disperse, leaving one resident in the family house, or from the stem family in which all live together but only one is married. In each case the brother or brothers may be living with the senior generation in a stem household. In Tibet however, residence is usually neolocal in the sense that each conjugal unit has its own house, giving more independence to wives and easing the burden of the mother-in-law for the new wife. On the other hand, the wider group may still constitute a joint undivided family (JUF) from the standpoint of property and to some extent production. And it may even continue to operate largely as a joint household (unit of consumption), at least to the extent that meals, if not always eaten in common, are often passed backwards and forwards between houses. Such a wide range of alternative forms of co-existing domestic groups may appear complex. But setting aside polyandry, they are by no means confined to Tibet, being found in contemporary Taiwan as well as in present-day India, where the varying forms are apparent around me in Gujarat as I write. Many of the misunderstandings about the nature of extended, joint or even stem and nuclear families to which I have already drawn attention (Goody 1972), result from a failure to understand, and even to categorise, the range of possibility involved, which must be a preliminary to comprehending the quality of interaction among their members.

Where the nuclear dwelling group is formed by the son (or daughter) taking over the family house and moving the parents into an 'old people's house', the likelihood is that the retirement of the senior generation is involved. Indeed, the same handing over may occur where they move to their own wing, apartment or room, although here the result will be a stem houseful (and not necessarily a household, especially where a retirement contract is involved).

In Tibet, then, marriage of the eldest son involved the retirement of the parents, with younger brothers participating in that marriage, entering a monastery, or marrying an heiress; the latter we would expect to find less frequently since 'fathers' with no male offspring are likely to be fewer where polygyny, the levirate or adoption are frequent strategies of the sonless; indeed among the Nyinba, Levine reported only 7 per cent of the marriages were filiacentric. In these circumstances direct vertical inheritance preserves the unity of the group of brothers at the expense of eliminating all but one from the standpoint of continuity, since the children of only one inherit the family property; on the other hand their sisters are endowed from the estate at marriage. Moreover, those younger sons remaining in the house are seen as participating in the one internal marriage allowed, a possibility that even remains open to sons who have departed.

The fact that some men do not marry while others take a common wife clearly keeps population growth in line with productive resources. It also means a plenitude of spinsters, a role which is characteristic of western Europe. Since divorce is rare, it is not as if a large number of women could experience a short spell of married life; the permanently single woman is a regular feature of society.

The extent of this problem emerges in Chen's study of the Khams of eastern Tibet (1949), although it deals with the unmarried rather than the never-married women alone. In his census, which included 544 households from nine villages, he found 39.53 per cent of all households had no married couple; most of the heads of these households were unmarried women who were also dependent on the 'big house' in that their holding was part of its estate, that is, the estate of the JUF. The percentage of husbandless women was of course even greater and showed interesting differences between the groups in the social hierarchy, being much higher in the lower as against the higher ones (table 5), a fact that is no doubt related not only to freer divorce, to the greater attraction of upper brides but also to the definition of marriage itself.

Polyandry is less common in the East and Northeast than in the West, perhaps because of the influence of the Chinese. The position of women in the developmental cycle of domestic groups is made clearer by reference to western Tibet. In Ladakh the houses dependent upon the 'big house' might include not only the small (or 'dower') house but also 'the still-smaller-one' (*yang-chung-pa*). If the parents of a main householder were still alive when his eldest son was ready to take over, then it was into the still smaller house that the senior generation moved, leaving the retiring farmer (or his widow) the dower house. But most commonly the smallest house was occupied by an unmarried sister or aunt of the main householder, or their illegitimate offspring. For a sister either was set up with her own house and land in this way or lived within the family house on equal terms. Many women lived as spinsters in their father's or brother's house because their chances of marriage were small (Carrasco 1959:31–2). But unlike the hypergamous situation that existed in parts of India, it seems that the daughters of the rich

Table 5. *Status and unmarried women among the Khams*

	Unmarried women in each group (per cent)
Rich peasant (*kral-pa*)	22.36
Monastic subject	50.00
'Side-dwellers' (landless labourers)	63.64
Servile classes (servants, slaves)	68.42

Source: After Carrasco 1959:69

were more likely to find husbands, either from their own group (where we would expect a higher rate of both polyandrous and polygynous marriages) or because they were attractive brides for those below them. The alternative explanation, which is suggested by some of the material on the Rajputs of India, is that extensive female infanticide obtained among the upper groups. But I know no reports of such a state of affairs, and it would be unlikely in a country where Buddhism was so strongly entrenched, although the high sex ratio found by Levine (1988) among the Nyinba (120 males to 100 females) strongly suggests the neglect of young girls.

The reference to illegitimate children serves as a reminder that the inability to marry (as an heir-producing wife) does not necessarily mean celibacy in the strict sense. Celibacy, in Tibet as elsewhere, occurs in two forms, the sacred and the secular. The sacred variety comprises the organised, cloistered celibacy of monks as well as of the priesthood. Not all monks are celibate; in Japan most Buddhist monks are married, and this is the case in one part of Tibet. Priests living within the community are less likely to be celibate, and the difference between a celibate monasticism and a married clergy is one that divided the eastern and western Christian Churches from an early period. Even those priests who have taken a vow of celibacy are less likely to live asexual lives than monks living in the more regulated environment of the monastery, and hence have been the main focus of discussions about the prevalence of concubines and illegitimate offspring, the concubinage and illegitimacy arising from the institutionalised rejection of marriage, and to a lesser degree of sex.

Celibacy in the Buddhist Himalayas means something very different for men and women. 'For women there is only secular celibacy. Women have no formal status in the religion and their remaining celibate has no ritual or religious purpose. These women are called *chomo*, meaning informally religious, but of course it actually means they are domestic servants. The majority live with their married brothers or elderly parents, but a number may live together independently and work for a monastery or live in the kitchen of a monastery and cook for the monks. *Chomos* are the source of much fun and ridicule' (A. Grimshaw, personal communication).

Celibacy and illegitimacy

Secular celibacy is found where marriage is 'delayed', or postponed altogether, for reasons that are often connected with the control of the number of offspring in relation to family resources. 'Delayed' or 'late' marriage for one sex, usually male, or for both occurs for reasons of labour, especially at a distance, or service in the army – living-in servants are normally unmarried, as distinct from those coming on a daily basis from their own homes. Or it may come about because of the accumulation of spouses, usually women, in plural marriage; given a normal sex ratio, polygyny is possible largely through the delayed marriages of men, and polyandry through those of women. In addition, there are those individuals who choose the status of bachelor or spinster, either because they prefer a union with members of their own sex or no union at all.

These 'voluntary' forms apart, secular celibacy, being 'enforced' and not the result of choice or a vow, is unlikely to be entirely asexual, however strong the external sanctions. Hence delayed marriage opens the way for primary illegitimacy, the birth of children to the unmarried, as distinct from what English law refers to as adulterine bastardy, resulting from an extra-marital liaison, distinct too from the offspring of a widow where they are required to be celibate, where no remarriage has taken place, or where there is no arrangement of the leviratic kind that automatically assigns paternity to the late husband's kin.

In societies where women marry early, such as India, Africa and China, primary illegitimacy remains at a low level and presents little problem. Indeed, in Africa the child of an unmarried mother may have a not altogether disadvantageous status in the family of its mother (see Goody 1956, 1962). In Asia the children of the concubine, which is a recognised status though below that of wife, may even inherit from their fathers; indeed the inability of the wife to produce a male heir is often the reason for taking a concubine in the first place.

In western Europe on the other hand, primary illegitimacy has long been a problem in that 'natural' children were excluded from material benefits (and often from immaterial ones). It would have been yet more of a problem had not the pregnancy of girls often been followed by their marriage, the reported rates being very high. But where the pregnancy resulted from a relationship between those of a different marital or social status, the usual outcome was of quite another kind; marriage was unlikely to take place, with the result that recourse might be had to abortion, infanticide or to the abandonment of children (and hence to the demand for institutionalised care), practices which, unlike the situation obtaining elsewhere in Eurasia, show little preference for one sex or another since they are rooted in the 'necessity' of getting rid of any child rather than in the 'selection' among them. Such differences in status between the partners, which provide opportunities for domination and submission, occur especially in societies with in-living servants; the dominant form of servanthood in rural Europe represented a movement between groups of similar status where the 'servant' was often a 'relative', but in addition there was the supply of servants from lower to upper classes which became such a major feature of the urban life of the bourgeoisie in the nineteenth century (Hobsbawm 1968:131).

In thinking of the fate of the celibates, whether men or women, we need to bear in mind that throughout Eurasia most agriculturalists were 'peasants' in the sense that neither their economy nor their social life were divorced from that of the towns, monasteries and other elements outside the village. Tibet, of course, enjoyed a literate culture over many hundreds of years, and while the women did not have the same option of running away to a monastery, though they acted as monastic servants (and in one area as wives), they could run away in other directions. In the first place, they might go to live with a labourer (or *dotul*), but by marrying down in a hypogamous union they forfeited any claim for maintenance from the family estate. Alternatively they could go away and work as (or for) a trader. The extensive network of trade with China and India, the problems of distribution in mountainous country, the difficulties that the terrain posed for wheeled transport (indeed there was none), the percentage of the population living in urban and monastic settlements, all this meant that a sizeable number of people were engaged in trade, transport and marketing; and some of these were 'unmarried' women. As in early modern Europe, late marriage encouraged women to leave the rural areas; they worked in towns which had a greater proportion of women, some of whom were accumulating their dowry. But in any case, since women were able to perform many of the agricultural tasks, they could exist economically on their own, especially since, as dependent householders, they had no military duties and could call upon their brothers' services for ploughing. It was the nature of these military duties far from home that, as has been argued for Sri Lanka (Tambiah 1958, 1966, 1973) and for Russia (Czap 1982), often made it desirable for a unit of production to consist of more than one adult male, whether polyandrously married or not, so that one of them would always be present on the farm. Tambiah notes that formerly in Sri Lanka, another Buddhist country, polyandry was seen as having the advantage of pooling labour as well as land (1966:298); one brother might engage in permanent paddy agriculture, the other in shifting cultivation. One could farm, one could trade. Above all, enforced military service for the king meant that rice fields would have had to be abandoned if there was only one man, and the same applied to corvée labour for public works, whether at the temple or the court, a rotation of duties that is associated with the rotation of cultivation and of wives within the joint family. The same holds true in the monasteries of contemporary Ladakh, where polyandry enables 'a brother to undertake labour service for the monastery without disrupting the agricultural production on the family plot. The brother left behind would have sexual access to the wife and ensure that in the absence of the husband she would not engage in other liaisons with village men' (A. Grimshaw, personal communication).

The nomads

We have so far looked at the agricultural areas of Tibet where the valleys provide richer possibilities for exploitation. But many of the same forms of family organisation are also found among the nomadic population, where similar practices have been adapted to quite a different ecology. Yet the situation is not entirely different, either on the level of family or of resources, as is indicated by the title of Ekvall's study (1968) of A Brog Pa, the high pasture nomads, namely, *Fields on the Hoof*, which draws attention to the similarity between pastoral societies and agricultural ones, at least those that depend upon permanent 'fields' rather than swidden.

In a system of production that has open resources and a limited technology based on the use of human energy, the differentiation in land holding is likely to be of relatively little importance. If land is more or less a free good, then labour is the differentiating feature; larger households inevitably cultivate more, smaller households less. Africa, for example, was largely dependent upon the labour of kin, for with adequate land for all, there were no landless labourers, except those forced to work under conditions of slavery.

With closed resources and an 'advanced' technology, there will tend to be the kind of differentiation in landholdings that existed in China. In order to limit such differentiation, a complex method of control is needed to restrict the size of holdings, for example, by means of the kind of 'communal' fields worked under the champion systems of western Europe or by the periodic redistribution of land in the Russian *mir*. Otherwise some holdings will get larger, others smaller, depending upon natural calamities, the depredations of the powerful, the number of children and the propensity of the individuals to save or to spend.

In this respect, the holdings of cattle by Tibetan nomads bear some relation to those of land under 'advanced' agriculture. Even more clearly than in the latter case, marriage involves a redistribution of property rights, to women as well as to men. For example, a man of position and wealth may take a second, younger wife, possibly a young servant girl with whom he has been sleeping. In this case he has to set up a 'little tent' having its own herd and management. This unit will be separate from the 'big tent', which often contains an 'extended family' since it may include parents and possibly other relatives. This physical layout represents the fact that a first wife brings dowry in the shape of a herd, whereas the servant girl may not, although the husband's herd is nevertheless split in order to provide her with the means of producing milk and other products. The splitting of resources is a simpler matter among the nomads, where capital can easily be increased by husbandry; so it is the rich who can afford polygyny.

Polyandrous families with two brothers (or even a father and son) sharing the same wife were common but appear to have been less resistant to fission than among the agriculturalists.

Quite frequently, two brothers decide not to divide the family herds and, since both sense and experience are against there being two tent mistresses, they agree to share one wife. This arrangement often begins when an older brother allows sexual access to his wife by his adolescent younger brother in the effort to keep the economic base of the tent intact. Such fraternal polyandrous marriages are quite unstable, due to sexual rather than economic reasons. The younger brother tires of the older woman and wants a younger one for his own wife. (Ekvall 1968:27)

The reasons given for the initial polyandry remind one of the position with regard to wives in other complex households, especially where they bring their own *peculium*, when they are viewed as potential foci of discord. Nevertheless, the polyandrous solution itself creates a problem because of the general tendency to individualise sexual access, especially when the wife is much older than the junior husband, which the existence of common herds as distinct from lands, common movables as against common immovables, is not sufficient to overcome. But dissolution of the polyandrous marriage does not depend upon the men alone; sometimes the wife herself will exercise a preference for one husband and drive the other out.

If a man has no sons, he may arrange a filiacentric union for his daughter, which is necessarily monogamous. These 'called-in-son-in-law' marriages are 'also devised to preserve family wealth intact' and resulted in an extended household of the stem variety. The son-in-law is usually brought in from a poorer family.

If he has a lineage 'bone' name or even 'house' name, he discards it and takes the lineage name of his wife, as a son of the tent, but unlike a real son, he does not have the right to set up his own tenthold apart from one of his wife's parents. It is assumed that mother and daughter can function in harmony as co-mistresses of the one tent. If the father dies early, the family may become polyandrous [polygynous], with mother and daughter as co-wives. (p. 27).

Normally division should occur only after the death of the father, when daughters who have not taken a dowry are entitled to an equal share with their brothers, although some property is retained for religious observances, chantry masses and for the maintenance of lamas and monasteries. Religious properties included lands acquired through gift, inheritance and insolvency. Chen estimates that in Kantze in south-eastern China, the lamaseries, which were much favoured by the state as a counterforce to local chieftains and which were centres of commerce and money-lending, owned 24 per cent of the cultivated land (1949:86).

On these various forms of marriage and family structure, Ekvall comments that 'economic considerations appear to take precedence over commonly cited reasons – sanctioned sexual intercourse and security for children – for the institution of marriage'. Since liaisons are common and children desired even outside wedlock, a full marriage consists of that form of union in which property is transferred to the wife in the form of dowry; should divorce take place, a woman is entitled to take away her herd plus any increase that has accrued (p. 28).

Family status is closely linked to resources in both the nomadic and settled populations, but it is in the latter that the maintenance of a fixed set is most important, not simply as a matter of survival, in order to sustain viable holdings in a situation where expansion from the valleys is difficult along an inelastic frontier. Given their fixed character, the aim was to maintain the position of the family by avoiding fragmentation. In some European cases it has been the goal of government or landowner, that is, of some collector of tax, rent or services, to insist that holdings are not divided. Here it was also perceived as in the interests of the families themselves, whatever the size or nature of their holding, to try and maintain intact the property that comprised the main basis of their social position.

This end polyandry, among other strategies, helps to achieve. By limiting the number of wives to one per sibling group, no proliferation takes place. The joint children of the brothers are all full siblings, one of another, and the sons among them can repeat the process in the next generation. But not all polyandry in Tibet is adelphic, even if all is based on strategies that are male-centred, whereas the 'polyandry' formerly practised by the matrilineal Nayar of Kerala was more female-centred in that a woman living with her brother in the natal home (*taravad*) received, from time to time, a series of 'visiting husbands' (Gough 1961). The Tibetan husbands were not always brothers in the case where a man's marriage was infertile and a second husband was brought in; while fraternal polyandry reduced the number of children of a sibling group, non-fraternal polyandry aimed to produce an heir. Other instances of non-fraternal polyandry occurred in the more hierarchical society of Lhasa where what was involved seems to have been the exercise of power and the imposition of one's will on a subordinate to whose partner one had access.[9]

Such arrangements find certain parallels in very different parts of the world. Among the LoDagaa of West Africa, when the first of twin boys marries, the second is said to have had access to his wife. Such a possibility arises from the very close social identity of the two siblings; and in rural Russia too we have reports of large households (Czap 1982) with brothers being allowed access to each other's wives, or a father having access to the wife of a young son who had been married in an attempt to adjust the land-labour ratio (R. Smith 1977:81).[10] In the event of an infertile marriage, the LoDagaa have an institution, discussed by Labouret (1931) under the rubric of polyandry, whereby the husband would call in another man to sleep with his wife after having made an appropriate sacrifice at the ancestral shrines.

In neither of these cases was 'marriage' involved and in neither was there any question of joint paternity. But they do represent situations in which the sharing of sexual access to one woman is permitted to two men at the same time. Among the LoDagaa such an act would provoke abhorrence at any other time whether or not the men were brothers; only after death does a man have access to the widow of his brother, for under the levirate it is an obligation on him to produce offspring to his name if there were none to succeed. Thus there is a kind of continuum from the high 'Hindu' ideal of the union of one man and one woman, which even death does not dissolve, to the African union which, except under special circumstances, excludes other males until death, when a union with the wife of the brother (or even of the father if she is not one's biological mother) is obligatory. The continuum leads from Africa to the practice of fraternal polyandry in which the union with the brother's wife is an obligation from the start, and finally to non-fraternal polyandry. In relation both to procreation and to power, socio-sexual dimorphism means that the situation looks very different from the woman's as distinct from the man's point of view, especially in the case of polygynous marriages. But there is nevertheless a continuum representing a kind of tension between the identity of same-sex siblings with regard to outsiders (even wives) and a general tendency to individualise rights of sexual access, more particularly to wives. Tibetan polyandry, indeed Tibetan marriage, clearly lies at one end of this continuum.

Finally let me turn to the range of regional and hierarchical differentiation which we discussed for China and will do so again for India. Regional differences were present in Tibet, with less polyandry in the east and north-east nearer to China; in Tibet itself cross-cousin marriage is prohibited but among Tibetan communities in Nepal it is allowed (as it is among the Hindu), and hence polyandry and polygyny involving different generations are forbidden. In Spiti there is little polyandry and much ecclesiastical celibacy, in Nyinba the reverse.

Hierarchical differences were in many ways yet more striking, as we have seen with regard to the percentages of unmarried women. Among the Nyinba of Nepal, Levine (1988) describes a situation that was hierarchically less complex than in Tibet proper but in which there was a division between masters and slaves or freedmen. While the former practised polyandry and over the generations formed what were effectively stem-families, the slaves had small, uxorilocal, monogamous households, occupying the small houses (*khang-chung*) behind the great house (*grong-chen*) of the master;[11] those of both sexes carried out women's work, so necessary to local agriculture, and thus supplemented the high sex ratio of the masters. Uxorilocality gave slave women a less disadvantaged status than their male counterparts; relations were matrifocal, divorce more common. Even in 1983, the mean household size of dependent freedmen was 4.8 as compared with 7.7 among the masters, that is, the 'citizen-landlords'. When the slaves were freed, they quickly adopted the norms of the dominant group, first virilocal marriage, then polyandry, as they became economically independent and acquired land, herds and pack animals, because, as the Nyinba see it, the only way to combine agriculture, herding and trade is by the occupational specialisation of brothers.

The same kind of hierarchical differentiation was found in Tibet itself. The wealthy 'taxpayers' (*trongba*) attempted to keep their holdings together by polyandrous marriage with divorced women occasionally living in adjacent households; beneath them the smaller serfs exchanged labour for land (or even wages), were taxed as individuals and lived in nuclear households. These differences were both normative and economic. That is to say, a value was placed on polyandrous marriage and members of lower groups tended to follow that pattern when they became wealthier and changed their status. On the other hand, the demands of a differentiated economy and of the state on male labour, as well as the felt need to keep the estate intact, were potent factors in the political economy that encouraged this unusual version of the solidarity of brothers.

II

India

Like China, India is a vast and populous area of the world with many internally shared cultural characteristics, largely the result of its religious heritage (for no over-all political unity existed until recently), although this ritual unity was supplemented by local cults and was broken on the national level as early as the fifth century BC with the development of Buddhism and much later the advent of Islam. Buddhism largely disappeared except in Sri Lanka, but Jainism and Judaism, Christianity and Islam from the West, all made their appearance to supplement local differentiation, even if Hinduism reasserted itself throughout. Some of the common features of marriage and the family are particular to the sub-continent, especially the exceptionally early age of marriage, particularly of girls, while others display a broad similarity with the mechanisms of continuity we have found in China. At the same time it is important to stress the internal differences, whether of town and country, of tribe and caste, of upper and lower and, most importantly, of religion and region. We shall try to specify some of these features and to link them, where relevant, with other differences in the social system, taking into account the past as it may have influenced the present.

In the context of the general continental similarities that are brought out by the often implicit contrast with Africa, we want to explore the difference between upper and lower in the hierarchy of caste and class, between North and South India, as well as that between India and China. In making these comparisons we will also be looking at common themes, at the way these different practices represent parallel mechanisms for dealing with general factors in the human situation of those living in civilisations based upon advanced agriculture of the kind developed in Eurasia. But attention will also be given to possible explanations for the differences as they emerge from recent discussions. In so doing we want to avoid treating 'kinship' as a special field for the application of formal analysis since such an approach tends to be dominated by terminological considerations, leading to a divorce of domestic life from the social matrix in which it is embedded – the modes of production, the system of communication, the practice of religion, the influence of the state and the control of the judicial apparatus.

The broad effects of religious adherence on kinship are seen very clearly in northern India where Hindus are enjoined to marry outside their lineages (indeed effectively they have to marry non-kin) whereas Muslims (throughout the North of the Indian sub-continent) practice father's brother's daughter marriage, so a spouse often comes from within the patrilineal clan or lineage,[1] although she may also be a cross-cousin as among Hindus and Buddhists in the South. Religious affiliation means that Bengalis on each side of the border with Bangladesh follow significantly different rules as to who they can marry, not to speak of adoption, divorce, polygyny and the levirate, on which the rules diverge substantially.[2]

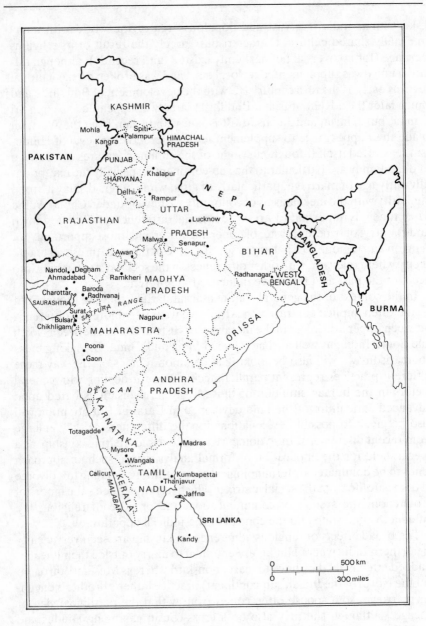

Map 2 India

On the other hand, both in the North and the South, in Muslim and in Hindu villages, India is a country, a sub-continent, where direct dowry exists side by side with indirect dowry or dower, that is, with the endowment of the bride by the groom and his family, called brideprice by many. Sometimes these transactions vary with the different strata in the same locality, with dowry being high status and brideprice low, but in many intermediate groups they run concurrently and a woman receives gifts of property both from her husband and from her parents, as well as from other kinsfolk, affines or friends. The timing of these transactions is important in various ways. The transfer of property from the husband to the wife at the time of the marriage (the indirect dowry) places some limited economic power in her hands. But more often this transaction (or the bulk of it) takes the form of a pledge of future support which is realised only when the marriage is dissolved by death or, in some cases, by divorce; only then can the promissory note be cashed.[3] Such is often the case with the Muslim *mehr* (*mahr*) in Pakistan where, if specified in the marriage contract, it acts as a kind of guarantee of the marriage and varies with 'the social position of her family and her qualifications' (Korson 1975:328); this prestation 'the wife alone shall receive' as with *jāhez*, which are gifts to the bride from family and friends consisting of clothes, jewellery, household goods, even property, and which remain her personal possessions (p. 329). Thus, argues Korson, Islamic marriage safeguards the rights of the wife and attempts to ensure her an economic status commensurate with her social standing (p. 329). High caste Hindus, on the other hand, accepted nothing on behalf of their daughters; marriage was ideally the gift of a virgin, accompanied by property. As with indirect dowry, the direct payment may be demanded and transferred on the spot; or it may remain a claim on a future inheritance, against the woman's parents or her brothers. But it comes from the bride's family rather than the groom's, even if the recipient is the same.

6

Marriage and the family in Gujarat

with Esther Goody

This chapter will concentrate upon marriage and the family in Gujarat, and is based upon short spells of fieldwork in India, discussions with the members of the Gujarati community in England and an examination of other studies of the region.[1] A more general reason for starting in the North, apart from the natural sequence following from Tibet, is that in recent years a number of influential analyses of marriage and the family in India have been based on the South and these have tended, at least among anthropologists, to set the themes for the study of the whole of the sub-continent.

Here we begin from a different vantage point, geographically and comparatively. In relation to our general theme, the most relevant works on Gujarat are those of Shah (1956, 1974, 1982) and Pocock on the Kanbi or Patidars (1972 and 1973), the major farming caste of the region. In the introduction to the first of his two studies, Pocock apologises for the lack of information on economic pursuits, indeed on the economy in general. Since he was dealing with a caste of working landowners whose activities were based on their title to that scare resource, land (and the water to irrigate part of it), a resource that was unequally divided between members of the caste, economic factors are clearly of considerable importance. That is especially true where the local productive system is based largely on domestic groups and where marriage involves the differential commitment of resources in order to establish a union among equals or better. In looking at kinship, marriage and the family specifically in relation to the economy, in the widest sense of that word, there is no question of introducing an economic 'determinism' to replace the 'religious' view of caste espoused by many scholars of India, as well as by the Brahmins themselves. It is a matter of righting a balance that is seen as tipped too far in one direction in order to account for our own particular experiences or to accord with a theoretical predilection for investigating the relationship between production and reproduction, that is, for extending the restricted kinship paradigm upon which we have earlier commented. But such an extension must also take into account religious, legal and political factors, as well as questions of centre and periphery, of differential contact with earlier inhabitants and of the 'compatibility' of institutions.

Nandol

Nandol, the village in which we lived during the rain season of 1977, was recorded as having 2,359 people in the 1961 census.[2] Situated on the banks of the Khari river, it had been known in the past for the craft of dyeing cotton sarees and other cloth. Nowadays, there is a small amount of dyeing work carried out, the bulk of the inhabitants working in agriculture, in service tasks or in jobs outside the village. For it was by no means an isolated settlement, being only a few kilometres from a railway station at the *taluka* centre of Degham, and some thirty from the great commercial city of Ahmadabad. The size of the households was small on average, partly because of the high rate of migration. In our Brahmin street half the houses were vacant; it is true that this section was something of a special case, but in the others too, except for those inhabited by groups heavily engaged in farming, namely, the Rajputs, the Patels and the Thakorda, the effects of migration were considerable.

Studies of Indian villages immediately bring to mind names like Brahmin, Nayar, Coorg – caste names that are often used as if they described 'peoples' or 'societies'. This usage arises mainly from the fact that the particular . named caste was dominant in the village under study, but also because the nature of the divisions between castes often made it difficult to work with more than one group at a time. Nandol presented a somewhat different picture from the many villages with a single dominant caste, since the Patels and Brahmins were almost equally represented in the village. Of course while the Patels were the main group of farmers and, after land reform, of land owners, in the ritual hierarchy the Brahmins were at the top, here as elsewhere. On arriving in the village, the first visitor we received together was a former member of the education department, a learned and friendly man called Kali Das. Sitting on the veranda, he refused the water offered him, saying, with little or no sense of apology, 'I only eat or drink in the house', by which he meant among his own section of Brahmins. Younger members of this caste were more willing to accept food from us, as well as from school friends or from members of their cricket team who were of lower ritual status. But in most other respects the barriers between castes remained strong.

In the past the Brahmins had probably been the dominant caste (or *jāti*) in terms both of numbers and of the ownership of land. Now they shared their numerical dominance with the Patels who belong to the same inclusive caste grouping as the Kanbi and Patidar of whom Pocock writes.[3] Known as the Patils in Maharastra, this is the main farming caste of the region. That is to say, they now own and farm (or supervise the cultivation of) the bulk of the village lands. In the past the Brahmins were also considerable landowners. But they rarely supervised directly the growing of crops (that is, 'farmed'), let alone used the plough. As a result of renting out their lands many were forced to sell them to their tenant farmers when the Gujarat Tenancy Act was introduced in 1957. Our friend Kali Das was caught in exactly this position. He had held ten acres which he let out in return for a proportion of the crop, that is, in one of the many forms of share-cropping. As with other Brahmins, the ground floor of his house contained large earthenware jars for storing grain. Now they were empty, for he held no land and lived off his pension, buying what grain he needed. In the section in which he lived only one Brahmin family farmed, and their acreage was quite small, about five in all. Unusually for that part of the village, a buffalo was tethered in front of their house in the evenings; during the day it was led away to graze by a herdsman, together with most of the milking herd of the village. Otherwise the Brahmin streets were totally unencumbered by animals, except for snarling dogs. This absence of farm livestock made a striking foil to the Patel sections, where in the evenings it was hard to squeeze down the narrow streets since at each house buffalo were being milked and fed with freshly cut grass, while all around their hooves had churned up the pathways which were bespattered with their dung. The picture of steamy, throbbing animal life contrasted starkly with the silent inaction of the Brahmin sections. Both groups, it should be said, were vegetarian in theory and very largely in practice; the animals of the Patels were for milk, dung and traction.

The orthodox hierarchy in the village consisted of Brahmins at the top, those specialists of ritual and literate activity, some few Rajput families from further North, the Patels who were the main farmer caste, the service castes such as Barbers, Goldsmiths, Potters and the like, then the main caste of landless labourers, the Thakorda, and finally the Harijan or 'Untouchable' castes. The nature of the distribution of castes in a village or small town is of course not random but related to (not determined by) the nature of livelihood activities within the village and between village and town (Shah 1982).

The Thakorda or Thakor are a subgroup of Koli, sometimes confused with the 'tribal' Bils, but who by the nineteenth century had established many small local chieftainships, the rulers of which adopted Rajput customs and married their daughters to the lower rung of Rajputs, thus taking their place in that hierarchy through hypergamy, although the hierarchy 'was very gradual and lacked sharpness' (Shah 1982:12–13). However, Shah suggests that this hypergamy, which was accompanied by Sanscritisation as well as by the adoption of 'a number of oral and literate traditions cultivated by specialists such as priests, bards, genealogists and mythographers ... provided an important mechanism for integration of the lower caste and tribal population into the Hindu society over the entire length and breadth of northern, western, central and even eastern India' (p. 14). While elsewhere Kolis claimed Kshatriya (warrior, ruler) status, the Thakorda of Nandol, whom I take to be recent immigrants, filled such a role in neither a political nor a ritual sense.

Many of the Harijans worked in the cotton mills in Ahmadabad, the first of which had started production in 1861, building on the earlier manufacture of hand-printed, hand-painted, and hand-woven cottons that had played such an important part of local and overseas trade in pre-European times. They were employed on shift work and travelled in groups by bus or cycle to the nearby town of Degham where they caught the train to the city. There they work mainly on the spinning side of the industry, and in one large mill where they are employed, they controlled recruitment to those sections of the plant. Before partition in 1947 the weaving rooms were staffed by Muslims, who now constitute only 15 per cent of the workforce, their jobs having been largely filled by migrants from Kerala.

Recruitment then is mainly within the group, indeed within the family. The shortage of jobs certainly encourages the desire to exclude 'outsiders'. But there are more positive factors at work. Young boys often come to the mill to bring their father's lunch (*tiffin*) box; when there, they may give their fathers a hand while they eat their meal, so that eventually they are in a good position to be taken on as workers, both from the management's interest in trained manpower and from the workers' view of hereditary occupation.

At the other extreme of the ritual hierarchy lies the Brahmin caste. Today, as in earlier times, their role is to perform religious ceremonies and to show others the right ritual and indeed ethical path. As in Islam, as in Catholic Christianity, many rites of passage are incomplete without the intervention of a priest, or rather of a member of the priestly group. In the former West African kingdom of Gonja any knowledgeable Muslim could perform the rites of the life-cycle, though senior ones from the division were essential for the major ceremonies in the annual cycle which, as elsewhere, carried a heavy political significance. In Nandol it was a special set of Brahmins attached to particular temples who performed the regular ceremonies; in all the major temples in Nandol 'poor' Brahmins acted as *pūjāri* (temple servants), not a high position but one that brought its own material and spiritual rewards. This was also true of other temples, such as that of the Barbers in Degham, that acted as centres for the devotion of members of a specific caste inhabiting a whole district. Only the Untouchables, that is, the Vankars or Dheds (Weavers) and the Bhangi (Scavengers), possessed temples which they looked after themselves, for they were not allowed into the places of worship to which the other castes had access (Gazetteer 1984:206). In Nandol the weavers' temple stood on top of the hill at the edge of the town where the houses of the Vankars were clustered, including many substantial buildings erected with money gained in the mills.

In addition, other Brahmins came to the temples at special times of the year and collected gifts and offerings from the congregation that they attracted. In year 1977 the intercalary month adjoined that of Krishna's birth and so doubled the length of this holy period of intense worship. The courtyards of a number of temples in Nandol were occupied by visiting Brahmins from other districts. Some built clay statues of deities, and decorated them (as deities should be decorated) with flowers, leaves and garlands, with vermilion powder (*konkor*) and with sandalwood. In the River Temple at Nandol, the visiting Brahmin had built a clay statue to Krishna. Every day worshippers, mainly women, came to leave him a little money, to have their hands spotted with sandalwood and to be blessed with prayers which were recited from the sacred book of ritual instructions that the priest had at his side. Each evening he carried this clay figure down to the nearby riverside and cast it in the waters, only to fashion a new one the following morning.

Apart from these village-wide public performances, Brahmins were needed for all individual rites of passage in the human cycle as well as for most occasional ceremonies. Unlike those for the Gonja Muslims, these services depended upon closed rather than open relations between a priest and his congregation or clientele. One afternoon we attended a *pūjā* in a nearby town, an occasion arranged by the university-educated wife of the electrical engineer. The reasons for the *pūjā* were obscure. We were told it was just a celebration for friends and neighbours, many of whom were present, but it was clearly more than that. For the first hour we sat there, nothing happened except talk and the handing round of food. A lot of important local people were kept waiting because the Brahmin, *their* Brahmin, had not turned up. It was impossible for them to call on another priest; knowing that such a *jajmānī* arrangement existed, no other Brahmin would have come unless he had been asked to do so by the *jajmānī* Brahmin himself.[4]

The word *jajmānī* has been employed in a more general 'service' context by Wiser (1936), Beidelman (1959), Neale (1957) and other scholars. However in Gujarat (and Bengal) the term was used for the association between a family and a specific Brahmin, not for service relationships generally, which were known as *vasváya*. Pocock, too, notes that he only heard the word *jajmānī* in answer to a query. In Nandol, it was employed more frequently but specifically for the relation between Brahmin and non-Brahmin, never for other relations of service that in some cases were very similar in form. However, as we will see in relation to the conceptualisation of rewards for services rendered, the two sets of activities are viewed in different terms.[5]

We have spoken of the position of the Brahmin as one of ritual dominance. However it seems difficult to argue that the hierarchy of Indian society was ever single-stranded. From the Brahmin standpoint, that is, from the ritual and (very importantly) the literate standpoint, this caste stands at the top of a hierarchy that even today one hears described in terms of the four traditional *varṇa* of the scriptural writings. However the total organisation of *jāti* was of course much more complex. In Nandol, as elsewhere, the extremes of this hierarchy are relatively fixed, with Brahmins at the top and Untouchables at the bottom, though neither of these groups is undifferentiated. The Patels came next to the Rajputs and they to the Vanias and then the Brahmins, and there were the usual disagreements among the service castes, Barbers, Potters, Goldsmiths and so on, plus a small section of Muslims who operated the mill for grinding oil. But while the Patels were located beneath the Brahmins in the ritual hierarchy, they were certainly not inferior either in economic terms (particularly now, as a result of changes in their position as landowners) or politically, since the name of Patel was then held by the Chief Minister of Gujarat, the chairman (*sarpañc*) of the village council and the previous chairman, and since that same caste occupied the majority of places on the council (*pañchāyat*).

The present numerical balance of Patel and Brahmin resulted partly from the emigration of Brahmins and partly from the immigration of Patels. We have already alluded to the emigration of Brahmins in contrasting the emptiness (of people as well as of buffalo) of their streets with the bustle of the Patel quarter. This emigration was based in large part on the Brahmin's command of literacy, for they quickly adapted to European education just as they had used their earlier skills in business and administration, but on a smaller scale.[6] We ourselves lived in a street of Brahmins in a house that was traditional in most respects but of considerable elaboration, being one of those many village houses in India which high caste emigrants had retained, sometimes to celebrate rituals, sometimes as a retirement home, but which are decreasingly used for either (Lardinois 1986b:283). It had been built in 1929 by a Brahmin who as a young man had left the village for Ahmadabad with a few pennies in his pocket, where he had made his money on the Stock Exchange; speculation on such things as commodity futures had long been an established feature of Ahmadabad life, at least as far back as the eighteenth century (Gillion 1968:51). Afterwards he invested some of his gains in an elaborate house in his natal village, with doors modelled on those of the Stock Exchange, to which he intended to retire in his old age. In fact, he stayed in Ahmadabad with his city-bred children who had now become teachers or had entered other professional fields. Success in the Stock Exchange (and failure too, both are much spoken about) was not unusual during the period that saw great activity in the Ahmadabad mills beginning with the 1860s, following the introduction of new milling technologies from abroad and roughly coinciding with the coming of the railway. Earlier commercial activity of a wide-ranging kind, and affecting life in the villages as well as the town, was centred on the production of hand-printed cloth for export to South East Asia, Indonesia, Africa, West Asia and to Europe, all these markets being in existence well before the advent of European powers to the Indian Ocean. Subsequently the British encouraged the export trade using cloth as a means of obtaining Indonesian spices and they promoted the commercial growing of opium and indigo for sale to China. Today, as in the recent past, manufacture, commercial crops and trade continue to have their effects on country as well as town. Every month the one Brahmin farming family in the next street to us was visited by the 'Bombay wallah', a restless wiry man, now retired, who had gone into the business of manufacturing brushes with an Englishman in Bombay, had speculated on the Stock Exchange, and still returned regularly, sometimes to offer a large *pūjā* on behalf of the Brahmins in the village. However most migrants were teachers and clerks who depended, even more than businessmen or financial manipulators, on their literate skills which they could exercise only outside Nandol.

The various gradients of differentiation and power, of ritual, economic and political kinds, found in Nandol were certainly not isomorphic one with another. On the other hand, the 'ritual' gradient was not unconnected with certain types of economic and political achievement even today, especially when we take into account success outside the village. But apart from that large and important body of the inhabitants working elsewhere, which included Barbers in Britain and Africa as well as Brahmins in Bombay and Untouchables in Ahmadabad, the internal hierarchy of the village, looked at from an economic point of view, depended largely on the relations of people to land. The main categories can be summarised in the following way: (1) major land holders; (2) craftsmen; (3) permanent labourers; (4) casual labourers. In all three lower groups, some of whom owned plots of land, others of whom rented fields, payment for services could be made in grain, in a proportion of the harvest, or in money wages. Share cropping, wage labour and the 'family' farm interlocked in complex ways but as the result of recent legislation tenants had been largely replaced by farmers who 'worked' their land, sometimes in collaboration with an absentee relative, an arrangement which could double their permitted acreage in the case of the rich. Legislation had changed the position of non-farming landlords but had had little effect on those who actually farmed the land. Nevertheless this economic arena was one in which class relations definitely supplemented those of caste.

This was also the case in the past. The earlier hierarchy within the caste was related to the holding of the land, as described by Nath for the nineteenth century:

Within a village there was differentiation of status based on land ownership. First, there were the Lewa Patidar lineages who were dominant and influential and who owned land under Patidari tenure. Second, there were the Lewa Kanbis who were also landowners but did not own land under Patidari tenure. Third, there were Lewa Kanbis who were tenants of the landowning Patidars as also of the landowning Kanbis. Finally, there were Lewa Kanbis who worked as agricultural labourers either for their fellow caste men or for other landowning castes in the area such as the Rajputs. (1973:390)

In the eighteenth century Patidars (the earlier name for the Lewa Patels of Nandol) owned land on the Patidari tenure. The cultivable land of the village was divided among the different lineages according to ancestral shares. Land revenue was paid by the village but the land itself was divided up on a genealogical basis. The Patidars kept genealogies for this purpose which were often written and printed.

Marriage transactions

The ritual gradient is more closely linked to marriage, to reproduction than to production; one does not marry outside the caste, though occasionally a union may take place between a woman and man of a higher group. But if the prohibitions on marriage are related to the ritual gradient, the practical policy of alliance is closely linked to the economic and prestige system, for it brings into the reckoning the resources of the man as well as what a woman takes into or receives from the marriage by way of dowry; through marriage the families of both men and women may be trying to better their position within the caste by seeking the most desirable partner they can get.

In his account of Patidar marriage, Pocock (1972) treats the dowry as a gift to the groom's family, just as he treats marriage as a gift of the bride. This view of marriage, and to some extent of dowry, is strongly influenced by the predominantly exchangist views adopted by Dumont from Lévi-Strauss whose approach was originally formulated in the analysis of Australian systems which constituted for him the elementary form of kinship. However it is also true that the notion of gift (but not of exchange), the gift of a virgin (*kanyādāna*), forms a specific part of the Brahmin ideology of marriage which has been developed in the corpus of written law (Tambiah 1973).

In his analysis of South Indian kinship, Trautmann draws attention to the relation at the ideological level between the gift of a bride (*kanyādāna*) and the religious gift (*dharmadāna*). In theory the Brahmin is the universal recipient (they alone can beg), while the king is the universal donor, a relation that Trautmann sees as being the central conundrum of Indian social thought, that between spiritual authority (*brahma*) and temporal powers (*kṣatra*), between the receivers and the givers of material things, who are themselves the givers and receivers in turn when it comes to spiritual gifts, a 'conundrum' that is 'resolved at the level of ideology' (1981:286); that is to say, it forms the basis of written (Brahmin) texts of narrative and commentary.

Without the ambivalence generated among the recipients, remarks Trautmann, 'the brahmin theory of the gift looks as though it might be explained as a simple conspiracy of priests' (p. 286). Clearly we are not faced with a conspiracy of a particular set of priests. But all priests depend upon gifts, now and in the past, unless they take to following the ways of conquest, commerce or production, the ways of the *Kshatriya*, *Vaiśya* or *Śūdra* respectively, which in normal circumstances fall outside the scope of their activity. It is not a question of conspiracy but of support, of gaining the means of livelihood. To obtain this end means transforming the notion of exchange into a gift for which there is no material return but which receives its reward in spiritual benefits. Just as the channelling of one-way gifts of material objects was important to the Catholic Church in Europe (Goody 1983), so it was an essential feature of the Hindu and Buddhist priesthood in Asia and the Muslim clergy in Africa.[7]

With regard to the application of the notion of gift to marriage, Trautmann summarises the classical concept as one that completes a man and enables him to become a sacrificer. The groom 'assimilates – I should rather say quite literally "incorporates" – to himself a wife who becomes his "other half", *aparārdha*, rendering her an extension of himself in which capacity she assists him in the rites'. For the woman 'it severs her from the family into which she was born, by the act of gift ... , and incorporates her to her husband and his family. His patrilineal ancestors become hers and, in some measure of tension with the basically cognatic nature of this as of all kinship systems, she is cut off from her natal ancestors and kin' (1981:271–2). But note that in this discussion of the incorporation of woman it is usually the girl's family that initiates the negotiations (Mandelbaum 1970:105) and it is of course from her home that the groom's party have to seek her during the wedding ceremony. Cutting off the bride may suit the notion of the one-way gift and the idea of the male receiver; but it 'mystifies' rather than represents the actual transactions.

There are obviously some similarities between these notions of alms and marriage; both are seen as gifts to superiors, non-reciprocating and permanent. But analytically the differences are equally apparent. The first is a gift to Brahmins, the latter a 'gift' between Brahmins; the first an object, the latter a subject, as least in the sense that she is a right- and duty-bearing person; as a subject, a human subject, she is not permanently cut off from the givers but maintains a significant link with them, part of a continuing brother–sister relationship of great importance that is never entirely broken by marriage, either in the North or in the South. Whatever the texts may argue, the 'transferability' of women, to which Trautmann refers, always has a double aspect. Parry notes this when he writes of women being transferred to their husband's clan and *sutra* at marriage. Yet, he adds, she 'never entirely renounces her moral right to the help and protection of her parental household . . . They observe mourning for her death and her brothers have their heads shaved' (1979:13). On the other hand, the responsibility for performing the mortuary rituals falls on her conjugal household, although, significantly, it is her son who is ideally the chief mourner.

Let us consider more explicitly the utility of the concept of gift as a tool for examining the range of Indian marriage practices. In discussing China there were good theoretical reasons to doubt the applicability of the *analytic* notion of giving or exchanging a bride in major and filiacentric marriage, if such a gift is held to imply that a woman gives up membership of her natal group and is exchanged as a totality. While such notions may or may not be applicable to aboriginal Australia, they seem inappropriate to the study of societies of a very different sort, that is, to more complex societies where the nature of marriage transactions is linked to the system of production as well as to that of exchange. For example, the appointed daughter who makes a filiacentric union is not given or exchanged in any way. Even if the argument is restricted to standard marriages, to major marriages, the data in Gujarat and elsewhere indicates that the gift is never made over to the groom in any absolute sense, neither in the shape of the dowry nor much less in that of the bride.

Pocock's own account shows (as does the work of Shah and others) that even after marriage a woman continues to relate to her natal family; above all there is the continuing brother–sister bond, the continuing gifts from her kin, and the continuing part played not only by the natal family of her father but also by that of her mother. For instance, when the groom's party comes to visit the bride's home, they receive gifts from her family. 'At this time', writes Pocock, 'the girl's maternal uncle is expected to make a rather more substantial gift than the others' (1972:112). Why the maternal uncle if the mother had already been given away at her marriage? In fact, these wedding gifts appear to pass between ranges of kin, bilaterally defined, rather than between clans (that is, unilineal groups) or villages, and this applies to the bride herself. It is at the time of this visit that the dowry is 'handed over' and only afterwards can 'the groom receive the final gift, his bride, whom he receives from the hand of her maternal uncle' (p. 112).[8]

The role of the maternal uncle at the wedding suggests that marriage cannot involve the complete handing over of a woman between groups, patrilineal or otherwise, since an emotional and jural interest in her is necessarily retained by the natal family of her mother as well as by that of her father, just as she retains her own sentiments, claims and memories about them. Similar limitations on the notion of 'gift' apply to the dowry, at least among the Patidars. Traditionally a girl did not immediately accompany her husband back to his village after the groom's visit but followed later on, carrying those gifts 'that it had been settled her husband should give her', clothes, bedding, ornaments and so on. After a few days she returned to her father's house and then went back again to her husband with some more clothing. Subsequently she goes back once again to her natal home and returns later on for a third time, in theory for her confinement as is the case in much of India (Lardinois 1986a:550) but in practice often arriving with her first-born. It is at this time that the most expensive gifts of all are presented to her. While all this is happening the gifts of the groom to his father-in-law become less important.[9] Even so there is no termination of the bride's own ties since her brother and maternal uncle continue to have obligations not only to her but to her children, including as we have seen the nominal ability of 'giving her away', as the English expression goes, when she gets married.

The gifts a girl receives from her own parents when she leaves home have no proper name.

They comprise clothing, jewellery, and vessels but in larger quantities than have been received in the *dej* (the gifts to the bride from the groom's family in which she has no permanent rights unless she produces children). Properly speaking the girl or, if she dies, her family retains rights in this property. Naturally as the girl has children and grows into her husband's family her interests and so her rights tend to be identified with his. If all goes well the woman will preserve her jewellery and pass it on to her own daughter when she is married. If times are difficult it is well understood that a husband may be obliged to sell part or all of this jewellery, but only a dissolute spendthrift would take such action without considerable thought. Ideally the husband should be in a position to augment his wife's ornaments, and this kind of investment in gold is traditional among the peasantry of India. (Pocock 1972:111–12)

What we find here is a transfer of property to the girl both by the groom (*dej*) and by her family. While in other groups part of the groom's gifts may go to the bride's father under conditions we will discuss, the bulk of the property is seen as belonging to the wife rather than the husband. The fact that under certain extreme conditions the husband may use the dowry without permission does not contradict the notion that, while the transfer is in most castes an intrinsic part of the marriage transactions, even the indirect dowry is essentially a gift to the daughter (or the handing over of her 'share' in the case of the direct dowry) rather than a gift to her husband. Of course its amount is always of concern to the groom's party, a larger dowry (as Parry shows for the Rajputs) often being expected with a girl of lower standing; indeed the element of bribe is not necessarily absent, although 'inducement' would better express the general notion. Such an interpretation certainly applies to Nandol, just as it emerges from the data that Pocock presents.

The Patels of Nandol live in their own 'quarters', a *pol* locked at night and entered by an arch which announces that they are Lewa (or Leva) Patidars (a name nobody now uses). They have built a new hall in the village which acts as the home of the local branch of the Cooperative Bank as well as the meeting place for the whole subcaste from the surrounding villages, those local groups that form the circle within which marriages can take place. This *nati gor (gol)* or 'agreed circle', is known as *bewandar gor*, the circle of fifty-two (most such groupings have numerical names), although in fact the subcaste had split into two new circles, this one consisting of only sixteen villages.

At marriage, the *sarpañc* declared of the Patels, we have one peculiarity (implicitly, *vis à-vis* the Brahmins). 'We give ornaments to our son's wives as well as to our daughters.' The first gift is a reference to what Pocock refers to as 'brideprice' or *dej*, a transaction often thought of as a prestation from the groom's to the wife's kin. The phrase I cite makes it clear that the gifts fall into the category of what I have called indirect dowry, a type of transaction that is generally regarded as lower in status than the direct dowry 'to our daughters'; that is to say, the Patels do it while the Brahmins do not. But note that in this case the gift from the groom's family is made specifically to the bride rather than to her father, a transaction of the *hedna* type found in ancient Greece, the *mahr* of Islam, and certainly not one which these Patels regard as a price or purchase.

Not all Patels act in this way. In the nearby town of Degham, Dr Dinubhai Patel, a Lewa Patel who belonged to a different circle known as Khosi, followed the 'upper', Brahmin way of accepting nothing from their in-laws on behalf of their daughters; and in this way the circle rose in the hierarchy. In the old days, he claimed, people 'sold' their daughters, meaning they allowed their husbands to endow them. His son-in-law worked with him as a doctor on two days a week but kept his fees for himself; Dr Dinubhai was careful to take nothing from him lest it be construed as payment or even a return gift, whether for himself or his daughter. The difference between an emphasis on direct or indirect dowry is not only a matter of caste hierarchy but sometimes of the relative position, including the age, of the husband and wife, for Lewis records that in the Jat village of Rampur near Delhi 'marriage by purchase' was generally resorted to by older men whose money was used to pay off a debt or to spend on a wedding feast (1958 [1965]:190), although the latter seems hardly an economical way of effecting a purchase. But in the case of the Patels, to refer to bridal endowments as 'sale' or 'purchase' is to adopt the upper Brahmin view; what is called in French 'le prix de la fiancée' is taken to represent 'objectivement l'achat d'une femme' (Lardinois 1986a:530). It is nothing of the sort.

According to Shah (1982:24), there were also groups in Gujarat, namely the Vanias, who provided no marital endowments, either direct or indirect. The absence of such transfers he attributes to their small, endogamous subcastes. My own limited contact with merchants of this caste suggests that they are equally concerned about the endowment of daughters. Could it be that devolution is postponed and that what is dowry for others becomes inheritance for them? Another possibility among groups that take the education of women seriously, is the replacement of dowry by the pre-marital expenditure on schooling.

Among the Lewa Patels of Nandol the bride received both a direct dowry and a bridal endowment, an indication of the intermediary position of the subcaste in the total hierarchy. Consistent with this position is the fact that they allowed their widows to remarry, although earlier that was not the case. The decision to change had been made at a meeting (*sabhā*) three years before when it was so agreed because 'we had many of them and could not spoil their lives, whatever the religious people might say' (GJ 78). In fact we heard of no case in which remarriage had taken place, but the possibility had been broached.

The amounts involved in these various gifts to the bride are sometimes considerable. The elderly wife of the doctor in Degham received a total of 600 *tolas* of gold, i.e. 6,000 grams, which in 1977 had a value of £24,000. Her husband certainly did not claim that this was given to him. In fact the gold was used for ornaments, for the marriage headdress, for bangles, for a necklace, and for decorations for the ears, fingers and the nose. These valuables were stored in the bedroom under lock and key, her key. They formed a standby, not used for investment; and her married daughter had already been provided with a dowry without delving into this reserve.

Our neighbour, another Dinubhai (a stranger, 'Brahmin', Thakur, living in rented property in a street of a different Brahmin subcaste), was a teacher at the local primary school. As literates, Brahmins gravitated towards the teaching, clerical and administrative professions;[10] indeed the first 'modern' school in the village had been held in the grounds of the nearby temple, no doubt emerging out of an earlier Sanskritic school or *parsallah*, and at the beginning the recruitment had been exclusively Brahmin. Of course other higher castes had been able to learn to read for many centuries, but the teaching of the Vedas is still meant to be confined to the Brahmins (Ingalls 1959; Staal 1961). Returning from the River Temple one evening, teacher Dinubhai explained that the minimum amount of gold for a daughter's dowry was 100 grams, which at 600 rupees (or £30) for ten grams, meant £300 in 1977; the value will have increased many times by now but even then represented a considerable amount in relation to his salary. 'This we save from our salary and buy ten grams at a time, as well as what you spend on education, and eventually it will be made into bangles and other ornaments. This we have to do in our station', he explained (GJ 11). 'If you have many daughters, you have to look for a man who has been unable to find a wife.' The dowry, he seemed to be saying, is required both for prestige and for protection; it is the girl's fortune which she herself owns. If there was not enough, she would have to make a less desirable (hypogamous or isogamous) marriage.

This view of women's property rights, expounded here by a 'Brahmin' but accepted beyond the confines of that caste, is given explicit expression in classical theory. Discussing what he sees as the complete assimilation of the bride in the family of the husband and the complete *dissimilation* from that of her natal kin, Trautmann writes:

As a woman she may not inherit landed property, and because she has been given away in marriage, she has no claim to her father for maintenance. Hence the bride is 'adorned' with a dowry of clothing, utensils, and above all jewelry, which constitute her property (strīdhana), as a kind of premortem inheritance. The bride adorned is but the first of a series of gifts that flow from the bride's people to the groom's. But the bride's people must accept nothing in return. (1981:291–2)

Note the bride may be 'given away' but her endowment, her 'premortem inheritance', remains hers.

It should be noted that some of the phrases used by Trautmann to indicate incorporation in a patrilineage, namely, 'the better half' and 'given away in marriage' (p. 292), as well as Gough's 'becoming one flesh', are precisely those that until very recently were employed of marriage in the English-speaking world where bilaterality, choice of spouse and conjugal love are supposed to have reigned more or less supreme. In Europe it would be hazardous, to put it mildly, to interpret the rule against divorce, still obtaining in Spain today (and universally in earlier Catholic Europe), as indicating the complete detachment of a bride from her natal family. Much less would it be possible to interpret 'the better half' or 'one flesh' as part of a unitary structure of concepts in an 'ethno-biology' of procreation or in a sociology of married life. We have to understand these usages (I hesitate to use the word 'metaphors') contextually. Becoming one flesh with another is perfectly consistent with remaining of the same blood as one's kindred. To suppose otherwise is to insist upon a too simplistically ordered view of human thought and metaphor, one that fails to allow for the 'contradictions' that are characteristic of oral usage and of customary practice, but which the written word often tries to iron out by its own hegemonic procedures (Goody 1986). A contrary supposition might arise were we to treat the text as reality, which of course it is, often having an important influence on behaviour, not of the reading classes alone. But the text is obviously not the whole of reality, to the other elements in which it may stand in some contradiction. As Trautmann perceptively remarks of the *Dharmaśāstra*, it is not 'simple customary law' but 'something new and highly wrought, originating in custom no doubt, but developing it to the point where we are often unsure what bearing the perfected doctrine has on actual life' (1981:294).

In Nandol the gifts to a bride from her natal family were called *dahej* (the *dej* in Pocock's account was used of gifts to her from the groom's family). As the Chairman (*sarpañc*) of Nandol Council described his own wedding, the transfer included money, household equipment, TV, scooter, steel cupboards, even a house. At first he said, 'This my father-in-law gives to me.' On my questioning him further (for his wife was not present), he added: 'gives both of us'. And he agreed that the wife would take these possessions away with her if the marriage was dissolved. He went on to explain that in contemporary law property, even the land, goes to the children of a marriage, both male and female, for all are equal. 'It is moral considerations that lead the daughter to make no direct claim on the land at her marriage, leaving it instead for her brothers, for she does not want to split up the farm itself, the basis of the estate. That is why the daughter gets such a big dowry' (GJ 79). Sometimes her restraint may be rewarded with an extravagant marriage ceremony. 'That is also why we help our sister at the birth of her child' (GJ 79). These comments show that, in his view at least, the 'presents' given to the daughter at her wedding, during her marriage and at the birth of a child (the sister's child) derive from the claims she can herself exercise as a child and as a sibling (that is, as an heir) – although the quantity of such 'presents' is linked to what she and her kin acquire at marriage by way of a husband, his wealth and his status. This interpretation is reinforced by considering the role of the mother's brother. What a woman gets at marriage is not the end of her claim on her natal family; her own daughter exercises some continuing call upon the resources of those kin, for she has some notional claim on her mother's brother, as it were, for that portion not taken by her own mother. This delayed claim has some structural resemblance to the one enshrined in the northern French costumals discussed by Le Roy Ladurie (1972), following Yver (1966), where an individual may either take the whole of his portion when leaving the family holding with a definitive allocation, or may be given only part, maintaining a claim on the rest to be realised when the estate is divided.

To return to the subject of dowry, the minimum specified in the Brahmin case (ten *tolas*) should be compared with the amounts suggested by a Barber friend, namely five *tolas* (i.e. fifty grams) plus seven sets of dresses. Such minimal payments are often exceeded when the families involved are well off, and the Barber caste of Nandol was engaged in running shops in East Africa and Zaire as well has having a colony in Leicester, England. So when our friend got married, his wife received from her father: twenty *tolas* (200 grams) of gold, in addition to one necklace, two chains, three bangles and three rings. Other relatives also gave her presents. Moreover the groom's father supplied some dresses, while the whole of his *vas* (quarter) offered her gifts as well. Some also flowed to the groom. From the bride's father he received a gold ring and a watch. This was neither a pure gift nor yet a calculated inducement to take the girl, but rather part of the total expectations involved in the marriage, one that was clearly set aside from the rest of the property listed above which the wife keeps for herself both as trousseau and as peculium, possibly to be handed on to her daughter when she married.

Who is it that a person can marry? Castes in this region are basically endogamous and there is little of the intercaste hypergamy reported for the Rajputs in the North (Parry 1979) or for the Nayar in the South (Gough 1961). But while they must marry within the caste, the Patels or Patidars cannot marry into their own local descent group, that is, the descent group located in their own village and to which they themselves belong. In addition they cannot marry anyone else of their caste resident in that village. Men are further prohibited from marrying into the particular local descent group from which their mothers have come or into which their sisters have married. In other words not only is marriage to the father's brother's daughter (FBD) prohibited (unlike Muslims in the north of the sub-continent) but all marriage to cross-cousins (XCM) as well (unlike the Hindus and Buddhists of the South). Prohibitions on marriage extend, as among the Tallensi of northern Ghana, to all 'kin' who consequently stand resolutely opposed to 'affines', to those whom one can marry.

At one level, potential spouses are positively defined, whereas among the Tallensi they are only negatively so. A person must marry not only into the same Patel caste but within a specific group of villages known as a *gor* or circle. The use of the term 'circle' does not indicate a system of 'circulating conubium', A to B to C, such as has been postulated for some other parts of the world. Nor yet, unlike the practice of some other groups in North India, including some Patidars and Rajputs, does it imply a step-wise, unidirectional flow of brides in hypergamous marriage (Mandelbaum 1970:239). The circle defines a range of possibilities. These circles, according to Shah, were never completely closed to hypergamous marriage, even though they were apparently organised to get relief from its inherent difficulties, 'so that almost every unit became loose in the course of time' (1982:16). But the system was unlike that of the Rajputs who practised hypergamy without any attempt to form small endogamous units.

Village exogamy means that all wives, though within the circle, are in another sense 'outsiders', with consequences that will become clear in chapter 8. However, the limitation on the number of villages in the circle means that the members will be known to one another as persons of the same kind; each potential bride is of the same generalised status as each potential groom. And, while the disadvantages are obvious, Mandelbaum notes that people in the North discuss the value of village exogamy in making it easier for young brides to adjust to their new situation (1970:102). By definition no endogamous subcaste was limited to Nandol itself, since marriage had to take place outside the village but inside the caste. Hence all subcaste relations spread outside the village, sometimes covering a large area and including, especially for the artisan castes, groups resident in the town of Degham.

I mean by the same generalised status that the partners are broadly similar socially as well as economically, for as Pocock observes a caste may be highly differentiated.

There are not only marked differences of economic condition but also differences of custom. Some Patidar assist at blood-sacrifices, eat meat, give bride-price for their wives and practise widow-remarriage. All these are considered to be signs of low caste by other Patidar who are strictly vegetarian in diet and worship, give dowry at marriage, and do not allow widows to remarry. (1972:2)

This same generalised status may include persons of roughly the same economic level, although there are bound to be differences within as well as without the circle, differences that will profoundly affect the marriages people make. Of these differences Pocock writes:

In India there are extremely wealthy and highly educated Patidar living in the countryside in their natal villages and in the cities of Gujarat, to say nothing of the large communities of emigrants in different parts of the world. There are also illiterate Patidars extremely dependent for their living upon labouring for others. These extremes can be found in one and the same descent group in one and the same village, and between them every grade of economic conditions can be found. (1972:1)

In an earlier paper on hypergamy (1954), Pocock describes a very similar situation among the Lewa Patidars of Charottar in the Kaira district. There had previously been a situation of free hypergamy of the 'kulin' (superior lineage) variety, in which daughters could be given to higher marriage circles, accompanied by a dowry, leading to the infanticide of upper daughters. In the lower groups on the other hand, the shortage of girls meant brideprice, marriage by sibling exchange, unions to lower castes and widow remarriage. However, the marriage circles did not constitute a formal hierarchy and only subsequently has there been a formalisation of these circles into *ekada* groups, so that now a man is fined and boycotted if he gives his daughter to a higher village (p. 198). Of course within the circle itself there were still attempts to marry one's daughters to the better (often wealthier) families.

Pocock is concerned to point out that Patidar 'marriage groups' only include village segments (*jāti*, a portmanteau term) of the same general status, those having the same customs. Since we know from the work of Srinivas and others that the position of one caste segment (whether the subcaste or circle, the local caste or those in one village, or the local caste subgroup, that is, descent group) in the ritual hierarchy of purity and pollution is often subject to efforts to increase its status by the process of Sanskritisation (and one should add, decrease it too under certain circumstances), the composition of a *gor* (or *nati gor*, agreed circle) is likely to change, that is, to undergo fission and sometimes fusion. But size also depends upon the occupational aspect of caste. The smaller the local caste groups, the wider the circle. The *gor* of castes like the Barbers, often with relatively few members in each village, will usually extend much further than that of a larger caste like the Patels. In both cases, the unity of the group centres not only upon common interests but on common property, in particular the possession of a temple, a meeting hall, or both.

One reason for this development has been the promotion of the marriage circles, which embodied homogamy, by the British in the nineteenth century because they saw hypergamy as connected with female infanticide. The practice of infanticide among the Patidars was related to hypergamy in an interesting way. For it was more prevalent among higher than lower groups, partly because men of the upper lineages often married well-endowed girls from lower ones, thus leaving their own sisters unable to find a husband (although polygynous marriages were also more common in those upper groups). Men in the upper groups gained twice by killing off their female infants. It left them free to take rich brides from below and it saved them having to endow their own sisters. One can look at the causal chain running in either direction but the result was that the poorer groups on the other hand were short of brides and had to marry outside the caste, enter into a union with a widow or a divorcée, or engage in an exchange marriage, all non-Hindu practices (Nath 1973).

While the remarriage of widows and divorcées may be seen as a means by which the lower groups coped with the lack of brides due to hypergamy

(Shah 1982:16), there are of course simpler ways of adapting, such as delaying the marriage age of men or advancing that of women. In contemporary rural Gujarat, where rates of hypergamy seem low, such practices are now more a matter of social definition in which the rejection of celibacy has a wider base in social practice and ideology.

This brief account of marriage in the Gujarati village of Nandol will serve as a backdrop to the discussion of India in more general terms. In view of our wider aims it should be stressed that many of those born in the village are scattered not only in India and West Asia but in Africa and Europe as well, where the activities of one small local caste range from shopkeepers in Zaire, policemen in Tanzania (alas, no longer), to wool-knitters and potato crisp-makers in Leicester. Little would have predicted an adjustment of the Barber caste to such a wide range of activities, yet in this vast span of accommodations to different languages, economies and political regimes, they have struggled to retain features of their familial and religious life, and especially those relating to marriage.

In these marriages and in others, the material from Gujarat provides little evidence of any absolute incorporation of women into their husbands' family or lineage if, by that, is meant a cutting off from the groups into which they were born. The absence of divorce, the idea of a lifelong union, has sometimes been taken as evidence of a total transfer. So too has the levirate, which is forbidden in 'upper' groups. But the most striking evidence of continuing ties rests on the strength of the brother–sister relationship which will be looked at again in connection with hierarchical differences, especially as this is one of the ties that seems little affected by social or economic variation.

Women continue these ties after marriage, for they are neither purchased nor given away in marriage but endowed either directly by parents or indirectly by the groom, emphasising their status as persons rather than pawns, even though that position of a new bride presents many problems. But these transactions too vary with their position in the hierarchy, which we examine in the following chapter.

7

The high and the low

The differences between hierarchical groups that Pocock noted for the Patidars of Gujarat and that obtain in other villages of the state, represent a trend that we see on a more general level in India as a whole; while there are some inversions and some exceptions (we do not expect to find absolute associations but rather statistical correlations), there are nevertheless significant trends. Take first of all the well-known situation regarding religion. High (ritually high) means abstinence from meat and often from other foods, while by and large low means omnivorous. Exceptions exist on a national plane, for while Rajputs are 'higher' than Baniyas, the former eat meat while the latter are vegetarian. The problem is that there is no single hierarchy of values or of achievement, the powerful are higher than the holy in some contexts, the rich in others. On the other hand, despite such apparent exceptions, this religious valuation of behaviour regarding food tends to prevail, partly because it is based on the authority of the written word as against that of the sword or of money. In the village of Ramkheri (in the Dewas district of Madhya Pradesh), Mayer noted that while the Vaiśya were below the Kshatriya in traditional (*varṇa*) terms, 'the vegetarianism of the former is said by many to make the Vaiśya equal to, if not superior to, the Kshatriya' (1966:141). This difference in valuation expresses itself in offerings to the gods as well as in consumption by humans. In the village of Totagadde in western Mysore vegetarian food is presented to the household deities of the Brahmins, blood offerings to the guardians of lower ranking households (Harper 1964).

Many other aspects of religious behaviour vary according to position in the hierarchy. Since they place great emphasis on descent, ancestral rites are more important in the upper groups (Mandelbaum 1970:42) as are some family rites such as those associated with twice-born status, including the tying of the sacred thread. Scriptural, transcendental aspects of religion are largely in the keeping of the higher *jātis*, the pragmatic aspects principally in the hands of the lower ones (pp. 223–4). The latter are more concerned with

179

Table 6. *Hierarchical trends in religious practice in India*

	Human diet	Offerings to gods	Gods	Communication
High	Vegetarian, restricted	Cooked food	Scriptural, married, ancestral	Mediated by books and their interpreters, priests
Low	Omnivorous	Blood sacrifice	Local, female, of the earth	Unmediated access, possession

local gods rather than with the major Hindu deities, with the female 'mother' goddesses of the village rather than the married deities of the text. At the same time, they are more likely to use possession as a means of communication between god and man, a practice tending to be opposed to the restraint, even impersonality, of the book. It is a situation that we can crudely indicate by means of the above table (table 6), which has many of the disadvantages of all such simplifying devices.

Such a hierarchical ranking of religious behaviour is firmly set within the framework of Hinduism and the culture of India. While in no sense exhaustive of that culture since those high on the scale of political, military and economic achievement are often lower by religious and textual criteria, explanations of behaviour have rightly to be set within that context. However there is another dimension that is highly significant for my analysis. In the first place some of these differences apparently represent changes over time within the Indian tradition; the earlier Vedic religion was 'essentiellement centré sur le sacrifice' (Lardinois 1986a:522). The Vedic literature is full of references to blood sacrifice which later disappeared among upper groups. But this development is not peculiar to Hinduism, for a similar change took place within the Judaeo-Christian tradition. Some of these hierarchical differences appear in other cultures, such as the contrast in Islam between the higher (written) tradition of the ’ulama and the lower tradition of the popular religious orders. In that same Christian tradition some of the ritually pure, such as Benedictine monks, adopted prohibitions against the consumption of meat, even if early Christians had rejected the vegetarian doctrines of the neo-Platonists claiming that all God's creatures were 'good to eat'. Regarding worship, it was the upper groups in Tibet who provided the literate lamas, the lower ones the inspired mediums. Similar comments could be made on other differences but these would be only partly relevant to the topics of marriage and the family. However, the examples given point to the general problem of explanation. Unless the relevance of a hypothesis of diffusion is accepted, analysis cannot be confined to factors that are particular to any single society but has to take into account wider 'structural' features. This need will become more evident when we consider kinship variables. Bearing in mind the necessary caveats, the material presented on Gujarat in the last chapter can again be laid out in the form of a table (table 7).

A similar distribution of family variables is found in many other parts of India and Ceylon. Dowry is high, 'brideprice' low. In Awan (Rajasthan), it is the twice-born castes that give dowries and the lower castes 'bridewealth', although the latter change when economic circumstances improve (Gupta 1974:76). Again, in the case of the Mahisya caste of peasant cultivators, the numerically and socially dominant caste in Radhanagar, a caste-elevating movement began around 1900 spreading throughout Bengal. First they changed their name to separate themselves from a fishing group; then they began 'to stop giving bridewealth and to begin taking a dowry' (Nicholas 1967:71). In earlier times, Nicholas claims, marriage transactions had passed from the father of the groom to the father of the bride; 'bridewealth' was called *kane paṇ* (*kane* is bride), dowry being referred to as *paṇ*, or *bar paṇ*, though nowadays the more elevated term *yautuk* or *dān* (gift) *yautuk* is used. The theory that is employed 'in agreeing upon the marriage portion of the bride is that she is entitled to a share of her family's property almost equal to that of her brothers' (p. 73). Such marriages are not related to hypergamy, though unions of this kind may occasionally occur. More frequently we find hypogamous marriages in which, as in China and elsewhere, 'a boy from a poor family marries a girl from a rich one' (p. 73), almost always when a man has no male heir and the boy comes to live as a *ghar jamāī*, 'a son-in-law in the house'. Sometimes, according to Nicholas, the daughter is virtually sent to seduce the boy; the father then complains to the village council or *pañchāyat* and the boy is persuaded to enter into the marriage with the promise of becoming heir to the agricultural land. This case of hypogamy is in fact what I have called a filiacentric union, discussed by Maine (1861:80) under the heading of 'the appointed daughter', the *putrikāputra* of Hindu law, 'the daughter treated as a son' (Tambiah 1973:79) that was so important a feature of the major Asiatic as well as of European societies (Goody 1976:73). In such unions, it is usually the lower group that 'gives', the upper one that 'receives'.

A similar range of hierarchical differences in family structure is noted by Khare in his study of a town in North India where he examines higher and lower caste concepts of marriage in relation to the strength and duration of affinal bonds. 'Unlike the higher caste version, where single marriage for women, and widower remarriage among men, exhaust the normative choices, the lower caste affinity is equipped with several more choices',

Table 7. *Hierarchical trends in family and marriage in Gujarat*

	Divorce	Marriage transactions	Widows	Domestic groups	Age at marriage	Position of women	Strategies of continuity
High	None	Dowry	Remarriage condemned	More complex	Lower	Restraint	More adoption
Low	Some	More 'brideprice'	Remarriage allowed	More nuclear	Higher	'Freedom'	More levirate

remarriage being possible for women. The Brahmin priests bring the idea of 'single, unbroken, life-long marriage' to their ceremonies, but the nature of those unions is different (1976:226). Women may return to their natal lineages; distinctions between categories of kin are more 'blurred'.

In the lower castes, and he is speaking of the town, dowry was only nominal, but with the coming of Western-type education, better-off grooms had begun 'raising their dowry demands' (p. 229). Earlier it was food, later a bicycle or a transistor radio. Khare gives a dramatic account of a wedding in which the groom and his party declined to eat the cooked rice (*bhāt*) until the future husband had been provided with money for a motor scooter and until some additional payments had been made to his parents' siblings and affines (mother's brother, father's brother and father's sister's husband). The meal was delayed a whole hour until a prestigious mediator persuaded the visitors to drop the demand. It is both 'normal and proper' for the groom's party to show initial reluctance to eat the rice until they have received more gifts, but in this case 'the game of competitive ranking, prestige and prestation' got out of hand.[1] While this particular element of the marriage prestations consists of the passage of property to the husband from the bride's family, the transactions as a whole involve setting up a domestic unit rather than providing a personal peculium for the husband, much less a circulating fund for use in a future marriage, as would be the case if this transaction were to be considered the precise counterpart of bridewealth, that is, as some form of 'groomwealth'.

In giving a final example of this differentiation in notions of family and marriage, let me emphasise again that the payments of dowry and 'bride-price' are part of the way the actors themselves view the hierarchy of caste. Of the Kangra Rajputs in the Punjab, Parry writes:

People also explain the status of caste by reference to its marriage customs and its diet. In the most prestigious form of marriage a virgin is handed over, along with her dowry, to her husband's family as a completely free and sacred gift for which no return whatever should be accepted. Marriage is regarded as an indissoluble union – which as far as the woman is concerned is also a monogamous union. As a corollary of this, widow remarriage and divorce are absolutely forbidden. In flat opposition to these ideals, the low castes – as well as low-status Rajput and Brahmin clans – sanction the inheritance of a deceased elder brother's wife, as well as other forms of widow remarriage. They also allow various types of exchange marriage which are considered to run counter to the notion of the gift, accept brideprice payments, tolerate divorce, and when expedient turn a blind eye to casual sexual liaisons. (1979:88)

It should be added that in this region even the Brahmins eat certain kinds of meat (but not others), so that hierarchical differentiation does not always apply in an identical way, although what you eat still matters as much as how you eat it and with whom. And of these the latter is perhaps the most important; in the past some higher groups such as the Nambudiri Brahmins of Kerala refused to eat even with those they sleep with, the Nayar mothers of their children.

In the rest of this chapter I want to discuss each of these hierarchical family variables, beginning with divorce since its absence is critical to the idea of a continuing life-long union held so firmly in 'upper' circles, and its presence to notions of the greater independence of women.[2] Later I briefly relate these points to the discussion of hypergamy and conclude by returning to the problem of 'the incorporation of women' in the contexts of the brother–sister tie. The problem of diet (in particular vegetarianism) I do not pursue, except in relation to the more general tendency of upper groups, especially in religious hierarchies, to advocate renunciation, even where they do not always practise what they preach. This matter is complicated by the obvious indulgences of some other upper groups (notably royalty and warriors) and at the same time by the attempts of the less powerful to distinguish themselves from lower groups by more restrained (polite, formal, punctilious, supercilious) behaviour; in India lower groups observe fewer fasts, talk more freely about sex and continue childbearing over a longer period (Mandelbaum 1974:65, 66). But in addition, as Pocock observed of food among the Patels, they may do in the fields what could not be done in the house, not necessarily because such behaviour is hidden from one's kin but because it belongs to a different domain of activity.

Divorce

As in China, the idea of a life-long union means that for women both remarriage and divorce were rare, indeed forbidden in the upper groups since according to the *śāstra* (the *Dharmaśāstra* is the orthodox juridical theory of Hindu India), divorce was not permitted. Marriage was one of the ten *samskaras* (a sacrament or purificatory act) necessary for men of the twice-born castes, and it was the only Vedic rite prescribed for women. Marriage, generally very early, is still virtually universal for both sexes and celibacy rare. For Hindus it is a sacrament performed in front of the nuptial fire accompanied by readings from the sacred texts; on completion of the ceremony the bond is irrevocable. For the Vedic and post-Vedic periods there is no evidence of divorce (Virdi 1972:19); marriage was a holy union of the mind, body and soul of the spouses. For the Sastric nuptials were performed only for virgins and the wife bound in this way was supposed to remain chaste even after the death of her husband, not even mentioning the name of another man. The union was perpetual and the notion was embodied in the ritual immolation of the widow on the husband's funeral pyre (*satī*). However, this practice, which was forbidden by British law in the mid nineteenth century, was always rare, and in Nandol at least, where the handprint of such a widow is pointed out with pride, associated with those who felt they had to attest their fidelity in some public way. Even if a widow had no son, she could never have children by another man, though mention is made of the practice of a widow producing an heir by her dead husband's brother in some Vedic sources, and in more recent times this form of union (the levirate) has been permitted by many lower groups.

In such groups, especially in non-twice-born castes (for example, in Rajasthan, Gupta 1974:142), divorce does occur. The general difference between higher values and lower practice is clearly laid out by Karve.

Divorce is not tolerated by the Brahmanic law books and has not the sanction of the priests. The Hindu law codified by the English with the help of the Brahmin savants also withholds recognition of divorce and yet divorce is a firmly established social institution all over India in all castes except a few which consider themselves the top castes, e.g. Brahmins, Kshatriyas etc. Divorce is granted in the Indian law courts and also in the caste-councils without recourse to the law courts and yet all castes combine in a conspiracy which denies the existence of this feature of the marriage customs of Hindus. This refusal to face facts is helped by certain linguistic devices. There are different words for the first marriage i.e., marriage of a virgin and for the subsequent marriages i.e., the re-marriage of a widow or a divorcée. When I made enquiries about the marriages of widows in a community I always received an emphatic "no" as an answer. When I persisted and asked if a widow or a divorcée never "made a new home", a reluctant affirmative came, followed by the explanation that that was no "marriage", it was but a Sagāi (Hindi), Karewā (Punjabi), Natrā (Gujarati), or Pāṭ (Marathi) according to the region of my enquiry.

The refusal to accept the existence of divorce has very far-reaching effects on kinship and caste organisation. One of the first steps which a caste used to take in order to improve its standing in the caste hierarchy was to interdict divorce and widow-remarriage. (Karve 1953:275)

Another, as we have seen, was to shift from 'brideprice' to direct dowry. Both were aspects of hierarchy.

Marriage transactions

In discussing China I suggested that what was often called brideprice was usually better described as indirect dowry or as bridal gifts, first because the transaction is very different from what has been called brideprice, or better, bridewealth in Africa and elsewhere, secondly, since the recipient is generally the bride, the question of a price does not arise. Of India Kane writes that *śulka* is 'the bride's fee or gratuity', the second term seeming to offer a much better translation. As Derrett explains, it is given first to her parents but afterwards 'to the bride herself' (Tambiah 1973:87); at the same time it often retains a certain distinctiveness from other types of *strīdhana* (woman's property, dowry), since at her death, if childless, it should go to her natal rather than to her conjugal kin. This fact Tambiah sees as indicating its earlier origin in an African-type bridewealth which the dominance of the conception of dowry turned into an indirect dowry.

Although it seems highly probable that over the long stretch of cultural history bridewealth has given way to dowry, direct and indirect, at some point in time, forms of endowing women have been found in societies of the same general socio-economic type as India ever since the Bronze Age, the age of 'civilisation', of the culture of cities, and I would regard such endowments as linked to the kind of stratification found there (chapter 10). Any initial change that occurred must have happened a very long time ago and for more recent periods it seems preferable to examine the coexisting forms of transfer in their own right as part of a set of marriage transactions.

While there are differences between these forms of marital transfer and while Kane's term is certainly more appropriate for the gifts sent to the bride, I prefer to substitute the phrase 'indirect dowry' for Gujarat and elsewhere in India in order to draw attention to the element of endowment (which does not exclude the possibility that part is acquired by her natal kin). So that table 7, presented above, is better read (with some qualifications) as:

High   Direct dowry
Low   More indirect dowry

although as far as most groups are concerned, the difference is one of emphasis. Not only do both types of transfer occur within the same society, they are often found within the same marriage.

It is the higher castes, for example, the Brahmins (and their law, the Law of Manu) who emphasise 'the gift of a virgin' from a man to the groom's father, accompanied by the gift of a dowry. As we have seen, this notion of gift has to be interpreted in context. For it is very clear in Srinivas' account of the Coorgs of Mysore (1952) that in general Indian marriage does not involve the total handing over of a woman but rather a transfer of certain rights in her, from one set of persons to another; at the same time the woman herself relinquishes some rights and duties, retains others, and acquires new ones.

In Gujarat the higher view of dowry was expressed by Dr Dinubhai Patel of Degham, when he remarked, 'I cannot go and eat with my daughter at her husband's house. Formerly we used to "sell" our daughters (referring to the indirect dowry), but now we don't do this. We refuse to take anything from our in-laws' (GJ 78). Not even hospitality was possible for the father, although her brother could be fed (Karve 1953:30; Dumont 1961:84ff.).

The same kind of differentiation found among the Patels occurs throughout the region. The Anavil Brahmins, numbering about 60,000, form the dominant caste in the Surat and Bulsar districts of South Gujarat, which were close to the important trading ports of the area in earlier times. While the Anavil are thought of as belonging to the Brahmin *varṇa*, they are not permitted to carry out any priestly duties, an instance of the division between priestly and lay Brahmins that is found in many other parts of India. One group, originally appointed as tax-farmers (*desai*) by the Moghul princes in the seventeenth century, became the local rulers (*rāja*), though their power was restricted by the central authorities under British rule. It was then that they participated in the process of 'Sanskritisation' (Srinivas 1962). Restricted in their exercise of political power, they increasingly conformed to the Brahmin ideal of dowry marriage; while this shift had important ideological elements, van der Veen claims it is primarily 'a matter of economics' (1972:37). The remaining Anavil, known as Bhathelas, continued to practise what, following the usual practice, he calls 'brideprice' and which he sees as having its economic rationale in the idea of compensation for the loss to the bride's family.

In her analysis of kinship in a village in Thanjavur (Tanjore) District, Gough (1981) also observes that there are significant differences between the Brahmin landowners and others. The *kanyādāna* form of marriage represents the Brahmin ideal, which she attributes first to their superior economic position (allowing gifts to be made, daughters to be endowed) and secondly to their religious values. Trautmann (1981:309) would prefer to reverse the emphasis. There is clearly no simple way of assessing priorities between these factors, especially as both relate to features of 'upper' behaviour; however, since the same kind of differences are reported in Buddhist Sri Lanka by Yalman and by Tambiah, as well as in other countries further afield, the more general formulation would seem to be the more appropriate.

I do not see any consistent evidence here that any greater or lesser quantum of rights in women or women's rights are involved in direct rather than indirect endowment, in dowry than 'brideprice'. However the question of relative wealth is undoubtedly important in these transactions. Even within the same local caste, richer families are more likely to allocate a portion of the parental wealth to daughters; poorer families tend to insist on a larger part of the endowment for their daughters coming from the groom's parents, and in part from the wider group of his relatives. Clearly both forms of marriage transaction require a transfer from the senior generation to the married couple, but direct dowry is the more 'honourable' form, not only in India but elsewhere in Eurasia, taking the problem of explanation (at least at this one level) outside the realm of particular local ideologies. Why is this so? I suggest that the high status of this form of dowry derives partly from the fact that it avoids using the daughter to attract wealth from outside her natal family (all is provided within, demonstrating the capacity to support one's own offspring), and partly too from the fact that indirect dowry can rarely include the most valued of all endowments, land; alienating family land to a 'wife' (except temporarily as a widow's dower) is very different from alienating it to a daughter. Nor can one use the indirect dowry as one can the direct form, that is, as a means of importing a son-in-law to provide labour or heirs.[3] To accomplish this physical movement of the groom, which usually occurs in the absence of sons or of male labour, and to emphasise the daughter's position in society, parental wealth has to be passed directly to her as the heiress, the brotherless heir, although her husband may have the management of the conjugal property. Whatever the reason, larger sums, permanent endowments, higher honour, greater dignity and religious merit, these are the necessary accompaniments of upper as against lower marriages in stratified systems of this kind (and here I refer to a hierarchy of control over resources other than those primarily at stake in the caste hierarchy of greater purity). Moreover these features are general rather than specific; that is to say, upper families have more to gain or to preserve through the direct dowry, since this helps to maintain their own status as well as that of their daughter.

Why is it necessary to struggle to maintain the status of daughters rather than, or in addition to, that of sons? The answer is first that the status of sons is involved in that of daughters; indeed in the Mediterranean and elsewhere they were often her major protectors, insistent upon her status, guardians of her honour, a refuge in extremity. Secondly, in virilocal marriages daughters left the house to live with strangers, whereas men stayed put and, outside the royal family or clan, were seen as enhancing, or at least as throwing a mantle over, the status of their wives, more commonly than wives over husbands. Thirdly, women tended to be more passive recipients of standing (although by no means in every case) as compared with men who could make more active efforts to change theirs, for better or for worse, by accumulation, by warfare and by gambling – though in terms of religious merit and piety, the roads were often equally open to women.

The interpretation of dowry that underlies this attempt to explain hierarchical differences is not the only one possible. In North India, Sharma treats it as a 'gift' rather than as a girl's portion. She assumes, for example, that the wealth changes hands between families and that the bride's dowry comes under the control of the mother-in-law. 'It is largely women, and especially senior women, who control the flow and pace of gift-giving both within the household and with other households' (1984:65). If this is so, then for any particular woman, the loss of control is a temporary affair, since the management not only of her own property but that of others will in the end devolve upon her. Sharma's argument depends upon the continuing co-residence of daughters-in-law and mothers-in-law. But how many women are in fact living with mothers-in-law at any one time? Given high mortality and frequent residential fission, the answer is 'not many'. Clearly fewer in urban than rural situations, possibly related to the smaller but more crowded houses. However, gift-giving is not the same as the alienation of an endowment. One critical aspect bearing upon the nature of the marital transaction and its resemblance to other 'gifts' has to do not with control (although this may be of great functional importance) but ownership. Are these goods retrievable by the wife or her family when the marriage ends? If so the, mother-in-law's powers are clearly limited.

While money often comes under the husband's control, there is plenty of evidence to show that ownership continues to lie with the wife and that the dowry is deemed by the Hindu themselves to be the equivalent of an inheritance, the daughter's share of the parents' estate. But, asks Sharma, 'are we obliged to view it in this way too?' (p. 70). Not necessarily, but it would be a dangerous precedent to ignore such an explicit statement of the *Dharmaśāstras*, particularly in favour of a gift-giving hypothesis the grounds for which are not all that strong: that it is not a fixed share of the estate, and that it is handed over to the husband's family. However the issue is not whether dowry is inheritance but whether both are part of the wider process of the devolution of property to women, to daughters. In India the present law of the land entitles women to a portion from the property of their parents, including land. This allocation is in part an innovation, but even in the North women were traditionally endowed with wealth other than land which they took with them into marriage: even if in some cases they lost control for a period, ownership rested with them in the long run.

The position seems to be clear from their historical power, at least in upper groups, to distribute property themselves. In the third century AD, the small Andhra kingdom of Nāgārjunkoṇḍa provides evidence of major donations made by royal women to Buddhist establishments; unlike North India, these were rarely land grants. The historian, Dutt, concludes that the rulers were Hindu, their women Buddhist, although wealthy merchants involved in the trade in *muslin* to the Roman world also made contributions (1962:128 ff.). But the substantial donations of women, which result partly from their greater longevity, partly from their earlier age of marriage as well as from their greater piety, may also indicate the control they themselves exercised over property.

As Sharma remarks, a daughter's 'share' was not always a constant proportion of the estate but varied according to whom she married, with the families of high status grooms asking for more extravagant transfers. This has long been an aspect of hypergamous marriages in India (Parry 1979) and elsewhere, although wealth is rarely the only factor involved. But the operation of this competitive principle in modern conditions has led to some important modifications, especially in urban areas.

Srinivas claims that modern dowry, as it has developed since the Second World War, 'imposes an unconscionable burden on the bride's kin group' (1984:24). One reason has to do with the growth of education and wage employment in which men participate more than women. An educated male can command a bride with a higher dowry than an uneducated one from the same family. For the bride's family it becomes an additional sum that has to be found and which in one way 'compensates' his family for educating him – or rather, *he* is compensated on behalf of *his* family by having access to *her* wealth.[4]

Since boys usually receive more schooling than girls, education often introduces of itself a hypergamic aspect to marriage. Within the same subcaste, girls may regularly have to marry up the educational ladder; they have had less schooling and have to contribute a higher dowry to marry an educated man, even when the families are of equal standing in other respects. While from one standpoint this contribution is a counterpart of funds spent on the education of males, it is necessarily a drain on the family's resources.

One problem is that there is a tendency, explicit in many legal decisions before 1930 that followed the *Mitākṣharā* rule, to regard income derived from an education which was paid for out of family funds as being joint family property. The situation was only changed in that year by the Hindu Gains of Learning Act which established such earnings as separate and distinct. But it should be remembered that in Europe, too, money spent on education was often regarded as part of an individual's share of family property; such was the case in fourteenth-century Ghent (Nicholas 1985), and such has frequently been so in much more recent times in Greece (chapter 16) and in western Europe generally. When schooling is largely confined to males, it may represent a man's endowment which needs to be met by the girl's.

But there is a more sinister aspect to which Srinivas calls attention in his dramatic claim that dowry is the *satī* of the twentieth century. This striking phrase needs to be put in context. Reviewing the data on Gujarat, his account of the distribution of dowry and 'brideprice' is similar in most respects to the one I have given above.

While the richer and higher strata of hypergamous castes paid huge sums by way of dowry to obtain desirable grooms, the poorer members of the lower strata were often required to pay bride price, or have recourse to marriage by exchange, either direct or indirect. Direct exchange was when two men married each other's sisters, and indirect, when other parties were also involved to complete the exchange. Thus the rich, land-owning Patidars of central Gujarat paid dowry, while poor Patidars paid bride price. Again the rich land-owning Desais (upper layer of Anavil Brahmins) paid dowry while the Bhatela, the poorer division of the Anavils, practised marriage by exchange, both direct and indirect. In the extreme south of Gujarat lived the Pardi Desais (also called Kay Desais) who were also Anavils but who were very poor until recently and had the custom of marrying by exchange. But during the last twenty years many of them became prosperous through the cultivation of new and profitable crops, and dowry has come to stay amongst them. There is a 'cargo cult' aspect to dowry marriages – the groom's kin regard his wedding as an occasion for securing, without paying a paisa, the many and much-desired products of modern technology. Among Tamil Brahmins, for instance, a video cassette record of the wedding is the latest demand made by the groom's kin. (1984:14–15)

The last remark calls attention to the more mercenary aspects of the dowry, what Srinivas calls the modern as distinct from the traditional dowry, that is, the *kanyādāna*, the material gifts that accompany the gift of the virgin daughter in the Brahminic ideal. He is eager to draw a line between the two, seeing the modern dowry as being 'entirely the product of the forces let loose by British rule such as monetization, education and the introduction of the organised sector', by which he means the sector of salaried and professional jobs. Certainly a number of institutions have been and are changing, now and in the recent past, and the dowry is one of these – a burning problem, he notes, because in the first ten months of 1983, 690 women died of burns in Delhi alone, a fact that he and others have attributed to the pressures placed on brides to produce more wealth; they are threatened and perhaps 'encouraged to die' so that another more profitable marriage can be arranged. But the death of young brides did not begin with recent social changes and were not earlier attributed to the material component of marriage alone. Pushed to desperation by the experience of an early marriage, they might try to commit suicide or become possessed. 'Throughout village India, instances are graphically told of women who drowned themselves in wells' (Mandelbaum 1970:91). Even the increased incidence of suicide that Acharya claims to have noted in Gujarat he attributes to the tension between mother-in-law and daughter-in-law related to the likelihood of the earlier separation of the junior couple (1974:180).

Complaints about the use or abuse of dowry have come down to us at least from Juvenal, and before that many similar problems over marriage transactions arose in the ancient Near East. There is always a commercial aspect to dowry; maintaining or advancing the position of one's son, daughter or family in a marriage implies some kind of a reckoning of benefits between the parties. Obviously the competitive element is greater in hypergamous marriages to outsiders and on any scale these can widely occur only in the northern (out-marrying) as distinct from the major southern (in-marrying) pattern of marriage in India. It is also more problematic when a wife is expected to bring back gifts every time she visits her parental kin, as is the case in three communities in the Gangetic Plains, Rampur, Senapur and Khalapur, studied by Lewis (1958), Singh (1957) and Minturn and Hitch-cock (1966) respectively. 'If she *fails* to bring such gifts, her security in the husband's household may be weakened, even endangered in some in-stances' (Kolenda 1967:176), especially in the early years of marriage before she has had children.

With the expansion of consumer products in recent years, the demand for material goods has become more explicit, more vulgar, more secularised, more commercialised, and the dowry items fall more closely under the husband's control with less protection for the wife coming from her own family. But this potentiality was always there, and even now the modern cannot be completely separated from the traditional, at least in the area of Gujarat in which we worked, nor yet among the Anavil Brahmins of the same province described by van der Veen in *I Give Thee my Daughter* (1972). Srinivas himself observes that in addition to paying the 'dowry', the bride's kin provide her directly with gifts of jewellery and expensive saris, which are normally included in the dowry process, in that aspect of devolu-tion occurring at marriage. As we will see later, 'dowry' in India has come to signify a particular aspect of marriage transactions, but of the daughter's direct endowment, Srinivas goes on to say:

it is difficult to state with confidence that the bride will have control over the jewellery. Traditionally, however, it was hers to dispose of, at least in south India, and she passed on as much of it as she could to her daughters. If the husband sold a piece of jewellery belonging to her to meet a crisis, he was expected to make good when his circumstances were better. (1984:12)

The situation is clearly acute among some groups around Delhi and other big towns where 'dowry' has nowadays become part of the black market economy. One problem is that black money, money made in illegal commer-cial transactions, has sometimes become the critical component of marriage transactions; deals are struck (or thought to be struck) and then renounced (or thought to be renounced) and the prime sufferer is the bride. It is also possible that the increase in 'dowry dealing' is related to the newly emerging system of stratification which is modifying the nature of marriage. Hypo-gamy was prohibited but now more girls of traditionally higher strata are marrying against the grain, that is, to boys of traditionally lower strata. At the same time dowry 'not only continues to be a symbol of status in the new hierarchy but is gradually replacing brideprice wherever it existed and dowry amounts are now reaching astronomical heights' (Shah 1982:27). This aspect is altogether new, and the desire to reform the institution of dowry goes back beyond the recent past, it having been prohibited under the Dowry Prohibition Act of 1961. In this Act dowry was defined as 'any property or valuable security given or agreed to be given either directly or indirectly by any party to marriage to the other party to the marriage or by the parents of either party or by any other person, at or before or after the marriage as consideration for marriage of the said parties' (Lardinois 1986b:287). However, 'any presents made at the time of marriage in the form of cash, ornaments, clothes or other articles as well as dower (or *mahr* in the case of a Muslim marriage) have been specifically exempted' (Sarkar 1982:352). Thus the legislation was aimed at 'gifts' *between* families, rather than 'devolution' *within*. Not only did the domestic nature of marriage transactions (like expenditure on funerals in West Africa) make enforcement difficult, but ambiguities in the legal definition of dowry itself made compliance or non-compliance virtually impossible to determine. So it is not surprising to find the law widely disregarded, as the discussion of dowry deaths would suggest.

In his comments upon the definition of dowry in the 1961 Act and upon subsequent modifications in its provisions, Lardinois' remark that 'the act meant prestations in money or kind by the bride's parents to the son-in-law or his family' (1986b:287,293) may be factually correct but the terms of the bill would also prohibit what he calls 'le prix de la fiancée', the indirect dowry practised by lower groups. The 1983 report of the Law Commission defines dowry in rather the same way as Lardinois suggests and Srinivas implies, namely as goods 'demanded from the wife or her parents . . . by the husband or his parents' without any legally recognised claim (p. 9). So that 'dowry' in the sense of *strīdhana* was specifically excluded. What seems to have happened is that changes in the nature of the system of production and consumption meant that women are pressed to bring to the marriage goods which can be used not only by the women or by both parties but some that are mainly employed by men, especially when they are marrying men of higher status as is more often the case in the North, and especially when new educational and occupational differences are added to the traditional ones. In traditional marriages the groom often received gifts from his in-laws, as in the case of marriage among the Nandol Barbers, but such prestations were quite distinct from the dowry itself, the property which continued to belong to the woman even though some of it was under the man's control. Changes in the patterns and items of consumption, the added value of educated and employed sons (and daughters too but they are less common) have led to a confusion of categories and to the manipulation of affinal and conjugal relations which constitutes the other face of arranged marriage. Of course, the fate of the new young bride in India was always uncomfortable at first, and a contributing factor to the imbalance of male–female deaths in early adulthood, but the pressures for increasing affinal gifts (rather than dowry itself) seems to have augmented the dangers in a more dramatic way than ever before.

It is possible that there is some difference between North and South India in respect of modern pressures on the dowry.[5] It was North India that traditionally had a high dowry in movables; since land was not included, women were endowed in other goods. In any case close marriages in the South seem generally to have required less dowry than distant ones, although land was more likely to be involved in the overall process of devolution. On the other hand a high dowry in movables given to outsiders (caste members but not from the village) made for a greater element of manipulation, for more hypergamous intent. Of course not all women can marry up. Indeed given universal but largely monogamous marriage, as many must marry down; and it was the case that although there were some exceptions to the monogamous tendency (Srinivas 1984:13), monogamy generally prevails, helped by the fact that widows remain unmarried, at least in the upper groups. But there are two other conditions to the achievement of an overall balance in movements up and down: first, the daughters of upper groups have to survive and marry; secondly, the criteria of a better or worse marriage have to be clear-cut and stable; that is open to doubt when what one partner sees as marriage up, the other may consider in the same light, as when beauty or even brains are exchanged for wealth, learning for rank, poor youth for rich age. However, daughters did disappear either through deliberate infanticide or through differential care; some Rajputs and Patels practised female infanticide in the nineteenth century, not as in much of China largely because of poverty but apparently because of an unwillingness among the males of the upper groups in hypergamous situations to allocate sufficient wealth or status to daughters to maintain their status after marriage or to allow them to live as celibates. Women do of course live as celibates when their husbands die, whereas the reverse is not the case; hence this too will tend to modify the balanced movement of partners in marriage as there will be fewer brides for the lower sections (the lower sections of higher castes, since in lower castes there is no bar on remarriage).

Marriage transactions vary not only according to strata but also in individual cases depending on whether these are up (hypergamous) or on the same level (isogamous); it is rarely admitted that a woman marries down. Such differences are particularly noticeable in North India where the higher family of a groom is to some extent compensated for marrying a girl from a lower group by the dowry she brings and the gifts that are made. Or to look at the situation from another point of view, the bride has to be heavily endowed to make her equal to the groom, but the contributions are well spent not only for the bride's sake but for 'equality' if that is reflected in future relations between the two groups. At the same time, brides who have to marry into lower groups require less dowry and a greater contribution from the husband, but there is still a feeling that she and her family are losing honour.

The family of a girl marrying a man of the same (or lower) general status may expect to receive a 'brideprice', that is, an indirect endowment. Economic and status considerations are in each case played off against one another and advantages accrue to both parties. The difference between marriages with direct and indirect endowment is therefore not only a question of differences between *jātis* or between families within a subgroup, but of arranged marriages. A well qualified son may attract a dowried bride; his unfavoured brother may need to endow a girl in order to marry at all. In Gaon village in Pune district, higher groups give dowries, lower 'brideprice', but even the higher groups may 'give' rather than 'take' if the son is disadvantaged or if the bride is very attractive (Orenstein 1965:50).

Transactions such as these may be seen as 'bribes'. No doubt that element is sometimes present, but such 'gifts' are also endowments made to support a daughter. The fact that a girl is differentially endowed, differentially accompanied by prestations on marriage to a man of higher status, is also a matter of establishing her position as an equal in her husband's family as well as of enhancing the status of her natal kin. In a study of the Pandit Brahmins of Kashmir, Madan found that the families rated highest were those most generous in their offerings (1965:137–40).

In some cases hypergamy of this kind takes on a collective aspect (Karve 1953:125; Mandelbaum 1970:103), meaning that in a general sense one subcaste or *jāti* is always superior to another, giving and taking wives in a unilateral direction. One such example is found among the Rajputs of Kangra discussed by Parry (1979), presenting us with a situation of group hypergamy that is unlikely to occur with the two-way (bilateral) cross-cousin marriages of the South, though it might of course be consistent with marriage to the mother's brother's daughter, as discussed by Fortune (1933), Lévi-Strauss (1949), Leach (1951) and Dumont (1957a); on the other hand we do find a rather similar 'marriage' arrangement among some Brahmin and Nayar groups of Malabar which I discuss in a later chapter.

Srinivas (1984) sees the co-existence of dowry (in upper groups) and 'brideprice' (in lower groups) as integral to hypergamy, and that is the case with forms of group or subgroup hypergamy practised in North India, especially among some Rajputs, Bengali Brahmins and Patidar of Gujarat. But the main incidence of hypergamy takes place within the subgroup, the *jāti* or local caste, which is generally homogeneous with respect to the particular attributes of marriage. Indeed the marriage circles of Gujarat divided precisely on this basis. If one segment of the circle allowed widows to remarry or accepted wealth for their daughters from the groom's family (which many call brideprice), then all the others had to do the same. Discussions on such issues were part of the business of caste meetings in the hall built by the *jāti*. On the other hand to reject 'brideprice' produced a rise in the status of the whole marriage-circle because the notion of the gift of a bride endowed by her parents approached the Brahmin ideal by way of the process of Sanskritisation that Srinivas and others have outlined. That is status-rising of a different sort, on a group basis. Nowadays we also find examples of what might be called status-lowering, lowering in terms of the Brahmin ideal.[6] The influence of reform movements has led some local castes that formerly forbade widow remarriage to allow it on what can be described as humanitarian grounds, grounds of social justice, although assuredly there are other factors involved. In so doing the group lowers itself in terms of traditional criteria and raises itself in relation to modernising ones.[7]

Something should also be said at this stage regarding Muslim marriage payments since these are often regarded as an extreme form of 'brideprice'. In Pakistan however there are two main kinds of marital transfer. With the *mehr* (*mahr*), nothing necessarily changes hands but the bridegroom promises to pay the bride an agreed sum in the case of death or divorce, specified in the marriage contract known as *nikahnana*; the delayed part of this transfer is a kind of dower. On the other hand the *jāhez* (the *dahej* or *dej* of Gujarat) is a gift received by the bride at the time of her marriage (Korson 1975:328). This form of transfer, which is mentioned neither in the Qu'rān nor in the Muslim Family Law Ordinance of 1961, consists of gifts to the bride of clothes, jewellery, household goods and of other property donated by family and friends; this dowry remains her personal property and may be listed as such in the marriage contract.

Among the very poor a payment from the groom's family sometimes goes to the bride's father at the time of the marriage but the husband still promises to pay the *mahr* in a contract which since 1961 has to be filed in the offices of the local Union Council. The amount depends upon the social position of the bride's family and upon her own qualifications, thus promoting isogamy. In this way, argues Korson, 'Islamic marriage ... safeguards the rights of the wife, and attempts to ensure her an economic status commensurate with her social standing' (p. 329).

Finally, one interesting aspect of the dowry, which derives from its role in stratified societies, is the merit that richer members of the community could gain by contributing to the dowry of poor brides, sometimes confined to girls of the same clan, family, caste or village.[8] In most cases property, often land, is left to an ecclesiastical (or secular) foundation, the interest on which can be used for the purposes laid down by the donor, in this case cash for the endowments.

Dowry and devolution in Hindu law

I have remarked that while it would be a grave error to overlook the views expressed in the *Dharmaśāstras*, at the same time it would be wrong to concentrate upon the higher view to the exclusion of wider analytic or observational considerations. It would be an error to overlook texts that were in effect the basis for many legal pronouncements as well as for some normative behaviour. On the other hand much normative behaviour differed substantially, not only among lower groups. It is also the case that the very attempt to formulate a written body of 'law' created both internal contradictions and attempts to resolve them, which have had their impact on discussions by jurists, anthropologists and others ever since. Let me briefly pursue this point before continuing to examine other hierarchical differences.

In the first place, unless it becomes highly descriptive, any 'code' has difficulty in coping with more than one level of normative behaviour, the level chosen being likely to centre upon that of the group for whom or by whom it is being formulated. For example, in considering the doctrine expounded by Maine (and others before him) that 'the Kshatriyas sprang from the Brahmanas' (Manu IX:321) just as the *brahmana* sprang from the Brahmin's mouth, the first born and the possessor of the Veda (Tambiah 1973:143), we should consider who originated the ideology or doctrine, to whom the statements were directed and in what context.

Hierarchical variation is not normally a feature of such codification for jurists often aim to establish certain general principles. However, the distinction between dowry marriage for the highest groups and 'brideprice' for the lower is in fact recognised in the religio-juridical literature, for while Manu allows for marriages based upon both 'gift' and 'brideprice' (*āsura*, indirect dowry), only the latter and other inferior forms of union are legal for members of the lower orders. One shashtric authority, who sees 'brideprice' as 'sale', permits such practices to merchants, farmers and servants on the grounds that these groups 'do not keep their wives under restraints, they having to do the work of ploughing and waiting upon other varṇas' (quoted by Tambiah 1973:69). In this way actual differences in practice become embodied in prescriptive injunctions.[9]

There is another aspect of this and other written codes which bears upon one of the central problems in the argument about whether dowry should be seen as an affinal gift accompanying marriage or as a woman's portion, and which in the Indian case seems embedded in the implicit contradictions in the *Dharmaśāstras* themselves. Let me discuss a specific case before returning to the general point. While the high form of marriage is seen as 'the gift of a virgin', the notion of *strīdhana* as 'a gift which accompanies the gift of the girl' appears to stand in opposition to the other idea of the *Dharmaśāstras* that *strīdhana* is female property. Tambiah (1973) has looked at the legal commentaries from a sociological standpoint, Sontheimer (1977) from a legal stance; both have emphasised the point, with Tambiah concentrating on changes over space and Sontheimer over time. I have no wish to duplicate their valuable remarks but there are certain aspects of the discussion which are particularly relevant to my present theme.

It is evident that the 'gift' may herself receive gifts. In the first place a bride receives Manu's sixth category of *strīdhana*, 'those made by the affectionate husband' (what I call indirect dowry), which reverses the general flow of prestations (Sontheimer 1977:48). According to the words of one early commentator, she was 'free to give it away and otherwise dispose of' this property.

In the second place, the *Dharmaśāstras* themselves indicate that the main *strīdhana* or dowry is considered to be the daughter's portion of the family estate, a compensation amounting to one quarter of a son's share according to some authors (p. 53). If any are unmarried when the father dies, then 'to the daughters should be given that much of their father's (estate) as would be required for their dowry'. The same *Asthaśāstra* goes on significantly: 'If a man dies sonless, his property shall be taken by his legitimate daughters of the same caste as himself *in the same way as a son*' (my italics). According to some authorities, a community of property was also implicit in the *Dharmaśāstra*, becoming explicit in a possibly spurious *Smṛti* that declared: 'Property is joint, or common between spouses', but at divorce or at the husband's death it was clearly designated as the wife's (pp. 12,79). At the same time this jointness during the couple's lifetime did not mean that the wife lost jural control. A thirteenth-century Marathi text (the *Lilacaritra*) tells how a man lost heavily playing at dice and asked his wife to help pay his debts with her ornaments. 'She refuses to do so – obviously quite correctly as her husband has no right in her property (*strīdhana*) in such a case' (p. 161).

The notions both of the jointness of the conjugal estate and of the wife's separable holding in it present problems for the legal concept of the 'Hindi Undivided Family' (or 'joint family'). On a practical level we have seen the threat of fission this posed in China where the wife's property formed the core of conjugal interests that might lead to a split among the brothers. The same kind of problem posed itself to the makers of codes; the idea of an estate in the hands of male coparceners alone comes up against the existence of woman's property whatever form this takes, but especially when the bride is accompanied by property, or claims to property, at marriage, thus modify-

ing the holdings of her parental and conjugal estates. Moreover, although
the bride may be spoken of as coming from the father, her dowry comes
partly from her mother. In any case, all would be resolved if the 'gift' had
brought no 'gift' with her.

The effects of women's property rights on the structure of a domestic
group are felt even more strongly when there are no brothers. Despite the
nature of the Hindu Undivided Family with its potential four generation
depth of coparceners, Tambiah points out that brothers are more likely to
divide when one among them has no sons since that man will call into play
the institutions either of the appointed daughter (and incoming son-in-law)
or else of adoption rather than permit his share of the inheritance to go to
collaterals by default (1973:78), thus setting aside the rules of male sur-
vivorship and reversion which are explicit in the legal conceptions of joint
ownership by male agnates. The preference is for the 'lineal before the
collateral heir' (p. 79).

It is true that some commentators have held that *strīdhana* was not *dāya*
(that is, family property), from which women were exluded. However the
customary tendency in early medieval texts was 'to consider the property of
the mother as part of the common estate' (Sontheimer 1977:100). Medhā-
tithi makes the basic assumption that there is common property between the
couple, related to his idea that 'husband and wife differ only in their bodies
and in all functions they are entirely united'. Such unity can be seen in the
important necessity for any male Hindu to have a wife in order to be able to
perform the essential religious rites; moreover the wife is not simply a
figurehead but has to agree to the necessary expenditures on worship.

In this medieval view the wife's dowry was part of the estate and a
daughter's birthright was well established in customary law. How else could
her father's property be transmitted to her children in the absence of heirs,
that is, as an heiress or as the wife of an incoming husband. For 'daughter's
sons had an interest in their maternal grandfather's property by the very
definition of *dāya*, though their ownership was under an obstruction' (p.
189).[10] It is this situation in particular that presented logical difficulties for
the *Mitākṣarā* and for subsequent Anglo-Hindu law. As in the case of
Chinese and Japanese Confucians (McMullen 1975), the formulations of the
written 'law' 'rationalised' the complexity of the situation by producing a
stronger agnatic model which played down a woman's legal claims – and
succeeded in practice to the extent that their injunctions were taken as
authoritative. The *Mitākṣarā*, the commentary written between 1121 and
1125 which came to dominate the legal life of much of India, stressed the
male core of the agnatic group, effectively excluding as coparceners, widows, wives (despite conflicting notions of their incorporation) or daughters
(despite the possibility of their being 'appointed'). For such a possibility

necessarily raised problems concerning the concept of the *strīdhana* and whether it formed part of the estate which would thereby be joint; this author leaves open the question of the community of property of husband and wife, while others insist on its immunity from the claims of agnates (Sontheimer 1977:132; Lardinois 1986a:522, 524). Given the premises, no satisfactory resolution was possible.

There is a similar problem regarding sons which was again treated by different schools in different ways. If the *dāya* is ancestral family property which is owned jointly by all members, each son could claim his own from the very beginning. Such was the teaching of the *Mitākṣarī* school, but the *Dāyabhāga* of Bengal taught that a son only received the right of inheritance at the father's death. There was in any case a popular notion that a son's birth tended to restrict the father's power in so far as he was no longer supposed to use the property for purely personal purposes. And if a son does force a partition it is legal but impure (Sontheimer 1977:93). The difficulty is obvious: if the son could demand his birthright when he liked, the authority of the father and the building of the joint household would be heavily undermined. As was the practice among lower groups, each marital pair would be able to set up house on their own, without permission, in contradiction to the Confucian injunction current in China, 'So long as parents are living, no enterprise must be undertaken without their counsel and approbation'. The actual distribution of the differentiated rights of adjacent generations in the family estate was as difficult to deal with in written form as were the differentiated rights of males and females.

It might be suggested that the *Dāyabhāga* code would be associated with the later fission of the household or the estate since it would prevent the sons claiming a share during their father's lifetime. When Kolenda (1967) examined this possibility in connection with the larger number of complex households in villages in the Gangetic plain, she found that these groups often subscribed to the other legal code. The approaches of these two codes represent solutions to widespread social and intellectual problems, often modified in practice. However, the discussion was not simply notional but 'real' in its effects since it has some affect on judicial decisions, especially for the upper groups. The solution brings out very clearly the complexities of trying to set down behavioural norms in writing and then using the resulting code as a source of law. The problem is not simply that the texts, whether *Mitākṣarā* in Indian or Confucian in China, present a picture more consonant with upper than lower groups and that this picture is more patrilineal for that very reason. Nor that any one written code may give more attention to male, political interests than to female, domestic ones. Nor yet that any one written code, especially in its earlier versions, is inevitably a simplification of oral complexity, with different codes concentrating on different aspects of reality, leading Renou to remark that the diversity was perhaps an illusion, 'affaire de philologie plus que d'adhésion au réel' (1978, quoted Lardinois 1986a:527). It does all of these things, as well as creating rather than representing those situations because of the pull of written norms not only among literate specialists but among those for whom and with whom they worked, especially when the written code and its composers have a sacred status.

But there is a further element. The code is also trying to rationalise what, at the level of practice as well as of principle, is a conflicting if not a contradictory situation, the position of an endowed woman in relation to a patrilineal descent group or joint family, whether this is her natal or her conjugal group (Lardinois 1986a:522, 527). For there is a measure of tension between the continuity of the second and the existence of the former, that is, between lineage and dowry. The notion of gifts to Brahmins has other roots that characterise priesthoods everywhere. But at one level the idea of the dowry as a gift can be seen as a way of avoiding the notion that a woman has any claim (certainly any further claim) on the estate of her male agnates.

The celibacy of widows

In a very general way, renunciation in India tends to be part of an ideology associated with the higher rather than the lower, although as far as remarriage is concerned it applies differently to women and to men. In the next street to us in Nandol lived an old lady who had been widowed at an early age before she had been able to bear a child. As a Brahmin she had remained in her husband's home and now lived alone, spending her time reading the *Gita* and the daily newspaper, and taking part in religious activities of a more public kind. The ban on widow remarriage fits with this higher ethic and in Nandol it was the rule not only among Brahmins but also among Patels and all those who followed the *Dharmaśāstras*. Recently however there was a threat of change. The Patidar marriage circle, based on Nandol, was under pressure from various 'liberal' elements (the local Patels vote Congress and control village politics), so they came together and decided that the fate of the widow should be improved. By so doing they reversed their earlier adherence to the 'high' position and agreed to allow remarriage in line with the recommendations of long-established movements of reform. In Ahmadabad itself the movement in favour of widow remarriage and against child unions was promoted by the Gujarat Hindu Social Reform Association as early as the 1860s (Gillion 1968:66). However, when we were in Nandol some years had passed since the Patels' decision had been made and no widow remarriages had so far taken place. Despite this reluctance, the decision provides an example of deliberate de-Sanskritisation, promoted by an alternative 'modernising' ideology but which was based upon conflicting practices already existing at different strata in the social system.

The capacity to maintain the ban on widow remarriage depends upon a certain level of economic activity, since a family may have to support a spare female 'outsider' over a long period, one who may perform no sexual duties by way of return. The widow is sexually neutralised and kept that way, partly by restricting her contact with the world. This the lower groups find less easy to do, and their celibates or widows, whether living as sisters or as wives, are inevitably more involved in that world. As with other features of the dowry complex, the ideal is more readily achieved by the rich than by the poor, by upper than by lower. Renunciation enters into the moral code of the comfortably off; the poor have to exploit other possibilities of social action.

This distinction extends to sex before as well as during and after marriage. As Dumont has noted, 'In India, there is an interesting difference in pre-marital sexual behaviour between the regime of castes and the regime of tribes; the former forbid, the latter permit' (1966b:110). But the difference also obtains within the caste hierarchy itself; lower castes such as the nomadic Rabadi are openly freer and more permissive than the upper ones; it is in their ranks we find the prostitutes rather than the nuns. In the village of Kumbapeṭṭai in Tanjore, Gough reports, the 'Original Dravidians do not value sexual asceticism' like the Brahmins, while their men are more ag-gressive (1956:84). Equally the upper groups choose among their foods, rejecting alcohol, for example, while the lower ones do not.[11] They are more eclectic.

The association between high status and the celibacy of widows, low status and widow remarriage is a widespread feature in India. Why? Once again the 'cultural' or purely religious explanation is not by itself sufficient (at least for the observer, though it may suffice for the actor), since a similar internal differentiation of the kinship system is found in other parts of Eurasia. Among higher groups in China widow remarriage, whether outside or inside the family was frowned upon or prohibited; the inheritance of widows by clansmen was strictly forbidden and any remarriage of widows was firmly discouraged. 'Neo-Confucian morality after the Sung period regarded re-marriage of a widow as disreputable as adultery' (Liu Wang 1959:92), though poor families did marry off widows and even collected money from the new husbands. But by remarriage a widow lost her right to support by the kin of her dead husband as well as all claim upon his estate; and it sometimes happened that unscrupulous clansmen would force a widow of one of their members to remarry in order to get hold of the property that had come under her control (p. 91). In other words, by marrying again she lost her dower, though she might retain her dowry. The ideal widow was one who remained chaste after her husband's death and by so doing retained an interest in the property, in the conjugal fund, established at their marriage.

Some later Hindu codes did allow a woman to take another husband under specific conditions, for instance, if the first husband became a religious ascetic or disappeared from her life in some other way; in the latter case she had to wait six years, twelve years if he went to a foreign country for the purpose of study. Nevertheless a stigma was generally attached to the twice-married woman, though the situation was somewhat different under custom and under 'law'. Custom too represents a source of judicial decision and the dissolution of marriage by custom was preserved in the Hindu Marriage Act of 1955 (Section 29:2). But in the past the 'law' worked for the upper groups whose ideological counterpart it was; for the lower groups the equivalent was oral custom, which sometimes permitted what the written law forbade.

Although widow remarriage was frowned upon by higher groups, it was encouraged not only by many reform movements but, for different reasons, by farming groups such as the Jats of Rampur, near Delhi. As a nineteenth-century observer wrote of the latter: 'He is, of course, far below the Rajput, from the simple fact that he practices widow remarriage. The Jat father is made to say, in the rhyming proverbs of the countryside – "come my daughter and be married; if this husband dies there are plenty more". But among widow-marrying castes he stands first' (Ibbetson 1903:76). In the 1950s widow remarriage in Rampur was in fact limited to the junior levirate, the widow being permitted to marry the husband's younger brother with whom, as a senior brother's wife, she had often joked, while all remarriage of widows was forbidden among the Brahmins (Lewis 1958[1965]:4). The avoidance of widow remarriage, as Shah (1974) notes in his study of Gujarat, puts a special obligation on the sons to look after their mother, though some young widows did return to their kin. One son, usually the youngest, stayed on in the parental home and in Brahmin groups the eldest son might actually remain unmarried; for the rest ties were inevitably weakened by a second marriage (p. 42).

So, while the custom of marrying (or having children by) the husband's dead brother in order to raise up seed to his name appears to have existed in Vedic times (Chattopadhyay 1922:25), it is strongly condemned by Manu (IX.64–8) and in other medieval texts, although it is widely practised in North India, especially in the form of the junior levirate. Chattopadhyay sees the preference for marriage to the husband's younger brother as connected with the existence of a unique set of terms that differentiate husband's elder from his younger brother (*jeth* and *divar*) in Gujarat; *divar* is elsewhere *dēbar*, meaning *de*, second, *bar*, husband. Or, to put it another way, the classificatory affinal terminology and the levirate are both associated with the common interests of the lineage.

In looking at the distribution of the levirate on the one hand and the ban on widow remarriage on the other, we are faced with a hierarchical difference, with regional differences, and with a possible change over time, each being features that we find in other societies, more particularly in West Asia. As with the high/low distinction, the change over time consists in coming to give preference to adoption as a strategy of heirship as against the levirate, and the same is true of plural marriage as against divorce and remarriage in general.

Why should this be? While disagreeing with the interpretation of Maine and Chattopadhyay of *niyoga* as widow *remarriage*, as distinct from the obligation to produce legitimate children to the name of her dead husband, Rose (1922:96) makes some suggestions as to the process of change that might have taken place. 'In primitive communities, Aryan or non-Aryan, failure of legitimate sons is repaired by practices like the *niyoga*, or the affiliation of sons like the *kānīna* or the *sahodha*. Then come the reformers who try to raise marriage to a higher level, and introduce adoption as a less degrading method of allowing a sonless man to obtain an heir than polygyny, especially second marriages with women of strange castes.' Why less degrading? The objection to the plural or successive marriages of women, even to close kin, must be viewed, in part at least, in the context of property relations.

I have argued elsewhere that the property relations involved in like marrying like (or better) imply an attachment of one person to a set of material objects (or to rights in those objects) in a particularistic way if only because that is what the transaction itself involves. There is a matching of one status against another in which property plays a major but not exclusive part. This rearrangement of interests in marriage establishes one of the many kinds of conjugal fund which may subsequently be augmented by kin but which begins to be dispersed when the children of the union first reach their majority or get married. The joint arrangements that have been made are tied to the marriage, and its dissolution by death or divorce involves a corresponding dissolution or modification of the fund. The larger the fund, the higher the status and the greater the productive resources; consequently the less easy it is to dissolve. Indeed the fund and in another sense the marriage may continue even after the death of one or both of the partners, since its future rests with the children of the marriage, either implictly by customary arrangement or else formally by means of an entail, a *majorat* or similar device. Readers of Balzac's *Contrat de mariage* will not need reminding of the elaborate financial game involved in marriage among the upper strata of French provincial society in the mid nineteenth century. The union of the Comte de Manerville with Natalie Evangélista led to drastic acts of revenge carried out by the party that deemed itself the loser. 'In most families', notes the author, 'the creation of marriage-portions and the respective contributions to be provided for in the marriage contract, engender embryonic hostilities, aroused by wounded self-esteem, by the lesion of diverse sentiments, by regret for enforced sacrifices and the desire to lessen them' (1897:109). So it was with this unhappy union, where the wife and her mother continued to hold a special interest in the fund that was established at marriage and which would have descended to the children of the union, had there been any.

In dowry systems the extent of property considerations often militates against the remarriage of widows in upper status groups more decisively than in the lower ones, especially when they thereby lose their dower. Concepts of honour and purity are also important in the context of particular sets of cultural values. But the wide distribution of this restraint on remarriage in upper groups also calls for a transcultural explanation which embodies some recognition of the measure of overlap between religious and politico-economic factors. Although significant discrepancies exist, most stratified societies are marked by stratified value systems, and by and large higher women are purer and more honourable than those of the lower status groups.

In lower groups other considerations come into play. Property is not so central an issue and remarriage may be necessary to support the widow and her children. Moreover, where the major emphasis is placed upon an indirect dowry, the conjugal fund is established out of the resources of the husband's family, those of the wife's having mainly an implicit significance, important in setting up the initial transaction but possibly never reaching the woman's own hands, even as inheritance. If the woman is entitled to a portion from her own parents, the handing over may be deferred until their death, yet further postponed for her own sons, perhaps abandoned altogether in favour of alternative claims on the brothers who remain; in this case the indirect dowry, the contribution of the groom and his kin, may in effect anticipate a woman's future patrimony which she hopes to receive by inheritance. At lower levels of society, there seems less difficulty in dissolving the union and in entering a new one, partly because less (sometimes nothing) is involved by way of property or prestige and partly because it comes mostly from one source, the groom's kin. In the Hindu Marriage Act of 1955, the high caste authors attribute the practice of remarriage to the 'low cultural level and high degree of illiteracy of tribes'. Low castes and aboriginal tribes tend to permit divorce and remarriage. However the same is true of Muslim societies, where the indirect dowry (*mahr*) may not be handed over by the groom's kin until divorce actually occurs (Ahmed 1984) and where the wife's own contribution usually comes from inheritance and may even then be delayed. The woman's right to inheritance rather than dowry often means that she retains a concrete interest in the natal estate and her siblings may continue to be responsible for her honour and in the last analysis her support, making the dissolution of the marriage arrangements and the return (or transfer) of the woman to her natal home an easier proposition.

Strategies of continuity

While the inheritance of widows, and even their remarriage outside the kin group, was frowned upon among upper groups in the major Asian societies, where it is clearly linked to objections to divorce and remarriage, in many parts of Africa it was encouraged in the special form of the levirate said to have existed in India in Vedic times. In Israel too a man was obliged to take the wife of a brother who had no heir, having a duty to produce 'seed' to the dead man's name. The situation was very different in post-Vedic India, as Karve points out.

> Though the system of levirate is found among a large number of castes it has not the sanction of the present-day Brahminic religion. The Smṛtis have all condemned it as a custom not suited to the present times, so that during the historical period one finds the custom of adoption coming into vogue. Higher castes and ruling families generally prohibit the levirate and prefer that the widow should adopt a boy. In a majority of cases however it is the man who adopts a child, if he finds himself childless in spite of marrying again and again. A very large amount of litigation arises out of the quarrels between the adopted child and both or one of his parents. Agnates generally prefer a widow to adopt a child from the agnatic branch, preferably a child of the brother or cousin of the deceased husband. Sometimes they wish to prevent an adoption as they hope to get a portion of the estate if there is no son as successor. It was said that one of the reasons why so many widows were forcibly burnt with their dead husbands was to prevent adoption of a stranger as a son into the family. (1953:133)

Once again, while the levirate may be condemned in the upper groups, it is accepted in the lower and 'the woman who lives with her brother-in-law is called Ghar-baṭhi. A widow may enter into the house of an unmarried man or a widower and force him to marry her. This mode of marriage is not uncommon among poorer people' (p. 133).

The complementary relationship between the levirate and adoption is brought out in some Indian commentaries where the adopted boy should be 'a reflection of a natural son'; a brother's son can be adopted because the adopter could have fathered the boy in question through the levirate (*niyoga*), that is, by his (dead) brother's wife. The argument is a little convoluted and reminds one of the Confucian discussions in Japan, China and elsewhere about the desirability of limiting adoption to a man's own agnates (McMullen 1975). But it also reflects the fact that these institutions often appear as historical alternatives, as 'strategies of heirship' or continuity, with the levirate tending to give way to adoption, although this never happened with Semitic-speaking societies who consistently practised the polygyny which the levirate might entail.

Alternative strategies of continuity, meaning the acquisition of offspring for labour or for heirship, include the acqusition of the additional children through adoption and of additional wives through polygyny. Although the Indian law books contain extensive discussions of adoption (Goody 1976), it seems to be relatively rare among castes in Gujarat; Shah notes only two cases among the 299 households of the central Gujarat village of Radhvanaj (1974:17), although there were some instances of widow remarriage, mostly of the leviratic kind. However the law books are full of discussions of its procedures and it is found widely throughout the country, always taking place within the same *jāti* and preferably within the same lineage. Clearly adoption becomes more important in those groups in which widows themselves cannot produce heirs by remarrying and where there is a substantial estate to be transmitted. In an irrigated village in Mysore, Epstein found that 10 per cent of adult males had been adopted, whereas the figure was only 2 per cent in a neighbouring, non-irrigated village (1962:179, 306).

In India, as in China, we find not only adoption but another form of continuity obtained through the resident daughter's children, the *ghar jamāī* (Srinivas 1984:23).[12] The articulated reason, Srinivas notes, is to provide someone to perform the ancestral rites, very much as in ancient Rome. As in China plural marriage is rare, one man, one woman being the general rule; again Shah (1974) found only one case in his sample households, although a higher incidence is found elsewhere among Muslims and even among some Brahmins.

Age at marriage

Before turning to other hierarchical differences, one feature of domestic life requires attention although, as we see in the following chapter, it remains fairly constant in the various castes. This is age at marriage which strongly affects, for example, the age at which wives become widows, but not the proportion of widows, since that depends upon the sex differential age at marriage. Very early marriage of women gives rise to the child widow who, in upper groups, is required to remain with her late husband's family without remarrying.

The single-mindedness – and even single-bodiness – that the ban on widow remarriage represents is associated with the idea of the perpetual union of a woman with one man (but not necessarily vice-versa, though polygyny is rare, except among some *Kshatriyas* and some Muslims) and hence, as in China, with the absence of divorce and remarriage. It is also linked with a tendency to the early betrothal or marriage of the partners, found in minor marriages in China although different reasons are given by the actors. Srinivas writes of the days in India when 'pre-pubertal weddings were the rule' (1984:11): a girl had to be married 'before she came of age'. The father of a girl was obliged by Hindu law and by the custom of the country to marry her before she attained puberty, though cohabitation was often delayed, an average of three years (thirteen to sixteen) being usual for girls at the end of last century when the age of marriage for men was twenty-one (Lardinois 1986a:531).

The extraordinarily early age of marriage in India was connected with religious doctrine in other ways. In 1901 the average age at which a woman joined her husband in Mysore (usually at formal marriage) was 14.1 (a considerable increase over the situation in 1891 when it was 13.5). In terms of religious affiliation the Jains had the lowest age (12.8), then Hindus (14.0), Muslims (14.9), Christians (16.9), but interestingly 'animists' were highest at 18.1 (1901 Census, vol. 24, pp. 238–40). Those not belonging to one of the major written religions were higher, nearer the level of age recorded for Africa (Goody, forthcoming a). Could it be that attachment to a major written religion actually tended to promote early marriage?

Age at formal marriage does not mean the beginning of a sexual relationship since this starts only after puberty, usually shortly after. In the Mysore Brahmin community studied by Srinivas, all marriages had to be consummated on the sixteenth night after the bride's puberty (1942:134–5). In the Nagara Brahmin community on which Mankad (1934–35) reported, a bride only visited her husband's home after puberty and took up permanent residence there six months later.

Even the early co-residence does not mean the beginning of childbearing, because it is generally agreed that menarche is followed by a period of adolescent infertility. In the data discussed by Mandelbaum (1954), the average age of puberty (actually the consummation of marriage) was 13.7 (Madras), and the average age of first birth 17.4 (Mysore), a difference of 3.7 years.

As we will see the situation is not so very different today. Marriage is relatively later for women, the sex difference in age has dropped and the delay in cohabitation has decreased. But marriage is still very early. The reasons given are religious whereas in China they are economic or familial, the groom's family often being anxious to pre-empt a bride for a son (possibly at less expense to themselves) and the bride's family anxious to divest themselves of a daughter (again, possibly at less cost). Some of these factors may also apply in India since the lowest ages of marriage are found among the Brahmins and among the *harijans*. Early marriage or betrothal places great powers of control in the hands of the senior generation, whether parents or collateral kinsfolk, both as regards the choice of partner and as regards the option for marriage itself. Equally it puts the bride in a very dependent position in her new household, where the result is a situation of multiple conjugal units at an early stage in the developmental cycle. That is, there is a greater likelihood of joint households.

Srinivas notes that 'Until a few decades ago marriage was the only "career" for a woman except among the landless labourers and other poor where women had to hire themselves out for daily wages' (1984:10–11). The description is perhaps a little harsh since with production concentrated within the domestic group (which is the core not so much of a mode of production as of a mode of organising production), all 'careers' are linked to marriage. Otherwise the point is well taken. Marriage is early and effectively universal for women and somewhat less early for men, partly because it is forced upon adolescents at an early age by their kin – since in principle they could have alternative careers in their parental homes if only as 'maiden aunts' or celibate uncles. As in Tibet, marriage tended to be earlier in the upper groups (at least among Brahmins) than in the groups immediately below them. However marriage is not necessarily more frequent among women in the upper groups, at least in those situations of group hypergamy where some higher women were left stranded without husbands and the lower men without wives.

The reverse situation is reported for parts of North India where there is a later age at marriage among Jat girls. But the situation is new and comes to resemble that found among silk workers in Kwantung in South China, although there the delayed marriage appears to have existed long before the advent of industrial reeling in the mid nineteenth century. With the development of agriculture involving intensified or differentiated production, families are better off, there is more work on the farm and hence more labour is needed in the house and related activities. Girls work at home for a longer period during which time they help to accumulate a dowry (Mandelbaum 1970:40). But here we are dealing with the farming castes, not with the Brahmins who were owners or even managers of farms on which they were often forbidden to work the plough.

Mandelbaum has claimed that 'the fear of barrenness is pervasive in most social strata' in India (1948:132). Since the ability to bear children is seen as an essential part of marriage in most societies, it is not surprising that internal and external pressures exist which make it desirable to test the potentiality and compatibility of spouses, especially women, at an early age.

Especially in a largely monogamous society where divorce is difficult, the family has to think about alternative strategies if the union does not produce children, and the sooner this is done the easier.

Early marriage has a number of consequences apart from the obvious one of reducing the span of a generation from, say, thirty to twenty years, which is important for a variety of familial arrangements (forming a joint family, parent–child relationships, etc.). It means more parental control of the choice of a spouse (and of marriage itself) which constitutes some defence against misalliance. Partners will be selected for their suitability while sexual attraction may be secondary. Early marriage clearly helps to protect a woman's pre-marital virginity. But early betrothal or marriage may also have something of the same positive effects on social relationships as the unions with fostered daughters-in-law in parts of South China. That is to say, it habituates or accommodates affines, in-laws and conjugal partners to one another at a period when one party is more malleable than is likely to be the case later on, although of course a rather similar effect may result from 'family marriage', by marrying a cousin or other close relative which is the practice in South India. There are obviously costs as well as gains. In a study of child marriage, Mandelbaum (1954; 1974:36) showed that the birth of the first child took place, on average, four years after co-residence; teenage fertility was generally low and Mankad's study of Gujarat (1934–35) suggested that earlier familiarity entailed a reduced role for sex (Kurian 1975:213). Accommodation and acceptance are not the same as affection, love and desire, although these latter may develop with time. Such early arranged unions may bring a reluctance to shift from an asexual to a sexual relationship, not the aversion that may be linked to the early contracts between children of three to five years in China, but nevertheless giving rise to problems arising from role reversal, even familiarity, and sometimes from lack of choice in opposition to the freedom idealised in much poetry. While I know of no direct Indian evidence to this effect, we have come across such cases of the reluctant bride in northern Ghana and the general ambivalence towards cousin marriage (it is good, it is bad) may relate to the same phenomenon (E. and J. Goody 1966). Is it possible that one element in the greater asceticism of the upper groups is also linked to early arranged marriage?

Domestic groups

I do not intend to look in any detail at the organisation of domestic groups, as distinct from particular relationships, except to touch upon the question of household size, especially as this is one of the features often stressed in the discussions about China, in the well-known but sometimes disputed (Wolf forthcoming) saying that the rich have extended families, the poor stem families (e.g. M. Wolf and Witke 1975:7). For there are some broad similarities in the developmental cycles of domestic groups (Mandelbaum 1970:95ff.), not only in the phase of growth (in which many of the mechanisms are similar – the early acquisition of brides, the strategies of continuity), but more particularly in the phase of family fission. In both countries it is possible (though rare) for sons to claim their heritage, which is literally a birthright, while the father is still alive. More usually, upper groups have collective arrangements which do not necessarily include living under one roof but which continue after the father's death until there is a petition (in India, Mandelbaum 1970:35) or a contract (in China, Cohen 1976) of division. Frequently the split is attributed to wives rather than to sons, and there are concrete reasons why this should be so, in particular those surrounding what is known in China as the wife's private money (*se-k'oi*) which she 'surrenders' to the conjugal estate only after separation (Cohen 1976:210–11; Baker 1979:20). But whether or not such attributions are correct, and with less reason they are as frequent in Africa as they are in Asia (Goody 1958), they help the men 'break an uncomfortable solidarity' with their agnates and then resume cooperative relations later on (Mandelbaum 1970:93).

Early marriage does not directly effect the size of minimal domestic groups since the acquisition of a bride in one house corresponds to the loss of a daughter in another. But it affects the composition, there being a larger number of wives. At the same time it has an important influence on interpersonal relationships since a young bride or groom is necessarily more dependent than an older one. Although size is not affected directly, complexity is since we find 'complex' households (that is, those with more than one 'elementary family') established at an earlier point in time and the birth of children taking place sooner. Generations in other words are shorter.

Here again, the hierarchical differentiation we have noted in ritual and marriage has parallels in household size and formation. We find a similarity with traditional China in the situation in North India, for example among the Jats and Brahmins studied by Lewis (1958[1965]:17). These higher families (that is, households) tend to be complex or 'extended' (66.7 per cent), while the lower castes have more simple or 'nuclear' households (64.8 per cent). In the Deccan, too, complex households are more common in the higher castes. Sons usually form separate households after marriage but domestic fission does not take place immediately and it is the earlier dispersal of sons among the lower groups that partly accounts for the difference (Dube 1955:133). Note that even though the sons are living separately, they are not necessarily divided productively or economically; in Nandol separate dwelling units or 'housefuls' continued to farm the land as one 'joint family' operation. The same is true elsewhere in India; in joint households all belongings may be held in common, with a common fund for living expenses, incomes and so on; however sons and brothers may have separate households, separate dwellings and yet still keep the land and property undivided.

A similar hierarchical difference in household composition was found in Wangala (Central India).

Most households in Wangala are composed only of elementary families: only 10 per cent of the total 192 households contain more than the members of the elementary family and an occasional grandparent. Elders complain of the break-up of joint-family living and attribute it to the selfishness of the young. In the course of collecting genealogies, I found ample evidence of the predominance of the joint family among Peasants and Functionaries, but none among Untouchables. The difference in family structure between Peasants and Untouchables in Wangala's past can be explained in terms of difference in economic organisation: joint families can exist only on the basis of jointly owned estates; Peasants had such estates, whereas Untouchables had only small land grants from the Government. On the other hand ownership of estates does not necessarily involve joint families. (Epstein 1962:176)

The same is true of Gujarat where Breman (1974) notes that at Chikhligam, it was the landowners who had joint families as well as the larger households. But the advantages of 'joint families' also accrue to other elements in the population of Gujarat.

It has been said that among high caste Hindus and among the Patels, where business and agriculture dominate, that the 'lineal and lateral joint family provides the much needed manpower – trustworthy and interested' (Acharya 1974:179). Such 'joint families' are not necessarily co-resident. Among the Patels, one brother might go into trade outside India, especially in East Africa, and send money to be invested back home. The adaptation of the managing agency system by local industrialists was a way of mobilising capital among kin, so that the joint family pattern was 'part of the economic organization' (p. 180), providing investment, recruitment and stability. But the 'family type that is in vogue is where property is joint but residence separate' (p. 181).

The tendency for upper families in India to have more complex families than lower ones has been carefully analysed by Shah (1974). In this study he challenges the assumption that in earlier times Hindu society was characterised by 'joint families', pointing out that this is an ambiguous concept sometimes referring to residential groups, or 'housefuls', sometimes to households, sometimes to kin living in adjacent or nearby houses and, more technically in law, to property-holding groups, that is, groups of coparceners in a Hindu (or Joint) Undivided Family. In Nandol a contemporary example of the latter was provided by the *sarpañc* who described how he and his brother, who was a university teacher working many miles away, had a joint bank account into which the one paid the profits of the farming enterprise (which were considerable as each brother had the maximum of fifty acres) while the other paid in his salary. From this fund both could draw. This intriguing description parallels arrangements in certain Israeli *kibbutzim* as well as in some communes in the West, whereby, after allowable deductions, the earnings of an individual who works outside are placed in the common pool. How it worked in the particular case of the chairman is obscure, but arrangements of this general kind are not uncommon.

Joint control over property, the family firm, is more likely to feature among upper groups than lower ones. But complex households are also more common at that level, a fact Shah considers to be due to Sanskritisation rather than wealth (1974:170) although it is not easy to separate the two factors. But since the same phenomenon is found in China it is difficult to accept the purely local explanation. Kolenda (1968:190) observes that in general larger households are found among the 'twice-born' castes as against the Untouchables, although Brahmins do not have a higher proportion than average, a point that Shah thinks is based on inadequate data (1974:224). Certainly in contemporary Nandol where they were more closely involved with the wage-earning economy, Brahmins do not have large households. As with age of marriage, it is those just below the Brahmins, and in particular the rich farmers and merchants, who are at the apex of the hierarchy of many family variables. Although neither Kolenda nor Shah see any evidence that landholding and joint families are correlated, most authors agree that 'people tend to remain in joint families [households] when economic factors favor such families. The poorest and the lowest tend to have fewest joint families, but even at these social levels, most families become joint for at least a time after a son marries' (Mandelbaum 1970:54). At the same time, higher groups tend to have fewer births than lower groups, not so much because of later marriage, but because of the earlier cessation of childbearing (Mandelbaum 1974:33).[13] On the other hand, the children they bear have a greater chance of survival.

Complex households are obviously created by early marriage and delayed fission. If sons establish their own household at marriage, there will be fewer complex ones. Again the number of single-person or 'subnuclear' households depends upon the prohibition on widow remarriage, or possibly on a particular type of polygynous arrangement where second wives are established on their own, and women allowed to head a household in both cases.

The situation has not altered much over the last century, despite modern changes. The average size of households in India lies between 4.5 and 5, and Orenstein (1961) has shown that if anything this figure slightly increased between 1871 and 1951, possibly due to demographic factors. There seem to be proportionally more simple than complex households in large towns and cities; in small and traditional towns and in the traditional sections of large, modern cities there are more complex units as compared with the villages (Shah 1974:163).

Hypergamy

The hierarchical differences in family structure that have been outlined are often considered in the context of hypergamy, the marriage of women to persons of a higher status, prestige or wealth. There are three aspects to this situation which may be linked but are often confused; these relate to individual roles, to families or lineages and lastly to castes. Some writers speak of hypergamy when a bride and possibly her relatives are considered, temporarily or permanently, to take on an inferior position with regard to the groom and his family simply by the fact of marriage. This situation is sometimes linked to the gender- or generation-based roles of inferiority, of women to men, of sons-in-law to father-in-law, of daughters-in-law to mothers-in-law; and often in India an association is seen with the notion of the 'gift' of the bride from inferior to superior, and with her incorporation in the lineage of the groom, the dowry being part of the accompanying gift. In other cases, hypergamy refers to a marriage of a bride from a family that is poorer or of lower standing to a groom from one of higher standing but within the same caste group or *jāti*. Thirdly, others refer to marriages between hierarchically arranged groups, neither individual families nor lineages but castes or classes.

Let me turn initially to the first of these usages which occurs in the work of Dumont (1966b), Vatuk (1969), Turner (1975) and others interested in kin terms and affinal gifts, whereby the bride's side (the wife-givers) are held to be inferior to the groom's side (the wife-receivers); hence every marriage is hypergamous, that is, upwards for the woman. These statements refer to supposed differences in the hierarchical arrangement of roles (father-in-law, son-in-law) that are found in the two groups or groupings involved in the marriage, which Dumont speaks of as local descent groups, Vatuk as kin groups, and Turner as kindreds. But the distribution of these roles in the context of a particular marriage has nothing necessarily to do with any permanent differences of status between these groups, since the relations established by one marriage may be reversed by those established at the next (Madan 1965:140; Turner 1975:268; Vatuk 1969:109). Indeed unilateral marital arrangements are rare.

The idea that hypergamy is encapsulated in the kin terminology has been rightly criticised by Fruzzetti and Östör (1976a) who find that these terms are perfectly consistent with exchange marriage. Not only do kin terms provide no guide to the presence of hierarchical marriage, they do 'not lead to any "groups"' (1976a:93); 'hypergamy as anthropological construct has nothing to do with terminology. If anything the logic of the nomenclature implies reciprocity.' In any case, they argue, hypergamy in the classic anthropological sense is missing from the Bengali scheme which they studied. Gifts flow from the bride's to the groom's side. 'But if this is "hypergamy" then it is something very peculiar.' To assess hierarchy we need to look at the wider social system. 'Without recourse to caste, locality, and marriage as elements extraneous to the terminology, an analysis cannot proceed very far' (1976a:92).

In the first case we have to look not only beyond the terminology but beyond the roles themselves. It is sometimes argued that the wife-givers are superior to the wife-takers on the grounds that the father-in-law is 'superior' to the son-in-law or because gifts travel in one direction rather than another. In a sense the first argument is true by definition, because it takes as a baseline the relations between generations; it implies nothing about the continuing ties between families or kin groups, at least in situations where the supposed flow of rights may be reversed at a future wedding, for the inequality will then be rectified. Another such supposed 'inequality' is seen to derive from the relative positions of the kin of the groom and the bride as a result of the location of the married couple, for with virilocal marriage, a wife moves into her husband's house. In this case the son-in-law's family, the receivers, are the superiors. But once again unequal roles and positions in marriage, whether of the groom and father-in-law, or of husband and wife, do not necessarily imply inequality between status or family groups; the two are logically independent since, even in a particular marriage, any inequality may be cancelled out by counterbalancing factors.

A similar notion is used by Parry in his analysis of Rajput marriage where the deference towards a married sister is seen as being an aspect of hypergamy as well as of her transference to her husband's clan and of her exclusion from her natal one (1979:137, 146). For following the wedding, the bride returns home and is worshipped as a deity by her brother's wives (pp. 147–8). But in fact all prepubescent girls of the lineage are *devis*. The worship takes place whether or not a marriage is hypergamous or isogamous, and therefore should not be interpreted as a manifestation of status differences between the families as such. In any case, the superiority and inferiority of particular affinal roles at the domestic level does not imply any over-riding status difference between the lineages of bride and groom. As Trautmann remarks of the Dravidian system of the South, 'it is easy to see that this differentiation of roles into asymmetrical wife-giving and wife-taking sets cannot be maintained if bilateral cross-cousin marriage is consistently practiced [indeed practiced at all] for it will then often happen that conflicting roles are assigned to several individual kinsmen' (1981:311).[14]

The second usage of hypergamy is that employed by Pocock of the Patidars of Gujarat when he declares: 'The good marriage is formally between families within the same castes; so people try to marry their daughters to wealthier or better families.' In this case, families try to find higher grooms for their daughters within the same group. In the Gujarat village of Nandol, as we have seen, kin are effectively proscribed as partners while marriage within the circle is prescribed. But within this circle, as Pocock points out, differences are great and marriage is 'a competitive affair' (1972:3), 'indissolubly connected with expense' (p. 2). Following Dumont, Pocock links this intracaste competition with hypergamy based upon the superiority of the groom's over the wife's family, the girl being laden with wealth and given to a superior (p. 3; Dumont 1964:89). This interpretation of dowry and hypergamy is not altogether convincing. I have already discussed the problem of dowry as 'gift' which, like the notion of sale applied to bridewealth, tends to reduce a qualified transaction to an absolute one, a total and irreversible transfer. And as far as hypergamy is concerned, we need to begin by distinguishing movement between castes from movement within, despite the possibility of more fuzzy boundaries in some areas where marriage occurs across the hierarchy of subcastes.

Thirdly, there is the intercaste hypergamy involved in the upward 'marriages' of Nayar and Kśhatriya women of Malabar to the Nambudiri Brahmins, as described by Gough and others. In the Surat region of Gujarat, it is also the case that poor Desai married rich Bhatela girls, demanding they bring a dowry, whereas Bhatela groups had to offer a 'brideprice' (Srinivas 1984:26; van der Veen 1972).

Most of the Gujarat cases do not involve intercaste unions since they occur between ranked groups *within* the larger unit. Near Baroda the Leva *jāti* is ranked in sections, with girls only able to marry into the higher groups, accompanied by a dowry. At the bottom of this hierarchy there is a shortage of possible brides; the lucky grooms have to provide an endowment ('brideprice'), while others remain unmarried or take girls from lower non-Patidar groups whom they try to pass off as Patidars (Mandelbaum 1970:107). In theory this arrangement should produce a surplus of unmarriageable daughters at the top, the cause for infanticide among some Rajputs and Patidars in earlier times.

The situation that Parry analyses for the Rajputs resembles that of the Patidars of Baroda, marriage being largely within the caste but between hierarchically arranged sub-units. Clans regarded as being of equal status in a general way form a single *birādari* within which they can marry, isogamously from the group standpoint. But whereas in Malwa (Mayer 1966:152) this group constitutes a marriage circle of the Nandol kind, here there is 'a tendency' (Parry 1979:201) towards hypergamy, that is, for men to marry into the *birādari* below and women into that above.

The Rajput hierarchy in Palampur consists of four such groups, the men of which (to simplify a more complex situation) marry women of the group below, a system that 'clearly creates a surplus of women at the top of the hierarchy and a shortage at the bottom' (p. 201). Since hypergamy was not 'mandatory', that is, prescribed between the groups, the extent of this surplus and the corresponding shortage depends upon the percentage of 'outside' marriages; Parry's figures show that 59.7 per cent were within the *birādari* and 37.7 per cent without, though the present trend is towards more isogamous unions.

The extent of this movement meant that there was an excess of daughters in the highest group and, since female celibacy was a dangerous and dis-approved alternative, the infanticide of girls was seen as the least disastrous possibility (p. 214). Statistical records for the year 1852 show that there was a sex ratio of 585 girls to every 1,000 boys in the top two Rajput *birādaris* of the present day Kangra and Palampur subdivisions, that is, 172.3 males to every 100 females; but this very extensive infanticide was largely confined to clans of the highest status.

Why could not the matter be resolved by marriage within the group? While accepting hypergamy as a major end of the system (as distinct from the possibly conflicting aspirations of individuals), Parry indicates an answer: 'there were many fathers of inferior *birādari* who were prepared to pay handsomely for the honour of a royal alliance. Unless he was to be hopelessly outbid by his subordinates, a substantial dowry – which made daughters a ruinous financial liability to all but the richest – had to be offered' (pp. 215–16). Given the obligation to endow daughters, the danger to infant girls is clear.

One alternative to killing off the surplus daughters of upper groups who are intent on pursuing what Tambiah refers to as the exchange of status for wealth, is to allow plural marriage or at least polycoity. As Hutton (1946) pointed out, this is one of the reasons for 'kulinism' among the Rarhi Brahmins of Bengal (Tambiah 1973:66); these polygynous brides stayed with their natal families (contrary to the higher norms) and were visited by their roving husbands, the children being brought up by their mothers rather like the matrilineal Nayars of South India. Hutton saw this as a preferred solution to infanticide by the non-violent Brahmins, whereas the martial Rajputs had no such scruples about taking life.

One of the incentives to the hypergamy that encouraged this practice is the fact that if 'lower' girls bring 'higher' dowries and marry higher, they raise the status of their natal families. 'A man gets rich, he . . . then tries to translate this newly achieved standing into the more durable sort of status of a prestigious marriage alliance' (Parry 1979:204), taking his family to a new level higher up the ladder, and presumably (although this is not said explicitly) changing his *birādari* in the process.

While at the top there were surplus women, at the bottom of the hierarchy there was a shortage of wives leading to high rates of celibacy or a later age of marriage for men (p. 227), which is also compatible with pressure for higher 'brideprice'. As a result of this shortage, some members of the fourth *birādari* were forced to marry Jat girls and thus transgress the ideal of caste endogamy (p. 229). Parry's figures show less than 1 per cent of such marriages but most of the sample came from the upper group of Mians. In any case the relationship between high dowry, infanticide and hypergamy is clear.

In his analysis, Parry puts the stress on family rather than group hypergamy, which he tries to relate to the 'role hypergamy' in specific marriages. 'The general point here, then, is that even within the *birādari* the asymmetrical and inegalitarian relationship between wife-givers and wife-takers has something of the same quality as the relationship between one *birādari* [group of clans] and another and between one caste and another' (p. 5). However in most other cases, and largely today among the Rajputs (since much of his analysis of hypergamy relates to historical times), any temporary asymmetry that may be established by marriage is perfectly consistent with general isogamy, certainly with marriage within the group. To Parry's suggested link of 'mandatory hypergamy' with the notion of the gift of a bride and with forms of prescriptive cousin marriage, I will return in the following chapter on North–South differences. The problem is to decide at what level the role of 'mandatory hypergamy' operated. If it was a continuing characteristic of the system, it could lead to a permanent distinction between wife-giving and wife-taking 'groups', although in the North no marriage is possible with the mother's group (and in the South this would imply a differentiation between cross-cousins as marriage partners). Neither of course is there any distinct term for a mother's brother's daughter (though there are ways of distinguishing them, e.g. mama's children) since like all other female (first) cousins, they are 'sisters'. On Parry's showing there is an oscillating equilibrium (or instability) in the system, a contradiction between the idea the brothers are differentiated into inferior and superior, as Leach would see it,[15] and the notion of the accumulation of women at the top and deprivation at the bottom, as Lévi-Strauss and Parry see it (p. 268). Moreover, the latest of the *birādari* reform movements tried to make isogamous marriage 'mandatory' (p. 314) even with the re-establishment of hierarchy, since only some 25 to 33 per cent of marriages took place outside the group, that is, were hypergamous.

The attempt to raise the status of one of the parties through marriage is a widespread feature of stratified societies and the particular form it takes in India is associated with notions of 'the purity of women'. But the very fact that women are endowed can create problems, since in the Rajput case higher groups are prepared to overlook lower status if the bride comes with other advantages. In this case, as Parry's argument makes clear, they may set aside potential wives from within their own group in favour of outsiders from further down the hierarchy. For the fathers of some daughters are unwilling or unable to provide for them as generously as others.

While these transactions may be conceived of as 'gifts' without return at an ideological or scriptural level, those who provide the large dowry gain advantages not only for their daughter but for the family as a whole. Equally the groom's family are seeking advantages. These may not necessarily be in the form of dowry but rather the prospects of inheritance, as when a man has a daughter but no sons (p. 273). Parry speaks of the role of 'more mercenary considerations' in this case; those certainly exist, but advantages and disadvantages come in many forms of which the mercenary aspect is only one, although always important since it helps to secure or improve the daughter's status.

Not everyone can hope to marry off their daughters in this way; not everyone has the resources. But it must surely be the policy of the respective families of both man and woman to arrange a match that is at least equal and at best better. The latter eventuality may involve hypergamy, or possibly hypogamy, depending on the outcome. Not everyone can win and the soundest policy may be to avoid loss, that is, to aim at isogamy, as van der Veen (1972) suggests is the case for the Anavil Brahmins. But at a very general level the basis of such marriages is a trade-off between the attributes of both parties, a trade-off in which each considers that they have gained, and which may in some cases affect the relations not only of individuals and families but of the broader groups to which they belong.

Interpersonal relationships

Parents and children

The differences we have noted on an institutional and demographic level have their counterparts in interpersonal relationships of which they are an intrinsic aspect. These latter turn on the greater freedom of the lower groups, partly in their work, partly in matters of divorce and remarriage; both aspects are linked to the absence of the constraining influence exercised by considerations of property, partly in the form of dowry but also because their separation from the means of production forces women as well as men to work for others outside the home. The nature of these differences emerge very clearly in Gough's account of the Tanjore village of Kumbapeṭṭai (1956) which displayed considerable differences in the social relations of both men and women, depending on position in the hierarchy. The sons of Brahmin landowners stayed on with their fathers whose authority remained strong; the sons of the Adi Dravidas, who were landless labourers, took jobs soon after puberty, had separate houses shortly after marriage and were less dependent on their fathers. Their sisters were independent both economically and socially, divorcing easily and frequently, remarrying as widows, working for wages in the fields and less isolated from their natal families. On the other hand it is reported that a husband's authority 'is more durably imperative among the higher and wealthier *jātis* than among the lower and poorer', where women can earn money and are therefore less dependent (Mandelbaum 1970:73), although the husband's superiority is regularly maintained at the formal level, even if in practice it is modified, sometimes greatly so. At the same time the shame about sex, so noticeable in upper groups, is less strong lower down.

The hierarchical differences in family life extend to sentiment, along the same lines that Fei perceives in China (1946; see above p. 100). Among the higher groups in India, Mandelbaum observes: 'Between father and son, relations are supposed to be formal and restrained and are often so in reality. Each may have great affection for the other, but after the boy becomes adolescent there should be little familiarity, intimacy, or demonstrativeness between them. This holds especially among landowners of high ritual rank' (1970:60). Among the Brahmins of Tanjore described by Gough (1956:835–8), a boy of eight to nine should touch neither parent and had to prostrate himself before them daily. Nevertheless the son's demand for partition, to which he is entitled under *Mitākṣarā* law as a coparcener at birth, may lead to a softening of the father's stern control (Mandelbaum 1970:61), indicating the relevance of property in personal relations, especially in matters of parental authority, and of course all property exists both in and as a relationship (Goody 1962: chapter 14). For in the families of the lower *jātis*, a son's dependence was less intense and protracted, while the father himself was less aloof, even he becomes more distant as the boy grows up (Dumont 1957b:212–13).[16]

The same differences in the structure of authority apply to that exercised by women. A high caste mother may continue to supervise her son's domestic life after marriage, even his sexual relations. On the other hand women of the middle and lower *jātis* working outside the home are less completely centred on their children (Mandelbaum 1970:62; Karve 1953:12; Gough 1956:838).

Brothers

It follows from the comments on paternal relations that those between brothers are likely to be more equal in the lower *jātis* (Mandelbaum 1970:64), if only because the elder brother is not required to take over the father's role in the same way.[17] Such equality could take a variety of forms. Among the Kotas, formerly among the Nayars and among some hill peoples of the Himalayas, brothers had the right of access to each other's wives, although usually only the younger could sleep with the wife of his elder brother;[18] indeed this practice is structurally and physically contiguous with the fraternal polyandry of those same hill peoples (Berreman 1962) as well as with the acquisition of the brother's widow after his death, by inheritance or by the levirate. But polyandry was by no means confined to lower or tribal groups; in Tibet as we have seen it was characteristic of landowners rather than the landless. Nevertheless in India, as with the paternal relationship, that between brothers tends to be influenced by the level of property the family commands. 'Brothers of a poor family of low *jāti* may have little to quarrel about. If they are all laborers or heavily dependent on an over-lord, they have little cooperative enterprise of their own. But those brothers who together manage and work the land or jointly provide goods and services are likely sooner or later to fall out' (Mandelbaum 1970:66), especially after the death of the father.

Grandparents

Relations between alternate generations are affected by similar factors. In poor families, the parents have less to offer, separation takes place earlier, so that grandparents and grandchildren are less likely to live under one roof. There are in any case fewer living parents or grandparents since mortality is higher and even if living they are more likely to be in a dependent position on their children, having 'retired' from the management of the household.[19] But in the complex households of higher groups, the grandfather may continue to wield authority, disapproving, for example, of visits of the grandchildren to their mother's home as being likely to spoil them (Madan 1965:212). Clearly the opportunities or lack of them that a woman has to visit her natal home will affect the substantive nature of the relation between her brother and her children, that is, between the mother's brother and the sister's children, although everywhere this seems to be relatively 'warm'.

Mother's brother and sister's children

Like Mayer (1966:223), Mandelbaum sees the tie between a mother's brother and the sister's children as being 'an extension of a brother's protective, beneficent relation to his sister' (1970:73), arising not out of affinity or even out of what Fortes called 'complementary filiation' (though that is involved), but out of the sibling bond, which is how various writers have seen cross-cousin marriage (the union between the children of brothers and sisters) and even marriage to the sister's daughter (Yalman 1967:351–2). Such oblique marriages are not all that uncommon. In one Mysore village they accounted for 7 per cent of marriages, whereas about 40 per cent fell within the cross-cousin range (McCormack 1958:36,39). In other areas they are even more in evidence.

These are problems to which I shall return in discussing the theoretical implications of the brother–sister relationship below. But first it is worth pointing to one general aspect of the differential hierarchy of kinship. With wealth a man can actuate many more ties, by presents at marriages and by entertainment generally, than can a poorer individual. Indeed of Ramkheri in Madhya Pradesh, Mayer concluded that kinship depends on wealth; through invitations a man is able to 'keep kin from growing cold', as they say (1966:249). The networks of the poor are narrower and thinner.

Brother and sister

I have singled out the brother–sister tie for separate treatment partly because it is of such central importance throughout the entire hierarchy, although there is clearly more (not necessarily closer) interaction when the brother and married sister are freer to communicate with one another. But the main reason lies in the relevance of this relationship to analytical notions of the incorporation of women and to the actors' notions (at least at the higher levels and in specific contexts) of the 'gift' of a virgin. Both, I have suggested, require some modification, partly by being put firmly in context.

The idea of the alienation of the bride by gift or sale runs counter to the heavy emphasis placed on the continuing nature of brother–sister relations despite the fact that in the North marriage requires them to live in different villages. That relation is celebrated and epitomised in the annual ceremony of *Rakshābandhan* in northern and western India.[20]

In 1977 this ceremony took place in Nandol on 28 August, the full moon of *Srāvaṇa*. Its name, *Rakshābandhan*, is cognate with that for marriage, *sambandhan*, where the common element, *bandhan* (Sanskrit *bandhá*) refers to the act of tying. The ceremonies are complementary. Marriage (*sam*, reciprocally) ties spouses; *rakshābandhan* ties brother and sister. The ceremony itself involves the visit of women to their brothers (that is, to the homes of their own fathers, their natal homes) on a specific day of the year when they tie a gaudy decoration on the right wrists of their siblings, which is at once a defence against misfortune (*rakshā*, protection), a symbol of mutual dependence and a mark of respect (Monier-Williams 1899:860). Today mass-produced decorations fill the shops for weeks in advance. The brother may wear it until it falls off, which may be only for a day or two, or right up to *Divali* some two months later when it is his turn to visit his sister and to give her a substantial present such as a *sari* or a watch in return. This close relation of the brother and the sister is well-brought out in the Maharastran marriage songs published by Karve whose sentiments she links to the separation of the bride from her home and to the inability of her parents to pay her visits, both more typical of the North.

The only person from the father's house who can and does go to the sister is the brother. He is her champion with whom she can talk about her joys and sorrows. He brings her the annual brother's gift but he too becomes a stranger when he marries and under the influence of his wife either forgets or wilfully neglects the sister.

The words of the songs run as follows:

Even more than a son I love my younger brother. He and I were constant companions in my childhood.

We two sisters are like two wells of two villages. The fine strong brother is like the fine green corn-field in the middle. (The jowar-corn is fine, being watered by the wells – The brother thrives because of the love of his two sisters who are brides in neighbouring villages on either side.)

The brother was on the point of drinking water, he had drawn from the well; but he did not, when he heard that the sister was cruelly treated at the father-in-law's house.

God has given me enough in the husband's house which is my kingdom; but brother dear, I still look forward to your annual present of a piece of cloth for my bodice.

The price which my brother pays for the piece of cloth he presents to me for my *choli* (bodice) is as high as that for a *sari*. Those who have no brothers wonder at this extravagance.

The beautiful black *sari* with red border and the end embroidered with the sacred name of Rama is the gift of my darling brother.

My eyes are aching and red by staring at the street in expectation of his arrival. I cannot understand how my own mother's son has become like a stranger to me.

The rain comes in torrents and vanishes as suddenly. My brother too has forgotten me since the birth of his daughter.

He gives a dozen excuses for not going to the village of his sister; but if he has to go to the daughter's village he immediately takes away the bullocks from the plough.

The brothers are mine own. What are the sisters-in-law (wives of brothers) to me? But I call them mine. Do we not string beads together with a precious amulet?

The brother was buying for me a *choli*-cloth (special cloth for bodice) for one rupee but his wife made him buy one which cost only half as much.

After the death of the parents the father's house is lost to me. Now if I go on a visit my brother's wife says please put up at the *sarai* on the outskirts of the town (*sarai* is a public building where travellers can live without paying anything).

In this age the brother no longer cares for the sister. The *choli*-piece which should be a gift for me is in his pocket but he is enquiring about the house of the younger sister of his wife. (1953:177–8)

Note how the brother's generosity is seen as restrained by his wife. She it is who is the sister's rival and she it is who, in a joint household, makes it impossible for the sister to remain celibate at home or even return later as a widow. When she does go back to visit her brother at *Rakshābandhan*, the wife leaves for her own natal home. In 1977 the festival in Nandol fell on a weekend, at which time there was a great deal of movement of women boarding the local buses for their natal homes. The street in which we were living was emptied of wives and filled by sisters who now had the opportunity of cooking for their brothers. Conjugality gave way to siblinghood, affinity to kinship. While the ceremony primarily concentrates on the relationship between full brothers and sisters, there is inevitably some degree of extension to wider kin, although mainly in upper groups and to important people. We were sitting in the ground-nut oil factory in Degham when a man came in, walked up to the boss sitting behind his desk and tied a decoration on his wrist. In return he was given a gift. The guardian of the River Temple came and left a wrist decoration at our house returning two days later for a gift, apparently a standard act by temple guardians who adapt the expression of kinship obligation and sentiment to their own support. Our neighbour's wife, Davidaben, also sent us a decoration, partly as a neighbourly act, but mainly because of our assumed importance in the community which had been demonstrated by the status of our visitors. In a well-off family in Ahmadabad, decorations were given to close cousins of the opposite sex as well as to siblings. As Mandelbaum notes: 'a man may receive charms from several donors, from his wife, from a Brahmin with whom he has dealings, or from others who can give him ritual protection. But usually the principal charm is that given by his sister, and the occasion is one when sister and brother should meet' (1970:68).

This continuing importance of a daughter to her natal family is well brought out in Das' study of Punjabi kinship (1976). During the time she was in the field, four brothers murdered their sister, a doctor, who wanted to marry a Tamil. When things are going well, the brother's role is that of gift-giver. But he also acts as protector of her honour; Das reports another case in which the brothers came to the house of their married sister when they heard she had been maltreated, saying 'We have come to remind you that N.'s brothers are not dead.' If a bride dies young, murder is suspected and her kin are inevitably involved in the ensuing accusations.

The continuing relationship is also seen in the giving of gifts. Gift exchanges are formalised in terms of the concept of *hag*, the right to receive as well as to give. A woman maintains the right to receive gifts from her natal kin, and at the next generation this right is continued in the gifts made by her brother at the marriage of her daughter. On the other hand in most upper groups, the bride's family will take nothing from the groom's when she gets married. The daughters of upper Punjabi castes are in the paradoxical situation of appearing to be 'incorporated' into their affinal households to a greater extent than women in lower groups. That is partly a function of the wealth involved and their status in affinal and natal terms, which obliges them to enter the permanent conjugal unions sanctioned by the dominant ideology. But it would be quite wrong to see such unions as cutting them off from their families of orientation, or from the wealth these provide.

Notions of incorporation are often expressed in exchangist terms and run quite contrary to the acknowledged strength of the brother–sister bond in Indian society. That relationship is durable partly because few rivalries are involved; it continues to be kept up after her marriage when a brother has a special relationship to her husband and especially to her children, to whom of course he is mother's brother.[21]

Considering the all-India scene, Mandelbaum makes the general point simply and directly. 'When a bride joins her husband's family, she becomes a member of his lineage for most purposes, ritual, economic, and legal, but she also retains some affiliation with the original lineage and some rights in it. Only rarely is a woman cut off from her natal lineage' (1970:137). Experience of Indian families in Gujarat, both in the village and the town, as well as among Gujaratis living in England, emphasise the continuing importance to the wife of her natal family, especially her brothers. The bonds between siblings are stronger than in comparable groups in Europe, measured by whatever criteria one chooses. While this tie is in a sense a lineage one, its continuing strength after marriage cannot be reconciled with any notion that there is a cutting off; even to talk of retaining 'some affiliation' seems less than adequate. Part of the importance of this cross-sibling relationship should perhaps be attributed to contemporary changes which diminish the strength of wider lineage ties under conditions of urbanisation and migration, although these latter have long been factors of Indian life. But even if this is so, the readiness with which the change has taken place tells us something about the structure of the 'traditional' Indian family.

In this chapter I have tried to examine the nature of marriage transactions in relation to other features that differentiate the higher from the lower groups, namely widow remarriage, divorce, the size of households, asceticism in diet and worship. In addition I tried to clarify the notion of hypergamy since, in the area of Gujarat in which we worked, both observations and hypotheses suggested that isogamy was the more usual form. Elsewhere some intergroup hypergamy is found, but while the brides may be lower in caste position, they are sought largely because of their greater access to property (that is, higher dowries) which balances the equation with status. Finally I turned to differences in interpersonal relationships and in the position of women, especially the continuing bond between brothers and sisters after marriage, which stresses that women are not simply given away, for their ties continue to be important not only for each other but for each other's children, as mother's brothers and as father's sisters.

There is one additional point to make about the differences between high and low. The practices of the lower groups interlock with various other aspects of their social life and represent a partially accepted facet of their existence, which the dominant ideology justifies in wider terms. But when their circumstances change for the better, they often attempt to adapt their institutions to those of the upper groups. Such upward movement is not universal, as we have noted; in the name of social justice Hindu reform movements, in particular the influential Arya Samaj, have advocated the adoption of the freer practices of lower groups. This too has been the general trend of much modern legislation, at least for divorce and remarriage. Nevertheless certain pressures for upward adjustment remain, not simply as aspects of Sanskritisation, whether the emphasis be placed on religious or social merit, but also because those practices, specifically that of dowry and the maintenance of the position of daughters, are themselves linked to the very achievement of a higher socio-economic status in the whole range of major Asian societies. A similar hierarchical distribution of practices is found not only in India but in China and West Asia; women of high status are entitled to a dowry which ensures their standard of living and demonstrates the wealth and position of their natal families who provide it.

To treat the dowry as part of the devolution of property to (or sometimes on behalf of) daughters in order to maintain or to better their position in life is to treat it as an aspect of diverging devolution whereby property is transmitted by parents, sometimes jointly, sometimes separately, to the children of the marriage. But while such an understanding implies that marriage does not totally alienate women from their natal family (and especially from their brothers) as subjects of a process of gift-giving or incorporation, this is not to suggest for one moment that their position is equal to that of their brothers, much less their husbands, nor that females are treated in the same way as males; the facts on infanticide, overt and concealed, show that there are radical differences from the very beginning. And the differences of course continue in later life because, as the Rajput situation brings out and as is emphasised by the religiously sanctioned injunction to marry off one's daughter before her first menstruation, a marriageable daughter is normally a liability, a marriageable son an asset.[22]

But while women's roles may be systematically inferior to those of men of parallel position, it is always important to maintain their standing, with respect to caste, reputation and standard of life, partly because any gain or lapse would reflect upon her natal family, partly for the sake of the woman herself. Her entitlement means that in the absence of brothers, of siblings of the same parenthood (and not in the absence of any male kinsmen of the lineage, as would be the case in Africa), she will be an 'heiress' and can continue the direct line as the appointed daughter, whose husband will be in certain respects inferior. So while the *Dharmaśāstras* may see dowry as a gift, and social reformers as a bribe, the aspect of endowment remains a significant component.

Once this point is acknowledged, the appropriateness of any idea, at the analytic level, of marriage as a gift without return must be questioned. In the first place, even hypergamous marriage clearly brings benefits for the bride's family. Secondly, the gift of dowry is made to her, to the conjugal estate and to its heirs, rather than to the groom's kin, or even to the groom. Thirdly, the transaction does not end with the wedding but continues throughout the marriage.

But there is also a further implication. Once admitted, the female endowment with parental property has to be seen as a variable, to some extent over time but certainly over space, social and geographical. Evidence of temporal variation, at least at the legal level, is provided by the earlier changes (not all in one direction) in Indian law, on which the more recent changes build.

Female endowment, I suggest, is not simply a dependent variable; the conception of women's rights has long been capable of expansion under internal pressures (as we see from the paradigmatic case of the daughters of Zelophehad in chapter 11) and contraction under external ones. But while I have drawn attention to the common features underlying variants in this huge area, and suggested that the adoption of one among the alternative mechanisms may be partly due to a realisation of the problems raised by another, we are not simply faced with structural drift. Both in the temporal and the hierarchical context, a comparison with other societies brings out directional factors. For India, the explanation of the hierarchical range involves, first, seeing the variations as a loose 'system' of the kind found in other major societies of Eurasia, that react to and impose a set of similar constraints and opportunities in the domestic sphere of production and reproduction, but which change over time. Some of the variations were consistent with and encouraged by the position of particular groups in the productive system. Others required the consideration of further factors, including the demands of religious affiliation, the nature of political domination, the degree of cultural incorporation and more specific socio-economic activities. Religious affiliation involved not only the consequences of adhering to Hinduism, Buddhism or Islam, but more generally how family life was affected by the problem of providing support for a temple organisation, by priestly role models as well as by ecclesiastical courts. Equally, gradual secularisation or the sudden rejection of religion may release individuals and groups from these constraints on domestic life. Political domination in turn may affect household production and composition if demands are made for *corvée* and military service; it may encourage the early transmission of property if inheritance is taxed, and influence the availability of men or women if sexual and other services are concentrated at the top. Cultural incorporation becomes a factor of importance when 'lower' groups are made up of tribal peoples that have only recently been brought into the main system, though the possibility of 'survivals' over a longer period cannot be ignored, even if more positive reasons than sheer inertia or attachment to custom have to be sought for effective resistance to the hegemonic forms that have changed so much else.

The regional differences that I explore in the following chapter involve a number of the same variables that appear in the hierarchical analysis, and their distribution raises not only general problems, for we find similar geographic variations in the context of dowry transactions in China and the Mediterranean, but also specific questions to do with ecology, mode of livelihood, extent of contact with autochthonous groups, core and periphery, about which a number of partly competing or contradictory but often convergent or complementary theories have emerged.

8

The North and the South

The discussion of the continuing importance of the brother–sister relationship in Gujarat and other parts of India is a convenient point at which to shift from a consideration of hierarchical differences to a comparison and contrast of North India with the South and Sri Lanka. Any such attempt raises an obvious problem. Many of the hierarchical differences we have noted are pan-Indian, particularly where Brahmins are involved, for example, in the southern village of Kumbapeṭṭai studied by Gough (1981), a main reference of the group is to a common set of written norms; people may interpret these differently, even setting them aside altogether but their very embodiment in a text means that by calling attention to such discrepancies, it is always possible for reformers to lead them back to more 'Sanskritic' ways. In other words, there is a certain dynamic tension between the *Dharmaśāstra* and the customary 'law' which results in a change in the balance over time.

But at any point in time differences always exist, both hierarchical and regional, and the problem is that in trying to point these out, one may inevitably overemphasise. However, the fact that differences do exist is widely recognised by actors and observers alike. Their importance is a matter for debate; nevertheless even their existence tends to be denied or played down by those approaches to the study of Indian systems of kinship and marriage that stress the unity of Indian culture, whether because they assume a common deep structure for the whole country (or sub-continent) or whether because they concentrate, explicitly or implicitly, upon the unity of written Hindu orthodoxy. But a recognition of the continental influence of the Hindu religion, especially in the fundamental area of caste, does not exclude the acknowledgement of important regional differences at the level of kinship.

Unity and diversity

The insistence on the unity of systems of kinship and marriage in India has been a prominent aspect of the work of Louis Dumont and is closely linked to his general approach to the study of society. In regretting the lack of interest in kinship studies, he maintains that 'in contradistinction to many others [other fields – he is thinking of 'social change' and no doubt 'economics'], here is a real, self-defining, system, I mean a system whose boundary is objectively given' (1961:76). He feels the average researcher is more likely to be successful and useful here than if he engages in more perilous undertakings.

One can sympathise with Dumont's desire for cumulative knowledge. But his approach towards the field of kinship seems problematic in general (not always in the particular) precisely because he does attempt to treat kinship and marriage as a distinct field, linked at times to modes of thought but virtually independent of modes of production, modes of communication and political systems. I would argue that we need constantly to explore the interconnections and only with these in mind can we make sense of kinship systems, either in the domestic or in what Fortes (1969) has called the politico-jural domain.

In the paper I have quoted, Dumont spends some time commenting upon an early article of mine (1959) on the relationship between the mother's brother and the sister's son, in which he opposes my so-called 'descentist' to his 'alliance' theory; in another context he calls the latter 'structural' as opposed to 'functional'. He then explains how he applied to South India 'a structural theory of kinship which concluded by bringing out what I called marriage alliance, that is to say the repetition of intermarriage through the course of generations – a repetition still more ideal than actual – by which the classification into two categories of kinsmen in several generations . . . might be understood simply' (1961:76–7). It is an extended notion of repeated marriage that he attempts to apply to the North as well as to the South, even though the terminology of kinship and the pattern of marriage are very different in the two cases. And it is in this framework too that he looks at the relationship between a man and his mother's brother.

It would be unprofitable to engage in a detailed argument if only because my point was that different social and economic factors had to be taken into account in examining the LoDagaa of West Africa on the one hand and the Pramalai Kallar of South India on the other. While these differences may have had something to do with the analytic frameworks adopted, to describe them respectively as 'functional' and 'structural' was to confuse theoretical approach with empirical differences. For this reason, I thought, his specific comments on Radcliffe-Brown's article, 'The mother's brother in South

Africa' (1924), seemed to miss the mark. They did so not for regional reasons, reasons of geography, but because there were basic differences in the politico–economic systems of the two areas which could only be ignored if one was concerned to concentrate upon certain very formal aspects of kinship (especially the 'terminology'), attempting to separate these from the social system as a whole in order to establish a distinct analytical domain of 'kinship'. Such an approach is especially problematic when we are dealing with matters to do with inheritance and devolution (including some marriage transactions) which constitute an essential part of the process by which a socio-political system reproduces itself at the domestic level.

Let me rather turn to the present situation. In discussing Gujarati marriage I noted that a woman's right to an endowment was associated (by the actors as well as by myself) with her position as a sibling and as a daughter, and that the continuation of these relationships was evident in visiting, especially between siblings, in gift-giving, especially from the mother's brother, and in rites of passage, both personal and annual. In other words the woman is not cut off from her natal group as the extreme version of exchange theory would imply. Indeed her continuing role as a sister (and of a man as brother) is very much to the fore, especially at the yearly ceremony of *Rakshābandhan*.

Dumont's interpretation of a similar situation in North India takes quite a different view. In an article entitled 'Terminology and prestations revisited' (1975a), the author comments primarily on the work by Vatuk, especially her paper (Gifts and affines in North India, 1975) which deals mainly with a newly urbanised community of Gaur Brahmins in western Uttar Pradesh.[1] In an earlier article (A structural analysis of the Hindi kinship terminology, 1969), Vatuk had based her analysis on Dumont's discussion of marriage in North as compared with South India. There he examined the relation of kin terms to ritual prestations and concludes that North India represents a kind of 'compromise between a "Dravidian" practice and an Indo-Aryan verbal heritage' (1966b:114), for despite terminological differences there was a common pattern of kinship practice, the central feature of which was the manner of conceptualising affinal relationships. In her own study Vatuk, like Marriott (1955), found evidence of 'the existence of a status differential between bride-givers and bride-takers and of an irreversible flow of gifts on informal as well as ritual occasions, "upward" from the former to the latter' (1969:110). Those 'above' were termed *dhyānā*, from the Sanskrit for daughter: 'no senior kinsman of the woman given in marriage (with the exception of the brother) may accept their gifts or hospitality' (p. 110). However, she goes on to remark that this is a 'conceptual framework' that does not result in 'any systematic ranking scheme' (p. 110); in other words at the group level hypergamy, in *sensu strictu*, is not at issue. In any case, as she points out, the groups concerned, that is, the 'daughter' groups, are not unilineal descent groups, which can be ranked exclusively, but rather 'kindreds' (pp. 111–12), which are overlapping, a fact related to the use of Hawaiian terminology which makes no distinction between cousins and siblings.

A comment by Dumont on this article is revealing, for it rests upon a boundary distinction between internal and external prestations.

> The gift of the maternal uncle or *bhāt* is a clear case of oriented internal prestation. It represents a sequel from a former marriage. A man had given his sister in marriage, and now that his sister's child marries, it is an obligation for him to contribute a substantial and complex gift, which will go for a part to the protagonists of the marriage themselves (that is, not only to the nephew, or niece, but also to his (or her) spouse: we note the presence of an "external" gift), and for another part – in the case of a niece – will enter into the composition of the *dahej* offered to the groom's side, and thus be "further given" (*āgedive*). This expression is precious for us, as it shows that the people have in mind a chain going from the former wife-giver, the mother's brother, through the natal family of the bride, to the new wife-taker's, the groom's side. (1975a:210)

This line of argument is completely in keeping with his questioning of Vatuk's perception of the married daughter as being the 'primary recipient' of her parents' gifts, in favour of viewing these as affinal gifts; the *dān-dahej* is the main 'crossing or external gift'. 'Dowry' is seen as an affinal prestation, a concept in keeping with brahmanical notions of marriage but quite out of keeping with sastric conceptions of *strīdhana*. Out of keeping too with the reports of ethnographers such as Nicholas who offers the following comment on marriage prestations in the 'Radhanagar' area of Bengal:

> the theory that is employed in agreeing upon the marriage portion of the bride is that she is entitled to a share of her family's property almost equal to that of her brothers. The stipulation which, in most instances, keeps her from getting an exactly equal share is that agricultural land is inherited by sons. Most of the property transferred with a bride to her father-in-law's house – brass utensils, bedding, clothing and a few pieces of jewelry – is supposed to remain, as it has in the past, in the bride's personal control and is supposed to be returned with her in case of divorce. (1967:73)

Inevitably, there is some ambiguity, since the 'affines', her husband or members of his family, may take possession: but ownership differs from possession; and remains vested in her and in the case of divorce the girl's father may sue for the return of the ornaments on these very grounds. While I would not wish to deny an affinal aspect, broadly interpreted, to these transactions, the conception of dowry as an external gift between affines, the exact counterpart of bridewealth, shows the limits to an interpretation based purely on exchangist terms. The problem is partly one of applying the notions of Mauss, appropriate to the Trobriands, to more complex situations. But it derives more directly from attempting to establish kinship as an independent system, and from ignoring the reproduction of productive resources (which at some point entails 'parental' redistribution) in favour of exchange. In his analysis of these transactions Dumont operates from the relatively static standpoint of the membership of continuing (descent) groups or in terms of the even more static chart of kin terms (or possibly of kin roles), without taking into account the changing perspective of the developmental cycle in which the brother–sister relationship of one generation develops into the bond between a man and his sister's children in the next. Obviously such a development is found in the South as well as the North and it is explicit in the actor's frame of reference. One of the southern ceremonies that are equivalent to the *Rakshābandhan* of the North is the *iNaiccīr* ritual performed at marriage in the Konku region of Tamilnadu (Beck 1972:239).

Proper regard for this connection is said to contribute to the prosperity and fertility of the brother's family, and many local folktales recount examples of how a pure and devoted sister can bring strength and good fortune to her brothers, especially if she is a virgin. At the same time, the sister has a claim on her brother's daughter as a wife for her own son. In the ceremony, she ritually requests a part of the fruits of his prosperity, a daughter, for the continuance of her own family through her son's marriage. (p. 240)

In this future marriage to the mother's brother's daughter, it is not continuing affinity that is stressed, the inherited claim of the wife-receivers to get a perpetual supply of brides from the same source, much less the hypergamous aims of the givers, but rather, as Srinivas argues for the Coorgs, and Yalman for Sri Lanka, the reaffirmation of the tie between siblings of a different sex, separated by their own marriages but united by the marriages of their children. And it is the sister that makes the claim on the brother for her son, not the husband on his brother-in-law.

Another indication of the weight placed upon terminology (and sometimes upon its fundamental categories) appears in the title of Dumont's early article, 'The Dravidian kinship terminology as an expression of marriage' (1953). Arguments from terminology have to be approached very carefully for a number of reasons, but one particular problem is the role/actor confusion which can result. In discussing marriage preparations in Lucknow, Khare (1976) calls attention, apparently in support of Dumont (1966b), to the role at marriage of the 'female affine' who scooped up some earth to be used for the hearth and for the ceremonial canopy. The female affine turns out to be the bride's father's sister (*man*). Since both the parents' siblings of opposite sex are placed in the same box as affines in the system of binary classification, it is hardly surprising to find him claiming Dumont's hypothesis that 'an affinal link always enters to rank and legitimize a crucial food transaction in marriage will be repeatedly confirmed in our description' (p.

196).[2] Make this assumption and there is no alternative. The question of whether or not the identification (MB=FZ) translates the local terminology (in fact this does not appear to be the case) is not necessarily critical for the outside observer, especially one working with those English concepts which have been transformed by disciplinary usage. But the contributions and intervention here described can surely be more parsimoniously understood in terms of sibling rather than conjugal or affinal ties, assuming (which I doubt) that it is necessary to opt for one rather than for the other, certainly not in the case of the South with its system of marriage to close kin.

The main commentator stressing the differences between North and South is Karve upon whose major work (1953) I have often relied. Karve claims that 'the Dravidian kinship organisation' of the South is 'fundamentally different' from that of the North (p. 228), the principle of immediate exchange being opposed to that of extended exchange and leading to 'a policy of consolidation, a clustering of kin group in a narrow area, no sharp distinction between kin by blood and kin by marriage, greater freedom for women' (p. 229), differences which she claims relate to the agricultural economy of the South and the (former) pastoral economy of the North.

Dumont's approach leads him to dispute Karve's interpretation of the differences between North and South (see also Dumont and Pocock 1957). Specifically he rejects the following contentions. First, that in the North, village exogamy is general; secondly, that married women there do not generally visit their kin; thirdly, that exogamous unilineal groups are absent; and, fourthly, that *sapiṇḍa* prohibitions prevent the repetition of marriage between local descent groups (1966b:90). Regarding the first point, village exogamy is certainly widespread if not universal. We may agree with the second and third objections while recognising that restrictions on a woman's visiting her home often exist and that the exogamous unilineal groups are of a spatial kind. With regard to the fourth, while *sapiṇḍa* prohibitions may not prevent the repetition of marriage between local descent groups over time, they necessarily prohibit the repetition of close kinship marriage in adjacent generations; as Dumont himself points out, 'cross-cousin marriage, preferred and we might even say prescribed in the South, is forbidden in the North (among Hindus); and it is extremely likely that people in the North marry at a greater distance, spatially as well as structurally' (1966b:90). However he considers this feature a purely negative characteristic, centring his own enquiry on 'the place and treatment of affinity in North Indian kinship' (1966b:91) in order to demonstrate the basic unity of the sub-continent.

The trend of Dumont's work, here as elsewhere, is to point to aspects of the North Indian pattern of allocating ritual gifts and ceremonial functions to 'wife-takers' (i.e. the daughter's husband, the sister's husband and the father's sister's husband), an allocation which he sees as reminiscent of the South Indian system of marriage alliance based on cross-cousin marriage. Despite differences in kinship terminology, structure and marriage rules, he perceives an underlying similarity in the conceptualisation of the nature of affinity (Vatuk 1975:156; Dumont 1966b:91–5, 113–14).

The attempt to assimilate the kinship systems of North and South India is based upon the examination of three main features:

1 Kinship prestations in general, and especially at the end of mourning, in the village of Rampur studied by Mayer (1966). Of this 'northern' situation he concludes: 'while we should as yet avoid the expression of marriage alliance, which supposes intermarriage being ideally or factually repeated from one generation to the next, it is nevertheless the case that affinity has something of a diachronic dimension' (Dumont 1966b:95).

2 Kinship vocabulary, where an attempt is made 'to extract from the configuration of the system of kinship terms the definition of the fundamental categories of kinship' (p. 96). The kin terms themselves obviously differ; unity demands that we move to a more inclusive level of analysis, which leads him to set aside (p. 103) the hypothesis that 'the centre of gravity of a kinship system lies in the terminology (or only when it is 'simple'), in favour of a search for 'fundamental categories' (which are underlying categories).

3 Marriage rules and intermarriage, where once again the significance of the obvious differences is questioned. Are these 'so-called "rules" ... a requirement of etiquette or an index of rank more than a functional item in kinship organization?' (p. 112).

The problem with the first statement is that affinity may well have a diachronic dimension in any relatively self-contained community or region, even if it requires a computer to reveal the connections. But intentional repetition at adjacent or even alternate generations is something very different, both for the actor and for the observer, from a loosely structured and possibly unconscious repetition over time of marriages within a certain range of individuals defined by kinship, locality or nationality. Either the thrust of our argument or our use of the computer may lead us to neglect the role of intentionality and to obscure, in Parsons' terms (derived from Weber), the differences between social action and behaviour. While this is certainly not relevant in every circumstance, it seems problematical to jump, as Dumont does in the second point, from the level of explicit to 'underlying categories' when the terminology is no longer 'simple', even if only because no limits are then set to the search. In his third point the author similarly suggests that by interpreting one set of marriage rules as 'functional' and the other as marginal ('etiquette') one can resolve the apparent difference between them. In each case the procedure by which differences are taken to be superficial (surface) and then ironed out in favour of a more profound unity (the deep structure) seems to be questionable both from an analytic and from a theoretical point of view.

As we found before, the same line of reasoning finally leads Dumont to apply the term alliance even to the North because 'affinity has something of a diachronic dimension: it does not, as with us or as is generally supposed, disappear into consanguinity for the next generation' (p. 95). This statement points a finger at an important problem in the study of kinship. The immediate context of his remarks is the analysis of the funeral ceremonies for a Brahmin who, since he has no domestic priest, has to have certain rituals carried out either by a sister's husband or by a father's sister's husband, involving a linking of roles which he understands as incorporating a 'diachronic' element in affinity. But this is surely a matter of the use of the analytic category of 'affines', and the manner in which this translation of the terminology chooses to insist on the relations between brothers-in-law in both generations, rather than of any handing down of affinal status. The general problem relates to perspective as well as to terminology and classification. Whether in Europe or in North India, my wife's brother becomes (or rather is) my son's mother's brother; the same individual is in one role (relationship) for me, another for my son, and the 'diachrony' has to do with reproduction, with the developmental cycle. Someone linked in one way to me (affinity) is linked in a different way to my son. Dumont's argument appears to confound ego's view of comparable roles in different generations with the view held of the same actor by individuals of different generations. It is confusion based on a failure to differentiate roles from positions (where an individual holder may fill a plurality of roles, but only one status).[3]

In a recent study of a community in North India, Parry (1979) claims that one dimension of 'alliance', the group dimension, does exist among the Rajputs of Kangra. While he does not specifically suggest that this demonstration strengthens the unity argument, his discussion brings out some relevant points which relate to the level of generality at which the analysis is pitched. He claims to have shown, contrary to the ideas of Dumont and of Tambiah (1973:93), that in this northern group there is 'a pattern of cumulative alliances between subclans' who marry hypergamously (Parry 1979:297).[4] Nevertheless there is no ideology of alliance and no apparent manifestation in the kinship terminology.

His demonstration of 'cumulative alliance' certainly holds. But it also holds for the work of Heritier on the Omaha system of the Samo of Burkino Faso (1981), despite the fact the Lévi-Strauss (1966:19) has referred to the 'perpetual turbulence' of systems with Crow–Omaha marriage rules. And perhaps, more surprising, it holds too for the work of Segalen on Brittany in the recent past (1985).

Such demonstrations raise two points. First, at this level we are dealing with regularities that are found in a large number of widely separated and relatively stationary communities. Secondly, it is important to insist upon the differences between the overt rules of the actor and the discovered rules of the observer, however one sees the two as linked at a deep structural level. As Parry suggests, in the Indian case we may be dealing with affinities of a very general kind (1979:286), referring to the relations between 'elementary' and 'complex' systems in general, which he sees as an over-rigid dichotomy (p. 312).[5] A very similar pattern of repeated alliances, he notes, is to be found in other systems with 'rules of exogamy' of the Crow–Omaha type; and he refers to the discovery that the Tallensi are a case in point, based on the earlier finding of Dumont that there is an alliance aspect to the mother's brother-sister's son (MB/ZS) relationship in West Africa (p. 312). But we are perhaps dealing on a level of even greater generality, of observer-oriented generality, at which most 'patterns' merge into an overall unity. In West Africa, whether we are dealing with 'Omaha' systems of the Tallensi type or Crow systems of the Lobi type, the actors obviously recognise that adjacent descent groups repeatedly intermarry, and that ego's wife's brother is his son's mother's brother, but it is also the different *rhythms* of repetition and the different *implications* for marriage choice (explicit, not implicit) that are present to the actors and that are communicated to the observers. In India too, there are important and significant differences related to these systems on which Karve (1953) and more recently Trautmann (1981) are right to insist.

Looking at the 'deeper' level of continent-wide unity, Dumont claimed to be initiating a change from a 'functional' to a 'structural' approach. Since that time a further shift in kinship studies in India claims to move from the 'structural' to a 'cultural' approach; to put the matter in more personal terms, the change is from Dumont to Schneider. Approaches that privilege the underlying in accounting for, or even discounting, the 'surface' are not limited to structural analyses. However, in every case these approaches assume a kind of directionality which is sometimes circular and often evaluative. In their study of Bengali kinship, a very different part of the North to those we have discussed, Inden and Nicholas speak of Bengalis as sharing an all-Indian 'culture of kinship' which stretches backwards in time to the ancient Sanskrit period (1977:xii) and includes even Muslim Bengalis (1977:90). Of course they recognise that change has taken place and that Muslims have their own pecularities, but 'a single coherent pattern of symbols' underlies the variants. Other accounts treat culture in more culture-specific terms. In another analysis of Bengal, Fruzzetti and Östör (1976a, b and c) claim that Schneider's contribution was to challenge the assumption that 'something called "kinship" exists in every society as a way of classifying people and groups through consanguinity, affinity, descent, filiation and the like . . . Kinship in these terms is the creation of the investigator, not the property of native social systems' (1976b:96). The problem is seen in the following light. 'Much of the anthropological corpus on kinship suffers from what Lévi-Strauss called, in a different context, the distortion of a semantic field. Until recently, it was generally assumed that kinship deals with basic social problems such as incest, the allocation of rights over the reproductive process and its results, and the division and classification of people, groups, lineages and so on resulting from these prohibitions and allocations. It was also held that different societies solve the same basic problems in different ways, and that this diversity can be analysed genealogically, if not universally in the same manner, at least in the particular social equivalents of genealogy' (1976b:96). This assumption, which is what Fortes (1969) had earlier called 'the genealogical fallacy', has been attacked, they claim, from several angles of which Schneider's cultural approach is the most radical of the attempts to come to terms with kinship as 'something other than the most exact, measurable, concrete and quanti-fiable field in anthropology' (1976b:96). But while holding that earlier views of 'kinship' are the creation of the investigator, these authors themselves assume that there may be 'domains of kin relations' (p. 96) in different societies which are susceptible to comparative research and analysis in cultural terms.

We find ourselves here in the middle of the *pons asinorum* of social research, the apparently irresolvable conflict between 'objectivist' and 'sub-jectivist' interpretation, a bridge which every investigator nevertheless manages to limp across in some way or other if only because he has to do so in order to carry out any type of enquiry, except perhaps one that limits itself to a recording on tape and a transcription of every conceivable interaction. The examination of the actor categories in their own terms is a worthwhile, indeed essential, task, but it does not exhaust the analytic possibilities. In trying to stay as close as possible to the native concepts, it is still necessary to make a rough translation of the terms (for example *bhai* into 'brother') in order to obtain a minimal degree of communication even with oneself. Exactly how the more general problem of crossing the bridge of fools is resolved will depend upon the questions we ask and their interest for future research. There is no indication that the 'cultural' questions raised by these authors have any greater validity or interest than the sociological, economic or political questions posed by other investigators. Certainly, the idea that in the domain of kinship there is a Bengali account, a thing in itself, which is independent of socio-economic or religious factors, seems highly debatable. It is a pity that difficulties with the muddles in the models (of which there are many) should have led to a reluctance to propose any models at all other than a 'cultural' one, in the elucidation of which every ethnographer is engaged, but in a task that can never be his only aim.

In their own enquiry Fruzzetti and Östör attempt to analyse the 'cultural' domain of kinship in a Bengali town. They make the point, as we have done for Nandol, that to describe marriage in general as hypergamous on the basis of kin terms and flows of gifts in each particular union, and from that description to derive status differences between actual wife-giving and wife-taking groups on the ground is to distort the evidence. Equal status may well be the result, even though every father-in-law sees himself as superior to his son-in-law (or vice versa, since cultural viewpoints are certainly not undifferentiated). For group relations are not necessarily affected by the role or status differences between individuals which may balance themselves over time, be cancelled out by other considerations or be largely irrelevant in yet other contexts. But while the attempt to specify Bengali concepts in the 'kin domain' is altogether admirable, it is not clear why this endeavour should present an alternative, radical or not, to more 'exact, measurable . . . etc.' studies, and why 'basic social problems' should be excluded. There is no one way in which the system 'really works'. Whose definition of reality would we be dealing with? At one point locality is declared to be 'an aspect of the Bengali domain of kinship' (1976b:127). The authors find that the Bengali notion confirms Dumont's statement (derived from what socio-cultural universe?) that 'locality is clearly subordinated to kinship' (Dumont 1964:76). But in this case we are comparing what is claimed to be Bengali ideology, translated into English academic usage, with Dumont's analytic statements. Nothing much seems to have changed.

Moving from a single cultural account of Bengali kinship, they attempt a comparison with Tamil Nadu in the South, based on an examination of 'ideologies' (p. 130). In so doing they are forced to work at a highly 'objectivist' level, 'not at surface aggregation . . . but at the level of structure' (1976c:160). At this level, they discover, 'the same kind of things passed between parent and child' (p. 160); and that there is a 'common stress and emphasis on alliance' (p. 160). In making these observations of the world, they claim to depend upon Schneider's methodological prescription: 'question every proposition that our own ideology places outside itself as "natural"' (p. 161). The injunction is sound, the results are meagre. In the first place the comparison remains at the level, whether of 'ideologies' or 'concepts', of high generality (as distinct from broad generalisation). Secondly, practice takes second place to 'talking about' practice. Thirdly, kinship again tends to be treated as a separable domain, setting aside the need to investigate the connections with other 'domains'. As a result, we are presented with a rather similar version of the unity of Indian kinship to that of Dumont. The comparison of ideologies, of the content of kin ideologies, is interesting up to a certain point. But it remains a comparison of sets of concepts, without asking questions about the role of controllers, creators and carriers of those ideologies, much less with what these systems of reproduction have to do with systems of production. Is dowry analysed? Is land or class discussed? This is where Gough's studies of kinship and modes of production in South India (1978, 1981), which we shall discuss in the next chapter, provide a necessary counterbalance, because they put kinship back into the context of history and of the comparative study of the past and present of social institutions and cultures. For there is no need to look upon 'functional', 'structural', 'cultural' and Marxist models as alternatives to one another; rather they are different facets of a comprehensive approach to marriage and the family – or at least they raise different hypotheses to be investigated. To view them as competing theories producing alternative answers is to misunderstand not only their nature but the nature of practical theory.

Siblings and property in Sri Lanka

Having reviewed some general approaches to Indian kinship that relate to the question of unity and diversity, let us examine the empirical material. The explicit differences between the South and North turn on a pattern of close marriages (in particular between cross-cousins) as distinct from the prohibition in the North (and in the main Hindu texts) on marriage to kin, certainly near kin, although of course in both areas marriages have to be made within the caste, or sub-unit thereof. That meant in the North an individual was prohibited not only from marrying close relatives within the unilineal descent group (as in China), but also under the *sapiṇḍa* system, members of the mother's and other related lineages. As it was put in Nandol, 'we do not marry "blood relatives" (*lohi sagai*)'. In positive terms, you had to marry members of your marriage circle (*gor*) who lived outside your village.

While this particular practice differentiates the South from the North, there is another feature relating to a woman's property that differentiates Sri Lanka from India, although some aspects of the customary situation in South India provide a bridge between the two. I refer to the rights of women in Sri Lanka, among both Hindu and Buddhist communities, to the same kind as well as the same quantity of property as their brothers, land as well as movables. Just as we have a close association between marriage rules and kin terminology in the first case, so here we have a firm link between women's property rights in land and bilateral forms of social organisation, as compared with their virtual exclusion from land and the patrilineal lineages operating in the North, a state of affairs embodied in the Hindu texts (Tambiah 1973).

There are clearly some links between these two sets of features. The notion of *sapiṇḍa*, promoted by the *Mitākṣarā* school of the eleventh and twelfth centuries which may have changed understandings of the system of prohibitions (Lardinois 1986a:524), presumes a patrilineal group of agnates (Sontheimer 1977:190): both cross-cousin marriage and a woman's rights to property are linked to the brother–sister relationship, because the union of the children of brother and sister in a sense re-affirms the bond that has been attenuated by the incest taboo and the insistance on marriage to outsiders. And one level at which this coming together works is on that of property, since sisters have a more or less equal entitlement to their brothers.

Before pursuing the range of these North–South differences and their links with other variables, I want to look at the nature of the critical brother–sister relationship in Sri Lanka, with particular reference to Yalman's valuable study of Sinhalese society (1967), partly because it raises some of the general issues with which we have been concerned, partly because it emphasises the different features of the South as a whole and attempts to apply the same kind of 'deep structural' analysis that lies behind many discussions of the unity of kinship in the sub-continent, and partly because it takes us ethnographically into the 'extreme' case of Sri Lanka on which the discussions of Leach, Tambiah and Trautmann are also based.

Yalman tries to explain the social organisation of communities in Sri Lanka and more generally in South India by reference to a 'traditional structure', a set of common elements, which is seen as being more 'basic' than the variations between these communities. The structure, which lies behind both thought and act, consists of 'a limited set of principles' (p. 376) whose 'logical permutations' produce the variations found in the range of social systems. Like language (a comparison that is often employed) 'the principles are clearly not embedded in the utilitarian particularities of specific social systems' but are 'fundamental principles of organisation'; social structure thus corresponds to grammar. It is deep structure, common structure, which undergoes a series of transformations to produce sets of variants.

Leaving aside the questions of the 'fit' of the linguistic analogy and of the approach to structure as a generalised 'genetic' model (whether this be seen mechanically as a camshaft or generatively as a grammar), what are these 'fundamental principles of social organisation' on which society is constructed? There are many references to particular principles, for example 'caste principles' (p. 375) which include 'the principles of caste endogamy'. Then there are the 'general principles of kinship' (p. 375) which include 'the emphasis on the connections between the children of the brother and the sister' (p. 374); as in the case of the Coorgs, the siblings are seen as separated by incest prohibitions and their children united by marriage, thus intertwining 'the double principles of consanguinity and affinity' (p. 374). And these double principles are themselves perhaps an aspect of 'those divine creative principles' (p. 374), male and female.

Turning to his more specific comments, the 'crucial indices' (that is, the fundamental principles) of this general structure are:

1 cross-cousin categories that are associated with the systematic Dravidian terminology and marriage rites.
2 the formally recognised rights and obligations between mother's brother and sister's son, father's sister and brother's daughter and between cross-cousins of either type. (p. 342)

These in turn can be reduced to 'the fundamental principles of organisation in the family, cross-cousin marriage, the insistence on the mutual claims of brother and sister on one another's children' (p. 333).[6] And these again, he suggests, can perhaps be reduced to what Dumont calls 'affinity', a term which he would translate, very differently it would seem, as 'rights and obligations between brothers and sisters' (p. 358). In 'affinity' we come to something very close to Radcliffe-Brown's 'principle' of 'the unity of siblings', as Yalman himself recognises (p. 359). Since most if not all sibling relations display a solidarity, equivalence, unity of this kind, the concept cannot carry much weight as an explicandum of the characteristics of particular societies, especially when it is difficult to assess the relative strength of that principle.

The problem involves one's general view of the analysis of social processes, whether this goes under the name of methodology or theory. That is to say, the question reaches down to the core of one's understanding of the three levels: social interaction, relationships and the socio-cultural system, as well as of the methods available for such an understanding. If I assume that what we are observing is a set of 'expressions of underlying principles', transformations of the elements of a deep structure, the product of the camshaft behind the jigsaw puzzle, if one adopts such a highly 'rationalist' approach, one is in danger of falling into the kind of analysis offered by Parsons, among many others, where the elements of the scheme seem capable of infinite proliferation, where abstract notions and invisible entities tend to get reified, and where the level of generality and ambiguity of central concepts makes the resulting accounts capable of fitting almost any situation. I am not concerned to deny all utility to these notions, but rather to assess their validity, to avoid circularity in their employment and to draw attention to what I consider their limitations.

There is an alternative. If we see notions like filiation or the brother–sister bond not so much as abstractions from the data but as interactive ways of examining those data, then what is at issue at any point is the nature and degree of abstraction or the adequacy of the concepts that are required for a particular explanatory purpose. Our 'principles' (such as the unity of the sibling group) become relevant for particular rather than for general tasks, at specific levels of the hierarchy of understanding. Of course as with the elements of deep structure, such notions may be imported at more or at less appropriate moments. But what is at stake is the way we understand such concepts, their epistemological status once we have imported them, and the consequences for the analysis and understanding of social behaviour.

Yalman draws attention to the differences in the mutual claims of brothers and sisters among the 'wealthy' and the 'poor', arguing that these 'turn on the attitudes toward women, and this is expressed in the daughters' rights in the inheritance' (1967:131). Let us be clear on what is being said. The difference between rich and poor 'turns on' differences in attitudes towards women (above it was the position of women), and this difference is 'expressed' in the way property is transmitted. Yalman goes on to show that 'in principle, all daughters share alike with their brothers in the estates of the father and the mother. In this sense the basic pattern for both rich and poor is bilateral.' In practice this is true only of the poor and in wealthy families only of daughters who do not marry out and take their dowry with them. Those who remain in *binna* marriage do not take anything from the estate, although their entitlement to do so remains and they are the ones who 'inherit'.

As Yalman observes, the significance of this point depends upon how much dowry a daughter takes with her at marriage. If it is a large amount, then she is more than compensated for not receiving any share in the inheritance at a later date. In reality, he says, there is no simple generalisation about how large the dowry will be, 'it depends entirely on the status of the son-in-law' (and vice versa). 'For our purpose the important point is that in wealthy families the size of the dowry is controlled by the father, or the brothers, and that, in terms of succession, the sons are thought to be the principal heirs of the intestate property.' He sees this as 'a distinct preference for patrilineal ideals' among the richer classes, which may even go as far as 'excluding the daughters from the property of the father'; that is to say, the father's property goes to the sons while the daughters are entitled to the property of the mother. This pattern (which he describes as 'sex-differentiated double unilineal') is however rare. But he views it as providing evidence of a greater agnatic emphasis among the upper strata where 'unmarried women are, as it were, "owned" by the groups of men'; it is 'men who control the fate of daughters or sisters for their own purposes, and men who decide the size of the dowry'. At the same time the situation is 'inextricably related to the ideas of caste and family prestige and purity' (pp. 132–3).

While there is certainly a difference in emphasis in the upper, propertyowning groups, Yalman like others (Tambiah 1973:131) perhaps overstresses the dominant role of the male as controlling women. The system of homoparental transmission, that is, father to son, mother to daughter, is not necessarily an indication of inequality or dominance, if women are entitled to the same share and kind of property as men: indeed as Tambiah points out (1973:134), this separation may provide a protection for a woman's children in the case of plural marriage, since it prevents what she brought in being dispersed among the offspring of other 'beds'. The absence of a dowry for women who stay in the house and make filiacentric unions (which they can do even if they have male siblings) puts them in the same class as their brothers; it may also be an indication of greater freedom of choice, which is certainly the case with those women who start as away-marrying brides leaving the natal house and then later return with their husbands, changing their relationship to the family when they do so (Tambiah 1973:131). Even in the former case (*deega* or away-marrying) a woman may not necessarily take her dowry at the time of marriage but may leave it with her brothers to be inherited later on, a feature that seems linked to the general flexibility of marriage, divorce and residence since nothing is committed, only promised, although in a highly advantageous marriage it is necessary to seal the agreement with immediate delivery.

If one were looking for a dominant (though not the sole) factor on which the system turned, the differences in rich and poor would seem to relate 'primarily' to property, the distribution of which affects or restricts certain attitudes; at the very least property and attitudes should be considered as co-ordinate with one another. Indeed Yalman says as much when he comes to deal with 'The position of the daughter among laborers'. The lower orders in Terutenne treat their daughters with much less care and attention than do the higher orders. The rich try to arrange suitable marriages for their daughters, but the poor, lacking property, are unable to engage extensively in such social maneuvers' (1967:133). In the absence of adequate property the difference between marriage at home (*binna*) and marriage outside (*deega* or *diga*) is lost, so all daughters share the same position with regard to inheritance.

If one views inheritance and dowry as being part of the same process of devolution over time, then from the standpoint of entitlements it does not matter whether a girl takes her portion at marriage or at the death of the parent. At another level the difference is important since a later transfer leaves the parents with greater resources in their hands and the wife with possibly less commitment to her marriage, in that less is committed to the conjugal estate or to the daughter herself. Clearly, the greater the property, the greater the attempt to control marital arrangements, by both mother and father. And since marriage involves some matching, or at least a comparison, of valued considerations, it is not surprising that here as elsewhere, and especially in the case of the rich, property may have to be committed at the time of the marriage itself. In many upper groups a woman tends to be granted her property earlier (at marriage) rather than later (as an inheritance), since it is often by the transfer of property that a good (or advantageous) marriage is made and sealed. The result may be greater initial control by the parents of the marriage arrangements. But the early transfer of wealth may mean more freedom for the daughter after the marriage has taken place, though less so than we find in the parallel case of the son when there has been the early handing over (premortem transmission) of rights in a farm. Because for a woman, greater freedom from parents may mean greater dependence on the husband, especially where property is involved; or to put it another way, the couple is less dependent if they have control of the capital resources of either spouse; the earlier transfer of wealth may well give the young couple 'a better start in life' since they can use an early endowment for investment as well as for consumption. The alternative is to base the marriage upon a promise (of an inheritance) rather than a transfer (of a dowry), giving rise to a lengthier dependency of the junior upon the senior, parental, generation.

These different arrangements may be linked to different attitudes towards women. But to imply that the latter constitute the independent or underlying variable, especially when they are so difficult to assess, seems tenuous. The situation emerges more clearly if we rephrase earlier discussions based on bilaterality, patrilineality and double descent in favour of one dealing with the differences in the possibilities and strategies for the acquisition and holding of property in particular socio-cultural contexts, and their relation to different interpersonal arrangements and attitudes, without however assuming that this constitutes the only relevant factor. Undoubtedly these possibilities are linked to the organisation of kin groups, as Tambiah (1973) has suggested for India, Sri Lanka and Burma in respect of women's property rights. But in discussing inheritance we need first to look at the domestic level and then take into account wider political and religious considerations. For example, the exclusion of daughters from their paternal property (that is, from their father's as distinct from their mother's possessions) is hardly of great moment from the standpoint of equality if one assumes that the marriage of the parents was arranged as a match with property in mind. If the parental contributions are equivalent, then a daughter can take her share from father, mother or from the joint estate without compromising her equal treatment. At least that is the case in most isogamous unions but not in those romantic cases where a poor and beautiful girl marries a rich or influential man, hypergamy but of a very different kind than that reported from North India and which bears some resemblance (though the distribution of wealth is reversed) to the impoverished European aristocrat marrying a rich American heiress. Otherwise the difference to the daughter may be small, although this sex-specific method of transmission has some importance in preserving a particular estate in agnatic hands. In the case of a virilocal marriage, the homoparental transmission of land (that is to say, the devolution of a father's property to his sons) ensures that the productive core of the estate has a greater chance of remaining intact. At the same time the daughter is perhaps more likely to marry a son of her mother's brother (that is, to agree to a father's sister's daughter's marriage) in order to retrieve her mother's portion which might otherwise be absorbed by her brothers, a possibility to which Yalman himself draws attention (1967:135).

If for the purposes of transmission (but not of management) the property of man and wife are kept distinct and not merged (what I call a dual rather than a joint conjugal fund), a feature that is linked to the bilateral transmission of land, there are important implications for 'the very concept of "marriage"' (p. 133). The relative looseness of the 'conjugal fund' is linked to the looseness of the union itself. In Sri Lanka, in contrast to the upper groups in India, marriage is not seen as a powerful, indissoluble bond; the concept of a marriage 'in which their separate properties are united and which clearly defines the heirs to the property as the joint heirs of the couple (to the exclusion of "illegitimate" children, for example) has no place in the Kandyan way of thinking' (p. 134). The exact relationship of man and wife is of no importance; neither is a woman's status as concubine or wife. 'The property remains distinct and the inheritance goes to all equally' (p. 134). Hence ordinary people can dispense with the marriage ceremony altogether. Note the relation of this distinct conjugal property to the freedom to divorce as well as to concepts of illegitimacy, a relation we have considered in the context of the tighter varieties of conjugal fund found elsewhere in the East.

A situation where women acquire land as part of their dowry or, to a lesser extent, as part of their inheritance, obviously creates difficulties for their natal families since it entails splitting the family estate, though the consequences of such division are modified when their entitlement is to what their mother brought, especially so where she is a close relative. If they marry nearby, the problems are fewer. When women in Sri Lanka marry at a distance, then two main possibilities exist. Firstly the land allocated to a daughter marrying away may be exchanged or sold: alternatively, the estate may remain undivided while the bride relies upon her brothers to cultivate her plot and to provide her with an income; in other words she forgoes her claim to the land itself (at least temporarily) in return for other benefits. This latter solution brings its own problems related to the joint family of coparceners. For 'the property may actually remain formally undivided among the siblings for many years after the death of the parent' (p. 134), even though the shares of each child are in principle separate. This situation often brings trouble, not only between the brother and sister but also between a woman and her husband, her children and her brothers (p. 135).

The position with regard to property clearly affects the quality of the tie between an individual and his or her maternal uncle. For this relationship acquires 'a special significance when property remains undivided between the mother and the MB. Under such circumstances there is the latent possibility for unresolved conflict between them' (p. 153). In other words, its quality depends upon whether or not the cross-sibling estate has been divided. The situation is somewhat analogous to the one described for Africa, both for those matrilineal societies where the property of the mother's brother is handed over to the sister's son only after death, and for those patrilineal ones where a man passes on virtually nothing to his sister's sons, that is, the children of the female members of his own descent or sibling group. These differences I have earlier attempted to analyse in terms of the position of the residual sibling, linking it to the differences in the nature of the tie of a man with his mother's brother.[7]

These two relationships, brother and sister, sister's child and mother's brother, are linked together on a much wider basis than inheritance alone. Looked at in developmental terms the one grows out of the other, depends upon the other, a view which in India is frequently expressed by the people themselves. A recognition of the fact must lead us to qualify the approach of some 'alliance' theorists that treats the relationship with the mother's brother purely in terms of affinity. One way of doing just that is to offer the same equation as Yalman, namely, affinity=brother–sister tie. But this translation seems an overly drastic tampering with common usage when other solutions are at hand.

I ended the last chapter with a discussion of the continuing bond between brother and sister in the North, maintaining that analytically it provided an indication that women are not completely cut off from their natal homes; they are neither 'given' nor 'sold', for they do not abandon ties of kinship in acquiring those of conjugality. In the North women did not normally inherit land. Nor did they take it as dowry – equally a form of devolution but occurring earlier in the developmental cycle. However, at least among the upper groups in Sri Lanka, a woman's dowry may include land which she can also receive as a gift. The inclusion of land is not only a matter of acquiring rights in the basic means of agricultural production, important as that may be. For the acquisition of rights in immovables, especially at marriage, has quite different organisational implications than those in movables. Unless she effects an exchange, or leaves management in the hands of a brother, their effective exploitation involves marrying nearby. The union of cross-cousins brings together in one conjugal fund the property as well as the sentiments that had earlier been dispersed through the out-marriages of a brother and a sister.[8]

Where marriage is predominantly virilocal, the devolution of land to women, whether they receive it as full or as residual (brotherless) heirs, creates logistic problems which can be partly relieved by marriage to a cross-cousin or by other forms of 'close' union. Of course, such consider-ations are not the only ones behind the distribution, the ideology or the practice of such marriages. They are found throughout the South and in many other areas where women do not receive a landed dowry. While I shall try to show that some similar considerations are involved in South India, it is difficult to envisage any satisfactory single-factor explanation of a human institution that is distributed as widely as this, whether we are looking at one society or at many. The inheritance of land by women can certainly occur without close marriage and vice versa. But there is evidence to show that some cousin marriages are made expressly to keep the property undivided and thus to reinforce the joint interests of the siblings.

I have suggested that similar factors may affect brother–sister relations even where the landed dowry is absent. In most landowning groups in South India it is only brotherless women who, as epiclerates, as appointed daugh-ters (*putrikā*), could acquire the land of their fathers, or rather who could act as intermediaries for the transmission of such land to their sons, to the sister's son (*putrikāputra*), by contracting a filiacentric union with an in-coming son-in-law (*ghar jāmāi*). But the very fact that, firstly, they receive movable wealth in the form of dowry and, secondly, that they receive (or transmit) rights in land under circumstances that are special but not in-frequent, means that they must in some sense be aware of a submerged claim that they have otherwise given up in favour of their brothers, an awareness that is well brought out in the biblical story of the daughters of Zelophehad which gives explicit recognition to this problem (Goody 1962:319). Even where they have a right to land as dowry or inheritance, women sometimes allow this claim to rest dormant in favour of more diffuse support from their siblings. When sisters forego, or are made to forego, their rights to land, they exercise a more continuing claim on their brothers and more generally on their natal families. On the other hand, by taking the land (that is, one's share, portion, lot), they may be seen to be cutting off the links that tie them and denying themselves any future support from that quarter. That must always be the extreme case, but in Sri Lanka no such formal breach occurs

since they have the 'option' of claiming a share in the inheritance by
returning with their dowry to their natal homes, a situation which from the
standpoint of property (but not of residence) is broadly parallel to that
obtaining under the optational system of the Parisian region of France under
the *ancien régime* (Yver 1966).

The question of reuniting what has earlier been separated affects the
wider South as well. Of the Coorgs of South India Srinivas writes that
cross-cousin marriage actually helps to overcome the breach in the brother–
sister bond caused by their obligation to marry out (1952:147; see also
Yalman 1967:153; Beck 1972:240); it may be said that the wound takes a
generation to heal. Such an interpretation of cross-cousin marriage is very
different from one that rests on the idea that women are exchanged between
male groups, but it seems more appropriate to the form of the practice found
in the relatively complex societies of South India, as distinct from the
hunting and gathering communities of Australia, whatever may be the
connections, real or assumed, between Dravidian and Australian systems.[9]
As I have remarked, practices of such generality change their functions with
changes in the productive systems and in a host of other factors.

The continuing importance of the brother–sister tie in matrilineal societies has been emphasised by various writers, especially by Malinowski on
the Trobriands of Papua New Guinea (1927), Gough on the Nayar of Kerala
(1961), Richards on the Bemba of Zambia (1950) and by Fortes on the
Ashanti of Ghana (1950). Others have stressed the importance of this key
relationship in bilateral societies (e.g. Pehrson 1954, 1957). But it is equally
clear from the evidence we have cited in the previous chapters that the same
is true of the patrilineal societies of North India. This fact must lead us to
modify the notion of those writers who speak about marriage as the exchange of women, with special reference to 'patrilineal' societies, and treat
women (in Lévi-Strauss' terms) as units of exchange between male oper-
ators (1956). Such a conception, such a practice, would leave little room for
any continuation of the brother–sister bond after marriage. Yet the evidence
for continuation seems very clear from India, although this is one of the
areas where these notions of 'total exchange' have been most vigorously
applied. In certain patrilineal societies in Africa we perhaps come nearer to
a brother–sister split leading some authors to refer to the incorporation of
women in their husband's kin group (Gluckman 1950; Leach 1957; Fallers
1957). However, there is a danger of confusing spatial separation (often
temporary) with the ending of a social relationship. Movement between
domestic groups is not the same thing as movement between kin; unlike
slavery and many forms of adoption and minor marriage in China, marriage
does not normally involve the dissolution (as distinct from the attenuation)
of earlier ties but rather the creation of new ones (albeit within a prescribed

pattern). Nor yet, as we have seen, does the prohibition on divorce (in China, India and Europe) or the presence of the levirate (among the Arabs and Israelites) constitute any indication of a wholesale transfer of women from one group to another.

The North and South

Unity and division

Having looked at the 'special' situation of Sri Lanka, let us pursue the question of the differences and similarities between North and South. Clearly there are many of each, because we are dealing with a huge area and a vast population on the one hand, and with the results of the advance of the Hindu (and Buddhist and Islamic) North, not only politically and militarily but in the dominating role played over at least two millennia by the written products of Brahmin scholars which are normative both as religious texts and as juridical and political guidelines. We are dealing at once with the problems of the hegemonic and the aboriginal cultures, as well as of the centre and the periphery.

Some are tempted to look upon the differences as 'surface' variations on a 'deeper' unity. This approach has been adopted not only by the authors we have mentioned but in different ways by Yalman for Sri Lanka (1967) and by Tambiah for a wider 'Indian' world that includes Burma and Southeast Asia (1973). But it is also possible to argue that this approach tends to overlook the fundamental nature of certain differences, especially when we are dealing with elements of family systems that anthropologists elsewhere have considered so central, that between what Karve calls immediate and extended exchange, between close and distant, endogamous and exogamous, marriage, which are associated with very different methods of classifying kin. The question of surface differences versus underlying similarities does not seem a very profitable one to pursue, especially given the values attached to those terms and the lack of any adequate theory of transformation; it seems a less important enterprise than trying to specify and if possible 'explain' the variations and similarities themselves.

There are many ways of looking at the regions of India (Crane 1967), including the dimension of plains and hills, which here as elsewhere correspond to core and peripheral areas of complex agriculture, the 'civilised' as against the refuge and tribal areas. But the choice of North and South has been dictated by the interest in systems of marriage and the associated terminologies which largely follow the linguistic divide, which in turn may be linked to some physical difference (Cohen 1967).

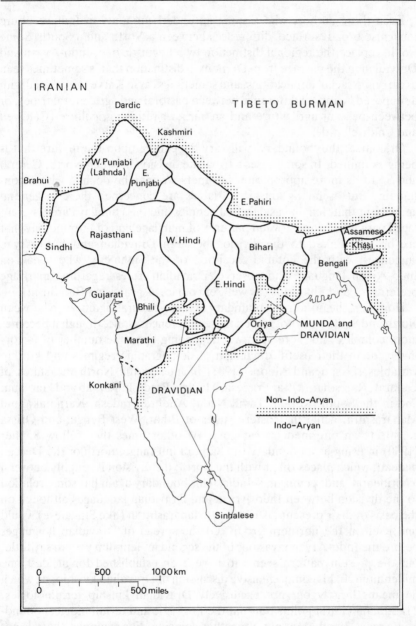

Map 3 Map of the Indo-Aryan languages

Even those authors who assume an underlying unity in Indian culture recognise broad 'surface' differences between a North and a South. Some would replace the regional distinction by a linguistic one, Indo-Aryan and Dravidian in the passage from Dumont, a distinction that is sometimes seen as carrying 'racial' implications, and sometimes (as in Karve) associated with a supposed historical difference between pastoral and agricultural tribes, or between peasant agriculture and an earlier shifting agriculture (Caldwell and Caldwell n.d.).

Of course, the 'boundary' will vary depending upon the feature that is being examined. In some cases a tripartite division between North, Central and South is more appropriate; in others we may be dealing with a continuum. But as far as kinship variables are concerned there is general agreement that, leaving aside tribal peoples and the Himalaya area, we are faced with a division between patterns of marriage and of terminology that are broadly linked to the division between Dravidian and Indo-Aryan languages, with the notable exception of the Sinhalese, who speak an Indo-Aryan language and observe 'Dravidian' rules regarding marriage preferences and kin terms (as well, of course, as practising Buddhism).

However, the notion of a boundary of socio-cultural significance between North and South does not rest on these differences alone, though it becomes more complex and more arbitrary depending upon the number of factors involved. In their useful discussion of demographic regimes and kinship variables, Dyson and Moore (1983) include in the North the states of Gujarat, Rajasthan, Uttar Pradesh, Madhya Pradesh, Punjab and Haryana; and in the South, Kerala, Tamil Nadu, Andhra Pradesh, Karnataka and Maharashtra, while the eastern states of Bihar, West Bengal and Orissa constitute an intermediary category. At other times they follow Sopher (1980) in using as a boundary the Satpura hill range, north of the Deccan plateau, which places Bihar with the North; the division is roughly between 'continental' and 'peninsular' India. This boundary again has some relation to the division between Indo-Aryan and Dravidian languages although on the basis of their present distribution, Maharashtran (like Sinhalese) would find itself in the northern group. Of the spread of Dravidian languages before the Indo-Aryan invasions of the second millennium we can say little, but the present pattern seems to have been established for at least one millennium. In his comprehensive discussion of Dravidian kinship, by which he means largely but not exclusively Dravidian kinship terminologies, Trautmann (1981) points out that the linguistic and terminological boundaries (maps 3 and 4) do not altogether coincide. For example, there is not only the case of Sri Lanka, but the non-Brahmin castes of Maharashtra, some communities in Saurashtra (Gujarat) and other groups (Konkani Brahmin, Baiga, Khond and Kurukh) in the 'frontier zone' use an Indo-

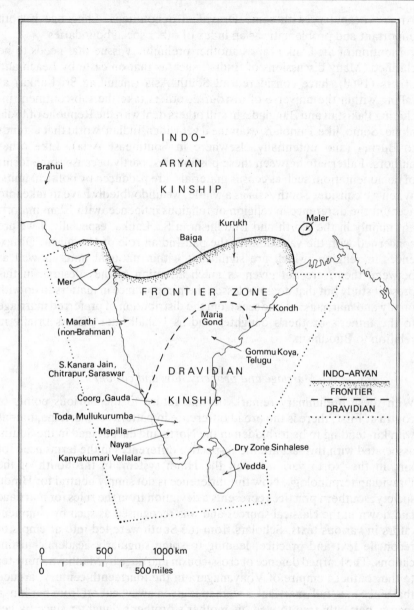

Map 4 Map of the Dravidian kinship region

Aryan vocabulary with some Dravidian denotations. Language is both important and problematic as an index of other social boundaries.

Mention of Sri Lanka raises another preliminary issue that needs to be clarified. Many discussions of 'India', such as that on caste by Leach and others (1960), have considered all South Asia (including Sri Lanka) as falling within the universe of discourse; others take the sub-continent including Pakistan and Bangladesh; still others deal with the Republic of India alone. Some, like Tambiah, examine a yet wider 'Indian' world that extends to Burma (and potentially elsewhere in South-east Asia). Like other authors, I alternate between these possibilities, partly because some forms of documentation, such as census materials, are produced by political units. When we consider South Asia as a whole, we undoubtedly have to take into account the difference in religion or religious influence, with Islam important mainly in the North and Buddhism in Sri Lanka, especially if we are concerned with the variations in the pan-Indian role of Hinduism. Differences in religion, which are significant within national units as well as between them, are not given as much attention as they deserve in this present study but that does not lessen their importance in matters to do with family and marriage, as one sees from the distribution of preferred marriage to the father's brother's daughter and as I shall later discuss briefly in relation to Buddhism.

Marriage and property: law and custom

With these preliminary remarks let me return to the obvious points of contrast. First, there is the broad difference in patterns of marriage, unions with kin tending to be forbidden in the North and encouraged in the South; associated with this fact are the respective differences in the terms used for kin, in the North variations on the Hindi system, in the South of the Dravidian terminology. Now this difference is not simply neutral for Hindu society; southern practice represents a deviation from the rules for marriage laid down in the classical sources and was recognised as such by commentators in various texts. Scholars from the South were led into attempts to reconcile text and practice, leading to some singularly academic justifications. The learned defence of cross-cousin marriage by Mādhava, minister to the southern empire of Vijayanagara in the fourteenth century, argued that since in a 'full' marriage a woman is given away, cut off from her kin, a man is perfectly free to wed his mother's brother's daughter since by her marriage his wife ceased to be related to her natal kin, only conjugally to his own lineage. The classical texts that explicitly forbid such marriages are held to refer to inferior unions in which the wife does not form part of a gift, but remains a member of her natal lineage and hence continues to fill the role of mother's brother's daughter (or sister's daughter or mother's sister's daughter, Trautmann 1981:304–5). This argument was conceivable because with respect to marriage (but not to death, impurity and inheritance), 'the *smṛtis* tell us two contradictory things at once: by gift marriage the affiliation of a woman (e.g. the mother) with her natal kin (e.g. mother's brother, mother's brother's daughter) is utterly severed: yet by the *asipaṇḍa* rule, the mother's natal kin are prohibited in marriage' (p.306).[10]

It was obviously not only legal commentators that recognised the divergence from Hindu writings; people in the South do so today, especially in the patrilineal Brahmin castes where the system of close marriage raises acute questions in the minds of many visitors from the North.[11] Nevertheless these differences have clearly persisted over the centuries, despite the teachings of the sacred books and the disapproval of northerners. The defence of the jurists rested on the idea of *brahma* marriage as a gift of a woman that separated her from her natal family and incorporated her in that of her husband. It is a curious argument, in that it assumes a marriage exists before it has taken place, an assumption that presents problems even for an analysis in terms of alliance or repeated affinity. It also depends heavily on the classical notion of marriage as a gift. I have already commented upon the analytic utility of this notion but it also presented problems for the actors as well as for observers. Despite the differences which he recognises between marriage in the North and the South, despite seeing a rough boundary between the regions, Trautmann argues that from Jaffna to Kashmir the ethnography records the diverse, local adaptations and workings out of a pan-Indian idea, that marriage is a pure gift (1981:315). The working-out is largely, but not exclusively, a matter of Brahmin practice and Brahmin texts which provide a cover for the different marriage rules in the South. That this idea of pure gift should be associated with the Brahmins is completely consistent with the (written) notion that it is only they, the teachers of the Veda and the officiators at sacrifice, who can receive gifts of other kinds, gifts which pass to superior beings and in expectation of no (visible) return, only a transcendental reciprocity. The religious gift (*dharmadāna*) is continuous with sacrifice and 'substitutes for it' (p. 279). The *Ksatriyas* on the other hand make lordly gifts to inferiors of the gains they have made through conquest, while *Vaiśyas* and *Śūdras* are involved in other forms of exchange, the former in commerce, the latter receiving wages for service. Forms of exchange correspond to the social hierarchy.

Giving to the Brahmin is to be preferred to giving to one's kin. In making an offering to the patrilineal ancestors, the only proper worldly recipients are the Brahmins who can transmit it to heaven. 'Food eaten by a kinsman (in the sacrifice) is indeed a gift to the goblins. It reaches neither the ancestors nor the gods. It wanders about this world only, having lost its power (to reach heaven), as a cow that has lost its calf wanders into the wrong stable' (Āpartamba Dharma Sūtra 2.717.4, quoted by Trautmann 1981:282). The significance of this ideology of gift-giving is clearly related to the position of Brahmins in the social system, as priests rather than as producers, and to the fact that it is they who compose and read the written text. Since they are interposed (or have interposed themselves) as intermediaries both with the other world and with the holy texts, they have to be supported (not paid) in their professional role.

There is a further difference between the North and the South that has to do with the status of women, *vis-à-vis* property and *vis-à-vis* men. In this case we do not find the sharp divide that marks marriage patterns and terminologies. It is more of a continuum which sees an increase in the rights of women culminating in the situation in Sri Lanka, among Buddhist Sinhalese and Hindu Tamils alike, in which sons and daughters have very similar rights to property, including rights to land itself, which a woman may receive either as dowry or as inheritance.

The question of the nature of the property to which women are entitled in South India is complex. Brahmin groups tend to follow North Indian practice and to obey the injunctions of the *Mitākṣarā*. But there are also local practices tending towards greater female rights in property, which Tambiah sees as related to the shift from 'unilineality and unilocal residence in India to bilaterality and ambilocal residence in Ceylon' (1973:136). The variant to which he refers occurs among the matrilineal Nangudi Vellalar where women have *strīdhanam* rights to dowry both in movables and land, the same being true of the Vellalahs of Jaffna in Sri Lanka as well as of the Kandyan Sinhalese. Among the Nangudi Vellalar of Tamil Nadu, one of the groups discussed by Dumont (1957b) and directly linked to the Tamil Vellalahs of Jaffna, the bride's parents provide a dowry composed of jewellery, land and household effects; property, including land, is transmitted separately between men and between women (father to son, mother to daughter), with houses being female property, residence being uxorilocal and father's sister's daughter's marriage preferred, the critical union for joining together what had earlier been divided along sexual lines.

But the tendency is more widespread than that. I have referred to Nicholas' comment that in a Bengali village a bride is theoretically entitled to a 'share' of her family's property 'almost equal to that of that brother's' (1967:73). That is in the North where land is usually excluded. But from the admission of such an entitlement it is but a small conceptual step to include in this equality land as well as movables.

Outside Sri Lanka such a move was made among the matrilineal groups referred to above. But elsewhere too women are not always excluded from rights in land. The Kammas, for example, sometimes gave land to daughters at marriage and the same is reported for Andra Pradesh (Reddy 1979). So too did even some of the patrilineal castes of Brahmins. Gough notes that dowry in Kumbapeṭṭai might include land (1981:209,242). In addition, of course, when a man has no sons, he could pass his land to 'a chosen daughter's son' (p. 209), a situation that might theoretically occur in as many as 20 per cent of families. If a man who had separated his property from his kin died without surviving children (potentially another 20 per cent), the land passed to his widow for her lifetime, after which it returned to her natal family unless a son was adopted, a possibility that sometimes gave rise to bitter disputes. However self-acquired land, like other property, could always be willed to a widow or daughter, although a man would usually pass this on to his sons. 'In these ways both married women and widows *frequently* became landowners' (p. 209; my italics) and were registered as such when, under the British administration, 'land shares' were turned into 'private property'; in 1897 12 per cent of registered landowners were women, in 1952, 20 per cent. That is to say, the implicit rights that women had in the earlier system often became explicit with registration.

Such transfers were contrary to the 'code' as embodied in the *Mitākṣarā*, which was accepted as law throughout the South with the exception of course in the matrilineal areas and in Sri Lanka. In general the courts themselves were reluctant to admit to any transfers of land to daughters, even small transfers made as gifts. When such transactions were upheld in the 1960s, they had to be small. But the fact that they came to court at all represents not so much a recent change in the situation but a recognition of customary tendencies which appear to have been somewhat more acceptable in some earlier codes.

Contrasting conceptions of family property in the North and South, Sontheimer (1977) claims that in the former such property is held to be vested exclusively in male agnates, whereas in the South 'the position was much more complex because of the simultaneous co-extensive interests of the family members in the common property'. Derrett (1958) too sees a difference in the concepts of women's property in the North and South, at least on the practical level, for the content of South Indian inscriptions points to the rights of control a husband obtains in his wife's property after marriage, the corollary of which was her greater rights in the marital estate, a half share going to her on divorce or on the husband's death. The distinction turns on the relative separateness of a woman's property in North Indian law. Certainly in the South, in Madras for example, custom ran contrary to *Mitākṣarā* and 'allowed gifts of a reasonable amount of immovable property to a daughter even after marriage', and the Supreme Court has recognised this moral obligation which Sontheimer attributes to the 'right of a daughter or sister to a share in the family property at partition which was lost by the efflux of time' but was nevertheless recognised by certain Shastric sources (1977:208–9).

In recent times there have been two important legal enactments in the South, one in the state of Kerala and one in Andhra Pradesh, reserving the rights of daughter. In Kerala an Act of 1976 abolished the Hindu Undivided Family, thereby wiping out the discrepancies between sons and daughters built into the *Mitākṣarā* system. In Andhra, more recent legislation has extended the traditional right by birth of the *Mitākṣarā* to unmarried daughters, thus bringing their rights on a par with those already enjoyed by sons.[12]

As we have seen, the trend in the South was towards not only female property (that existed in the northern dowry, even in Muslim areas, even where purdah was most extreme) but towards the allocation to women of relatively equal rights in property, including the basic means of production. This is seen most clearly in Sri Lanka, the (Buddhist) Sinhalese part of which was obviously not directly subject to the Hindu Law Codes deriving from the North, nor yet to the direct effects of Muslim conquest which affected much of the rest of the South at different times, for example, in the plundering of its temples. But female rights to land were in fact recognised not only in the Kandyan code but also in the *Tesavaḷamai* (*Thesawalamai*) law of the Hindu Tamils, which is 'customary' in relation to the classic written code. The dowry was 'an essential part of the property belonging to the couple and would include immovables unlike in the patrilineal, exogamous family of the Dharmaśāstras' (Sontheimer 1977:78). It was common property until divorce or widowhood. 'In a nuclear family it constituted . . . the nucleus for a community of acquisition' (p. 79).

Thus the South diverges from Hindu orthodoxy both in its patterns of marriage and, in parts (Sri Lanka, and in a lesser way, some of South India), in the kind of property that can be allocated or given to women, specifically whether or not land is included. Both of these divergences are the subject of legal discussion, justification and compromise, and both are of continuing importance at the 'customary' level, the level of 'practice'.

Let me stress that the endowment of women is not at issue, but whether it includes the basic means of agricultural production, to the implications of which I will return. There may be a general difference between North and South in the proportion of a family estate which is allocated to a daughter; on this I have little information, except that some orthodox commentators declare that a dowry is notionally one quarter of the share of a brother (Sontheimer 1977:53). However, among the Brahmins of Kumbapeṭṭai in the South, a daughter's share might be even larger than that of her brothers.

Families were evaluated financially in terms of the land they owned and the amount they paid in dowry and marriage expenses for their daughters. Marriage expenses included lavish feasting, gifts of clothing or valuables to prominent affines, the services of a group of musicians, and a taxi to transport the bridegroom. The dowry necessarily required silk and cotton clothing for the bride, considerable gold jewelry, and brass vessels: the bridegroom's family might also demand in the contract a gift of one or more acres of land to the bride or even a cash sum to be paid outright to the bridegroom. When marriages took place between cross-cousins, a man and his sister's daughter, or other close relatives, the dowry of jewels and vessels could be limited and no special gifts to the bridegroom would be demanded. The dowry had, however, greatly increased in the previous twenty years with the increase of marriages to strangers or to more distant kin of similar socioeconomic rank. In Kumbapettai in 1952, the total cost to the bride's father of a Brahman marriage, including dowry and wedding expenses, ran from about Rs.1,000 to Rs.12,000. It therefore usually equalled, or even exceeded, the amount a son could expect to inherit on his father's death. (Gough 1981:242)

Dowries in Kumbapeṭṭai were undoubtedly heavy and were the chief cause of indebtedness in the late nineteenth and twentieth centuries, creating bankruptcy among Brahmins with many daughters. Like others, Gough attributes this situation to 'the new, competitive economy of private enterprise' which caused them to spend more than they could afford in order to attract 'suitable' husbands of appropriate education and wealth (pp. 200–1). While a measure of competition seems characteristic of dowry systems everywhere, the increase in the range of marriage and the advent of mass consumer goods undoubtedly made for further difficulties. But so too did schooling, since the lack of female education meant that this expenditure on the achievement of males had to be compensated by added dowry.

I pointed earlier to the logical connection between cross-cousin marriage and the allocation of substantial rights to women; the greater the woman's claims to property, the greater the pressure towards this form of close marriage. In discussing Sri Lanka, such marriages were seen to be linked to the allocation of rights in land to women; here we are dealing not only with immovable resources, not only with the basic means of production, but also with the special heritage values that are so often attached to land and other family items. These heritage values are linked with the sacralisation of the soil as an element of production, as the locus if not of the disposal of the ancestors at death (cremation does not have the same call for graveyards but it often has for places of memorial) at least of their daily lives. Certain forms of close marriage help to retain or reunite rights to particular segments of territory, heritage territory.

Writing from a legal point of view, Sontheimer had no hesitation in linking cross-cousin marriage with the retention of property within the family, or at least with isogamous marriage.

In Kandyan law marriage with the maternal uncle's daughter, or a paternal aunt's daughter was desirable and even obligatory. In some customs the person refusing to marry the cousin forfeited his or her right to the share or the dowry in favour of the party who was prepared to marry. One of the purposes of such marriages was to keep the landed property within small kinship groups. (1977:86)

After giving an example, he concludes:

The consequence would be that the property of a family would potentially belong to all descendants of all the families of the kinship group and would in fact be circulating within the kinship group. Even where cross-cousin marriages were not followed or where such marriages were not advisable, e.g. because the family of the partner to be married had become impoverished or because there was no marriageable partner, marriages would take place with affinal relations who were of equal status so that kinsmen by marriage and descent became often the same. Marriages were thus concluded with the aim to retain kinship ties between people of comparable wealth and ritual status.

This he associates with the fact that 'the land which was received by a couple as dowry and as an advancement to the son would . . . eventually form the property with the help of which the people would set up their own descendants'. The families connected by marriage continued to have 'some residual interest', especially as the effect of continuous intermarriage among kin meant that 'property which went out by marriage would return by marriages' (p. 87). Thus customary law in parts of the South differed from the sastric pattern, a circle of relations having interests in 'the estate which consists of property derived from the father's ancestors and the mother's dowry plus acquisitions of the couple' (p. 84).

How far is this process explicit from the actor's point of view? In his account of the Jaffna Tamils, Banks (1957) notes that the advantages of cross-cousin marriage are usually thought of as ensuring purity of caste or status, as creating a stable marriage between those of known background, and 'as enabling the recombination of the properties of a man and his sister through their children' (Tambiah 1973:119). While the first two features are also claimed as present in North Indian marriages, the third is characteristic of the South alone. And the epitome of the process of recombination is when a woman's property, separated from that of her natal family at marriage, is brought together once again by a further marriage (to the father's sister's daughter). And this is more dramatically the case when her dowry includes land.

The same considerations do not apply with equal force to movable property, although some heirlooms fall into a rather similar category. But a close marriage is also 'good' in that it largely avoids the problem of marrying down which hypergamy inevitably entails (marriage 'up' for women means 'down' for men, though more usually the advantages to one are traded off against the benefits to the other), and which is also associated with the possible absence of appropriate husbands for upper women and the shortage of brides for lower men, as well as with the consequent infanticide, deliberate or by neglect (Karve 1953:132), or alternatively the kulinism (plural marriage) of some parts of the North. Nevertheless, property remains one of the important factors. First, because even where a woman does not normally acquire land, she does at least act 'like a son' in the absence of brothers, a situation which in other parts of the world encourages close marriage and sometimes close adoption, that is, adoption within the clan. Secondly, the same pressures exist whenever women are treated more or less equally with men regarding shares, that is, where they receive a direct endowment, since the indirect forms do not carry the same implications. And direct dowry and inheritance are found predominantly in upper or middle groups, those who have status and property to conserve, as was the case with the Konku families examined by Beck. In the context of marriage to the sister's daughter (ZD) which like other investigators (Karve 1953:187) she found to be more frequent than marriage to the daughter of either the mother's brother or the father's sister (1972:253, table 5.9), she writes 'the genealogies I collected bear out a pattern of especially tight intermarriage in households of middling economic status, particularly among those families that have inherited special rights that they wanted to preserve' (p. 252).

I will return to the question of the interrelation between dowry and close marriage at the end of the chapter. Meanwhile it is important to consider other aspects of North–South difference and similarity before taking up more fully the problem of explanation.

Differences in relationships

Wife and husband

An interesting point related to a woman's entitlement to land emerged in the discussion of Sri Lanka, where a critical factor was the whole question of marital residence in the determination of which women play an important part, even when they have brothers. The flexibility of residence is linked to the flexibility of conjugality. Among the Kandyan Sinhalese forms of conjugality exist which simply involve cohabitation, a 'laxity' remarks Tambiah that is paralleled in the ease with which unions are dissolved (1973:130). Easier divorce is not limited to Sri Lanka but is characteristic of the South, especially of the matrilineal groups; in this and in other ways, there is a general resemblance between practices in the South and those of 'lower' groups in the North, both of which from one point of view represent divergences from Hindu orthodoxy.

Looking at the broader arena, the most outstanding difference between the South generally (as distinct from Sri Lanka alone) and North, is that between close and distant marriages. This feature formed the focus of Karve's valuable study in which she drew out many of the implications for interpersonal relations and specifically for the experience, feelings and position of a woman as a wife, that is, of what to anthropologists is often a purely formal aspect of social structure, namely, patterns of marriage or alliance.

The effects of being compelled to marry outside the village in the North are vividly and sensitively described:

Early marriage out of the native village to a complete stranger is a terrible crisis in a girl's life. In India marriage is a sacrament and no normal man or woman must die without receiving this sacrament. It is a custom among many communities that if a woman dies a spinster, a marriage ceremony is performed with the corpse and the woman is then burnt with the honours due to a married woman. There is greater freedom for man, but if a man who has gone through the initiation ceremony dies without marrying, he is supposed to become a ghost. To die childless is not to attain heaven. This firmly established belief would make a girl unhappy if she is not married. The marriage ceremony is pomp and fun and yet the moment of parting from the mother is poignant. The whole of the Northern Zone reflects this in the number of pairs of words for the father-in-law's house on the one hand and the beloved house of the father and mother on the other. Hundreds of folk-songs bear witness to the agony of a girl at parting for ever from her parents' home. The husband is a shadowy figure, the real people are the parents-in-law and from an indulgent home she has to go to strangers who are ready to find fault with her at the slightest gesture. In the husband's home there is the ever present fear of the husband bringing another wife. Only when a girl becomes the mother of a boy does she feel completely at home in her husband's house. The sentiment existing between the two families joined by a marriage is well reflected in the custom according to which a respectable man does not take food at his daughter's husband's house when he goes on a visit. He is among strangers. The relationship is that of givers and receivers. One who gives the daughter should not receive anything. A father rarely visits a married daughter. He may go only on extremely formal occasions but the brother may go often and hence in Northern folk-songs girls sing always of the Bir (the brother) who comes as a beloved visitor and brings news of the parents. (1953:130)

Contrast this with the close marriages of the South:

A man does not bring a stranger as a bride to his home, a woman is not thrown among complete strangers on her marriage. Marriage strengthens existing bonds. The emphasis is on knitting families closer together and narrowing the circle of the kin group, a policy exactly the opposite of the one followed in the north. The whole tone of the southern society is different. The distinction between the father's house and the father-in-law's house is not as sharp as in the north. A girl's behaviour in her husband's family is much freer. After all, her husband is either her uncle or her cross-cousin and his mother is either her own grandmother or her aunt. Neither is she separated for long periods from her parents' house.

The custom of marrying close kin results in girls being given in marriage to families living not too far from their houses and there is much visiting between the two houses, and the girl goes often and on long visits to her parents and almost always for her confinements. (1953:228–9)

In fact we have seen the range of marriage in the South has tended to widen with modern changes, which is perhaps partly the reason for reports of 'dowry deaths' there as well as in the North. Moreover, according to a recent survey (Prasad 1987) the pressure to produce 'additional dowry' after the wedding, which may be due to unfulfilled promises as well as to increased demands (see Kolenda 1967) comes primarily from the husband and only secondarily from the mother-in-law, perhaps because he wants to set up on his own. But he is scarcely a shadowy figure.

The effects of the range of conjugal ties continue in later life, for in the North a wife is a stranger, in the South a kinswoman. Karve sees this linked to purdah restrictions which appear to be more severe when wives are strangers. Like the extended use of the veil, purdah is a practice which was associated with the Muslim influence that made itself felt in the North over such a long period.

In the whole of the north women rarely go out of their houses, or take part in marriage processions. In the central and the southern zones women in their coloured *Sāris* and rich ornaments are the most conspicuous members of marriage processions. In the north the women's sphere is much more isolated from that of the men than in the south and this is due to the fact that the family is not only patrilineally oriented but dominated by the patrikin and where girls are always given in marriage to people with whom they are not acquainted. The southern patrilineal families on the other hand prefer marriages of cousins so that the orientation is not entirely patrilocal. (1953:135)

A woman isolated among affines clearly lives in a more restricted social milieu. The fact that marriage occurs so early in adolescence means that she experiences more deeply the absence of her own kin and subjects her to the domination of her husband's, especially his mother, whose 'harassment' is sometimes the cause of much unhappiness. But the situation is one which age and motherhood can alter, especially after the birth of a son. 'Generally a woman is so dominated by the affinal kin or by the husband that she rarely makes a positive impression except as a mother. It is not rare to see women, who were nothing but meek nonentities, blossom out into positive personalities in their middle-aged widowhood, or boss over the weak old husband in the latter part of the married life' (1953:135).

Otherwise the conventions on behaviour are more restrictive:

The northern joint family is a status group where husband, wife, parents-in-law, daughters-in-law, sons, daughters, sisters-in-law and brothers-in-law have each a definite place assigned to him or her *vis-à-vis* all others. The work which each has to do, the pleasures each will enjoy are more or less fixed by conventions, and the important thing one has to learn are these conventions of kinship behaviour. A man behaves in a deferential manner to all elder relatives of his wife and jokes with her younger brothers and sisters. A man may marry the younger sister of his wife during the life-time of his wife or after her death. Many folktales exploit this situation in the relationship of sisters. (p. 135)

Marriage outside the group (or kin range) as practised in North India is more consistent with hypergamy in its various forms since bilateral cross-cousin marriage is likely to lead to the movement of partners between closely related families of equal rank, rather than their alignment as higher and lower; while the latter might occur with mother's brother's daughter's marriage, it would do so only in very rare cases (see Goody 1959). That means the partners to a marriage are more likely to be differentiated in terms of status on the man's side and wealth on the woman's, although in fact a kind of isogamy (or balancing of attributes) is nearly everywhere the predominant form, even in the North. Marriage outside is also more consistent with the idea of restricting a woman's access to her natal group and hence of children to their mother's brother. So it is understandable that the practice of the wife returning to her natal home to give birth is less frequent in the Hindi-speaking North (Mandelbaum 1970:89–90; Karve 1953:233). Srinivas, who sees the differences as lying between continental and peninsular India, quotes Marriott's words about the North; 'Behind this organization of marriage is the feeling that one's daughter and sister at marriage become the helpless possessions of an alien kinship group' (1955a:112; Srinivas 1984:9). Hence you heap gifts on their heads to secure their good treatment. While this may be an actor's view, in fact there seems little or no evidence that women receive more endowment in the North than in the South, just the opposite.

A woman in the North was more restricted in other ways, having to cover her face in front of older males in the house; in the South it is only in the higher groups that she has to give formal expression to the inequality among brothers by veiling herself in front of her husband's elder brother (Mandelbaum 1970:64–5). At the same time, the wealth of her natal family, which she was less likely to visit, or her father to visit her (p.83), was of greater importance, for in the upper groups they were considered as perpetual donors. In parts of the South, it is thought that the groom's family should be the wealthier, although any such discrepancy is compensated by the fact that the bride is frequently closely related and comes as a bearer of property. But 'bridewealth' (indirect dowry) appears to be more often a part of such transactions than in the North (Mandelbaum 1970:106).

In the North widows of the higher castes do not remarry but in the lower ones they may. It goes without saying that among orthodox Hindus even in the South a widow is not allowed to marry either the elder or the younger brother, real or classificatory, of the husband. In other words the levirate (the inheritance of an obligation to breed in the name of a dead brother), or anything approaching it, is forbidden. Karve considers that a change has taken place from ancient times when the levirate was preferred to adoption as a strategy of heirship. But the 'customs of levirate and begetting children by engaging the services of a stranger fell gradually into disrepute and were condemned by later Smṛtis' (1953:84). There was an increased value placed on chastity, on renunciation. 'It seems that the emphasis on woman's chastity and individual inheritance and marriage gradually made levirate an obsolete custom though it never vanished entirely from India' (p. 85). Widow remarriage certainly did not disappear from the lower groups, and in the South it is generally permitted, though not in the leviratic form. It is possible that there is correspondingly less adoption in the South, but the remarriage of widows does not in itself provide heirs for heirless males and in any case is part of the more general loosening of constraints on women's freedom of action. For in the South 'women enjoyed greater independence' and 'divorce and remarriage of widows were widely practised'; indeed in the *Tesavaḷamai* remarriage is visualised as common (Sontheimer 1977:147). All these features are against Brahmin rulings and more typical of lower than of higher groups in the North.

Sister and brother

In attempting to modify certain widespread notions of marriage in 'other cultures', I have discussed at some length the continuing importance after marriage of the brother–sister tie throughout India. Given the bluntness of the concepts and the inadequacy of the resources at present available to us, it is difficult to make any adequate assessment of similarities and differences in the quality of these relations. Obviously brother and sister interact more frequently in the South, where marriages are closer and less constraining, especially in Sri Lanka where their joint interest in land may bring them physically together in the same house. But this in itself is an explosive situation after marriage and it is true that the more loaded a relationship is with such interests, the more room for dispute. One of the strategies of a woman marrying out is to leave land with her brothers (as potential inheritance or as an exploitable concern) rather than taking it as dowry, thus maintaining an open claim for support; at the same time she keeps the property outside the possibly disadvantageous control of her husband.

In the North, brothers and sisters meet relatively rarely so that from the standpoint of interaction the relationship is thinner. That does not prevent it being intense when they do see each other, and possibly less encumbered with conflicts because they do not have the same formal claims on one another. Indeed the very isolation of the sister tends to increase her feelings of dependence on the brother.

Although the relationship continues after marriage, over much of northern India the brother is said to become 'inferior' to his sister's new family, at least in the higher castes. In some Tamil groups in the South the bride's family is also thought to be inferior but Dumont comments that this inferiority centres upon the marriage ceremony itself and passes away in time (1961:84), so that there is no asymmetry at the lineage level. That is also frequently the case in the North, except with the kind of *jāti*-hypergamy found among some Rajputs, Maharashtrans and among some Patidars. Even then, this 'inferiority' (which is often a matter of matching higher 'status' with lower 'wealth') appears to have little effect on the relations between the siblings themselves, at least those that had survived and made a marriage. However, the sisters of some of those men at the top of a hierarchy who made hypergamous marriages were strongly affected by the actions of their fathers and brothers, since as children they might have suffered from neglect or worse, and at best were condemned to remain unmarried or to be second wives. Among the Nambudiri Brahmins of Kerala, where only the eldest son could marry in the same caste while the others took matrilineal Nayar women as consorts, many of their sisters remained spinsters. 'Relations between brother and sister were never close; indeed there was a tendency to regard sisters both older and younger, as simply a drain on the family resources' (Mencher and Goldberg 1967:95, 101). So that this suffering was inflicted in the cause of maintaining the status of the family as a whole.

This theme will be taken up once again when we come to look at differences in mortality between males and females (below, p. 279ff.), but the relation of a sister to her brother tends to differ relatively little on a North–South axis as compared with her position as wife, and the same seems to be the case with the relation between a man and his sister's children. Clearly marriage patterns have some effect, not only closeness and distance but also hypergamy, so too do systems of devolution. But the major difference occurs in matrilineal regimes which vary in the way property is handed down but always organise its transmission through women, a fact that has some influence on their position as sisters and usually as wives.

Mother's brother–sister's son

The relation between mother's brother and sister's son is linked in obvious ways to the brother–sister tie, since it involves her children's relation with *her* brother, as with cross-cousin marriage. Where such marriages are encouraged, or actually built into the kinship terminology as in the South, there may be no terminological distinction between parent-in-law and the parents' siblings of opposite sex. Karve characterises the difference between South and North as follows: 'The categories of kin are not blood-relations and in-law relations as in the north, but blood-relations whom one may not marry and the blood relations whom one may marry' (1953:228).[13] Terminological differences are seen by her as related to married life as much as to marriage itself.

The North has separate words for 'daughters' and 'brides' in each regional language, with a double standard of behaviour and sometimes of morality for each category. The custom of local exogamy cuts the women of a local group into two sharp divisions: the 'daughters' of the village and the 'brides' of the village. The daughters of different local families are very friendly with each other and enjoy each other's company whenever they come back to the village from their father-in-laws' houses. They all constitute a sort of spy service to watch the behaviour of the 'brides'. Folk literature singles out certain pairs of relations as natural enemies. *Nanand-Bhojāi* i.e. a woman and her husband's sister is one such pair. *Sās-Bahu* i.e. a woman and her husband's mother is another. *Nanand* (husband's sister) is the daughter of a house, *Bhojāi* (brother's wife) is the bride. The *Nanand* has to leave the house in which she is born and finds that a complete stranger takes her place. *Sās* is the mother-in-law, the ruler of the joint family. *Bahu* is the young daughter-in-law. Though both are 'brides', i.e. women who have come into the family through marriage, the *Sās* being the mother has established certain rights. The *Bahu* is the stranger, who is the present slave and the future mistress. The rivalry between *Sās* and *Bahu* is the rivalry of two generations of women between whom, in the course of time power is transferred from the old to the young. (Karve 1953:129)

Contrast the situation in the South where those whom you marry are already kin or are turned into 'kin', the husband and wife being 'cross-cousins' and the parents-in-law being mother's brother and father's sister, there being no terminological distinction.[14] Where marriage takes place with the sister's daughter, a marriage which Karve (1953:187) reports as being more frequent than that to cousins among some groups,[15] the mother-in-law is the sister and grandmother for the husband and wife respectively, while for the wife the mother's brother is also the husband.

In certain formal, ceremonial situations, no such radical difference appears in the relations of mother's brother and sister's son and, like that between brother and sister in similar contexts, it bears strong resemblances over the whole sub-continent, giving some grounds for the unity hypothesis. For example, despite the great differences in marital arrangements in North and South, especially in hypergamy and marriage rules, 'the role and gift-giving obligations of the mother's brother and other close affines are remarkably similar' (Tambiah 1973:92). The continuance of 'affinal gifts' and the mother's brother's generosity are consistent in his view both with the North Indian rejection of and the South Indian preference for repeated marriage. In other words, one might add, they are independent of them, the 'generosity' being perhaps more explicable in terms of the common fact of 'complementary filiation' (the duality of parenthood and the cross-sibling relationship) rather than the variable institution of 'alliance'. But the gift-giving referred to by Tambiah does not, of course, exhaust the transactions that centre on marriage and the family; and here he and others have pointed to significant differences, at least in Sri Lanka, in the nature of the property allocated to women, and through them to their children.

Similarities of course exist, both in cultural detail and at a more general level of analysis. But on the latter plane the similarities are not confined to the Indian sub-continent. Some years ago in an attempt to compare the mother's brother–sister's son relationship in India and Africa, I examined material from a selection of monographs dealing with kinship and marriage. The results showed more similarity than I had anticipated, despite the differences between the major transactions at marriage, dowry in one case, bridewealth in another, as well as in other, more general, features. Certain differences cross-cut the continents, and in both Indian and African societies the situation varied substantially depending on whether one was dealing with groups that inherit patrilineally or matrilineally (Goody 1968).

Looking at the 'patrilineal' peoples of North India, the role of the mother's brother is very prominent on ceremonial occasions, especially at marriage, which is a much more elaborate ceremony than in Africa. His role is important even in Muslim communities in Pakistan; among the Punjabi of Mohla, the mother's brother of the groom gives him some money, a horse or a buffalo. Again a portion of the bride's dowry is provided by her mother's maternal house (*nanke*) who thus contribute to the welfare of their sister's daughter (Eglar 1960:80). In other words the relationship of a mother's brother to a sister's son or daughter is essentially one of non-reciprocal gift-giving; 'to her children he is a loving *mamūn*, maternal uncle' (p. 98). The relation parallels that to the father's sister's husband, who may play this role in default of a mother's brother. According to the author, it is the relation of brother and sister that is critical. The special position of the paternal aunt (*phuphi*) derives from her relation with her brother; and the relation of the father's sister's husband is also seen as an extension of the cross-sibling bond (p. 97). If the child of one of her brothers does not have a maternal uncle and if there is no one to represent the *nanke* when this child marries, 'a sister will see to it that her husband fills the gap' (p. 98). He, the *phuphar*, the father's sister's husband, will make up for the missing maternal relatives.

We find a similar situation in Central India.

The mother's brother should give to the sister's son without thought of return and count it as a meritorious . . . act. The relation is closely connected to that of a man with his sister. Here, the brother regards himself as his sister's protector . . . It is in fact an extension of this tie which covers the sister's son. I was told several times that the mother's brother takes more interest in the nephew while his sister is alive. (Mayer 1966:223)

An individual can also get help from his father's sister's husband but he will first expect aid from his mother's brothers. At a wedding this relative is set apart from all others by the type of present he gives (p. 233) in addition to which he has to entertain the wedding party. But the parallel relationship on the paternal side with the father's sister and her husband is less strong: 'The sister has a firm attachment to the brother, but this does not extend to such an extent to his children.' Gifts and aid from the father's sister (*phua*) carry some merit, but are not seen to be so essential (p.223).

The mother's brother appears in a generous role in Indian societies but we do not find the same kind of snatching that occurs so often in Africa. This practice has been the subject of some general discussion (see bibliography in Goody 1959, reprinted 1968, Dumont 1961) and the empirical features can be understood by referring to Fortes' account of the Tallensi of northern Ghana. In former times,

when people moved about less freely than now, a man passing through the clan settlement of his *ahɔb* could seize any guinea-fowl he saw and collect any guinea-fowl eggs he came across irrespective of which member of his mother's brother's clan they belonged to . . . An *ahɔŋ* is still at liberty to cut himself a few heads of guinea corn or millet from any farm when walking through the settlement of his *ahɔb*, if he is feeling hungry. (Fortes 1949:306)

In India the relationship appears to be equally warm. On the other hand, the transfer of property is done in a more open way; the sister's son is entitled to expect help from the mother's brother, he does not have to assert a claim by snatching at festivals and other occasions. If, as I have earlier suggested, this behaviour is connected with the absence in Africa of any overt claim of a woman to the same property as her brother, then we should not expect to find this institution in India where, even in patrilineal societies, both sons and daughters acquire wealth from their parents and where after the death of the father, a brother becomes responsible for the provision of his sister's dowry. And in the absence of brothers, the daughter or her son becomes the full heir.

Whether or not this suggestion is correct, the maternal uncle plays a similar role in a number of other respects despite the difference in the direction of the flow of goods at marriage. Among the Lugbara of East Africa, both the husband's family and the wife herself send regular gifts to her father. Among the Tallensi, as among the nearby LoDagaa, a son-in-law has to bring parties to help on the farm of his wife's parents. Again at the funeral, the obligations of a daughter's husband are much greater towards his wife's dead father than the reverse.

In India the flow of gifts is largely in another direction, linked to the nature of affinal relations and of a woman's property. In Central India, according to Mayer, a husband will not visit his wife's people for three or four years after marriage. He goes there of course to conduct his bride back to his home, but afterwards sends his brother to accompany her on returning from one of her periodic visits; in the Deccan, affines do not maintain close contact. And in the North India village studied by Lewis (1958 [1965]), neither the father nor the elder brother of the bride could visit her at her new home. One reason for this came out in a remark made to us in Nandol. Among upper status groups (including upper Patels) you receive nothing for your daughter, and after marriage just to feed at her home might be taken as a return payment, even as a purchase. Gifts theoretically flow from the bride's family, although as we have seen not so much to the father-in-law, rather to the bride herself. In lower groups some gifts go in the same direction as in Africa, but most of them go *to* the bride, not simply *through* her. However, at all hierarchical levels the contributions of the mother's brother to his sister's children plays a prominent part.

While referring to this 'survey', of a far from systematic kind, I would remark upon two other aspects that we found to characterise domestic relationships. The deference due from a wife to her parents-in-law and her husband did not greatly differ in the Indian and African societies, and in both cases diminished after the birth of children (e.g. among the Lugbara). But in Africa with its high rates of polygyny, a woman's main rivals were her co-wives, and there was little tension with the wives of her husband's brothers or with her husband's sisters; among the Tallensi these latter are described as friendly. In India on the contrary the relations with both are very different. In the Punjab (Eglar 1960), a woman's main rivals are the wives of her husband's brothers; her prestige depends upon the gifts she receives from her own home, which sets up a competitive situation. In Central India (Dube 1955; Mayer 1966) the same rivalry exists with strong relations of inferiority and superiority between the wives of the husband's elder and younger brothers respectively, while the tension with the husband's sister is brought out in many accounts of Indian life (Karve 1953:129). As was noted for Sri Lanka, the coresidence of the sister and the brother's wife made for fragile unions.

If the relation between the mother's brother and sister's son is broadly similar in Africa and India, whether North or South, despite the significant differences in marriage patterns, in marriage transactions and in the type of political economy generally, this is presumably because its character is predominantly linked to the brother–sister tie which again displayed many similarities.

Once again, the major differences here lie not between North and South

India but rather between patrilineal and matrilineal systems. Where the mother's brother is guardian of the sister's children, as in some traditional Nayar households (Karve 1953:260), where he exercises authority over them, and where office and property are transmitted from one to the other, the role of the maternal uncle loses 'its relaxed and generous' character and conflicts are more likely to arise.

Some tendency in this direction is found in Sri Lanka where brother and sister have common interests in a landed estate. We have already noted that relations between brother and sister tend to be closer when she does *not* make any claim to the land for her dowry; in return it is open to her to call upon his help in other ways, whereas to exercise the right itself brings discord. The sister's children are clearly involved in this relationship, since their mother's failure to insist upon her claim affects their own position, as indeed does any dispute that arises between their mother and her brothers.

It is possible that other aspects of conjugal and domestic relations are affected. With close kinship marriage, one's in-laws are one's kin, a fact that may influence the structure of sentiments, of ties and cleavages, of tensions and attachments. For example, Shah (1974) remarks upon the tensions between the wives of elder and junior brothers and suggests that things might be different in South India where cross-cousin and uncle–niece marriages are frequent. In conclusion, while the position of a woman as wife varies considerably between North and South, this is less true of the brother–sister tie and to a large extent of that between mother's brother and sister's son.

Group differences

At the level of social groups, the emphasis of northern practice is towards a more patrilineal form of social organisation, consistent with shastric formulations. By patrilineal I refer to the transmission of the membership of descent groups through males, which exist throughout India. By 'more' patrilineal I refer to the relative importance of these groups, including the subgroups of undivided agnates (the Hindu Undivided Family) consisting of males and unmarried daughters with wives having a qualified attachment that normally excludes them from rights in land. Reckoning in terms of such groups is also more important for *sapiṇḍa* rules of marriage than it is for cross-cousin unions, an importance that seems to emerge in the greater role of genealogists. Several authors (e.g. Shah and Shroff 1958) have remarked upon the part genealogists play in northern India where their activities represent not simply a 'reflection' of lineage ties but an important constituent of them, as well as a contributor to the preservation of pedigrees, especially as they were not only recorders of social relations and events, but praise-singers as well. 'Those whose patriline was thus kept fresh in memory and green in glory, have been inclined to form their action groups with their patrilineal kinsmen more commonly than in South India' (Mandelbaum 1970:141). While lineages are widespread, being involved in marriage arrangements and the settlement of disputes as in China, they seem to have been more extensive among the upper groups, especially in the North, and in some lower groups such ties are little elaborated (Mandelbaum 1970:145).

I have said little, here or elsewhere, of the contrast between urban and rural practice, which was sometimes considerable. But in relation to our discussion of Chinese lineages it is worth remarking that in India it was the urban castes of the North that tended to have property of the corporation type, 'usually in the form of the *Vādis* (large buildings used for holding feasts and festivals, accommodating wedding guests, and holding meetings), huge utensils for cooking feasts, and money received as fees and fines. Frequently each such unit had a patron deity with elaborate arrangements for its ownership, including a large shrine' (Shah 1982:19). Conflicts over the management of this property sometimes gave rise to fission, for marital (*roti vyavahār*) as for commensal (*beti vyavahār*) relations.

The difficulties of making any exact assessment of the quality of interpersonal relationships does not render them less relevant than any other differences that are recognised to exist. While these interpersonal differences are particularly dramatic in the case of the matrilineal peoples, especially the Nayar (Karve 1953:258ff.; Gough 1961: Mandelbaum 1970:55–6), we find definite trends between North and South, especially in the relationship of a women with her conjugal and natal kin after marriage as well as with the non-familial world itself. In the North, a woman of the upper groups is committed to her conjugal family, even as a widow; in the South, divorce and remarriage, even returning home, become more possible as outcomes, especially in Sri Lanka where a woman's rights in the property of her natal family are effectively the same as her brothers' and make return to the parents' home another option. These and other related factors strongly influence the dynamics of family relations. Parent–daughter relations are affected by the barriers placed in the way of fathers visiting their married daughters, hence the greater dependence on one and the same person, son in the first case and brother in the second. Conjugal relations again are radically affected by whether or not a man or woman is marrying a kinsfolk or a stranger, not only the relation between the spouses but with in-laws as well. Other ties remain broadly similar, except in matrilineal societies where those between mother and children, brother and sister, mother's brother and sister's children, a close set of largely uterine-based relationships, are strongly influenced by the overall system of residence, inheritance and descent.

Demographic variables

Let me now turn to consider some other aspects of marriage and the family about which it is easier to make a quantitative assessment since the data derive from the census and similar surveys. A recent statistical analysis of variables contained in the latest census (Frenzen and Miller 1988) concludes that 'the regional differences in Indian household patterns, marriage and kinship systems; and the sexual division of labor coincide closely enough to delineate two distinct zones of domestic organisation in rural north and south India'. The former have higher proportions of households (housefuls) with extended family members, higher levels of village exogamy and lower proportions of women working outside the household, providing two different situations for examining the determinants of fertility. For our own particular analysis, a convenient starting point is age at marriage, which as with household patterns, we considered earlier as a hierarchical variable.

Age at marriage

The average marriage age in India has long been low and remains so, particularly for girls. Early marriage is certainly associated with ideas of maintaining virginity, and a girl is supposed to be married, that is 'betrothed', before she reaches puberty. According to the scriptures, she should marry while still naked (Kapadia 1955:138). As a result the birth of illegitimate children is virtually unknown. Moreover, it means girls have little or no say in the choice of partner, since the union is arranged, and in the South 'prescribed' or at least preferred; for example, there was nothing to stop her being married off to an old widower (though everything was done in the upper groups to prevent even a young widow marrying at all, for women were forced to be renouncers, whereas men as usual never gave up the possibility). Since 'religious' considerations are to the fore, it is not surprising that the average marriage age for girls is lowest in the ritually highest ranking caste, although it is less easy to suggest why the next lowest should be found at the bottom of the hierarchy. It has been observed that less dowry is given when the bride and groom are young (Sarkar 1982:352), but it seems doubtful if this consideration affects Harijan groups.

Attempts have been made to control the age of marriage by law for nearly a century. In 1891 the Age of Consent Act placed the age of consummation of a marriage at twelve. In 1925 this figure was raised to thirteen, and under the Child Marriage Restraint Act (known as the Sarda Act) of 1929 it was raised again to fourteen for girls and eighteen for boys, with sanctions provided for failure to comply. The Hindu Marriage Act of 1955 increased these ages to fifteen and eighteen respectively, and in 1978 they became eighteen and twenty-one. However, even though registration was provided for in the law, none has yet been introduced. The average age of marriage continues to be well below the minimum in many parts, even though individuals and groups have pressed for reform and the Gujarat Suicide Enquiry of 1965 saw child marriages and forced marriages as being important factors in the suicide of young girls.

Despite the generally low ages, there is some difference between North and South India. The figures given by Agarwala (1967:27) show that the southern states have a higher age of marriage. This was already apparent in the 1891 census, and has remained so with some variation until 1961. However, in all the states except Kerala the average age of marriage for females was below fifteen years in 1891; much later on marriage below fifteen was legally proscribed, but unions are still often contracted before that age. Indeed Agarwala (1966) presents a table derived from the Demographic Year Book of 1955 showing the average age of marriage for females in India to be 14.51, and for males 20.05, whereas the comparable figures for Sri Lanka (Hindu and Buddhist) are 20.05 and 26.09, much closer to Muslim North Africa (Tunisia, 19.77 and 26.24) and Christian Europe (UK, 21.85 and 25.15).[16] With the exception of Sri Lanka, the figures for the female age of marriage and for the percentage of never-marrieds in South Asia are the lowest in Asia (P. Smith 1980). For men the country and regional variations are much less for marriage age but greater for the percentage of never-marrieds which recent data show as varying between 10.0 per cent in Taiwan, 7.9 per cent in Sri Lanka, to 2.8 per cent in India (roughly the same as in Japan, although there the mean age at marriage is later), 1.1 per cent in Bangladesh and 0.3 per cent in South Korea.

For women the Indian situation is very particular and we have to reckon on the influence of the religious ideology. However, important as religious factors are, Sri Lanka, which is mixed Hindu and Buddhist, shows an overall difference, in keeping with the trend towards later marriage in the South (especially in Kerala) but much more marked. At the same time Muslim Pakistan and Bangladesh are much closer to northern figures, indicating the presence of other factors than religious ideologies. One of these is presumably the mother-in-law's desire to 'mould the character' of her son's wife, and the wish of the father-in-law to have his line continued earlier rather than later, making it easier to pursue alternative strategies in the event of initial failure, and successfully enabling him to build up a joint household, with which the average age of marriage is strongly and positively associated (Kleinman 1973).

Some of the corollaries of a later age of marriage for women and men have already been discussed; they include the possibility of more work opportunities for women, of more education, of more say in the choice of spouse and of a different initial relation with one's partner, possibly one's children, certainly with one's parents-in-law and parents. At the same time it is associated with less complex, simpler household structures and more 'individualisation' of conjugal units.

Fertility

The age of marriage is directly linked to fertility. In Taiwan, South Korea and Japan, the falling rates of fertility are associated with later marriage, and the governments of China and Israel, the Catholic Church and, in principle, India, all try to encourage later marriage with this aim in view.

However early marriage does not necessarily imply the immediate start of childbearing. A study carried out by Mandelbaum showed the first child to be born between seventeen and twenty, that is, some four years after the beginning of co-residence. There seems some evidence that child marriages are less fertile but also that sex plays a reduced role with early familiarity.[17]

In a limited study of child marriage in Kerala, Kurian (1975) reported that girls who married early at first played together with their husbands like any other children, but at about fourteen became shy and aloof, partly because of 'ridicule from older people which was obviously meant to keep the youngsters apart so as to avoid sexual contacts at too early an age' (p. 211). While both girls and boys married early, and even took up co-residence, they were strongly discouraged from having children until later. There was also the spouses' own relationship to be taken into account: he concludes, 'it is likely that sex played only a secondary role in the life of these people, since marriage took place at such an early age that personal bonds between husband and wife developed quite intimately outside the influence of sex . . . In other words, familiarity as such for a number of years from childhood reduced the primary significance of sex in their lives' (p. 213). Nevertheless most girls agreed that they were happy in their new home and that their marriage had been a success.

Whatever the overall effect of these factors, it remains true that those women married between fifteen and nineteen are likely on average to bear 0.5 to one extra child than those who marry later (Agarwala 1967:132). Hence the later age of marriage is presumably related to slower growth rates in the South. But was it also linked to other aspects of the social system? Dyson and Moore (1983) see the pressure towards early marriage and greater fertility in the North as being related to the rule of exogamous marriage, whereby women move to new communities in which their major role is as mothers, especially with purdah and with less participation in the outside workforce. It would appear as if the 'prescribed' marriages in the South may place marginally less pressure on parents to find a spouse for their child by early betrothal than the distant systems of marriage in the North. The search for high status husbands and rich wives outside the immediate range of kin possibly makes an early 'match' more desirable. However, the example of Sri Lanka on the one hand and Pakistan and Bangladesh on the other suggest that we need to look not so much at the difference between so-called Indo-Aryan and Dravidian systems of marriage but rather at variables connected with woman's access to property and to other rights and freedoms.

The situation in Bangladesh and Pakistan is complicated by Islam. Families cannot use full adoption to plug demographic gaps, since this is prohibited by Islamic law (Abdul-Rauf 1977:88–90: Cain 1986:379). In an analysis of living arrangements in rural areas in Bangladesh and India, Cain found only one case of adoption in the former sample (ninety-four parents) and indeed there were 'few' in the non-Muslim Indian one (n=114). He sees this limited use of adoption as being partly due to the restriction in practice of the pool of possible candidates to the children or brothers and sisters. But that seems doubtful as the reason, especially since Hindu law permitted adoptions from a wider range.

At the same time, women in Bangladesh and Pakistan are less independent economically since the practice of *purdah* confines them to the house and makes it difficult for them to participate in the fields or the market place. The seclusion of women also affects the Islamic areas of North India where Islam penetrated but, as in other parts of the world, the phenomenon tends to be limited (at least initially) to the upper groups.

In Islam not only *purdah* (an upper practice generalised) but also the remarriage of widows and divorcées are permitted, viewed elsewhere in South and East Asia a distinctly 'lower' activity. So too is plural marriage, a less-frequent solution to childless marriages than divorce. These strategies of heirship are preferred to adoption and to filiacentric unions and they may well result in fewer cases of childless or sonless marriages, since the Hindu one-for-always union offers less possibility of producing one's own children, either for males or for females. But it means a greater call to adopt those of other people, for which they may well have to depend upon kin even if there is no formal restriction to the children of relatives.

In many traditional Islamic societies these features are correlated with high fertility rates. Cain (1986) sees these rates as linked to the fact that since women are economically dependent, they need adult sons in order to survive. For those without sons are subject to higher mortality risks. But it is also the case that under Islam and Judaism, widows were not required to remain in an unmarried state (nor did wives have to remain in a particular marriage, especially if childless), and this may have had some effect on the difference in fertility.

An interesting aspect of Cain's table (1986:378 table 1) is that 76 per cent (81 per cent of women) of the Indian and 78 per cent (88 per cent of women) of the Bangladeshi sample of people over sixty were living with adult sons (that is, over fifteen years of age), while a further 4 per cent (2 per cent of women) in the first case and 13 per cent (9 per cent of women) in the second had sons living in adjoining houses, giving totals of 80 per cent (or possibly 81 per cent) and 91 per cent respectively, that is, 83 per cent and 97 per cent of women. Of the remaining cases, there were only 7 per cent and 6 per cent living alone, with a spouse or with minor children, the difference in the Indian case being made up by 6 per cent living with a married daughter and 6 per cent living with other kin. The Bangladeshi families appear to be remarkably successful in producing adult sons; only 3 per cent of those over sixty have no adult son compared with 16 per cent in the Indian sample and 17 per cent or 18 per cent in a demographic model. Cain suggests this can only be due to higher mortality of sonless elderly in Bangladesh; because of this, there is less occasion to look to adoption or filiacentric union for support. Given the quality of the age-specific data and the size of the sample, this must remain a suggestion. But it is also possible that the strategies of continuity prevalent in the Islamic world were more successful in providing children to support the elderly (which of course is only one way of securing that support).

Comparative studies of the causes of high fertility have tended to concentrate on two kinds of variable, the cost of children (e.g. Davis 1955; Caldwell 1987) and the status of women (Dyson and Moore 1983; Cain 1986). The problems of determining these variables are great, especially as cost and status have to be measured against particular scales and conditions; the cost of children is quite different where productive resources are relatively open, while status is usually assessed in somewhat ethnocentric terms – locally it may be higher status for women not to work.

Family planning

One interesting aspect of the higher fertility of the North is the greater difficulty social workers have experienced in getting people to adopt family planning. Easier acceptance in the South is correlated with the greater participation of women in the labour force, with less purdah, higher rates of literacy and the larger percentage of births attended by a medical practitioner, a network of relationships that is brought out in the valuable analysis of North–South differences in demographic and cultural variables by Dyson and Moore to which I have referred (1983:49, table 5, here table 8). The last two of these factors may be seen as recent aspects of

Table 8. *Selected state-level indexes related to women's status and acceptance of family planning*

Region/state	Per cent of couples protected by family planning[a]	Female labour force participation rate, 1971[b]	Per cent of women practicing purdah[c]	Per cent of females literate, 1971[d]	Per cent of births medically attended[e]	Index of son preference[f]
South						
Kerala	28.8	13	4.3	54.3	25.7	17.2
Tamil Nadu	28.4	15	4.9	26.9	21.9	11.5
Andhra Pradesh	26.5	24	9.4	15.7	12.2	8.9
Karnataka	22.4	14	5.4	20.9	15.9	11.2
Maharashtra	34.7	20	16.7	26.4	7.5	18.4
North						
Gujarat	20.1	10	41.8	24.7	9.7	20.8
Rajasthan	13.0	8	62.2	8.5	4.1	n.a.
Uttar Pradesh	11.5	7	46.4	10.7	2.5	25.0
Madhya Pradesh	20.9	19	42.9	10.9	5.1	21.9
Punjab	25.0	1	44.6	25.9	11.3	31.3
Haryana	30.1	2	72.6	14.9	15.3	20.7
East						
Bihar	12.2	9	29.6	8.7	2.8	24.3
West Bengal	21.2	4	n.a.	22.4	n.a.	18.4
Orissa	24.4	7	27.7	13.9	6.8	15.7
All India	22.1	12	n.a.	18.7	n.a.	20.2

Source : From Dyson and Moore 1983:49
[a] Statistics are cumulative to 1979; source: *The Monthly Bulletin of Family Welfare Statistics*, Evaluation and Intelligence Division. Department of Family Welfare. New Delhi, September 1979.
[b] Source: Census of India, 1971, *Series I—India*, Part IIA (ii), Union Primary Census Abstract, New Delhi, 1976.
[c] Source: Committee on the Status of Women in India. *Towards Equality: Report of the Committee on the Status of Women in India* (New Delhi: Government of India. 1974).
[d] Statistics include the population aged 0–4; source: Government of India. *Pocket Book of Population Statistics* (New Delhi, 1972). Although the statistics relate to the absolute level of female literacy, it is worth stressing that their relative literacy (i.e., *vis-à-vis* males) also tends to be substantially lower in the main northern states. The same point is applicable to labour force participation.
[e] Source: Government of India, *Pocket Book of Health Statistics* (New Delhi, 1975).
[f] Source: J. C. Bhatia, "Ideal number and sex preference of children in India," *Journal of Family Welfare* (Bombay 24, no. 4 (1978)). An index of zero would imply equal preference for sons and daughters.

development, although high levels of literacy have long been well established in Kerala despite the fact that attendance at school, especially for girls, is likely to be restricted by existing cultural factors. The positive role of medicine and education is demonstrated in Jain's analysis of regional differences in infant mortality (1985) where a path analysis of multiple regression data indicates these as the independent variables. It is becoming widely recognised that this complex of features, together with those aspects of family and marriage that differentiate the North and the South, bear directly upon the problem of regional differences in the performance of family planning programmes (Shariff 1985).

Differential infant mortality

The over-all Indian sex ratio for the total population is 107 (males to 100 females, 1981), which is about the same as the sex ratio at birth of European populations. However, since the mortality of males in Europe is greater, they are overtaken by the female population giving an over-all sex ratio for the British, for example, of 93.5 in 1971. As there is no effective registration in India, birth ratios are virtually undetermined, except for particular samples (Goody *et al.* 1981a and b), but it appears to be roughly the same as for European populations, that is, in the range 104 to 107 (Mitra 1979; Miller 1981). In other words, the figures for all India show an absence of the usual excess of male deaths, arguing for a greater than expected mortality of females. In the past, part of this mortality may have been due to infanticide, especially in the northwest and among Rajputs, but the basic trend probably resulted from a neglect of female children, or, rather, from the differential treatment of males and females (Miller 1981). An analysis of the causes of death shows that between the ages of naught and four years, girls are more liable than boys to the twenty most fatal diseases (Mitra 1979:24), perhaps because they are given less favourable treatment at home or are taken later to the hospital.

This divergence from the expected sex ratio goes back to the census of 1901. And contrary to expectations, the position of women in this regard has got progressively worse, except in the state of Kerala. In that year the overall sex-ratio was 102.8 males per 100 females whereas in 1981 it was 107, a substantial increase in the masculinity of the whole population. This increase has taken place throughout the country. Nevertheless the census figures show a constant North–South difference, the North having higher ratios in favour of males than the South.[18] The birth ratio is maintained or even increased in many northern states, the extreme being 114 in Haryana, compared with 97 in Kerala.

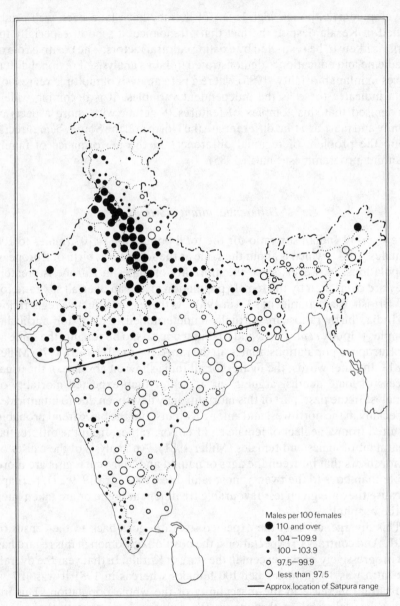

Figure 5 Sex ratios by district, for children aged 0–9, 1961

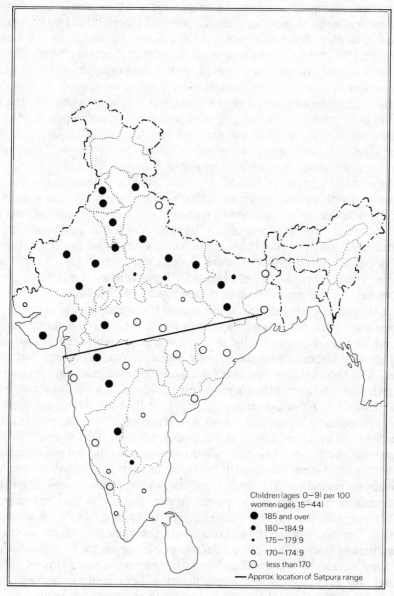

Children (ages 0–9) per 100
women (ages 15–44)
● 185 and over
● 180–184.9
· 175–179.9
○ 170–174.9
○ less than 170
—— Approx. location of Satpura range

Figure 6 Child/woman ratios, by administrative division, 1961

In their attempt to consider the North–South differences from a demographic and cultural point of view, Dyson and Moore (1983) take as their point of departure Visaria's study of interstate differences in sex ratios between 1901 and 1961, which were consistently higher in the North (figure 5). That author saw the prime reason for this state of affairs as lying in sex differences in mortality, the lives of women being more precarious in the North, although child mortality as a whole was greater, possibly because of earlier motherhood and a lower level of general social development. At the same time fertility (overall and marital) varies in much the same way as mortality, the rates again being higher in the North (figure 6). Larger numbers of children go with a lower age of marriage.

As we have seen, this situation goes back a long way and is only partially connected with modernisation variables, such as literacy rates, as is suggested by the evidence of a worsening mortality situation. The highest rates of female literacy are 54.31 per cent in Kerala, followed by 26.86 per cent in Tamil Nadu and virtually the same in Maharashtra, Gujarat, Punjab and West Bengal, the last two of which figure among the states with low sex ratios. The literacy rate for all India is 18.70 per cent for females as against 39.45 per cent for males (Census, series 5, part 1A, p. 144).

Taking up an earlier theme, it might appear contradictory to suggest that women are both advantaged in terms of endowment and sometimes discriminated against partly for the same reasons (e.g. among the Rajputs), but in fact most discrimination takes place against females as infants and children. The Indian data shows that for adolescents discrimination, measured in terms of mortality differences, is less (Caldwell and Caldwell n.d.:31): 'the female relative disadvantage' is 'rather small' at ten to fourteen years of age, 'particularly high' from twenty to twenty-nine, then disappears after thirty-five. The main danger is to infants after the first months of life, especially during the first year when one-third of the excessive female mortality occurs, another third in the next four years, and one-third over the remaining period (p. 31). So it is infants who are most at risk from this discrimination, as one would expect from a hypothesis that linked such behaviour with the expenditures required to be made in future on their behalf, especially in the upper groups with the transfer of direct dowry or inheritance. Once girls achieve a definite personality in the household, they become objects of pride and no longer subject to the same kind of differential care. However the ages of childbearing are difficult for them on other grounds, partly physical related to childbirth, partly social related to the position of the new bride, especially where she is under pressure to produce a greater endowment from her natal family.

Widows

The age of death of men, combined with the differential marriage age, determines the age of widowhood. Between 1951 and 1961 the mean age of widowhood for Indian women under fifty was 38.3, whereas in 1901–11 it had been 36.2, with higher figures for the northern states of Uttar Pradesh, Madhya Pradesh and Rajasthan compared with Madras, Mysore and Kerala. To what other factors this was linked is hard to say, especially as in the more recent period these regional differences in the age of widowhood have disappeared. But they were consistent with the greater masculinity of the North, and with the possible concealment of first widowhood by remarriage (possibly including the levirate). Today remarriage is becoming more frequent throughout. In a survey of Delhi and Pune, Agarwala found that 38 per cent to 25 per cent of widows, who themselves formed 20 per cent of ever-married women, had remarried. Few of these were of the higher castes. The non-leviratic marriages were largely confined to the childless, while the leviratic unions were not referred to as proper marriages but as *karena*, an institution whereby the husband's brother, who might be younger than the widow, put bangles around her wrist and offered her protection (1966:82). This form of marriage is practised by Jats and Gujars in the North and by some Rajputs and Anheers, as well as by the Muslim population. All forms of widow remarriage were more frequent in the South, where they formed part of the greater freedom of women from Hindu and Sanskritic norms. As Srinivas remarked, 'Sanskritization results in harshness towards women' (1962:40), although perhaps as Sabean (forthcoming) observes for Germany in recent centuries, women were less dependent than the legal codes suggested. As one might anticipate, legal codes sometimes supported women as daughters and sometimes harassed them as wives.

Female autonomy and female property

These demographic differences between North and South tend in general to be linked to differences in development on the one hand and on the other to the socio-cultural variables we have discussed in the previous sections. In the southern states of India, there are more town-dwellers, greater female participation in work, higher female literacy rates, greater access to doctors, more use of family planning and less preference for sons as against daughters (Dyson and Moore 1983:49; Shariff 1985:3–4). A number of these factors are linked to the greater seclusion of women in the North, especially in the Muslim-influenced form of purdah, to the greater strength of patrilineal reckoning in various forms, and possibly to the larger number of joint households, although this last association is a matter of dispute.

Dyson and Moore opt for 'female autonomy' as the independent variable, defined as 'the capacity to manage one's personal environment', which is typically characterised by several of the following features: 'post marital residence patterns and behavioral norms that do not rupture or severely constrain social intercourse between the bride and her natal kin: the ability of females to inherit or otherwise acquire, retain, or dispose of property; and some independent control by females of their own sexuality – for example, in the form of choice of marriage' (1983:45). This complex they see as distinctly southern. In a previous paper, Moore tried to relate these differences to the agrarian ecology, in particular to the far greater value of female labour in the rice-based farming systems of the South (1973), but it is now argued that there are problems in reconciling 'the notion of economically determined "culture areas" with the fact of enormous socio-economic differentiation and widely differing material conditions' (p. 47). For today, no clear spatial correspondence is seen between cultural variation and agrarian ecology, so that one should look to the selection of a cultural variable as the primary determining one. However in the rice-farming areas of both India (Miller 1982) and China, women seem to play more part in field agriculture, partly no doubt because of the nature of the technology. Or to put it another way, partly for geographical reasons, they were more resistant to the pressures for the adoption of seclusion from North India and of footbinding from North China (at least among the Hakka).

The hypothesis of Dyson and Moore regarding female autonomy has been criticised by P. and J. Caldwell first, because half the features they regard as major differences are not 'cultural' in that they did not exist a generation or two ago and follow from 'recent relatively high levels of female education in the South' (n.d.:18); however they admit that this feature nevertheless requires an explanation and in fact literacy may have been higher over a much longer period (Gough 1968). Secondly, the belief in the difference between North and South comes from the Indian community itself and academically from Karve's pathbreaking study, *Kinship Organization in India* (1953), about which they appear to accept the 'scathing attack' of Dumont and Pocock (1957). I have already presented some reasons in favour of Karve's account of the differences in kinship systems, although the correlation with Aryan and Dravidian languages and indeed with demographic variables is complex and remains open to question. But in any case it remains doubtful if the Caldwells' alternative hypothesis is any more satisfactory, since the contrast (of what factors?) is seen as lying between 'the heartland of an ancient peasant civilization and the periphery'; the upper Gangetic Plain was the original area of development of 'closely settled peasant societies with sedentary farming and a closed frontier' and displaying the segregation of age and sex that marked North China, the Middle East and the Mediterranean. It was a system marked by 'a very definite internal logic based on chains of command, internal segregation, and greater returns to those at the top of the hierarchy – with considerable similarities to the modern firm' (p. 20).

The Caldwells are referring to a system of advanced agriculture with marked social stratification, which I have argued is the background to the development of a specific set of variables in the domestic domain. These variables are in need of further specification than 'relations of age and sex' alone. The chains of command on the other hand seem to characterise a much wider range of organisations, as suggested by the comment on the firm. Nor is it easier to see these factors as being relevant to the differences between North India and China in contrast to the South (and to South-east Asia). The latter, it is claimed, have 'long been less rigid' but have 'long been slowly adopting the dominant model as remnants of matrilineality, uxorilocality and polyandry are submerged'. While a number of scholars have argued for the continuing influence of matriliny in these areas (although matriliny persists just as firmly in the North-east of the sub-continent), there is little reason for thinking that its persistence is functionally linked to the supposed absence of sedentary farming at an earlier stage; as Gough (1961) has argued, once established, matriliny persists in a number of 'evolutionary niches'. The Caldwells claim that the area in which they worked in Karnataka had been settled by sedentary farmers only within the last thousand years. That is by no means typical of the South, most of which has long practised various forms of intensive agriculture. Even if it were, any functional hypothesis would presume an adaptation well within these thousand years. More immediate influences surely need to be sought for the supposed difference in 'female autonomy'.

I return to the possible influence of agrarian factors in the following chapter, without implying for one moment that the choice is between 'cultural' and 'economic' determinants but trying to assess the strength of the influence of various factors and their inter-relationships. The conclusions of Dyson and Moore are broadly in agreement with Tambiah's treatment of North–South variation and with the kind of considerations I have myself had in mind relating to the greater strength of the women's property complex. These suggestions are not inconsistent with one another, nor yet with the greater weight placed upon women's access to property in the intensive rice-growing areas. On one point, however, clarification is called for. In the course of their analysis they point to the position of women in the North who 'generally do not inherit property for their own use, nor do they act as links through which major property rights are transferred to offspring' (1983:43), yet where the dowry is important. In contrast in the South, 'women may sometimes inherit and/or transfer property rights', while 'Neither marriage nor dowry is necessarily very important' in the case of marriages between close kin (pp. 44–5).

The lower dowry in close marriages, which is noted by Gough (1981:242), does not however mean that nothing is transacted at other marriages and at other times; it may simply imply that the major transfer is delayed until a later moment in time. For a woman's dowry is often counted as her inheritance, both in the North and in the South. In any case, dowry is important in southern marriages, as Gough's account of marriage in Kumbapeṭṭai brings out, although it should be remembered that part of her evidence concerns Brahmins who, as Dyson and Moore remark, tend to conform to northern patterns. Upper groups in Sri Lanka also give dowries and although other groups may not, they nevertheless transmit similar rights by devolution at a later stage (Tambiah 1973:133).

It is certainly the case that there is no broad contrast between dowry in the North and bridewealth in the South, although the emphasis on indirect and direct dowry respectively may be stronger in the respective regions. If this were so, and if we are right in seeing both dowry and female inheritance as aspects of diverging devolution, then the difference would be a matter of the timing of the transmission and the origin of the property, rather than in the incidence of 'female property' as such. However, one general difference does emerge in the access of women to real property; the fact that land is included could be associated with the tendency to delay its transmission, since the constraints on 'immovables' are inevitably greater than those on 'movables', quite apart from its constituting the basic source of livelihood. If (as Gough suggests) dowry is lower in the case of (close) cross-cousin marriages, this provides another example of delay rather than denial.

In his analysis of 'dowry and bridewealth and the property rights of women in South Asia', Tambiah examines the forms of marriage transaction and inheritance of women and concludes by seeing southern patterns as variants on the 'dominant Indian pattern'. 'Both in India and Ceylon women have noticeable property rights. But the shift from bilaterality and ambilocal residence in Ceylon appears to be related to the strengthening of female rights in property in Ceylon' (1973:136).

The question of whether or not we see Sri Lanka (and Burma, which Tambiah includes) as variants on a dominant pattern or simply as variants of equal status need not concern us here. But in terms of (northern) Brahmin ideology, Sri Lanka and the South are deviants rather than variants, a fact that may be connected with an imperfect assimilation of Brahmin norms, with the strength of alternative historical (Dravidian) patterns or with religious ideologies (Buddhism in the Sinhalese and Burmese cases). While it seems correct to think of the dominance of Brahmin norms in much of the South in the same way that we speak of a dominant caste in a village, there are other occasions on which the idea of dominance is less useful. Tambiah suggests that the dominance of the idea of dowry in India served to transform 'bridewealth' into dowry, that is, into indirect dowry. Some such process of change may well have happened in the very distant past but the evidence suggests that in early West Asian societies dowry, direct and indirect, were already well established as coexisting institutions (or better, as interrelated transactions) during the Bronze Age; indeed I would suggest that both were intrinsically linked with the economically stratified systems that emerged at that time (1976). So that any such transformation took place a long time ago and what we see today can hardly be attributed to any recent change and has to be analysed not as a palimpsest but in its own right.

Variations exist and cluster in two ways, some with Dravidian marriage patterns (the South generally) and others with women's ownership of land (in Sri Lanka and some South Indian groups). Tambiah's account, concerned with women's property rights, deals with the latter, Dyson and Moore's with the former. One set of variations is interpreted in terms of women's property rights, the other in terms of women's control of their personal environment, of which inheritance is a constituent element. The interrelationship is clear.

Logically, I have argued, there is a connection between cross-cousin marriage and women's property rights through the brother–sister relationship. Both Tambiah and I (1973) have pointed out that even in the North, women have rights in their conjugal estate in the shape of the dowry which is seen by the actors, by the shastric texts and by us at least, as part of the process of devolution and as linked to that of inheritance. Even if women are not normally entitled to inherit, they may act as residual heirs (indirectly rather than directly) when in the absence of brothers, they pass on the estate to their sons.

Great significance should be given to this institution of the 'appointed daughter' who acquires a marrying-in husband or an adopted son. Because once the claim of a brotherless daughter is admitted, and it is an extension from her claim on movables in the shape of the dowry, the door is opened for women to share in the family lands themselves even when they have male siblings (Tambiah 1973:131). And indeed women's claims to land, and possibly their claim to equal shares, do emerge more strongly in the South, especially if we take into account the 'gifts' of land that they may receive from their parental families. In other words this is not a question of the difference between northern patrilineality and a historically matrilineal South ('historical' at some undetermined time), as Hutton (1946) and Gough (1978) have suggested, but rather of the fact that while throughout South Asia women are endowed with property, in Sri Lanka this claim extends to landed property, representing the fuller working out of the 'bilateral' division of wealth, that is, the diverging devolution which maintains the status of females as well as males in a hierarchical society. One may remark that the caste system itself does this in a general way (Yalman 1967). But on a more specific level, a daughter's status requires maintaining or, better, improving, within the caste, a major mechanism for which is the allocation to her of wealth, whether at her marriage or at the parents' death, or at both.

To other factors behind the North–South differences, whether on an Indian or South Asian basis, we will return later. Here we have tried to point out the dimensions and establish, where possible, a logical coherence among them. While in the main we consider other features, we must not lose sight of the religious element, either in the shape of the influence of Hindu law or of the contribution, which sometimes takes the form of opposition, of Buddhism. In his valuable comparison between Sri Lanka and Burma, Tambiah tends to set aside the Buddhist influence in favour of the idea that what we find in those areas can best be described as a weakened form of the dominant Indian pattern. I doubt if this is possible, especially if one extends the comparison to Japan. It is not possible partly because of the different positions taken by Hindu and Buddhist texts, but also because Hinduism is a religion whose 'priesthood' consists of landowning Brahmins, committed to maintaining and increasing the resources of their lineages, while in Buddhism the 'priesthood' consists of monks, many of whom dwell in monasteries. Hinduism has but few such establishments, developed in response to Buddhism, although it has many non-monastic temples, especially in the South. But these two religious systems inevitably take up different attitudes towards family life and encourage different norms (Lancaster 1984:144), which are related to their modes of ecclesiastical livelihood and to their requirements of support and endowment.

Brahmins in general did not require the support of continual gift-giving, since they had already been allocated land which they had farmed on their behalf. Temple servants of course did need gifts, so too did the temples themselves. But there was not the permanent establishment of celibates to maintain, no role models for the unmarrieds, no monasteries to acquire endowments and no need or incentive to alienate family property to the Church, sometimes in such quantities that the development of that organisation posed a threat to civil society, leading as in Tibet to an ecclesiastical take-over of the government.

In Sri Lanka, as in Tibet, Buddhism was dominant, a fact that may have exercised an influence on the situation regarding women's property. As a monastic religion, it needed to acquire wealth in a different way from the Hindu temples, which are found in greater numbers and better endowed in the South where they escaped much of the predatory pillaging by Muslim rulers (Majumdar *et al.* 1953:305). In Sri Lanka, on the other hand, the Buddhist monasteries were dependent upon endowments from the faithful. While these contributions often came from royalty, they were also provided by merchants and other laity. Regarding the similar situation in Europe I have argued that the allocation of property to women was implicitly and sometimes explicitly encouraged by the property-holding church, since especially as widows they were more likely to give material expression to their faith than men. While I have no evidence that this was so in Sri Lanka, women did control more property than in the North, including land.

There are other dimensions of difference to which I have not referred here, especially the contrast between the societies of caste and tribe, or the 'Brahminical' and 'tribal' cultures (Bose 1975:5). However, a number of the differences to be found between these groupings are similar to those that distinguish high from low as we see from Bose's account of the Mundas and Oraons of Orissa, who practised animal sacrifice, meat eating and the drinking of liquor, as well as displaying relative freedom between the sexes.

Another dimension of difference is that between town and country; it is not only today that the urban middle class display significant values of their own, although the gap has been widened by increased education and the assumption of foreign models. However these same factors of difference have been present since towns existed, and that is some four thousand years in India, for those towns have always been foci of interaction with other cultures, including some with long-standing written traditions. That is, with the very societies, Egyptian, Israeli, Arab, not to mention Greece and Rome, that we will consider in the later sections of this book.

In this chapter I have tried to establish the general character of differences between North and South India. In particular the shapes taken by marriage arrangements and the women's property complex had important implications for a number of other aspects of kinship. But what brought about these differences themselves? I will return to this question at the end of the next chapter in which I want to discuss Gough's attempt, at a more local level, at linking certain variations to systems of production and polities, and to enquire into the relevance of such an approach for the data we are considering.

9

Kinship and modes of production

In the three previous chapters on India, I have discussed marriage and the transmission of property to women in one locality, then looked at the distribution of this and other family variables in the hierarchy and finally examined their regional spread in North and South. Before finally reviewing the status of theoretical approaches to these differences, I want to consider an attempt to discuss differences of a more specific kind that gives prominence (but not exclusively so) to modes of production. At the same time, I want to provide a link back to Tibet and forward to West Asia. To do this I turn to Gough's analysis of kinship in two areas of South India, Thanjavur (1981) and Kerala (1961), which is especially valuable as she looks at a region of the country on a comparative and historical basis in a way that emphasises the wider interdependence of castes in relation to state organisations embracing both town and country, subject and ruler.[1]

There are broadly two types of possible explanations of differences: the historical and the sociological. I use these terms advisedly, since they are neither alternatives nor yet completely distinct; any enquiry needs to take into account both the past and the present. But, quite apart from the selection of the significant factors, there is the question of how far into the past one should search. Moreover, when we isolate historical factors as potential elements in an explanation, we still have to show their relevance to the ethnographic present, to the analytic moment. In core areas of human affairs, survivals do not merely survive; they are made to survive. Any explanation that invokes 'custom' has to consider the mechanisms that reproduce that custom and the forces that try to change it; to remain unchanged under changing conditions is likely to indicate a peripheral or at least an autonomous status.

Gough has effectively linked some of the earlier differences in kinship and marriage within the South to differences in the systems of production by examining them in a regional rather than a village or caste setting. Like others, she has also pointed to the radical changes caused by recent shifts not

290

only in production, although this remains a key variable, but also in the educational and political domains. How much did such factors have to do with differences between the South and North?

Let me begin by reviewing the nature of the competing theories. In the preceding chapters, we have looked at certain similarities and differences in marriage and the family which are related to hierarchy and to region. Part of this variation is linked to the wider patterns of hierarchical differentiation found in the major states of Asia. But regional differences were also a marked feature of the sub-continent, sometimes cross-cutting the particular socio-cultural groups which anthropologists often take as the universe of their investigations. This turns out to be the case not only with the North and the South but also at a more local, regional level, and in her paper on 'Dravidian kinship and modes of production' (1978), Gough sees some of these differences as associated with the productive system itself and the roles played by particular groups, often caste groups.

However, first of all she discusses the more general question of the uniqueness of the South, one dominant feature of which she sees as persisting from a past form of social organisation. This is the Dravidian kinship terminology and she interprets the division between kin and allies (affines) as suggesting the earlier existence of a moiety system, a dual division of unilineal descent groups, perhaps matrilineal. Dual divisions, both patrilineal and matrilineal, have existed in recent times among a number of groups in the Tamil, Telagu and Kerala regions, and these are seen by her, following Hutton (1972:vii-viii), as the possible remnants of a much more widely distributed pattern. However, there are always problems of evidence and relevance with this type of explanation which I will discuss later, but in any case one could also regard such dichotomous divisions as specific developments occurring in particular places emerging out of a more widely distributed pattern of kinship and marriage of which the terminology is a part.[2]

Nevertheless Gough is surely right to argue that 'we have to abandon the notion that there is one single mental pattern underlying all or most of the present and recent Dravidian kinship systems, expressed in a common terminology' (p. 2), even though she does consider that in the past such a pattern once existed but disappeared with the formation of states. Reduction to a single pattern, as we have seen, is the approach taken by Dumont in his work on Indian kinship and by Yalman in his study of Sri Lanka (1967). Certain features are indeed widely distributed across many communities of varied structure and diverse origin, whether we are looking at India, the South or Sri Lanka. But in the case of India, some of the similarities are overlaying rather than underlying, that is, they pertain to the dominance of Hindu law and religion. In the case of the South, most groups display a preference for bilateral cross-cousin marriage and the terminological equations appropriate to such unions. But Gough also finds variations in the terminologies which she maintains 'reflect social institutions' (p. 3).

I have earlier queried the weight that many anthropological analysts of marriage and the family place upon kinship terminologies as indices of relationships, sentiments or structure. While there is clearly some link with other social institutions, terms can be very similar even where the related behaviours differ greatly; the tolerance is wide, although certain statistical relations do exist, for example, between types of nomenclature and types of kin group (Goody 1976). Exceptions to these correlations cannot simply be attributed to 'cultural lag'; a culture may have no need to refurbish its terminology when social changes occur if it is possible to utilise or modify the existing terms for new purposes. Or the terms may not be sufficiently closely linked to those changes to warrant any alteration, as appears to have been the case in England from the Norman conquest. Despite the many changes in family life and in socio-economic organisation, the terminology remained substantially the same from, say, 1200 until the present day (Goody 1983).

The use of the Dravidian terminology in Australia and South India cannot only be explained on the basis of divergence from a common origin, from a common historical root. That is one possible scenario. But as with cross-cousin marriage, this terminology can be found in societies located in many parts of the world and at many different junctures in human history; it is not compatible with a single mode of production or reproduction alone, nor yet with one 'mental pattern' or with any single aspect of social organisation. For example, some 'alliance theorists' have insisted upon the way that terms reflect marriage, but Dumont (1966b) himself reverses the argument when dealing with North India since he wishes to present the case for the unity of Indian kinship systems as a parallel to the unity of the Hindu religious system and the caste hierarchy.[3] On the basis of terminologies, these same authors are led to equate kinship systems, sometimes even 'social structures', that appear vastly different to the naked eye, such as those of the Australian aborigines and of South India. Overall similarity is assumed as the result of concentrating upon resemblances in kin terminologies, which are held to express marriage rules and these, in turn, are seen as critical to social structure. Equally some so-called 'descent' theorists deduce similarities by assuming that terminologies reflect, say, clan organisation. In both cases such approaches are valid up to a certain limited point. But clans, lineages, unilineal descent groups, vary in important ways in different regions under different conditions. While there are some links with types of terminology, there can also be great differences in other aspects of kinship, marriage and the family, some of which relate to the ownership and transmission of the forces of production. In other words terminologies may predict little (except perhaps in the Crow-matrilineal case), so that to take them as indices of either a common origin or of a common deep structure is often to overstress the nature of their entailment. We have little adequate evidence on the long-term changes in terminologies and kinship, but the European case hardly gives grounds for optimism in any of these particular directions. It emphasises that specific terminologies adapt to a wide range of social action and while changes do occur, they may arise from cultural or hegemonic reasons rather than from structural factors.

Gough attempts more broadly to associate differences in kinship systems with different 'modes of production' and 'social formations'. This inevitably leads to the consideration of important comparative and historical factors which take the enquiry beyond either the particularistic, event-dominated analyses of most historians or the universalistic, concept-dominated analyses of many anthropologists. It tries to give an organised specificity to general hypotheses, at the same time as linking them with major historical trends and utilising the notion of systematic relations between social forms, an approach that is at least as important as, but not necessarily exclusive of one that privileges relations at the deep structural level.

Starting with terminology, Gough observes that there is a variation on the Dravidian system of cross-cousin marriage that 'goes with' marriage to the sister's daughter (1978:3), one of several alternative forms which also include an accommodation to an occasional marriage to the mother's sister. As in other parts of the South, the main form of oblique marriage was common in Thanjavur (Tanjore), centred on the Kaveri (Cauvery) delta in South India which saw the rise of what Ribeiro has called a Theocratic Irrigation State (1971:55–64), a concept based on Marx's notion of the Asiatic Mode of Production, and what others have more loosely designated a tributary system (Gough 1981:105). It is in this complex society that we find marriage to the sister's daughter (1978:8), which for the girl, represents union with her mother's brother; in addition there is cross-cousin marriage, under which the maternal uncle becomes the father-in-law, not the husband.

This form of close marriage has to be seen in the context of the social organisation of Thanjavur. This I examine at somewhat greater length, partly in order to link Indian polities with those of China on the one hand and the Near East and Mediterranean on the other, partly for the more specific comparison with ancient Egypt, the paradigmatic case of close marriages, and partly to bring out the contrast within the polity of the Kerala region. 'It was a large, centralised kingdom with an elaborate bureaucracy. There were . . . departments of irrigation, justice, taxation, domestic affairs, of the auditing of accounts of prebendal estates, of charities, palaces, intelligence, the army and the navy, as well as bureaucratic staffs for each of the four levels of local government.' Leach (1959) has argued that Sri Lanka presented an example of a less centralised irrigation system than Wittfogel (1957) assumed in his analysis, again based on Marx, of Oriental Despotism. However Thanjavur, while in no sense 'despotic', had irrigation works that were supervised and organised by the state; the major dams dated from the first century AD and permitted the intensive cultivation of wet rice, though this was greatly extended between the ninth and twelfth centuries when the technique of transplanting seems to have developed here and in South China. The importance of water control is seen by the fact that in the eighteenth century enemies sometimes prevented the king from repairing the dam, as a result of which famine and chaos spread throughout the realm. The king and his government were a fundamental part of the productive system, organising labour not only for irrigation but for other purposes as well. The large labour force required for all these works consisted of part slave and part labourer (or 'peasant'), the same force that built the vast temples, forts and palaces of the kingdom.

In each village the land was managed collectively by the elders of the whole local group belonging to the dominant caste (what Yalman calls the micro-caste) which was usually Brahmin or Vellalar (Gough 1961:106ff.). 'In some villages the land was cultivated jointly by slaves or by peasants of the dominant caste itself or of some subordinate tenant caste. In other villages, which by the eighteenth century formed a majority, the village lands were redistributed by the governing committee to households of the dominant caste every one, three or five years according to custom' (Gough 1978:4). In these latter villages, there was a measure of joint ownership on the part of the 'managerial households'. Originally equal, according to Gough, the shares had ceased to be so by the eighteenth century since private ownership and inheritance of shares, together with their sale in the market, increased as mercantile capitalism penetrated the economy. While land was no doubt increasingly subject to sale over time, leading to a decrease in common rights, any notion of a general shift from communal to individual tenure under mercantile capitalism requires considerable qualification. In the first place the major states of the Eurasian continent had practised the sale of land from a very early period, long before the development of mercantile capitalism, if by that we refer to developments in the post-Renaissance West. The sale of land was common in England in the Middle Ages. Yet far being an example of the distinctiveness of the English or of the absence of 'peasantry', transactions that involved the exchange of land rights for forms of money were found not only on the continent but throughout Eurasia at a much earlier period. In ancient Rome and Greece, records of land sales abound. In *Works and Days*, Hesiod commented on this process in early Athens:

please the gods . . .
. . . so that you may buy the lands
Of other men, and they may not buy yours.

In Roman Palestine, Judas Iscariot bought land with his pieces of silver. In China, literate bureaucrats invested in land and wealth they had made in administration, as we see from that informative novel, *The Scholars* by Wu Ching-Tzu. But the evidence exists for much earlier periods. In ancient Egypt land was freely bought and sold (Pestman 1961). And many of the earliest written tablets from the ancient Near East record transactions in land. In the British Museum series, *Writing in Ancient Western Asia* (1963), the first two tablets reproduced are accounts of fields and crops from Jemdet Nasr, *c.* 2800 BC and from Lagash, *c.* 1980 BC. The third, an Old-Babylonian contract with its envelope, was a deed of sale of land, the envelope bearing the same text as the tablet. Sillī-Ištar, son of Ilī-sulallī, and his brother Awīl-ilī, have bought a plot of land from Sīn-imguranni, son of Pirhum, for two-thirds of a shekel of silver (that is, about one-sixth of an ounce). The parties swore by the gods Nanna (the Moon-god), Šamaš (the Sun-god) and Marduk (the patron god of Babylon) and by the reigning king Samsu-iluna (Uruk, *c.* 1750 BC). According to Sastri (Gough 1981:425), such transactions were common in South India, although restrictions on the transfer of land certainly existed. While the frequency of sales no doubt increased over time, the practice was clearly well established at an early date.

The other point has to do with the advent of mercantile capitalism. This is not the place to review the case for the 'seeds of capitalism' in South India any more than for South China. Yet the argument concerning certain similarities in the Eurasian family is linked, in a loose way, with that concerning systems of production. While the mode of organising commerce and manufacture was certainly different in South India than Europe at the beginning of the sixteenth century, the former was hardly behindhand in terms either of proto-industrial manufacture, for example of cloth (to name the most prominent product) nor yet of its active export to foreign countries throughout the Indian Ocean (Ramaswamy 1985). Is it not in hindsight, thinking of later industrial capitalism, that we associate Europe with the advent of the mercantile form? Were such activities not already well advanced in the Near East as early as 1500 BC (Goody 1986:177ff.)? In fact neither the commerce nor yet the manufacture are stressed in Gough's account but rather the extraction of the agricultural surplus, which certainly played the greater part in the sphere of kinship. It is the production, the extraction and the use of the surplus, on which we need to concentrate.

The state of Thanjavur was maintained not only directly by *corvée* labour but also by a large surplus derived from the agricultural work of others;

'from one third to half the gross produce was claimed by the state as its "upper share". The local managers retained only about a quarter of the produce after the state-supervised grain payments had been made at each harvest to the village servants, to any cultivating tenants, and to the slaves' (p. 5). Thus the type of so-called *jajmānī* system reported from the North emerges here as a state-organised method of payments to the lower orders in the hierarchy. The officers themselves were differently rewarded. 'The state paid its officers, especially those of the upper ranks, mainly through the allotment of all or part of the "upper share" of prebendal estates or *inams*, accorded to ministers, army officers, bureaucrats, members of the royal family, temples and monasteries, and to some lower functionaries' (p. 5).

The army was originally drawn from land-managing Vellalars and their Padaiyacchi tenants, but it took on more recruits from immigrant Naidus and Kallars who later became the dominant, managerial castes as a result of the way in which the military were allocated (or sometimes seized) land rights in return for services rendered. These groups provided the professional army which was quartered in barracks at strategic points throughout the kingdom. While in the earlier Chola period the government was predominantly 'a theocracy with a divine kingship and a Brahman bureaucracy' (p. 5), more posts were now allotted to military governors, although the Brahmins remained the core of 'the state class'. At least from Chola times, many villages had a resident caste of collective non-cultivating land-managers as well as a large caste of slaves who did most of the work of rice production, so that in some villages there seems to have been no free peasant caste at all. These managerial castes were closely interlocked with the cities which had a more complex division of labour and where the elaborate external and internal trade raised much additional revenue for the state.[4]

Some anthropological studies present a picture of the Indian village in terms, first, of its hierarchy of caste, defined very much in the context of Hindu religion, secondly, of a self-sufficient, cooperative socio-economic system in which one caste contributed towards the good of the others, either in an elaborate division of labour (Leach 1960) or in ritual co-operation centring upon joint participation in the village festivals (Srinivas 1952). While Gough acknowledges the relevance of these notions, she insists that for earlier times they must be seen in a wider context of the relations between town and managerial caste, the role of the state in irrigation and the extensive nature of trade. Castes operated not only locally but within the wider socio-economic system of the state which in turn had an important influence on the kinship systems of those castes and of their constituent local groups. An analysis of kinship in South India cannot be based on local studies alone, without reckoning with the complexity of social organisation, and the widespread links between town and country, as well as between different levels of the economic, political and religious systems.

In Thanjavur, 'the flat dry terrain permitted extensive roads, wheeled vehicles, mobile armies and the regular removal of the agricultural surplus to storehouses of the state and its officers' (p. 6). The point about the terrain and the transport is important in relation to surplus and its uses. Coquery-Vidrovitch (1969) has argued that while the possibility of a surplus existed in Africa, the demand was absent. I have suggested to the contrary (1971) that under existing conditions the possibility of surplus was in general small, but in any case its productive deployment was limited. In the savannah regions it was small because of the limitations of the farming technology and the distribution of water. Forest agriculture gave more abundant rewards, especially where the plantain was available. But everywhere the absence of wheeled vehicles (and in the forest the difficulties with pack animals because of tsetse) made the movement of bulk produce extremely difficult. Cereals were easier to move than yams or plantains, but without the extensive water transport that served the main Chinese cities, without the wheeled carts and barrows so widely used in Eurasia, often without even the energy of animals, the idea of maintaining a large, highly differentiated town on the basis of an agricultural surplus is difficult to imagine. In the agro-towns of the Yoruba of West Africa, most of the inhabitants grew their own food in distant farms, headloading back what they needed for their own consumption. It is true that in pre-colonial times, as we find in the Gonja town of Salaga, the household's own slaves might provide part of its wants, with the active participation of the masters. Nevertheless, the widespread movement of basic goods, as distinct from valuables, was difficult, even with the use of slave labour. And while some food was sold on the open market, this remained small in quantity.

It is sometimes claimed that if the 'demand' or 'need' had been present a surplus could have been obtained and transported. Such an argument may appear acceptable, even enticing, from the peak of our present technological achievement. Proposed alike by Althuserian Marxists as well as by formal economists such as Hopkins (1973), it is profoundly ethnocentric, failing to give sufficient weight not only to the nature of ecological constraints (such as the tsetse) but to the uniqueness of many transforming discoveries (such as writing or the plough), to the developmental stages of technological growth (a prime object of 'social evolutionary' theory and one that is characterised by accumulated knowledge), and most importantly to the social requisites and organisation involved in the production and maintenance of, say, a plough, not to mention the negative factors that resist such potential changes. It is these positive features that provide man with the capacities to exercise his skills on the one hand and his abilities on the other, not simply a decontextualised 'demand'.

In Thanjavur, suggests Gough, the economic and ecological situation was consistent with the fact that the main kinship groups were neither house-holds nor lineages but large in-marrying micro-castes within each village, composed of between six and thirty households, living on one street and receiving customary shares from the produce of the village lands. The 'corporate' mode of landholding among the dominant castes she sees as differing from the more individualistic systems of East Asia and of South India in the recent past. 'In the managerial caste, whether Brahman or high non-Brahman, the elders usually distributed the land to the lineages of the micro-caste' (p. 6) who then divided it among the households. But in other cases the land was directly cultivated for the managers by peasants and slaves. In addition they 'directed much communal labour connected with digging channels, transplanting, and harvesting, governed the lower castes, ran their own and the village temples, and carried on a highly integrated social and religious life' (p. 6).

The lineages of the managerial caste were segments of dispersed, exo-gamous patriclans; members used kinship terms and shared birth and death pollution as well as jointly carrying out certain temple tasks. Bilateral cross-cousin marriage occurred, but kin terms were asymmetrical, empha-sising lineage solidarity. However, the lineages themselves were equal, in other words there was no hypergamy; it was just that '*within each generation* wife-givers and wife-takers were distinguished both behaviourally and ter-minologically' (p. 7, my italics). Thus wife-givers and wife-takers are defined from an ego-oriented, not a lineage, standpoint. At this level inequality is inevitably present so that this kind of hypergamy or hypogamy always exists. As we have seen this problem lies at the bottom of much literature on 'alliance'.

But while Gough stresses the 'corporate' nature of land holding, the dominant forms of law were the Hindu codes we discussed in the previous chapters. Moreover, the main kinship groups for many purposes were the households which were usually 'a patriarchal linear or stem family, dividing every generation. It had no fixity on land or even in a house' (p. 7). On the other hand they were the main units of production and consumption, and it was they who arranged for the transmission of individual property and the marriages of its members. This point is yet clearer in the lower groups, despite the collective responsibility for some tasks.

Among the lower castes of Thanjavur, the patrilineal groups were weaker and the micro-castes stronger. 'Nuclear or stem households were the norm, with occasional linear households of short duration' (p. 7). At the same time land-holding within the village was highly differentiated as in pre-Revolutionary China, but by caste as well as by family; the early system of joint, even common, ownership with equal shares applied only to the managerial class. 'Land was sometimes distributed to individual nuclear families of tenants for cultivation, but on an annual or seasonal basis; sometimes it was cultivated in common by all the tenants. Slaves received tiny allotments of land, and on prebendal estates village servants had small service tenures for their maintenance. But most village servants, tenants and slaves, lived mainly from grain shares meted out to them at harvest time on the village's threshing floors. Slaves were part of the collective property of the village establishment, and in most villages were redistributed to the managerial households every one to five years along with land and cattle' (pp. 7–8). There was no permanent attachment of a slave to a master; in any case much of the agriculture was done in collective gangs drawn from the micro-caste as a whole.

This account presents a highly corporate, 'egalitarian' view of land-holding among the managerial castes which is not altogether compatible with the award of land for particular services nor with its accumulation by successful entrepreneurs, as evidenced in the records of gifts to temples. It has its parallels in other redistributive systems of land tenure in the Near East and in Russia, but it would clearly be vulnerable not only to the sale of land but to the alienation of rights for any particularistic purpose whatsoever. And in any case it is to the managerial castes it applies, not to the tenants or the landless.

The analysis has links with Marx's notion of the Asiatic Mode of Production. Up to a point Gough accepts the idea of the local 'self-subsistence community' and herself speaks of 'village communes'. But she also stresses the interrelations between town and country, and certainly does not see Indian society as condemned to perpetual stasis. For, despite these communes and despite the bureaucracy, 'there seems to have been nothing inherent in this system that would prevent the expansion of empires, the increasing division of labour and the growth of specialised urban populations, of manufactures, and of trade' (pp. 5–6). From the economic standpoint the preconditions of capitalism were almost complete. The one exception was the firm control kept by the state over manufacturing, trading and other private wealth, 'so that it seems doubtful that capitalism would have developed without European intervention and eventual conquest' (p. 6). On this view, the difference in preconditions can hardly have been great, since India was not without its entrepreneurs nor Europe without its state intervention (which has been seen as a critical factor in the development of Japan, for example); moreover, the respective contributions of these two factors is always difficult to measure and their impact difficult to assess. On this view, again, colonial intervention is seen as opening the way for capitalism by creating a breach in the control of the earlier state; others on the other hand have claimed that colonialism prevented the indigenous move to capitalism. But on both views capitalism might well have developed first in this part of the world rather than in Europe; both seriously challenge Marx's idea of the uniqueness of the West in the formative period.

Production was based upon the intensive cultivation of wet rice. As in other highly irrigated parts of Tamil Nadu, we find nucleated villages settled on small stretches of dry land among the paddy fields. The village was divided into streets of land-managers, tenant-peasants, artisans, service workers, other village servants connected with maintaining and protecting the irrigation works and the slave castes who lived outside the village proper. How was this hierarchy connected with the question of marriage? Among the lower castes, unions take place not only to cross-cousins and to the sister's daughter, as among the Brahmins, but also to the mother's younger sister, an oblique marriage in a genealogically upward direction. 'Unlike the Brahmans, the lower castes also favoured marriage to the mother's younger sister or classificatory sister if she was younger than the bridegroom' (p. 8). In this context the mother and sister were clearly 'affines' as well as kin.[5] The major type of oblique marriage takes a daughter not only from the descent group to which the mother has been 'given' but from the very family, the antithesis of any hypergamous arrangement affecting social groups. The secondary type of oblique marriage, practised by lower groups, involves taking from the same source as before, in fact, taking the nearest relative of one's own mother. A man's marriage to the mother's sister is the equivalent of a woman's marriage to the sister's child, whom Brahmin men are already permitted to marry. Both these unions fall into the class of closest possible marriage, leaving aside only that between a brother and a sister themselves. In these same lower castes that permit unions with the mother's sister, divorce and remarriage occur, with a married woman retaining considerable claims on her natal household. In other words there is little of the so-called 'incorporation' among the poor that is reported for the upper castes.

Among these poorer groups there were no dispersed patrilineal clans; instead each man 'was strongly bound to his wife's natal household and to the conjugal households of his sisters. Correspondingly, relations with the mother's natal household were as significant as with the father's; mother's brothers, in particular, had a claim to marry their sisters' daughters or to give them to their sons' (p. 8). But this type of marriage (to the sister's daughter) was also important among the Brahmins, indicating that there too the mother's house was of continuing importance for a woman, especially as it might also be her conjugal home.

Gough raises the question of whether the marriage to the sister's daughter was limited to the 'hydraulic bureaucracies with their weak and shallow patrilineal groups and their tendency to override generations' (p. 9). Since there is no difference in this particular form of marriage as far as low and high castes are concerned, whereas the high castes have stronger patrilineages, we should perhaps look elsewhere for a possible explanation, taking into account the interesting link with complex irrigation states. Marriage to the sister's daughter has some of the same consequences as that to the father's sister's daughter or even to the bilateral cross-cousin, which tends to pull back at the third generation what was divided at the first. But with sister's daughter marriage, the return suffers only a limited delay by comparison (figure 7). If a woman is provided with land as her dowry, then marriage to her daughter will re-integrate the fixed element of the family estate that was dispersed (at least in terms of claims) when she married.[6] Even if land is not included, what went out of the sibling group at one generation returns at the same level, whether this be endowment, status or other inheritable attributes (which may include heirlooms, learning, 'blood' and beauty).

The marriage itself comes close to a union between siblings. Instead of his sister, a man marries her daughter. Interestingly enough, the only case of widespread brother–sister marriage, a union that is critical for most theories of incest, occurred in another irrigation civilisation, namely ancient Egypt. Why irrigation? It is a question to which I return in discussing Egypt in the next chapter but one common element, under high investment and high productivity, is the great value placed upon land, with which is connected the extent of social differentiation, the wish to maintain by endowment the position of daughters as well as of sons and a pattern of marriage which prevents dispersal or reunites the divided estate.

There are three further points to which I want to call attention in the

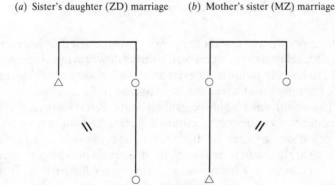

(a) Sister's daughter (ZD) marriage   (b) Mother's sister (MZ) marriage

Figure 7 Oblique marriages

analysis of Thanjavur. The first concerns the redistributional function of the managerial economy, and especially the rotation of land, cows, slaves. The redistribution of land was also practised in the Russian *mir*, as well as in Ottoman Palestine among cultivating Arabs. In these cases at least, the institution must be seen not as the remnant of some earlier egalitarian system, an example of what Radcliffe-Brown called 'distributive justice', but rather as the result of efforts of the state and of land-owners to control the size of the holdings of those who worked the land. As with some European systems of primogeniture, the landlords were interested in maintaining farms of certain dimensions rather than allowing a fragmentation, which quite apart from raising the question of viability or return, would have broken up the system of service or even of tax, diminishing existing responsibilities and increasing the difficulties of collection.

Secondly, the allegedly communal nature of these aspects of its land tenure is not related to so-called 'primitive communism', but rather to the character of a complex state based on irrigated agriculture as well as to the element of rotational distribution. Of course, some common lands exist in all socio-economic regimes and their extent is partly related, as we see in contemporary Greece, to the nature of the economy, pastoralism in particular. Again in pre-industrial societies, joint rights in land are often held by kinsfolk of various degrees of inclusiveness. While these forms of tenure may well undergo profound changes with the growth of mercantile or industrial capitalism, that does not mean to say that all land was held in common nor that individualised rights (to buy, sell or otherwise dispose of and exploit) were not already well established. The error into which many writers fall is illustrated in Issawi's statement about the last two centuries in the Near East: 'Another necessary change took place in land tenure . . . the communal or tribal forms of tenure that prevailed in most of the region were slowly replaced by private ownership' (1982:4). But a kind of 'private ownership' of land involving sale has been known in those parts for millennia.

Thirdly, upper women appear to be more constrained than lower ones. Is this difference related to the stress on the direct dowry at marriage, while the lower tend to have an indirect, or even a delayed, dowry which merges with inheritance among those who have little to pass on?

While Thanjavur was a highly centralised state, Kerala was very different. 'In the sixteenth to eighteenth centuries Kerala had some nine to dozen feudal states of varying sizes' (p. 10), the largest being situated round a port. 'The state's surplus, much smaller than in Thanjavur, came mainly from taxes on overseas trade and only secondarily from village tribute, for there was no land survey and no regular land tax'. The contrast, highly significant from the standpoint of the structure of the state, is between one built on exchange revenues and one built on production revenues, a distinction that goes to the root of the nature of 'despotic' authority. For 'liberalism' tends to characterise the former and control the latter, if only because overseas trade depends more directly upon individual initiative and upon some accommodation with outsiders. Kerala was not a major area for agricultural production. The terrain was mountainous, with few roads and wheeled vehicles, a heavy rainfall, only minor irrigation works, and mostly rain-fed gardens. 'The plough was much less used than in Thanjavur, and oxen were not used for threshing or irrigation' (p. 10).

The Nayars of Kerala had the right of overseeing the villages in which the Tiyyars were the cultivators; slaves were employed in wet-rice cultivation and the same service castes were present as in the south-east. The region was characterised by what Leach (1959) calls 'hydraulic feudalism' [7] or, in Fox's phrase (1971), by a collection of 'kin-feudations'. There was almost no central bureaucracy, land being parcelled out among Brahmin temples and Nambudiri Brahmin households, the former having their own internal bureaucracy and maintaining a complex system of accounting. The Brahmins possessed what almost amounted to private estates guarded by Nayar lineages acting as military vassals, while the Tiyyars held lesser tenures in coconut gardens, providing in return tribute and labour for the Nayars as well as for the nobility. Village servants held plots of land but were also paid in grain by the households they served. Slaves were granted their own small gardens in return for cultivating paddy for the Nayars and Brahmins, that is, for the gentry. The ubiquity of such tenures and the weakness of the state meant stronger lineages, linked by either hypergamous or egalitarian marriages. As Fox argues, in simpler states large kin groups can be adapted in the service of state formation.

Royal lineages stretched back some twenty generations and were marked by the lateral transmission of office in contrast to the primogeniture of Thanjavur, the sideways succession often found in the less-centralised states of Africa (Goody 1966). 'Matriliny also persisted among the Tiyyar peasants in regions where plough agriculture was insignificant. In Central Kerala, however, where the plough was more prevalent, the Tiyyars had patrilineal households which apparently date from the late sixteenth century' (p. 12).

While the Nayar and slave castes bred freely, 'the elite patrilineal caste of Nambudiri Brahmans . . . kept its birthrate down and conserved its family estates by the well-known device of having only the eldest son marry in the caste and beget children for the family. Younger sons found consorts in the matrilineal castes of royals, temple servants and Nayars. Thus although the eldest Brahman son might have as many as four Brahman wives, many Namboodiri Brahman women remained unmarried' (p. 13). In other words, we find a domestic pattern similar in some ways to that of Tibet, with marriage being permitted to only one brother (of the upper group) while the others took consorts outside the caste, morganatically rather than polyandrously, with the result that the sisters often had to remain unmarried, since they could not marry 'down'.

The Malayálam Brahmin system was characterised by Mateer as 'primogeniture run mad' (1883:176). The account of the Portuguese traveller, Barbosa, dating from the sixteenth century, described the situation in the following words: 'They marry only once, and only the eldest brother has to be married, and of him is made a head of the family, like a sole heir by entail, and all the others remain bachelors and never marry. The eldest is heir of all the property' (1866:121). A local writer of the last century described these arrangements in the following terms: 'The younger brothers are to remain unmarried, to aid the increase of the family estate as much as possible, and to honour and obey the elder like a father.' The property can never be divided, but if the younger brothers wish to separate, the elder will give them a regular allowance for food and clothing. They may then 'form connections, which entail no proprietary consequences, with Nair women' (Simcox 1894:i,555).

It is also the case, according to Barbosa, that even the royals took mistresses rather than wives. 'These kings do not marry, nor have a marriage law, only each one has a mistress, a lady of great lineage and family, which is called nayre, and said to be very beautiful and graceful. Each one keeps such a one with him, near the palaces in a separate house, and gives her a certain sum each month, or each year, for expenses . . . And the children that are born of these mistresses are not held to be sons, nor do they inherit the kingdom, nor anything else of the king's; they only inherit the property of the mother . . . ' But 'The king sometimes makes grants of money to them, for them to maintain themselves better than the other nobles.' The king's sisters, whose sons succeed him after his full brothers, 'do not marry, nor have fixed husbands, and are very free and at liberty in doing what they please with themselves' (1866:105–6).

Two points should be noted. Writing on Malabar, Logan remarks that while his children were not his heirs, nevertheless 'natural affections' led the king to make a suitable provision for the mother and the offspring, sometimes in the form of a grant of territory (1887:154). 'Similarly it was observed at the beginning of the last century that the Rajahs were generally poor at their accession, because their predecessors were careful to distribute all their property before death among their nearest relations, to the exclusion of the heir' (Simcox 1894:i,550). The Nayar themselves were matrilineal in that property and position were inherited from the mother's brother rather than the father, so that the relationship between the groups was mutually compatible. At the same time the social and physical separation between husband and wife was profound. In earlier times the matrilineal Nayar themselves 'married' polyandrously, except that unlike Tibet, the system was woman-centred and the sibling ties with the brother received more weight than the tenuous relation with the visiting husbands to which some have denied the term 'marriage', reserving this for the formal *tali*-tying to a ritual partner which a young girl underwent at puberty. In her earlier study of Kerala, Gough (1961) suggested that this form of matrilineal social organisation may have evolved at a much earlier point in time, before the advent of an advanced type of agriculture, and that once established the system continued to adapt and be adapted to changing circumstances, but displaying a certain measure of structural autonomy of the kinship system from the political economy. That interpretation seems correct; northern norms, incorporated in Hindu texts, were of course brought in or adopted by Brahmin and other groups in the South, while many of the indigenous peoples maintained aspects of their earlier forms of social organisation. Nevertheless this process represented no simple survival but an active adaptation to the new order which it influenced, as it was itself influenced. Aspects of the matrilineal situation fitted with general developments in the South that saw parallel adaptations in patrilineal groups.

Events over the last century have made greater demands on the system that brought out the internal tensions in the matrilineal organisation created by individual conjugal ties. Even when Simcox was writing in 1894, the Nayar were changing. 'Now that a Nayar usually marries one wife, lives apart with her in their own house, and rears her children as his own also, his natural affection comes into play, and there is a strong and most laudable desire for some legal mode, other than those at present recognised, for conveying to his children and their mother all his self-acquired property. At present he can only convey to them his property by stripping himself of it, and making it over to them in free gift during his own lifetime' (p. 553). An early handing over to the children, who are not even the legitimate heirs, means there is the possibility of having to endure considerable hardship. If this way of getting round the provisions of an institutionalised system of inheritance was general, it would present the same inherent difficulties that are intrinsic to any early transmission, whether to avoid tax or to seal a marriage, difficulties that are well brought out in the tragedy of *King Lear*. But that was not the case. Many matrilineal fathers continued to transfer some property to sons, and in Kerala the aim was to hand over to them *self-acquired* rather than inherited property instead of leaving that property to go to uterine brothers or sisters' sons, who were already entitled to the family holdings. If the sons had taken those as well, the whole system would collapse. Simcox notes: 'In an Arab description of the peculiar marriage customs of the Nairs in the sixteenth century, it is stated that the object of not allowing the children to inherit their fathers' estates was to prevent the alienation of the family property' (1894:i,552). Interestingly Simcox herself relates this general problem of the brother's son and the sister's son to the situation in ancient Egypt which I review in the next chapter. There men conveyed all to their wives and then married their sisters, which she appears to see as a partial solution to the matrilineal puzzle, that of looking after both the offspring and the heirs (p. 553).

Among the Brahmins younger sons were effectively eliminated from the inheritance, while their sisters often remained unmarried, as a result of which they received no dowry but did have support. A more radical solution to this latter problem was that of the nineteenth-century Rajputs who killed their infant sisters, apparently for similar reasons (Tod 1920:ii,741). A more merciful strategy was found among the patrilineal Tiyyars and artisans of Central Kerala who used fraternal polyandry to keep their households small and united, a similar mechanism to that adopted in Tibet.

The internal stratification of marital assigns follows the pattern we have already seen in the North, direct dowry among upper groups, more indirect dowry among the lower ones. 'In patrilineal castes such as the Nambudiri Brahmans ... where the wife was removed to her husband's home, the bride's family provided a dowry of jewelry, vessels, and even cash, cattle and slaves' (Gough 1978:13), though land went only with men. 'Among the lower castes such as Tiyyars and artisans, as in the lower castes of Thanjavur, the bridegroom's family made a counter-payment which remained with the bride's family, in addition to contributing to the expenses of the marriage' (p. 13).

Gough sees in this more even balance of the assigns a recognition of the value of the wife's labour (which was not used in upper castes) and of her powers of procreation, providing an addition to her right to property from her natal family. In the matrilineal castes of Central Kerala there were no marriage payments (and no real marriage), both men and women retaining rights in the ancestral lands of the *taravad*. Women continued to be strongly attached to their natal group. But those endowed sisters of the Nambudiri Brahmin caste who were married to eldest sons she sees as being totally cut off from their natal families. While there is certainly some relation between marital transfers, position in the family and the economy, I have argued that women are rarely if ever completely disestablished in this way; on the other hand, the absence of major material transfers at marriage in the matrilineal groups seems generally associated with the minimal transfer of rights that marriage or cohabitation involves, so that greater emphasis is placed on inheritance. For lower groups, a woman's productive labour is certainly more important but it is often difficult to see these counter-payments as compensation since they are usually passed to the wife either directly or indirectly as an endowment.

Marriage arrangements bound together not only individuals and families but whole lineages, especially in the upper reaches where we find hypergamous unions between castes. The lineage of the King of Calicut (Zamorin) had liaisons with women of the Nayar group whose brothers were soldiers. Royal sisters married Nambudiri Brahmins, creating a kind of feudal hierarchy of conjugal unions. But there was a strong separation even between sexual partners which left untouched any change in property rights. 'The lower-ranking wife and children were forbidden to eat with or normally to touch the high caste husband' and the wife might not enter his house after his death. 'For in these aristocratic lineages with their valuable properties and their specialised political ranks and functions, it was imperative that the personal attachments of marriage and fatherhood not "spill over" and mar the highly restricted and political character of affinal ties' (p. 15). Or to put it another way, by having second-class wives, they limited the claims to property and office. It was a particular sort of concubinage, not the concubinage that supplied children when one already had a barren wife, as in China, but the concubinage that provided sexual and domestic but no genetricial rights, as was also the case with monogamous, morganatic unions, extending to the yet looser ties, with no rights involved, of the companions of priests of the Christian Church in the early Middle Ages, three forms which we might distinguish as legitimising, morganatic, and companionate concubinage.

Before returning to the general discussion it is worth commenting on the contemporary changes in some of the features we have reviewed since the evidence on North–South differences is often of more recent date. A general decline in the number of complex households occurred between 1949 and 1964 in Kerala (Gough 1975) and between 1951 and 1976 in Thanjavur. In the village of Kunbapeṭṭai in Thanjavur over that period the percentage of nuclear households rose sharply. The Brahmins still had a smaller percentage, but there the change was particularly dramatic (57.7 per cent increase);

Brahmin	45 to 71 per cent
Non-Brahmin	70 to 80 per cent
Harijan	76 to 90 per cent

Whether or not this represented a similar decline in 'Hindu Undivided Families', that is, in effective property-exploiting groups, is less certain since division does not automatically follow from physical separation. However, in upper groups separate residences do at least suggest a decrease in the authority of the elders and, in the case of virilocal marriages, of the mother-in-law over the daughter-in-law. As spatial distance between kin increases, there is a falling off in cross-cousin and other preferred marriages, combined with more frequent unions to strangers. At the same time early pre-puberty marriages tend to disappear along with polygyny and polyandry, the sororate and the levirate, though these latter were always features of lower rather than upper groups. In Kerala there was again a yet more significant increase between 1949 and 1964 in the proportion of nuclear households among the Nayars (and matrilineal servant castes), that is, 82.7 per cent; among the Harijans, the increase was 51.2 per cent and among the Izhavars (Tiyyars), Christians and village servants it was only 5.9 per cent. These differences are significantly related to the varying levels of complex households at the start. For example, the Nayars had only 29 per cent of nuclear households in 1949, being much more 'feudal' in certain ways.[8] However, 'joint households' continue not only in agriculture and in business but also among the propertyless, partly out of sentiment but also because, in the absence of public welfare services, 'juniors are still expected to take care of aging or disabled kin' (p. 266).

These developments are linked with wider social changes, especially with the increase of wage-earning and market production which tends to individualise the interests of members of family groups. Improved communication and public education have widened the potential range of social relations while a democratic political regime has led to a loosening of primary group loyalties. As in China and Japan (Cartier 1986b; Beillevaire 1986), the spread of reformist doctrines, stimulated by contact with the ideologies of the West, has influenced society at all levels, at the same time as the changing demographic and economic situation has led to a reassessment of family strategies. Of course, much has continued, particularly the kin terminologies, and although they no longer have the same prescriptive pull, cross-cousin and oblique marriages are still given some preference.

Returning to the question of traditional unions, in South India and Sri Lanka marriage was permitted, indeed prescribed, with close kin (especially cross-cousins and sister's daughters), in opposition to North India, where all close marriages are forbidden. This is not a difference between exogamous and non-exogamous clans, since cross-cousins always fall outside these groups. In China, 'clans' (patronymic groups) are exogamous, but one can nevertheless marry cross-cousins, although there is no apparent preference for close kin marriages as distinct from close kin adoption. In North India on the other hand one is forbidden to marry any kin, however related. In the South one has to marry close relatives; indeed marriage turns any partner into a close kinsman. Dravidian kinship is marked by a terminological distinction between 'kin' whom you cannot marry and 'allies' (or 'affines') whom you can. In fact both are 'kin' and an outstanding feature of the domestic life of this irrigation society, and one that runs contrary to the Hindu norms observed in the North, was the closeness of the marriages one made, almost as close as the permitted marriages in another great irrigation society, that of the Nile Valley.

In drawing attention to these very close unions, I want to recall the fact that we are not dealing with a primitive tribe just emerging from 'nature' to 'culture', that is, not the Australian aborigines but one of the most advanced economic systems of the time in which the intensive, irrigated cultivation of rice was combined with an active mercantile and craft economy. Differentiation was great and land highly valued. Yet we find a form of marriage apparently approaching the pole of nature rather than culture. And while it might be said to involve 'exchange' (of rights rather than persons), the exchange is between minimal units and smacks more of reclamation than exchange, reclaiming what one has parted with by way of loan or debt.

What light does the discussion of the relation between kinship and modes of production throw on the general issue of North–South differences? It will be recalled tht Moore had at first presented an interpretation in terms of the contrast between wet-rice production in the South and cereal cultivation in the North; others such as Karve have seen the explanation as connected with the earlier pastoralism of the North and the agriculture of the South; some others, like the Caldwells, looked to the yet earlier intensive agriculture of the North and the shifting agriculture in the South, to the difference between the northern centre and the southern periphery, and to the continuous influence of 'aboriginal' cultures of a matrilineal type in the South. Others again have pointed to more 'cultural' factors, based upon a contrast of Indo-Aryan and Dravidian languages, and to some extent peoples, even 'races'.

As I have remarked, there are two broad types of competing theory, one of which privileges historical variables, another which privileges sociological ones, the past and the present. There is no fundamental opposition between the two, and much depends upon the data being used and the questions being asked. Problems arise with both. A particular type of numerical data can lead to forms of factorial analysis which can elucidate functional and causal relations. In default of such material, the alternative is a comparative method. Historical discussion is often more concerned with 'origins', always a tricky problem even when the documentation is adequate to the task. But most of our authors adopting such an approach fail to explain the persistence of some features over time and the supposed discontinuity of others, why one factor was submerged by Hinduism and not another.

That is basically the case with the argument that the South differs because it had earlier been matrilineal, or is closer in other ways to 'aboriginal' culture. For example, the Caldwells see the 'traditional peasant society' of the Gangetic plains as marked by great segregation of age and sex as against the peripheral areas which have been more influenced by matriliny. As in

China, northern peoples moving to dominate the South certainly met up with local groups who had different practices regarding marriage and the family, and some of whom were matrilineal (as indeed were some in the North-east of the sub-continent). The difficulty in offering an explanation in these terms is that we have to provide some account of why these particular features and not others should have continued over the long term – in Sri Lanka, for example, where other aspects of culture, the language, the religion, the political and economic systems, underwent such radical changes.

At the political level, the Caldwells refer to the system of marked social stratification in the North which we have seen as associated more widely with advanced agriculture and in turn with a particular set of variables in the domestic domain. It is true that as in China the early centre of this civilisation was in the North, which has gradually spread its culture to the South. That process may even have been linked to the early contact of the Indo-European with the Dravidian speaking peoples. But for many centuries, the South has been more developed in a number of ways. It had long ceased to be peripheral in a religious sense, ever since the Muslim invasions at the end of the twelfth century. Major Hindu kingdoms continued to exist in the South even after the North had succumbed to Muslim rule, although by the fourteenth century Muslims dominated the coast and the trade routes to South-east Asia (Stein 1980:39). From the standpoint of production, the South was highly successful over a long period, both in terms of the extensive trade and cultural expansion to South-east Asia, and in terms of local agriculture. The intensive wet-rice cultivation of the South was highly productive as early as the medieval period, the surplus being a prerequisite for hierarchy and a support of the Brahmin caste (Stein 1960; 1980): tens of thousands of stone and metal inscriptions record gifts (*dāna-śāsana*) to Brahmins or to temples from wealthy and powerful persons or groups in a locality, giving rise in the thirteenth century to a temple-generated urbanisation.

Part at least of these gifts came from women, as was also the case in the North. The access of women to property is seen most clearly of course at the highest level. At the centre of Sārnāth near Benares, where the Buddha is said to have preached his first sermon, twelfth-century inscriptions record the donation, possibly of land, of Queen Kumāradevī, praising her maternal grandfather as well as herself; 'The *vihāra* (monastery) is described as an ornament to the earth, which consisted of nine segments' (Dutt 1962:208).

Some of the similarities looked at in earlier chapters are linked in a very general way with productive systems. So too are some of the variations. But in general the latitude for selection between alternatives within a particular productive system is wide, and the particular set of practices that emerges as dominant out of the total range of possibilities may depend upon factors of a religious or political kind; they may represent an adaptation of an earlier state of affairs, reacting in turn to the nature of contemporary social action in the sphere of production and reproduction; or they may even result from the relatively 'free' shift between the different potentialities. In some cases the latitude of adaptation of reproduction to productive systems is wide and as Gough has argued for the matrilineal Nayar and for Thanjavur, kinship relations may not change 'more than they are compelled to do so', compelled not only by economic and political factors but by religious and ideological ones as well. Nevertheless, there is continuity as well as change in the paths societies and religions follow as we will see brought out in the area for which the history of kinship stretches back longest in time, namely, West Asia.

Before turning to that area, let me call attention to some remarkable similarities with China, not only in terms of hierarchical but also of regional differences. There too the equation, North:South :: upper:lower, holds for many factors. In India the first six features of the summary table of regional trends in table 9 mirrors the hierarchical distribution in table 7. Yet more surprisingly, it bears a considerable resemblance to that in China, not only in the distribution but also in the explanation. For in both societies

Table 9. *North and South trends in India*

		North	South
1	Divorce	Less	More
2	Marriage transactions	More direct dowry	More indirect but more inheritance to women
3	Widows	Less remarriage	More
4	Domestic groups	More complex	More nuclear
5	Age at marriage	Lower	Higher
6	Position of women	Restraint	'Freedom'
7	Marriage (a)	Distant	Close
	(b)	More hypergamy	More isogamy
8	Husbands and wives	Strangers	Kin
9	Descent	More patrilineal	More bilateral
10	Fertility (overall and marital)	Higher	Lower
11	Mortality (of women)	Higher	Lower
12	Sex ratios	Higher	Lower
13	Family planning	More difficulties	Less
14	Development	Less education, literacy, medical treatment	More
15	Female labour	Less	More
16	Cultivation	More cereals	More rice
17	Devolution	Less land to women	More land to women
18	Ideology	More orthodox	Less orthodox

attention has been drawn to the greater strength of matrilineal organisation in the South, which is again a measure of its distance from the original centres of Han and Brahmin learning respectively, even though the protected position and the later riches of the area, associated with rice production and overseas maritime trade, brought about a subsequent shift of academic centres.

The causal and functional factors involved are clearly complex and can be determined, if at all, only by more extensive and systematic comparative analysis, towards which this study makes a preliminary attempt. Factors related to the economy and more specifically to production clearly cannot be set aside. In the first place we have posited an association between 'advanced agriculture' and 'the woman's property complex' which is supported by wider surveys (Goody 1976); and the latter notion would cover many of the variants in both North and South. On the other hand there is also a strong link between upper groups and direct dowry, ideologically (in the Hindu frame) and practically. The kind of increased productivity associated with the development of wet-rice agriculture in the eleventh century might well have served not only to increase the amount of transfers to women but possibly to increase the amounts contributed to daughters by way of direct dowry; that at least would be one logical outcome. Increased 'female autonomy' can be seen as an aspect of this process.

The same differences can be interpreted in terms of the centre–periphery argument, although we have to see the centre as constituted not only by the 'original' point of dispersal (if there was one) but by the many centres in which Hindu learning and its practitioners were concentrated, not only in the North but throughout the sub-continent in those nodes of Brahmin culture in the towns and in the country wherever this group was dominant in the local caste system. Upper groups throughout were more linked to these centres and it was they who preferred a direct endowment of their daughters, a procedure that was enshrined in Hindu texts. But the existence of a similar upper–lower difference in marriage payments among other major societies in Eurasia suggests that we need to look further afield than the particular ideology and examine certain structural features associated with the allocation of property to daughters in upper groups, the extent of which is increased by the greater circulation of goods. Not that this is the only relevant factor; all forms of endowment are consistent with advanced agriculture and the stress on one aspect may be followed by the stress on another as the result of the working-out of internal contradictions. Nevertheless increased productivity is more often accompanied by an increased emphasis on the property transmitted directly to women as daughters, and this in turn by the kind of very close marriage that we find not only in South India but also in the Near East, especially in earlier times.

III

The Near East

In the sections on East and South Asia I have been mainly concerned with the recent past and with the analysis of material derived from field studies. But in turning to the Near East (including West Asia) attention shifts to the past rather than the present. This change in focus is partly because it is on this earlier period that discussions about broad changes in forms of family and marriage have often concentrated. And partly too because the richer evidence enables us to look at the relevant facets of kinship associated with the kinds of agricultural regimes, intensive and pastoral, found in a period long before Europe played a dominant role in world history and so tended to treat as marginal, peripheral, even 'primitive', the civilisations of the East. As we will see, these societies of the Near East raise problems which are not only of particular interest but relate closely to those practices found in the other major Asiatic societies, especially regarding the endowment of women, close unions, monogamy and concubinage, as well as regarding other strategies of continuity such as adoption, filiacentric unions and the levirate, evidence of which already exists in the earliest documentary material on the human family that we possess, namely, that on Mesopotamia (Glassner 1986).[1] There we see some reference to large-scale kin groups (p. 103) but their structure appears to be basically bilateral. At the domestic level the emphasis fell on the 'nuclear family' as the core dwelling unit, although there were some stem-households where a son remained with his parents, as well as some examples of brothers living together in an expanded household or frèreche (pp. 111–12), neither of which features are surprising in view of the early marriage that is reported. More relevant is the fact that we find not only a dowry but at times landed dowry (Johns 1904:153); although women might not always claim these rights it was presumably when they did not do so that brothers acted as their sisters' trustees (p. 161).

Dowry inventories are found in the Armana letters, listing ivory, boxes, spoons and furniture. In the north Mesopotamian centre of Nuzi a girl was entitled to inherit unless she had received dowry, when she was counted as 'paid off', although not equally with the sons (Grosz 1981:165). Indeed Skaist has argued that 'all intergenerational transmissions of property including the dowry given to a woman can be regarded as advance payments of the inheritance' (1975:243; Paradise 1980:189). Dowry contracts show this property, which could include land and houses, to be transferred to the bride herself (p. 169), later to be passed on to her children. She also received an indirect dowry, possibly when the marriage had proved fertile; that is to say, part at least of the movables sent by the groom's family were given to her and this transfer was symbolised by the silver thread in the hem of her garment. Right from the very beginning of written records in the ancient Near East we find ourselves in the presence of a system of endowing women, which was especially prominent in that great contemporary of Mesopotamia, Egypt.

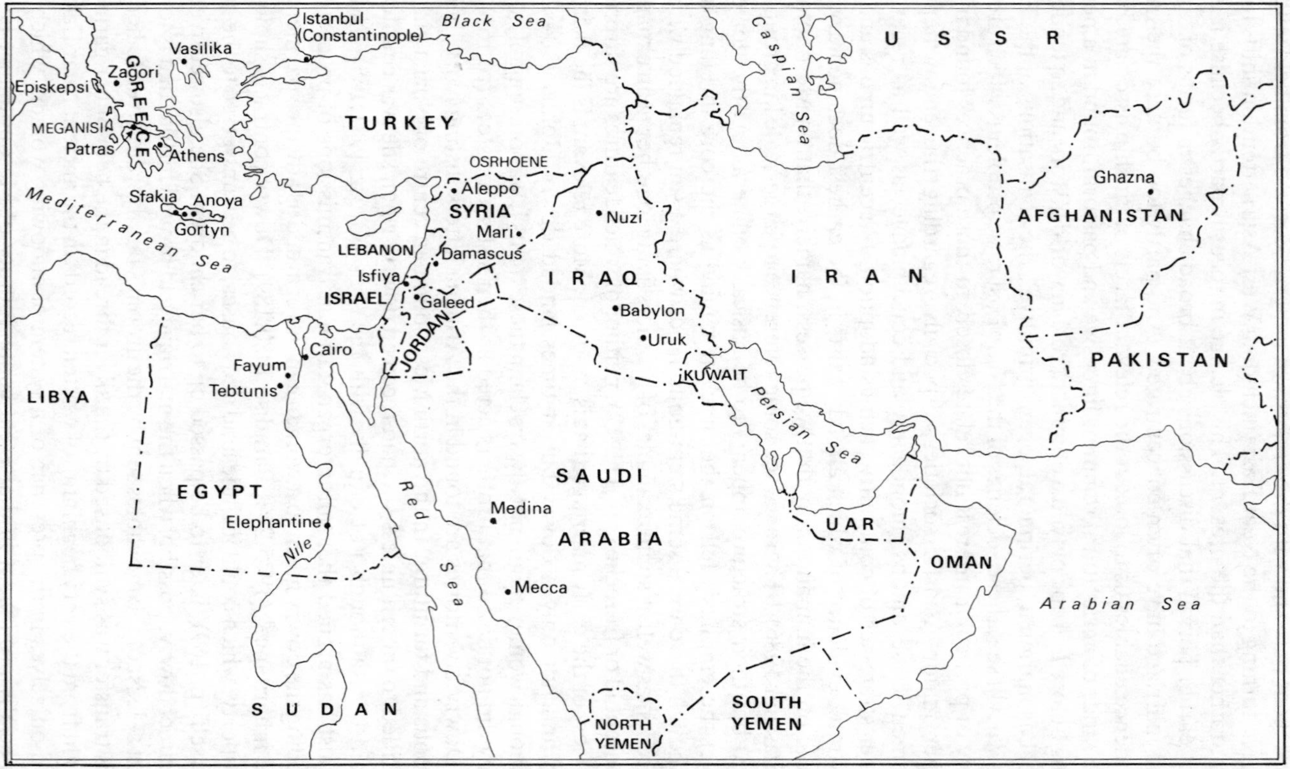

Map 5 West Asia

Of course the role of dowry was greater in the upper groups, those in which a woman could receive land. Around 1780 BC Shibtu, the 'chief wife' of one Zimri-Lin at the northern Syrian town of Mari, came from Aleppo and some of her land there may have been part of her patrimony or dowry (Malamat 1971:12). Such endowed wives played prominent roles, as is revealed in the noteworthy class of letters consisting of the extensive correspondence by women. Of one woman it is said she 'entertained the king's utter confidence, representing his interests during his absence from the city and exercising considerable influence in her own right' (p. 8). At this level at least the system was not organised around males alone.

One indication of the position of women in terms of devolution is the fact that, in the absence of sons, a daughter was entitled to inherit the entire property of her parents (Paradise 1980; Ben-Barak 1980), although this sometimes entailed marrying an 'adopted' son-in-law. Moreover a daughter could be an heir along with her brothers, but in any case she received a dowry (*mulūgu*) from her father which might include land, buildings and livestock (Paradise 1980:199), and which was given 'to provide some financial security for the daughter and her children' (p. 204). Ownership of the property therefore remained with the daughter, although usufruct might be either in her hands or those of her husband, depending upon whom it was agreed should make the return gift to her father at the time of the marriage. But a daughter might also be endowed from the prestations given by the groom (*terhatu*), which was to be used if the woman was divorced or widowed. Similar practices obtained in other parts of the ancient Near East (Ben-Barak 1980).

One of the general problems has to do with the continued predisposition to interpret the evidence on marriage in the early Near East as indicating a shift from brideprice to dowry; indeed the element of purchase, or at least of the exchange of objects (including women), continues to play its part in Western understanding of marriage in the contemporary Arab world where it is seen as closely linked with the question of the status of women under Islam and of domestic slavery both in a literal and in a metaphoric sense. This view of Islam contrasts with that taken by some earlier commentators on ancient Egypt and Mesopotamia where the position and possessions of women were considered to be very different from that under later dispensations, with ancient Israel representing a half-way house. However the institutions and traditions of these societies need to be looked at in relation one to another, not only because they shared a broadly comparable range of historical, ecological and social conditions but because their traditions were linked in the same way as their social life. This fact is brought out for the eleventh century AD in the remarkable collection of Geniza documents which shed so much light on the way that Muslim, Jew and Copt interacted in

Cairo and in the course of trading links with the western Mediterranean on the one hand and western India on the other. Much earlier the Bible, recounting the story of one 'tribe' located among many different groups, shifts its focus from Egypt to Sinai, from Syria to Babylon, from pastoralism to agriculture to urban life, in a way that vividly demonstrates the relationship of peoples and places to one another.

10

The abominations of the Egyptians

The civilisation of ancient Egypt developed in the fertile valley of the Nile where a natural form of irrigation was provided by the annual flooding of the river. The land was highly productive, yielding an agricultural surplus which permitted the growth of temples, palaces and an abundance of crafts, including that of the scribe. But the area of cultivation was limited in extent, the division between the desert and the sown being very sharp and allowing little room for the expansion of agricultural activities, and not much for hunting, gathering and pastoralism, except of a very extensive kind.

This society was marked by some features that bear directly upon our discussion. Differentiation was great and based largely but not exclusively on the control of land, a highly scarce resource. Yet as in Sri Lanka, land was inherited not only by men but by women, associated with a similar 'bilateral' system of kinship, an absence of important unilineal descent groups such as clans and lineages. At the same time the position of women was in many respects very favourable. But one striking feature of domestic life was that marriage was permitted, even encouraged, between brother and sister, whose union has often been considered prohibited by a universal taboo on 'incest', that is, on sexual relations within the elementary family of father, mother, daughter and son.

Incest and Egypt

It is unnecessary to go into the types of theory on incest. I have already published on that topic (1956), although a great deal of work has been done since then. Some demographic theories (e.g. Slater 1959) have tried to suggest that such unions were virtually impossible. On the other hand, the reluctance of those brought up together on an Israeli kibbutz to marry one another has led to a revival of the Westermarck theory (1891) which attributes the prohibition to the difficulties of sexual partnerships among those jointly brought up together at an early age. The theory has sometimes taken a socio-biological form (e.g. Shepher 1971) although others have given greater weight to sociological factors (Spiro 1958; Talmon 1964). In chapter 4 we discussed Wolf and Huang's detailed analysis of *sim-pua* marriages in Taiwan (1980) where they reformulate the Westermarck theory in the light of the evidence of subsequent difficulties actually experienced by marriage partners when they have been brought up together. This work has had some interesting support from animal studies carried out on Japanese quails who appear to favour mates that are similar but at the same time different (Bateson 1982; 1983).

My own contribution to the discussion was to plead for what might be called a cultural approach to incest, but which I would prefer to designate a refined analytic approach based on cultural categories. I argued that it was difficult to isolate any general phenomenon called incest, especially from the standpoint of finding a universal explanation. The English word itself is derived from *incasta*, unchaste, and at various periods during European history this notion extended to intercourse with fifth cousins on both sides, indeed to anyone with whom one reckoned kinship of any kind, 'natural', affinal or spiritual. Even if we restrict our attention to the prohibitions within the elementary family, it is necessary, both from a cultural perspective and from a more general analytic one, to distinguish sexual intercourse within generations from that between generations. Many of the standard explanations of these widespread prohibitions, like the aversion among those growing up together or the necessity for the exchange of potential mates, apply mainly to sex between brother and sister rather than to sex between generations, that is, between father and daughter or between mother and son; parents and children grow together in a very different way, with a different pattern of dominance and subordination. Hence what are put forward as universal explanations of universal phenomena are nothing of the kind. That is not to say they are entirely wrong. Recontextualised, one theory might apply to one set of relations in one set of societies, another to a different set in another.

This statement is of course true of a number of anthropological and sociological discussions, and it is for this reason that the disciplines tend to flounder between the cultural particularity of thick description and socio-logical overgeneralisation of thin theory. One finds a proliferation of articles on specific peoples with whom the writers have worked, set (in the better cases) in a context of some very general statements of a quasi-theoretical kind which would often be more at home in a philosophical debate. The links between phenomenon are assumed; the evidence for them is not forth-coming; and hypotheses of the middle range are overlooked. As a result we are faced with a severe lack of substantive theory.

In my earlier article, I implicitly accepted – like most anthropologists of that time and this – the universality of the incest taboo, by which was meant the prohibition of sexual intercourse between brother and sister, and between parents and children. The assumption that these are universal lies behind not only the Tylorian position (further developed by Lévi-Strauss 1949) that regards the ban on brother–sister unions as promoting external ties but also behind the Parsonian treatment of the ban on parent–child relations as a prerequisite for successful socialisation within the family. For Tylor (1889), Freud (1938), Parsons (1954) and Lévi-Strauss (1949) the incest taboo was the basis of culture, the root of the moral order; it was a fundamental prerequisite for human social life itself. Exceptions were explained away as the peculiarities of royalty or the license of the gods, categories of social person who were privileged to do what was forbidden to lesser mortals. But in making these claims we tended to overlook certain cases which earlier writers, less concerned with universalistic theories, had frequently discussed.

A wide-ranging nineteenth-century work of scholarship by A. H. Huth entitled *The Marriage of Near Kin* (1875) begins with the following sentence: 'The Egyptian, the Greek, the Jewish, the Roman, and perhaps in a smaller degree the Persian, were probably the only ancient civilizations which have affected our marriage law' (p. 9). Of these societies, he goes on to show, all except the Romans were said to allow the marriage of brothers and sisters. 'The Egyptians', he writes, 'were accustomed to marry their sisters from the earliest times of which we have any record' – that is on the authority of Diodorus. Several Greek authors claim that the Persians, especially the Magi, the priests of Zoroaster and eponymous 'inventors' of 'magic', married their mothers and daughters as well as their sisters.

The situation in early Iran is obscure since our sources are external to the society, deriving from those who regarded the enemy, the barbarians or the pagans as having appalling manners. 'Such like is the whole barbaric race,' wrote Euripedes, 'father with daughter, son with mother weds, sister with brother: kin the nearest wade through blood: their laws forbid no whit thereof' (*Andromache*, 173–6). It is only clear that Persian texts approve of close marriage. 'I praise at once . . .,' runs the *Avesta*, 'the Faith of kinship marriage', and although one eighth-century reformer objected, the practice was as enrooted here as elsewhere in the Near East. So the earlier comments on yet closer marriages among the Magi cannot easily be dismissed in view of the situation in the region generally. Indeed in earlier Mesopotamia we hear only of the ban on sexual relations between a mother with her son and a father-in-law and his daughter-in-law (Glassner 1986:118). The legitimate spouses of the Archaemenid kings of Persia were chosen from among his sisters and cousins, one of whom became the queen and wore the crown, being differentiated from the other wives and concubines of the palace.

Cambyses had three wives, two of whom were his sisters; Darius married two daughters of Cyrus. Nor were such unions confined to royalty. Close marriage was prescribed, and the closer the kinship between husband and wife, the more praiseworthy the union; not only did sister marry brother as in Egypt, but the father his daughter and the mother her son, at least among the Magi.[1]

Cyril reports the Emperor Julian, Julian the Apostate, brother's son of the great Constantine saying, in the course of an argument against the Christians, 'There is a greater difference in the laws and manners of men than in their speech. For what Greek will say that it is proper to cohabit with a sister, a daughter, or a mother? This, however, is judged to be good by the Persians' (Huth 1875:14). Despite the above quotation the earlier Greeks themselves certainly married their half-sisters, as well as practising oblique marriage (BD) and obligatory marriage to a close agnate such as the father's brother's son in the case of an heiress. Before the time of the Mosaic laws, the Jews too married their half-siblings; the patriarch Abraham took his half-sister, Sarah, to wife.

She is the daughter of my father, but not the daughter of my mother; and she became my wife. (Genesis 20:12)

While Lot's union with his daughters hardly constitued a legitimate union, there were other cases of oblique marriage between a man and his brother's daughter. Moses, who was himself the product of a union between a man and his father's sister, changed all that. Indeed the Mosaic prohibitions not only differed from those of Egypt, from whence the Israelites had fled, but may have served to set the tribes of Israel apart from their neighbours. Before laying down the Levitical rules, the Lord spake unto Moses saying:

After the doings of the land of Egypt, wherein ye dwelt, shall ye not do: and after the doings of the land of Canaan, whither I bring you, shall ye not do: neither shall ye walk in their ordinances.

Ye shall do my judgements, and keep mine ordinances, to walk therein: I am the LORD your God. (Leviticus 18:3–4)

The laws he laid down require the Hebrews to reject the forms of marriage they had practised among the Egyptians whose 'abominations' included brother–sister marriage. It was the earlier practice of Abraham as well as the oblique marriage of Moses' own parents (i.e. of a man to his father's sister) that the new dispensation specifically set aside (18:11). What was not of course prohibited was marriage to cousins, parallel as well as cross; indeed the union of Christ's parents, Joseph and Mary, may have been a marriage to the father's brother's daughter (Huth 1875:33).

Most of the later arguments against close marriage were put forward by theologians who supported the wide prohibitions of the established Christian Church, although some had already been propounded by classical authors. What is interesting is that many of these justifications closely resembled the theories of later anthropologists. Trying to resolve his doubts about the English, St Augustine of Canterbury wrote to Pope Gregory I who claimed that such marriages were bound to be sterile (Bede 1.27). Thomas Aquinas took a more sociological approach, arguing that if marriage were permitted among those living under the same roof, it would inflame their passions (*Summa* 2a2ae.154.9); at the same time he considered out-marriage to be important as a means of extending the range of friendship to a larger number of persons by way of affinity, a view put forward both by Aristotle (7 Politics II.1.1) and by St John Chrysostom, commenting on Leviticus (18.6) concerning marriage to the wife's sisters (1718–38:X,315).[2] Out-marriage widens and mixes. While recognising that like would marry like, Plato declared that if everyone married whom they most nearly resembled, there would be no mixture of characteristics and property, which could give rise to political dangers (*Laws* vi, 773 a–e). In-marriage confuses. The Protestant theologian, Theodore Beza, held that were all marriages to be permitted, relationships would become confounded.

Others looked to more concrete reasons, and it is to these arguments that I want to draw attention in the Egyptian and Indian contexts. In the ancient world objections were raised against close marriages because they generally took place between an old man and a young woman, as in the case of marriages between uncle and niece; that is to say, oblique marriages may exploit relationships of trust in the form of either wardship or tutorship. And Luther, who was so hostile to the extensive prohibitions of the Catholic Church and saw no actual harm in cousin marriage, considered such unions inexpedient on the ground that people would marry without love merely to keep the property in the family, while poor women would be left spinsters (Huth 1875:152, following Reich 1864:135). In these latter cases it is the role of close marriage, particularly oblique unions, in keeping property within the family that stands at issue.

To return to the ancient World, Egypt was the oustanding exception to the general rule by which intercourse within the elementary family was prohibited. Although largely neglected by the anthropologist, a great deal has been written about the question in oriental circles from the very beginning.[3] The existence of brother–sister marriage among the ancient Egyptians was already the subject of comment by their contemporaries. Diodorus Siculus (fl. 44 BC), who had travelled widely and wrote a world history in forty books entitled *Bibliotheca Historica*, considered this practice to be related to the fact that in the mythological world the siblings Isis and Osiris were married, but he also linked it with the high position of women in human society:

The Egyptians also made a law, they say, contrary to the general custom of mankind, permitting men to marry their sisters, this being due to the success attained by Isis in this respect; for she had married her brother Osiris, and upon his death, having taken a vow never to marry another man, she both avenged the murder of her husband and reigned all her days over the land with complete respect for the laws, and in a word, became the cause of more and greater blessings to all men than any other. It is for these reasons, in fact, that it was ordained that the queen should have greater power and honour than the king and that among private persons the wife should enjoy authority over her husband, the husbands agreeing in the marriage contract that they will be obedient in all things to their wives. (1, 27; Diodorus 1933:85–7)

In his comment upon this passage Wilkinson claimed that 'an allegorical fable' was insufficient to account for such 'a very objectionable law', pointing out that in the time of the patriarchs, as shown in the case of Abraham and Sarah (Genesis 20:12), and as among the Athenians, it was possible to marry the daughter of the same father but not of the same mother (1837:ii,63).

In Egypt, under the Old Kingdom, a woman had full rights of property. She obtained not only a direct dowry at marriage but also an inheritance on the death of her parents. In addition she received a gift from the groom after the marriage had been consummated, an intercourse gift equivalent to the Teutonic *morgengabe*. Moreover, her dowry was augmented by a share of the joint earnings arising out of the marriage partnership, her funds being managed by her husband. Divorce, though possible, appears relatively rare and polygyny seems to be excluded by the terms of contract, although the Pharaohs had large harems, with a sister as senior (or only) wife.[4] As Hobhouse notes: 'It seems clear that in this period the position of the wife depended on the bargain. This might, in fact, be varied by a post-nuptial contract. In point of fact these contracts secured the wife by a money penalty against arbitrary divorce, and her children in their inheritance' (1906:xx).

Much new light has been shed on this problem by Keith Hopkins in a study on brother–sister marriage in ancient Egypt (1980). He begins the latest version of his essay (forthcoming) with this quotation from Sextus Empiricus, a second-century physician:

If we did not know about the custom of brother–sister marriage among the Egyptians, we would have asserted wrongly, that it was a universal opinion that men ought not to marry their sisters. (*Outlines on Pyrrhonism* 3.234)

In the original version he quotes from a favourable horoscope in an astrological handbook of Graeco-Egyptian origin, surviving in a late Latin translation. 'If a son is born when the Sun is in the terms of Mercury, he will be successful and have great power . . . He will be brave and tall and will acquire property and moreover will be married to his own sister and will have children by her.'

The Egyptian data provide evidence of brother–sister marriage as far back as eleventh dynasty, 2000 BC. Černý (1954) considered such unions to be frequent but in a study of almost 500 he found only six cases (and the most that can be proved was that they were half-siblings). In Greece, the Athenians allowed paternal half-siblings to marry and the Spartans permitted the union of maternal half-siblings; on the other hand there are few known cases of either. Things were decidedly different in the Egypt which the Greeks conquered in 332 BC. One of Alexander's successor, Ptolemy II, divorced his wife, although she was not barren, and married his full sister, Arsinoë, who became known as Arsinoë Philadelphus, Arsinoë the Brother–Lover. Some contemporary writers compared this marriage to that of the Greek gods, Zeus and Hera. Others were not so complimentary: a court poet cited by the anthologist, Athenaeus, remarked, 'You are thrusting your prick into an unholy hole'. According to Pausanias, Ptolemy rejected the Macedonian custom in order to follow that of Egypt. And of the next eleven kings of Egypt, seven married their sisters. It also seems that royalty may sometimes have engaged in father–daughter unions (Forgeau 1986:143).

What about the extent and incidence among the common people? As the quotation from Sextus Empiricus shows, some literary sources indicate that here too such marriages were allowed. But the most valuable evidence comes from census returns. The practice of numbering the people, closely connected with internal taxation, is known from the Palermo stone as far back as the First Dynasty, c.3000 BC. Although the Greeks followed this practice, the surviving records from Egypt date only from the Roman conquest in 31 BC. Of the available returns, 172 are good enough to use, listing 880 people over three centuries. While the sample is drawn from a wide area, a large block (63 per cent) comes from the Fayum region which was artificially irrigated and very fertile. Nevertheless it appears to be fairly representative in terms of class, sex and age.[5]

Of 113 marriages in which both partners were living and still married, twenty-three were between brother and sister (seventeen certain, six possible), that is, between 15 and 21 per cent; of these, nine to ten were between full siblings, eight between half siblings and three unclear. In addition there were another thirteen brother–sister marriages among the ascendants of household members. Since only about 40 per cent of families were likely to have both brothers and sisters who reached a marriageable age at all, the percentages are high, between 37 and 53 per cent of possible cases. It is apparent from marriage contracts, wedding invitations and genealogies that such unions were considered normal.

Women and property

This extraordinary situation occurred not in some marginal forest tribe but in one of the most advanced societies of the ancient World. Moreover it was one in which the position of women has been seen by many scholars as being exceptionally high. The Greeks certainly thought of Egyptian women as being freer than their own; they went to the market and traded; wives seem to have offered advice to their husbands; queens played an important political role; according to Forgeau (1986:155, 159) there was no exposure of female children, as happened in Greece and Rome, but in fact a famous letter (Papyrus Oxyrhynchus 744) from a Hellenised Egyptian advises the exposure of a female child, although there is little evidence that this was a common practice (Hopkins 1980:317). 'Surprisingly modern' is the phrase Hopkins uses for some aspects of the marriage contracts (p. 334), while at the beginning of this century the sociologists Hobhouse in *Morals in Evolution: A Study in Comparative Ethics* (1906) and Westermarck in *The History of Human Marriage* (1891) both regarded the position of women in Egypt as outstanding from a legal and a personal point of view.

The legal position was closely tied to the rights over property a woman acquired at marriage from her parents and from her husband, as well as at the death of those same individuals. 'In Ancient Egypt', writes Hopkins, 'women commonly owned property; they could legally inherit property and also testate it to others; they could hold property independently of their husbands; they had the same legal capacity to transact business as men; in sum, the status of women was high' (1980:346). In the last millennium BC, some wives were given substantial rights in their husband's property which they preserved at his death or if either party divorced the other without fault; now divorce was not uncommon (Forgeau 1986:147). Nor were such rights confined to the privileged, although some women in the upper groups obtained considerable control over property. Indeed this may have been one reason why the parents encouraged them to marry a brother.

The evidence about the nature of property relations between the spouses comes from a series of marriage settlements which have been analysed by Pestman (1961) who suggests they should really be called settlements rather than contracts since they do not appear to be obligatory. Indeed some of these documents were made after the marriage had been completed, a statement of what had been done rather than what was to be carried out. They refer to four components of matrimonial transactions:

1 *šp* . . , provided by the husband,
2 *nkt.w*, 'goods of a woman', brought by the wife,
3 s'n*ḥ*, goods brought by a wife, then handed over to the husband but returnable on divorce,
4 *ḥd*, 'money to become a wife'.

The deeds themselves, which were drawn up as a proof of rights pertaining to property, belong to two main types. Those of type A stipulated the amount given (or promised) by the groom (*šp*) and what was due in the case of divorce. The amount of the bridal gift was modest, but if the husband later repudiated his wife he gave her an additional sum as well as returning her own goods. In other words the indirect endowment was split, as is often the case with the contemporary Arabic *mahr*, into a definitive payment at the start of the marriage and a conditional one at the end, depending on conduct. In Ptolemaic times the payment at marriage disappeared, leaving only the one at divorce, together with the return of the direct dowry; but the same formula continued to be used, leading Pestman to suggest that this refers to 'a fictitious property brought into the marriage' (1961:15, fn.7). Following other precedents, that author assumed even the earlier trans-action to be a survival of a payment by the groom to the bride's father 'in order to marry her'. As he himself admits, of this there is no proof whatso-ever (p. 16). The first settlements were entered into with the wife's father, although later on they were made with the wife herself (p. 180). But the fact that the settlements were made *with* the wife's father gives no indication of the destination of the goods, that is, whether or not they went *to* the wife. The contracts may well specify the negotiator rather than the recipient and so provide no substantial evidence of any shift from 'brideprice' to indirect endowment.

Deeds of type B record the property brought by the wife (*ḥd*) and offer further documentation on the maintenance provided by the husband. Sig-nificantly that support continued even after the divorce in those cases where the husband did not return the money and goods to which she was entitled; control of the direct dowry was closely tied to the obligation to maintain the woman on whose behalf it has been allocated.

Quite apart from the gifts that passed at marriage and that were listed in the settlements, other aspects of a family's property might need to be reorganised at this time. One woman of the twenty-sixth dynasty 'requires from her father, when marrying, a house and a share in the income of a priestly office' (Pestman 1961:143). In any case the fact that a woman had received a gift on account of marriage did not exclude her from further inheritance, which was the case under Graeco-Egyptian law when a wife received a *pherne* for her portion. Otherwise the woman was not paid off at marriage as happened in some other systems, with endowed sons as well as dowried daughters.[6] To be paid off, as son or daughter, was to free the estate and its heir from further claims, but not in Egypt.

The situation, Hopkins notes, changed over time. The Graeco-Egyptian marriage contracts from the first two centuries AD are 'concerned solely with property' (1980:341). The receipt of the dowry and trousseau was acknowledged; in return, the husband was to provide clothing and other necessities. The couple were to live together 'blamelessly'; in the case of divorce, the dowry and trousseau were to be returned within a given number of days. The elaborate provisions of the earlier Egyptian demotic contracts about the rights of widows and children had disappeared.

During the Byzantine period, in the sixth century AD, a new type of marriage contract emerged under Christian influence which Hopkins sees as restricting rather than as expanding the rights of women. Moral obligations were elaborated; a bride was accepted only after virginity had been confirmed; she was expected to 'love, cherish and serve' her husband as well as 'to obey him', while the obligations on his side had been reduced. 'Subservience had replaced reciprocity' (p. 341). 'In the course of fifteen-hundred years, Egyptian marriage contracts moved from no-fault divorce with significant compensation for the divorced wife, through community of property and reciprocal if unequal moral obligations between husband and wife, to virgin marriage in which the wife was bound to subserve her husband under threat of legal and religious penalties' (p. 342). While the position of women hardly improved over this period, the Christian wedding formula and the requirement of virginity can perhaps be seen as a formalisation of existing expectations rather than as indicating a total break with the earlier situation. Others have argued that the position of women under the earlier Christian Church was not all that unfavourable and ecclesiastical norms were in some ways better than the emergent civil codes (see Goody 1983). Moreover, in significant ways as we will see, Byzantine codes were based on earlier Greek practice.

In sum, the eighty-two demotic marriage settlements analysed by Pestman fell into the two main types, A and B. In the first (which he assumes to be the older) the groom hands over a bridal endowment ('brideprice' or indirect dowry). In the second, the bride's father or guardian gives a dowry in return for which the husband contracted to maintain his wife at a certain level, usually measured in wheat, oil and money. Hopkins sees this dowry as 'paid' to the husband just as Pestman sees the earlier indirect dowry as paid to the father, but this description seems to require some modification since the wife can certainly claim the amount back again. Here too concepts of sale and purchase seem inappropriate, even though it is claimed that the notions were used by the actors. 'Dot ou achat, l'alternative se retrouve dans la langage juridique des contrats rédigés au 1er millénaire, reprise codifiée de coutumes plus anciennes' (Forgeau 1986:139). As we have argued earlier, such statements may well conceal problems of usage, metaphor and translation, but even if these were solved, the substantial analytic issues remain.

However, instead of succeeding one another, these types of settlement appear to have co-existed. On the other hand there is no evidence of variations by geographical region or hierarchical stratum, such as we find in India and elsewhere where dowry tends to mark 'high' transactions and indiret dowry ('brideprice') 'low' ones. Here, in whatever group we look, up to the sixth century BC the settlements (but not necessarily the payments) were made between the husband and the wife's father, but later on these were concluded with the wife herself.

In addition to the Egyptian data, we have a set of Greek marriage contracts which were very similar in character. As in mainland Greece, these included restrictions on the sexual rights of both partners. 'And Philiksos shall not bring in another woman besides Apollonia, nor keep a concubine nor a boy-lover' (Hopkins 1980:341). Community of property was explicitly recognised and became even more strict in the Roman period, much more so than in Roman Italy in that the wife's agreement was needed before the husband could sell property. And the marriage contract lay between the groom and the bride, not with her father as in Greece itself.

As so often, the nature of the contract emerges when the marriage comes to an end. In Pestman's sample ten out of the eighty-two marriages terminated in divorce. If the husband was at fault he might have to pay certain penalties. In seventeen out of the fifty-four 'bridal endowment' contracts, 'the husband made over at least one-third, and sometimes one-half, of his property to be surrendered to his wife in case he divorced her. Husbands usually but not always . . . excluded the property which they brought into the marriage, just as wives also retained their own property independently of their husbands' (Hopkins 1980:336). If the wife was divorced from her husband, with no fault on her side, she was entitled to part of the joint estate, but if she left, she sacrificed this claim, which was not available to the majority of those who received a bridal endowment (pp. 336–7).

Marriage contracts involving a direct dowry 'created a community of property, in the sense that typically the whole of the husband's property was held as security for his wife's dowry and was committed to the children of the marriage (to the exclusion of children by any remarriage)' (p. 337). Hence the husband had to get the permission of the wife and eldest son to dispose of parts of his property. Such contracts were enforceable in law, which was presumably the intention of putting them in writing.

These contracts have many close relationships to those found among the Jewish communities in medieval Cairo discussed in the next chapter. By and large their content bears out Hobhouse's early comment that they give evidence of the privileged position of the wife in the contracts arising largely from considerations of property and inheritance. As later in Judaism and in Islam, post-marital contracts helped to support the position of the wife which 'depended on the bargain', for they 'secured the wife by a money penalty against arbitrary divorce, and her children in their inheritance' (1906:184). Hopkins provides us with an example of the kind of contract drawn up at the marriage of a brother and a sister. Horos acknowledges that he has received the sum of twenty drachmae from his sister in silver. He guarantees to provide 'all necessities and clothing and everything that is befitting to a wedded wife according to his resources . . .' (p. 323). If he leaves her, he has to return the dowry within thirty days of being asked. In other words even a brother and sister have separate claims on the estate if the marriage breaks up. In another case, just before the marriage to her brother, a bride-to-be registered her vineyard and two slaves given by her mother with a local official (p. 323). Note that land is involved as well as slaves. At divorce, which as we have seen was not uncommon, she was entitled to claim her share. One deed of divorce of a brother and sister survives: Kronion and Taorsenouphis agree to live apart. By chance we also know that two years earlier the father of the pair had made a will virtually disinheriting his son for having behaved very badly towards him throughout his life. He left the major part of his estate to be divided equally between his two other sons and his granddaughter by the sibling marriage (p. 323). This coincidence stresses the very close relationship that existed between the various forms of transfer from one generation to the next (devolution), whether these occurred at marriage or at death, that is, whether they constituted dowry or inheritance, whether going to the children or to the grandchildren. The same point is made by Hopkins when he notes that dowries 'counted as part of the daughter's inheritance' (p. 339). In the present instance the grandchild apparently benefited from the shares of both mother and father, uniting in her person what had been split in two at the previous generation. This view of the process resembles that of cross-cousin marriage among the Gonja of northern Ghana and the Coorgs of southern India as held by the actors themselves (Goody, E. and J. 1966; Srinivas 1952); it ties together what would otherwise be separated.

Wills

Marriage contracts are only one aspect of devolution, wills being the other main instrument of transfer. Here the situation of the wife emerges equally clearly in the various provisions that were made from time to time and may have been personal rather than general statements of custom or law. A widow who was pregnant when her husband died received only her dowry, released all claims she might have on her husband's estate, and in return 'secured the rights to expose her baby' (Hopkins 1980:339). Consider this point. There is no insistence on adding to the husband's descendants after his death. Instead the mother is given, by this act of renunciation, the power of life and death over a child, even when the child is conceived before her husband's death but born afterwards. The phrase itself indicates the child's attachment to the mother's family, a shift of *potestas* as happened in the reverse direction in *manus* marriage under Roman law. But as in Rome the right to destroy her own offspring may also indicate a desire to control the output of children, especially female, not simply to bear as many as one can, which so often seems the strategy in Africa where the man–land situation was relatively open. Egypt, on the other hand, was virtually closed, for the Nile valley did not even provide the option of second-class land that could be exploited by additional children; there was the irrigated land on the one side and the desert on the other.

Some wills make explicit the potential life interest of the widow in the conjugal house; and in one instance a widower too acquires such an interest, perhaps through a filiacentric union. In another example a widow's maintenance, comprising food and pocket money, is conditional on her staying 'irreproachably' at home (Hopkins 1980:339). This is a provision widely found in Europe, and associated elsewhere with the ban on widow-remarriage, where the wife is entitled to support as long as she remains chaste and does not form any other union. Presumably unchastity does not lose her control of the dowry she has brought into the marriage, but she does forfeit the indirect endowment her husband should provide.

Another will shows a widow holding the property in trust for her children while drawing upon the usufruct during her lifetime. In yet another instance, which has an even more contemporary flavour (Goody 1987), a married couple leave the property to the surviving spouse but always in trust for their children (p. 339).

Of the widows who had received a bridal endowment (or 'brideprice'), only the minority got a third share, the widow's tierce. Of those who received a direct dowry, the property was either held in trust for, or, especially in the later period, inherited by, their children, with the eldest son receiving the largest share. If the children were young, the widow looked after the property. But though there were variations in the wills, it generally devolved directly to the children. If the couple were childless, the widow sometimes only received her dowry back again. Otherwise she was in theory dependent upon her children, as they had earlier been on her.

In different societies the nature of the conjugal fund, often very complex, varies in important ways. In ancient Egypt, it is clear that a married woman could carry out all sorts of transactions with regard to her property without the assistance of her husband; she could even lend him money. Those marriage payments placed under his control, even his disposal, remained her property and the equivalent had to be returned at the dissolution of the

union. In addition, from the time of the New Kingdom, the directly endowed wife had a right to one third of the property acquired during the
marriage, for they were judged to have gained it jointly (Pestman
1961:151–3). At the same time any woman could perform 'all conceivable
legal acts'.

> The woman's legal position is not weakened because she enters into a marriage; on
> the contrary, in many cases the husband draws up a deed for his wife by which he
> allots important rights of property to her . . . while furthermore law or custom also
> grants certain rights of property to the wife . . . her right to a third part of the property
> of her husband. (p. 182)

Her position in this respect is firmly established.

Explaining brother–sister marriage

In attempting to seek an explanation of brother–sister marriage, Hopkins,
like Diodorus, begins by considering the religious factors. Recognising that
many religions have myths of initial incest, often incorporating stories of the
dashing activities of gods, he observes that the relationship between Isis and
Osiris, who were at once brother and sister, husband and wife, did provide a
legitimation of this type of union:

> O Great Bull, lord of passion
> Lie thou with thy sister Isis . . . (1980:344)

A certain hymn to Isis runs:

> You have made the power of women equal to that of men. (p. 343)

While these statements may provide supernatural support for the practice,
the ways of gods only too often represent the obverse of the ways of men. In
any case, if the gods are to be regarded as the imaginative creations of men,
their deeds alone cannot provide a total explanation for human conduct,
especially where some societies attempt to follow, others to reverse their
ways of doing things.

Another suggestion, also an early one, is that the prevalence of such
marriages may be a possible 'solution' to the payment of dowry since the
expense of making such a provision was saved if it occurred within the same
family. Hopkins at first rejects this explanation. 'If we assume that on the
whole husbands married wives of equal wealth and status, then giving a
daughter in marriage to someone outside the family would cost a dowry, but
equally the son's outside bride would bring back a dowry into the family. So
also when the parents died' (p. 322). However, dowry is not only a marriage

transaction, it is also part of the devolution of property to women over their whole lifetime. Of this, the portion transmitted at marriage may be but a minor constituent. In the village of Tebtunis, for example, a median transfer was of eighty drachmae, that is three months' subsistence for an average-sized family (p. 342), but there was considerable variation between the poor and the prosperous, the range running between 18 and 1,600 drachmae. In addition brides brought a trousseau (*parapherne*) 'which varied from simple to extravagant'. But while the dowry itself may not have been large, the parental estate as a whole was divided between the children of both sexes, though not always equally. Such a bisexual pattern of inheritance might have favoured close marriages on the same grounds that have been put forward for dowry: both are aspects of diverging devolution and some Egyptians may well have seen advantages in brother–sister marriage in retaining posses-sions and status within the family. It is in this context that Hopkins draws attention to the similar ideas of the village heretic in Montaillou in the medieval Pyrenees:

If my brothers Guillaume and Bernard had married out sisters Esclarmonde and Guillemette, our house would not have been ruined because of the capital (averium) carried away by those sisters as dowry; our ostal [house] would have remained intact. (Le Roy Ladurie 1978:36)

Nevertheless Hopkins considers this argument invalid because of what he sees as the reciprocal nature of dowry transactions; if each married an equal, then it did not matter to whom or who took what. If daughters took their dowry with them on marriage, sons' wives brought the equivalent back again, assuming that most marriages represented a match.

As we have seen, Srinivas (1984) has argued that quite the opposite is true for India, at least with regard to the 'modern' dowry. This transaction in cash and valuables he sees as linked to the hypergamous status-climbing tend-encies of the North, where families are trying to maximise (and hence differentiate) their receipts, with women aiming to marry up, men as a consequence down, that is, down in status but up in possessions. Whether or not this constitutes an adequate description is beside the point. The match involved in dowry marriages is often a matching of different values; in hypergamous unions one may use the daughter's share to acquire the man's status, for her, for her offspring and in a reflected way for her natal family. In this respect we have seen there was a difference between North and South India; in the North women tried to marry up and out; in the South, they married across and in. Egypt approached the southern rather than the northern pattern, indeed represented a more extreme instance of the tend-ency to in-marriage.

However this may be, in a number of instances of close marriage, some-

times with bridewealth as well as with dowry marriages, the actors offer
explanations of an economising kind. Marry close and save the expense.
Marry close and save the dowry. Why should this happen if there is always an
equal exchange of goods? The answer lies at several levels. First, not
everything can be exchanged in the same way: immovables such as land
create problems unless the marriage is close at hand. Secondly, no match
provides an exact balance of goods, services or of partners. Thirdly, even
when their value can be totted up in some quasi-objective way, family jewels
and family lands mean more to descendants than to affines. And fourthly, if
one can avoid the act of splitting and reconstituting the family estate at
marriage, that in itself constitutes a major gain. Let us consider these points
in greater detail. First, the nature of the assets, including the view taken of
them by the actors. If women receive land, either as dowry or later as
inheritance, what is given may, from the family's point of view, be much
greater than what it received. A premium accrues to a particular piece
depending upon its location; in general terms one parcel may be equal to any
other but it acquires added value if it lies adjacent to the main estate, indeed
if it is part of that estate. Conversely, land has less value if it has to be
exploited from afar. Obviously a woman cannot physically take her holding
with her at marriage; if she marries at a distance, she may have to leave its
exploitation to her brothers or else it has to be sold or exchanged and the
money reinvested.

If her assets include family jewels, these too are inevitably 'endowed' with
a special virtue, the mana of the ancestors, the sacredness of tradition. On
the market, they may be equal to any other set. But not for the owners; the
strictly economic argument fails to reckon with the heirloom factor. And the
same may be true of blood, especially blue blood, royal blood. To conserve
it has a special value for those in whose veins it flows. An exchange of such
sacra with another family always has its risks; less so with a known family,
but even of these one may be more critical (and more suspicious) than of
one's own closest kin.

Regarding the fourth point, the offer of a dowry in cash may also involve
the splitting up of family assets, selling some property, mortgaging the farm.
Indeed under some circumstances the same may be true of bridewealth and
indirect dowry (or 'brideprice'), although in the latter case the sum is either
brought back physically by the wife or its transfer delayed until the marriage
is dissolved; even where it is received by or contracted to the bride's father as
'compensation', it usually ends up in her hands rather than his. Any such
transaction is likely to entail an effective transfer of rights from senior to
junior generation. Close marriage, even between first cousins, would thus
tend to prevent early disruption by delaying the division of the main estate,
for claims may be held in suspense or never made, especially if they can be

passed on intact to the grandchildren in the third generation. A similar effect may be partially achieved by the late marriage of both sexes, such as occurred in Europe and which can there be viewed, from one point of view, as a functional alternative.

The explanation which Hopkins himself offers for the appearance of brother–sister marriage in Egypt turns on his analysis of the domestic unit and relates to certain considerations that were reviewed in the case of China. From the census records the size of households, which have to be distinguished from the dwelling groups, was not large, having an average of 5.1 persons. Kin and neighbours assisted one another in the fields and additional labour could be hired temporarily or purchased on the longer term in the form of slaves. Land was rented and sold in a vigorous market, so that households could add to or dispose of resources to match their changing requirements. In one area in the fourth century AD, 28 per cent of all landowners changed the size of their holdings by more than 5 per cent over a period of about eight years (Hopkins 1980:343). It was a market that was probably stimulated by partible inheritance, cash dowries and taxation, as Habbakuk (1950) has suggested for Europe.

Slaves constituted about one tenth of the population, being present in one sixth of all households, almost half of which had only one. It is significant that slaves are found more frequently in simple than in complex households, especially those ravaged by death and having dependent children. So that 'slavery appears not so much as a mode of production, but rather as a method of recruiting supplementary labour, particularly to help a family in the medium term through a crisis caused by death or by the needs of dependent children' (Hopkins 1980:331). As in parts of Africa, slaves were used to plug a demographic gap (Goody 1979).

In Egypt sons were sometimes unable to marry or to gain access to a farm before the father died, in contrast to the situation in other communities, including parts of Europe, where there was a more regular handing over during the father's lifetime entailing a sort of early retirement, usually at the marriage of the son or daughter who was to take over. However, through the market in Egypt sons could purchase land before their father died; others took up different jobs, while 'some Egyptian fathers apparently distributed land before they died'. Multiple households were common (despite the small average size) indicating that some married sons did stay with their fathers, while after his death, brothers sometimes continued to live together even until they had grown sons of their own over fourteen, for there seems to have been an advantage in having a somewhat larger labour force, especially on irrigated farms (Hopkins 1980:332).

Following up Hajnal's thesis about the European marriage pattern (1965), Hopkins points out that in most of the pre-industrial world women married young (though as we have seen this was not the case in Tibet, in Japan, nor even among the Nambudiri Brahmins of India). However in Egypt the marriage age of women could not be regarded as early; in the age group 20–4, only 43 per cent of women were recorded as married. However by the age of 30–4 years, all women were either married or had been widowed.[7] Contrast this with the ages recorded on Roman tombstones where the median marriage age for girls was only 15.5 years (Hopkins 1980:333–4), although if we look at provincial tombstones outside Roman Italy, commemoration patterns might suggest that the average age at marriage may have been higher because daughters dying in their later teenage years were typically commemorated by parents not husbands (Shaw 1987). In Egypt husbands were approximately three years older than their wives, the median age of male marriage being in the mid twenties; however the differential increased with the age of the couple, probably as a result of second marriages. As elsewhere, older men often married younger wives, while older women usually remained widows. Nevertheless the possibility of remarriage did exist, although an effort was made to control it by means of marriage contracts. Why should the Egyptians, like the upper groups in China and India, wish to control remarriage at all? One reason is made clear in the contracts themselves. These documents allocate the wealth that was brought together at marriage to the children of that union, not to any others; their rights continued to be safe-guarded even when the marriage had been dissolved by death or divorce. While the partners were then free to remarry, a new union inevitably created the problem of 'the second bed'. That problem concerns the way the property should be divided among the children of the different marriages. Equity suggests that the children of the first union are entitled to the property which father and mother have brought to the union plus that which has accumulated to their joint account. On the same basis the children of the second union should be entitled to what the husband contributed and the new wife brought, plus later acquisitions. But quite apart from the impossibility of assessing the husband's different contributions to the two unions, except on a purely arbitrary basis (so much to each child), there is always the possibility of the alienation of property in favour of the children of the later marriage, that is, the problem of the 'wicked step-mother' who attracts to her own offspring what should have gone to the children of her predecessor. This danger exists only with 'serial monogamy', that is, where remarriages occur in societies that are basically monogamous and where specific conjugal funds are established by each couple. And it provides one reason why many societies forbid or discourage the remarriage of widows, although the fact that few extend the ban to widowers means there are other factors at work. But even with this freedom an Egyptian widower might take a concubine rather than a wife to look after his household (Forgeau 1986:157), and such a move would avoid the whole problem of property.

Looking at the composition of Egyptian households, Hopkins raises the issue of whether brother–sister marriages can be seen as one way of dealing with the problem of the marrying-in daughter-in-law. In Taiwan and in traditional China, as we have seen, the mother was visualised as tyrannising her son's wife who, reacting in a humble fashion, nevertheless tries to split the family by using her influence over her husband. One way of inhibiting this tendency lay in bringing into the household a young girl who would eventually marry the son as a *sim-pua* and who would be raised into obedience to her mother-in-law. It is suggested that marriage to the sister might have played the same role for the Egyptian family, avoiding premature fission and allowing later marriage.

To this consideration we have to add another which we discussed earlier. Hopkins notes that a further reason in support of close marriages adduced by parents in many parts of the world is that a bride 'would not need a grand dowry or an elaborate trousseau (*parapherne*)'. The wedding ceremony need not cost a fortune and any subsequent allocation to the daughter by way of inheritance would not fragment the family's estate. Most importantly, in his view, a daughter married to her brother would be inhibited from using her considerable legal powers as a wife to split her property from that of her husband (Hopkins 1980:352). By combining this argument with that about fission Hopkins aims to supplement 'property interest with intra-familial dynamics'; in this aim he is correct, but a women's control of property remains an important factor in those very dynamics, for the split itself is promoted by the endowment she receives.

'Family marriage' was largely limited to that taking place within the nuclear family. Although marriage to cousins might seem to be an alternative when no sibling was available, it appears to have been infrequent.[8] Hopkins links the infrequency of such marriages with the absence of wider kin groups (although of course the range of recognised kin included cousins). In the absence of kin groups, households were aggregated directly into the village which 'was quite steeply stratified and internally differentiated' (p. 342). Land was bought and sold, for the economy of Roman Egypt was highly monetarised, partly as a result of taxation; the whole body of census records that Hopkins employs originated in the system of internal taxation. In northwest Ghana one of the first pressures to induce people to sell additional yams and corn on the market was the tax demands of the colonial administration; indeed the provision of food for its employees was seen as an important function of the head tax.

While an active market and the absence of wider kin groups (both features of later Europe) may have had some influence on the relative infrequency of kin marriages outside the sibling group, family strategies may also have dictated that some marriages should be out rather than in. This is the situation that Bourdieu (1977:30ff.) has outlined in Arab countries where there is a preference for father's brother's daughter marriage but only for some siblings. In other words the 'preference' is conditional; once having been put into effect, the best strategy for the family may be for the next marriage to be of the opposite type, one with an outsider to strengthen political or other ties. Only a tyrannical notion of the rule, of structure, fails to recognise this role of strategy. Given this situation, the high proportion of brother–sister marriage may have satisfied the immediate demand for marriageable kin and at the same time reduced their availability; to marry one's sister is to deny her to a cousin. For example, the percentage of first degree parallel cousin marriages among the Druze of Isfiya (n=184) was 19.5, that is, involving nearly one of every two marriageable parallel cousin pairs, 30 per cent being within the patronymic group (Atran 1985b:679). If sibling marriage is at 20 per cent, then the number of possible pairs is halved. But this is not simply a matter of numbers, which are often surprisingly similar across a wide range of Arab societies with differing modes of life and livelihood. Such a union, writes Atran, 'does not primarily serve the interests of a lineage, tribe, patronymic group or village, but rather the camp or household and is a matter of preserving the patrimony, including land'. If this has already been done by sibling marriage, then few unions are likely to take place between cousins.

In connection with strategies Hopkins presents an interesting example of a princess who loved her brother but thought her father would marry him off to the daughter of another general 'in order that the family might be enlarged and so we should be separated'. In other words, there is a recognition of the possible advantages of out-marriage in creating ties, which was in this case defeated, Hopkins remarks, by 'romantic love'. The presence of these alternative strategies seem to be a characteristic feature of many reported cases of cross-cousin marriage, in northern Ghana for example (E. and J. Goody 1966); the union may be recommended as desirable, but only for some.

Much has been written in recent years about the difficulties of close marriage, even to the point of positing a certain innate aversion among those brought up together in opposition to Freud's notion of a natural sexual attraction to other family members. The Egyptian material must lead us to modify generally accepted ideas about the universality of the incest taboo, whether seen as counteracting desire or reinforcing aversion. To this extent the ball is back in the sociological court and the game is a matter of identifying contingencies that may over-ride widespread tendencies. What is especially interesting from the standpoint both of general theoretical assumptions and of more specific hypotheses is that whatever contribution brother–sister marriages in Egypt may have made to lessening affinal tensions and conflicts over partition, they cannot simply be regarded as arrangements made to suit either the senior generation or the 'collectivity' as a whole. So much is clear from the fact that 'love' played a prominent part even in 'family marriage'.

Love and marriage

'Love letters', as we have seen, were written by brothers to their sister–wives. Love poems and mummy portraits leave the impression of a vivid individualism which, Hopkins suggests, seems incompatible with subordinating self-interest to the collective concerns of the household, if that was what brother–sister marriage required (1980:352–3). Did the household make this requirement? If one is dependent upon the family estate rather than being a wage-labourer, there is no sharp dichotomy between self-interest and collective concern at the level of the domestic economy. So that highly 'individual' people are equally capable of internalising either a desire for their sisters or the absence of such a desire.

Such appears to be the import of the love poems which were written much earlier than the census records, about 1300–1100 BC and suggest 'a high degree of mutual regard and affection between men and women, of romantic love both before and after marriage' (p. 346). This sentiment Hopkins regards as 'rare' in pre-industrial societies, if one excludes relations with courtesans. Where it occurs, romantic love between men and women has been connected, Hopkins suggests, 'with women's control over property (as for example in Heian Japan or in Rome in the first century AD)'. In ancient Egypt, as we have seen, women commonly owned property, could transact business and, in sum, 'the status of women was high' (p. 346).

Gluckman (1956) has argued that love serves to separate both spouses from their kin (and kin groups), uniting them into a conjugal team (see also Goode 1959, Lantz 1982); this is an aspect of love in the modern Western world. A similar comment can be made about the establishment of a conjugal fund, or conjugal property interest, when both male and female inherit or acquire wealth. As we have seen the creation of these funds weakens the corporate nature of the lineage, where these exist; at the same time, it clearly establishes the conjugal unit on a more intimate, more solid footing, which again tends to separate the unit from lateral ties. The Chinese wife is often given as the reason for the separation of brother's property, though such separation is consistent with lineal persistence on the shape of the stem family.

The point about the high status of Egyptian women was made by moral-

ists, historians and sociologists at the beginning of the century. But some of
the implications of these remarks apply to other cultures as well. Despite the
role of arranged marriage, love poems exist in the Sanskrit (Brough 1968)
and more recently India is certainly not lacking in the techniques or actuality
of love. China and Japan, too, are full of stories of the loving relations of
men and women, in and out of marriage. It is not an easy matter to define
romantic love, for it is a subject on which even we as actors are remarkably
unclear. But some evidence about the nature of conjugal relations (and let
us concentrate on that side of it) can be gathered from looking at works of
art. In India, Mesopotamia and Egypt, men are very often depicted with
women, kings with their consorts, brothers with their sisters, Krishna with
the handmaidens. But in African sculpture, and here we are dealing with
wooden sculpture which presents some particular problems of technique,
women very rarely appear with men. Does this indicate the same kind of
separation of the sexes that the seventeenth-century Dutch trader, Bosman,
early remarked for inheritance and other matters in his encounter with the
inhabitants of the West African coast and which I have posited as a major
difference associated with the productive and reproductive systems of Eurasia and Africa (1976)? For under the extensive systems of production in
Africa, where the individual or familial ownership of land was of little
significance, where differentiation in productive resources was in general
small, and where political considerations put a premium on marrying-out,
all women had roughly the same value and did not share in male funds;
under the more intensive regimes of Eurasia, with their greater surplus at
stake, with land holdings differentiating individuals, families and strata,
with the politics of marriage often developing around marriage within, then
women as daughters and wives were as differentiated as men, and hence
were differentially endowed from the family estate at marriage, creating a
kind of conjugal fund. 'Love' can be interpreted as a specific form of the
close conjugality (and extra-conjugality) that one finds under diverging
devolution.

For in spite of all the attention given in Egypt to supposed 'matrilyny' (see
Forgeau 1986:157) and to brother–sister marriage, the conjugal family was
well established. ' "Si tu es un notable, fonde un foyer . . . et chéris ta femme
dans ta maison comme il convenient", enseigne le vizir Ptahhotep à son fils
dans une des plus anciennes *Sagesses* . . .; la littérature égyptienne didac-
tique abonde en des éloges similaires de la félicité conjugale' (p. 136). In
Egyptian sculpture husband and wife are constantly depicted side by side,
and often as equal in size, an iconography that is virtually absent from
Africa. Women appear closer to men, wives to husbands, than in Africa
south of the Sahara and I would tentatively link this conjugality to the nature
of conjugal funds and the position of women in their families of birth and

marriage in a hierarchical system, households which are small and compact. Forgeau sees households as even smaller, more nuclear, than Hopkins. She claims that founding a household, making a marriage, meant in many cases constructing a new house (p. 138). Houses contained a 'nuclear family' (p. 154) while extended (*étendus*) domestic groups under the same roof were rare except for a lone parent (*esseulé*), usually the mother. High mortality and late marriage meant that the overlap of generations was brief (p. 155), the average lifespan of males being thirty four and of females thirty.

Whatever the exact composition, we find a domestic economy based on a relatively small household (there is even some suggestion of contraception) and evidence of similar strategies of heirship as appeared in Asia. In the absence of children adoption was practised (p. 159); old men disinherited sons who did not look after them in their old age (p. 158); widowers might take a concubine rather than a wife, displaying ambiguous feelings about a second full marriage in this generally monogamous society. However both divorce and plural unions seem to have played their part in securing an heir.

There is a little evidence about hierarchical differences in practice; the type of dowry did not seem to vary, although its size did; households were larger (slaves included) in richer than in poorer families (p. 186). Other hierarchical differences no doubt existed, for despite its apparently extreme form of marriage, Egypt was not all that far removed from Southern India on the one hand, and Arab and ancient Hebrew society on the other, much as their neighbours may have wished to distance themselves on particular issues, such as the nature of rules of marriage. But close marriage was a feature of all these societies and Egypt has to be seen as another variant on a general theme widespread throughout the Near East and eastern Mediterranean.

11

Jacob's marriages

Mosaic law about marriage was formulated in opposition to that of the Egyptians. But it modified the ability, indeed the injunction, to marry close kin very little, only in respect of siblings by the same parents, the uterine form of which had been permitted to earlier Israelites. By a curious twist of fate a code which allowed close marriage and, at least in the incident of the daughters of Zelophehad, associated this with the retention of property allocated to women, was utilised by later Europeans to prohibit those very unions. As a result of the spread of Christianity the code became part of the ideological umbrella of European religious law and to a lesser extent of secular practice. Canon law and popular debate both refer to Biblical precedent, usually that of the Old Testament since the New provides relatively little by way of guidance on this aspect of family life. But despite the common ideology, patterns of marriage in early Israel and in later Europe were very different and any account of the development of European family and marriage has to begin by recognising this fact (Goody 1983). In this chapter I want to trace out the situation in ancient Israel with regard to marital transactions, the devolution of property to women and close marriage, linking this with certain aspects of the domestic domain that we have examined in previous chapters.

In discussing Egyptian marriage I argued that it was important to look with great care at the evidence put forward in accounts that assume a general shift from 'brideprice' to 'dowry'; in that particular case, the question of 'purchase' was always marginal, given the recognition accorded to the position of women, the nature of brother and sister marriage (hardly purchase, hardly exchange) and the intimations of ancient matriliny discerned by Margaret Murray and others. Not that speculations about general developments of this kind should be entirely banished; most scholars assume some overall shift from 'elementary' to 'complex' forms of kinship involving such changes. But it is the form of the shift, as well as its timing, that is open to argument. Many nineteenth-century accounts were based on totally insufficient evidence, which we have tried to supplement, as well as a confusion of terms, which we have tried to clarify. The latter encouraged an acceptance of over-rigid unilineal schema of development which were often based on inappropriate or misunderstood examples from 'primitive' societies. The situation in Biblical studies regarding marriage and the status of women was (and to some extent still is) an outstanding example of just such a confusion.

In earlier chapters Chinese marriage was examined in order to see if (as is often supposed) this presented an example of the extreme version of an uncompromisingly 'patrilineal' situation where a woman was always incorporated at marriage into her husband's family, lineage or patriclan. I argued that if by incorporation one meant that a woman's membership of an *exclusive* segment was transferred lock, stock and barrel, then the notion was incompatible with the fact that in major marriages she continued to retain personal ties as well as explicit rights and duties with regard to her natal kin. Her role at the marriage of a brother or a brother's daughter, and a man's at the naming ceremony of his sister's child were striking aspects of this continuing relationship. Moreover in Chinese society, which was often said to value woman at a low rate, she acquired property of her own. As a wife she took property into her own marriage, some of which came from the bridal gifts of the groom, constituting part of a fund over which she exercises continuing rights, and at times control. On bringing this property into the marriage she acquired the inalienable right to perpetual support. What looks like incorporation can also be seen as the setting up of a conjugal fund which cross-cuts the boundaries of the patrilineal descent groups and which arises out of the fact that women are bearers of property into marriage.

In the shape of the related concept of purchase, the same question about incorporation has frequently been discussed in connection with marriage in ancient Israel. The article by Benzinger on Hebrew marriage in the *Encyclopaedia Biblica* (1902) serves as an example. He begins: 'To betroth a wife to oneself, meant simply to acquire possession of her by payment of the purchase-money'. And the 'purchase money' is seen going at first to the girl's father as brideprice and only at a later date (as in the Koran) to the bride herself.

Benzinger admits that mention is made of gifts to brides at marriage, but curiously maintains that this 'is no "dowry" brought by the wife to her husband; such gifts remain the personal property of the wife. Conveyance of property cannot strictly be made simply because daughters had no right of inheritance.' Such statements take a very restricted view of 'dowry' since they exclude those cases where the woman manages her own property; they also fail to appreciate the relationship between dowry and inheritance as aspects of the same process whereby the diverging devolution of property occurs through members of both sexes, and argue quite wrongly from the absence of one to the absence of the other, a typical case of the over-generalisation of legal 'principles' found among practitioners of the written word.

The supposed progression from brideprice to indirect dowry is seen as a falling away from an ancient patriarchy, following the same reconstructed sequence by which Fustel de Coulanges (1864) had tried to account for much of the history of domestic life of early Greece and Rome. The Patriarchal Theory, elaborated by Maine (1861), has had a long and not altogether salutary influence upon classical studies, nor was it a great improvement on the Matriarchal or even the matrilineal alternatives. The problem is that while we need to avoid the earlier (and still current) anthropological stand that denies the validity of proposing any sequences of development in such matters by dismissing them as 'pseudo-historical' or 'evolutionary', we also need to re-examine these old schema in the light of more recent empirical evidence and of the theoretical implications deriving from contemporary cross-cultural research as a prelude to proposing more satisfactory alternatives. The pitfalls are many and the kind of problem to which such schema can give rise is illustrated in the next sentence of Benzinger's article, 'The man who owns his wife as a chattel can on the same principle own as many as he pleases.' One has only to apply the reverse argument to Tibetan polyandry to see its weakness. In any case polygyny, the role of which in the Old Testament is much debated, is not to be understood in such simplistic ways as suggested by the terms, the seller, the buyer and the bought. That is to take a highly Eurocentric view of plural marriage which has little relationship to reality, outside that of the slave mart where humans of both sexes were items of commerce, commodities produced for the market.

The nature of marriage transactions in ancient Israel is by no means clear, since the time-span is great, the evidence small and what exists often prejudged by attempts to apply such over-determined schemes of development. A further difficulty arises because the Hebrew word usually translated as 'brideprice' is *mōhār*, whereas in the English version of the Bible the translation is given as 'dowry'. Both words are also used to render the cognate Arabic word, *mahr*. However, although the *mahr* may originate with the groom, its offer does not represent the purchase of a wife; indeed the transfer of part and sometimes all of the sum may be delayed, taking place only if the wife has been repudiated by her husband in order to ensure her continued support. As such, the amount of the transfer, negotiated at marriage, relates to the 'worth' of the bride but matching her status for support not for purchase. It is thus a variable sum, different from the classic cases of bridewealth in Africa where amounts are relatively fixed. While the former may look more like a 'price', the position is rather that where women are endowed, directly or indirectly, less commonly with the latter, the payment is more likely to be variable. On the question of variability the Bible provides contradictory evidence. In the story of Shechem, the daughter of Leah and Dinah (Genesis 34:12), the anxious suitor remarks, 'Ask me never so much dowry (*mōhār*) and gift, and I will give according as ye shall say unto me; but give me the damsel to wife'; the reference is to a wife that the suitor had previously 'defiled', so is hardly typical. On the other hand, Exodus (22:16–17) declares that if a man lies with a virgin who is not betrothed and if the girl's father refuse to accept him as a groom, then 'he shall pay according to the *mōhār* (dowry) for virgins'. This passage refers to the special value (in monetary and in other senses) placed upon virginity which is brought out in the post-consummation ritual of the blooded sheet observed in many Semitic-speaking communities; in such cases a standard addition to the marriage transactions may be paid over and above the variable bridal endowment. Indeed many Jewish marriage contracts (*ketubbah*) continued to refer back to the Biblical payments for the next two-thousand years, a fine example of the conservatism of the written formulae, especially ones originating in the Holy Book.

Both fixed and variable marriage prestations are found in the Near East today. In some parts the higher the status of the wife, the higher the *mahr*. This prestation shows a certain element of conspicuous display on the part of both the partners; a large gift declares that this is what I (the groom) can afford and this is what I (the bride) am worth. But the important point to note, and one that must modify any notion of purchase is that, as in China, where the prestations are handed over at the marriage, at least a portion of what is given by the groom's kin is then passed to the girl to take to her new home, to their conjugal home. 'Part of the bride price', writes Patai, 'and occasionally all of it, is spent by the father of the girl on her trousseau. Silver and gold jewelry – earrings, nose rings, bracelets, anklets – form an important part of the outfit received in this manner by a girl from her father' (1959:57). The word 'trousseau' is somewhat deceptive since this jewellery is not merely a matter of decoration but of security; it forms a pool of wealth, a bank, upon which the wife can call in an emergency and which she controls independently of her husband. An instructive example from India is given in Satyajit Ray's film, *The Glass Mirror*, where the bankrupt Bengali landlord, the decadent owner of a dying estate, attempts to use his wife's jewels to raise money to pay his debts, an event which leads to the departure of both the wife and her son. In the Near East, as in North India, the gold and jewellery a wife brings into marriage are not legally available to her husband without her express permission; this element may be very loosely attached to the rest of the conjugal fund.

While these gifts are status indicators, they also constitute an endowment of the wife. A woman's value may vary according to 'family, face and fortune' and what she receives in this indirect form may be related to the wealth of the groom, but the value is vested in her. Otherwise why would the sum be transferred at all, if it were simply returning to its starting place in the same condition as before?

Precisely because of this variability, marriages often involve a complex set of negotiations concerning property; a man of much property tends to marry a woman of much property and to bring such arrangements to fruition the services of an intermediary or match-maker, a role found in many Eurasian societies, may nowadays have to be employed, especially outside the range of kin, outside the 'family', since for close marriages they are hardly required, either here or in South India.

Often the payment of the *mōhār* was delayed or split. At best only two thirds of the indirect dowry was sent by the groom before the wedding; the remaining third was retained by him and only paid out if he divorced his wife – it was a 'reserve on which the wife can count' (Patai 1959:57). For it provided her with a dower in the event of separation from her husband, the high incidence of which suggests that it constituted not so much an effective sanction against divorce but rather a protection from the consequences. Any property arrangements that establish a joint fund or endow the wife on separation may have an inhibiting effect on divorce which involves a dissolution of the fund, although the rights of the offspring are normally protected. But the earlier transfer of a dowry at marriage seems to be a more efficacious instrument for this purpose than the delayed transfer at dissolution. Dissolution can come in two ways, by death as well as divorce, and the dower (or 'inheritance') received by a widow from her husband is similar in certain respects to the endowment she receives at betrothal, marriage or divorce. It enables the woman to support herself, under some circumstances to establish herself independently as a *feme sole* and possibly to increase her attraction as a conjugal partner if remarriage is permitted. But where death intervenes, access to the late husband's property often depends upon the continuing 'fidelity' of the widow, thus reducing her capacity to be 'merry'.

But a woman in ancient Israel received not only an indirect dowry from the groom but also a direct one from her parents and there is no evidence that one preceded or precluded the other in the period covered by the written records. Indeed we know very well that this was not the case either in ancient Mesopotamia or in ancient Egypt, although the indirect dowry may have been more common among lower than higher groups, and among pastoralists than settled agriculturalists. Among the latter, as elsewhere in the ancient Near East and in South India and South China (but unlike North India and North China), a Hebrew woman could obtain rights in land. 'She considereth a field and buyeth it: with the fruit of her hands she planteth a vineyard' (Proverbs 31:16). Purchase apart, she could obtain land at marriage, often as part of the direct dowry, and it was this very ability to acquire landed property, especially when he had no brothers, that was linked to the pressure on women to make close marriages within the 'tribe'.

Endowment through bride service

There were other ways to acquire a partner besides producing a direct or indirect dowry. As in various other parts of the world, service to the future father-in-law could achieve the same end. When Saul's daughter fell in love with David, the father asked for the foreskins of a hundred Philistines in place of a *mōhār* (an indirect dowry). Saul himself was presumably prepared to endow his daughter from his own funds in return for military aid. A more usual case is that in which a poor man, who was in no position to ask for an endowed bride, acquired a wife by service on his father-in-law's farm rather than by producing property of his own. Such services often involved an initial stage of residence at the wife's home, but not in the form of a uxorilocal marriage (since it is not the norm, the dominant form) nor yet a filiacentric union of the kind we have found so widely distributed in Eurasia. For the husband initial residence at the wife's home may be simply a means to eventual bride-removal and hence resembles the pattern of early conjugal cohabitation found for example among the Bemba and in some other matrilineal societies (Richards 1950). At the same time the father-in-law regards it as a way of increasing his supply of labour, which would be particularly important if the bride had no brothers. But even when she had brothers, for example when they are young boys, the husband's labour services may become essential to the running of the 'family farm' and he may be induced to prolong his bride-service by various means.

The point is well illustrated in the story of Jacob's marriages which also brings out a number of general aspects of the kind we have been examining.[1] It will be recalled that through the intervention of his mother, Rebekah, Jacob stole the blessing of his father, Isaac, from his elder twin, the hairy Esau. The words of the paternal blessing, which represents the complement of filial *pietas*, ran:

> Therefore God give thee of the dew of heaven,
> and of the fatness of the earth,
> and plenty of corn and wine:
> Let people serve thee,
> and nations bow down to thee:
> be lord over thy brethren,
> and let thy mother's sons bow down to thee:
> cursed be every one that curseth thee,
> and blessed be he that blesseth thee. (Genesis, 27:28,29)

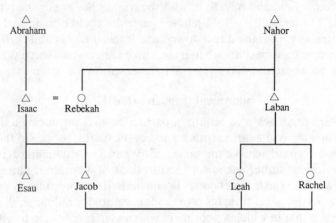

Figure 8 Jacob's marriages

With the words of this blessing in his ears, Jacob set off, propertyless, to far Mesopotamia, where he made for the house of his maternal uncle, one Laban, a Syrian. Having no money, he could afford no *mōhār*, so he set to work for his mother's brother in return for the promise of his daughter, declaring, 'I will serve thee seven years for Rachel thy younger daughter' (Genesis 29:18). However the arrangement did not work out so straightforwardly. For when the seven years were up, Laban deceived Jacob by introducing his eldest daughter, Leah, into the wedding chamber. As in many parts of the world, including Europe in recent times, it was felt that the eldest daughter should be the first to marry. Undaunted by this setback Jacob set to work for a further seven years in order to acquire the younger daughter as well. There was a kind of poetic justice (or even structural homology) about the situation, since his mother had substituted Jacob for his brother in order to secure their father's blessing before he departed. In the end Jacob spent a further six years, making twenty in all, with his mother's brother and at the end of this time he expressed an understandable wish to go 'unto mine own place'. So he came to an agreement with Laban to continue to look after his herds for a while in return for all the brown sheep and the spotted and speckled cattle and goats. When this was agreed, Jacob set to work to make Laban's flock bear as many of such animals as possible, partly in retaliation for his father-in-law's earlier deception. Seeing him accumulate their father's property in this way, Laban's sons grew jealous and God persuaded Jacob to leave for the land of his fathers. As a result of this supernatural guidance he spoke to his wives, telling them a tale about how the speckled flock had been miraculously increased and asking them to leave their father's house with him. 'And Rachel and Leah answered and said unto him, Is there yet any portion or inheritance for us in our father's house? Are we not counted of him strangers? for he hath sold us, and hath quite devoured also our money' (Genesis 31:14–15). In other words, these daughters saw 'all the riches which God [through Jacob] hath taken from our father' as being theirs – 'that is our's, and our children's' (Genesis 31:16). It was their entitlement.

Jacob loaded his wives and children on camels and set off secretly. Hearing of their departure, Laban and his brethren went after them and overtook the fleeing party at Galeed, 'the heap of witness'. Laban protested at the stealth of the departure (as well as at the loss of an image), to which Jacob answered, saying he fled because he thought his father-in-law might have refused to allow him to take his wives along with him. Laban replied that since these daughters, their children and the cattle all belonged to him, the father, how could he harm them. So he suggested that they build a heap of stones as a cairn and enter into a solemn covenant, an agreement which was in effect a mutual oath with God as witness. The main point of this agreement was expressed in the following words: 'If thou shalt afflict my daughters, or if thou shalt take other wives besides my daughters, no man is with us; see, God is witness betwixt me and thee' (Genesis 31:50). Appealing to their different gods, the God of Abraham and the God of Nahor (Laban's father), Jacob slaughtered an animal in sacrifice and they broke bread. After this Laban kissed his children with the kiss of peace and the two parties went their various ways.

This account suggests that when a man served for his bride, she received a portion of her dowry out of the increase resulting from his labour. In other words, the suitor was working both for his wife as well as for her father. When she had been granted her portion, the daughter was in a sense paid off, since she had nothing further to receive from her 'patrimony'. That is why the daughters saw themselves as 'strangers', as having been 'sold', which was obviously very far from the whole truth since they remained at home and were even partially 'endowed' at marriage. It was when they left, following their husband, that they agreed to take the animals, feeling that their father had not given them enough by way of endowment.

The property interests that formerly united the group of cross-siblings now split the brothers from the sisters who wanted to take their own share and leave; the sisters allied with their husbands, the brothers with their wives, a similar situation to that observed in the Chinese family but rather different from African cases like that of the LoDagaa and the Tallensi. Nevertheless this fission of the herds or of any other components of the 'patrimony' did not totally alienate a woman from her natal kin; this much is clear from the words of the covenant entered into by Laban and Jacob, and indeed by the very fact that Jacob went to visit his mother's distant kin in the first place.

The livestock they received from the work of their husband was not their only endowment. While Laban's daughters made no mention of it in effecting their escape, they had already received some property from their father at the time of their marriage. For it is elsewhere stated that he 'gave unto his daughter Leah Zilpah his maid for an handmaid'; and to Rachel he gave 'Bilhah his handmaid to be her maid'. These maids, handmaids, slaves, were clearly property of considerable value and ones which stood the women in good stead.

The manner of her marriage, her surreptitious introduction into the marriage bed, did not augur well for Leah's relations with her husband; she is described as 'tender eyed', whereas Rachel was 'beautiful and well-favoured'. Leah was the 'hated' one, while Rachel was the 'favourite' wife. However, the terms *senua*, the hated one, and *ahubah*, the loved one, were not personal but common epithets for the first and second wives and refer primarily to the husband's shift of affections to the younger wife. But there is also the question of the bitterness that is often seen to exist between co-wives. In Arabic, the word *darrah*, in Hebrew, the word *sarah*, mean both co-wife and enemy; in Africa the root for 'jealousy' often forms the basis of the word for co-wife.[2] Indeed, as we have seen in Tibet, the sororal polygyny illustrated in Jacob's marriages may represent an attempt to lessen the hostility of two women married to one man, a hostility which emerges in the witchcraft accusations between co-wives that are common enough in polygynous societies.[3] But it may also represent a compromise with a general resistance to plural marriages (as distinct from subsidiary unions with handmaids or concubines), which is seen in the words of the covenant between Laban and his son-in-law, 'if thou shalt take other wives besides my daughters'.[4] The taking of other wives would have been an affront to their status and to that of their kin. But it could also mean a diminishing of the interest of their children and themselves in the conjugal fund, in the property which they and their husband (in this case through them) had brought into the marriage. They might be partly displaced by a new 'favourite' over whom they had little control, and who would enjoy the estate that they had helped to build up. Under these circumstances, a family would prefer their daughter to be married in a monogamous union, but if there had to be a second wife, usually because the first was barren, then it was better that they were sisters.

In this case God saw that Leah was the hated one and it was her womb that he first opened, while Rachel remained barren. As in Africa, wives, whether hated or loved, were slept with in turn; Jacob, it is said, 'fulfilled her week' (29:27). So all had more or less equal opportunities for (or exposure to) pregnancy. Leah bore Reuben, Simeon, Levi and Judah, and then her child-bearing ended. Meanwhile Rachel 'envied her sister', begged her husband to give her children, and angered him as a result. At this point she turned to him and said, 'Behold my maid Bilhah, go in unto her; and she shall bear upon my knees, that I may also have children by her.' The act of giving birth upon the knees of her mistress indicated the substitute role that the slave is called upon to fill as her husband's concubine, a role that is legitimated by the actions of the wife. Leah too used her handmaid, Zilpah, for the same purpose, and then later on, after the incident of the anthropo-morphic mandrake root which Rachel begged from her in return for giving up her place on the marriage bed, she began to bear again. 'God hath taken away my reproach', she declared.

There is much discussion about Jacob's marriages that draws attention to the similarities with the situation in Nuzi in Mesopotamia, especially in relation to so-called *errūbu* marriage whereby a man, usually without sons, 'adopts' a son who marries his daughter in what I have called a filiacentric union. But despite the claims of Burrows (1937) and Gordon (1937), there is no Biblical evidence of adoption or that Ruth and Leah were without brothers at the time of their marriages. In rejecting this notion, van Seters (1969) interprets the incident much as I have done, calling attention to other aspects of Mesopotamian marriage transactions which suggest a rather similar set of prestations obtained in much of the ancient Near East.

When he looked at the nature of such marriages in ancient Israel, Benz-inger saw them as part of a general development from brideprice to dowry and therefore assumed that the practice of dowry was not an ancient one. So he was forced to argue that the case of Pharaoh's daughter, for example, was evidence for Egypt alone; and that the parting gifts a bride received (much less the handmaids given to Leah and Rachel) were not true dowry because they 'remain the personal property of the wife', although he did recognise that after the exile true dowry was found. Earlier I made a broad distinction between the situation where the woman's dowry is amalgamated into a common fund and one where the conjugal property is kept in separate parcels, the husband's and wife's; though in the latter case the property of the spouses is in one sense brought together through the marriage into a joint fund, the parcels are in another sense distinct. In some instances, as in medieval Cairo, a woman had her own personal property, gained either by gift or as a result of her earnings, as well as her interest in the dowry proper, which came from both her parents and her in-laws. Indeed in any one society different kinds of property or different kinds of gift (as we will see very clearly in the case of Rome) may be amalgamated or kept distinct. The situation is variable within societies and over time. For example, a change from one to the other appears to have occurred in early Roman law.

Nevertheless both can be seen as types of diverging devolution, or at least as types of the status-weighted endowment of daughters; whether they co-exist or succeed one another over time, they should be looked at in this context rather than as representing a shift from 'brideprice' to dowry.

It is the same with direct and indirect dowry. Some authors have seen the apparent shift of emphasis in Europe after AD 1000 from the morning-gift supplied by the husband to an endowment on the wife as a general one from 'brideprice' to dowry (Hughes 1978), while others such as Herlihy (1974) see it as a reversion to Roman custom. How far this practice had disappeared is a moot point, especially since the written record is not always a good indicator of customary gifts (in much of the Near East the *mōhār* or indirect dowry was legal, the direct dowry customary). Nevertheless such changes of emphasis over time are not unusual. Broadly speaking the richer, settled groups tend to stress direct dowry, while poorer, pastoral or 'tribal' ones (such as the ancient Germans) made more use of the undirect form, paralleling the hierarchical differentiation found in India. In a general way such forms can be seen as alternative methods of endowing women, with different implications to be sure, but they are often complementary and in any case have to be seen in a different developmental perspective than is provided by many of the analyses of marriage in the Near East and other parts of the world which were based on archaic theories and ethnocentric views of the world.

There are several further aspects of Hebrew marriage which relate to my general theme. The first has to do with the binding character of the betrothal. Secondly, there is the stress on pre-marital virginity. Thirdly, we find the differentiation of types of union, marriage and concubinage. Fourthly, a considerable pressure exists towards monogamous unions. Fifthly, bills of divorcement involve the use of writing[5] and may be required by law (Deuteronomy 24:1ff.); marriage contracts appear to have derived from these (Tobias 7:14). The written form facilitated the distribution and return of property when such arrangements differed, in quantity at least, for each individual, unlike the relatively standardised payments we have noted in the oral cultures of Africa. The necessity of producing a written bill may also have placed some restriction on the ease of divorce. So too did the religious idea that a wife is the mother of the 'seed of God' so that to put her away is hateful to Jehovah. Sixthly, unlike upper groups in India and China, the remarriage of divorced or widowed women is not prohibited, though the levirate, like plural marriage, seems mainly aimed at producing a legitimate heir;[6] adoption on the other hand was rare and as in Islam and some other societies the two possibilities appear as alternative strategies. One operates at the level of adding wives, the other of adding children (usually sons), but both recruit mainly from within the existing range of classificatory 'wives' and 'children', and thus tend to strengthen ties within the kin group. This strengthening of kin ties is one aspect (heirship is another) that may lead to the condemnation of these practices by sectarian or non-kin interests (Goody 1983).[7] In any case, as we have seen in India and China, the levirate is likely to be condemned by those upper groups and societies that tend to stress the unique combination of man, woman and property in marriage. Seventhly, while there were no match-makers in ancient Israel (as distinct from modern Jewish communities in Europe),[8] marriages were usually arranged in one sense of that word. Eighthly, women not only received a dowry, but they could also 'inherit' in the absence of sons. There is little evidence of hierarchical differences in the sources, but the 'receivers' of marrying-in sons-in-law were generally richer than the givers (although not necessarily higher on the scale of learning, as in India), and the higher possibly placed greater emphasis on direct dowry than poorer groups and pastoralists. Finally in the story of the daughters of Zelophehad we gain a very clear picture of the relationship between diverging inheritance and endogamy, for inheriting daughters were not allowed to marry outside the tribe (Numbers 27:1–11). And while property was not involved in this instance, one of the first acts of the Israelites on their return from Babylon was to purge their sin of marrying 'strange wives'.

'Now when these things were done, the princes came to me, saying, The people of Israel, and the priests, and the Levites, have not separated themselves from the people of the lands, doing according to their abominations, even of the Canaanites, the Hittites, the Perizzites, the Jebusites, the Ammonites, the Moabites, the Egyptians and Amorites. For they have taken of their daughters for themselves, and for their sons: so that the holy seed have mingled themselves with the people of those lands: yea, the hand of the princes and rulers hath been chief in this trespass' (Ezra 9:1–2).

The pressure to marry within was partly political, partly 'sectarian'; for the religion was at this time 'tribal', an affair of the lineage descended from Abraham. The sectarian aspect of in-marriage, or rather endogamy since it was incorporated in an explicit rule or injunction, is made clear in the case of King Solomon who 'loved many strange women, together with the daughter of Pharaoh, women of the Moabites, Ammonites, Edomites, Zidonians, and Hittites; of the nations concerning which the LORD had said unto the children of Israel, Ye shall not go in to them, neither shall they come in unto you: for surely they will turn away your heart after their gods; Solomon clave unto these in love' (I Kings 11:1–2). As a result he fell into apostasy and followed other gods to whom he burned incense and made sacrifice. But at another level the problem was that of the daughters of Zelophehad. When they were given permission to inherit the lands of their father, they had to marry within the tribe. Inheriting daughters could not be permitted to marry outside and take their entitlement with them. What is crucial is the fact that women could and did have rights in the 'patrimony', or more accurately in the conjugal fund of their parents.

In ancient Israel the situation regarding marriage and the entitlement of women is difficult to unravel because of the poverty of the evidence and the possibility of outside influences in the written record, although my general thesis would suggest that we can exaggerate the importance of such contacts as distorting factors in view of the regional similarities and the constant interaction between groups. Such was the case with the development of Islamic law, as we see in the following chapter, and such too was the case in medieval Cairo on whose Jewish community the remarkable collection of Geniza manuscripts has thrown so much light.

According to some of the Talmudic sages, the most important task of the Almighty after the creation of the world was to arrange marriages. 'This was no easy feat, and "matching them is as difficult as splitting the Red Sea"' (Friedman 1980:90). First of all there was an engagement contract, then a betrothal, stages that were often combined. The betrothal was binding; indeed the couple were legally husband and wife, although consummation of the marriage was delayed to the final stage, a delay that sometimes created legal problems (pp. 193–4). The union involved a marriage contract, often beautifully decorated, which the groom had made specifically for the bride since it was largely protective of her rights and her property. For it listed, first, the minimal marriage gift from the groom to the bride which followed a Biblical formula. Indeed one of the characteristics of these documents is their formulaic conservatism; phrases like 'Be to me a wife according to the law of Moses and Israel' are repeated for 2,000 years. More important financially was the additional marriage gift (also *mōhār*), of which part was made immediately but the larger portion was delayed, usually until the marriage was dissolved, and was therefore sometimes known as *ḥōv* or a debt. Finally the contract (*ketubbah*) listed the direct dowry or *nedunyā* which was given to the bride by her parents, mostly from the mother's personal property, and her bridal outfit all assessed at their worth, and all or half of which was returned to them if she was childless, depending on whether they were Karaite or Rabbanite.

There is no doubt that all these gifts were made to the wife, some forming part of an integral conjugal fund, others not, and that their listing in the marriage contract by the notaries was a way of protecting the property of daughters and their natal lines. Aramaic marriage documents from the Jewish colony in the Egyptian town of Elephantine in the fifth century BC each have detailed dowry lists, a procedure which, it has been suggested, originated among West Semitic peoples (Friedman 1980:292). These lists are frequently the largest and most interesting part of the *ketubbot* from the Geniza, giving a record of the answer to that ancient question, 'How much will you give to your son? How much will you give to your daughter?' 'The sons will inherit', runs a *midrash*, 'the daughters will be provided for' (p. 356). Fixing the relative size of the gifts was an essential part of the marriage negotiations; especially the daughter's part which was often larger than the *mōhār* and other marriage payments, 'frequently several times so, by five to thirty times' according to Goitein (1978:129). In order to arrange a good match, the bride's family had to present her with a large and expensive dowry (Friedman 1980:289). Indeed some men might give away all their possessions to this end, leaving little for the sons, a situation which, as in Byzantium, led to attempts to control excessive dowries. At the same time a rich man could perform 'a meritorious act of charity' by providing a dowry for a poor girl.

The extent of the direct endowment made things hard for fathers and led to the hoarding of precious metals for the protection of daughters (Goitein 1978:139–40). However these items could also be used as collateral for loans by the husband, especially in lower income families, so that they were not entirely removed from more productive activities. Indeed the woman herself could invest her personal property in various ways, but the general uncertainty of life made jewellery portable, easily concealed and readily exchangeable for other goods or services.

The possessions a bride took into marriage consisted of two categories, the 'iron sheep possessions' for which the husband assumed full responsibility for the duration of the marriage, and *melūg* property which he administered but which remained in her possession.[9] One of the items sometimes provided by the bride's kin at this period was a house or apartment for the new couple, reminiscent of later Greece, although sometimes the real estate was used as an investment for the wife rather than as a residence.

The provision of a dowry including real estate, especially marked in the Palestinian contracts, meant a heavy strain on the bride's parents, so that the gift was often conditional on their being allowed to live there themselves. This was a kind of future retirement contract which interestingly enough displayed the same elements of distrust between the generations as we find in the case of Europe (Goody 1983). 'Experience taught them not to rely on filial piety' (Friedman 1980:301). Absent husbands were very precise in the amount of food allocated to their wives (Goitein 1978:189). It was also the case that partnerships between brothers might take an exact, written, legal, form, while even fathers and sons working and living together were not necessarily partners, for the latter might be on a commission basis like an agent rather than automatically sharing in the profit and the loss (pp. 34, 40). Unlike the situation in later Ashkenazi communities in Europe, men were not meant to marry until they could be independent and, although some couples did live with parents, separate living quarters were considered to be 'more conducive to good family relations' (p. 40), so too were separate purse strings. One of the difficulties of having more than one couple, as we have seen in China, is the potential conflict surrounding the taking of a new wife, especially between her and her husband's sister, a conflict that acquires more serious proportions when she remains in the house. Even when she marries, the sister is never entirely cut off and remains the *dhimma* or responsibility of her brother. That was the case more generally in the Near East, and Goitein calls attention to the women's dirges that were so popular in pre-Islamic Arabia and which, like the songs from Maharashtra, were directed towards brothers rather than towards husbands. For even after marriage a woman remains, to some extent, a member of her paternal family, and still today, in an Arab village in North Palestine, a married woman will say to her brother's wife, 'You cannot prevent me from taking food from my brother's stores. It is not your money and not even his. I eat from my father's possessions' (Goitein 1978:21).

While in Biblical times the *mōhār* may have been transferred to the bride at the marriage itself, during the early Talmudic period the emphasis was not on a payment made immediately at marriage but on an endowment pledge written into the *ketubba* or marriage document and collectable on the dissolution of the marriage (Friedman 1980:239). The pledge was intended by the rabbis not only to take care of the divorced wife but to make the man less likely to initiate such a procedure, 'so that he should not think lightly of divorcing her' (p. 258).

As we have seen, the *mōhār* consisted of two payments, an advance to the bride and the delayed endowment. In some cases the first could amount to a considerable sum and her power to make use of it reflected, in Friedman's view, 'the elevated social position of the Jewish wife and her *relative* economic power' (pp. 277–8). In fact the same situation existed in Arab communities even before the coming of Islam (p. 273). Like their neighbours, Jewish women owned real estate and were granted the right to administer and dispose of their property (p. 303).

While Goitein is very explicit about the medieval Jewish *mōhār* as a gift to the wife, he offers quite another view about the Islamic *mahr* of contemporary Cairo. 'The Arab–Muslim *mahr* was essentially a bride price, a payment to be made at the wedding, but one that could be deferred to one or several later installments', which were fixed in the marriage contract (1978:120). The grounds on which the differentiation is made between gift and price hardly justify the radical distinction and seem to reflect a measure of ethnocentrism, rare in this distinguished scholar. Analytically there is little to be said for such a view of Islamic marriage, which represents a hang-over from the earlier discussions of Near Eastern unions by European writers.

In his discussion of the Geniza material, Friedman draws a distinction between the Babylonian and Persian traditions of the *ketubba*, the latter representing the practice of those Jews living in Islamic societies. But both sets of documents show that the position of women was 'more advanced in some respects than one would have imagined' (1980:viii). 'Marriage was considered a partnership. Husband and wife undertook mutual obligations, and each party was assured the right to terminate the marriage if he or she desired.' As a result the documents place great emphasis on 'possible interruptions of the marriage and its dissolution', a feature that resembles Islam but is quite at odds with the Chinese, Indian or European traditions. The likelihood of divorce strongly influences the nature of marriage contracts and the payments they lay down. At the same time that possibility does not reduce the importance of the family and Goitein (1978) has stressed the role of the nuclear unit in this society. Women are no less important as wives but the whole system of endowment brings out the way that as daughters, too, they are treated with regard to property. While these various features may represent in part the urban ways of life in Cairo, it is impressive even in that context and is certainly not unique since in significant respects it continues the earlier traditions of Egypt and the Near East to which we have called attention.

Such features should lead us to question widespread ideas about the uniqueness of European institutions in these and later times. It is worth remarking upon the role of love in marriage (Goitein 1978:165) as well as the need for regular conjugal sex, on the Friday for Jews (for two weeks in the month), Thursday for Moslems, Saturday for Christians, before taking one's bath and going to synagogue, mosque or church (p. 168). Each of these ecclesiastical institutions, supported by charitable gifts or foundations, assisted the poor, the destitute and the hungry, especially widows and orphans. For the west had no monopoly on 'public charity' which was made possible by gifts from women as well as from men. For wives, who were spoken of as companions (Malachi 2:14), owned real estate, went to court and conducted business, even entering into *commenda* partnerships (p. 348).

In all this the dowry played its part, since it allocated property to women, some of which such as the first marriage payment, inheritances, and gifts from the family remained outside the common pool (p. 179). For the better off these gifts consisted largely of gold from her husband and furniture, jewellery and houses from her family. While the husband had control but not ownership over the common pool, he had to mortgage his own property against an assurance that he would pay back both what she had brought and what she was owed (p. 123). So that in effect she had a right of veto, especially if she were an epiklerate, over the disposal of goods even from the common conjugal fund (p. 179), as well as being able to decide about her own *peculium*. 'A woman invested mainly in real estate, she lent money, concluded partnerships, also sold and bought textiles, jewellery, and other items included in a bridal outfit, but she was not in the mainstream of the economy – the larger-scale production and exchange of goods' (p. 332). Nevertheless, they could buy and sell, rent or lease houses, stores, workshops, flourmills and other types of urban real estate as well as taking care of their own maintenance (p. 326). As Goitein remarks, 'the middle-class dowry and other possessions of the wife made her position quite comfortable' (p. 180). But women of 'all classes' possessed immovables (p. 326), while those that were destitute could apply for means-tested charity by 'uncovering her face', charity to which the upper groups had contributed property, much of which was in the control or possession of women. In this way, 'the dowry represented a strong bond between the spouses and gave them a constant opportunity for cooperation' (p. 180).

The dowry that was then and is now so widespread among the settled Semitic peoples of West Asia persisted in the Jewish communities of Europe until very recent times. Of course as in medieval Cairo farming land and flocks were rarely involved in the marriages of the diaspora since Jews were often forced, sometimes chose, to adopt a more urban, more commercial, way of life. In the Jewish communities of eastern Europe (Zborowski 1949, with E. Herzog 1952) there were three main criteria of status: learning, family and money. The ideal combination was learning and wealth, these two together ensuring *ikhus*. The typical daydream of a mother, as expressed in a folksong, was to have her son a '*talmid khokhom* (a wise student) and also a clever business man' (Zborowski 1949:91). A family acquired a learned status through educating its sons, for to study and to learn is a *mitsva*, that is, a deed commanded by God. But that could also be obtained through marriage; Jewish parents dreamt of marrying off their daughter to a learned youth or their son to the daughter of a learned father.

Two consequences followed. The arrangements leading to a marriage had to be carefully weighed. Through the dowry payments learning, even inherited, could be linked to property. The marriage-broker, who was very important in the *shtetl* or small town, had in his notebook detailed accounts of the *ikhus* of the boys and girls, including all the learned men in their families. The greater the background of learning, the better the match. For the Talmudic sages had said 'a man should sell all he has in order to get for his son a bride who is the daughter of a scholar'.

The dowry of a girl was proportional to the scholarship of the prospective bridegroom. Very rich Jews went to the *yeshiva* to ask the head of the college for the best student whom they would then seek out as a prospective son-in-law.[10] An outstanding student would receive not only a bride with a rich dowry but a given number of years of *kest*, that is, of board in order to support him in his studies.

Marriage among Orthodox Jews in Eastern Europe continued to be governed in minute detail by the book which the Christians read but rein-terpreted very freely on this subject. Marriage to any kin or affines was forbidden to Catholics, but the Jews followed the letter of the law. If a man did not take his dead brother's wife in a leviratic union, he had to perform the ceremony of the boot. This practice harks back to an incident in the Old Testament. When Boaz took as his wife Ruth, the widow of a kinsman, the closest relative of the deceased, his redeemer and potential husband of his widow in a leviratic union, could not 'redeem' the kinsman's land, and he drew off his shoe to confirm that he had passed over that right to Boaz.[11] The new husband then declared the purpose of the marriage in the following words: 'Ruth the Moabitess, the wife of Mahlon, have I purchased to be my wife, to raise up the name of the dead upon his inheritance, that the name of the dead be not cut off from among his brethren' (Ruth 4:10). What he 'purchased' was in fact the field (the inheritance) rather than Ruth herself. In due course Ruth gave birth to a son, Obed, who in turn beget Jesse; Obed was nursed by Naomi, the mother of her late husband. In this way the mother of the 'social father' became the social mother in the eyes of the world, 'for thy daughter-in-law, which loveth thee, which is better to thee than seven sons, hath born him' (Ruth 4:15).

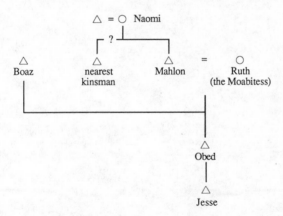

Figure 9 Ruth's marriages

Thus, in earlier times, marriages could be concluded among close kin as well as with affines; written contracts of marriage and divorce specified what claims women had on the property, including the land, they had brought as dowry or had accumulated during the marriage. While these were often arranged, relations between men and women were certainly not loveless as the Song of Solomon amply testifies. Monogamy later became the norm but even in earlier times polygyny (as distinct from polycoity) was relatively rare; like the levirate (but unlike adoption which as in Islam was not an effective option) it remained a possible strategy of heirship for ordinary folk, although among rulers and merchants it could also be a matter of the conspicuous consumption of sexuality. Certainly there is little evidence for the kind of developmental sequence from brideprice to dowry, from purchase to qualified freedom, that has been posited by many. The 'woman's property complex' has been a feature from the period of the earliest records, not only in this but in other societies throughout the ancient Near East.

12

Marriage and property in the Arab world

The Arab world constitutes a vast domain in time and space, but one which displays some remarkable similarities through the application of Islamic law and custom. Nevertheless there are considerable differences not only among the various schools and regions but in particular between the nomadic Bedouin of the desert, with their 'tribal' organisation based on the solidarity of the lineage, and the settled populations, the peasantry in the villages, some with tribal affiliations, and the merchants in the towns. Clearly different strategies of heirship obtain among nomadic peoples, where land was indivisible and held largely in common and where livestock are easily split up into smaller but self-reproducing parcels, than in rural or urban situations where rights in land, in houses or in enterprises have to be reallocated in rather different ways.

This tripartite division of the population is neither new nor confined to the Arabs, but goes back to the coming of agriculture to West Asia, long before the coming of Islam. Both the continuity and the diversity have to be borne constantly in mind when thinking of kinship, marriage and the family among the Arabs from, say, the fourth century AD. For there is once again a tendency to foreshorten the historical sequence, and in particular to look upon Mohammed himself as a point of transition between the tribal and the settled, between the solidarity (*'asabiyya*) of the desert lineages and the domestic, familial patterns of the town and even of the settled, farming hinterland. The notion of such a change is intrinsic to Islamic faith which looks back to the Prophet as the great reformer, but it also forms part of many European views of social evolution in the Near East (Mundy 1988). Of course, transition was always taking place because the inhabitants of the desert, the fields and the town constantly faced one another over the millennia, with the results that Ibn Khaldun analysed in so dramatic a way. Individuals and groups moved between one situation and another while at the same time there was a long-term trend towards the extension of farming and increasing urbanisation as trade grew and populations expanded. The

361

trend was often slow and uneven. In greater Syria, agriculture expanded between the fourth and eighth centuries, during the fifteenth and sixteenth centuries and from the late nineteenth onwards. Urbanisation in the Near East increased greatly in the twentieth century. But there had been important urban and farming components in the life of the area over several millennia so that to study the initial phase of the transition, one would need to go back long before Mohammed, even for Arabia, back at least to the time of the patriarchs. And even then we would find nomadic herders and settled agriculturalists developing contemporaneously in some loose symbiosis rather than succeeding one another in any unilineal fashion.

Because of the search for this transition, the study of Arab kinship and marriage has long been dogged by the same kinds of assumptions about the pattern of long-range changes that we noted in the case of Hebrew marriage. Brideprice was said to have been followed by dowry, matriliny by patriliny. It was this sequence that Robertson Smith claimed to have found in his classic study of *Kinship and Marriage in Early Arabia* (1885) and one which continues to be put forward today, in the full form by a few writers (e.g. Ahmad 1986; Coulson 1964), and by others in the modified form of a shift from brideprice to dowry. Leaving aside the question of evidence for what has been called the superimposition theory (Powers 1986), there are two theoretical difficulties lurking behind this discussion, both of which derive from a similar source, namely, the tendency to treat social groups and social institutions as self-contained boxes. Regarding social groups, clans and lineages are seen as boundary-maintaining units to which people are assigned and in which all (or most) of their relationships are largely contained. Evidence of relations running between these units are often interpreted as anomalous, as inconsistent with the ideal type and therefore as representing a possible shift to or from another form. Regarding institutions, these tend to be tagged by labels such as patrilineal or 'brideprice' which are then held to be characteristic of particular states of human society following each other in a predetermined sequence.

It is not so much a question of totally rejecting such an approach but of refining the categories, replacing them by variables where necessary or where possible, of discerning trends rather than unilineal sequences, and of recognising that 'patrilineal' groups, for example, may co-exist with their presumed opposites, matrilineal ones. Pure agnation is a figment of the imagination, not a state through which all societies once passed and therefore something to be searched for and discovered in the shaky evidence on early societies.

Under the superimposition theory, the ideal type of clan is seen as an exclusive, boundary-maintaining group which allows of no cross-cutting relations. Among the Arabs clans are recruited by 'patrilineal' descent, now and in the discernable past, and Robertson Smith concluded that, because some recognition was given to relations with the mother or her kin, 'male kinship had been preceded by kinship through women only' (1907:xi). The premise is that male (reckoning of groups and relations) excludes female and vice versa. At the same time 'descent', eligibility to a clan, is quietly identified with the whole range of kinship and marriage. On this basis, and following the lines proposed by his friend McLennan in *Primitive Marriage* (1865), he attempted to sketch out a hypothetical picture of the development of the social system over time (1907:xiii).

There is little point here in laying out the evidence Robertson Smith and others put forward for this earlier state of matriliny, namely the presence of female eponyms (pp. 28–32), the role of the mother's brother and the presence of filiacentric unions, nor yet in considering alternative explanations.[1] Since he assumes there has been a general move from matrilineal to patrilineal institutions, any practices of an 'intermediary' type are interpreted as showing signs of a transition from one to the other or alternatively as survivals of an earlier state. But contrary to his central assumption, there is no single organisational form for unilineal descent groups, nor is there any over-riding necessity why in any given society the systems of descent, succession and inheritance, to use the triad of Rivers (1914), should always be homologous in character. While there is certainly evidence of some strain towards consistency in these three areas, the patrilineal recruitment to descent groups, whether in China, India or Arabia, is perfectly consistent with the transmission of property to women as well as to men, that is, with diverging devolution. To talk of patrilineal societies or institutions without further differentiation obscures this critical point; it makes for an inadequate analysis of particular societies and regions as well as a distorted understanding of long-term developments.

The basic problem in Robertson Smith's study is that his adoption of inadequate categories and simplified sequences leads him to expect homologies and to perceive contradictions in Arab marriage, which he then attempts to impose or resolve by a series of speculative propositions and imagined reconstructions. For example, in discussing the operation of the feud in Arabia, he points out that 'the blood-wit is distributed to the kin of the slain within the limits of inheritance' (p. 65). Inheritance and blood-revenge were two sides of the same coin, the latter being clearly dependent upon clan membership; following Baidawi, he remarks that 'none can be heirs who do not take part in battle, drive booty and protect property' (p. 66). Since women did not take part in the feud, they did not inherit. 'The exclusion of women from inheritance was not therefore confined to Medina, and ... was probably nearly if not quite co-extensive with marriage by contract or purchase. The same law seems to have existed in other Semitic countries along with marriage of the same type. The Mosaic law gives daughters a share only in default of sons, and even this law is one of the latest in the Pentateuch' (p. 66).

His description of the situation, for Israel as for Arabia, is highly debatable. Inheritance and descent are presumed to be organised in the same fashion, both being related to participation in tribal war, although as we have remarked trade and agriculture had long been part of the productive activities of the Arabian peninsula. But that was not the case even for pastoralists. The assertion about the lateness of the law allowing women to act as residual heirs to their brothers is purely an assumption, and an unlikely one at that given the Mesopotamian evidence. But whenever the right of the heiress was instituted in ancient Israel, women also received a dowry, direct and indirect, the first indicating their claims on the parental estate, the second their entitlement to hold property. Moreover under later Islamic law, all women had an explicit right to inherit; while under Sunni rules they were only entitled to a reduced share compared to that of their brothers, they also received an endowment at marriage (or divorce). Part of this endowment came from the husband and it was this element that Robertson Smith appears to pull out of the devolutionary complex and refer to as a 'purchase'. On the other hand he does not go on to draw the conclusion that women are incorporated into their husbands' patrilineal group by this transaction, although that might be thought a logical implication of the notion of purchase. Indeed he contrasts Arab with early Roman marriage in that 'a married woman did not change her kin' (p. 77), the substance of which claim we will examine later; for she had then, as she still has today among the Bedouin, the right to return to her kin and to be protected by them. After marriage the protection of her honour rests with her brothers, unlike the Turkish tribes where it becomes the responsibility of her husband (Bianquis 1986:569). In many Arab societies today, a woman retains her family name after marriage, implying that the maintenance of the status of the family is a function of the status of daughters as well as of sons (Mundy 1979:176). Cuisenier (1975) regards this retention of daughters as an index of a more rigorous agnation than existed among the Romans where a wife (at least in *manus* marriage) is said to enter the lineage of the husband, but the opposite is equally plausible. The point about whether retention or transfer is a mark of strong partriliny (or agnation) has been argued by anthropologists (e.g. Gluckman 1950; Leach 1957; Fallers 1957; Lewis 1962), but the terms of the debate need to be rethought. At the societal level, I have found no adequate ethnographic evidence of complete transfer or of complete retention. Single diagnostic features such as the use of natal or conjugal names need to be carefully examined in context in order to decide upon their relevance; the disappearance of a woman's natal name at marriage in Britain as compared with Spain or America would not appear to indicate a greater degree of incorporation or of patriliny in one society as against another.

In the course of his search for sequences, Robertson Smith also points out that there were instances where a woman would contract a marriage with a man who then lived in his wife's home (pp. 79–88), that is, in a filiacentric union. For when a man sought the protection of a tribe other than his own, it was normal for him to be given a wife. He suggested that formerly this marriage may have been of the temporary *mut'a* variety, where the contract specified how long the union would last. This form of private marriage, though retained in Shi'i law, was condemned elsewhere in Islam as 'the sister of harlotry' and Robertson Smith assumes that, as in the *binna* marriage of Sri Lanka, the offspring belong to the mother's family, although that did not necessarily follow. It is the position of the woman in these marriages which he sees as anomalous. He then tries to explain the discrepancy by a developmental hypothesis that assumes a general shift from matrilineal to patrilineal institutions which has left some survivals in its wake. But, as we have seen, filiacentric unions of this kind are very widespread in the major European and Asian societies, and their presence can also be explained in terms of strategies of continuity and the structure of the sibling group as well as the provision of wives for refugee strangers. For they occur not only for ancient Israel but also in medieval Islam and indeed today. If a woman in Highland Yemen has no brothers, her husband would 'marry into the house', setting up the 'prince consort' situation on a humble level. If she marries within the *'asabah* (the group of agnates), and possibly even within the same property-owning group, then the name is kept on the land by means of a marriage to her father's brother's son (Mundy 1979, 1982). The case that Robertson Smith describes has a political rather than a property base, but such marriages are also the result of the choices and strategies inherent in a system in which daughters as well as sons transmit status and property by diverging devolution. They can never simply be considered as the survivals of an earlier mode of social organisation.

The assumption that Arabian society had passed through three phases, the matrilineal, the patrilineal and the modern, the last being a form of compromise, structures much of Robertson Smith's thinking about Near Eastern society. For example he claims that the two words for marriage prestations in Arabic, *sadaq* and *mahr*, are synonomous in Islam, although originally they were quite distinct, *sadaq* being a gift to the wife (also referred to as *jahāz*) and *mahr* to her parents. He goes on to conjecture that the first type of prestation was again associated with *mut'a* marriage which he links to the matrilineal phase, the second with 'marriage of domination' in the later patrilineal stage. So he excludes altogether the possibility that these forms of marriage had coexisted functionally from an early date and were both

associated with the capacity of women to hold property. Yet already in the
Syro-Roman law books of the period just prior to Islam (Crone 1987), there
is plenty of evidence of the contemporary existence of multiple forms of
marriage that relate to the nature of women's property.

In a marriage of domination the price alone was seen as inducing parents
to part with their daughter. However, such an interpretation is inconsistent
with the fact that in medieval and in modern Islam, the prestations did not
usually go to the parents but to the bride; or rather some went to her at
marriage, the rest if she was divorced (Bianquis 1986:574). Because of his
erroneous view, and in opposition to other scholars such as Wilken, Robertson Smith considered that the marriage contract remained a purchase, albeit
a purchase of marital rights.[2] It is clear that women were no mere objects of
exchange, but the notion that rights over them were purchased also presents
analytic and empirical problems. For they themselves held rights over
property which included rights over the so-called purchase price itself. Even
on his own evidence there were parts of pre-Islamic Arabia (let alone in the
later period) where women could hold property, for there are references to
their ownership of herds; a form of divorce existed whereby the husband
declared, 'Begone, for I will no longer drive thy flocks to the pasture' (p.
116). Setting this testimony on one side, Robertson Smith claims that in
Medina at least, women did not inherit until the time of the Prophet, though
he does allow that they received valuable gifts and that in Mecca their
position was better than elsewhere. It was there that the widow Khadija,
who offered herself to the Prophet as a wife, engaged in a lucrative caravan
trade and presented her daughter Zainab with a house. Women in the towns
of Mecca and of Medina, like those of Damascus and Byzantium, enjoyed a
certain liberty and played a part in their own as well as their husband's affairs
and in historical events more generally; it would be wrong to assimilate their
role to an imaginary tribal model of Bedouin behaviour.

While Robertson Smith continued to regard Arabian marriage as one of
purchase, even after the time of the Prophet, he also notes that 'by a humane
illogicality the price becomes the property of the woman' (p. 121, my italics).
Even if his analysis were correct, it would certainly be illogical to give the
name 'price' to an 'indirect dowry' for the bride, but throughout this work he
tried to fit a bilateral peg into a unilineal hole of a kind he has made for
himself, one in which women, or rights over women, have to be bought and
sold. For while the system of descent (that is, eligibility to clans or patronymic groups) is unilineal, the system of devolution (that is, the transmission
of property) is diverging. But his commitment to a box theory of institutions
and social groups prevents a proper appreciation of the facts. Yet the critical
aspect of these payments is clearly brought out in the incident he recounts of
a suitor asking for a girl's hand in marriage. 'Yes', replied the father, 'if I

may give names to all her sons and give all her daughters in marriage.' 'Nay', answered the suitor, 'our sons we will name after our father and uncles, and our daughters we will give in marriage to chieftains of their own rank, but I will settle on your daughter estates in Kinda and promise to refuse her no request that she makes on behalf of her people' (p. 124).[3] In other words the wife is endowed by the husband during the course of the marriage arrangements, though part, even the major part of that endowment, may not be hers until the marriage is dissolved: hardly a 'price', certainly not a purchase. However, it sometimes happens that a portion of the prestations received from the groom, known as *shart*, does go to the bride's father. But this gift has to be taken in the context of all the other transactions, not singled out as a relic of a bygone age. It is linked to the various transfers between father and daughter (*jahāz*), as well as being accompanied by a prestation from the groom to the bride (*mahr*). It partakes neither of the character of bride purchase nor yet of bridewealth, at least in an African sense, for it is not part of a significant circulating fund that permits brothers to get wives out of the funds received at the marriage of their sister. And it may well constitute a fund on which the bride can later draw.

Even if we substitute the term 'indirect dowry' for 'brideprice', we have to be careful as to how we interpret types of dowry as indices of societal organisation, whether historically or comparatively. It is possible that some societies have experienced a general shift of emphasis from *mahr* to dowry, that is from indirect to direct forms of endowment. We have suggested that a much earlier shift from bridewealth to dowry was related to the development of hierarchical societies which tended to stress direct dowry in the higher groups and indirect in the lower. In India and elsewhere, increasing wealth in those lower groups has led to the growing use of a direct dowry. But we cannot overlook the way these forms function in the same society at the same time either on a hierarchical basis (as in India) or as alternative types of contract available across the board (as possibly in ancient Egypt). Indeed there is a third alternative. The German tribes were said to have given an indirect endowment to their brides but, as with the Egyptian *šp*, the gift was often a 'fictitious' one, delayed until the dissolution of the union by divorce or by the death of the husband when it became a widow's dower or *douaire*. It has been claimed that later on there was a shift to dowry from 'brideprice'. Of emphasis, perhaps. But in England the widow's claim on the dead husband's estate continued to be a specific feature of marriage transactions; during the course of the wedding ceremony, the husband declared 'with all my worldly wealth I thee endow'. The offer represented a delayed indirect dowry, a 'brideprice'. But it was no mere survival from an earlier state of society, rather a promise of support for the wife when the marriage ended. Affinal endowment of this kind is not an alternative but often an accompaniment (albeit delayed) to parental endowment, since it matches gift (or rather promise of a gift) with gift. There is no contradiction between the two forms of endowment, though they may be differently timed and stressed in different situations.

The stratification of marriage transactions is not simply a question of amount but of type. Where ethnographic evidence exists, there are definite indications that direct dowry characterises upper, richer, groups, and indirect dowry ('brideprice') the lower, poorer, ones. Such is the case in Sri Lanka (Yalman 1967:172–7) as well as among settled Arabs in the Yemen (Mundy 1979:166). In Hindu law the high status marriage is the 'gift' of the daughter, where the father rejects any notion of 'price' or even of reciprocity. But to be in a position to endow one's own daughter at marriage, one needs to have sufficient resources. So that there is not only a 'class' element but possibly an 'evolutionary' one in the different emphasis on 'indirect' and 'direct' dowry, though the progression is never a simple linear matter. Nevertheless we can never regard all 'mixed' types as transitional cases for to do so would simply reflect the crude abstractions that we made initially.

Let me turn from considering the superimposition and box theories associated with Robertson Smith and many writers before and after him, to more recent evidence of a different type derived from historical enquiries and from ethnographic observation (Mundy 1988), to see what light can be thrown on marital assigns and on the whole process of devolution to women, including inheritance.

Historically there is no evidence for the exclusion of women from property in South Arabia in pre-Islamic times (Beeston 1957:103), nor is this suggested by a careful reading of the *hadith*, with the possible limitation on their ownership of agricultural land in Medina (Stern 1939:158–68). That is what we would expect from the evidence not only of the contemporary law-codes of neighbouring peoples (Byzantine, Syro-Roman, Sassanian and Jewish) but also from the evidence of their own practices as revealed by documents and inscriptions. For pre-Islamic Arabia had been heavily influenced by Roman–Byzantine law, with scholars travelling from the peninsula to study in Beirut. In the separation of property of the spouses, in the endowment of a woman from both natal family and marital family (and in the negotiations concerning this property in case of divorce), and in the case of delayed payment in the implicit tendency to equate these sums with claims on the respective estates of father or husband, we find institutions of Roman–Byzantine law not without points of comparison to the formulations of Muslim jurists (Mundy 1988:29). There were also some differences. Under Islam only the indirect dowry (*mahr*) was essential to complete the formalities of marriage, but that of course did not mean that women were not directly endowed by their parents, at least in the richer urban and peasant strata. Despite the differences, in broad terms 'the texts can belong just as well to the general environment of written law of the period' (Mundy 1988:29).

In post-Islamic times the situation was changed by the intervention of a religious text. While the position regarding women may not have changed all that much, the general legal situation altered because of the nature of sectarian activity; in early Islam as in early Christianity (Goody 1983) 'allegiance to the new sect both entails a break with anterior social bonds and yet builds upon kindred notions – of social brotherhood and of individual power to alienate property – in forging a new social community' (Mundy 1988:32). The situation also altered because of the very existence of the text and its commentators. Islamic law does not emerge directly from the religious text. It took shape only after long discussions of legal scholars which were embodied in *fiqh* and which absorbed local custom as well as developing particular lines of argument to form distinct schools.

Both these elements affected the law of inheritance which was the subject of the earliest extant *fiqh*. The difficulties entailed in understanding the verses of the Qur'an referring to inheritance and succession gave rise to a number of differing interpretations associated with the main schools of Islamic law, Hanbali, Shafi'i, Hanafi, Maliki, and their component groups and scholars. Some of the differences arise from attempts to work out general principles, leading in turn to juridical disagreements. One such early debate is recorded in the *Risalah* of al Shafi'i where a passage runs, 'Indeed, if you divided the inheritance only according to the closeness of a relationship then the relationship of the daughter to her father is exactly the same as that of the son'. Such uncompromising reasoning from physiological to social 'closeness' carries implications for the division of property, although clearly 'closeness' may be differently defined for different purposes – for inheritance and for descent. But as we see in Europe, once graphic representations of kinship have been established, they become in some measure decontextualised; what began in late Roman law as a guide to inheritance (which was inevitably bilateral because of the form it took) was later applied to prohibited degrees of marriage (Goody 1983). As Mundy points out, one of the constant problems in Islamic jurisprudence, and its interpretation by outsiders, is the failure to appreciate that different 'rules' may be applied to inheritance (which is bilateral) and to descent (which is unilineal); it is a problem that we have found in both China and India and which we will encounter again in Roman attempts to transfer the oral to the written.

But such differences were not purely dependent upon ambiguous formulations. External factors intervened. For example the way in which Maliki law allows the Muslim community to share in cases of intestacy 'suggests the development of doctrine as the sect was transformed into institutional faith and during the ensuing contest between state officials and kin groups over inheritances' (Mundy 1988:45). It was a process that was carried out in a yet more radical fashion in Christendom some centuries earlier; in Islam this change occurred in the late third century of the Hegira, in Christianity in the late fourth century AD.

This same inability to contextualise 'general principles' may have influenced the stress which later scholars gave to agnation. 'If anyone, it is the *fuqaha'* [the lawyers] who lie behind the re-introduction of the agnatic group as a legal principle in the Sunni codes', suggests Mundy (1988:47) because they were attempting to restrict the fluid devolution of property that had been associated with a conquering 'tribalism' which assimilated the conquered, first as dependents, then incorporated them as kin. The authors of the law attempted to limit the demands of the state treasury, to insist upon the rights of the family but to allow personal disposition not through mere bequest but 'within the institutional form of religious endowment, in *waqf* beyond the easy reach of the state' (p. 47). That is to say, they employed those 'general principles' in ways that supported the religious rather than the political establishment.

The notion that the community or the state should be entitled to a share of an individual's wealth at his death, especially if he was reduced to creating (fictional) heirs or wished to bequeath his property by testament (which amounts to the same thing), is widespread. This was the Anglo-French doctrine of escheat. In China when the failure to utilise one of the various strategies of heirship led to the extinction of the direct line, the government would confiscate the estate, although only in the case of larger holdings (Ebrey 1981:123). Under Islam, Schacht has suggested that the ability of an heirless man freely to alienate his property to 'social kin' was restricted to one third of the total upon the insistence of the State, which would otherwise lose the whole estate (Mundy 1988:34), or rather fail to draw any benefit from it. In fourth-century Christendom, similar restrictions on testamentary freedom were introduced in the interests of children, to prevent parents from handing over all their property to the church for religious purposes; it was a restriction on the power to disinherit legitimate heirs (Goody 1983:94). On the other hand freedom of testimony clearly benefited the new sects, especially when the transfer to 'social kin' was restricted. Such a transfer could be carried out by adoption as well as by bequest. Under Hanafi law, a man can adopt an heir when he leaves no living relative; in this case escheat to the state or to the religious community is avoided. But in other schools of Islamic law, adoption was prohibited. It appears to be only in the later Islamic schools which developed as the result of the institutionalisation of the third century after the Hegira, that religious communities established a claim on inheritance by enlarging the notion of escheat, a process that had its parallels in early Christendom of a similar period.

Reverting to our main topic, we may sum up by saying that there seems to be little evidence that Islam brought any major change in the relationship between women and property. In settled areas throughout the Near East marriage transactions already appear to have included a settlement by the husband or parent upon the wife, who was also entitled, at least after the Prophet, to a share in the inheritance of her parental property. Let me now turn to the ethnographic studies which represent a range running from urban merchants to rich farmers to pastoralists. Obviously the possibility of the transmission of land occurs only with the first two groups in which there seems to be a greater emphasis on the direct endowment of daughters.

The general position regarding women and property becomes clearer when we look at a much later period in the history of Islam through the eyes of an author who had no particular developmental axe to grind. Lane's account of Egypt in the middle of the nineteenth century (1871) described an urban society rather than the Bedouin pastoralists of Libya or the agriculturalists of Tunisia, Lebanon or the Yemen which I discuss later. Both in town and in country, Sunni law recognised two kinds of rights of a woman to property. First she was entitled to a portion of the inheritance equal to half that of a male of the same degree of relationship to the deceased (Lane 1871:i,129). If there were no sons, the daughter became the recipient of the bulk of the property.[4]

But although daughters were otherwise entitled only to a half share of the inheritance they also received a dowry at marriage. This dowry came from two sources, indirectly from the groom and directly from her parents. The amount of the groom's contribution was the subject of pre-marital bargaining and was specified in the marriage contract known as the writ (al-kitab), though it was not always written down. Two-thirds of this amount was generally payable immediately before the marriage contract was made; the remaining third was held in reserve to be paid to the wife if she was divorced without her consent, or in the case of the death of her husband (Lane 1871:i,202); as we have seen, it was a kind of dower.[5]

Partly because property was involved, partly because of the urban environment, marriages were often complicated to arrange, and Lane provides a graphic description of the go-between or khatibeh conducting female relatives of the groom around the woman's quarters to look for a girl who was both beautiful and rich enough in jewellery. Neither of these facts could a man belonging to the higher orders easily discover for himself, since women who were his equals always appeared veiled in public; even the groom himself had to provide a special gift before lifting the veil from the face of his new bride.

Among the villagers the groom also had to provide an indirect dowry for his bride, which sometimes raised a barrier to a man getting married, just as the direct dowry among upper groups in India sometimes made it problematic for a girl, the Muslim difficulty relating to polygyny and the later marriage age of men, the Hindu one to infanticide and the earlier disappearance of women. On the other hand in nineteenth-century Egypt a man could marry a divorcee or a widow with about half the amount needed to endow a virgin wife; alternatively he could acquire a slave as a concubine, for her children were automatically legitimate while the mother herself became a free woman on the death of her husband and master.

While plural marriages were allowed (the Prophet himself had many wives), only about 5 per cent of the married men had more than one wife; moreover polygyny, Lane claimed, was even rarer among the higher orders than the lower, partly because the poor women work while the rich do not. 'A poor man may indulge himself with two or more wives, each of whom may be able, by some art or occupation, nearly to provide her own subsistence; but most persons of the middle and higher orders are deterred from doing so by the consideration of the expense and discomfort which they would incur' (1871:i,231). If Lane is correct, the situation is atypical of Arab societies not in the percentage of plural marriages, which is often lower, but in the hierarchical distribution of polygyny, which is elsewhere found to be more frequent among the rich, or nowadays among the middle classes (Goody 1976). Both among rich and poor, polygynous marriages usually occurred when the first wife was barren, though she always remained 'the great lady'. Because of this differential status the father of the new bride, or the bride herself, might insist the husband divorce the first before marrying the second. In any case, among the higher orders each wife had a separate house and there were no joint households in the physical sense. A rich man might also take a slave as a sexual partner; he could not approach a female slave of his wife's without her express permission, but the very possibility is reminiscent of the domestic life of the Hebrew patriarchs.

When we turn from nineteenth-century Egypt to the twentieth-century Near East, field studies show that, despite the important features common to the Arab world, considerable differences in domestic life and kinship organisation exist, especially as between the major groups of town dwellers, agriculturalists and pastoralists. Among the settled agriculturalists of the Yemen (Mundy 1979), we find the larger patronymic associations ('asaba, habl or bayt) that are called lineages in the terminology of many ethnographers but which need to be clearly differentiated, especially in their relationship to land, from the lineages of pastoral societies or indeed from those of societies with simpler agriculture like the Tallensi or LoDagaa of West Africa. Among both the latter types of society, some communal and joint rights in land existed, for herding in the first instance and for shifting agriculture in the second. But in the societies of Highland Yemen that practise intensive agriculture, members of patronymic groups are not joint holders of real property in the same sense, although one '*asaba* may make common cause against another in a political fight or an irrigation dispute. The major exception to domestic ownership, reminiscent of the 'strong' lineages of South China, arises from the charitable provisions of Islamic law and their manipulation for familial ends; the placing of land in trust was a way of keeping it out of the hands of rulers who might confiscate large fortunes (Bianquis 1986:598) since the ends of the foundation were religious in the broad sense. A family *waqf*, as distinct from one directed to the religious life itself, meant that a man could endow his less fortunate descendants as well as provide benefits for the other members of the kin group. Mundy describes one large group with about seventy-five adult members in which land was held jointly and remained undivided. But otherwise land not subjected to trusts was redistributed per capita. As a result women were entitled to the same share as a man provided they married within the '*asaba* (1979:183), a practice that is again reminiscent of the inheritance provisions for an heiress in the Old Testament. As in Sri Lanka, a woman's ability to acquire rights to parental land was linked to her making a close marriage, although as we shall see the rights they acquired were not always activated.

In southern Tunisia, too, women have a claim on land, although some have argued that this right is found in Islamic law but not in custom. However the distinction is less a matter of law and custom and more a matter of whether an individual, male or female, lays claim to a specific share on departing from the house. Most of those leaving are women at marriage, for they leave even when they marry close kin. While a woman is entitled to claim a share of the inheritance, to do so 'would be tantamount to isolation from kin, clearly against a woman's interests if marital problems emerge. Hence most women prefer to leave their claims on the parental house dormant, to be exploited by the dominant brother from whom they receive some recompense' (Sant Cassia 1986:41). Later on, the claim of women may be exercised by or 'through their adult sons, who replace their brothers as resources, should marital problems emerge (such as the importation of another younger wife)'. So a woman's failure to make a claim can be seen as a positive rather than a negative act, the banking of resources which can be withdrawn in times of difficulty. In Tunisia it was mainly those married to distant kin or to very poor men who made early claims; otherwise the rights passed down to their sons, the sister's sons, who might act as residual heirs. By then the fragility of the marriage is no longer a major issue.

A similar handing over often occurs in the case of the widow, but here it is accelerated rather than delayed. Even if she does take possession of her husband's estate, she will usually pass on her land as a 'free gift' (*nidhc*) to the son with whom she is living. Not really as a 'free' gift, for it is a pre-mortem transfer made in expectation of support. It is a pension, a *pension*, in the literal sense of the word, in return for the provision of which the co-resident son or daughter is offered some benefit, temporary in China, permanent in Europe.

The 'banking' of claims to property seems to be linked to the frequency of divorce and that with polygyny. This also appears to be true of the delayed payment of part of the indirect dowry (perhaps of the indirect dowry of *mahr* as such), as well as the postponement of part of a woman's parental portion to an inheritance at their death rather than receiving her 'lot' at marriage. But in the present case a further postponement involves inheritance rights which are passed on to their sons, who then claim from their mother's brothers what the sisters had chosen not to take from their brothers. At the same time the delayed claim of the bride to parental property highlights the importance of what the groom brings to the marriage, that is, what he receives as a son, although here again part of the family contribution, including the 'brideprice', may also be delayed until a later date. Such delays stress the need to see these transfers in a developmental framework, at least over the individual life-cycle, rather than as static, individual, once and for all, transactions. To do otherwise may lead to a concealment of the elements of stratification and of strategy involved.

The Yemen study brings out very clearly the position with regard to indirect dowry of the paternal kind going first to the father rather than of bridal kind which goes direct to the daughter. In 1976 legislation was enacted that tried to stabilise the cost of marriage. Members of the community argued that if the *gimah* (the 'price or value of a woman') was reduced, then the price of clothing and food should also be lowered. The reason given was that the father, who received the payment, was responsible for providing support for his daughters, formerly in kind, on the occasion of certain festivals that mark the cosmic and human cycles. In other words the two transactions were seen as inter-related; 'the payment made to the father is not some free purchase price for the girl' (Mundy 1979:166), it is a contribution to future expenditure on his daughter's behalf.

Apart from the *mahr*, among richer groups the parents provided a direct dowry as well as other gifts on the occasion of the marriage. The result was a balance of transactions in favour of the daughter at all levels. 'Even among relatively simple people the woman's father may in time return to his daughter more than he received as *shart* (the part of the payment that goes to the father, as opposed to the *mahr* which goes directly to the bride)' (p. 166). This amount he pays out in installments over her lifetime, making the point that even if her husband's family is not treating her well, he himself will continue to do what he can to help. In one sense the continuing support is dependent upon the wife not having taken up all her legal and jural rights on the family land by claiming a direct dowry. In an interesting case a woman quarrelled with her young daughter, threatening to return to her own natal family. '"But you can't go home", said the girl. "You took the land from my uncle (*khali*)"' (p. 167). Taking her full entitlement meant the breach was complete. Most women therefore allow their brothers to cultivate their land, receiving a relatively small return. On the other hand they expect support and security in the event of life crises, especially when threatened with repudiation by their husbands. 'Only later in life, when a woman is truly secure in her marital household, with grown sons to support her in old age, will she have her sons press her claim' (p. 169). When this happens, 're-lations between brother and sister are unlikely ever to be as close again'.[6]

I do not wish to claim that the nature of marriage transactions in Arab societies is identical; far from it. Some authors dealing with Palestine have asserted that the gifts from the groom's family are said to be used by the bride's family to acquire their own brides (Granquist 1931; Rosenfeld 1958; Peters 1980). Nevertheless in most parts of the Near East that is not the case. What goes to the father enables him to meet the costs of supplying his daughter with her dowry. Of the rural areas of Iran, not of course Arab but Islamic, Mir-Hosseini (1989) claims that such payments are a matter of 'reimbursing the bride's father for his outlay in providing a dowry'. During the various ceremonies leading up to the wedding, gifts pass in both direc-tions but mainly from the groom's family, consisting of cloth and jewellery for the bride and food for the wedding feast which takes place at her house, the cost of which is largely repaid by a collection taken among her kin. On the final day she leaves her home in procession, preceded by horses bearing her dowry. That dowry consists partly of the *shirbaha* or 'milk price' which is cash provided by the groom and given to the bride's father to buy a *jahiz* or dowry of household items for the bride, to which he is expected to add at least the equivalent cash element. Indeed mothers may start collecting such items when the daughter is still a child, while the bride herself may weave the carpet which is often the most valuable piece. The increased expectations of recent years have meant that less is provided for the wedding expenses and more for the material goods required for the household, which the bride sometimes does not even bother to unpack until she and her husband set up on their own.

There is a third payment, the *mahr*, which Mir-Hosseini characterises as a 'delayed dower', and which has become more important in rural areas in recent years as they have adopted town practices and as marriages between kin become less common and daughters therefore require greater protection against repudiation.

Mahr is an inherent part of every Muslim marriage and is sanctioned by Islamic law. It consists of a sum of money, property or any valuables which the husband either pays or pledges to pay to the bride upon marriage. According to the Islamic law, even when a definite *mahr* is not stipulated in the marriage contract, the bride is still entitled to a *mahr al mithal*, that is, a bridal gift befitting her family position and her qualities. Muslim societies differ greatly with respect to the practice of *mahr*; in some it consists of two parts, immediate and deferred. The immediate portion of *mahr* is given to the father of the bride or the bride herself prior to or upon marriage. The deferred portion of it is usually paid in case of an unwarranted divorce.

In Kalardasht, nothing is paid at the time of the marriage; it is a pledge written into the marriage contract in which a husband undertakes to pay a certain sum to the wife on her request, but in practice she receives it only if she is divorced. In this form the *mahr* is directly comparable to the European dower.

There are two aspects of these marriage transactions that relate to wider issues. Frequent divorce has been a fundamental feature of Arab society over a long period, with rates as high as those in Europe in the 1980s, which are often regarded as evidence of the dissolution of the family. Divorce, which may take place early and usually when a marriage is infertile (Fargues 1986:342), is more problematic in urban than in rural settings because a woman does not have the same solidary kin group to which to return (Maher 1974). Hence the element of dower in marriage transactions, that which a woman receives after the end of the marriage, would then seem to become more important, perhaps to prevent her having to accept more transitory unions with men when her marriage is dissolved. Prostitution was a major problem in the towns, perhaps more so here than elsewhere as one inevitable aspect of polygyny is the shorter length of married life experienced by men rather than by women. Men remained bachelors for longer than women remained spinsters, which means a high differential marriage age. While marriage is virtually universal, the average age at present is twenty three for women in Lebanon, twenty two in Egypt and eighteen overall in the Arab world; for males it is twenty nine in the first two cases and twenty eight overall, a gap of ten years. Thus in the Near East the age of marriage for women is comparable to Europe but much later for men (Fargues 1986:340).[7] Despite the relatively late age of marriage of the women, there are few illegitimate births, presumably resulting from the strong social pressures against pre-marital intercourse, the control and support they give to their sisters, evidence of which is provided by the requirement of the bloodied sheet in the wedding ceremony; and in any case legitimacy is the *sine qua non* for an heir. But the defence against pre-marital intercourse and the late age of men's marriages suggest either prostitution or adultery.

Late marriage is not simply a matter of the unavailability of females which is aggravated not only by polygyny but by the greater than expected mortality among infant girls.[8] Part of the gap could be made up if women married at an earlier age. The fact that the groom has to acquire or accumulate a substantial indirect dowry for his bride tends in itself to delay the marriage (Bianquis 1986:577; Fargues 1986:342). The transfer of this sum is too often postponed, but some kind of gage has to be provided. Late marriage puts them in a better position to take on responsibilities for a union in which part of the wife's dowry may also be delayed. But on the other hand the men retain the usufruct of the property of their sisters.

In pastoral societies women also have certain rights to the basic productive resource, livestock. While they may not inherit any animals directly from their father's flocks, they can acquire these indirectly at marriage. But even these bridal gifts from the groom may be stored with the brother rather than the husband. 'In lieu of the portion in inheritance, a part of the bridewealth (i.e. indirect dowry) was later paid to the wife rather than to the father and was kept with the flocks of her brothers until such time as she might transfer this to her sons' (Mundy 1979:185, referring to Peters 1978:326). The deliberate transfer of property the bride has received at marriage from the groom to her brothers is a precaution against maladministration or ill will on the part of her affines; for it remains with her natal kin until such time as she has adult sons of her own and is secure in her conjugal family. It also throws another light on the father's part in these transactions, since the retention of property by her kin can be considered a matter of protection rather than sale.

Leaving land or livestock in the care of one's natal family ensures a continuing, active relation between brother and sister; withdrawal of the custodianship is linked to the withdrawal of support by the brother but it brings benefits to his sister's offspring. The relation between brother, sister and sister's son in Yemen comes out very clearly in a case where two sisters were being paid an annual sum by their brother in return for the use of their land. Later on one sister transferred her land to her sons. 'Their parts in the family property had been marked off and deeds of ownership given them at the time of the division of their father's estate, but in the records their land falls under their brother's name' (Mundy 1979:173). So a woman's claim to her father's land is 'a real one' although she may not always wish or be able to assert it. Sometimes she made no bid, for 'a woman's leverage to negotiate in marriage depends upon her retaining a claim on the resources of her natal family. In this sense a woman's share in the family estate may be more a promise or a symbol of her status in the family than a marketable asset she can freely manipulate' (p. 166). However at other times she was denied her entitlement; 'at the base of many complex and wealthy households was the refusal of a powerful man to divide the joint family patrimony' (p. 164). Men and women alike could suffer, especially when the father had died early and the male parental role had been taken over by his brother or his wife's brother, either of whom might, in the absence of a written document which could be taken to court, usurp the property. It is a typical 'wicked uncle' situation (Goody 1976:54–6,63). It should be added that, apart from land, some women in this region inherited considerable property from the mother, especially housing and jewellery, as well as lesser amounts from a husband, brother or sister. But 'land came almost exclusively from the father' (Mundy 1979:182).[9]

Pastoralists have different interests and different norms from agriculturalists, and these are often thought to bring them closer to the exclusively patrilineal model. Closer they may be but there is nothing exclusively patrilineal about their position regarding their natal and conjugal lineages, which has been carefully examined in Peters' studies of the Bedouin of Cyrenaica (1965; 1966; 1978). He points out that, in contradiction to many popular ideas as well as to some theoretical thinking, Bedouin women certainly do not 'occupy a position in complete "unmitigated servility" dominated by men' (1978:311–12). While they have important roles to play in their husband's camp, they are not cut off from their natal kin. It is true that the Islamic law of inheritance allocating male property to women is not always followed to the letter but as we have seen there are alternative strategies. And in any case women do acquire flocks which they leave to their sons; whatever the case with inheritance, they have some access to property rights through marriage transactions. As the result of negotiations, agreement is reached that wealth will be transferred from the kin of the groom to the bride's father. The amount of this transfer, which takes place only after the marriage has been established, depends upon the birth of children. In fact only a small fraction of the amount promised ever reaches the bride's father but against the outstanding remainder the wife herself can extract 'gifts' from her husband following a conventional pattern of behaviour. 'A wife, as a result of a quarrel with her husband, in which he has insulted her, or particularly if he struck her, goes back to her father in anger . . . she refuses to return until she is placated with a "gift" ' (Peters 1978:326).

These gifts might consist of a valuable pair of silver amulets or a sheep, and as among the Rwala Bedouin are sometimes very substantial (Musil 1928; Lancaster 1981), always representing a redirection of property in favour of the wife (Peters 1978:326). In his later years her father, knowing that further payments of the indirect dowry are unlikely to be made, will formally renounce all claims by requesting that the outstanding sums be 'put in front' of his daughter.

It is not given to her outright, but she insists on marking an agreed number of sheep with her father's or brother's brand and holds the right to nominate an heir, among her sons, to this property . . . In some cases, women amass sufficient property in animals (their silver armlets and anklets they tend to sell for animals as they reach old age) to affect significantly the distribution of inherited wealth among a man's sons. (pp.326–7)

A woman from a wealthy family may bring within her control relatively large amounts of wealth, though the wife of a poor man is pinned to his status and the wealth she controls is little because the wealth against which she can claim is small.

Among the Arabs too we find a hierarchy of practice, which is much more marked in the agricultural and urban communities (table 10). I have already commented upon the fact that the association 'direct dowry high, indirect dowry low', a matter of emphasis, is repeated in Yemen. So too is the tendency 'rich families, joint families; poor families, stem families', where 'family' stands for the unit of production or even of ownership. 'Those with small holdings (and whose houses were usually much smaller also) rarely could maintain undivided holdings of property by such large family groups. The land was not there to hold them: at lower economic levels a man's property was most often divided among his heirs before or soon after his death' (Mundy 1979:163). As Lane noted for Cairo one hundred years before, women in poorer families played a more active economic role, leaving the equivalent of purdah for the rich. Since they did not possess the capital for 'a relatively self-contained family farm or enterprise', such women often participated openly in market transactions; 'distance from the market place was a sign of high status and an expression of the power and autonomy of the household to which a woman belonged' (Mundy 1979:182–3).

Let me turn to some of the other topics discussed in earlier chapters. Unlike the other societies we have treated, marriage is not monogamous, although less than 5 per cent of marriages are polygynous, often undertaken when the first wife has been infertile, that is, as a strategy of heirship; in Africa on the other hand the average is above 25 per cent. Among the other mechanisms of continuity in Islam the levirate is practised but not adoption;

Table 10. *Hierarchical trends in Arab communities*

	Higher	Lower
1 Marriage transactions	direct dowry stressed	more indirect dowry
2 Size of households	larger ('joint')	smaller ('stem')
3 Partition	later	earlier
4 Plural marriage	usually greater	usually less
5 Position of women	more seclusion, less participation in market	less seclusion, more market activity

filiacentric unions made to acquire grandsons are rather rare, which makes divorce, remarriage and polygyny correspondingly more important for such purposes. Great stress is placed on pre-marital virginity and marriages are mostly arranged within the same property-holding strata, often within the same clan, the preferred spouse for a man being the father's brother's daughter; once again close marriage and diverging devolution appear to be linked together. This was so even in medieval towns, as revealed by the Geniza documents from Cairo (Goitein 1978) where there was little to distinguish the families of Muslims from those of Jews and Christians. But the former were the only ones to practice polygyny and were criticised for the ease with which they could repudiate a spouse. On the other hand both Muslims and Christians forbade oblique marriage to a niece, though they differed in their attitude to other close marriages. All the groups valued virginity before marriage and fidelity within; moreover the duty of protecting the honour of married women remained with their brothers (Bianquis 1986:564), like their property. Of course, the continuing responsibility of kin did not mean the absence of ties, indeed of affection, between husband and wife. Historical sources from the thirteenth century testify to the passionate attachment of a tribal chief for his wife and to the devotion of a mother for their sons. If such documents paid more attention to the solidarity of kin groups than of conjugal or maternal relationships, that was because, according to Bianquis, 'la chaleur effective maternelle ou conjugale allait de soi' (p. 562).

The incidence of marriage to the father's brother's daughter, in a classificatory sense, continues to be high, especially in many rural areas; it has been introduced into the regions where Islam has spread, though it does not appear to have the authority of Holy Writ. One of its immediate advantages is that less dowry has to be raised at the time of the marriage (p. 571; Cuisenier 1975); not that such women necessarily receive smaller amounts in the end, but a marriage between close kin is one between trusted partners, with a reduced element of competition. And if one aim is to keep property together, there is little point in dividing it on the occasion of the marriage. In this way close, intra-clan, marriage parallels the close, intra-clan adoption practised in China and India; the Arabs forbid adoption, the latter forbid intra-clan marriage. In ancient Greece the father's brother's son was a preferred partner for an heiress, an epiclerate, a girl without brothers, for by this union her heritage would be retained among the closest kin ('within the family'). It was the same with Sassanian law where 'the institution of succession by the son-in-law, that is, in the absence of a son by the husband of the appointed daughter, was bound up with the practice of marriage within the agnatic group' (Mundy 1988:29). As in ancient Israel, individuals were not free to alienate their shares of family property to anyone outside the agnatic group (Perikhanian 1983:644). The link with the daughters of Zelophehad is close, suggesting that the non-exogamous nature of agnatic groups in the Near East among Arabs, in Israel and in Persia, and their virtual absence in Greece and Egypt, should be linked to the need for at least some women to marry in because they were carriers of family property. In a historical and regional context, this form of marriage is part of the area of close unions that we noted in the Near East, and of which the most extreme example was represented by the unions between brothers and sisters not only in ancient Egypt but in Roman Mesopotamia and Osrhoene as well (Lee 1988), where not only sibling but parent–child marriages seem to have been practised until the time of Justinian (AD 527–565). In this sense Tillion (1966) was right to see marriage of this kind as involving 'l'obligation de l'inceste'.

I began this chapter by considering the kind of developmental sequence posited by Robertson Smith for Arab kinship and found it wanting in various respects. Clans tended to be treated as box-like units, 'brideprice' and dowry payments as incompatibles associated with different modes of social organisation. We found the direct and indirect forms of dowry to co-exist although they were differently stressed depending upon position in the hierarchy, the economy and the region. The great extent of the Arab world makes matters of family and marriage difficult to examine as a whole. There are obviously many common elements, but which of these exist in practice, which purely at the level of the code, are never easy to judge. Indeed the very existence of these written codes on the one hand and custom on the other raises two further questions we have touched upon in considering East and South Asia, and which will become yet clearer when we look at ancient Rome. In his discussion of how later jurisconsuls distorted the ideas of Mohammed, Bianquis remarks that women were turned into an object (1986:573). Part of the analytic problem we face comes from the fact that written 'codifications' tend to change the nature of jural concepts, or rather they present a particular picture of social facts, in part because of the process of decontextualisation to which they subject behavioural norms. Moreover lawyers, commentators on the law, tended to come not only from the towns but from environments that have provided them with an education in many ways far removed from the sphere of everyday life. At the same time, and this is the second point, written resources as a whole tend to deal with the public level of lineage, patronymic or even patriarchal relations rather than the conjugal, domestic world dominated 'par des présences féminines constantes et bienfaisantes, la mère, les soeurs et les tantes célibataires ou répudiées, les servantes' (Bianquis 1986:578).

Turning from law to society at large, we find a tension, especially among pastoral groups, between the solidarity (*'asabiyya*) of male-oriented structures on the one hand, the patrilineal lineage, the joint agnatic household, even to some extent the conjugal family, where authority and the continuity of the enterprise lie in the hands of the males, and on the other hand the need to maintain the status of women in a hierarchical structure. Women are entitled to a share of the patrimony, whether living in urban, agricultural or pastoral situations. Both past and present evidence suggest that property was in principle devolved on women at marriage (often indirectly through the *mahr*) as well as at death by inheritance (albeit a half share). If this division of the property was often postponed or even avoided in rural areas, that was associated with the continuing obligations of brother towards their sisters, of particular importance where divorce was frequent. Women were not absolutely transferred at marriage from one group to another, but a shift of relationships took place which involved no cutting off of ties; with the emphasis placed on marriage to close kin such separation would have been impossible from the outset. But even in more distant marriages, brothers might remain the protectors of their sisters, sometimes looking after their property and ready to receive them back in the case of divorce. As with other societies in this region, the continued ties between brother and sister are often associated with close marriage on the one hand and the distribution of property on the other. The notion of the purchase, indeed even of the exchange, of free women is foreign to such social systems. Rights in both men and women are transferred at marriage but notions of sale applied only to slaves as individuals, and to prostitutes and others for short-term services.

Even in Robertson Smith's day there were no real grounds for the exclusively patrilineal view of Islamic society. Its rejection did not have to await either recent ethnographic studies or modern historical research. In the late eighteenth century a French scholar wrote:

Inheritance is not a temporary grace when there are sons, it is a right; and a right that daughters have for goods acquired ... Indeed one even finds Governments passing to the son-in-law through the rights of the daughter. (Duperron 1778:172–3, Mundy 1988:5–6)

And his Danish contemporary, C. Niebuhr, puts the general situation in yet more uncompromising terms:

The Europeans are mistaken in thinking the state of marriage so different among the Mussulmans from what it is with Christian nations. I could not discern any such difference in Arabia. (1972:ii,212, quoted Mundy 1988:6)

The Arab world was by no means homogeneous; the nomadic peoples tended to give more emphasis to the indirect forms of endowment, but nevertheless in certain central ways Niebuhr was right.

IV

Greece and Rome, yesterday and today

The history as distinct from the prehistory of Europe effectively begins with the advent of writing in Greece, continues with the development of the Roman Empire and then with the coming of Christianity diverges into the tradition of the Western Church based in Rome and the Eastern Church based in Constantinople. In my analysis of the development of marriage and the family in Europe (1983), mainly medieval Europe, I discussed some aspects of the inheritance from Rome. Both Rome and Greece had important influences on the social life of the Near East, of Egypt, Israel and the Arab world. In the next section I want first to consider the situation in ancient Greece, then in ancient Rome, finally returning to the subsequent history of marriage and the family in the Eastern Mediterranean in order to provide a link with the structure of domestic relations in rural Europe in pre-industrial times. In this way I hope to draw together some of the threads that bind societies in the Far and Near East, between East Asia on the one hand and the Mediterranean world on the other, to indicate some of the points of similarity between the structures of kinship, marriage and the family in the major societies of Asia and Europe.

In discussing Greece and Rome I will take the same approach as in the previous section where I have tried to bring out some of the changes that have taken place in the understanding of Western scholars regarding marriage, endowment and lineage in these societies. It may seem strange to begin with the works of scholars writing at the beginning of this century or before. It is not only a matter of the history of ideas. I use these authors, as well as more recent authorities, partly because earlier views still persist, partly because some of the reconsiderations have often taken place since I began this undertaking, but partly too because many social scientists are locked into views expressed by Sir Henry Maine or Fustel de Coulanges, to take only two authorities, because they played such an important role in the thinking of scholars like Durkheim and Radcliffe-Brown, and are still used as teaching material to this day. *Ancient Law* and *Ancient City* are important books by any standard and deserve to be read widely. But their notions on the nature of marriage and the family often need to be radically modified in the light of later empirical evidence, and above all in the light of a comparative, theoretically oriented consideration of the practices of these societies.

The reader who turns directly to these chapters because of a greater interest in the European past may be worried that I am employing certain terms such as 'conjugal fund' and 'lineage' in ways that are sometimes unusual in considering Greek and Roman law. I have indicated the ways I am using the terms earlier in the argument. I continue to do so here because I regard the resemblances in the relevant institutions as being sufficiently close, certainly in relation to my contrast with other, especially African, systems.

13

The heiress in ancient Greece

From a consideration of Arab and Hebrew marriage and property I turn to that of ancient Greece, partly to make the link with Europe, but also because these institutions display some striking similarities and at the same time have undergone similar misinterpretations, especially regarding the position of women with regard to property and kinship. While some writers have claimed a priority for matrilineal descent in early Greece (e.g. Thomson 1949), most have seen the kinship system as firmly patrilineal.[1] Fustel de Coulanges' study of *La Cité Antique* (1864) takes a strong stand upon this issue.[2] For him, as for Maine, religion was the key to early institutions and the domestic cult was transmitted from male to male.

This was owing, no doubt, to the idea that generation was due entirely to the males. The belief of primitive ages, as we find it in the Vedas, and as we find vestiges of it in all Greek and Roman law, was that the reproductive power resided exclusively in the father. The father alone possessed the mysterious principle of existence, and transmitted the spark of life. From this old notion it followed that the domestic worship always passed from male to male; that a woman participated in it only through her father or her husband; and, finally, that after death women had not the same part as men in the worship and the ceremonies of the funeral meal. Still other important consequences in private law and in the constitution of the family resulted from this. (1955:39)

From this supposed need for the homologous organisation of religion and kinship, the author derives the notion of *patria potestas* and ideas about the position of women, just as Robertson Smith did with feud and kinship in Arabia. His reconstruction of her fate at marriage, at an unspecified period, runs as follows: 'She must abandon her religion (the domestic fire) . . . she must give up the god of her infancy . . . the wife belongs entirely to her husband's family . . . divorce was almost impossible' (pp. 43–8). Fustel de Coulanges wrote of this transaction as 'sacred marriage' and in its sacredness lay both its indissolubility and its monogamous nature.

We have seen that, having posited a similar set of strong, box-like agnatic

386

units for the ancient Arabs, Robertson Smith goes on to argue that the only means of getting the woman from the domination of her father to the domination of her husband is either by capture or else brideprice, which was the interpretation he gave to the *mahr* accompanying Arab weddings. There was no shortage of scholars who were prepared to argue in a similar way for early Greek marriage.[3] Clearly the situation in fifth-century Athens or Sparta, like the later forms of marriage in Israel or Arabia, gave little support to such theories. So a similar procedure was adopted of harking back to the early period where the evidence, necessarily thin, was picked over for traces of sale or purchase, indeed for signs of any transactions that passed property from the kin of the groom to the kin of the bride. But even a casual glance at the classical sources emphasises the continuing relationship between a wife and her natal family, especially with her brother, the maternal uncle of her children (Bremmer 1983).

In his survey of the theories of Köstler and other writers, Finley convincingly rejects the idea of purchase and points out that such transactions may have quite other implications. Instead of representing a sale, they can be seen as part of the network of reciprocal prestations that characterise many aspects of the social relations of pre-industrial societies. Hence there is no contradiction between the passage of gifts (*hedna*) to the bride's kin and the passage of dowry (*dōra*) in the other direction. One gift provokes a counter gift. A bride bringing many gifts is described as a *polydōros*, gifts which he sees as being given to the husband Finley is surely correct in seeing these transactions as existing simultaneously in one society (as they often do today) so that their presence provides no basis for any assumption that one is a survival of a process of an overall change in the organisation of society and in its marriage arrangements from 'brideprice' to dowry. Finley was careful to deny he was dealing with tribal societies but does not the analysis rely too strongly on notions of the dominance of reciprocity in pre-industrial systems derived from the general studies of Polanyi, the theoretical work of Mauss and the particular accounts of anthropologists of Africa? Were the *hedna* really a reverse payment? Were the *dōra* really a gift to the husband?

In extending Finley's argument, Lacey (1966) has sketched out a number of forms of transaction that are closer to those we have found in other major Eurasian societies. Part of the problem arises from the fact that the earliest evidence from Homer deals with chiefs and warriors alone, so we have little knowledge of hierarchical differences. Nevertheless, he delineates two patterns of marriage. In the first, the wife joined the husband who had earlier offered *hedna*. However on two occasions, the bride's family is said to prepare *hedna* for a well-loved daughter (Odyssey i, 277–8; ii, 196–7), both cases referring to the already married Penelope returning to her father's house before entering upon a second marriage, her earlier one having been assumed to be dissolved. Finley's conclusion was that the term describes 'things given at marriage' by either side, though it could be argued that it might have meant both the direct and indirect endowment of the bride.

In the second type of marriage the husband joined the wife, especially when she was of higher status. A *basileus* could also attract a son-in-law to his own house or his realm by a form of marriage in which accepting a bride meant accepting a position as man-at-arms whose duty was to fight for the king, whether or not the bridegroom was, like Bellerophon or Tydeus, going in the end to succeed to the king's estate (1966:60). These are essentially filiacentric unions characteristic of societies where women inherit or act as channels for status and wealth, particularly as heiresses whose sons have a special relation with their maternal grandfathers.[4]

Lacey argues that *dōra* and *hedna* are rarely the same in Homer, the latter being a technical term, the former a very general one. A father or other guardian (*kurios*) could be approached with *dōra* and with offers of *hedna* for his daughter or ward. The *dōra* would be accepted from all the contestants, and on the basis of the offers made and of his own judgement, he would select a son-in-law whose *hedna* would then be accepted; Homeric society being what it was, the size of the offer would normally be a material factor. In due course the bride would be sent off with what part of the *hedna* her father thought fit (or had perhaps agreed to give) in the light of his own self-esteem and that in which he held his son-in-law. If the marriage ended for a cause other than her death or that of her husband, there was liable to be a claim for the return of *hedna*. Homeric society, however, with its code of gift-giving, also provided for *dōra* by which the goodwill of the parties was manifested.

The position differed from that of Finley who saw the *dōra* and *hedna* of Homeric times as being essentially countergifts; he found no evidence for the suggestion that the husband's gifts were handed back to the bride as security and spoke of the *dōra* as being given to the husband. For him a statement of Agamemnon leaves no doubt that the dowry went to the husband when he speaks of such a gift 'as no one yet ever gave along with his daughter' (1955:184). But the sentence has several possible interpretations; it is perfectly consistent with the dowry accompanying the wife on her movement to her new home, with it remaining in her possession (even if under her husband's management), and with the property of the husband and wife forming a conjugal fund. Working along similar lines to Polanyi, Finley is committed to a view of Homeric Greece as being a society in which gift-giving and barter predominated to the virtual exclusion of sale (except by foreigners). Bride-purchase could not have existed because there was no sale.

While the first part of this assertion is correct, the second is questionable.

Sale was certainly present in much of the Mediterranean and it would be strange if Homeric Greece were either so 'backward' or so isolated as its absence would suggest.[5] But the rejection of the purchase theory of marriage does not rest upon the notional state of the Greek economy at that period. Even where we find ample evidence of 'sale', even where the actors themselves apply the same term to marriage transactions (which was not the case in Homer), the equation, 'marriage = sale', is inadequate, especially for the later classical period when it is quite clear that women are being endowed (with a 'dowry') and that full marriage never involves a complete transfer of a person from one group to another. Finley is correct in rejecting the idea, but the grounds of his criticism, that we are dealing with a totally different form of *exchange*, namely gift-giving, made it difficult to take into account that aspect of marriage transactions involving intergenerational transmission, *devolution*. And I refer here not simply to what the bride receives as *dōra* (which I take to be the direct dowry) but to *hedna* (assumed to be the indirect dowry) as well. While it is unlikely that all the prestations from the groom went to the bride, part certainly did and much more may have done; the subtle nature of some of these transfers is apparent in Arab marriages. In any case, given the existence of direct dowry, it is always difficult to work out the balance of the transactions between father (or rather parents) and daughter at any one time, especially as devolution occurs during the overlapping lifetimes of the adjacent generations and, as we have seen in discussing Arab marriage, even when a handing over occurs a father or brother may act as 'banker' for a sister or a daughter. An acceptance of the fact that marital assigns are involved in the complexity of devolution enables us to appreciate and perhaps account for some or all of the ambiguities in the use of *hedna* to which Finley refers in trying to establish *dōra* and *hedna* as part of an 'exchange of gifts' (pp. 185–6).

However this may be for the Homeric period, by classical times there was certainly a dowry system in operation in Greece. Marriage in Athens was preceded by a betrothal (*engyē*) or, where an heiress (*epikleros*) was involved, by a court-judgement. Such agreements were virtually binding upon the actors and specified the amount of the bride's dowry. They might be made at an early age to pre-empt the choices of a propertied partner; the sister of Demosthenes was betrothed at the age of five and the dowry paid over at once. But marriage was more often postponed until about thirty for men and eighteen or nineteen for girls, a differential age of marriage equivalent to that found in parts of the polygynous Near East.

The late age for men was related to the passage of control of property from one generation to the next. Old men retired from 'the headship of (or at least from economic responsibility for) their families in favour of their sons, and the son's marriage was an appropriate moment for this to occur' (Lacey

1968:106–7). The father might then be considered as a child not yet capable of performing legal acts, for like lunacy, old age was seen as the cause of a man's incompetence at law and hence a reason for setting aside a will; an individual could be prosecuted for being 'out of his mind and wasting his property' (p. 125). So the aged entered their second childhood in a legal although not necessarily in a behavioural sense. In this respect the situation loosely resembled the system found in parts of Europe whereby a man married at the time he took over his parent's farm, resulting in a combi-- nation of late marriage and early retirement. In all these cases it was of course the obligation of the children to support the aged parents, more usually the mother for demographic reasons (Schaps 1979:83), and in Europe written contracts often laid down precisely what had to be provided for their maintenance.

A bride was endowed by her family at marriage, the amount being specified at the time of the betrothal, together with her ornaments and outfit. But while the dowry was managed by the husband on a day-to-day basis, it remained the property of the wife, as is the case in Greece today; it had to be accounted for separately since in the event of divorce it became vested in her nearest male relative, as did her own custody. For she never broke with her natal family as long as she lived (Wolff 1952:17; Levy 1963:141). In Athens the husband had to provide security for his wife's property; he had rights of use during her lifetime, but at her death it passed to her children alone, or, in the absence of any male issue, to her guardian. So too it did if the husband lost his status as a citizen, for then the marriage was rendered null and void. While dowry was a necessity in Athens the law saw a woman as always under the guardianship of a man (Sissa 1986:190) especially if land was involved; but this insistence was perhaps more a matter of law than of custom.

In Athens the dowry itself was in cash, and in order to provide a proper sum, noble families sometimes ran themselves and their estates into debt, for interest rates sometime stood as high as 18 per cent. In Sparta the dowry included real property and by the fourth century BC Aristotle complains not only about its size but because nearly half the land in Laconia was owned by women. In Gortyn daughters appeared to have shared with their brothers in their father's will rather than receive a dowry, and this delay may have made them freer, at least as married women, since they had all to look forward to (Schaps 1979:88–9).[6]

The Athenian dowry was a woman's portion and so she did not normally inherit in addition (Erdmann 1934:37). However if there were no male heirs she had an absolute right. The entitlement to property entailed a selection of mates according to proper qualifications, while the dangers of misalliance were reduced by the relative seclusion of rich wives and the close protection of others. Brotherless daughters were obviously of special attraction; in such cases the retention of property within the family and the continuity of the line became of major significance and was accomplished by two mechanisms, uxorilocal or rather filiacentric marriage whereby the husband moved into his wife's home (as in certain unions in Homer) or by the marriage of the heiress to a close kinsman, especially the oblique union with the father's brother as well as with the father's brother's son, though we also hear of marriage between half siblings by different mothers in Sparta, and of different fathers in Athens (Harrison 1968:23). She herself was known as *epikleros*, 'upon the estate', for she went with the property (or rather the property with her), her husband taking over its management for the benefit of the sons she might bear (Levy 1963:138). Such a woman could be claimed by her nearest agnate who could even divorce his present wife in order to engage in such a marriage. In this way he became the custodian and manager of the estate until the woman's eldest son reached the age of eighteen, when, as representative of her direct agnatic line, the son became the rightful heir. If the nearest agnate failed to marry the heiress, he was responsible for arranging a marriage which would produce an heir for the *oikos*, in other words, for arranging a filiacentric union. However even a woman who was already married elsewhere could produce such an heir for her paternal line if her son was adopted by his maternal grandfather. Indeed she could produce such an heir without marriage, by intercourse with a chosen relative (Lacey 1968:104).

Close marriages were 'extremely common' (though few cases are recorded), half-brothers to half-sisters, uncles to nieces; 'the mother of Hagnias was also his second cousin; Isaeus could also argue that it was a sign of ill-will that a father of two daughters married neither to a first cousin' (Lacey 1968:106). From the man's point of view, an uncle–niece union constituted a marriage to the brother's daughter; in relation to the retention of the property within the woman's kin group, it has the same structural significance as marriage to the father's brother's daughter (*bint al-'amm*) so widespread among the Arabs, and as the restrictions placed upon the daughters of Zelophehad when, in the absence of brothers, they gained residual rights to their father's patrimony (Numbers 27:4),[7] that is, they could not marry 'strangers'. While marriage to an heiress was usually an attractive proposition financially, it also had a considerable cost for the husband whose relative position in respect of his wife was often a function of the disparity in their wealth.

In classical Greece, as in Asia, the category into which a woman fell as sexual partner depended upon the transactions that took place when the union was initiated. A plurality of sexual statuses co-existed side by side. Between wife and mistress or courtesan (*hetairai*) lay that of concubine;

'Mistresses we keep for the sake of pleasure, concubines for the daily care of our persons, but wives to bear us legitimate children and to be faithful guardians of our households' (Demosthenes, *Against Neaera*, 122). The fact that a concubine came without a proper endowment affected the rank of her children as well as her own, for they were free but not fully legitimate. Nevertheless, she was not completely without rights, and where the guardian of a young woman gave her to a citizen as a sexual partner, as happened in poorer families, some kind of settlement was made to prevent her from being turned away without maintenance.

The effect of Pericles' law of 451 BC was to confine *conubium* in Athens to citizens. The children of unions between members of different status groups or with outsiders were illegitimate (or rather *xenoi*) like the offspring of slave-girls and concubines. They inherited only when a man had no children by his recognised wife. As in medieval France and England, the illegitimate sons of great men formed a category of persons who had nothing to lose but their bar sinister; they typically became mercenaries or military adventurers. This role of bastard is also connected with the dowry complex, though only indirectly; it arises out of the differential sexual status that propertied marriages involve, implying a concept of illegitimacy very different from that which obtained in Africa.

As in China the stratification of sexual statuses was associated with the system of social differentiation – the division between citizens and non-citizens; the absence of *conubium* meant a restriction on social mobility between the two. Only as the result of costly military campaigns were the restrictions of monogamy and *conubium* temporarily lifted in order to increase the future supply of manpower (Lacey 1968:105). Even among the citizens themselves a man's position on the roll formally depended upon the amount of property he could call upon.

An interesting aspect of inheritance emerges in the context of the use of wills. The law proclaimed that a man might dispose of his property by will if he had no natural, legitimate sons. In fact this was not the full picture, since daughters had their rights as *epikleroi* and men with heirs did make wills, apparently to clarify the extent of their holdings. Otherwise testamentary inheritance was a means of specifying an 'outsider' as heir. What many discussants of the *oikos, gens* and joint family have often overlooked is that the use of this formal procedure (or of similar heir-appointing acts) is highly significant, indicating as it does the nature of the wider kin group. In Africa next-of-kin inherit automatically, however distant he may be. In this sense the members of a kin group hold joint rights in each other's property. In the Eurasian societies we have examined the kin group is not corporate in the same way; joint rights in property are highly attenuated; inheritance was predominantly vertical, rarely horizontal, that is lineal, rarely lateral. Moreover lineal females were generally preferred to horizontal (or collateral) males, and in their absence a testament, or adoption, might be necessary to specify an heir even among close collateral kin; there was nothing automatic about the process.

Some other aspects of the Greek situation demand our brief attention. First, even for the Homeric period, Avezzù finds the distinction between extended and nuclear families of little use for analysing the earliest Greek households (as illustrated in the *Iliad*), especially when the notion of the nuclear is seen as opposed to the joint family in being the unique setting for conjugal love arising from the individual choice of partners (1983:87). Nuclear families were certainly present, one possible indication of which (though in my view its status as evidence is dubious) was the absence of a 'classificatory' terminology in Morgan's sense (Longo 1984), that is, one that grouped lineal and collateral kin in one category, suggesting the presence of 'clans'. The influence of 'clans' is small and elementary households are as much in evidence as extended ones. Secondly, there was a 'fanatical emphasis' on pre-marital virginity (Lacey 1968:107); according to Solon's laws an unmarried Athenian girl who had been seduced could be sold into slavery or remain at home unmarried. Thirdly, adultery was strongly condemned and any offspring of such unions were designated bastards. Fourthly, marriage was monogamous and concubines, whose children were legitimate, were found mainly when an established union had proved infertile. Fifthly, a further solution to the problem of providing an heir was adoption which could be practised only when there was no son (Sissa 1986:174) and often involved close kin; among the twenty-seven examples from Athens, four involved a sister's son and one a sister's daughter (Bremmer 1983:183). Sixthly, marriages were almost always arranged; it was a man's duty to find a husband of the right kind for his daughter or his sister, and for this purpose an endowment was required.[8] Seventhly, although some emphasis was placed upon lifelong marriage in religious discourse, divorce, which was initiated by either party, was 'easy', according to Lacey, although probably less easy for the woman, who had to appear in public.[9] It was especially easy when there were no children (Sissa 1986:195); the dowry was returned and used to support the divorcée. The problem of guardianship, which was also of great importance in early Rome, may well be associated with this turnover of marriages, particularly in towns where, as we have seen among the Arabs, kin groups were in certain ways less strong, less capable of taking care of women, the disentangling of whose dowry arrangements was in any case a complicated matter. Eighthly, widow remarriage is said to have been frequent, a function of the differential age of marriage, but there was no levirate to provide fictitious offspring for the dead man. Finally, we have mentioned various ways in which practices varied depending upon position

Table 11. *Hierarchical differences in ancient Greece*

	Higher	Lower
1 Type of marriage	more full marriage	more concubinage
2 Age of marriage	earlier	later
3 Position of women	seclusion	freer
4 Strategies of heirship	more filiacentric unions	fewer filiacentric unions

in the social hierarchy. While the evidence on these is thin, the points made are summarised in table 11.

A large disparity in the average ages of marriage for men and women carries a number of important implications for family life. These concern the relationship between the spouses, the wife being a junior partner in every sense, the relationship of children with an older father and a younger mother, and possibly the question of adultery and extra-marital sex, as a result of the younger age of the wife; the husband had his freedom before marriage, the wife after, especially when he was dead. One must expect a higher proportion of young widows (and hence relatively free women), a larger number of children with dead fathers (semi-orphans), an increase in the step-parental situation if remarriage is permitted, and a different generation span for men and women. All these factors were pointed out by Tait for the Konkomba of northern Ghana (1961), although in that case step-parenthood was replaced by the proxy-parenthood arising from the levirate which placed the woman more tightly under the aegis of her husband's kin. In a dowry system a widow would have her independent fund or dower which could be used to contract a new marriage in those societies or strata where widow remarriage is permitted, although limitations are often placed upon her access to the husband's contribution should she do so; on the other hand under the bridewealth system, a widow received nothing and unless she married leviratically, her new husband might even have to send the original marriage payments to the kin of the dead man so they could repay her earlier affines.

The allocation of family property to women, as epitomised in the epiclerate, resembles the situation in later Europe. But in ancient Greece the heiress had to make a close marriage, amounting to a kind of 'adoption' of close kin, and in this respect the pattern of marriage differed radically. While ancient Greece did not provide a main source of European law nor serve as a model for domestic conduct in any very significant way, Rome did; yet we find a similar reversal. While close marriage was not encouraged in the same way, it disappeared in favour of distant unions when Christianity developed and enforced its own rules at the end of the fourth century.

Despite this difference, many similarities remain between ancient Greece and later times; in the Byzantine period, an heiress could attract an incoming husband, the 'summoned man', and he continues today in the form of the *soghambros* (Beaucamp 1985:197).

To summarise, whatever the situation in Homeric times, the direct dowry was well-established in classical Greece and represented the contribution of the bride's family to the funds of the new conjugal unit. 'And we are not to reckon up which of us has actually contributed to the greater amount, but we should know of a surety that the one who proves the better partner makes the more valuable contribution' (Xenophon 1923:vii.13). In Sparta such a contribution to the 'communauté de biens', 'a common treasury', might well include land as well as other property (Hoffmann 1985:276). Dowries were sometimes provided for poor girls (p. 190), legal restrictions were placed upon their excessive growth (p. 189) and those giving the dowry protected themselves against the possibility of its non-return, in the case of divorce for example by taking out a 'hypothèque' on the husband's property. While the dowry represented the part of the patrimony that went to a daughter or her children (p. 191), it came under the day-to-day control of the husband. In some regions, such as Gortyn in Crete, it constituted a fixed proportion of the estate; elsewhere it varied with the status of the groom and the other attractions of the bride. In parts it included land, in others the land was maintained intact while the daughters received movables. At times, as during the Homeric period and possibly in Sparta, an indirect endowment seems to have been given greater emphasis than the direct component.

Certainly there were differences in the relation of women to property in Athens, Gortyn (in Crete) and in Sparta. It was of the latter that Aristotle commented upon the large dowries and the many *epikleroi*, which resulted in almost two fifths of the land belonging to women. In Gortyn too women appear to have been more independent, able to inherit (or take as dowry) half their brother's share and to retain it as their own. In Athens on the other hand, the dowry may have been smaller and came under the control of the husband (or father) as *kyrios* or guardian.

Despite these apparent differences, women in Athens do not seem to have been overwhelmed by the legal restrictions, however different these were from other parts of Greece. Schaps posits the opposite kind of process to that we have seen in China, India and in West Asia, where uniform religious or judicial codes cast their mantle over a large number of regional variations in marriage and the family, although I have tried to show that many of these belong to the same system repertoire, which is 'cultural' only in a limited sense. But for Greece, Schaps assumes a cultural unity among the immigrant population which gradually became differentiated at the level of codes of which each *polis* created its own. 'Among the various possible understandings of an institution, the law may choose one' (1979:91) and hence each code will emerge with a different 'choice of principles'. That is certainly a possible outcome, especially if one posits the recent migration of a homogeneous population; in the following chapter I return to the point, discussed for India, of the discrepancy between law and what is not simply practice but other sets of norms. However we must also recognise that these norms may embody alternative emphases of the kind we have discussed for China and which mark local life in Greece even today, despite centuries of attempted enforcement of uniform national and religious codes. For instance, there is a contemporary difference in the emphasis given to marriage transactions, on indirect dowry in the North and on direct dowry in the South, which appears to be the opposite of what Xenophon perceived. That suggests we find continuity in the range of variation (and no doubt in the pressures for alternation) rather than in particular practices in particular places. To the question of this distribution and of 'continuity' I will return in considering Greece in recent times. I want first to look at the other major society of the classical world, ancient Rome, which provided such powerful models for later Europe, both in the West and in the East.

14

Monogamy, property and control in Rome

In considering marriage prestations and inheritance in China, India, the Near East and ancient Greece we have seen little evidence of that extreme patriliny which is said to involve the complete assimilation of a wife to the agnatic group of her husband either by purchase or by some other form of transfer. In this chapter I look critically at another society, that of Rome, which, at least in its early stages, has often been taken as an extreme example of the incorporation of females combined with strong patriarchal authority (*patria potestas*) exercised over a joint 'family' of living agnates and their dependants.[1] Knowledge of the early period is necessarily fragmentary and uncertain, and has been subject to many changes of interpretation over the past hundred years, the general trend of which I want to sketch out in the way that has been done for ancient Greece, Israel and Arab societies. In seeking to qualify, as others have done, ideas about the position of women regarding property, I raise the question of how far reconstructions of the earlier state of affairs reflect the emergence of written 'laws' as distinct from already existing oral norms. I also want to indicate certain general features, mainly during the Empire, that seem to me broadly characteristic of the major societies of the Eurasian continent when contrasted with Africa; thirdly, I try to bring out some analytical points related to differences in 'conjugal funds' which were raised earlier in a general way, as well as in the norms of monogamy, in concepts of 'concubinage' and in notions of illegitimacy; fourthly, I attempt to take the enquiry a step nearer to the social institutions of Europe in the recent past and in the rural present by looking briefly at the structure of domestic groups including the 'elementary family'. For it is central to my argument that certain aspects of the system of marriage and property rights that characterise the main stream of societies in East as in West Asia, both anciently and in the recent past, are closer to the European and further from the African pattern than has commonly been supposed. In some other respects, in particular the ban on close marriage, adoption and other strategies of heirship, later European marriage patterns diverge significantly from earlier European and most Asian ones. But in order to understand this point we need to clear away a number of mis-apprehensions that derive in a large measure from the earlier approaches of comparative sociologists and comparative jurists.

Early Rome: forms of marriage

We have first to consider the position under early Roman Law as laid out in the Twelve Tables (451–50 BC) and in the practice of the following centuries of the Republic, bearing in mind the general poverty of evidence. There are sometimes said to have been two forms of marriage at this time, marriage with *manus* and marriage without. The latter, misleadingly called 'free marriage' by modern jurists, was the type which later became prevalent; its establishment was a matter of consent alone, for while there was a bridal procession, no state ceremony took place and the wife retained rights in her property, although the *dos* itself came under her husband's control for the duration of the marriage. As for inheritance rights, she was entitled to a share equal to her brothers; however, at least in historical times, a testator had the power to disinherit, and it was easier to do so with a daughter than with a son, especially if she had already received a dowry as her share. In *manus* marriage (*manus* is the hand), the woman was said to have been taken out of the power of the father and placed in the hand of the husband; indeed as far as certain legal rights were concerned, many have maintained that she stood to him in the position of 'a daughter' (*filiae loco*) (for example, Bryce 1901:ii,387, who represents our point of departure), although the contemporary historian, Dixon, sees this as a later juristic reading (Gaius 3.3) since the wife also appears to have been referred to as *materfamilias* (1986:127). Moreover at marriage she took with her a dowry in which she retained rights that were similar to those she held in the other forms of marriage (Watson 1975:75). However at this early period she appears to have inherited from her husband rather than from her father (Dixon 1985b:521), or to put it in more recent terms, the transfer of the dowry entitled her to a dower; in this sense at least she was cut off.

Not all marriages were of this kind and indeed they became less common as time went on. It has been suggested (Volterra 1955) that there was only one type of marriage which could be contracted by voluntary agreement of both parties, and that the *conventio in manum* was a separate institution established by a series of discrete acts, namely *confarreatio, coemptio* and *usus*. The first took place in the presence of the chief pontiff, and its main feature was a sacrifice to Jupiter, with the eating by the bride and bride-groom of a cake of a particular kind of spelt (*far*), whence it was called *confarreatio* (Watson 1975:11). According to Bryce, it was originally confined to members of patrician houses (1901:ii,388).

It is the second form of marriage, *coemptio*, that has led to many misconceptions. Writing from the standpoint of the evolutionary notions earlier this century, Bryce described it as:

a purely civil act, and consisted in the sale by the bride of herself, with the approval of her father or her guardian . . . to the bridegroom, apparently accompanied (though there is a controversy on this point) by a contemporaneous sale by the bridegroom of himself to the bride. The transaction was carried out with certain formal words and in the presence of five witnesses (being citizens), besides the man who held the scales with which the money constituting the price was supposed to be weighed. The price was of course nominal. (1901:ii,388)

So, we may conclude, was the 'sale'. However this does not stop Balsdon like many earlier commentators from describing *coemptio* as 'a survival of primitive bride-purchase' (1963:179), a statement that has no standing at all, especially since, as was so often the case in Roman law (Dixon 1984:80–2; Watson 1975:15), this sale was mutual and 'fictive'. The kind of claim arises out of nineteenth-century reconstructions of cultural history which display little comprehension of the complexities of marriage transactions. But the notion lingers on, not only in the works of Balsdon and in the usages of some anthropologists, but even among legal historians. Jolowicz (1932:115), for example, argues that since bride-purchase was so common among other races 'it would be almost surprising if the Romans had not known it'. There is less of a tendency nowadays to adopt this view; Watson sees any purchase at the time of the Twelve Tables as already being 'fictitious' (1975:15), although he earlier claimed that this *imaginaria venditio* was originally 'a proper sale' (1967:24). If any such change did take place, gratuitous assumptions of survival tend drastically to foreshorten the span of possible events, bringing the Classical world far too close to the 'primitive', only too often a fundamental flaw in the application of anthropological data for comparative purposes.

There was yet a third institution, known as *usus*. For even without these ceremonies and transfers, a woman would pass under the hand of her husband after a year of 'marriage' (*anno continua nupta*) providing she had not absented herself from his house for three consecutive nights (*trinoctium*) during that period (Balsdon 1963:179–80; Watson 1975:16), although this result could be avoided. The argument concerning the number of marriage types is an academic one which Watson sees as 'fundamentally sterile' (p. 19). It does not matter whether we think of two or three forms, or even of one kind of marriage followed in some cases by the *conventio in manum*, a consequential arrangement that carried important legal implications, which the other institutions did not (except that later they affected gifts between husband and wife). The immediately relevant questions Volterra raises are whether the *conventio* implies a change in membership of a descent or family group, and how this relates to the position of women.

Manus marriage did not take place between members of different status groups but only between full Roman citizens, for they alone had *conubium*, the exclusive right of inter-marriage. In the Twelve Tables marriage was prohibited between patricians and plebs, although there was less opposition to hypergamy, that is, to the man marrying down. *Conubium* was essentially an aristocratic right (De Visscher 1952:412) and there was an aversion to (even a horror of) mixed marriage. 'Le *conubium*, droit exclusif d'intermariage, constitue l'instrument essentiel de leurs alliances, et le meilleur garantie de cette domination aristocratique sur le Latium' (p. 413). So although the wife came under the Hand of her husband and took the name of his *gens*, the union was of a very different kind from the incorporation of a slave. The 'less free marriage' was high rather than low in status; from the woman's standpoint it was more rather than less respectable. The situation is not dissimilar to that in China and India where it was the daughters of the rich who entered into what some observers have thought the severest form of conjugal 'servitude'. This being so, early Roman marriage raises important general issues. First, how were types of marriage related to the system of inheritance, or rather to the transmission of property? A Roman woman was the recipient of property from her parents. In *manus* marriage a daughter took an endowment in the shape of a dowry which came under her husband's control but which gave her rights over the conjugal property if the marriage ended by divorce or by death. In 'free-marriage', however, she retained the right to inherit from her father and such personal property as she received remained very much her own; she could not even give it to her husband, although she could make him a loan. In contrast the Hand or *manus*, according to Bryce, 'gave the husband all the property she had when she married. It entitled him to all she might acquire afterwards, whether by gift or by her own labour' (1901:ii, 387), and even enabled a man to pawn his wife. On the other hand there were corresponding gains for her as well. 'In compensation for these disadvantages the wife became entitled to be supported by her husband, and to receive a share of his property at his death, as one of the "family heirs" (*sui heredes*), whom he could disinherit only in a formal way' (p. 387; Jolowicz 1932:123ff.). So the coming into the Hand of the husband carried rights as well as duties, and was of major benefit to the wife as a widow. While it linked her property more firmly with the husband's estate, that estate was modified as a result; from the standpoint I have taken in this book, it is possible to see marriage as establishing some kind of conjugal fund, or at least funding, upon which the wife and her children had a continuing claim. She was entitled not only to support in his lifetime, partly from what she had brought, but to a share in her husband's property in the event of his death, not while the marriage lasted. That is, she was so entitled under the conditions of 'intestacy', under what we may perhaps regard as the customary practice of the mass of the people; it is true that in historical times she could be disinherited or left only a smaller share in a will, but wills generally mean 'an interference with the legal rights of a man's family' (Jolowicz 1932:126) and were probably subject to public sanctions (pp. 126–7). Indeed in the last century of the Republic, about 50 BC, there grew up the 'complaint of the undutiful will' which entitled any claimant to seek to modify a will; whether this represented a qualification of earlier legal principles or a recognition of custom is a matter for conjecture, but it did put limits on the process of disinheritance, which like most legal processes of the time, reflected the norms of the aristocracy.

Such a state of affairs differs from that found in most simpler societies, where women, according to Benedict (1936), do not generally have any claim upon the estate of their dead spouse, even in bilateral systems. A woman is supported by her late husband's kin if she is taken in leviratic marriage or by widow inheritance, but she has no independent claim on his estate; she may have to depend in the first instance either upon her children or upon her siblings. Leviratic marriage was virtually ruled out by the rigorous monogamy of Roman unions. But with a high differential marriage age in favour of men (less perhaps among the aristocracy), widowhood was frequent. In *manus* marriage a woman's continued support was ensured, at least in custom, by making her an heir of her husband, and in this sense his 'daughter'. Conjugal inheritance was linked to the establishment of a conjugal fund, which came under his effective control, when the wife brought her 'portion' of hereditary property into the marriage. As an unmarried daughter she inherited a share from her parents; married, she inherited a share from her husband and thus regained control.

Manus unions, then, took place within the framework of the diverging devolution of property, with the setting up at marriage of a conjugal fund upon which in the end both the widow and the children could draw. It signified not so much the total incorporation of a wife into her husband's descent group or family as the total incorporation of her property into a newly established conjugal unit. The dowry came directly from the wife's parents or their heirs. There was no contribution by the groom, much less any 'purchase of a bride'. 'Les anciens Romains ne connaissaient pour régime patrimonial des conjoints que la *dos*, c'est-à-dire les biens que la femme apportait à son mari à l'occasion du mariage.' *Donatio propter nuptias*, 'les arrhes des fiançailles', *sponsalicia largitas*, these gifts appeared only later, Volterra claims, when Rome came under the influence of oriental law (1955:366). In any case such gifts do not normally constitute a bride-wealth, much less a brideprice, but rather an indirect dowry.

Later on, *manus* marriage virtually disappeared so that for almost all purposes a married woman retained rights in her own property, whether acquired by gift, bequest or by labour. The correlative of this change was that she now received only very limited rights of intestate succession to her husband's property whereas under *manus* marriage she had succeeded to his entire estate, or shared it equally with his children (Bryce 1901:ii, 391). A wife took on the status of the husband unless either had been a slave, but whereas before she had taken the name of his *gens*, she now retained that of her own in addition to her personal 'first name' (*praenomen*), although these latter were rare enough.

The changes that occurred between the Republic and the Empire were not so much to do with the marriage tie itself, but rather with the property rights of the spouse. The wife in *manus* pooled her property with that of her husband who acquired managerial rights. The fund so established was eventually destined for her children as well as for her own support in the event of her husband dying first. That the institution of *conventio in manum* was used to define the wife's position in a society which devolved property to the children of both sexes is indicated by the whole tenor of Bryce's description, despite his view of marriage as incorporation. If the wife was referred to as *filiae loco*, this was a contextual usage which did not imply that she was entirely cut off from her natal family or descent group, as we see from his comment on the power the husband could exercise over her. 'He could control her actions. He sat as judge over her, if she was accused of any offence, although custom required that a sort of council of his and her relatives should be summoned to advise him and to see fair play' (p. 390). The subsequent statement that 'He could put her to death if found guilty', clearly requires some modification. We cannot take the provisions of a legal code as indicating the whole jural position; in this case custom required consultation with the wife's natal kin, while statements about the 'power of life and death' are notoriously difficult to assess and rarely represent guides to everyday action. As Bryce himself remarks, 'It would be difficult to understand how such a system worked did we not know that manners and public opinion restrain the exercise of legal rights' (p. 391). We can see this process as one of public sanctions modifying private power, but it is also a question of jural practice in conflict with legal formulae.

In other words, we can see *manus* marriage as involving the shift of rights over persons and property rather than the complete transfer of the woman herself from one group to another. For while in major marriages she moved physically, she continued to have relations with her natal kin who were still concerned with her welfare as they were with her children's; for instance, the mother's brother often played an important role in their lives, in legend as well as in practice. The fact that a wife took the name of the *gens* of her husband in *manus* marriage is a doubtful criterion of incorporation, as we have seen in other cases. One might equally contend that in contemporary Europe a woman enters into her husband's family when she accepts his name. I doubt if any adequate criteria for a complete change of membership are possible but clearly this form of naming is not one. In any case the interpretation of early Roman marriage as involving the alienation of women looks more dubious in the light of later developments where the evidence is much richer. For when *manus* no longer occurred, a wife remained, for all legal purposes, a member of her original family and not of her husband's (p. 391). The difference, I suggest, was one of degree rather than of kind.

This once-fashionable interpretation of early Roman marriage had affinities with the bride-purchase theory of the early forms of marriage in Arabia (e.g. Robertson Smith 1885), in ancient Israel (e.g. Benzinger 1902) and in Homeric Greece (e.g. Koschaker 1950). A strongly patrilineal, even patriarchal, pattern was posited for the earliest known phases of the society, for which the evidence is necessarily thin, and that included the total transfer of women in exchange for a brideprice. But if we look at the later, better documented periods for each of these societies, we find an emphasis on endowment rather than 'purchase', on 'bilateral' (or diverging) rather than purely agnatic devolution, and at least in the upper status groups, a stress on the role of women in setting up some form of conjugal corporation of property.

Even today, some scholars see Roman women as totally transferred from one set of agnates to another, accompanied by a dowry which passed into the ownership of the husband. In discussing this view of early Roman society, Dixon (1985c) refers to Leach's description of 'primitive marriage': 'In the great majority of societies a woman at marriage is a pawn in a contractual arrangement between men', a phrase that recalls Lévi-Strauss (1967:59–61), although the following sentence adds a significant modification. 'She is treated as a bundle of valuables *some of which* [my italics] are transferred from one guardian to another in exchange for appropriate payment' (Dixon 1985c; Leach 1971). That is to say, the woman is no longer seen to be transferred as a jural entity (as is the case in much exchange theorising). However in Rome she was married with a dowry which can be seen as her intestate portion granted in return for ceding any claim to her own family's estate (Dixon 1985c:359), since an unmarried daughter is an heir of her father, a married woman an heir of her husband. In other words not only was she the subject of transferable rights, but she was also the holder of such rights; rights in property, rights in her husband. She is not simply the object of an exchange, a pawn in a male enterprise. Indeed the logical corollary of the earlier argument is that by transferring a payment (the dowry) a women is acquiring rights in a man, but the notion of the transfer of property like that of women also needs to be modified.

One concept that tends to give rise to such notions is that of *patria potestas*, whereby the woman is seen as passing from the power (*potestas*) of the father to the hand (*manus*) of the father-in-law. But of course her husband was under the same *potestas* and equally lacked 'the capacity to own property' during his father's lifetime unless he had been emancipated. Emancipation is equivalent to the separation or division that sometimes occurred in China and India within the father's lifetime, although in most cases it took place after his death when it included an allocation to the unmarried daughters. In this respect the wife's position with regard to the dowry was not very different from that of her husband with regard to his portion. While the property of a married woman might have been merged with that of her husband or his family, she acquired a claim 'on par with that of her children to the whole of the estate when her husband died' (Dixon 1985c:359), although a will could be used to modify or set aside these benefits. Since divorce at this early period was 'very uncommon', the question of the repayment of the dowry rarely arose. But one of the problems concerned with the remarriage of widows, which was generally disapproved of by the upper classes, was that it would lead to a division of the estate (p. 360). In the case of the so-called 'first divorce' at Rome in 230 BC, the actions of the husband seem to have been generally condemned partly because he had not explained the reasons before a family council, in particular why he had not returned the dowry. This suggests that not only was there provision against arbitrary action but that if he was to blame, reimbursement of the dowry was required, as one would expect from the practice of other societies. In other words, the transfer 'to the husband' was highly conditional and the wife continued to hold rights in the property.

Mention of the family council raises an important issue which relates to the evidence and its interpretation. In early Roman law property is said to have been treated 'as a joint family holding' (Dixon 1985c:359), although few scholars now consider that we generally find three-generational families living and working together. Nevertheless Roman law assumed the existence of a 'block' holding administered by the *paterfamilias*. But the early evidence on practice is slight, so that our information on these matters comes largely from a reconstruction of the fifth-century Twelve Tables on the basis of later quotations. Their very name suggests that such a source, which does not mention dowry though it was certainly present (Corbett 1930; Volterra 1955), was highly limited in its scope; even if it had been intended as a 'code', it could not have accommodated the wide range of 'law' on the family. In any case many of the essential decisions were made in unrecorded councils; it was at that level that such disputes were often discussed and settled.

The notion of *patria potestas*, the authority of father over son, is often seen as linked to that of the extended patriarchal family, and this in turn to the nature of the lineage. Many of the propositions about these and other aspects of family life in the later periods come from the studies of legal historians whose major sources are the statements of Latin authors concerning rights and duties that themselves formalise the ideas behind everyday practice, the complexities of which are sometimes better conveyed in imaginative literature. Writers such as Daube (1969) have followed those early authors in seeing Rome as being dominated by *patria potestas* to the extent that a son, even if living separately, would have to refer his bills to his father for payment (Thomas 1986:213). Doubt has been thrown on this strong version of the father's powers by social historians such as Crook (1967a) who regards the assertion of the power of life and death more as a way of conceptualising paternal relations and filial dependence, without any necessary implication of actually putting children to death (Saller 1986). Comparative evidence supports this view, for the idea of fathers (or their equivalent) exercising such powers over children is not confined to Rome. Some years ago, I reported a similar case, certainly not unique, from West Africa. In practice fathers did not go about killing their children. The saying had much more to do with the kind of authority supposedly exercised by dead fathers over their living sons, which in turn buttressed the milder authority that existed within a household (1962:408). Even where it is reported, it was never a matter of arbitrarily putting an individual to death, but of taking responsibility for the actions of one's descendants, agnatic or uterine, in the face of the wider society.[2] If contemporary practice does not mirror proverbial 'wisdom' even in this oral society, the discrepancy is likely to be even greater when that 'wisdom' is decontextualised by being expressed in a written form, especially in the very abstract one of a written code. It is true that by the very process of setting it down, the idea of paternal authority may acquire a greater normative force. But this idea largely operated at a notional level (except perhaps in the decision to expose or let live a new-born infant). Historical demography has been called in as support. Saller (1986, 1987) points out that low life-expectancy and the late age of marriage for men, less for upper men, minimise the numbers of people with living fathers. Only a quarter of those marrying in their late twenties would still be under *patria potestas*; the others would be free to choose their spouses. Women married earlier and were therefore more likely to have marriages arranged for them by their kin. But even those under *patria potestas* (and the demographic argument has more to do with numbers than norms) were certainly not necessarily excluded from the paternal estate; they were entitled to inherit up to an equal share of the patrimony (Saller 1986:15). If daughters acquired paternal property, as women they were not entirely without power.

Whatever the earlier situation, in the later Roman Republic the dowry was general (Watson 1967). A bride also brought into her marriage a trousseau (Balsdon 1963:186) which, among the better off, included her treasures of gold and precious stones of which she might possess large amounts. These jewels were at once items of conspicuous expenditure and stores of value. The amount of the dowry itself was fixed after a process of bargaining between the two parties. Early on the sum is said to have been relatively small, but by the Empire a million sisterces was the sum one very rich family in the top half of the senatorial aristocracy had to produce, to be paid after the marriage in three annual installments of cash, though land might also be included (p. 187; Hopkins 1983:77, fn.60). Some of this amount might be kept by the wife as a distinct fund to meet part of the costs of her own household but more usually that obligation fell upon the husband. As in Greece the dowry was not necessary to establish the validity of a marriage,[3] but the dotal pact was an important aspect of the arrangements, though affecting the two parties in different ways. For the woman it was testimony of her status as wife rather than concubine. But the amount of property brought into the marriage might place her in a higher position not only in relation to less fortunate women but also to her husband. In Plautus' *Mostellaria* the audience is addressed in the following words: 'You know she's right, most of you who have dames at home for wives, that bought you with their dowries' (1924:315). The image of purchase exaggerates the position, but it is certainly more correct in these cases to speak of the purchase of men rather than the sale of women, or even of rights over women, between groups of men. Money talks, even in marital affairs.

The nature of the conjugal fund that was set up by endowed marriages in later Rome has been the subject of much discussion. While Crook sees no *patrimoine conjugale* along the lines of the community of property of the Napoleonic code, 'there were mechanisms, arrangements, strategies for dealing with that fact' (1988). And while he sees the dowry as coming wholly under the ownership of the husband during the marriage, that ownership was qualified by two facts. First, it was returnable since one function was to provide a woman with a fund when the marriage dissolved. Secondly, in some documents at least, the dowry is seen as formally constituting a woman's share of the patrimony, the interest on which was to be used for the *onera matrimonii*, her maintenance as a wife, which may have been recorded in the pact or simply been the subject of a tacit accord.[4] But what is particularly interesting, thinking again of similar arrangements made in China, is that the dowry may only be promised (Crook 1988: documents 19–21), not actually handed over. However the father still paid the interest on what he had notionally allocated and this money the husband then used to maintain his wife. In these cases a married daughter continued to exercise a claim, through her husband, to maintenance at an appropriate level from her parental estate.

The case of Turia, dating from the last decades of the Republic at the end of the first century BC and recounted in the funeral eulogy spoken by her husband, is particularly revealing. While her property came under his management, he was clearly not the only decision-maker. 'With joint zeal we have preserved all the patrimony which you received from your parents. Entrusting it all to me, you were not troubled with the care of increasing it; thus did we share the task of administering it, that I undertook to protect your fortune, and you to guard mine.'[5] Her effective power is plain from the fact that she educated some daughters of her relatives at her home (she was herself childless) and provided them with dowries so they might 'attain to a station in life worthy of your family'; that is, married women continued to be involved in the affairs and status of their natal families. In so acting she had her husband's support. 'Gaius Cluvius [her sister's husband] and myself, by common accord, executed your intention, and approving of your generosity, in order that your patrimony might suffer no diminution, offered our own family possessions instead and gave up our own estates to provide the dowries settled upon by you' (p. 485). So not only did her jewellery remain under her control (she used it to help her husband escape), but her patrimony stayed notionally separable within the 'conjugal fund' managed by her husband. So confident was she about her continuing claim on this property that she had no hesitation in fighting to increase it. Once she had avenged the murder of her parents during her husband's absence in Africa, she left her father's home and went to live with her mother-in-law. There she fought against her maternal relatives who tried to set aside her father's will on the grounds that he had entered into a *coemptio* or fictional sale with his wife. Under the will she and her husband were heirs ('instead of you alone taking possession of all the property') whereas she would otherwise have entered under the legal guardianship of those relatives and her sister would have been excluded from inheriting because she had been transferred into the power of Cluvius, that is, had made a *manus* marriage. Nevertheless Turia declared that she would in any case divide the property with her sister, for since there appear to have been no brothers, the daughters were heiresses.

From the third century BC the dowry was recoverable under conditions that were gradually widened in scope. The claim to recover these sums on the part of the divorced wife or the widow (*actio rei uxoriae*) was made in order to establish a fund she could use for her subsequent support or for another marriage. The husband could retain part of the dowry if the dissolution of the marriage was deemed to be due to his wife, partly for punitive reasons but also because he continued to have custody of the children who would be its eventual recipients. The assessment might also depend on his ability to pay (Watson 1967:67); the *dotis aestimata* meant that particular items did not necessarily have to be returned, by the husband or the wife, since the equivalent could take its place as the dowry had been valued.

The supposed change in the lineage or family membership of a married woman and in the husband's authority can also be looked at in terms of a shift in the relations of women to property, one that occurred within the overall framework of diverging devolution. Under *manus* marriage a woman took her dowry and was no longer entitled to inherit from her parents; as elsewhere her future 'prospects' lay with her conjugal family. In free marriage she took her dowry in a similar way but was entitled to have this made up by inheritance from her natal family, to the equivalent of a son's share.

Since the dowry, in a free marriage, was very often a delayed payment handed over in three installments possibly during the course of many years (Dixon 1984:88) and did not necessarily represent the whole of a daughter's endowment, it may well have been relatively smaller than in a *manus* marriage. Or was it that in the latter the contribution from the husband's side was greater? Saller (1984:202) has written of the modest size of dowries under the Principate, representing only one year's income of the estate, suggesting that they were employed not for production but for household expenditure, meeting the *onera matrimonii* in accordance with the wife's position. But the difference may represent the changing focus of the evidence or of the timing rather than a diminution of the total amount devolved on daughters. In any case we are dealing with the richest city-dwelling families; among farmers, with whom we have been largely concerned in earlier chapters, there may have been immediate demands on the wife's entitlements which were more likely to be held in productive property.[6]

The implications of the endowment of a woman at the death of her parents rather than at marriage are several. As I have observed for Arab societies (1976:61), delayed transfer is more compatible with the high frequency of divorce and remarriage of later Roman society (Saller 1984:203), in which the remarriage of widows was more frequent than that of divorcées, except in high society. The same suggestion has been made for Rome where among the upper classes the rare divorce and *manus* marriage of the early period gave way to frequent divorce and the separation of goods (Dixon 1985c). Evidence from the sub-continent of India as well as from Europe and Japan provides some further support for the hypothesis, but the separation of goods is a matter of timing and of degree. Of timing because in 'free marriage', women probably took a further portion of their property as an inheritance to add to a smaller dowry; at marriage among the lower groups there was little to join except possible expectations. Of degree because the dowry was still controlled by the husband although owned by the wife in the sense that it was returnable; moreover, despite the possibilities of disinheritance, testamentary freedom and legacies, the bulk of the property of both partners went in practice to the children of the union.

While marriages of this kind may have less chance of enduring, a union with a woman who has 'great expectations' is obviously advantageous to the offspring, even if the husband himself has less to gain, and it is therefore to the long-term benefit of the 'family' line whether or not it ends in divorce. In some cases property was left directly to grandchildren (Corbier 1985), especially by women to whom they were on average closer in age than to male ascendants. However, given the high levels of mortality, some three fifths of women would have lost their fathers by the time of their marriage, though less so in aristocratic circles where both men and women married earlier (Saller 1987:32) and where marriage was more likely to be arranged. So that women would often have been dowered with their inheritance; the two major points at which devolution occurred, marriage and death of parents, were often closer together than the demographic structure of contemporary populations would suggest.

Law and change

A general view prevails that there was a substantial change in the access of Roman women to property between the institution of the Twelve Tables in the mid fifth century BC and the end of the Republican period, despite the fact that there were few alterations in the law itself. Indeed Finley has argued that there was no great change between the Republic and the Empire (1963:25). When the first literary evidence becomes available at the beginning of the second century BC the situation of women appears in a very different light than most interpretations of the reconstructed Tables suggest. In the upper groups they were entitled to inherit on the same basis as their brothers, were allocated a returnable dowry at marriage (which was managed by their husbands), and could receive substantial assets by gift or inheritance even when not *sui iuris*, free from tutelage (Dixon 1985a:168), which was increasingly the case over the last two centuries BC (Hopkins 1983:90), that is, from the period of the first literary evidence. The view of Roman woman as 'the paradigm of oppression' was upheld by a 'bare reading of the law' which was 'quite contradicted by literary and documentary evidence'.

This was even so with *cum manu* marriages which continued to be practised until the time of Nero (Watson 1967:23). While such a wife could not institute divorce proceedings nor in theory have property of her own, she had the right to inherit that of her husband if he died intestate. And 'it does not follow that in practice such a wife was necessarily in an inferior position' (p. 28). Plautus' Demaenetus married a much wealthier woman *cum manu*, at least partly for her money, but she managed to keep control of her dowry, was free from the domination of her husband, and indeed tyrannised over him. Yet legally all her property belonged to him (p. 29). But there were some explicit advantages, connected with the avoidance of taxes, and a woman could enter into *manus* at any time, by choice. Under other forms of marriage a childless spouse stood to inherit very little, but when they came into *manus*, they would inherit all.

It is possible to interpret a gap between 'law' and 'practice' as the result of a change over time, as many authorities have done. But such a gap often exists as a matter of course, especially when 'codes' are initially written down (Goody 1986: chapter 4). In the first place the intention of these documents is rarely to make a complete digest of laws, which comes about only much later. As Bottéro (1982) has insisted, the aim of the 'Code' of Hammurabi was not that of a code at all. In Rome, the primordial status of the Twelve Tables is illustrated by the fact that students learned them by heart as part of their formal education (Dixon 1985b:520ff.), suggesting that their function was more 'biblical' than legal.

Of course once formulated, such writings have 'real consequences' for social action. They necessarily form one of the sources of law, however peripheral they may be for legal judgements. And even if they initially represented a 'distorted' or simplified view of reality, they place constraints on human intercourse: in court proceedings (and even beyond them) a woman might be defined as an agnate because she 'inherits' a dower from her husband rather than her father; or she might find her husband gaining greater control of her property after marriage because the legal formulae did not build in the capacity of kin to take counteraction in the case of misappropriation. As a result 'legal reform' may take a long time to catch up with an earlier state of affairs; the history of such movements may look like a continuous process of rationalisation, of modernisation of 'primitive law', whereas their very existence stems from the initial failure of written law (perhaps because of particular interests, perhaps for more neutral reasons like an inadequate understanding, or inadequate tools for understanding, the complexities of the present situation) to encompass or reflect the process of actual decision-making. However the making of jural decisions is not totally thrown out of joint by the advent of a written 'rule', since families may take formal steps to get round its provisions (as with the marriage settlements of eighteenth-century England), they may simply try to ignore the 'law', or they may be ignored by it in the sense that most social action only meets up against the 'law' under certain specific conditions which may be largely irrelevant to the family life of ordinary people.

In the second place, the written code is only one source of law; custom and equity always play their part while the actions of individuals are subject to more than legal sanctions alone. The gap between 'law' and practice is not simply a question of deviation from the norm; the written version may have been inadequate in the first place or directed to some other end. The effective law may not only lie outside the courts because there are none, that is, in 'convention' supported by the kind of social sanctions on which many societies rely, but even with judicial decisions, the courts themselves may pay more attention to what is *not* written down since this may provide a fuller statement of the applicable norms. Dowry or marriage may be inadequately represented in the written, not because they necessarily fall into the private rather than the public domain, but because the social sanctions surrounding them may be of a quite different order, subject to different modes of judgement, different forms of sanction.

Thirdly, what is written may well be only a crude and peripheral representation of the total jural reality. The problem with regard to early 'codes' is partly a matter of the initial difficulties of giving a written form to social action which until then has been conducted solely in the oral channel. While it would obviously be a mistake to see the latter simply as practice, since such behaviour always has a normative component, this 'ideal' element may take a very different shape under oral conditions where the statement of 'rules' will always have a more precise contextual frame. Indeed the 'rules' may often be implicit rather than explicit, regularities rather than norms. Even if explicit, they may display a plurality that permits choice (as with sets of proverbs that offer a selection of partially contradictory advice) or they may allow more room for contextual applications. The scribes, on the other hand, were aiming at a more abstract and general formulation (and eventually a statement of 'principles') since they were inevitably dealing with law in a more decontextualised way. As a result they encountered many initial difficulties in reducing a complex situation to a written formula, which was rarely simply a question of transcribing a spoken norm. So we cannot presume that the difference between the Twelve Tables and the legal or literary texts of Republican or Imperial Rome necessarily represents a substantial shift in the overall situation, even though the scale and complexity of society changed dramatically over this period. It may, in part at least, represent a problem of 'transcription', of formulation, which can never be entirely resolved. For instance, the written formulations may have to treat as alternatives what are in practice two aspects of the same situation. In her study of Scipio's affairs, Dixon remarks that 'At the banker's or before a praetor a man might, quite properly, designate "his" the property he elsewhere termed "my wife's"' (1985a:164). The analysis constantly runs up against similar 'ambiguities' that arise out of the nature of the situation, the fact that a woman is under tutelage, yet acts as if she were independent (an ambiguity possibly reflected in shifts of emphasis in the law); that she both belongs and does not belong to the families of her husband and of her father, that the law of inheritance does not adequately represent the network of rights and obligations since it takes into account only one moment in the process of devolution. These problems may arise out of a changing situation but they may also represent not simply the inadequacies of early legal writings when treated as codes, but the difficulties that all decontextualised codes have in coping with aspects of social life that need to be treated contextually or that are replete even with concurrent ambiguities. The fact that the written law selects one possibility rather than another (for example, concerning a woman's membership of a kin group) may well push the total system in a certain direction, but if the initial 'ambiguity' is too embedded in social action, it may also lead to a layering of law and custom, creating the possibility that the balance may shift once again sometime in the future. As Dixon remarks of agnation and the question of whether a woman belonged to the lineage of her husband or of her father, 'technical change made little difference to the Roman conception of the obligations imposed by "blood" relationship (*cognatio*)' (p. 169). A woman in a *manus* marriage is said to have been seen as an agnate of her husband's kin, although by whom and in what context is not clear. Nevertheless 'jurists later decided that woman were only regarded as the "nearest agnatic heir" (*proximus agnatus*) in the case of sisters, because of a legal quibble about the original wording of the Twelve Tables on intestate succession' (Dixon 1985c:361). Note the way that these legal relations are defined in the single context of inheritance, whereas agnatic relationships obviously have a wider importance. But more significantly note the possibility (I do not say the actuality) that this was not necessarily a deliberate change of law but, either in the first or in the second ruling, the jurists may have made an error, as the result of misunderstanding the meaning of the highly condensed Twelve Tables, whose status and content were themselves questionable as the sole source of judgement for the reasons we have suggested. It would not be the last time this had occurred.

It is not only a matter of error but of usage. Written scholarship selects in favour of concepts that have 'universal' significance. As readers we expect 'agnation' to have the same meaning in each context. But while early Roman law considered all relatives traced through males to be agnates, the term was also used more specifically to refer to those agnates outside the category of *sui heredes* (which included a man's children, his sons' children and his wife), that is relatives through males beyond the immediate degree of 'heirs' (Dixon 1985c:361–2). The top of the list were *sui heredes*, the next group was *proximus agnatus*. We can see that the problem turns on whom to choose, in a particular context, among a list of agnates. Agnates are thus inclusive of heirs in one context and exclusive in another. This ambiguity is not simply a casual or even a careless usage, but one grounded in the fact that a wife does have a claim on the property of her husband (and to a lesser extent on his *consortium* or Joint Undivided Family when he is 'unemancipated', 'unseparated'), not because she has been incorporated in his agnatic group but because she has been allocated property for a conjugal fund over which she has little direct control, though the allowance she received from her husband was roughly in line with the scale of the dowry (Crook 1988). As Dixon points out, it is through bringing her parental endowment (her dowry) into the marriage that she acquires a claim, at least a moral one, on her husband's estates; he gives a compensatory allowance in her lifetime and an endowment at death. Or to put it another way, power is not simply the *potestas* of the husband/father; it is also the power of others, including women, to inherit from him, a man (Dixon 1985c:361). It is the complexity of this situation that gives rise to some of the predicaments in legal writings, whose interpretation we then tend to read back as 'the law' in a substantive sense.

Why should these early writings have been able to solve problems of this kind straight away, since it was not a simple question of transcribing *themistes*? In the matter of marriage and lineage, as we have seen elsewhere, the notion of diverging devolution is not easily reconciled with the continuity of a fixed estate. If women are endowed and marry out, a contradiction inevitably arises. Again, are children (of whatever sex) to be limited to the pre-mortem transmission of property or do they have a further claim as heirs at death? Does their claim entitle them to the basic productive resources as well as to movable assets? What is the relation of their endowment to the estate of their spouse and his natal family? If the husband 'separates' physically at marriage, as in the case of many neolocal peasant families in western Europe (and apparently as in Rome), the latter problem is relatively easy to solve. So too if he takes over the management of his parental estate at this point in time. Even so, there are many modalities turning on the degree of the husband's control over his wife's dowry and the extent of her ability to acquire and hold property outside that specifically committed to the marriage, a liberty she possessed under Roman law (Dixon 1985a:156–7; Crook 1988, cases 6 and 9) as well as under the later Justinian code operating in the Byzantine empire, where Beaucamp (1985) speaks of *'non-specifiques biens'*. But the problem is of a different order when the husband remains unseparated at marriage. Despite the possibility of neolocal residence, and important as this may be for the quality of personal relationships as well as for domestic arrangements, if no separation of the Joint Undivided Family had taken place, the senior generation maintained general control of the undivided property, as is often the case in India or Taiwan today.

The dual position in which women are placed in all those situations in which they physically move to the home, country or workplace of their husband is well attested, facing towards their conjugal group the bulk of the time but always retaining ties with their natal family. It is the same with men (allowing for a measure of socio-sexual dimorphism) in cases of filiacentric or uxorilocal marriage. But the existence of agnatic groups such as patrilineages gives another twist to the situation, since these unilineal units are by definition exclusive. Physical movement and group membership have sometimes been seen (above all by outsiders) as coincidental, a woman giving up membership of her natal 'group' on leaving to join her husband's. But the various groups and groupings to which one belongs are differently constituted. One can leave a household without ceasing to belong to the lineage with which it is associated, just as one can join the domestic group of one's spouse without joining his or her lineage. And it may have been partly to meet these contextual points that, in relation to filiation rather than affinity, Roman law elaborated the contrasting but concurrently applicable concepts of agnation and cognation, although, as we have seen, one use of the term 'agnate' was for those relatives who fell outside the category of *sui heredes*, that is, not so much outside the minimal lineage as the joint undivided family.

The problem of the written reductionism of oral complexities also affects the question of change. A 'bare reading of the law' may see in Cicero the earliest evidence for the obligatory return of the dowry of a widow or a divorcée even when she had been *in manu mariti*. Yet literary accounts make it clear that the practice was already current at least by the mid second century BC (Dixon 1985a:169). When we learn that in principle women remained in life-long tutelage (*tutela*, a concept again linked to inheritance) although custom and formal erosions eventually made this a nominal limitation on the scope of their actions (Dixon 1985c:363), we do not know if the earlier legal formula was substantive or a function of drafting.[7] Again, was the legal insistence on the husband's 'ownership' of the dowry, despite the application of successive limitations, despite the recognition of its returnable nature in the case of divorce, the accountability of the husband, and the distinction between the property of husband and wife (Dixon 1985c:364), all of which run counter to the notion of his ownership, was this a matter of change in substance or in literary expression? Were the 'successive limitations' an adjustment to customary norms that underlay the written law?

Such examples throw some doubt on the notion of radical changes in the later periods, as envisaged by Veyne (1978). But they also suggest that the earlier written law may never have provided an adequate representation of the jural or even legal life of the community, especially with regard to the complexities and contradictions in the position of women. For in conformity with what has been suggested for China and India in respect to the static, territorially based, androcentric view of the significance of corporations consisting of agnatically related males, Dixon observes that 'women represented a dangerously dynamic element, for on marriage they took part of the family holding with them in the form of a dowry' (1985a:149), mostly in cash, it is true, but still 'disruptive' of the family finances. It was this situation, linked to the maintenance of the status of all members of the family in a hierarchical society, that early legal systems, like later historians and anthropologists, have had such difficulty in conceptualising, or rather in putting down in black and white.

Women and property under the Empire

As in the case of testaments and legacies, the establishment of the complicated and variable arrangements that are often arrived at in dowry systems derives some support (perhaps even its existence) from the presence of a written record that specifies the details of the settlement made between the two parties, for it was in the interest of both that the transaction should be clear and enduring. After the guests had assembled at the house of the bride's father, the marriage contract or *tabulae nuptiales* containing the agreement about the dowry was signed by a number of those present. Two such contracts from Egypt survive on papyrus, probably from the first century AD; both documents contain a full list of the bride's jewellery and one of her clothing as well.

Under Augustan legislation a written form was sometimes used to prove the act of divorce and carried the seals of seven witnesses. Divorce entailed the return of all or part of the dowry. An extreme instance of the link between direct dowry and divorce is illustrated in the reply of Emperor Marcus Aurelius when it was suggested that he divorce his wife, the younger Faustina. 'What' he said, 'and return her dowry?'. The dowry was the Empire itself, for he had succeeded his father-in-law.

The fact that women were carriers of property gave them value as widows, as divorcées and as heiresses. The rich widow was a characteristic feature of Roman society, attracting the attention of confidence tricksters as well as of potential mates (Balsdon 1963:222). So too was the rich heiress. Since any individual's claim to wealth was decreased by having to divide it with siblings, an only daughter was a particularly valuable prize. Such a situation was more common than might be thought. It has been argued that a process of natural selection was at work in the upper strata in favour of small families (Last 1947), leading to its gradual disappearance. However this may be, there does seem to have been a tendency among the wealthy to restrict the size of the family for economic reasons. What Polybius noted for Greece in the second century BC was also true for Rome; in order to maintain the same standard of living for their children, richer families in Greece 'deliberately refrained from having – or at least bringing up – more than one or two children' (Balsdon 1963:197). Such a small number was not always sufficient to protect the family against the ravages of disease or the misfortunes of war, so it might have to seek an outside heir; while we have little idea of the relative frequency, the emphasis seems to have been upon adoption, upon bringing in a substitute, rather than upon taking a supplementary wife, although divorce and remarriage was also used for this purpose. By the time of the late Roman Republic divorce and remarriage were very frequent among the aristocracy. This was not the case in the second century BC and in general before Augustus; and the motives included the formation of political alliances as well as the search for family security.

In a recent and more thorough study (1983), Hopkins has analysed the turn-over in the ranks of the more successful senators (the consuls), who had a very low rate of hereditary succession. He sees this as due to the expenses involved in becoming a member of the Senate, especially after the increase in eligibles with the expansion of the Empire and the overall growth in wealth. 'The inheritance of property, split equally between all surviving sons and daughters, diffused wealth away from the agnates to relatives by marriage' (p. ix). The costs of producing a senator, the necessity of dividing the property equally, led to a delicate balancing act between biological continuity and social survival, the outcome of which it was impossible to calculate exactly, given the high rates of mortality. It was dangerous to have too many children (that is, more than two) but at the same time easy to end up with too few (p. 117). There were alternative strategies of heirship such as adoption, but rates were as low as 4 per cent among the consulate in 250–49 BC (p. 49), although filiacentric unions, where a son-in-law took the family name of his wife, represented another possibility, an attractive one in the case of an epiklerate. In these ways the problem of the Roman aristocracy is central to the theme of this study.

Considerations of property and status were among those that led to the arranging of marriages as in China and the Near East, especially among the higher social classes. It was generally the father who arranged the marriage of a son or daughter, though in the latter case the mother was also consulted (Balsdon 1963:174). Suitable matches were achieved by discussion among friends when the factors taken into account were largely 'family, face and fortune', so that a poor man had little chance of getting a rich man's daughter, unless he was a poor noble with ability and prospects.[8] Any husband who married up by means of a hypogamous marriage put himself at risk. While there are dangers in using literary evidence, especially from the pens of satirists and comic writers, there are other dangers in neglecting views that derive from non-judicial sources. Juvenal's comment seems to ring true: a man who took a very rich woman as wife ('that husband with an ample portion bless'd') was allowed to enjoy her wealth only on condition that he permitted her the utmost freedom in her private life.

> She writes, nods, whispers, while her lord can see,
> Of all which favours she has paid the fee
>
> Who needs the husband whom her purse invites,
> Preserves, unchallenged, all the spinster's rights
> (Juvenal 6:173–6)

Since the transfer of property was virtually essential to a full and equal conjugal union in all except the lowest groups, some might have to delay their marriage so that the family could accumulate the right endowment. However since upper marriages were usually arranged by the parents, a suitable pair, suited in terms of both property and status, might marry right after puberty (deemed to be fourteen for a boy) and the betrothal could even take place at a considerably earlier date, at the age of seven, by which time the children were taught to understand the nature of the ceremony.[9] Consequently the age of marriage among the rich was substantially lower than among other groups.

In early Rome betrothal had the same binding character we have found elsewhere and it was then 'bilaterally actionable' in the sense that either party could sue for breach of promise. By the end of the Empire a man of the upper classes might have to make a substantial gift to his fiancée, known as *donatio ante nuptias*, which became part of her dowry, an indirect dowry. On the other hand gifts between husband and wife, which were valid during the Republic, became invalid at the end, an aspect of the strict separation of property within the framework of a matching of funds. But even if there was no community of property in *sine manu* marriage, where women could keep at least part of the dowry, we find what Gaudemet has called 'a community of use and enjoyment' (1961, after Crook 1988). While betrothal was never absolutely binding until the fourth century AD, it became increasingly subject to political considerations which could lead to abrupt changes in marriage plans. In 59 BC the daughter of Julius Caesar was on the point of marrying Servilius Caepio when the engagement was broken off and she was married to Pompey to further Caesar's political interests.

The emphasis on arranged marriages may aggravate the tensions between the generations since the reasons behind a particular choice of partner may not weigh equally with all parties. The result may give rise to difficulties not only between the spouses, a much-reduced adult version of the problem Wolf found in China between those partners brought up together from an early age (the extreme case of arranged marriage), but also between those who arranged the marriage and those who were forced into it. Experience elsewhere suggests that such attitudes were rare but may be more common where a man can take only one wife at a time, unless a wider range of sexual partnerships are available. In Rome, as elsewhere in the ancient World and in urban Eurasia generally, a rich man had access to his slave-girls or kept a courtesan; he may sometimes have patronised the prostitutes who worked in brothels, though these establishments were mainly the resorts of the poor, of travellers or of rich young bachelors.

Unlike China (although even there it was relatively rare), concubinage does not seem to have been practised by married men (Balsdon 1963:232); a man could not have a wife and a concubine at the same time, a concubine being a woman with whom one set up house but with limited legal consequences (Watson 1967:10). In further contrast to China, the children of concubines were not fully legitimate; on the other hand neither were they bastards (*spurii*), being known in later times as 'natural children' (*liberi naturales*). Concubinage was a lasting sexual union of lesser rank, the resort of those who could not legally marry such as legionary soldiers, or of persons of different social status such as a senator and a freedwoman (Balsdon 1963:232). A union of this kind meant that no dowry had been given. Even a woman of the same status as her husband might have to contract a concubinate union if she could not be properly endowed. Such at least is a possible implication of some literary comments. While a dowry was not legally necessary for either Roman or Greek marriage, there was 'a strong moral duty' (Watson 1967:6). So that not to provide a dowry would create an impression of concubinage, even as early as the plays of Plautus which provide the main evidence for the situation at the beginning of the second century BC (p. 14). In Plautus' *Trinummus*, Lesbonicus was in the position of being unable to provide a dowry for his sister: 'with people passing word around how I gave you my own sister for a concubine, more than wife, in case I did give her to you without a dowry, whose name would be put above mine as a rotter? And in case you did take her without a dowry, all this spread-the-word would glorify you and muddify me: you'd get the honour and glory, I'd get something for them to throw at me' (1938:165).[10] Property considerations are closely linked to the idea of honourable behaviour so characteristic of Mediterranean societies (Peristiany 1965): a brother acquires honour by properly endowing his sister, and shame by failing so to do.

Roman concubinage differed from the Chinese where it was an additional form of low prestige, polycoital union with no necessary effect on the children's status. In Rome, on the other hand, the offspring were not heirs, the woman was usually but not always of lower status, and the union, though less prestigious, was not a polycoital adjunct to marriage of the same kind but rather an alternative. Some men rejected the idea of marriage altogether and deliberately entered into concubinate unions, even though no status barrier was involved. Widowers sometimes took this course of action if they already had heirs: the emperor Vespasian considered concubinage preferable to remarriage and Marcus Aurelius took a concubine when his wife died because he did not wish his children to suffer from a step-mother. The role of the step-parent is clearly critical in dowry systems, since it complicates not only personal but property relations as well.

The point can best be made in contrast to Africa. If a LoDagaa marries a woman who has already had children (or vice versa), there are no particular grounds for conflict over property (though there may be other reasons for tension) between the male offspring of the different fathers. They share in their own fathers' possessions while the females have some interest in the mother's estate, usually very small. A second marriage has little effect on established property relations though interpersonal ones may certainly be affected. When the mother dies, the children may suffer as 'orphans' but hardly as step-children; in any case a polygynous family has no one step-mother and any hostility tends to be widely diffused. The situation of the 'second bed' does not impose itself, especially as land is not involved in inheritance in the same way. In dowry systems, on the other hand, a woman's property is divided between the children of her various marriages, and a new husband will tend to prefer his own offspring to inherit rather than those of his predecessor. Likewise a stepmother may wish to benefit her own children at the expense of her husband's earlier offspring. Such were the reasons that moved people to worry about step-relatives, a sentiment that Juvenal expresses with magnificent exaggeration.

> From stepsons by concocted poisons slain,
> And their domestic treasons, I abstain
> (6:163–4)

One reason for the preference for concubinate unions under such conditions was that they produced no additional heirs to share in the inheritance (and hence were especially attractive to emperors). Another was that they could be dissolved with ease; partly because there was no property to be divided, the woman could simply be sent off home more easily than a wife. The presence of a dowry might place difficulties in the way of divorce but in any case it was some safeguard for the wife, and not merely an instrument of her subjection; this protection arose out of the property arrangements involved in the marriage settlement which were binding on both parties.

> Now, if by marriage contracts firmly tied,
> You neither hope, nor wish to love your bride
> (Juvenal 6:241–2)

Men were thus not only monogamous, there was even some feeling against a widower remarrying; that is to say, in exceptional cases, he might take a concubine or a 'slave mistress' if he had heirs. While remarriage became increasingly frequent, there was some notion of the uniqueness of the marriage bond (at least for women and while the union lasted) which appears to be related in a very general way to the fact that the partnership of the couple rested on property as well as on generative sex, and which contributes one element to the kind of companionship in marriage reported for some patrician unions. The first marriage of a woman is widely recognised as the most important she makes and the full rites are often performed only on this one occasion; for it is then that she takes on the new role of wife and changes her position with regard to her family of orientation. But where elaborate property arrangements are involved, where a conjugal community or even partnership is established by means of a direct dowry, the first marriage is ideally the last. A man would boast that his wife was *univira*, a one-man woman. While divorce became more common in Rome, it was virtually absent in the early period.[11] This absence did not reflect the wife's incorporation in the husband's family or lineage, as has sometimes been suggested, so much as the nature of conjugal arrangements and the sanctions that surrounded them. So too did the tendency for widows not to remarry.[12] In later periods a high value continued to be placed upon the woman who had married only once, even though remarriage was not proscribed; indeed Augustus made people re-marry, women as well as men. But when the marriage feast had ended, the bride was led in procession to her husband's house where a miniature bridal bed had been prepared for the spirits of the married pair, the *genius* of the groom and the *juno* of the bride. After the *epithalamium* had been sung and the bride escorted to the bed-chamber, it was the *univirae* who undressed her for the bridal bed. The symbolism and the ideal are self-apparent.

The elementary family

Whatever the make-up of the household, whatever the importance of agnates, whatever the rule of intestate succession (and in Rome a woman's intestate heirs were her brothers if she had neither children nor parents), it is clear that the emphasis was on viewing 'the nuclear, conjugal unit as the proper focus of material loyalty' (Dixon 1985c:363). As Crook remarks, 'the husband-and-wife relationship is at the very heart of family strategies'

(1988). Dixon herself sees this trend as accompanying an increase in those marriages in which women were not 'transferred' to their husband's agnatic group. That increase was in turn related less to the emphasis on natal ties than to 'a visible strengthening ideal of conjugal attachment and nuclear identification that was evidenced not only in literary and sepulchral celebrations of married love and family life, but in the transmission of property' (p. 362). The development of such orientations is attributed to the late Republican period (p. 356), at a time when marriages were still arranged (as they continued to be for a long time to come in the upper groups of Europe) but divorce was easier to obtain (a situation that was later to change in Christian Europe).

The claim is not that nuclear or elementary households or families first developed at this time (although this is often taken to be the case by those who see women as having been earlier 'transferred' between agnatic groups) but that we find a strengthening of conjugal bonds. Nuclearity and conjugality are sometimes confused; while they may be connected, the notions must be kept distinct for the purposes of analysis, otherwise our conclusions simply tend to confirm our expectations.

The elementary family consisting of husband, wife (in some cases a plurality of spouses) and children exists in virtually all known human societies, but not necessarily as a residential unit. In most societies some dwelling groups consist of elementary families, some of more complex ones, and increasingly some of one-person households, but the extent of variation in the size of dwelling groups (housefuls) and units of production (farming groups, in the agricultural sector) and consumption groups (households, in which housekeeping and cooking groups may again be different) occurred within fairly narrow limits (Goody 1972). As we have seen, more complex households exist, and yet more extensive joint undivided families (property-holding groups), but these larger units always include smaller conjugal ones which form the foci of eventual fission. In this process of splitting, the establishment of a conjugal fund by means of diverging devolution plays an intrinsic part, as we have tried to show for East, South and West Asia. That system of devolution had already existed in the Fertile Crescent from an early period, being connected with the hierarchical nature of societies with advanced agriculture. So that we would expect to find throughout the kind of emphasis on conjugality, and on nuclearity, of which we see evidence in Egyptian and Mesopotamian sculpture and painting. Greece and Rome may have been different in the very earliest periods of their development, for their entry into 'civilised' society, the society of cities, came later than other parts of the eastern Mediterranean. But any enquiry needs to begin by adopting a sceptical attitude towards such trends owing to the paucity of the evidence and its literary nature. We need to ask if the trends are substantive, if the argument is *ex silentio*, and if the existing evidence is a function of attempts at written legal formulation.

Whatever conclusions are reached about the earlier changes, we need also to remind ourselves, and historians of the family generally, that the evidence on the priority accorded to the 'nuclear, conjugal unit' as 'the proper focus for material [and emotional] loyalty' is early and widespread, and that its existence has little or nothing to do with the kinds of sociological, demographic or historical reasons that contemporary Western authors have often suggested. For the importance of this nuclear unit long preceded the coming into being of the modern or industrial world, not only in Europe but elsewhere. That is to say, in considering either the presence or absence of 'family' (i.e. household) models of a nuclear, stem or communal (*communautaire*) kind (Burguière 1986), or the geographical typologies spelled out by Hajnal (1965) and Laslett (1983), we have to recognise that we are not dealing with the invention, discovery or appearance of the elementary family as a social unit. Conjugal units and even nuclear households already existed in Rome just as they did in Asia; while the latter were proportionally less common in earlier times and in other cultures, larger households were potentially more frequent when marriage was early and universal.

The general point is reinforced by Saller and Shaw (1984), who, in their comments on the theses of Le Play and Laslett concerning the supposed progression from extended to nuclear families (that is, households), remark that whatever the linguistic terms indicate, 'on the basis of the tombstone inscriptions we have come to the conclusion that . . . the nuclear family was the primary focus of certain types of familial obligations' (1984:124). The same point is made by Thomas (1986), as well as by Veyne (1978) who sees the Roman family (that is, household) as 'nuclear' from the second century BC; by this he means something quite specific, that among the aristocracy a newly married couple set up its own house (p. 35), even though the couple would remain within a joint undivided family from the standpoint of the control of property (Crook 1988). In earlier Rome not everyone, Veyne asserts, 'married in the formal sense, since marriage had one objective, to transmit the patrimony to one's descendants' (p. 40). Later on, major marriage is seen as spreading to the plebs, although clearly they must previously have had some form of accepted union. It is in the diffusion of this 'high' form that Veyne sees the key to the advent of the 'conjugal family', with affectionate relations between the partners, despite the high divorce rate; on the other hand he did not think of his argument as necessarily extending to affection between parents and children. These comments reflect the contention of many historians and sociologists that the relationship between the elementary or nuclear family and modernisation is linked to the notion of the conjugal family as the focus not only of material interests but of a special degree of affection between spouses and towards their children.

Conjugal affection

Historians of Rome like Veyne (1978:37), writers on Classical Greece like Avezzù (1983:87), and scholars of Roman Egypt like Hopkins (1980) have at times insisted on the resemblances, beginning in the period with which they are dealing, between the family in the society they study and the one in which they live. For Rome Veyne speaks of 'une totale transformation conjugale et sexuelle durant les deux premiers siècles de notre ère; on est passé d'une sexualité aussi exotique à nos yeux que, par example, celle de l'ancien Japon, à une sexualité et une conjugalité qui était encore les nôtres à une date toute récente' (1978:37). He sees this transformation as occurring later than the time suggested by Dixon but before Christianity had become influential in this sphere. Indeed Christianity is said to have adopted changes that had taken place in pagan morality, changes that Veyne speculates happened in the course of the shift from a competitive aristocracy to one based on service; the service aristocracy 'invented a conjugal and sexual morality' to provide themselves with an exterior discipline which they had lost. 'Il invente le mythe de l'amour conjugal, afin qu'on lui obéisse par amour, sans qu'il ait à commander' (p. 37). It was the Antonines (AD 96–192) who were the true inventors of the Christian sexual morality prevalent among the nineteenth-century bourgeoisie.[13] Previous to that, affection was weak, children were disinherited, parricide prevailed and marriage was only for those who wanted to pass on their property. With the Antonines, all that changed.

Once again it is interesting to learn that the Roman family of that period had some of the same characteristics as later Europe. Veyne insists that we can find there the kind of affectionate family that Shorter discovered in England in the nineteenth century, Stone in the seventeenth and eighteenth, and Macfarlane in the Middle Ages. His insistence is a salutary reminder that affectionate elementary families, characterised by individual emotions, already existed at this earlier period and should lead us to modify if not set aside altogether both the ethnocentric speculations of those historians of later Europe who have been as much concerned with explaining the present as the past, not to speak of the more imaginary theses about sex and the family in the ancient world (for example, Foucault 1984). What is problematic about Veyne's argument is the assertion that it was during the Principate that these 'fundamental changes' were 'invented'. Both the timing and the nature of change are at issue. Other scholars have claimed that changes took place much earlier in the organisation of the family and the lineage; whereas at first the woman in a high status union was endowed at marriage and came under the *manus* of her husband and his agnates, in the early Empire she inherited and controlled her property, while remaining under the *manus* of her father. Others have also put forward different suggestions for the way in which the organisation of lineages changed over time, but there seems little evidence of the early exogamy posited by Thomas (1981) outside the body of mythology (Saller and Shaw 1984:135); in this respect West Asia and the Mediterranean differed from East and South Asia for as long as history recounts.

Whatever the status of such supposed shifts, which hark back to nineteenth-century theories of social development, the evidence is overwhelming concerning the position in the late Republic. In a speech to her husband, Brutus, Porcia is reported as saying, 'I, daughter of Cato, was introduced to your household not as a concubine, to share only in bed and board, but as an equal partner in your prosperity and your troubles'. The idea of sharing in both riches and poverty was of course intrinsic to the notion of marriage in the Catholic Church. These facts should lead us to qualify 'the usual, rather evolutionary view of the historical development of conjugal love and companionate marriage' (Dixon 1985c:373). It is perhaps not so much a question of qualifying an evolutionary view, even in the sense of long-term development, as of specifying the nature of the change and its timing. While the evidence casts doubt upon the way that historians of later Europe often perceive dramatic changes of this kind as occurring during the periods in which they are interested, the relocation of those changes in Rome itself is even less satisfactory. Veyne's proposal seems dubious in terms both of substance and of explanation. In terms of substance because different historians seize on different chronologies and different characteristics. In terms of explanation because the basic change in family structure is attributed to the replacement of the violent, rival oligarchs of the Republic by the faithful state servants of the Principate. But as the funeral monuments show, the conjugal family was already well established in the early period of the Republic (see also Treggiari 1981; Thomas 1986:209). In other words, there appears to be no adequate evidence for any over-all move from extended to elementary, no general extension of sexuality, love or affection (Thomas 1986:227). Whatever happened and when, it was on a different scale than such claims suggest.[14]

Affection for children

In standard accounts of the European family, love of children is often seen as the counterpart of companionate marriage. Rome does not seem to have lagged behind later Europe in its attachment to children, if not to childhood.

Such sentiments were expressed in the memorials for young children which brought out both the affection and the grief of the dedicator (Saller and Shaw 1984:126; Hopkins 1983:217ff.). The funerary monuments reveal substantially more dedications from parents to children than vice-versa. For those interested in the supposed shift in the value of children and its relation to demographic change, this fact might be taken as a reciprocal counterpart to the upward flow of services from children to parents on which 'traditional' societies are said to rely; on the other hand it is also consistent with a supposedly 'modern' structure of sentiments where the flow of transactions is held to run downward. Neither proposition fits with the general theory that relates the direction of such flows to the demographic transition, since the kind of affection that Ariès sees as developing in the early modern period already seems to be a feature of Roman society. But the problem is not simply one of finding a point farther back in the European past in order to question ethnocentric theories about the modernisation of the world. We have to look much more widely and ask what evidence exists anywhere for a category of human society that lacks such an affectionate orientation to children. The answer runs yet more sharply against the whole trend of such hypotheses. Neither conjugal love nor parental affection were born in the West, neither under capitalisam nor under the Roman Republic.

Age at marriage

There is one other feature of marriage which demographers and historians see as characteristic of modern Europe, that is the late age of marriage for males and females. Later marriage too is sometimes linked to greater child care (by older parents) and to conjugal love (by older partners), as well as the servanthood of the young (before marriage) and the retirement of the senior generation at the marriage of the junior. Here there is certainly a substantial difference. In Rome the age of marriage of men seems to have been around twenty-five to thirty for the bulk of the population, but, as is not unusual, somewhat earlier in the upper groups (Saller 1987:30).[15] Women on the other hand married earlier than men, possibly not as early as has been suggested by Hopkins (1965) but in the late teens or early twenties (Shaw 1987). This typical 'Mediterranean pattern', which Smith (1981) discerns in the data from fifteenth-century Tuscany analysed by Herlihy and Klapisch-Zuber (1978) but which was earlier distributed through the romanised west (Saller 1987:30), is described as one of late male and early female marriage. From a comparative point of view the female marriage age was hardly early, but it is the gap between the two that presents an important difference with later Europe. Herlihy (1974) saw this gap as being opened up during the central Middle Ages but, as Saller (1987) remarks, it already existed a millennium before (p. 23).

Later marriage means longer generations. For women the generation span was clearly shorter, but the longer generations of men implies fewer male-based three-generational families and in actuality the evidence for ones headed by males is small. So too for households in aristocratic circles, even though marriage was substantially earlier for both men and women, in the town and in the country, but where sons often moved out before marriage, though sometimes remaining within the 'house'.[16] Among 'lower' families, on the other hand, the paucity of such extended families was due to the lateness of marriage for males which meant longer generations, higher mortality and so less likelihood of three generations co-existing at all.

Hierarchical differences

In ancient Rome decisive evidence for the same kind of divergences between upper and lower groups that we have observed elsewhere is difficult to come by. One of the problems is that much of the data for the study of Roman society is insufficient to enable us to make an exact assessment and what is available comes mainly from aristocratic sources. But not all; tombstones were erected for a wide segment of the population (Saller and Shaw 1984) and literary sources give some evidence of 'lower' practice in the towns (Rawson 1966). In the aristocracy marriages (or at least betrothals, Thomas 1986:224) were substantially earlier for both men and women. Aristocrats had lineages, others not (p. 201); they were locked into agnation. The notion of legitimacy, which as in Greece was so essential to inheritance and citizenship, was characteristic of 'upper marriage'. Rawson (1966) suggests that possibly only a third of the population entered into a full union and according to Thomas (1986:200) the poor practised 'promiscuity' and children took the name of their mothers. Such views about the poor represent those of the top echelons of the society; certainly others would have their own notions of what constituted legitimate parenthood. It is suggested that rates of divorce were perhaps lower among lower groups (Dixon 1985c:356), while the remarriage of widows may have been freer, and adoption and concubinage less frequent. It is also suggested that there may have been little difference in rates of infanticide in the form of the exposure of children, which occurred among rich and poor alike (Thomas 1986:196), although the reasons may well have been different in the two cases. Inadequate as the statistical data are, a number of differences seem to have been present in the relations of property existing between men and things (table 14), which can be tentatively associated with the relations of production.

Table 12. *Suggested hierarchical differences in ancient Rome*

		Higher	Lower
1	Type of marriage	*manus* ('free' later)	'free', *usus*
2	Marriage transactions	direct dowry (plus indirect later)	
3	Widow remarriage	disapproved (common later)	freer
4	Divorce	disapproved (common later)	(lower rates later)
5	Choice of spouse	arranged	freer
6	Age of marriage	earlier	later
7	Legitimacy of children	important	less important
8	Adoption and concubinage	more frequent	less frequent
9	Kin groups	lineages	none

The changes over time display a specific pattern, with certain practices of the upper groups coming to resemble those of the lower (items 1, 3 and 4, table 14). In these respects the position also became similar to that in the Near East, although it seems doubtful if the change can be attributed to an orientalising process. In other respects upper and lower groups continued to be differentiated in significant ways.

To return to the theme with which I started this enquiry, even societies such as China and early Rome cannot be regarded as ones in which a wife relinquished the membership of her natal descent group in order to be totally incorporated ('as a chattel') in that of her husband. This was the case even where a woman was given her 'lot' at marriage. She changed households, and in ordinary speech the actors might well employ the same word for household as for family or lineage; but that did not imply a transfer of her membership in a descent group. In any case, unlike women in Africa, she was entitled to share in the property of her own and indirectly of her husband's 'house', creating an additional problem for marital organisation, namely, whether the property a woman brought into the marriage or received as inheritance should be pooled or retained in a separate package, distinct from that of the husband but nevertheless in some type of joint fund as far as the children are concerned. However it took place, transmission to women had an important consequence for the lineage since the property of its members was being redistributed at each generation, some of it going to women who were marrying out, some to men who were leaving the family home. While descent was unilineal, inheritance was bilateral or diverging. While descent, that is, eligibility to the membership of descent groups, embraces daughters as well as sons, in a patrilineal system it is only passed down through the latter, and in a matrilineal one through the former. But the property of the members of a descent group is not necessarily subject to unilineal transmission; allocate goods to both sexes and these will diverge down all lines.

Where the property transmitted to both sexes consists of movables, the physical shift of one spouse that most systems of marriage require does not create any overwhelming problem for the family, lineage, or descent group; that unit can still retain control of the basic productive resources if it can manage to raise other funds for endowment. But when land (or cattle) in an agricultural community are included in a woman's 'portion', then a dispersal of the means of production takes place, or does so in the absence of very specific mechanisms which have their own far-reaching effects on the society. Delay is possible; a woman's portion may be handed over at the parent's death or even later (sometimes not all). Or her endowment may consist largely of support coming from the groom's family, possibly in the form of a delayed dower at his death or at their divorce; and in this case the property does not get dispersed, since even if it is handed over at marriage, it accompanies the bride when she joins her husband.

Land was not a regular feature of a woman's dowry in ancient Rome. But she was endowed at marriage, even in the early period, and retained rights in that property even if she did not always control it. In later Rome her degree of control appears to have increased but at no point had she simply been a pawn of men, an object of purchase or exchange. As in the other societies considered to represent the extremes of patriliny, of the incorporation of women, of the *potestas* of men as fathers and husbands, the situation in Eurasia turns out to be more complicated, not least because of the relation of women to property under a system of diverging devolution.

15

Dowry, continuity and change in the eastern Mediterranean

In our examination of the woman's property complex (which is the short-hand name I give to the cluster of variables linked to diverging devolution), we have found broadly three ways of devolving property on women, all of which were found in rural Greece, sometimes one receiving more stress in one region at a certain time but all present in the repertoire of the system if not of a local area at any one point in time. At one pole, the most male-oriented end, we find the stress placed on marriage prestations from the groom which were used, at least in part, as an indirect dowry for the wife; such practices vary according to the proportion which is retained by father and daughter respectively. In some codes, such as the Law of Manu, it was strictly forbidden for the father to retain or even transmit anything at all; the indirect dowry was out, not because it entailed 'bride-purchase' but because transfers from the groom implied that the father was unable to provide support for his own daughter.[1] In some circumstances a man may keep back some of these payments, though at the same time he makes prestations to his daughter which may well be seen as 'balancing the books', or the daughter may allow her property to rest under her kin's control for the sake of protecting it. In most upper groups emphasis is placed on the direct endowment of a daughter at marriage. Again, there is devolution of property on women at the death of their parents as a primary right (e.g. in Muslim law) or as a residual right (as with the brotherless daughters of Zelophehad in ancient Israel).[2] These methods further vary in the nature of the goods transmitted to daughters (e.g. whether land is excluded or included), secondly, in the share of the estate passed down to women (e.g. under the Sunni Muslim law of inheritance, a woman receives half a man's share, though she may already have been endowed at marriage; indeed under Shia law (e.g. Iran), a daughter takes all the estate in the absence of sons), and thirdly, in the nature of the arrangements for managing and organising the property of the conjugal pair. Moreover these methods are by no means exclusive. In Islamic societies all three may be involved in the same mar-

429

riage. But different communities and the different groups within them tend to give different emphases to the transactions, partly depending upon the position of the spouses in the hierarchy, partly upon the provisions of religious or national law, partly upon changing custom over time, all three being subject to local pressures. In Greece today the transformation of the economy, of the rural–urban balance, of the nature of employment, and of associated notions about family life, have led to further changes of a more distinctly directional kind, first towards an increased emphasis on *prika* (direct dowry) and the woman's share (Couroucli 1987:338ff.), which some see as based on the Aegean model, others as intrinsic to the process of urbanisation and commoditisation; secondly, among the urban population, away from marital assigns in favour of an educational endowment plus inheritance much later on.

Most of this range of variation apparently existed within the boundaries of ancient Greece and was still to be found in Greece and the Balkans in recent times. Greece belongs to that part of Europe, together with the Mediterranean countries of Italy, Spain, Portugal, and Malta, that has retained the practice of dowry, which exists in rather a different form under the 'communauté de biens' of the Napoleonic code. The transmission of property to daughters has not disappeared in other European countries, but it has gradually shifted away from marriage, first in the working class, then in the bourgeoisie, a shift related to the adoption of industrial modes of production and of educational endowment.[3]

The variations within any particular region may be influenced by ecological adaptation as Schneider (1971) has argued in the case of the related concepts of honour and shame. The mountain peoples of Europe appear to display a greater agnatic emphasis than those in the valleys, a fact that is related to their pastoral activities as well as to their relative isolation and their need for protection. This difference has often been regarded simply in terms of the 'backwardness' of those who were thought to have retained an 'earlier' form of social organisation: that has been claimed of the 'isolated' islands of Corsica and Sardinia, as well as of the Ionian Islands. There may well be some measure of truth in this assertion; however these differences are a matter not only of the past but also of current practice in land tenure and farming, especially where those 'isolated' regions place more emphasis on pastoral activities.[4]

A hill settlement in Albania

I want to look at three studies of rural communities in this area, one pastoral, one of mixed mountain farmers and one of farmers in the plain. Despite ecological and other differences, women in each of these groups were in some sense endowed. While this took a variety of forms, which may be related to ecological as well as to cultural factors, there was also a common element. In the final section I look at these problems in the wider historical and geographical framework of Greece but also in relation to general factors that have affected many other parts of Europe – western, eastern, northern and southern – in the recent past.

I begin with an account of mixed farmers from the hill areas of Albania in the 1930s, since these mountainous regions of Europe had a quasi-tribal organisation in which a form of patrilineal descent group often played an important part, as they did in other communities peripheral to the main agricultural areas. The persistence of such an organisation was often related to the absence of effective central authority; law was largely a matter of feud, vengeance and self-help, so that the level of violence was high and such 'political' activity was dominated by males. It is therefore not surprising to find that as far as devolution was concerned the society tended towards the mode of homogeneous (male to male) inheritance, while marriage was accompanied by a payment from the groom or his family to the bride or her family, transactions which approached the male-oriented end of the continuum. Even so, a woman received more than a token quantum of property at her marriage. Bedding was brought as part of her trousseau which included the contents of her dower chest (Hasluck 1954:60), an object of great symbolic and practical importance that is found widely distributed from India to Scandinavia where it existed as the *patari* and the *brudekiste* respectively; this is a transaction that has been devalued in some recent studies, partly because of its decreased importance in Anglo-American marriages. In addition she was given pocket-money, wedding presents, livestock and other possessions, all of which remained in her charge. This was a domain with which the master of the house, described by Hasluck in strongly patriarchal terms, had nothing to do. She wrote:

In astonishing contrast to the penniless men, all women had their own money and controlled it absolutely. Called *pekul* [a word that also appears in Ottoman areas] from the Latin *peculium*, and essentially pin-money, they spent it on kerchiefs, gewgaws, and even clothes and shoes. Each received the first of it on the morning after her marriage, when her relatives filed past her in farewell and dropped money into a plate for her.[5] Afterwards her father or brother might slip a coin or two in her hand when he visited her. In the tribal districts of the north her father also gave her on her marriage as much as half of the money which her husband had paid him for her. (p. 42)

The idea of 'paying for' is not altogether consistent with the return of a good part of this payment to the bride herself, and it is clear she was effectively endowed both indirectly by the groom and directly by her kin. Women had the *pekul*. Contrary to many theoretical assumptions, money appears to play a greater part in relations between kin and affines than among strangers. The transfer of money or jewellery provides the wife with a kind of bank, especially among the urban middle class, but those items received from the in-laws are more likely to be sold for support whereas those coming from the parents tend to be regarded as heirlooms.[6]

This money given to her father had often to be raised by the groom himself and in order to get the necessary cash he frequently had to become a wage labourer (p. 44). That the servant or hired-man was often a person trying to raise the marital prestations for himself in this way again suggests that the payment by the groom served a different kind of function than bridewealth in traditional Africa, where the income from the daughters makes it possible for sons to get married, as the exchanges tend to be self-financing.[7] In Albania the payment did not come from a fixed pool of circulating wealth. The family estate might get dispersed at each marriage when part is handed over to the bride. To prevent this sums were raised anew for each event and often by the groom himself. The more he accumulated, the larger (and richer) the choice he had. But as his contribution came back with the bride, his labour helped towards setting up their new quarters, even if it delayed his marriage. Since kinship reciprocities make it everywhere difficult to get paid at the going rate within the household, a man went to live in another house as a hired hand. As in pre-industrial England, the proportion of servants per household was high;[8] in Europe it was women who worked for their direct dowries rather than men for an indirect one, but of course the gains made by men also helped to establish the new households they set up at marriage, which nearly always involved providing separate accommodation.

The position of the hired-man is also interesting from the standpoint of the life of the household. For in Albania he took on a quasi-kinship status in his master's house; and the employer was responsible for avenging his death. Terminologically the master was referred to as 'father' and his children as 'siblings'; it was deemed 'incestuous' to seduce the daughter of the house, though that was a less heinous sin than sleeping with the wife. In the latter case the servant was killed immediately, but in the former he was sometimes allowed to go. Fornication did not incur the same punishment as adultery, neither for the man nor for the woman. The girl was married off to her existing fiancé as soon as possible; indeed if the fiancé had already handed over some of the marriage prestations, he would have killed her father had he been refused her hand and the marriage not been completed. But if the 'incestuous' relationship had produced a child, it would be sent to the father who, instead of acknowledging paternity, would abandon it to the elements, as in the case of the Roman *spurius*.[9]

While seduction was 'incestuous', marriage itself was not prohibited. To marry the boss' daughter was always possible, but to seduce her was not; it was a betrayal of trust. Such a marriage was particularly likely where the master was a Muslim and the servant a Christian who had agreed to change his 'lower' religion in return for a 'higher' wife. To convert the heathen in this manner was an act of piety on the master's behalf and a means of social mobility for the servant.[10]

A wife received an endowment at marriage. But she later added to this by making articles which she gave to her father or brother to sell, 'never to her husband or grown-up son, for they would not let her even see the money'. But in any transaction made on her own account she had to pay cash, 'for the law forbade her to pledge either her husband's or her father's credit' (p. 42). In this way she built up her own independent fund which complemented that managed by her and her husband. These sums she could let out at the usual rate of interest, which at 30 per cent was more than enough to compensate for the want of security; and in the less-developed north she could invest it in sheep, plough-oxen, or even houses, which she hired out on the 'half-and-half' system of *metayage* or share-cropping. Before she died, a woman gave some of her *pekul* to her daughters, most went to her sons and nothing to her husband. In other words we have an example of conjugal partnership with separate accounts in addition to a joint conjugal fund (p. 43). The difference resembles that between the operation of joint or separate bank accounts by married couples in western Europe, though there the matter is one of personal choice rather than institutional complementarity. The fact that the wife had her separate account in this hill area may be linked to the fact that she was entering into a 'joint family' situation at marriage. In China she merged her separate fund with her husband's when they 'separated' from his own family estate. On the other hand, in many parts of Europe personal property was widely distinguished from the fund itself.[11]

As in the other societies we have examined, a woman might also inherit the whole or part of the conjugal fund established at the marriage of her parents when she was 'the sole survivor in her family'. This practice was perhaps more important in Christian Europe where adoption and other mechanisms of continuity were effectively prohibited by the Church (Goody 1983). Inheritance of any kind occurred only within the undivided farming group. These co-resident domestic groups in the Albanian hills were larger than among Greek peasants to the south (Friedl 1962) being about the same size as the co-operating labour groups of the Sarakatsani shepherds which Campbell (1964) describes. Since farming in the hills was both pastoral and agricultural, one man could hardly carry out all the necessary tasks. Indeed he could not even tend the cows and oxen, ewes and lambs, which were pastured in the hills. So the most viable labour unit was larger than an elementary family, though here, as with other Mediterranean peasants, that constituted a basic unit with husband and wife co-operating together in the fields. Of course, in most societies husband and wife have complementary activities in the production sphere, but in this case the emphasis was on co-activity. Peters (1966:53) sees this joint activity as the important difference between Lebanese Arab farmers and the pastoral Bedouin, more important than differences in inheritance. However both participation and inheritance relate to the complex of property relations relevant to the mode of livelihood; pastoral societies are characterised by male dominance in the economic sphere of livestock herding.[12]

Another factor militating in favour of larger domestic and lineage groups was the absence of a strong government presence in the hills. The relevant law was the law of *talio*, so that the more guns the stronger the house. 'Separation', ran the proverb, 'ruins a family', not only for economic reasons but also for the ability to engage in self-help. While the break-up of dwelling groups was an almost inevitable aspect of the developmental process, it rarely happened before the father's death. If the unit did divide early, the father stayed on with the youngest son. Even first cousins sometimes lived together and in the earlier part of the century it is said that a single dwelling unit could consist of as many as sixty to ninety people, a veritable *zadruga*.[13] But under the more peaceful conditions of the 1930s, houses were smaller since it had been defence rather than farming that kept them large. After the father's death the brothers might divide the property equally, except that, as so often, the mountain pastures remained a common resource. The house itself might be split and a new entrance constructed on the opposite side to the existing one.[14] It was when a separate 'household' or apartment had no male heir that a woman inherited the parental fund: the larger 'houseful' was no longer an inheritance unit.[15]

Even in the Albanian hills we find a number of the general features encountered further east; the woman's endowment, her role as residual heir to the sibling group, the direct transmission of property. While Muslim Albanians were not monogamous, the extent of polygyny was very limited and betrothal was certainly binding; Christians on the other hand generally forbade the close marriages and the levirate permitted by Islam, as well as adoption which Muslims rarely practised.[16]

The Sarakatsani shepherds

Other communities in this region place more emphasis on the direct dowry pole, especially among the farmers, but I first consider a group of Greek shepherds, the Sarakatsani, an account of which is given by J. K. Cambell in his book, *Honour, Family and Patronage* (1964). The community he studied consisted of some 4,000 people. During the summer months they were found in Zagori, a district in the Pindus range of the province of Epirus; in the winter they moved down to the coastal plain where they led a more dispersed existence, living in houses scattered among the farmers.

The pattern of social groupings was simple. The most important unit was the family, 'whether in its elementary or its extended form' (1964:8). Once again, the economy brought into play wider groupings.

To this small group the individual owes almost exclusively his or her time, energy, and loyalties. However, the family group is normally unable to manage its flocks, without some assistance from outside and, in these circumstances, two, three, or more families related by kinship or marriage, associate to form 'a company' (*paréa*) or *stani* . . . , which for functional reasons must include at least four adult males and generally numbers between 15 and 50 persons of all ages. But the duties which the individual assumes as a member of the 'company' are specific and have an obvious relation to the welfare of his family. (p. 8)

While the company constituted a work group for certain purposes, the elementary family remained the unit of property control, which leads Campbell to speak of it as a 'corporate group' (p. 36), though he admits that it did not have the characteristic of perpetuity which Maine saw as essential. For Sarakatsani 'families' were limited to a life of some forty years, that is, the period which normally elapsed between a man's marriage and the division of the joint household by his married sons (pp. 36–7).

The family broke up soon after the marriages of the sons and daughters, since it was then that the property devolved upon the younger generation. In fact, this process was continuous since a woman received her dowry at the time of her marriage and took it to her husband's home. At the same time other obligations were transferred between the parties. Henceforth it was the husband, no longer the brother, who had to protect a woman's honour, a situation more reminiscent of Turkish than of Arabian communities where such responsibility continued to lie with her natal kin. The transfer of this particular responsibility may look like the incorporation of a wife into her husband's kingroup and has been so interpreted in the case of the Somali (Lewis 1962) as well as among the Kachin of Burma (Leach 1954). However a Sarakatsani woman could return to her father if she was widowed before giving birth to children; in this and other ways marriage certainly did not cut her off altogether from her natal kin. Indeed a son too went through a rather similar process after marriage, though it happened more slowly. For in a sense he too was cut off from his family of birth (or orientation) when he received his portion of the herd and became 'incorporated' in the newly created family of procreation (or marriage) constituted by himself and his wife. 'It is significant', writes Campbell, 'that after his marriage and even before the birth of his children he is unlikely to undertake a vengeance killing for a murdered brother or a dishonoured sister. Eventually, after five to ten years, but often sooner, he parts from the extended family and from all his remaining categorical rights and obligations as son and brother' (1964:54). Both for men and women marriage leads to a shrinking of obligations even between close kin.

However, among the Sarakatsani some co-operation between kin continued at a more inclusive level even when the property was constantly being divided between the sons and daughters. For with direct lineal inheritance, the group within which property is actually transmitted (as distinct from the maximal group within which property rights are seen as being held) must necessarily be small; concepts of the Village Community and the Joint Family need always to be considered in this light.[17] And when lineal inheritance is combined with the diverging transmission of property, the 'corporate group', in a property-holding sense, is no longer simply a group of brothers (even where there are patrilineal kin groups) but rather the conjugal pair of husband and wife, at least after the partition of the husband's 'joint family'. It is true that if land is kept out of the hands of women, the brothers can maintain solidary arrangements, but these are always threatened by the conjugal pair and the marital fund that female endowment creates on its behalf. The formation of such a cross-cutting unit is implicit in marriage outside the group, but among the Sarakatsani the handing over of the property, flocks rather than land, was delayed until all the sons had found wives; elsewhere the division takes place at or after the death of the father. But since the marriage age was late, twenty-eight to thirty-two for men and twenty-four to twenty-nine for girls, the father was already well advanced in years by the time he handed over control of the flocks (p. 83); the late age of marriage is clearly coincident with a policy of 'early retirement'.

There are no wider unilineal kin groups among the Sarakatsani and the bilateral kindred can never itself constitute a localised group, certainly not when marriage within is prohibited, which was the case both under the Eastern and the Western Church. Here 'the kindred . . . includes only those blood kinsmen of a man (or woman) who are formally recognized for social purposes' (p. 36). By this the author means 'all cognatic relatives as far as the degree of second cousin'; that is, all the descendants of a man's four grandparents and their siblings were his kin, excluding the children of his second cousins, the grandchildren of his first cousins, and the great-grandchildren of his siblings; these are the specific cut-off points, some form of which always has to exist in any system of bilateral kinship which would otherwise proliferate without end or boundary. Following the teachings of the Church the Sarakatsani defined this grouping as prohibiting marriage, but unlike the villagers of Catholic Europe, there was no way in which property could be retained within the kindred by means of close unions obtained under ecclesiastical dispensation.

These kinsmen gave support and help in many contexts of social life, when money was needed or more generally at times of crisis, and they were also 'indispensable in the delicate negotiations of "match-making". Before a girl is sought in marriage, very careful inquiries have to be made concerning her virtue, industry, health and temperament. A kinsman who lives near the girl's family will be in a position to give accurate details' (p. 39). It is because so much is involved in the marriage – work, fertility, property and honour, and because trust may be lacking, that such careful enquiries have to be made on behalf of the parents, and in this the marriage-broker plays an important part.

While the company or *stani* may well have a core of brothers, it also includes other kinsmen who live nearby and who are often linked by ties of foster-brotherhood. Though it is not a property-holding unit in itself, it is involved in co-operative production in a different way than the farming groups of many agricultural societies. I am thinking here of the groups that co-operate in the clearing of new land, in weeding and in farming for in-laws, under the extensive hoe farming systems of Africa. Plough farming demands different forms of co-operation, which will again depend upon the type of plough (whether it is the light Mediterranean plough or the heavy plough of northern Europe pulled by a team), as well as the nature of the land, climate, labour and other socio-economic factors. On the peasant farms of the circum-Mediterranean, the basic unit was a man and wife, who worked together in the fields. The work-group among the Sarakatsani takes its shape from the way in which the flocks are divided for herding purposes. Campbell observes that they are deeply concerned about three things; sheep, children (particularly sons) and honour. In winter and spring they 'divide their animals into four flocks. The most important of these divisions is the flock of pregnant ewes or, after lambing, the milking ewes . . . In the second flock are the rams, and the sterile ewes which were not successfully mated in the summer . . . The third division is a small stock of last season's ewe lambs . . . And finally there are the goats' (p. 19). The herds consist of the sheep of all the families in the *stani*, and they are split up in this way because natural pasture is not all of a piece, the best grass having to be reserved for the most productive and delicate beasts: the prosperity of the *stani* depends upon the crop of lambs and the amount of milk that is sold to the cheese merchant. To each of these categories of flock, an adult man has to be assigned, requiring a minimum of four adult men.[18]

The property of the Sarakatsani, which comprised mainly sheep and goats, descended both to sons and to daughters, though the flocks went mainly to men. This devolution occurred both at marriage and at death, influencing in important ways the choice of spouse. This choice was approached with considerable deliberation. 'Many personal qualities of a prospective bride are taken into consideration but invariably the crucial question to be debated is the quality and prestige of the girl's family and close kin' (p. 43). In this process of selection, great weight was given to the maintenance (or increase) of status, and if one spouse was lower than the other, he or she was said to destroy the 'vein' of the partner. In marriage the material wealth, like the immaterial prestige, was pooled from the resources of both partners.

The corporate property of a family is a common stock of animals, money and goods, from which sons and daughters must be endowed. Daughters receive their portion as dowry at the moment of marriage, but the married sons normally continue to live in an extended family group where family wealth is still held in common. In the eventual partition of this joint household and its property, which is delayed until all the daughters have been married, and generally occurs five to ten years after the marriage of the eldest sons, equal shares of stock and other assets are received by each son; but in the case of the youngest an extra half-share is provided for the maintenance of each surviving parent who by custom remains in the household of this son. (p. 44)

Here as elsewhere the 'responsible son' receives a larger share, giving rise in this case to preferential ultimogeniture. While the other sons are allocated more stock than the daughters, both sexes are seen as 'endowed' out of the common fund.

The amount of wealth devolved at marriage was considerable. At the time the value of a dowry was about £150 or the equivalent of fifty sheep (Campbell 1964:44). But since 1945 the practice had grown up of demanding from the bride's family about forty additional sheep or their equivalent in gold sovereigns. In addition the bride herself received gifts of valuables direct from the groom and his kinsfolk, which formed the 'indirect' part of her personal wealth; these marital prestations from the groom did not pass through her father but were placed directly in her own hands (pp. 302–3). The direct and indirect endowment of the bride are both part of the same system.

Campbell observes that 'it would be wrong to think of the dowry merely as a payment made by the bride's family to obtain a husband for her' (p. 44). While calculations of family prestige did enter into the amount paid, and while a girl with physical or moral deficiencies might have to produce a larger dowry, 'each side contributes one of its members and a certain amount of property' (p. 45). 'The implicit purpose of the dowry is to complement the wealth with which the new family is or will be endowed by the husband's family' (p. 45). The husband provides the flock, the wife provides the furnishings; the result is a conjugal fund, a joint enterprise.

So in this community of shepherds we find: (1) arranged marriages with dowry, direct and indirect, associated with strong concepts of honour and shame, and (2) small property-holding groups centring around the conjugal pair, expanding as children grow up, contracting again as they marry, but always as part of wider co-operating units. In addition a third feature associated with diverging devolution is present, namely, filiacentric unions. Where a man had no sons, he married his youngest girl to someone who was willing to live in the home of his father-in-law. The groom brought with him the share of his own family herd to which he was entitled, although 'the property of the wife's family of origin, which may be considerable, does not formally come under the control of the new family until the wife's father has retired from active work' (p. 45). But when he did so, the conjugal pair emerged as a new property-holding group.

It is true that, as in many other parts of the world where it is the woman that goes to live with her husband's family in virilocal marriage, the position of the new bride was a lowly one. The wedding ceremony brought out the consequences of physical separation from her parents, for the induction into her husband's family included the performance of acts of humility, learning the proper use of terms of respect and carrying out the hardest of the household chores. But this low initial position changed over time, partly because she eventually became a mother and a mother-in-law, but also because of the property with which she was endowed and with which, in the absence of brothers, she could draw a husband from his own natal group to reside in her own (Du Boulay 1986). Despite the agnatic and male-oriented ideology that permeated much of social life, diverging devolution created a substantial breach in the patrilineal system by comparison with Africa. Once again property talked, even in the hands of women.

Farmers in southern Greece

The two communities we have so far discussed were located in hill areas and placed a strong emphasis on pastoral activities. Both facts tend to emphasise patriliny or at least the role of males. In every continent pastoralism was closely (though not absolutely) associated with agnation and with the dominant part played by men in the economic and political spheres. At the same time the nature of the hill farming often brought it closer in some ways to the shifting agriculture of Africa than to the plough cultivation of the plains or river valleys characteristic of the major societies in the Eurasian continent. Under conditions that are peripheral to intensive agriculture we would expect diverging devolution to have a less pervading influence than in the lowland farming areas of Greece to which I now turn.

Writing about the Boeotian village of Vasilika in the 1950s, Friedl (1962) saw dowry as part of the system of inheritance whereby women as well as men shared in the estates of both their parents. Vasilika may not have been an altogether 'typical' plains village, even in the 1950s, for it was oriented more towards the town than most, both in the marriage of daughters and in the education of sons. It was a relatively recent settlement whose inhabitants came from a nearby mountain community and a quarter of whom were still shepherds. Both the urban orientation and its relatively recent establishment may have influenced the fact that provision of dowries which 'function as inheritance' (Friedl 1962:64) tends to follow the national legal framework regarding equal inheritance more strictly than may be the case elsewhere.[19]

Of great importance was the fact that in this part of Greece, in contrast to the northeast, their rights in this estate applied to land as well as to movables. Consequently while there was some continuity of ownership in the male line, the lands so inherited constituted only part of the holdings of any particular domestic group. No man owned or farmed exactly the same holdings as his father before him; indeed, because of the extent of marriage outside a village, he might well have to work lands in dfferent communities.

Since the rules of the Church and society forced people to 'marry out', they often had to marry outside the village. It was difficult for the newly married couple to exploit fields that were at some distance from one another, so they might exchange or sell those the wife had received as a dowry. But as a widow, she retained the dower right in the lands that were purchased with the proceeds of what she had originally brought in, and she lived on the benefits of these fields with one of her sons who at her death would receive an extra allocation of property as a recompense for looking after her old age.

If they quit the family farm, men as well as women were 'endowed'. For not all men wanted to stay on the land; some had been given a higher education in town schools and the cost of providing this training was deemed equal to a share of the patrimony. In the past there were distinct advantages to the village and its constituent households in having some of its 'sons' situated in the town, but since the Second World War changing socio-economic conditions have turned the trickle into a roaring torrent.

The dowry system had various corollaries that have been noted in other agricultural societies with diverging devolution. First, filiacentric marriages were made with heiresses. A marrying-in husband, known as *soghambros* (or inside groom), was someone who had married a brotherless daughter or a young widow with no grown sons; the latter arranged a second marriage for herself with a man who was willing to work the holdings of her first husband together with her own original dowry lands, a practice not dissimilar to that found in China.[20] As elsewhere the role of in-marrying spouse (and to a lesser extent, of remarrying widow) carried a measure of social stigma, since such a man was not thought of as 'master in his own house'. However such a marriage provided a way in which a poor man could better himself, so that even his 'inferior' status in marriage represented some improvement on his earlier position. Status mobility was not the only reason. A man may make such a marriage in order to move to a different village and in Corfu would bring with him the right to the land to which he is entitled as an endowment and which also is known as a 'dowry'.[21]

Girls too might 'rise' by means of the dowry. The larger the dowry, the better the husband; an extra endowment might compensate for the lack of other attractions. The inhabitants of Vasilika, 216 in all, generally had to marry outside since the prohibition on marriage up to a third cousin, together with the same ban on marriage with affines and spiritual kin (god-parents), put most of the village in a tabooed category. In recent years the farmers of Vasilika favoured marrying their daughters to husbands from the town rather than to those who had often come to be regarded as country bumpkins. The fact that some of their sons had left the land and that farming incomes had improved meant that they could offer larger dowries for their daughters than in earlier times. Between 1949 and 1959 the marriage of every girl whose father was in the upper half of the income range was with a man of respectable occupation who lived either in a provincial town or in Athens itself (p. 65). In the course of this process dowries had increased rapidly in size, from $3,000 dollars for an ordinary town husband in 1950, to $4,500 for a spouse of the same type ten years later.

As a consequence the dowry was no longer limited to an equal share of the inheritance; sons were even willing to give up part of their property in order that their sister might 'live well', a situation from which they might benefit in other ways, helping them to get a more valuable wife or providing them with useful contacts in the towns. A further consequence of the rise in dowry was the increasingly late age of marriage for village girls, especially for the upwardly mobile. 'It takes farmers longer to accumulate the larger amounts of cash for the dowry, and the prospective groom longer to attain a position of income at least partially commensurate' (p. 66). Girls who married in the towns were between twenty-five and thirty years, but those from poorer families marrying in the country were in their early twenties. Moreover town husbands were increasingly reluctant to take land as part of the dowry, since it had to be left in the hands of the wife's kin. They preferred either cash or a town house. So some Vasilika fathers, anticipating their daughters' requirements, had started to build such a house for them when they were quite young and gradually completed it over the years.

All this accumulation and preparation entailed further delay which was not altogether displeasing to the parents.

Besides the property costs of the dowry, a father loses the labor of his daughter both on the farm and in the household. If he has no farming son who can bring in a wife, or has only a young son who will not be ready to marry for several years, and a single daughter, this cost may be considered great enough to delay the marriage of the girl. If a man has one daughter left at home and a wife who is ill, this may again delay the girl's marriage, for the cost of losing her services is too great. Finally, there is a psychic cost to the parents, particularly to a mother, at the marriage of a daughter. She loses the companionship of a friend, confidante and working partner. Since, among the more prosperous farmers, girls marry increasingly late, i.e. between twenty-five and thirty, mothers have many years of continuing cooperation in the house and fields with grown daughters and the wrench at parting is seriously felt. They commonly speak longingly of how much they miss their absent daughters. (p. 122)

Such delays tend to increase the dependence of the filial upon the parental generation; a 'boy' remains a 'boy' (as in Ireland), a girl a girl, for a substantial period of their adulthood, a situation more reminiscent of the western European marriage pattern (Hajnal 1965) than of the eastern type often characterised by early marriage.

In her discussion of attitudes to the dowry system, Friedl points out that while men found the raising of daughters full of tribulations and expense, they did not see their sons bringing any comparable gain. This comment provides some indication of the difference with the role of bridewealth in African societies where the receipts from marriage transactions roughly balance the outgoings; here on the other hand parents pay out both to sons and to daughters as part of the process of early devolution; the more offspring they have, the smaller the shares. While there is some 'gain' from incoming spouses, what a woman gets remains hers in the end, not her husband's or her father-in-law's, only her children's; it provides her with security and support and guards against the dangers of a shiftless spouse. It is an aspect of intergenerational transfer rather than exchange in the strict sense of the word.

The provision of the dowry by men is a responsibility whereby they acquire honour. Peristiany and Campbell have both stressed that Greek men gain honour through protecting the chastity of women, to which Friedl adds the payment of dowry as an alternative source of male pride. Both these sources of self-congratulation interlock since the control of chastity is especially important when marriage is delayed as it is considered essential in finding a suitable husband. A girl lacking in 'virtue' requires a larger dowry, although some couples manage to elope to the mountains and establish a home without one. While it would be a mistake to impose any exclusive interpretation on so widespread a feature of human societies (Pitt-Rivers, forthcoming), honour in the circum-Mediterranean region 'can be thought of as the ideology of a property holding group which struggles to define, enlarge, and protect its patrimony' (P. Schneider 1969; J. Schneider 1971:2).

The endowment of women in time and space

These three studies of communities in Albania and Greece give some idea of the distribution of practices under different forms of socio-economic life. Direct endowment, which included land and even a house, prevailed in the south, indirect dowry in the north, especially among pastoralists. A consideration of other more recent ethnographies, for example, those of Handman (1983) and Couroucli (1985b) on Thessaly and Corfu respectively would have widened the spectrum of family and economy. While island maritime communities in the Aegean place even more emphasis on the transmission of houses through women by means of the dowry, in the olive-growing areas of Corfu the notion of an agnatic group is given much greater importance. But in all these cases some form of endowment, direct or indirect, is provided for daughters, varying in different places and at different times but all belonging to a similar repertoire of social acts. The continuity of this repertoire over time is obvious from a comparison with the earlier chapter on ancient Greece and has been stressed by several authors (Friedl 1959, 1963; Lambiri-Dimaki 1983:158). A recent volume of essays (Piault 1985) brings out a number of other aspects of this historical continuity. But this is not so much a continuity of specific practices in specific places as a continuity of the means available for organising the arrangements of socio-economic systems that are marked by diverging devolution and the associated mechanisms of management and continuity. Not of course that everything has continued just as it was. Regions that were already differentiated in earlier times were later subjected to different pressures. Some economic, political and religious factors have influenced the whole area. Developments in Christianity put out of court certain practices of the Classical period, close marriage and close adoption; the Turkish occupation introduced further constraints and important economic changes have affected the whole of the rural economy over time. Nevertheless the system of marital assigns and inheritance continued to operate in a broadly similar fashion from the early period to the recent past, partly because inheritance practices were embodied in ecclesiastical codes of law but also because the general system of marriage transactions was not simply a function of a particular culture (it extended too widely for that), but of a type of domestic organisation and economy which has, in some areas, continued down to the present.

In this final section I want to consider some of the points brought out in these village studies in the context of more general, more historically oriented discussions of women and property, dowry and inheritance in Greece in order to provide a preliminary pulling together of ideas prior to summing up the main themes of this enquiry.

The variability and flexibility of shares

If dowry is seen as part of a set of exchanges between families, then it tends to be visualised as passed to the groom or his family as some kind of gift or bribe accompanying the bride. Influenced by analyses of the role of exchange in the simpler societies based on the work of Malinowski and Mauss, some authors write in this way of Greece. But they are brought face to face with the fact that, legally at least, the dowry is passed from parents to daughter in whose ulimate possession it remains, whatever degree of control the husband may exercise during his lifetime. In contemporary Greek law, the position is contradictory. While dowry movables are said to be the property of the husband, they are returned to the wife in the case of divorce. But cash is clearly more manipulable than land; tales of husbands who abandoned their wives with the dowry money in their pockets are legendary among the poorer strata of rural immigrants to the big cities. In any case a man who asks for cash rather than fields in the village is thought to be planning to establish himself as a professional or as a store-keeper.[22]

The allocation of *les apports nuptiaux* (marital assigns) depends on the kind of marriage that is made, for the amount of the direct dowry is in general linked to the status and expectations of the groom and his family (or alternatively to the lack of status and attractiveness of the bride) as well as to the desire of the bride's family to marry her well and ensure that she maintains her style of life. So the amount transferred is not necessarily a fixed share but often a variable portion, the size of which may impoverish the estate in the interests of getting the daughter 'properly' married (Loizos 1975:82). Directly the notion of a variable portion takes root (and given the difficulties of equal division the practice is perhaps always implicitly present), the family of the bride becomes open to pressures to increase the endowment, especially that part consisting of consumer goods, furniture or accommodation used by the entire household, that is, the common consumer items, as distinct from productive or potentially productive property and from the bride's trousseau or personal apparel.

So to speak about the endowment of daughters is not to assume they get a share equal to that of sons; in most cases it is clearly not the case. Where women's shares are notionally fixed, either as dowry (direct or indirect) or as inheritance, these are usually smaller than those of their brothers who among farmers are more likely to have the responsibility of looking after aged parents as well as the family estate. But social pressures on marital assigns may alter the balance in favour of women, laying more emphasis on what she brings into the union rather than what she receives from her husband's kin. Moreover, the increasing number of male labour migrants in towns means that more responsibility falls on women, for the estate as well as for parents, leading to higher percentages of filiacentric unions.[23]

In theory the fixed (though often unequal) share would mean less competition between siblings and between families; that is to say, such competition would be less likely to take a monetary form, rather to depend on the selection (usually parental) of the bride or groom in which some will do better than others. For even where there is a notionally fixed share, it usually pertains to inheritance rather than marital assigns. Potential pressure exists on individual families to raise the endowment during the negotiations; if, as we see from some cases in present-day India and even earlier in Sung China (Ebrey forthcoming), pressure may continue even after marriage, open conflict may arise, especially where the rapid growth of expectations accompanies the increased demand for and, availability of consumer goods. But what is required for a daughter's marriage may also vary with the attractiveness of the bride and the qualifications of the husband as well as with these general consumer pressures and market conditions. Especially where land is included, a woman's eventual share may be equal to, and, in some cases, even greater than that of the man's, leading as we have seen to claims about the impoverishment of the family holding (Loizos 1975a:510). Such claims are sometimes overstated, being made by men in their capacities as brothers. However for every man who has provided an apartment for his sister (or for his daughter), there is another who has benefitted as a husband (or as a son). The objection can only be to ownership, not to enjoyment or control. The distribution of property through the endowment of women has important consequences for particular family estates and the accumulation of such wealth in the form of houses may affect the wider economy by limiting the funds available for more productive activity; but it does not directly lead to any overall difference in levels of riches or poverty, since one man's loss is another man's gain, or rather a gain for the conjugal pair. And even if a woman is entitled to a portion of the family estate, she may not always assert her claim; rights over land may be relinquished on leaving the village, necessarily of course where those rights are 'common', for example, use rights to pasture livestock rather than rights capable of being broken down on an individual basis.

The fact that marital assigns are not necessarily a fixed proportion or an equal part of the total heritage has led some authors to reject the idea that they represent a pre-mortem devolution. The difficulty appears both in the analytic view and in the actor's perception (Hughes 1978). But the notion of a daughter's portion does not depend upon the question of equality between siblings nor yet upon an entitlement to a certain proportion of the whole. In any case equality is always difficult to arrange, especially where advances are made and then have to be reckoned, generally or specifically, against how interest and opportunity have affected the earlier payments, against the profit or loss that has accumulated to the estate. Moreover the idea of marriage as a 'match' may lead to pressures that result in an overall increase in the allotment to one person or sex as compared to another. However the absence of fixity or equality does not prevent the transfer also being regarded as an endowment out of family funds and hence, along with inheritance, as an aspect of 'devolution' between the generations.

The self-accumulated dowry

Dowry may be provided directly by the parents, indirectly by the spouse's family, and in some limiting cases by the spouse themselves. In a general way the provision of an endowment among groups where family labour is important may well be linked to the contribution children have made to the estate; the later they leave, the more they contribute, the greater their entitlement. In Africa responsibility for the payment of bridewealth is often linked to labour contributions (Goody 1962); in recent times, those who go off to work outside the realm of domestic production often have to contribute the bulk themselves, unless they have paid all their earnings into the family coffers, a highly unlikely contingency. A similar transformation took place in Europe, leading to a disappearance of dowry in the traditional sense. But at an earlier stage women (and to some extent men) were sometimes viewed as helping to accumulate their own endowment. Even then, there seems to be a greater tendency for women to regard such wealth as their own *peculium* rather than as conjugal or family property. The immediacy of the relationship between their labour and its product altered their views of its nature; it was no longer considered a parental endowment but a personal acquisition.

Clearly the last possibility depends upon the ability to accumulate property outside the family by working temporarily on another farm as a domestic servant or hired hand in some rural industry such as silk-production in nineteenth-century China (Stockard 1988), or in town either as a servant or in some manufacturing or trading enterprise. All these opportunities are available at much earlier periods than is often imagined; all are attested in Europe in the sixteenth century and elsewhere in Eurasia well before that. Such 'life-cycle workers' may also have been target workers in the sense that they were working mainly to make their own contribution to the new household they would establish at or after marriage (Hajnal 1965:133). Whether or not this process is viewed as working for a dowry, as is the case among some Greeks in Cyprus (Roussou 1985:293), Australia (Bottomley 1985:315) and in Greece itself (Lambiri-Dimaki 1983:172), or simply as an individual contribution to the new home, as elsewhere in western Europe, depends largely upon whether the property acquired is seen as an intrinsic or an optional part of entering into marriage. The marriage based primarily on the personal encounter (love) stresses the latter, the arranged marriage the former; that is to say, the more the family is implicated, the greater the emphasis on an institutionalised provision. Obviously it will at first tend to be in the 'poorer' families where that provision takes the form of a self-acquired dowry, as is often the case with the promise of a future dower by the husband. Such families may be poorer because of the number of daughters, the early death of the parent or even the difference in comparative status rather than in estate alone, so that we might expect to find one or more members having to work for a dowry for themselves or for another of their number. But what was once a lower practice of those who had to sell their labour to acquire capital became generalised upwards with the growth of wage labour under a changing system of production. In 1965 a study carried out in Athens concluded that the great majority of single girls who had emigrated to Germany, Belgium and other northern countries did so to increase their earnings and build up a dowry, although some of them also claimed to want to live in a society where their marriage prospects no longer depended on what property they brought into the union (Lambiri-Dimaki 1983:172), an attitude which Sant Cassia sees as part of a 'vocabulary of justification'.

Self-accumulation tends to delay the marriage of women. Or to put it another way, the later marriage of women may be related to the independent accumulation of wealth by various forms of wage employment, hence to their greater independence as well as to the greater prosperity of the estates of their parents, who now need their accumulated funds to support themselves when their children have left. But that is a more recent scenario and it was more likely in the past that self-provision was made necessary by the paucity of family resources, because of relative poverty or because of the increase in the goods needed to set up a consumption or production unit, rather than because families no longer control those resources in the same way when the total domestic economy has shifted to wage labour. Poverty has existed throughout the history of the types of economy we are examining and the failure to raise a dowry has sometimes been met by local bequests that provide money for the dowry of poor girls (Kalafati-Papagalani 1985:227), a practice with a long-standing and widespread distribution in ancient Greece (Mossé 1985:191), in China and elsewhere. But the possibility of self-provision is clearly a potential stimulus to economic activity, or alternatively it may be stimulated by existing opportunities for wage labour. While some opportunities of the kind have existed in most societies with settled agriculture, their great extension came predominantly with the development of larger-scale manufacture and industrial production, although in some areas the growth of services and urbanisation has had similar effects. This in turn had an explosive effect upon attitudes not only to wage-labour, which eventually lost some of its more servile connotations, but also attitudes within the domestic group, now largely a unit of consumption rather than of production. Greater independence for the individual resulting from external employment opportunities means earlier independence from parents; since the latter could no longer rely on their children's support, which came more or less automatically when they had worked in the same domestic enterprise, they could no longer afford to disperse the family estate by early endowments. Forced to supply their own 'pension', they tend to shift to inheritance rather than endowment as a means of transferring property between the generations.[24] This pension is all the more necessary because of their greater longevity, and the transfer is perhaps less necessary for the children if their marriages are later. In any case the children are more likely to have received an educational endowment to help set themselves up independently. In effect, endowment is earlier, inheritance later. This greater longevity is a marked feature of the contemporary as distinct from the earlier period. In the years 1820 to the 1850s in Episkepsi, Corfu, three out of four men had no living father at the time of their marriage, so that there was a low possibility of 'grand families' of the three generation type; on the average men inherited from their fathers at roughly the same time that women brought in their dowries, that is, about the age of marriage. Today children generally inherit around the time their own offspring are ready to marry, or even later.[25]

Age of marriage

The later age of marriage, however associated with self-accumulation, is at first likely to increase worries over the virginity of women and lead to the possible rise in illegitimacy. It is also related to the later division of the family estate, for even if the dowry is limited to the allocation of movables, its provision may result in indebtedness or the sale of property. On the other hand, for the men in agricultural production land is bound to be involved; if there is more than one son, marriage may also lead to a division of the estate, or to the endowment of the departing brother. While such a division may be 'earlier' in Europe and 'later' where married brothers continue to work together, fission is eventually likely to occur and the actual span of joint activity across the generations will depend upon the age of marriage and may vary little as between joint and nuclear households.

Interest in the labour of daughters, a desire to prevent the splitting of the estate and the intention to retain control of one's property rather than entering into an early retirement encourages a delay in marriage (Just

1985:179). Delayed marriage means longer generations (that is, the average span of ages between parents/fathers and eldest children/sons) and hence less likelihood of the senior generation having to retire before death. Equally the existence of 'extended' families, that is, of three or more generations, is critically dependent upon the marriage age; the greater the generation span the less the possibility of (lineally) extended families as against (laterally) expanded ones; the earlier the marriage age the greater the likelihood. Delays in marriage were pleasing to the parents in Vasilika as in Germany (Sabean forthcoming), just as they were in the Pearl River Delta of China when times were good (Stockard 1988); indeed in the first case delays were partly brought about by the rise in the value of the dowry and perhaps the shift to its direct form, which requires more parental investment. I do not see any necessary relation, only evidence of the two horns of the dilemma: to keep a daughter at home for reasons of emotional, economic or practical support; or to get her married off so the sons can then marry.

The content of dowry

The dowry in Cyprus, in some Aegean islands, and now in the urban centres generally consists of a house situated near that of the bride's parents, together with some land, while for urban marriages, especially during the last few decades which have seen so strong a movement to the town, there is the 'apartment-dot'. Unlike those parts of Europe where movement to towns meant selling out or being forced off one's land, in Greece in recent times one could retain one's rights, or at least exchange them for a dwelling in the city, a fact that has had a significant effect on the changing structure of the economy.

To own a piece of land and then build one's house or apartment upon it is an overriding goal for almost all urban residents of Athens or Salonika ... To be an owner of property was, in village life, the *sine qua non* of full status in the community. It seems clear that this feeling, transferred to towns, has sufficed to distort the pattern of Greek economic development ever since the Athenian building boom began in the early 1950s. (McNeil 1978:223)[26]

Although no cadastral survey has been carried out, the dowry is nonetheless usually set down by the notary as part of a written contract which becomes of greater importance when the transaction includes house and land (Saulnier-Thiercelin 1985:47–8). Clearly a heavy payment of this kind is a great burden on those families where daughters exceed sons, or indeed those with a number of children of both sexes, even where the new house in the country (unlike the apartment in town) can be constructed with the help of reciprocating labour. Such families may well fall into debt (Roussou

1985:291,295) in the attempt to provide the newly married couple with their own house, but nevertheless the loss to one family or generation is always a gain to the next. In some areas such a burden has long been accepted but elsewhere it has resulted from the escalation of the women's share due partly to recent changes in consumerism and male-dominated education, but there is also a more general pressure arising from competition and comparison on a local basis ('we cannot do worse for her than the Jones'). Once started such inflation is difficult to stop except by external fiat (the 'sumptuary' legislation of Church or State) or by the participants themselves contributing to their own dowries, a process that if it becomes sufficiently generalised with wage labour leads to the eventual disappearance of these assigns, though functionally they continue as 'voluntary contributions' to building up the home, when they are no longer seen as an aspect of devolution but reflect an overall shift in employment and the disappearance of the domestic group as a unit of production.

Internal differences

In Greece the transfers made at marriage in the recent past have varied considerably. Couroucli (1987:329) defines four broad types of rural family structure, that of the pastoralists with extended families, where brides could receive a trousseau at marriage, that of the continental farmers with nuclear families, where women may receive land as well as a trousseau, the island farmers with agnatic lineages but neolocal residence, where women received only their trousseau and small parcels of land of little importance, and the seafolk of the Aegean, where residence was uxorilocal and the houses were passed down from mother to daughter. But it was also the case in Attica, the Peloponnese as well as the Aegean Islands, that the bride received from her parents a house, fields and a trousseau according to their means. In the North it was either money (golden coins) or furniture, although in some parts it was the groom who had to provide an indirect dowry (referred to as *le prix (achat) de la fiancée*), while among some shepherds nothing at all was expected.[27] In practice there appear to have been three sorts of 'indirect dowry' coming from the side of the groom. The first is the promise of a future dower; the second is usually given to the wife at the marriage itself and belongs to her from that moment. A third seems to provide greater justification for the word 'prix' since it went to the bride's father. It seems clear that in the nineteenth century the northern emphasis on a gift from the groom to the bride's father, the *agirliki*, follows Turkish practice, as the word itself indicates (*agirlik*, 'for the weight of the bride'). But it was a gift to enable him to provide the *çeviz*, from the Arabic *jahāz*, the trousseau or in a larger sense the equipment (Couroucli 1987:333–5).[28] It is also characteristic of the agro-pastoralists of the north, whereas in Epirus south of Macedonia and Thrace, we find the other kind of indirect dowry, the *progamiaia doréa*, the antenuptial gift which goes directly to the bride (Couroucli 1987:355). But the difference is perhaps not so marked as might appear since it is not clear whether in the first case the father passed the gift to the bride, used it to purchase her trousseau, regarded it as compensation for what he had already given her, or kept it as a potential dower. For these types of prestation co-existed in the same local as well as cultural repertoire and were not alternatives, even at one point in time and space. In any case in more recent times all those differences have tended to disappear in favour of the direct dowry embodied in the Civil Code of 1946 (Handman 1985:237–8), at least in the increasingly dominant urban situation.

Such differences have been linked to economic practices; in the north of Greece mixed agriculture was dominant and the aim of a household was to preserve the land or herds in the hands of the group of brothers. Other areas were dominated by the dynamic trading communities situated around the Aegean Sea, where women were often the transmitters of land and especially of houses. For unclear reasons this North–South difference seems to repeat itself in Italy as in India. In India and the Mediterranean, indirect dowry tends to receive more emphasis in the North and a direct dowry, sometimes including land, in the South.[29] In many of these regions and over a long period the North has had more connection with the pastoralists and the land routes, and the South with the sea. The North has often been poorer, the South richer – but there are too many exceptions to suggest anything but trends.

The central difference is first the matter of the relative stress placed on indirect or direct dowry, and secondly of whether or not land is included in the goods devolved to women. Its exclusion means that in an agricultural society the basic means of production are kept in the hands of related males who, with virilocal marriage, form the basis of a local group, for example, in a lineage or descent line. In the case of pastoral societies, it is the herds and the pasture that tend to be reserved for men (though livestock are more readily divisible), agricultural land being less central. In some mountainous areas of Crete, farming land could be devolved on women who are nevertheless excluded from rights of pasturage and the ownership of herds (Saulnier-Thiercelin 1985:55). Indeed since herding rights to territory are normally held communally rather than severally (which constitues one of the important differences in social organisation between livestock and farming), one is more likely to find lineages in pastoral societies (or pastoral subgroups), even where devolution is diverging since they guarantee access to pasturage. In any case the passage of a few beasts to women does not affect the estate in the same radical way as the passage of a portion of the land; the reason has to do with the difference between movables and immovables, as well as between livestock that increases and land that does not (though the crop does). Even with land it is possible partially to isolate 'lineage' holdings by transmitting to the daughters in dowry the land brought into the conjugal union by their mother, as reported for Corfu (Couroucli 1985a) and other Ionian Islands – for example the island of Leucade (Kalafati-Papagalani 1985:225), where women were entitled to a dowry even if they remained unmarried. But the variability of the form and composition of sibling groups must always make such a procedure hazardous as a deliberate policy, especially in those considerable number of cases where there are no male heirs. For the epiclerate then inherits all the parental property from both father and mother. Note that lineal daughters always have preference over male collaterals.[30] As far as devolution is concerned, lineage or kindred links come into play only in the absence of daughters, and even then wider links can easily be set aside by making a testament, often in favour of a religious establishment (Beaucamp 1985:202).

Bilaterality, land and the rights of women

One of the problems of analysis is the frequent use of the terms bilateral (or bilineal or even matrilineal) for a division among sons and daughters, and patrilineal for a division among the sons alone. But a man's daughters are equally his patrilineal descendants, even though by definition they cannot pass on that 'descent' to their children. Hence the retention of property over time within patrilineal groups implies its transmission to males and through males, that is, homoparentally. If there are no sons, then other males have to be drafted in if the estate is to remain intact. That is not what happens in Anoya or in most of Greece. If there are no sons, a daughter inherits. This practice is, I have argued, an index of qualified bilateral transmission or, if we include the life-time transfer of rights (the dowry at marriage as well as the inheritance at death), of diverging devolution.

What is basic to the maintenance of a 'corporate', physically united group of male agnates (whether part of a patrilineal descent group or not) is the retention of rights over land, not only because land constitutes the basic means of production in an agricultural society but also because common residence involves some control over territory, over rights of settlement. Hence problems arise if land is included in the dowry in order to maintain the status of daughters. The alternative is to allocate them movables alone, but even such a content-restricted transfer of a direct dowry constitutes a demand on the estate, unless it is limited to the mother's property (held distinct), to self-accumulated goods or unless brides are provided with an indirect dowry by the groom, the loss to whose parental estate is initially compensated by the fact that the bride usually brings along most or all of what he has supplied; it is only 'lost' in the case of the dissolution of the marriage, although it effectively changes hands, at least in generational terms.

Two problems are posed relating to bilateral organisation generally and to the nature of the estate. Where landed property is devolved to women there is likely to be less stress on unilineal ties. The diverging devolution of land militates against the formation of lineages or *lignages* and encourages the bilateral reckoning of kinship ties. We have to be careful of applying the notion of a general shift from lineal to bilateral which is sometimes linked to that from indirect to direct dowry. In Crete 'bilaterality' was anciently established in the east of the island as well as in the towns (Saulnier-Thiercelin 1985:57); elsewhere in the west it is more recent, associated with national law, and families still try to 'exclude the daughters from the family patrimony'. That statement turns out to mean that 'the daughter's part' was always smaller, even though it sometimes included agricultural land; shares but not equal shares are said to be more 'patrilineal', although more 'male favouring' would be a better description. The bilaterality of the east is undoubtedly linked to this access of women to landed property as earlier emerged in our discussion of studies of the Tamil and Singalese population of Sri Lanka by Tambiah (1973), Yalman (1967) and Leach (1961), and as is brought out by Saulnier–Thiercelin (1985:53) herself. A bilateral tendency operates throughout the Mediterranean. While vestiges of lineage and clan remain in the older islands of Sardinia, Corsica and in parts of the Balkans, 'kinship is decidedly bilateral, and the nuclear family is the most significant political as well as economic structure' (J. Schneider 1971:8). The author is referring mainly to pastoralists, but among cultivators too the autonomy of the nuclear family is an important feature (p. 12), as is the prevailing absence of lineage structures in the core areas. But it is when women become carriers of land that 'bilaterality' is most marked.

Women's control

The allocation of land to women may define their status but does not automatically ensure their continuing control over that property. One perpetual problem of dowry, arising out of virilocal marriage and sexual differences in domination, is the extent of managerial control exercised by the husband or his family. The question was openly discussed in the Byzantine Empire in the eleventh century. According to the collection of practical judgements known as *Peira*, since the sixth century sons and daughters had been entitled to share if no will had been made. In the absence of either children of the marriage or of a testament, the property reverted to the respective kindreds, the so-called 'lineages', of the husband and the wife. That property was of two kinds, matrimonial, consisting of the dowry (*proix*) brought by the wife and the marriage donation promised by the husband as a dower. Together these formed 'une sorte de patrimoine commun du couple', consisting largely of the wife's contribution but managed by the husband. Both of these elements functioned as advances on the inheritance (Beaucamp 1985:200); neither were essential to marriage and each had to be 'returned' if the partner wished to participate as an heir in the family estate.

But the inheritance a woman or man later received was considered as 'falling outside the dowry' and was totally controlled by the recipient who theoretically could not even make a gift of any part to the other spouse. Unlike the 'joint fund' which went to the surviving spouse in the absence of children (and even then the surviving spouse was entitled to a child's portion), the separate properties reverted directly to the natal kindreds.

In other words one way of ensuring a daughter's control of parental wealth was by the later transmission of property, which secured its effective retention in the hands of her natal kin in the case of childlessness. A recurrent question centres upon the daughter's share, whether it should be limited to what she is given at marriage, or whether she should have the additional right to inherit, possibly by returning her dowry to the pool. The notion of the 'dowry as share', the total share, obtained under the Ionian Code of 1841 (Kalafati–Papagalani 1985:215), but the alternative was practised in Patras on the mainland where a wife continued to be entitled to her *legitima*, her prescribed share of the estate (Sotiropoulos and Dimitropoulou 1985:254). While the second procedure also emphasises the 'bilateral' element, it retains the direct interest of a daughter in her parental estate and at the same time delays its eventual partition.

The timing of the transfer

Obviously the timing of the transmission is not permanently fixed over the long term. In Rome the notion that dowry constituted the whole of a woman's lot seems to have given way, at least at the level of the written word, to one in which she shared both in the dowry and then in inheritance, as was the case under the later Byzantine law based on Justinian's Code. Such dual entitlement is also characteristic of the optative devolution found in the sixteenth-century costumals from the Paris region of France (Yver 1966) whereby those men or women who had received an early endowment at marriage or, like Dick Whittington, on quitting the family house to make their fortune elsewhere, could later 'return' what they had taken to the pool if they wished to share in the inheritance. Contemporaneously in southern

France there existed the system of *preciput* whereby one son or daughter received the whole of the farm or enterprise at marriage in return for supporting the parents and compensating the siblings; here the distribution was definitive, made once and for all.

In some cases these different procedures are contingent but in others they have crystallised (possibly with the help of a code or costumal) into institutionalised alternatives, each with its own wider implications. The definitive distribution seems more appropriate with a stem household and with early retirement, and hence with an early handing over, while the optative one goes with the continuing interest of the sibling group in the estate and in the parents, together with the later handing over of responsibility for both.

Responsibility in Greece normally rested with the older generation until they died, although retirement remained a possibility providing there were contractual safeguards (Kalafati-Papagalani 1985:219), the kind of safeguards embodied in many such systems. Clearly the timing of the transfer may be affected by a variety of factors, the desire to allow a daughter to make a proper marriage, the desire to encourage a son to stay on the farm rather than to migrate elsewhere, or the desire to escape inheritance taxes with the onset of old age (Goody 1987b), all of which lead to earlier transmission. Equally the fear of 'ingratitude', the departure of children to town or elsewhere, later marriage, all these delay the process of handing over.

Some of these factors are related to the productive system (Goody 1962:327), others to politico-legal constraints, some to religious practices, but yet others depend upon individual personalities or intra-familial relationships (Saulnier-Thiercelin 1985:55–6), all of which affect not only the timing but the nature of division. For instance, in contemporary Crete we find a system not dissimilar to that of pre-Revolutionary China, where land is partitioned among the heirs, each type of land being divided separately and the choice made by lot. If there were many sons the resulting shares would be small, so that those who left the village might well give up their claims in favour of those who stayed behind, not only in the case of sons who had taken up occupations other than agriculture but also of those who had moved in with their wife's family in a filiacentric union. If the division happened during the active lifetime of the father, he kept back some land and livestock as 'the old man's part' which was shared equally among the heirs at his death.[31] Until that happened the parents lived with their youngest son who took over the house and the headship.

The timing of the handing over was obviously affected by the age of marriage of the younger of the spouses. Since this was normally the wife and since the differential age was often considerable, widows without children might retain control of property for long periods, and even those with children would do so during their minority. The question of the transfer of authority and control between widow and children was necessarily a delicate matter, depending very much on personal relations as well as on legal provisions. But in a working farm or similar enterprise, decision-making and management effectively shift to those most actively engaged. Among those classes where the estate consists of monetary income derived from others, such as rents and investments, transmission can be more gradual, and a proportion can be distributed without loss of control.

Division or impartibility

An apparent difference with China is that the heirs include daughters who are entitled to an equal share, including land. In western Crete, this equalisation is the result of recent legislation which has also changed the situation in China in the same direction. But according to J. Schneider (1971:16), the relative equality in devolution between siblings of both sexes extends throughout most parts of Mediterranean Europe. When the property consists of animals, division presents few problems, but with land the matter is much more complicated, leading to difficulties between fathers and children. As we have seen, even within the island of Crete considerable regional variation existed. 'Bilaterality' was said to be an ancient practice in the east and in the towns, while the west was 'patrilineal'. The terms are misleading. What is meant seems to be that at the beginning of the century sons received double the portion of daughters, at times more, although women might inherit some agricultural land. In the east, however, equality prevailed. Recent legislation had tended to emphasise equality of inheritance between sons and daughters, omitting any consideration of earlier endowments. But the more general notion of equality was already present in other parts of the continent. One rare type of sexual equality occurs in combination not with equal shares but with primogeniture, and is found in the Pyreneean region of France and Spain. While in most places primogeniture, *le droit d'ainesse*, usually privileges the male, especially where it is linked to sucession to office or military duties, here it is the oldest child irrespective of sex who receives the house and who brings in his or her spouse. Since girls marry on the average two years earlier than boys, the co-residence of couples and the handing over of the farm, either in anticipation or in actuality, took place earlier than where male primogeniture obtained and much earlier than where ultimogeniture was practised (Burguière 1986:646).

The notion of impartibility (Fr. *indivision*) found in the Pyrenees is often associated with the stem-family (*famille souche*) or with the three-generational extended family that Le Play called *la famille patricale*, that Burguière calls *la famille communautaire* and yet others the grand family. As we have seen, in this context 'family' is an ambiguous usage and it is preferable to refer to complex domestic groups, especially to housefuls/households (of which the kin-based variety is by far the most widespread) since it is households on which the bulk of the data exists. How ambiguous the term can be is illustrated by the fact that the members of many so-called 'joint undivided families' in India reside in simple households ('nuclear families') and their activities are 'joint' (undivided) largely in respect of property interests. While dispersed 'undivided' families ('houses') of this kind were not characteristic of western Europe, sons who left for other occupations or other places often retained claims on the parental estate; those who remained, married and occupied adjacent dwellings, might continue to share equipment or services, although frequently subject to an explicit or implicit process of internal accounting. In general where partition occurred, it took place automatically at death as the result of written wills and testaments which aimed to settle all.

The notion of 'impartibility' is not always as straightforward as it might appear, since individual claims may be implicit in the allocation either to one sibling alone or to the siblings (or brothers) jointly. The ambiguous nature of the concept is illustrated in an account of the frequently quoted case of the complex household of Guittard–Pinon visited by Legrand d'Aussy in 1788.

Jamais, dans aucun cas, ils [les biens] ne sont partagés . . . une Guittard sort-elle de Pinon, pour se marier, on lui donne 6,000 lires en argent; mais elle renonce à tout . . . Il en serait de même pour les garçons, si quelqu'un d'eux allait s'établir ailleurs. (quoted in Burguière 1986:645)

'Les biens' are visualised as the immovable portion of the estate; however the total capital (fixed plus working) is of course divisible because an endowment is given both to daughters and to sons when they leave, the first to establish themselves in marriage, the second in work. But such an allocation is made as a quit-claim on the understanding that their entitlement ceases at that moment. While the allocation to daughters could theoretically come from the 'dowry' of incoming wives, the demographic lottery always makes for difficulties in balancing income and outgoings. Moreover departing males have no bridal counterparts. In any case it is clear that 'impartibility' applies to immovables alone and that those who leave are entitled to a 'share' of the total estate.

In talking of an estate, I do not intend to confine attention to the property of large landowners but refer to that body of interests attached to an individual, a conjugal pair or a group, the control of which has to be devolved between the generations, ultimately because of death. Nor do I wish to imply that any absolute value is necessarily placed on holding together the particular set of assets which have been accumulated by the senior generation, although there will always be an emotional attachment to what they possessed and often some practical benefit in keeping it together. The allocation of land to all departing children, its sale for reasons of indebtedness or to make an alternative investment, these outgoings have their counterparts, not of course leading to balance in every particular instance, in the acquisition of land through incoming spouses and its purchase when circumstances permit. While such transactions do not allow an individual estate consisting of specified goods to be transferred indefinitely over the generations, they are not inconsistent with the notion of a family fund or estate, continuing but changing, which provides for the daily needs of its members or, in other circumstances, out of which the children are educated and then set up to work, whether or not they marry. Such an institution is fundamentally weakened only when the state (or an alternative body such as the Mormon Church) takes over the education and the establishment in work of each and every member of that society. Even then the take-over is rarely complete. In the first place the most paternalistic of welfare states and the most communitarian of religious groups may find it advantageous or even necessary to encourage the saving, investment and extra work which the possibility of family accumulation can provide, not for ideological reasons but in order to benefit the wider economy.[32]

The rights of the widow

At the time of division of the estate, one important consideration is always the protection of the position of the widow where she has contributed her endowment or with indirect dowry is entitled to the benefits of 'dower' acquired in the marriage arrangements. Characteristically the surviving spouse is entitled to be provided for out of the conjugal estate which in the absence of adult sons she may well control. Characteristically she loses such benefits if she remarries, except for that portion she has herself brought as dowry (Kalafati-Papagalani 1985:220), although her position varied in different parts of the country. The 'custom' of 1830 of Sfakia in Crete ran: 'When the husband dies and leaves a widow, she will have the use of his fortune, as long as she wishes to dwell in his house' (Saulnier-Thiercelin 1985:62), an arrangement that existed in other parts as well.

A widow's rights can be protected in one of several ways. When her parental endowment is incorporated in a joint conjugal fund, she may be entitled to draw upon that fund for maintenance and support. Or her dowry or inheritance may be retained, conceptually at least, in a separate account for her to use more independently. Or in the course of the marriage arrangements the husband may, in combination or not with such endowments, set aside or mortgage his own property as a future dower. Even where a woman goes into marriage with nothing, her husband's 'fortune' may nevertheless come under her control during the minority of her sons, that is, unless she remarries or moves elsewhere. From one point of view such a woman is worse off in not bringing an endowment of her own. But she could enjoy that endowment only by some dispersal of the estate of her natal family. In individual cases she may choose the path of denial, but in societies where she has no direct claim upon kin after marriage, the benefits her husband can confer are correspondingly greater and divorce seems less frequent, partly corresponding to the loss of independent control over her claims on property.

Changes in the dowry

The transmission of property at marriage, the endowment of men and women at this moment in time, has to be seen as part of the overall process of devolution. But it is a process that is under constant pressure from the fact that the amounts involved depend upon a series of negotiations surrounding the departing members. For women, the critical point is the wedding; the size of her 'share' becomes subject to the status-raising ambitions of the bride's family (that is, to considerations of hypergamy), to the demands of the groom and his kin, and to the desires of both parties to conclude an arrangement, all three considerations tending to lead to inflationary tendencies. It is partly because of these internal pressures that there is continual tendency for dowries to rise. For such inflation of the 'trousseau' is not confined to India or China alone, being reported from contemporary Cyprus, Greece and Australia. Whereas in Crete handsewn cloth used to be a main component, now it is furniture, including a gas cooker, refrigerator, television set and so on. But this phenomenon is not entirely new, for the same process happened in earlier times. Rising dowries are reported from Epiros as well as in Athens in the seventeenth century. As a result attempts were made by the Orthodox Church to control their size, but not altogether successfully, for even under Byzantium in the eleventh century some daughters may have received larger portions than their brothers because of similar pressures (Beaucamp 1985:204). Throughout the Aegean, in Cyprus and in parts of southern Greece, a daughter came to acquire a house and lands as part of her dowry, not to mention the occasional addition of a monetary payment referred to as 'dust in the eye' (Shapiro 1985:303), a phrase that carries the notion of deception.

Part of this perception of the increasing pressure on dowries has to do with a 'golden age' view of the past (Maropoulou 1985:110), although perhaps more with the dominance of urban life and of town culture, which encourage the spread of elite norms in line with changing class relations; part has to do with the general process of inflation over time and part again with the increasing circulation of consumer goods, all three more or less permanent features of human society. But the demand for consumer goods is, in the last analysis, associated with the rise of the mercantile classes, with manufacture in mass and this eventually with a change in the mode of production, whereby the bulk of the population live by wage labour and no longer exercise direct rights over the productive resources. In recent changes in the system of rural dowries in Greece, negotiation was a powerful factor; there was a shift from land to cash, to negotiable wealth that could be used to acquire houses in the town, partly because of the enormous pressure of urban migration in the post-war period, although contact with the cities has always been of value to better-off farmers involved in the market and in transactions with specialists. Since it was women who received property at marriage, while the men had to wait until the death of their fathers, it was the bride's dowry that often served to establish the young couple in the non-agricultural sector. Hence there was pressure from both husband and wife to increase this component (the direct dowry), partly because migrants had to set up in the town, partly because of the general rise in consumer demands. As a consequence, contemporary Greece is experiencing an inflation of dowries which now form the main means of passing down wealth between the generations. Since women retain ultimate title to this property, although husbands have certain rights of use and control, a greater proportion of worldly goods falls under their ownership and tends to be transmitted between females, from mothers to daughters (Allen 1979:150).

The increase in direct dowries also represents a shift in the timing of inheritance, the stress being placed on pre-mortem transmission in order to maintain (or augment) the status of daughters at marriage, but often as a result of pressures from the younger generation. In some cases this leads to the 'semi-impoverishment' of the parents and Allen vividly describes the retirement of aged parents to 'mere hovels' (p. 149), a situation that is yet more marked in rural Cyprus where the aged may be living in tiny mudbrick houses surrounded by the lavish reinforced concrete mansions of their sons and daughters, who by increasing their command over consumer goods achieved higher status on the backs of their parents. But these little houses are described by Loizos as 'purpose-built' (1975:64) and would seem to bear a strong structural resemblance to the accommodation for old people provided in other parts of Europe, the West Room of Ireland, the *Alternteil* of Germany, as well as the 'small house' of Tibet, found in the Aegean Islands in the form of the *gerontiko*, 'the old people's place' where the parents go when the daughter is given the mother's house at marriage. Early transmission of this kind, which tends to give rise to the *Lear* situation, is part of the general repertoire of systems of devolution. For not all the cards rest in the hands of the senior generation; various pressures over the centuries have led to the emergence, and no doubt the disappearance, of early trans-mission. And as for the accumulation of property in the hands of women, Aristotle was already complaining of that some two millennia before. When this property takes the form of houses, apartments or even land, place of residence is increasingly determined by women (uxorilocally) rather than men (virilocally).

It is interesting to note that legal formulations may have in fact promoted the inflationary trends. I have spoken several times of the problems involved in embodying custom or practice in law. But the effect of legal enactments is more radical than the notion of incorporation implies, even when the written formulations are clearly mistaken. One example of the influence of legal drafting is provided by the Greek Civil Code of 1946, which defined dowry as 'the property which the wife . . . gives to the husband in order to alleviate the burdens of marriage' (Lambiri-Dimaki 1983:166). However the husband did not possess the power to alienate this property which had to be returned to the wife in the case of divorce, so that, as Lambiri-Dimaki remarks, 'it is only too obvious that the dowry is not a gift to the husband' (p. 167). But once on the books such formulations acquire a kind of 'normative' force of their own since they may be the basis of judicial decisions backed by the power of the state.

The effects of judicial statements which are out of tune with local practice may be limited by a variety of tactics. The deliberate rejection of the written contract in Crete under Ottoman rule was to avoid having the disputes or dispositions of Christians brought under Muslim law (Saulnier-Thiercelin 1985:49), although such a way out was more difficult in urban and agricul-tural areas where more use was made of notaries public than in the moun-tainous, pastoral ones. It was the adoption of such methods of getting round the charges introduced into written law by various regimes that meant the dowry system maintained a roughly similar character throughout the mini-mum of twenty-four centuries it existed, although finally urbanisation and other contemporary changes seem slowly to be reducing the significance of marital assigns. The dowry was part of what a daughter was legally entitled to 'inherit' from her parents. But the (mistaken) legal formulation of 1946 has a life of its own, and perhaps its notion that the dowry was given to the husband may have coloured the perceptions of some actors and hence stimulated demand.

The inflationary endowment of urban women is related to the movement to towns under conditions that differ materially from the type of expropri-ation that frequently drove western European peasants off the land, as well as to the factory situations they found there. But the shift to wage labour has something of the same effect, in making self-accumulation not only possible but even essential for some, and hence loosening part of the bond of dependency and support that characterised social life in earlier times. None of these features were totally new, but the change in scale is beginning to transform social life.

The reported changes observed in Greece take two apparently contradictory forms, first, the inflationary pressures on the endowment of women at marriage, and secondly, the partial shift of emphasis from endowments tied to marriage to endowments for education; in the latter case the husband and his family are not directly involved, personal endowments tend to replace joint funds at marriage (although not those that are subsequently constituted by the proceeds of the marriage itself) and the obligatory nature of inter-generational transfers, at least those between the living, undergoes a modification in favour of voluntary gifts.

Changes in the productive system are linked to the increased importance of a woman's non-domestic occupation and ultimately to the decreased importance of transfers at marriage. When women are differentiated less by property than by training, the parental investment goes into education. If a woman has to accumulate a dowry herself by entry into employment, she becomes less dependent not only on the senior generation but on formal marriage itself. To acquire such urban employment women increasingly need education, beginning with basic literacy skills.[33] That is true of both sons and daughters who married into town or went to work there. Those who had received an education, whether sons or daughters, had this expenditure counted against their share. In this way Greece is increasingly following the path of the 'technologically advanced societies' where 'a woman's "dowry" is her education and her work' (Lambiri-Dimaki 1983:179). From the standpoint of the parents the pre-mortem devolution of property to children for the purpose of establishing themselves in a job, in a house, or in both, is still the critical factor. But since the transfer is no longer tied to marriage, it no longer serves to promote that institution in the same manner nor does it directly govern the choice of spouse; children's prospects are affected by the unequal distribution of wealth in less obvious ways. People are freer to remain single, to divorce, or to establish other types of partnership with members of the same or different sex. Of course, such independence does not come primarily from the modification of the dowry but from the same cluster of causal factors, namely, the gradual decline of the 'domestic mode of production' and indeed of any continuing family enterprise, except in a few areas. The widespread decline of the dowry first occurred among the nineteenth-century working class in northern and western Europe, then among the bourgeoisie and rural farmers. But among these latter groups there are always property relations to regulate. Educational transfers are made well before marriage which becomes more a personal and potentially less-permanent arrangement, and the wedding is less relevant as a point in the major transfer of property. However, even well-educated couples still expect help to set up on their own, and the more a girl can bring, the better the husband she is likely to get. Apart from money for education and possibly for house purchase, such transfers are more likely to be delayed until death (Kalafati–Papagalani 1985:219) or often the approach of death since all early transfers, including dowry itself, may have an aspect of tax avoidance if, as is often the case even in simple states, death becomes the major occasion for collecting revenue on wealth on the grounds that individual need is no longer present and family control is at its weakest. On the island of Patras resort was occasionally made to the 'simulated sale' from senior to junior generation (Sotiropoulos and Dimitropoulou 1985:255) as a means of early transfer. Such transfers amount to a kind of early retirement and are accompanied by contracts that specify precisely the oil, flour and other products needed by the older couple. The growing tendency to enter into such 'sales' appears to represent a further shift of the transfer away from the wedding itself. Sometimes it is when the birth of children is thought to provide a firmer basis for a union that a major transfer takes place, intended for the purchase of a house or for other purposes. Such transfers are increasingly viewed as voluntary 'help', as in the Ionian island of Meganisi (Just 1985:177), while the notion of the dowry, of a more or less obligatory transfer at marriage, is disappearing under the pressure of salaried labour which individualises the income of household members at an earlier point in their career. Later transfers too are no longer essential to the family's income, since its capital no longer takes the form of a working estate but of a house (or its tenancy), a job, a personal holding plus a stake in a pension fund (state or private). Under such circumstances the problem of the protection of the woman's endowment (Bottomley 1985:148) takes on quite a different aspect since its transfer is no longer part of the marriage transaction but bears a greater resemblance to what, in the context of eleventh-century Byzantine law, Beaucamp calls *les non spécifiques biens* of the husband and wife. Since these fell outside the scope of the marital assigns (*les apports nuptiaux*), each individual exercised greater control, for example in respect of their testamentary freedom which was limited only by the birth of children. In their absence, and in the absence of a will, the property returned to the natal kin of the respective partners (1985:200–2) and not to the surviving spouse, although this is not part of current developments.

Byzantine law demonstrates the long-established existence of transfers ('goods outside the dowry' or side by side with the dowry) that were not directly tied to the marriage. In some rural communities such as the mountain village of Anoya in Crete where the term dowry (*proix*) has come to signify a money payment, even those transfers made to a daughter as part of her entitlement, which may include land as a marriage gift (*cadeau de noce*), are viewed as 'help' for the new household rather than as 'dowry' (Saulnier-Thiercelin 1985:58). The question of terminology is not simply a matter of distinguishing between kinds of property (money from land) but of the nature of the transfer itself, which now takes on the character of a 'free gift' rather than a semi-obligatory payment. The difference is of course a matter of degree, both in terms of the timing and the recipient of the transfer, of when it takes place and to whom it goes (whether this is the daughter, the couple or possibly the groom's family). But that degree is important both from the actor's and from the observer's standpoint since it bears on questions of hypergamy, of control and of the position of a married woman. In Anoya marital property may come from both sides in varying amounts, depending upon their resources; and unlike other parts of Greece, no allusion is ever made to the amount of dowry at the time the marriage is agreed (p. 59).

The changing situation under rapid urbanisation, the large-scale disappearance of the family farm (rented or 'owned') that England underwent in the eighteenth century, has only been experienced in the eastern Mediterranean in the last few decades. Even today these countries still retain some aspects of a domestic system that dominated not only Europe but also Asia over the last two-thousand years, the global implications of which I shall discuss in the last chapter.

16

Asia and Europe

Let me try to recapitulate the main themes that have been discussed in the context of the issues raised at the outset. In the last chapters on the eastern Mediterranean I aimed to link aspects of the processes of production and reproduction in Europe with those of Asia. Following a course from East to West, I have looked at the major societies of Asia, that is, China, India, the Near East, attempted to draw out some general aspects of devolution and marriage, then tried to connect these patterns not only with the earlier Europe of the Classical world but also with more recent studies of part of the same area, that is, of Greece and Albania. I deliberately came to Europe from the direction if not necessarily the perspective of the East in order to try to avoid some of the assumptions about the Uniqueness of the West that have dominated both the popular and the academic approach to family, kinship and marriage. Despite the changes that Christianity and Islam brought about there are significant continuities in some of these practices, not only across Eurasia but also between the ancient and modern world. Indeed religious practices and beliefs are in an interesting way part of that broad continuity.

Women as property

I began this enquiry by discussing the position of women in relation to property in the major societies of West and South Asia, leading on to the ancient and modern Near East. My aim was to review the claim that women in major or normal marriages were bought or exchanged between families against a brideprice and so incorporated in the lineage or family of the groom. Associated with this notion was that of the supposed shift in historical or proto-historical times from brideprice or wife purchase to dowry, a developmental sequence based on nineteenth-century schema which should have long been modified if not discarded. From China to Rome, we have run into evidence of how this same idea has influenced the analysis of kinship

465

systems. Especially for the early Mediterranean, the sparse material has been ransacked by countless scholars to provide traces of this supposed change in the nature of marital assigns. Even when these transactions went in both directions contemporaneously, as in Homeric Greece, one set was often interpreted as a survival from the past, the other as a presage for the future.

With regard to the ancient world of the Mediterranean this notion has been largely set aside by more recent studies most of which have been undertaken since I first began this enquiry some twenty years ago. But although discussions concerning purchase and price should by now have been modified, they continue to crop up in discussions of ancient Egypt (e.g. Forgeau 1986:139), of classical Greece (Schaps 1979:93) and of Rome, not to mention China; of China in the pre-Revolutionary past, Levy wrote that a bride 'ceased to be a member of her biological father's family. She became a member of her husband's family' (1949:102); ownership changed. And similar notions have been promoted by certain trends in the writings of classical economists, of palaeo-Marxists and even of one branch of women's studies. The counter claim is not that the purchase of rights in men or women does not take place but that 'major marriage' is not best understood in this light.

The difficulty is three-fold. First, there is the use of the term 'price' with its connotations of purchase. That such a notion persists is shown in a valuable account of Weber's ideas about the family where the author claims that in horticultural societies the possession of many women is 'merely a form of wealth; in these societies women are most likely to be acquired by paying a brideprice', to which a note is added saying that this is 'sometimes euphemistically referred to a [sic] bridewealth, a term that obscures the nature of the transaction' (Collins 1986:292). It may well be true that the term 'price' is appropriate for some relationships between males and females not in one but in all societies, but we should not take the exceptional for the norm and overlook the critical distinction in English between wealth and price. Price can only be defined in terms of exchange, normally some form of market; that is not at all the case with wealth, which may be without actual or potential exchange value, an accumulation of valued items which may be 'priceless' because they fall outside the realm of the normal spheres of market activity. On the other hand price is associated with the notion of a complete and absolute transfer of ownership, an idea which in any case is more representative of our ideological rather than our actual present, much less our historical past.

Secondly, ideas of the complete incorporation of a woman in the family or lineage of her husband at marriage overlook the continuing relations that she and her children have with her natal kin.

Thirdly there is the failure to distinguish African 'bridewealth' from what has been called 'brideprice' in Eurasia but which usually represents an indirect endowment of the bride, even though there are instances where part of the transfer may be retained by the bride's father. Finally, a further problem lies not so much with the crude form of purchase theory, but with the more refined and subtle form of exchange theory whereby women are seen as passed 'like pawns' or 'objects' between groups of men. The legal systems of the societies themselves may embody such notions of handing over. So too may patterns of speech, for until recently in Europe itself, characterised over a long period as it was by bilaterality, dowry, the conjugal family, choice of partner, a father nevertheless 'gave away' his daughter in marriage. Why this notion should be counted as evidence of a survival of an earlier state of affairs in Classical Greece (Schaps 1979:74) and not in western Europe is far from obvious, except from the understandable standpoint that everything earlier is nearer the 'primitive' origin of things and the less understandable view that we alone were different from everybody else, at least in the historical past.

The notion of the sale of women for marriage in these early societies (seen as abandoned in capitalist ones, for marriage but not for sex) goes against the idea, propagated by K. Polanyi and others, that earlier societies were dominated by reciprocity and gift. Indeed it is partly for the latter reason that anthropologists such as Radcliffe-Brown and Evans-Pritchard adopted the usage 'bridewealth' for the prevalent form of marital transaction in Black Africa. But we need to be more specific. There are no grounds for dismissing the possibility of commercial transactions in simple agricultural societies; that supposition stems from an attempt to create over-precise boundaries to socio-cultural systems, to over-compartmentalise human behaviour. Equally well, the existence of commercial transactions does not mean that everything is always subject to sale, even in monetised capitalist societies. The vast majority of societies practice transactions of both kinds, but the 'sale' of women into domestic slavery in more than a metaphoric sense nowhere characterises the dominant forms of human marriage.

This misunderstanding is not simply a technical question of the nature of marriage or of endowment. It relates to the way we see certain central socio-economic processes in Asian and earlier European societies, especially those connected with farm and family, with the continuity and management of resources by the basic unit of production, the farm family. And that again with our understanding of the nature of these economies, the domestic as well as the political. For those misunderstandings entail drawing too sharp a distinction between ourselves (either as members of industrial societies or of European ones) and others, leading to a primitivisation of the Orient. *Their* marriage has to do with sale, the absence of affection, with immobility, extended families, and so on. Whereas we were not only different after the development of industrial capitalism at the end of the eighteenth century but were so beforehand. We had the seeds of further growth already dormant in our fertile soil, they had to await their implantation from elsewhere. And according to some, it was precisely this uniqueness of the West at the level of the family which encouraged or made possible the development of capitalism.

The units carrying out these marital transactions were usually seen as clans, lineages or other forms of wider kin group. So this approach meant that a continuing emphasis was given to such unilineal collectivities in the organisation of society, by so-called descent and alliance theorists among others, at the expense of the domestic groups, in the broadest sense, that form the nerve centre of most productive and reproductive activity. 'Clans' were seen as part of the distant past of western and the present of eastern societies and hence a feature that preceded the rise of the nuclear family or household. The view is similar to that which considered these societies as dominated by extensive ties of kinship to the virtual exclusion of the elementary family, ties that were manifested in more complex households which disappeared with the advent of modern society. A related analytic interest has focused attention on forms of cross-cousin marriage at the expense of other aspects of marriage, a transfer of the 'elementary forms' of Australia to the hugely complex societies of Asia. These efforts have all leant in one direction, emphasising the strangeness of that society, the need for 'anthropological' models to interpret its practices, in other words towards the 'primitivisation' of that society and in some cases of the European and Near Eastern past.

Women and property

How do these considerations affect the position of women? In the first place the extensive economic differentiation in Eurasia means that women were never equal to one another, any more than men. They are not simply 'exchanged' for their sexual and reproductive services against fixed quantities of goods. Nor indeed were they exchanged against *variable* quantities. They enter into marriage bringing (or, in the case of indirect dowry, attracting) variable quantities in order that they and their children may be sustained at the level that befits or improves their position in their families of birth and marriage. Regarding the position of women in marriage, I argue that in the major Eurasian societies daughters are endowed either directly by their parents or indirectly by their husbands, often by both, and sometimes in the poorest families by neither. But in any case women were differentiated economically both as wives and as daughters because they came from economically differentiated families who tried to preserve or increase the status of their children and themselves by means of marriage. What is often called 'brideprice' and seen as evidence of primitive forms of the 'exchange' of women, that is, their sale or transfer to their husband's lineage, is very much part of a form of marriage which characterised Europe until recently, and still does in many places. True, in some situations fathers may retain some of the marital assigns; in others the bride may lose control of the endowment while the marriage endures. But the two critical points to look at are what happens to the property when a woman has no sons but only daughters, and again what happens to the dowry (or dower) when the marriage is dissolved by divorce or death.

In most of the major Eurasian societies, the absence of sons gives rise to filiacentric unions, whereby a daughter can attract a husband to come and live with her and her parents and so continue the ability to work and transmit the farm to their children. That is but one of the mechanisms of continuity. The attempt to isolate a series of mechanisms of heirship, of management and even of expansion at the domestic level has had the aim of demonstrating the similarities and variations that exist across the Eurasian land mass. We can look upon these as strategies of continuity, immediate and long term; the first are strategies of recruitment of personnel, but to the family as a whole rather than for wage labour alone; the latter are strategies of heirship. What is the object of the continuity? There is plainly a personal element here; even among the polyandrous Tibetan Nyinba of Nepal, each brother wants to be accredited with a son; so too in the Jewish levirate. But in their absence daughters can substitute for sons and in any case if they survive to marriageable age they have to marry fittingly; the family's status depends upon them both. But it depends principally (though never entirely) upon the estate which provides support, so that continuity is a matter of securing the personnel to exploit and maintain the property as well as the offspring to inherit rights in it. What we are talking about is a type of domestic group, a family, referred to as a 'house' or JUF, which is not necessarily a household nor yet a houseful since individual members may be working abroad, but a group of variable size having claims on a particular estate by virtue of ties of filiation, of marriage and of their variants such as adoption and concubinage. Unlike a household or a houseful which may include lodgers, servants or slaves, this group consists of kin who have rights in the property derived from birth or from sex (or again from their substitutes). And at the heart of the group of kin lie one or more conjugal families, elementary, polygynous or polyandrous, within whose bounds the transmission of property tends to take place, through daughters in the absence of sons, and partly even in their presence, a fact that constantly influences its decision-making despite the dominant authority role of men

Table 13. *The geographical distribution of mechanisms of heirship*

	China North	China South	Tibet	India North	India South	Ancient Egypt	Ancient Israel	Arab	Ancient Greece	Ancient Rome	East Med.
Filiacentric unions	Y−	Y+	Y		Y	Y	Y	Y(rare)	Y	Y	Y
Close kin marriage allowed		Y(cc)	N/Y(cc)	N	Y(cc)	Y(sibs)	Y(½-sibs →pc)	Y(pc)	Y(½-sibs →pc)	Y(rare)	N
Plural marriage	N(rare)	Y	Y	Y→N	N	N	Y→N	Y	N	N	N
Concubinage	Y	Y	Y		N	Y	Y→N	Y	Y	Y	N
Levirate (widow remarriage)		$\frac{N}{Y}$	Y	Y	$\frac{N}{Y}$	Y(rare)	Y	Y	Y	Y(rare)	N
Adoption	Y+	$\frac{N}{Y}$	Y(rare)	Y	$\frac{N}{Y}$	Y	N	N	Y	N→Y	N
Divorce	Y−	$\frac{N}{Y}$	Y		Y	Y	Y	Y	Y		N

→ change over time
$\frac{X}{Z}$ higher groups / lower groups
Y yes

cc cross-cousin marriage
pc patrilateral parallel cousin marriage
N no

within but especially outside the *oikos*. For while the position of the wife may be ambiguous, that of the daughter is not.

Associated with the diverging devolution of property to women as well as men are a series of mechanisms of continuity by which conjugal pairs and the wider 'houses' attempt to perpetuate the relation between personnel, who are kin or fictive kin, and resources, which are fixed or movable. In each of the societies we have examined, a series of such mechanisms has emerged which are characteristic of the type of political economy dominant in the major Eurasian societies, in broad contrast to Africa. These mechanisms are differently distributed between and within the various societies, and have changed over time in response to various outside pressures and internal contradictions. The overall spatial distribution I have summarised in table 13, which also provides a general indication of the way Europe 'diverged' under Christianity. But before discussing what that distinction implies, a general point needs to be made.

I have earlier spoken of these features as 'strategies of heirship' and so under many conditions they are, but even in the present context, adoption, polygyny, marrying-in sons-in-law (filiacentric unions) are not concerned with inheritance alone, nor only with the provision of a successor who can propitiate the ancestors, two features that are often seen as interconnected. For there are other, wider aspects of all these institutions. A man with an elder daughter and a much younger son may have to arrange for her future husband to reside with the family in order to get the labour needed to make viable the farm or the herd; Pehrson's account of the Lapps (1957) brings out very clearly this aspect of continuity or management which is tied to the particular birth order and ages of a group of siblings. But such practices attract other motives and other outcomes. Some men marry more than one woman or take a concubine even when their wife is fertile. In Japan adoption was used much more frequently than demography would demand. Even in societies where the fate of the children or the personal satisfaction of a barren wife were not the major concerns (as they often are in the contemporary West), adoptions take place for a variety of reasons.

Despite those other uses a major factor in the distribution of these practices remains recruitment for continuity, the employment of strategies that include the provision of heirs. For example, the Confucian prohibition on non-agnatic adoption (and the consequent favouring of the agnatic variety, the brother's child or at least the clansman's) is said to have 'originated in the ancient Chinese cult of ancestor worship. In practice, in both China and Japan, it concerned almost exclusively the adoption of a male heir by families whose line was otherwise threatened' (McMullen 1975:137).

If adoption had wider implications, other purposes, that was even more true of features like close marriage, polygyny and divorce. Nevertheless I

Table 14. *Trends in the hierarchy of family variables*

	Higher	Lower
Marriage transactions	more or all direct dowry C,I,A,R	more indirect dowry
The position of women	more restraint C,T,I,A,G	more 'freedom' (more concubinage)
Divorce	less or none C,T,I,eR	more
Widow remarriage	less or none C,I,R	more
Adoption	more C,I,R	less
Giving away or selling members	less C,T,I(N),G	more
Plural unions	more C,T,A	less
Size of domestic groups	more complex (later division) C,T,I,E,A	simpler (earlier division)
Lineages	more complex C,I,R	less complex, more bilateral (Sri Lanka, Japan)
Written norms	closer C,I	more distant

Legend:
A   Arab communities   C   China   eR   early Rome
G   Ancient Greece   I   India
R   Ancient Rome   E   Ancient Egypt
N   North   T   Tibet

have included them in table 13 because their absence closes a possible door
to continuity. Taking a second wife or, in a monogamous society, divorcing
one and marrying another, both render possible the acquisition of offspring
to provide personal, parental, and perhaps social continuity.

Broadly speaking, status endogamy prevails; even where hypergamy is
practised, there is a balancing of attributes. But whereas in the East (C,T,I),
you have to marry outside the patrilineal clan (and in North India outside the
range of bilateral kin), in the West (E,Is,A,G,R) marriage occurs within the
agnatic unit. That is, the clans are not exogamous units whereas in the East
they are. Or to put it another way, in the West patrilateral parallel cousin
marriage is possible (with the father's brother's daughter), whereas in the
East close marriage is with the cross-cousins who are by definition outside
the descent group. But marriage in the West takes even closer forms,
'incestuous' by our standards, namely the brother–sister unions not only of
Egypt but of ancient Israel, ancient Greece and ancient Mesopotamia,

where their incidence should make us question the universal applicability of most biological and sociological theories on the subject.

Other features display general trends in the distribution between upper and lower groups, which I have attempted to summarise in table 14. For upper groups plural marriage is permitted on any significant scale only in the Near East (A,I) and Tibet, although secondary unions such as concubinage exist throughout; but as far as both the levirate and other forms of remarriage are concerned, lower groups often practice what is forbidden to the high. Interestingly, where plural marriage (including the levirate) is practised, adoption tends to be prohibited; elsewhere the latter is favoured by upper groups, and in India and Rome there seems to be some evidence of a shift over time from levirate to adoption. In general the acquisition of children marks higher status than the acquisition of wives, giving rise to fewer problems of the type of the second bed. It is in some of the areas where plural marriage is permitted that divorce is frequent (T, A), although it is also found with monogamous marriage. Like the inheritance of widows it is found in the lower strata even when forbidden by the upper. We also find that direct dowry is given more emphasis in upper groups (C,I,A,R,), while upper women tend to be under more restraint than lower ones; 'freedom' is an attribute of the 'low' (C,T,I,A,G). In some cases the restraint, which characterises the religious as well as the secular life, includes an outright ban on or resistance to the break up of a marriage by divorce (C,I,eR), and even the remarriage of the widow; that of men is rarely restricted, although in Rome and Egypt (Forgeau 1986:157) widowers in higher groups might prefer to take a concubine rather than a wife in order to limit the complexities entailed even in successive marriages of a major kind. Where the remarriage of widows is prohibited, it follows that the levirate obviously is, since it is a form of the same institution, but like divorce the prohibition falls upon upper rather than lower groups in China, India, and early Rome. In all these respects, the practices of upper groups tend to be closer to written norms than those of lower ones (C,I), whether those norms are formulated by Church or by State. Exceptions exist, for conquering aristocracies may see themselves as free to disregard the rules of their predecessors or of the country at large, and with the ecclesia established as a distinct organisation in its own right, there are frequently differences between the religious and the secular, between the Church and the State, over the interpretation of the injunctions of both. Nevertheless the leaders in both the religious and political spheres qualify for upper status and often find themselves acting in ways that contrast with the customary practices of the lower orders. But the difference is not simply a matter of deviance from upper norms. As I have argued in the case of Europe (Goody 1983), the norms of lower groups are more appropriate to their socio-economic situation as well as reflecting their looser attachment to the written word, to 'orthodox' religion and to political power.

There is a general trend in favour of monogamy and against plural marriages (C,I,E,Is,G,R,M); Arab societies are the exception, but the rates are low in comparison with Africa, particularly among lower groups. Men and especially women widely expected to make not more than one full marriage, a parsimony that was related to the nature of property relations arising from the direct endowment of women and the establishment of some variety of conjugal fund. The ideology of one flesh takes various forms which include a high value placed on the *univirae*, the fidelity, especially of women, that lasts beyond the grave and finds its fulfilment in the funeral pyre. But such notions of the uniqueness of the marriage bond are qualified by the ability of men to remarry or to take a concubine. Concubinage as an addition to marriage is found more frequently among upper groups (C), as is the case with plural marriage where that is allowed (A,T); but as an alternative to full marriage, concubinage tends to be practised among lower groups (G,T). That is to say, lower groups are less likely to go through the elaborate and often property-oriented ceremonies that dominate the lives of upper families, being prepared to face the consequences of 'illegitimacy' (I,R) which matters less for them in the absence of transferable property because they tend to avoid a resort to the courts for family affairs, through lack of money to meet the costs or through a fear that they will be handed down judgements from the establishment. But they may also be more attracted to unions of the *usus* rather than the *manus* type, since those are easier to enter, easier to dissolve, possibly easier to reduplicate.

Higher marriages tend more frequently to be arranged by parents rather than to be left to the choice of the partners (R), once again because more is involved; marriage tends to be earlier (I,G,R), although in India the age at marriage for women displays a 'U'-shaped curve since the *harijan* also marry very young. In China marriage is earlier for males in the upper groups, but it tends to be later for females. While the incidence of the very early *sim-pua* marriages of Taiwan does not seem to be greatly influenced by socio-economic status, Fei argued that the difficult economic conditions in the Yangtze valley in the 1930s produced a situation of 'crisis-fostering' (E. Goody 1973) which affected the poor more than the rich. Lower groups tried to get rid of female, and sometimes male, children in order to reduce the burden of bringing them up, the kind of situation that in famines in West Africa was met by a form of 'domestic' slavery. In China one aspect of early marriage or fostering was its role as a constructive alternative to infanticide.

It is not only marriage in India that has a bimodal distribution, but infanticide as well. While the differential treatment of female children in the major Asian societies still results in a greater masculinity of the population, upper groups among the Rajputs and Patels earlier practised the deliberate infanticide of girls, in this case partly because of their potential claims for endowment from the family estate as well as because the men aimed to marry rich women from the next step down the hierarchy. In China too infanticide among the rich appears side by side with the infanticide of the poor, but it is the latter that seems to have been much more prevalent.

Clearly the family's holding will influence which strategies of heirship it follows in terms of the supply and demand of personnel. Lower groups supply more heirs and concubines, upper groups receive them. The upward movement of women as sexual partners and of both sexes as servants does not simply represent the conspicuous consumption of upper groups but rather their accumulation of political, economic or religious power. On the domestic level it is they that have something to exploit and pass on, it is they that need workers to produce and heirs to inherit. Thus the higher you are, the more likely you will be to receive marrying-in sons-in-law who tend to come from lower (but often just slightly lower) groups. The same is true of adopted sons (C,I,R), which in China means those adopted from within the clan according to Confucian norms, a strategy that tends to be preferred to entering into filiacentric unions. In India, too, priority is given to recruitment within the clan, just as in ancient Israel, ancient Greece and in Arab communities, an heiress had to recruit a husband (filiacentric or not) from within the clan (just as a widow did her leviratic husband), so that unlike the East such units were never exogamous.

Given that notions of descent and filiation are likely to grow in strength with the greater flow of property, it is hardly surprising to find agnatic lineages more in evidence among the upper groups in China and Rome as well as in all India. This is especially true of the charitable foundations of lineage type ('corporation lineages') that we find in southern China and under Islamic law, since their funds came from the more rewarding kinds of activity, whether in the economic, political or religious spheres. But it is more generally the case that where lineages, and in the present context virtually always patrilineages, are more important in upper groups, then lower ones are more bilateral in their kinship structures (e.g. Sri Lanka, Yalman 1967; Japan, de Vos 1984:29). Yet more widespread is the association of upper groups with 'joint undivided families', and the poor with stem households (C,T,I,E,A). In China at least this difference is associated with the equal division of property among sons in upper groups, whereas in lower strata, one son takes over the productive concern and compensates the rest as best he can. As we have seen the proportion of complex domestic groups is increased by early marriage, which reduces the span between generations, as well as by the later division of the estate (C,I,A).

These various trends we have isolated need in turn to be examined in the

context of the geographical distribution discussed earlier, since certain
practices which are rare or forbidden in upper groups in China, India and
later Europe, were generally allowed in the Near East; divorce was and is
frequent in Arab populations, so too was plural marriage and the levirate. In
these linked respects the Near East approximated to the lower pattern
prevailing in those other societies.

The presence or absence of these features is not simply a matter of
statistics, of creating a list. They affect the nature of family life and conjugal
unions in fundamental ways. It has been remarked of China that upper
families place more emphasis on fraternal ties and lower groups on conjugal
ones. While it would be a mistake to underestimate the role of the wife in
upper families, as we see from many literary and historical texts, a common
property interest promotes close fraternal interaction; where partition takes
place sooner and marriage later, brothers become independent of one
another at an earlier phase in the developmental cycle, and are consequently
more likely to depend upon conjugal ties, certainly as far as the management
of the house is concerned. That is to say, in respect of conjugality, the
lateness of marriage and parenthood, and hence less complex domestic
groups and less grandparenthood, in respect of the ability to choose and to
unchoose one's partner, of the relative freedom of action, in all these
respects lower families come closer to the model of the post-industrial family
than do upper ones. The reason is clear. In neither case is marriage the
major focus for great transfers of property. In the first case, lower families
have less to transfer; in the second, post-industrial families consist largely of
wage-earners who make their transfers as 'voluntary' gifts during the course
of the life cycle rather than as obligatory prestations at marriage, retaining
or investing what they need to support themselves in old age rather than
drawing upon the proceeds of a joint estate with their children. The patterns
converge, just as the disappearance of dowry in the English working-class of
the nineteenth century is followed by its decline among the bourgeoisie at
the beginning of the twentieth. The fact that this event, which can be seen in
a shift in the meaning of the word 'pension', occurred at roughly the same
time as the dramatic fall in the birthrate and in the number of infant children
in the family may or may not be significant. For the fall in the birthrate can be
regarded as a long-term readjustment to the rise in numbers a century
before. But it is also the case that the rise in numbers of those employed in
industrial and other spheres not only reduces the significance of the joint
family enterprise but renders each individual a distinct economic actor on his
own account, capable of sustaining a kind of livelihood, single, possibly with
a spouse, but no longer directly dependent upon children (though often
dependent upon social reproduction in a wider sense) to maintain him or

herself in old age, at least with the advent of 'forced' savings in the form of pension schemes.

There can be no universal, single factor theory of 'upper' and 'lower' practices in Eurasian societies. But some specific trends are linked to the greater endowment of daughters in higher groups, which encourages restraints on their sexuality before and after marriage, tending to limit divorce (already inhibited by the nature of the joint conjugal fund) as well as the remarriage of widows. On a different level, restraints on sexuality tend to characterise upper religious groups and a similar ascetic attitude may emerge with regard to the consumption of food, in the rejection not of all but of certain categories, especially the flesh of animals. In the religious hierarchy, enthusiasm, prophetism, cultic practice are by and large the mark of the low rather than the high which is more attached to the priesthood and the text, that is, to orthodoxy. In other hierarchies a parallel restraint is often expected of the establishment in many formal situations (though they may experience great difficulties in controlling their own, especially their young, as Duby (1977) shows for France in the Middle Ages). Such restraint among the upper classes is not only a matter of conformity to the existing order that supports them but is a mark of social distance from those who maintain that privileged position in a more specific socio-economic sense.

The differences I have discussed are not only a matter of societies and strata, but also of differences within regions and of changes over time. I have argued throughout that some of these represent specific functional alternatives within a general type of productive and reproductive system based on a hierarchy that is economically more profoundly differentiated than the state systems of Africa, especially in relation to the transmission of holdings in land over the longer-term.[1] But the cross-cultural similarities in the hierarchical differences among the major Eurasian societies suggest we are in the presence of more particular compatibilities between class, mechanism and strategy. If so, it is not surprising we should also find some similarities in the direction of changes over time, not simply because lower groups are imitating upper ones, but because they are *able* so to do. And one factor here is the general tendency for standards of living to rise, for increased quantities of goods and services to be produced and circulated.

That seems especially true of the tendency for a shift of emphasis to take place from the indirect to the direct elements in dowry, whether we are dealing with medieval (Hughes 1974) or early modern Europe (Sabean forthcoming), with Song China (Ebrey forthcoming) or with contemporary India.[2] But similar factors may be behind the trend in India whereby the polygyny and the levirate of Vedic times gave way to the Hindu norms of monogamy and adoption. In ancient Israel, too, polygyny retreated in favour of monogamy, and in both societies the 'freedom' of earlier sacrifice gave way in parallel fashion to the restraint of prayer and meditation.

In discussing local and regional differences I tried to distinguish in principle between those that result from internal shifts, those that interlock in some degree with other kinship variables, and those dependent on contingent factors of another kind, all three being essential to take into consideration. I have evoked all three in various contexts, but in looking at local and regional differences, especially ones between North and South, I have called attention in particular to the role of what can be loosely called modes of production, as well as of modes of communication, including distance from the centres of the production of written norms. Both of these general categories of factor seemed important in contributing to North–South differences in China and India, which once again displayed a number of similarities.

Wider kin groups and the written law

My intention was not to develop a single-factor theory but to pursue the comparative analysis of systems of marriage and the family in a wider framework than has been the case in most anthropological, sociological, historical or demographic studies. Whereas the study of Chinese kinship has often been dominated by the shadow of the lineage, India has been dominated by that of alliance (Goody 1985). Not only do these two frames need to be brought together, but we need to widen them in a number of ways to take account of historical developments where this is possible, and of demographic material on the household, age of marriage and rates of celibacy, where these exist. But above all we need to consider the features of each socio-cultural system in a sounder comparative framework.

In this work I have been dealing with the relation of domestic groups to estates, that is, to resources and specifically to land, in order to lay out the similarities and variations in systems of devolution and marital assigns on the one hand and in the repertoire of strategies of heirship and the strategies of management on the other. To point out the similarities at the domestic level is not in any way to deny the important differences at the level of wider kin groups, whether kindreds, lineages or clans, nor yet the consequences of those differences in many contexts of social action. But in Eurasia generally we are not dealing with the same kind of descent group we find in Africa. While among pastoral tribes such groups frequently have important political functions (and to a lesser extent in sedentary ones as well), while they are important for the regulation of marriage in China and North India, and for the remarriage of widows in the Near East, they are widely subject to the process whereby their resources are split between men and women, by endowment or inheritance, that is, by diverging devolution. The extent of its effects, the degree of internal fission of the lineage and the cross-cutting solidarity of the conjugal pair, will depend upon whether endowment is direct or indirect, early or late, upon the equality of the division between siblings of the same and different sex, whether basic productive resources (in particular, land) are included, and whether other procedures inhibit departing siblings (in particular, women) from exercising their claims. At times women may deliberately leave or place their property in the hands of their kin, partly as a general safeguard (particularly where divorce is frequent), partly to keep it out of the hands of their husbands; but such procedures may well have only a temporary effect on maintaining the unity of the estate, since their rights are usually transmitted, albeit in a weakened form, to their sons. One institution that appears to have a strengthening effect on the lineage is the family trust which both in China and in Islam results in bolstering the agnatic organisation by providing a 'perpetual', indivisible, common fund whose benefits are enjoyed by the descendants of its founders in the male line, often only by the males themselves. The Islamic *waqf* tended to exclude women and the same appears to be true of China; indeed such exclusion is virtually bound to occur since eligibility to membership of the lineage (descent) is defined differently from devolution, and property is in effect withdrawn from transmission within the sibling group. The rough division that we see runs parallel to Fortes' distinction between the two domains of kinship, the domestic and the politico-jural, which some authors have seen as representing the female and male spheres of action respectively. The difference is more subtle and complex than that. The joint interests of the conjugal pair are inevitably a threat to any system that selects one sex as the medium for transmitting important rights. But when women themselves are vested with such rights to property, then the problem is greatly magnified in agnatic systems, and vice versa in the case of men in uterine or matrilineal ones.

Conceptually as well as practically, this divergence at the level of conscious aims or of implicit workings between the bilaterality of devolution and the unilineality of lineage (and in the main of estate management) gives rise to problems, especially when custom comes to be formulated as written law, for the latter cannot easily endure or encapsulate the ambiguity, the contextual pluralism, of oral discourse. A single 'rule' is likely to be laid down in writing, which initially tends to give increased pre-eminence to the line of males, reifying the agnatic genealogy and playing down the woman's entitlements, a situation that is apt to become even more extreme when jurists try to understand already decontextualised 'rules' in terms of yet more abstract 'principles'. Such at least seems to have been at the heart of some of the discussions in Hindu family law over the last thousand years, and possibly of some of the differences between the North and South in the Indian sub-continent. So too with the Confucian norms, which ran counter, in an agnatic male-oriented sense, to much that was happening not only in Japan but in China too. So too perhaps in Islam; some have argued that law is more 'liberal' than custom, but the conflict is present, certainly in English Common Law, where the written text also made the situation worse for women than the oral utterance.

It is not simply the fact that law and custom differ. I have been concerned with the way in which, at least in the earlier stages of legal codes, they almost *have* to differ. Nor is this a difference only of the general and the particular, the Common Law of England being different from the Custom of Kent. It is a matter of the difficulty in formulating in writing what are often contextual differences in the part played by domestic groups, conjugal estates and even family funds in which women are involved, and on the other hand those aspects of lineage or clan affairs from which there is an attempt to exclude them. Anthropologists like Firth, Fortes, Gluckman and others have drawn attention to the way that ties through the mother modify patrilineal relationships; the web of kinship cuts across the membership of exclusive, boundary-maintaining groups. The situation we are dealing with is one in which women in a hierarchical society are also carriers of property as well as of sentiments, ties and relationships.

The same kind of contradiction occurs at the lower level of the joint estate (the basis of a joint undivided family) or even of the conjugal fund, which is both its beginning and its end. Here we are dealing with a group of living individuals of both sexes who marry and inherit, processes that operate according to a different set of norms than those on which the lineage is recruited and organised. In differentiated societies of this kind, these norms derive from the pressure to preserve the status of daughters, economically and in other ways, as well as that of sons.

The wider kin groups differ in structure in different societies. In pastoral economies they tend to play a more extensive role than under settled agriculture since they are more often concerned with social control, with defence and offence, with common rights to territory. They also differ depending on the level of agriculture, whether shifting or permanent, 'horticultural' or 'agrarian', for under plough cultivation (and indeed under any intensive, capitalised form), rights in land tend to be of a more 'individualised' kind. However in China and under Islam we find lineages that are not simply corporate in the usual sense but act as corporations under the special provisions of state or religious law. It could be said that while corporate groups have to be recognised as such by each other, corporations have to be recognised by the state. Because of their foundations, they are highly differentiated one from another, quite unlike the relatively homologous units of a segmentary system, or indeed of the politically distinct lineages in an African state such as the Asante of West Africa or the Bemba of the South-east. Both in China and in Islam such corporations were at once religious and political. So too of course were those partly autonomous institutions, the 'great organisations' of the Christian, Islamic and Buddhist churches which were the recipients of donations from their clients and congregations, donations which they put to general charitable ends as well as to particular ecclesiastical ones in a different way than the distribution of accumulated offerings by local shrines, and it is in this context that the re-orientation of 'sacrifice' in favour of more permanent gifts becomes significant. Somewhat in opposition to such corporations were the family foundations, which also involved notions of charity, indeed sacred charity, that is, the giving of assistance to poorer members of the descent group; and in Islam such family *waqf* are a variety of the religious trusts directed towards maintaining ecclesiastical institutions, temples, schools, hostels and hospitals.[3]

By this means kin groups were strengthened in important ways, providing benefits for individuals and families even when other political and economic activities have been taken over by centralised bodies, and then in some cases devolved on the lineage, as an act either of policy or of necessity. In China the corporations were exogamous, in Islam endogamous (or rather in-marrying since there is no overall rule). In the North of India, too, lineages are exogamous. But in areas where women acquire land as well as movables by devolution, either at marriage or at death, in-marriage appears to be allowed, and under some circumstances encouraged. The transfer of the basic productive resources to women as well as to men is inimical to the maintenance of the estate of a unilineal kin group in its original form, or indeed of the groups themselves; it rather promotes an emphasis on bilateral reckoning. However the nature of the wider kin groups influences but does not determine that of the narrower ones. For if we shift from one level to the next, from 'lineages' to 'families', the picture differs. While there are important variations between systems and between cultures, a number of similarities exist, at least in terms of possibilities and potentialities, which arise from the close links forged at the domestic level between the processes of production and reproduction.

In calling attention to similarities at the domestic level of production and reproduction, I am in no sense opposing a domestic to a lineage mode and both to one based on mercantile capitalism, petty commodity production or proto-industrialisation. In pre-industrial society all of these elements had been present since the Bronze Age, concurrently at one and the same time. It is true that household production was at different times and at different places supplemented by the *corvée*, cooperative farming, the workshop, the plantation, and forms of out-work employing free, semi-free or servile labour. But neither the lineage, the *latifundia*, nor the manor replaced domestic production altogether but rather added to or temporarily displaced it in specific contexts. Until the coming of industrial production, the *oikos* remained the dominant context of economic activity in human societies, at least in the sense that the homestead was the norm to which individuals returned. But the centrality of the *domus* did not inhibit relationships of all kinds stretching well beyond it, through market activities, through the recruitment of labour, through marriage alliances, through tax and tribute, through migration and immigration, through war and trade.

Differences of course there were between earlier Europe and Asia as between earlier Europe and later Europe. But they rarely, if ever, lay at the levels that most historians and anthropologists have discussed. Moreover, they neither prevented the development of a mercantile capitalism in Asia long before it made its mark in western Europe nor did they prevent the development of exhaustive proto-industrial activity in China and India. Nor again have family variables done anything to inhibit the very rapid industrialisation in East Asia – indeed there is much evidence that its progress has been assisted by joint undivided families, the 'house'. That suggests either that kinship variables are of minor importance or that domestic structures of the major Eurasian societies are much more similar or more malleable than is often supposed. I suspect that both these propositions are true but my own analysis in the present volume has concentrated upon the latter.

In seeking evidence to support or revise such contentions the relevance of fieldwork and the use of observational data become clear. First it provides evidence of the way different institutions interlock in actual practice. Secondly it produces quantifiable information which has been collected for analytical purposes. Thirdly in its absence one is forced to rely on documentary evidence alone, often composed with specific purposes in mind, religious, political, or legal. Such 'legal' statements may take a number of different forms, some very far from what we think of as codes. The written word can play a very variable role with regard to custom and practice, including largely ignoring them.

Western and eastern families

The existence of such links at the domestic level immediately raises a fundamental problem about the role of the family, marriage and kinship in social change, and more precisely the hypothesis that the English or western European family was particularly adapted to the development of capitalism, or alternatively that the family structures of other countries inhibited capitalism. The second thesis is associated with Weber, the first with those historians who think England unique in bringing capitalism into being and in the nature of the family. Both approaches find causal relations or 'elective affinities' between the two.

Weber's position regarding the family was complex and not altogether consistent. In his account of the religion of China he sees the sib or kin group as effectively throttling the development of capitalism, while in India the caste played the same role. The great achievement of the ethical religions, and 'above all of the ethical and asceticist sect of Protestantism', was to shatter these fetters (1951 [1916]:237); by ethical he referred to those religions that derived from the Near East. But religion was not the only possible breaker of the chains of kinship; indeed neither in Judaism nor in Islam did wider kin groups disappear in the way they did in western Europe, partly for reasons connected with the different nature of religious organisation and charitable foundations. Apart from religion, he also sees the state, , charismatic leadership and even Eastern creeds as capable of breaking down the bonds of the wider kin group, a process he considered essential to the development of rationalised capitalism as distinct from the 'internal booty capitalism' of China. Not the breakdown of the household, for his earlier studies had shown him the importance of family capitalism in agrarian state-societies such as northern Italy in the Middle Ages (Collins 1986:269). It was rather the wider kin groups, that is, clans, lineages and castes too, which he thought had to be destroyed and the fact that this had happened in the West rather than the East was a central key to the development of the new socio-economic order.

Weber's constant preoccupation was with the conditions for the growth of modern capitalism and for him the Chinese clan and the Indian caste were candidates for inhibiting factors. In fact they did not prevent, and may well have assisted, the great extension of external trade and internal manufacture that took place in both those immense countries in a period well before the expansion of Europe. These developments raise one of the topics which I have inevitably left on one side and which I need briefly to mention. The differentiation of the economy, rural and urban, meant that many productive units did not have to depend entirely on the farm alone. Or to put it another way, not only did the farm produce food for sale on the market (incorporated in the definition of a peasant economy in its relations with the town, the Church and the state), not only could commodities be purchased with the proceeds (incorporated in the definition of craft production), but the rural economy depended upon the hiring of labour, in and out, in the country and in the towns, together with the renting of land as well as participation in manufacture, above all of cloth. The extent of such diversification varied; compared with most of Africa, that in Eurasia was relatively high but compared with contemporary Taiwan or rural Europe today, it was low. References have been made to the domestic production of silk in rural China, to trading in Tibet, to cloth in India. Some of this extensive and varied activity disappeared with the advent of industrial production; with the coming of the cotton mills, the spinster tended to become a factory if not an urban worker. At the same time new activities emerged in the countryside, wage-earning or trading migrants sent back remittances, the elderly retired home after working away. So that both earlier and later, rural strategies were rarely based upon the exploitation or transfer of land alone even though agriculture provided the basic means of livelihood in most of the areas we have considered. For in all of them there were strong artisanal, commercial, trading and even manufacturing sectors which, as in Europe, prepared societies, groups and individuals for the changes that were to come with industrial production. Proto-industrial activity was not confined to Europe alone nor was the petty commodity (or the petty capitalist) mode of production restricted to East Asia. Within the category of the major pre-industrial states of Eurasia differences in systems of production have influenced the systems of kinship, but not to the extent of justifying the radical division between East and West that is so often made. Instead it is preferable to draw a tripartite contrast of pre-industrial Eurasia with on the one hand, the domestic arrangements prevalent under extensive agriculture such as we find in Africa, and on the other those that are closely linked to the urban industrial society of the modern world. At this level our analysis would support that of authors like Eric Wolf (1982) who have argued against the division between a 'feudal' mode of production in the West and an 'Asiatic' mode in the East, proposing a 'tributary mode' that comprises both. Indeed, it would go yet further, because as we have seen in discussing marriage and the family in ancient Egypt, Greece and Rome, some core similarities exist on a yet wider canvas, that of post Bronze Age, pre-industrial, literate societies, that is, those based upon an agricultural system that harnessed the energy of animals, controlled the flow of water, constantly improved the strains of crops and livestock, and developed a strong artisanal sector.

Weber perhaps underestimated the capacity of such wider groups to adapt to new circumstances, indeed to operate in rather a similar way to the banking families of northern Italy by providing trust, labour and capital where it was needed. True, such operations were not always carried out by the caste or kin group as a whole (though common investment did occur with some charitable foundations in South China and common economic action with some local caste segments in South India) but they often centred upon an 'extended family' very different from the isolated nuclear unit of capitalist mythology, let alone the yet more isolated individual encapsulated in the 'history' of Robinson Crusoe and the legends of the Log Cabin. Weber understood the role of the 'household' in such activity, but in Asia he saw the domestic group as dominated by wider kinship relations. Naturally the smaller units had to operate within the framework of more inclusive structures, but the way they did so was much closer to the European pattern than Weber's discussion allows. For in his effort to pinpoint the Uniqueness of the West, he too tends to primitivise the nature and role of kin groups in the more complex societies of Asia, failing to allow for the variety of forms such groups may take or for the comparative flexibility of the relations between the levels of organisation that could develop not only in urban and commercial situations but also in the context of production and manufacture in the country.

Despite this qualification, the work of Weber, like that of Marx, is more suggestive than that of most other historians and sociologists, partly because they employed in their analyses more complex modes of differentiation than the variations on the folk dichotomy of simple and complex, of them and us. Marx was in no doubt that a series of stages existed between primitive communism and capitalism, stages that included ancient society, feudalism and, as an offshoot, Asiatic society characterised by the static oriental mode of production. While at times moving closer to a dichotomising approach that differentiated modern and traditional, Max Weber was never in danger of confusing Africa or the Pacific with the major oriental societies whose religious ethic he so profitably compared, or rather contrasted, with the West. It is however, the more simplistic dichotomy that has dominated so many studies of family, marriage and kinship, and which has led to the drawing of over-rigid boundaries as well as to the foreshortening of the course of historical developments.

The 'we' and 'they' takes not only the form of Europe and the Rest, or here specifically Asia, but also that of national contrasts. Side by side with the differing notions of European and Asian scholars are those, for example, of the historians of France and England regarding family variables such as conjugality, attitudes towards children and their contribution to modernisation, rationalisation and the other processes in which Europe was supposed to have taken a lead. National claims are not the issue here; nor yet the more subtle cultural presumptions of difference that I have touched upon elsewhere, at least implicitly (1983). What is at stake are the kinds of claims made for Europe as a whole. For example, the influential work of Ariès (1960) sees a new constellation of sentiment emerging in the sixteenth century, not only regarding children but the whole family. These contentions have been roundly criticised by medieval historians like Herlihy and Nicholas. But more importantly, since it takes us beyond the Christian tradition of western Europe, the evidence for earlier Rome casts further doubt on this thesis. A number of authors have pointed to the importance of the elementary family and conjugal relations which have recently been the subject of an analysis by Saller and Shaw (1984) based on a series of inscriptions on tombstones. Ariès (1983:230) saw the rise of funerary commemoration on stone in the late Middle Ages and its spread downward to the common people as 'the expression of a *new* feeling, *the sense of family'*. 'But clearly', remark these authors, 'vast numbers of people over equally vast areas of western Mediterranean Europe had already felt this "new feeling" centuries before the novel development noted by Ariès' (p. 146). The point is well made. But it was not only in medieval Europe and in ancient Rome that elementary families existed (sometimes but not always in separate households) and were marked by a constellation of emotional relationships between their members that were reasonably similar to our own (though differing in some ways too), that there was affection between husband and wife (even when they had little hand in the choice of a partner) as well as between parents and children (who had no choice at all). These features extended over a much wider area altogether. Without straying outside the bonds of Eurasia, families in ancient Greece, ancient Egypt, the Near East, India, China and (*pace* Veyne) Japan display characteristics of this kind that would qualify them for 'the sense of family'. In other forms this hypothesis is related to the notion that the Uniqueness of Europe resided in the development of the elementary nuclear family (or household), the presence of bilateral institutions (kindreds) rather than unilineal ones (clans), in the late age of marriage of males and females (which supposedly encouraged independence), to the living-in servants (which supposedly encouraged mobility), and the closer relations between parents and children ('parental love') and between the couple themselves ('conjugal love'). Each of these features of domestic life can be found among some of the societies we have studied. While it can be argued that only in western Europe were they found as a particular cluster of weighted variables or relations (a statement that is necessarily true), there was no question of any being unique to, or probably 'invented' in that region. While none may have been as dominant as they were in 'modern' Europe, these features existed in other societies where they were capable of being developed into 'modern' structures should the occasion give rise.

Indeed, surely that is precisely what is happening in those areas outside Europe where capitalism is most vigorous at this moment, that is, in Japan and the four 'Little Dragons'. There is no evidence that features of their family, marriage or kinship have inhibited that development, now or in the past. We may attribute this fact to the irrelevance of such features, to their malleability or to the overall similarity between the basic structures of domestic groups in the West and the East. In the present context it is the latter point I want to emphasise, in order to reverse the stress that has been placed on the differences between the advanced Western and the primitive

Eastern family, even before the advent of capitalism. And if not 'primitive' in the anthropological sense, at least considered different enough in its traditional hierarchies, its systems of alliance, its castes, its clans, its stagnation or its torpor, to prevent the kind of breakthrough to the modern world that happened in the West. At the end of the twentieth century there is much less justification for these views than there was in the middle of the nineteenth.

Notes

Preface

1 The problems and necessity of comparison have been excellently put by Finley in Generalizations in ancient history (1963).

1 The nature of the enterprise

1 I reserve the term 'in-marrying' or 'in-marriage' for marriages within the group or grouping, however defined. Many writers refer to this as endogamous marriage but I use the term 'endogamy' in what I take to be its original sense, namely, the rule or practice by which all members of a group marry among themselves. Thus Arab lineages are in-marrying but not endogamous nor yet are they exogamous. There is no general obligation to marry out or in, although there are preferences that often differ for different siblings. A marrying-in husband on the other hand is one who joins his wife at marriage. When such a union takes place in a predominantly virilocal society, I speak of a filiacentric union, since the place of marriage, and much else, is determined by the prior residence of the wife/daughter. I use the terms virilocal and uxorilocal for systems where there is a general obligation, rule or practice of marriage whose locus is determined by the husband and wife respectively.

2 I am thinking of the use of 'civilisation' in the work of N. Elias (1978), although the usage goes back to many nineteenth-century writers.

2 The incorporation of women and the continuity of the 'house'

1 The 'strength' of lineage ties is difficult to measure and has been the subject of much debate. In China some authors claim that lineages were present in the South and absent in the North. But Wolf has drawn attention to the existence of genealogical structures of the lineage type throughout China, where his recent survey showed roughly half the villages consisting of single surname groups. Although those in the North do not hold common property, he suggests that this very absence seemed to be associated with greater 'solidarity' of a more general kind; for example, cousins tend to wear the same mourning dress, whereas in Taiwan even brother's sons are differentiated (personal communication). The solidarity of the 'corporation lineages' of the South is partly a matter of common

property, whereas that of the northern lineages depends more upon co-activity. Despite the difficulties, I shall continue to contrast the 'stronger' lineages of the South with the 'weaker' ones of the North, simply because the latter have fewer features in common (see table 1).

2 The sale of the children of impoverished farmers as servants in seventeenth-century Japan provided an alternative to infanticide (T. C. Smith 1959:14–15). Such servants (*fudai*) were sometimes called 'Bought and Saved'; their 'sale' was a matter of adjusting the size and composition of the domestic group, with the servant becoming very much part of the household of the master who assumed the responsibility of the father. Similar arrangements were found in the upper groups. The Lady Nijō, thirteenth-century author of the fascinating *Confessions*, lost her mother while still an infant and was taken into the palace at the age of four; ten years later she became the concubine of the Emperor, GoFukakusa.

3 For a parallel distinction between 'crisis' and more extensive forms of fostering, see E. Goody (1982).

4 This kind of affinal cooperation was notably absent among peasants in the Teng lineage of Hong Kong (R. Watson 1981) and appears to be connected with the nature of the corporation lineages, most of whose members are tenants rather than land-owners (in contrast to contemporary Taiwan).

5 Ebrey (forthcoming) prefers the term 'betrothal gifts' either to the traditional 'brideprice' or to 'indirect dowry'. Certainly it avoids the question of whether such gifts go to the bride or the father; on the other hand the fact that the term contains no indication of the donor or the recipient is also a disadvantage; the gifts could go to anyone in either direction. A further problem lies in the specification of the occasion, the betrothal. Looked at in a wider perspective, betrothal gifts to the bride (the so-called 'brideprice' of the Near East) are often promises to pay rather than actual transfers, mortgages on a man's property, which a woman, as a dowager, may eventually take in the form of a dower. The term 'indirect dowry or endowment' does not include those parts of the marriage transfers that go to and remain with the bride's father, and are in excess of what he has given her (a difficult assessment). But otherwise the phrase seems more satisfactory, even for China.

6 Hsu made the same point for West Town. See also 'The myth of Chinese family size', *Am. J. of Sociology* 48 (1943), where he emphasises 'the potential cleavage in a family containing more than one married couple' (p. 555). On the role of the wife in family fission, see Baker 1979:19ff. A similar situation is found in India, but in polygynous Africa it is more often the mothers of siblings rather than their wives that provide the initial focus for differentiation.

7 As Freedman notes (1958:96ff.), this form of marriage is not so widespread as some analyses suggest (e.g. Lévi-Strauss 1949; Leach 1951). In West Town, one informant claimed they constituted 70 per cent but Hsu doubts the figure is as high as this. In other areas cross-cousin marriages are rare.

8 On the importance of the exchange of the red cards, see A. H. Smith (1899).

9 Of Taiwan in the same period it has been said that 'it took years for families of laborers to set aside enough wealth to obtain a bride for one of their members' (Sa 1985:292), hence one attraction of minor marriage. Following the line of western-oriented reformers, the Communist regime tried to change marriage procedures in mainland China. One reform was the attempt to discourage 'wasteful' expenditure on these and other rituals (Baker 1979:175ff.). But in recent times there appears to have been an escalation of marriage costs.

10 'The terms "payment" and "sale" only apply under circumstances of extreme poverty such as the marriage of girls to mainlanders, who in some cases present the cash and other gifts expected from the groom's side, but receive very little in return' (Cohen 1976:172).

11 In Hong Kong a prostitute was sometimes given a present in addition to the madam's fee and this was known by the same name as a married woman's private savings (*ssu-fang ch'ien*) (Hershatter forthcoming; R. Watson 1984:4–9).

12 On the use of private money by women to purchase land in Shantung, see Yang 1945:79. It seems as if land also played a part in some dowry transactions in Honan (Henan). See also McAleavy (1955:546 and note 18).

13 M. Wolf regards the property as belonging to a woman's 'uterine family' (that is, to the wife and her children), Cohen as belonging to the conjugal couple. The two formulations seem to me reconcilable if one regards the rights of the children as being derived not only from the mother but from a particular marriage she has made (Cohen 1976:186; M. Wolf 1975:135).

14 On the importance of the difference between first and second marriages, see A. P. Wolf (1985b).

15 On the importance of the first wife, see Baker (1979:36).

16 On the importance of matrilateral and affinal ties among the Chinese in Taiwan, see Gallin (1960, 1966).

17 Cohen's diagram (1976:157) represents what I have elsewhere called 'an ascending kindred', consisting of all ego's direct cognatic ascendants, traced through males and females.

18 It is obvious that both adoption (including adoption by a widow) and large endowments provide alternatives to the remarriage of widows that is often disapproved of (Dennerline 1986: 201).

19 Cohen notes that this phrase can also be used of the inheritance of property by agnates when there are no heirs to an estate.

20 Fei refers to affinal-type adoption in his study of a central mainland village (1939:71) while Yang says this form is specifically excluded in an area in North China (1945:84).

21 On the burdens of filiacentric unions during the Song, see Ebrey (forthcoming:43).

22 In fact Wolf (personal communication) notes that in Taiwan and Szechuan (Sichuan), land is sometimes included in the dowry in order to provide an income for the bride. In one wedding a cart carried a load of soil in which a notice had been stuck, announcing that it represented the bride's dowry. The existence of such a practice brings out a point on which I elaborate in the Indian case, that the existence of even limited property rights for women (in movables or as a residual heir) opens the door to their extension under a number of other circumstances, leading perhaps to the regional variations we often come across in India, Greece, Italy and other parts of Europe. But in China the transfer was to the daughter for her personal support; even if she died leaving children to follow her, the land returned to her natal kin.

23 There were twelve such marriages in the Yangtze village which had a population of roughly 1,500 people (density 1,980 per square mile), that is, roughly 3 per cent of all unions.

24 There was only one such marriage in the village.

25 In the Yangtze village virtually the whole of the contributions of the groom's family went to the bride as 'dower' (Fei 1939:43).

26 Fei insists that traditionally women had no right to inheritance and quotes the Kuomintang law of 1929 that reversed this situation (1939:79). While that may be the case, we cannot disregard both the property devolved on them at their marriage and their role as heiresses when there were no sons.

3 The lineage and the conjugal fund

1 Barclay's figures (1954) show that over 10 per cent of households in Taiwan had female heads.
2 On the residence of divorced, orphaned and widowed royal clanswomen in Halls of Extended Clanship during the Song, see Chaffee (forthcoming:206).
3 I am indebted to Rodney Hilton for his help on this point.
4 On indigenous bookkeeping in China, see Gardella (1982) and further references on p. 69.
5 In Yunnan the division often occurred earlier. 'An adult son may, when he marries, demand a share of the family property to establish his own house.' This division is indeed a 'common practice' (Fei and Chang 1948:114–15). But the ideal remains of a large-family system, at least in the minds of the senior generation. 'It is natural that the father should fight against the disruption of the unity of the group of which he is head, for it has both economic and emotional consequences' (p. 115). In this he is supported by the written ethic of the literati.
6 Freedman himself speaks of a married woman having 'no further economic claims on her natal family (although she may well receive gifts from it)' (1966:95). Of Taitou in Shantung province Yang writes that when the division takes place, money is put aside for the dowries of unmarried daughters (1945:83). At this time a mother gets a share and can choose to live independently 'if her portion is adequate for that purpose', otherwise she resides with her married sons in turn.
7 See Goody (1962:326) for a discussion of preferential ultimogeniture and primogeniture.
8 The split has nothing necessarily to do with residence and hence statistics on compound size are relevant only in a negative way. The same is true of China.
9 Already in the Song, dowries might be invested in a going business or used to start one (Ebrey forthcoming:158).
10 'Dispersal of families into separate households did not lead to family division, but rather was accompanied by continued social and economic ties between related households, and large flows of remittances to sending communities' (Greenhalgh 1985:9).
11 The notion of joint responsibilities for parents has obvious affinities not only with equal inheritance but with the rotation of the managers of the lineage trusts.
12 It is not of course always the case that a woman's portion has to be matched immediately by the man's, even when it includes land. In parts of Greece, for example, a woman obtains land as dowry but her husband may only do so by inheritance.

4 Differentiation, hierarchical and regional

1 In fact modern Chinese historians date individual land rights to the reforms of Shang Yang, about 350 BC (Cartier 1988:18). This is only the earliest recorded date: in any case discussion of transfer depends upon whether one is talking of underlying (*gen*) or surface (*pi*) rights to land.

2 For an earlier, eleventh-century account, see Elvin (1973:151). The expansion of trade and traders was connected with what he calls the 'revolution in money and credit'. Merchants had their own guilds, like the well-known Co-Hong of Canton. On guilds or firms of merchants, see Ng (1983:16).

3 The term merchant fills a wide semantic field. 'To speak of *ching-shang* is to speak essentially of the whole non-agricultural economy, just as *shang-jen* [merchant] can include traders, brokers, manufacturers, bankers, financiers, and managers in the service and transport industries' (Chan 1977:1).

4 Like the 'merchants', the 'gentry' were divided among themselves. Scholar–officials of the eleventh century had little sympathy for aristocratic life styles, and indeed philosophical criticism of such styles was a feature of much earlier writing.

5 On the overlapping categories of shopkeeper, broker and merchant, see Ng (1983:167ff.). Merchants in Taiwan and elsewhere could also be landowners; merchants were recognised as scholars, scholars became merchants.

6 This suggestion is broadly supported by the data on Fukien, where the amount of 'brideprice' increases with social class, but the amount of dowry increases yet more rapidly. In Shantung on the other hand, the amount of 'brideprice' decreases with social class but that of dowry still appears to increase (A. P. Wolf 1985a).

7 According to Freedman, the offspring were not wholly equal co-parceners. One son, usually the eldest, took on the special responsibility of supporting the parents and received an extra share as a result; and the sons of the wife usually got more than the sons of a concubine (1966:53). However it seems more usual that this extra share was allocated not permanently but only during the parents' lifetime.

8 The relationship between resources, especially land-holding, and the developmental cycle has been reviewed by Croll (1985), including the relation to recent policy changes. While there is some disagreement about whether to consider the 'rich' and 'poor' modes as one or two cycles (Cohen 1976:65ff.), and about the extent of the high and low category at particular places and times, the general situation is not in dispute.

9 On the demographic benefits of high status in China, see Naquin (1986:24) and Harrell (1985).

10 A. Wolf (1985b) sees no evidence of the intentional control of population in China, apart from female infanticide, because the fertility curve is normal.

11 On the existence of class differences in affinal relations see R. Watson (1981) and Dennerline (1986:186).

12 I rely mainly on personal communications with R. Watson, who refers to the large peasant dowries reported by Parish and Whyte (1978:181), Yang (1945:79,110,113) and M. Wolf (1985). M. Cohen's recent work north of Beijing brings out the continuing importance of the parental endowment. I am also indebted to the remarks of M. Cohen, S. Naquin and H. F. Siu.

13 Concubinage is another alternative but I do not know of any data showing its regional distribution. However there was clearly a class difference, as in the case of the possession of bondservants (Sa 1985:281).

14 On strong lineages and the lack of government control in Fukien, see Ng (1983:32).

15 Most of these nomads were Buddhist, including the Manchus and the Mongols, although of course some of the Great Horde were Muslim. But the influence of Islam in what is now north-west China was considerable and traders also brought

the religion to the trading ports of the South. On 'the Islamic thrust into the empire', see Kwanten (1979:46ff.) for the Tang period at the beginning of the eighth century, pp. 60–2 for Transoxania in the tenth century, pp. 206–7 for the accession and conversion of Ghazan in the thirteenth century.

16 On the other hand Wolf and Huang (1980) give the 'family size' for three villages in Taiwan in 1935–36, as 8.2, 10.6 and 7.6.

17 They were cheaper to arrange for the men. On the other hand dowries were often higher for widows, ex-concubines or ex-courtesans, who needed additional attributes in order to make a good marriage.

18 These figures are calculated on the assumption that divorce occurred only with first marriages; the total figures should be lower (Barclay 1954: table 64, p. 221).

19 Arranged unions are not of course confined to early marriage; but such arrangements are obviously easier to make if the partners are young, and if the opportunity to divorce is restricted. Despite a later age of marriage in Europe, arranged unions were common until this century (despite the Church's emphasis on consensus and the literary stress on love), although there was always some resistance. At the time of the French Revolution easier divorce was advocated as a way of checking the kind of union celebrated in song:

> Jeune brebis douce et gentille
> Tombe à vieux loup garou
> On met du dur avec du mou
> Pour l'intérêt de la famille . . .
> (Bertaud 1983:178)

20 I am endebted to Ernest Gellner for pointing out, among many other things, the similarity between marriage rituals and monarchy discussed by Jamous (1981). It is at once striking and consistent with my main theme that while major Asian societies draw an important ritual idiom for marriage from royal display, in Africa royalty draws its idioms of accession from funerals (E. Goody 1973). Display and ceremony are as intrinsic to African funerals for reasons touched upon in our discussion of Harrell and Dickey (1985) and earlier in my own analysis of death (1962).

21 On the perpetuation of common ritual sequences in funerals in North China and in marriage, see Naquin (1988:15ff.). Part of this continuity is seen to depend upon the uses of writing and written documents.

22 For an account of near contemporary marriage ceremonies in the New Territories of Hong Kong, see R. Watson (1981).

23 Note that pre-marital pregnancy increased enormously over time and was always much higher in the case of filiacentric unions, which of course mainly involved brotherless daughters and were entered into at a later age.

24 The sample is different in this case (Wolf and Huang 1980:185–6). These figures are based on simple percentages; a more sophisticated analysis based on age-specific data puts the probability of divorce in minor marriages as the highest in eleven out of thirteen communities in the Hai-shan area (A. P. Wolf 1985c).

5 Land, polyandry and celibacy in Tibet

1 Punjab, *Gazetteer of the Kangra District*, vol. 2, 1883–84, p. 21, quoted Carrasco (1959:33). It should be said that among the Tibetan Nyinba of Nepal (Levine

1988), the retirement of the senior generation is a much more gradual process, not so closely linked to marriage which for women occurs in the late teens, early twenties. But the social organisation is very different, labour requirements being supplied by ex-slaves.

2 There is a difference of opinion, and no doubt of fact, about when the eldest son does take over (Carrasco 1959:34).

3 For a comprehensive bibliography on polyandry, see Levine and Sangree (eds.) (1980).

4 Dr Grimshaw comments: 'In some cases the celibate monk in the monastery is an extension of a polyandrous marriage and family property holding. Monks are endowed when they enter a monastery and I was told that abbots in Tibetan and Ladakhi monasteries may take wives and produce offspring in order to retain the monastic wealth within a particular family. Another common arrangement, as in Sri Lanka (Evers 1967), would be for the son of an abbot's brother to enter and thereby "inherit" his uncle's monastic wealth and influence'.

5 Levine's figures for the Nyinba show 44.7 per cent of monogynous marriages, 49.3 per cent polyandrous and 6 per cent polygynous.

6 Punjab, 1883–84, *Gazetteer of the Kangra District*, vol. 2, Kulu, Lahul and Spiti, Calcutta (see Carrasco 1959:36).

7 Among the nomads sororal polygyny has the same advantage in keeping the tent together as do the rare cases of mother–daughter polygyny (Ekvall 1968:26).

8 This is also the case among the herders, e.g. the nomads of A-Mdo. A wife brings animals with her as dowry and these can only be disposed of with her consent; in the case of divorce, she returns to her natal kin together with her animals (Carrasco 1959:73).

9 One might argue that considerations of power are often involved in marriage, but I refer to political power of a sexual kind over men and women involved in securing access to their wives or to their daughters, for example, in *jus primae noctis* or, in a less structured way, in workplace relations between a dominant employer, doctor or teacher and a subordinate secretary, nurse or pupil.

10 The case of joint sexual access across the generations makes for radical divisions of opinion. Just as for the Hindu commentator, brought up on the ideal of the unique sexual relationship, Tibetan polyandry was disgusting, so the inhabitants of Birifu (LoWiili) who inherited their brothers' wives regarded as 'incestuous' their neighbour's practice of inheriting their fathers' wives other than their own mother. In Tibet we find reports of a father and son having legitimate access to the same woman while both are alive, as well as mother and daughter to the same man; the first may occur when a man is widowed, his son married, and both wish to avoid two conjugal groups in the one house; the second may occur when the daughter of a widow 'calls-in' a husband. I do not think we find permitted unions of a man with his daughter or a woman with her son. On the other hand father–daughter marriage appeared to occur among royalty in ancient Egypt alongside the much more widespread unions between brother and sister.

11 Among the Pahari, on the other hand, richer men tended to acquire additional wives, while the poor were restricted to polyandry (Goldstein 1978).

Part II India

1 Muslims in South India, however 'generally live by cultural practices close to those of local non-Muslims' (Dyson and Moore 1983:53; Mandelbaum 1970).

However, the continental role of Islam needs always to be borne in mind in considering discussions that stress the role of the Hindu religion as a unifying factor (De 1966).

2 There have long been distinctly different demographic regimes in West and East Bengal (the latter now Bangladesh). The West was more affected by malaria and hence higher mortality; the East has higher fertility (Dyson and Moore 1983:53,59; Geddes 1947–48).

3 Pestman refers to the Egyptian *šb* as being a fictitious transfer (1961). The same sometimes appears to have been the case with *morgengabe* in Europe (Goody 1983), while in Bangladesh too the *mahr* is often given to the woman only when her marriage is dissolved (Ahmed 1984).

6 Marriage and the family in Gujarat

1 In this fieldwork the major part is played by Esther Goody.

2 The average size of household in all-India was 4.91 (1950 Census, Shah 1974); in the Degham taluka the 1980 census shows an average size of 5.26.

3 Patel is the title of a village headman. Patidar is the term for a system of land tenure (Pocock 1954:195).

4 The domestic priest is known elsewhere as the *purohit*. Dumont reports that at funerals he has special functions such as impersonating the deceased at the close of mourning, after the ending of impurity (1966b:94).

5 For a general discussion of *jajmānī* relations see Kolenda (1963).

6 The situation is in some cases similar to that in Badlapur, a village of approximately the same size (3,000 in 1954) described by N. G. Chapekar (1955). In 1924–25, 17 out of 2,000 inhabitants, nearly all Brahmins, were employed as teachers or revenue assistants. In 1954, 116 people were employed, 38 of them Brahmins; extra-village employment opportunities had spread to the other castes.

7 Each of these forms of 'priesthood' differs substantially and each has its own type of support system. The reference to Africa is to fieldwork carried out by Esther Goody and to a lesser extent by myself among the Gonja of northern Ghana, where at the major annual festival of Damba, held on the Prophet's birthday, the members of the locally established Muslim estate read a prophecy from the Book of Years which calls upon the chiefs to shower large gifts upon their Muslims, some of whom (the 'spokesmen') are represented as their 'wives'. The giving of (free) gifts, *sadaaq*, is strongly emphasised in the Islamic tradition.

8 On the continuing role of the maternal uncle among the Rajputs of northwest India, see Parry (1979:238).

9 For a less elaborate 'coming and going' among the Rajputs of northwest India, see Parry (1979:23).

10 Thakurs were in fact Rajputs but ones who had emigrated as teachers (see Kolenda 1967).

7 The high and the low

1 This duelling for position however is nothing new, especially when the parties are about equal. A wife's account of a marriage in Maharashtra in about 1880 tells how her husband-to-be was encouraged to sulk until he was promised a ring, but

he soon tired of the tactic and joined the wedding party. In certain respects this behaviour can be seen as equivalent to the 'institutionalised reluctance' with which brides often enter marriage in Africa, sometimes tearfully and with shrieks of protest.

2 Significantly when Kolenda (1967:173ff.) considers factors that might explain the smaller proportion of joint families in some southern (and tribal) villages in comparison with those in the Gangetic plain in the North, she turns first to divorce and remarriage.

3 However in Burma, where marriage is often initially uxorilocal, the husband brings what Spiro designates a 'dower'; when the marriage is dissolved it is divided by mutual agreement but allocated to the wife if she is divorced without cause (1977:194–5). This is essentially a pre-mortem devolution to the groom at marriage and has to be considered in relation to the fact that, while the bride may not receive a direct dowry at marriage, she is entitled to an equal share of the parental property and is especially likely to inherit the house (p. 78). In towns she will receive a dowry.

4 Similar changes are reported in Sri Lanka by Tambiah (1973) and in Burma by Spiro (1977).

5 See Dyson and Moore (1983), discussed in the next chapter.

6 Secularisation, especially noticeable among upper castes, is a related but not altogether identical process that has been described by Majumdar as 'deritualisation' or 'de-sanskritisation' (1958:334–6).

7 Such structural ambiguities, combined with the search for personal gains and losses, are at the heart of the riots against privileged admissions to the university for scheduled castes and tribes, an issue concerned with positive discrimination which India under the Nehru dynasty has in many ways faced more directly than most other societies.

8 For twice-born castes in India, see Srinivas (1984:25); for China, usually in the lineage, see R. Watson (1985); for Europe, see Goody (1983); it also occurs in the Islamic *waqf*.

9 The 'brideprice' (*śulka*) form of marriage is a non-*kanyādāra* form, known as *āsura*, defined by Manu (3.27–34, Bühler's translation) as: 'When (the bridegroom) receives a maiden, after having given as much wealth as he can afford to her kinsmen and to the bride herself, according to his own will'. It is a form of marriage which contains an element of indirect endowment but which to some commentators approaches closely to notions of purchase and sale, although others argue vigorously against this view. In any case it is forbidden to the Brahmins and according to Trautmann, 'both its special identification with the commercial class and the low esteem in which it is held derive from the general theory of exchange' (1981:291). At one level, that of the text, this is undoubtedly true. Trautmann seems correct in his suggestion that whereas the exogamous provisions in the *Dharmaśāstra* are related to Northern, Indo-Aryan custom, the classical *kanyādāna* idea seems much more 'the refined product of the jurist's thought that has spread directly through the prestige of the brahmanical tradition' (1981:298). But what my comparative survey seeks to show is that certain limited features of marriage in the major Asian (indeed Eurasian societies) are found (at least as significant trends) across different societies, different cultures, different religious systems.

10 For a similar interpretation of the potential claims of a sister's son, see Goody (1959).

11 A fascinating parallel to this hierarchy is reported by de Vos (1984), discussing the work of Koh (1981) and Harvey (1979). Comparing the background of women who became nuns and shamans, Koh shows that the nuns were all of upper middle-class status, the shamans from lower middle-class families. While the nuns placed a high value on chastity, the shamans 'had been more expressive sexually and had developed liaisons which sometimes brought them into social disrepute'. The latter assumed the role of economic provider when their spouse could not do so (pp. 31–2).

12 See Mandelbaum (1970:97) for other references; Madan (1965) describes these institutions among the Pandit Brahmins of Kashmir. According to Tambiah (1973) the notion of the appointed daughter is now obsolete, having been displaced by that of the incoming son-in-law by whom the 'breaches in an otherwise patrilineal–patrilocal edifice are repaired' (p. 84). However these practices, which are in effect two sides of the same coin, are only effective as repair-kits by virtue of a woman's claims to property, albeit secondary.

13 There are some exceptions but it remains a general trend for upper women to have fewer births but more survivals.

14 Referring to more general discussions of mother's brother's daughter (MBD) marriage, Trautmann observes that only this form ensures that 'all wife-giving kin are distinct from wife-taking kin' (1981:311). In fact even prescriptive MBD marriage only produces this result under very special conditions where all the group's mother's brothers are to be found in one and the same outside group (Goody 1968).

15 Parry also sees it this way (p. 315) and indeed stresses, as against Dumont, that the notion of equality, of brotherhood, exists in opposition to that of hierarchy. He illustrates this point by referring to land tenure. But one can also discern the contradiction working in certain Bakhti movements and in conversions away from Hinduism.

16 Compare China; 'by the time the boy reaches the age of fifteen, the father assumes a more dignified attitude toward him and is frequently severe'; indeed there is much mutual avoidance (M. C. Yang 1945:57–8, quoted Baker 1979:17).

17 In China, too, brothers in peasant households are reported to be more equal (Myers 1970, quoted Baker 1979:13).

18 In poorer families in China only one son might be able to get married; while the others might stay, there is little evidence of 'polycoity' (Baker 1979:9). For a parallel discussion of 'stem households' in Europe, see Homans (1941) and comments in Goody (1962).

19 In a survey in Nagpuar District, Driver found over one quarter of coresidential elderly couples living in a subordinate position, but this occurred at all social levels (Mandelbaum 1970:79).

20 'In South India this affirmation [of the brother–sister tie] occurs as part of other rites' (Mandelbaum 1970:68). See Beck (1972:239) for an account of a Tamilnadu ceremony.

21 For a wealth of references from throughout India, see Mandelbaum (1970:67).

22 André Beteille, to whose comments I owe a great deal, made this point to me.

8 The North and the South

1 See also Vatuk's fuller study (1972).
2 Elsewhere both the daughter's husband and the sister's husband are described as *man* relatives (Khare 1976:208).
3 See Goody (1959); we could call this the role/actor confusion for short.
4 Dumont does recognise that 'north India is not universally averse to the repetition of marriage' (1966b:106).
5 My worry about the contrast in the Indian case is that from the sociocultural point of view, both North and South are equally complex.
6 On p. 344 of Yalman's book (1967) the general structure is the fundamental categories of cross-cousin marriage and the basic principles whereby sexual relations, marriage, joking behaviour, avoidance and so on can be organised within the family.
7 I am aware that I have at times used 'residual' in two senses which require to be better distinguished. In the case of siblings I refer to the sex omitted from the reckoning of descent, inheritance or succession, and hence from passing on membership, property or office to that individual's children. In the case of heirship, I refer to the subsidiary category of person who inherits when there are no available members in the primary category (e.g. a woman may inherit when she has no brothers).
8 I have elsewhere (1962) discussed the way in which marriage to the father's sister's daughter or to the 'bilateral' cross-cousin (the double cross-cousin) reunites the property or other relatively exclusive rights which were dispersed between or through the sexes at the previous generation. For example, in the system of double inheritance which often accompanies the presence of double descent (i.e. membership in both patrilineal and matrilineal 'clans'), such a marriage means that a grandson will belong to the same two clans as his grandfather and hence have the same claims and obligations. The technical reasons for this were first pointed out by Fortune (1932) but they also lie behind Lévi-Strauss' analysis of restricted and generalised exchange (1949). Father's sister's daughter marriage, in which rights over women pass first in one direction and then, at the next generation, in the other, is the prototypical case of restricted exchange. However, if claims to property and other rights are not sex-linked, as in dowry systems, then that consideration does not apply. Any type of cross-cousin marriage on either side will 'heal the wound', to use Srinivas' expression, although there may well be other reasons (repeated hypergamy, for example) to prefer one form above another.
9 However see Fortes (1969:109) referring to the work of Hiatt (1965) and Radcliffe-Brown (1930–31).
10 Sontheimer (1977:147–8) also notes that Devana admits that such a union is permissible if it takes place under the approved, *brāhma* form rather than the *gandharva* or *aśura* forms, the latter being common in the South, because it involves no 'gift of the bride' so that her relationships with her natal family remain unbroken.
11 André Beteille, personal communication. Sarkar comments that 'while marriages between maternal uncles and nieces definitely fell within the prohibited degrees of marriage and therefore were not permitted, in certain communities in the South such marriages are prevalent and even today are regarded as valid' (Sarkar 1982:349).

12 I am indebted to André Beteille for his information (5 July 86), and indirectly to B. Sivaramayya, a lawyer of Andhra Brahmin origin.

13 The term 'blood-relative' is less happy than consanguine, providing the latter is used in a broad sense of 'relative', 'kin', 'parent' (in French), as opposed to 'affines' and providing one does not allow oneself to fall into any of the associated 'genealogical fallacies'.

14 For example, in the terminologies for Tamil, Andhra and Kannada given by Karve (1953:196ff., but see Trautmann 1981 for a more scholarly account); MB=(with some modifications) HF=WF, and FZ=HM=WM.

15 'In a large number of castes the first preference is given by a man choosing his elder sister's daughter as a bride' (Karve 1953:187).

16 Median age at marriage, estimated by the Hajnal method.

17 The history of Gandhi's marriage is one such example. He was married at the age of thirteen while still at High School to Kasturbai, a girl of the same age who had her first child at eighteen. He continued to refer to 'the cruel custom of child marriage'.

18 Punjab, Haryana, Jammu and Kashmir, Uttar Pradesh, Rajasthan, Assam, West Bengal and Nagaland had lower than average ratios, while Andhra Pradesh, Mysore, Tamil Nadu and Kerala were higher (Census of India, 1971, Gujarat, General Report, Series 5, Part 1A, p. 124).

9 Kinship and modes of production

1 I have referred mostly to Gough's own summary paper, but she has provided much more detailed accounts of Thanjavur (1981) and of Kerala (1961).

2 Dual division did not shape the extensions of the kin terms in Kerala but were apparently universal among the lower ranks in the great irrigation states of Andhra, Mysore, Tamil Nadu and Sri Lanka.

3 See Dumont's *Dravidian et Kariera: l'alliance de mariage dans l'Inde du Sud, et en Australie*, which consists of earlier articles published in English. The collection of articles on the South of India and Australia is to some extent a refutation of Radcliffe-Brown's material on the 'Australian-Dravidian type of terminology'. However he too remains on the level of vocabulary, which is what he means by, for example, a Kariera system.

4 On an early recognition of pre-Renaissance trade and its importance in various continents, see William Robertson, *An Historical Disquisition concerning Ancient India*, first published 1791 but reprinted in the complete edition of his works, London, 1824.

5 On this discussion see also Yalman (1967), Beck (1972), but for the contrary, see Tambiah (1958).

6 Sister's daughter marriage resembles father's sister's daughter marriage. Note that it was the lower castes who stated the marriage preference as father's sister's daughter marriage (in fact bilateral), while the upper groups with patrilineal lines stated it as mother's brother's daughter marriage (as did the matrilineal groups of Kerala).

7 The feudal comparison has some interesting aspects. The *jus primae noctis* existed in both regions; however 'sexual familiarity on the part of landlords with the women of the tenant and labourer castes has decreased' (Gough 1978:18).

8 I am extremely grateful to Kathleen Gough-Aberle for having re-calculated these figures for me (letter, 5 April 1988).

Part III The Near East

1 In Mesopotamia we find adoption (Glassner 1986:127), filiacentric unions with an heiress (*kallatum*, p. 118), but neither the levirate nor the sororate (p. 119). The direct dowry (*sheriktum*) consisted of slaves, jewellery and furniture, but an indirect dowry was also provided which the literary evidence seems to suggest was transferred to the bride in an earlier period, but later to her father, a reversal of the usual sequence proposed for Egypt and elsewhere. Both sequences may represent changes of emphasis and evidence rather than of substance, but in any case the situations are both explicable in terms of the argument I have developed. The sale of land existed as early as the second third of the third millennium.

10 The abominations of the Egyptians

1 Maspero (1899:588-9, 745). There seems little reason to doubt the comments of classical authorities who call attention to this practice of close marriage, whatever their motives, whatever the frequency, whatever the exact relationships, since when these areas later came under Roman jurisdiction the conquerors were forced to take into account an actual rather than an imagined situation.

2 *Epist, prim, ad Corinth*, Homil. xxxiv, para. 4. For other references see Agathias, *Agathiae Myrinaei Historiarum* (1828, Lib.ii.c.24, pp. 116-18), who says that Zoroaster introduced incest; for Zoroaster, see Du Perron, *Zend Avesta*, vol.ii, pp. 556, 612; according to Al Beidâwi these practices of the Magi were condemned by Mohammed (Sale's Koran, p. 59); Theodore Beza, *Tractatio de Polygamia* [1651], and *Tractatio de Repudiis et Divortiis* [1569]; for Plato, see *Laws* iv, 721a-722b; vi, 772d-774e; *Republic* 458c. Most of Huth's references depend upon Wilkinson's *Ancient Egyptians* (1837) and W. Adam, Consanguinity in marriage, *Fortnightly Review*, 1865, vol.2; they require checking in greater depth than I have done here.

3 J. Bidez and Fr. Cumont (1937) *L'Egypte des astrologues*; M. Hombert and C. Préaux (1949) Les mariages consanguins; H. I. Bell, (1949) Brother and sister marriage in Graeco-Roman Egypt; J. Černý, (1954) Consanguineous marriages in pharaonic Egypt; M. Henne, (1954) Du mariage entre frères et soeurs dans l'Antiquité, H. Thierfelder, (1960) *Die Geschwisterehe im hellenistisch-römischen Aegypten*.

4 Herodotus (ii, 92) claims that the Egyptians, like the Greeks, had a single wife. But Westermarck comes to the conclusion that polygyny was permitted but unusual (1891:iii, 40). See also Griffith (1915:vol. 8, 444). As far as royalty was concerned the great wife or queen was differentiated from the other wives as well as from the concubines. The queen was rarely a foreigner, being nearly always a daughter of Râ, a princess 'born in the purple', as often as possible a sister of the Pharaoh who, 'inheriting in the same degree and in equal proportions the flesh and blood of the Sun, was the best qualified to share the bed and throne of her brother' (Maspero 1895:i, 270, 50). As queen she had her own followers, showed herself in public and played an important role in state ritual.

5 The sex ratio was 107:100, showing that infanticide could not have made much difference. But that some sex preference was involved is clear from the letter of Hilarion to his sister Alis. 'Do not be anxious . . . take care of the little one . . . As soon as we receive pay, I'll send it up to you. If by any chance you bear a child, if it is a boy, let it be; if it is a girl, cast it out.'

6 For the optional systems of France, see Yver (1966).
7 Forgeau suggests a very much earlier age of marriage in the Graeco–Roman period. The desire to get children to work on the farm or to contribute in other ways is indicated in the injunction, 'Take a wife when you are twenty so that you will have a son while you are still young' (Forgeau 1986:155); similar sentiments were expressed in China. Late marriage may be a good contraceptive but it is bad for the harvest.
8 Among the Nubian Kings, conquerors of Egypt in the eighth century, marriage with the sister by the same mother and father or with the patrilateral parallel cousin (FBD) was a widespread custom (Forgeau 1986:143).

11 Jacob's marriages

1 In this account I am clearly indebted to J. G. Frazer's study of Jacob's marriages in *Folklore in the Old Testament* (1919), which presented a pioneering study of cross-cousin marriage. It should be added that some authorities regard the story as reflecting ancient Mesopotamia rather than ancient Israel. For example Speiser (1964:250–1) claims that the stealing of the *teraphim* gods may have been copied by the Israelite scribe-redactor without fully understanding its meaning. For more recent contributions to the discussion see Burrows (1937), Greenberg (1962), Gordon (1937), and van Seters (1969).
2 See R. S. Rattray, *Ashanti* (1923:34); the same is true of the LoDagaa of northern Ghana and of many other peoples.
3 Were figures of divorce and accusations more common and more reliable, it would be possible to test the hypothesis that in polygynous societies the lower the frequency of divorce (or rather separation), the greater the tension between co-wives, since they have no escape from continued interaction. The Zulu would provide a useful case for such an investigation, were it not that rare divorce seems to be a thing of the past.
4 Some writers have maintained that monogamous marriage was the Jewish ideal (Abrahams 1915). But polygyny though rare was not prohibited by Talmudic law (nor yet by the early Christians), and there was no discrimination among wives as distinct from concubines (Mielziner 1901:30; Westermarck 1921:iii, 41). However, marriage contracts that prevented the husband from taking further wives were a common feature of the Jewish community in medieval Cairo (Goitein 1978).
5 Raquel gave his daughter, Sara, to Tobias as wife and then called his wife Edna 'and took a paper, and did write an instrument of covenants, and sealed it'.
6 For the levirate, see Neufeld (1944) and Burrows (1940).
7 It seems to have been possible, despite the conspicuous absence of clear legal texts in Exodus and Deuteronomy, to transfer heirship under certain circumstances, as in the case of Abraham's Eliezer and Jacob taking Menasseh and Efraim as his own. Close relatives would take in orphaned children just as couples without children might be given the children of close relatives to look after. Orphaned girls are characteristically provided with dowries in Jewish communities from special foundations, sufficient to marry within their own status level (H. Goldberg, personal communication; see also Feigin 1931).
8 See Zborowski (1949, 1952).
9 The fact that the direct dowry of the Talmud (*melūg*) has been traced back to the Mesopotamian *mulūgu* is itself suggestive of the prevailing situation during the

intervening period in Israel (Levine 1968). *Mulūgu* is generally seen as a gift between father and daughter.

10 Zborowski calls attention to the role of learning even in small Jewish communities, all of which have their *kheder* where the young children are taught, or their *yeshiva* for higher studies in the law.

11 In the sale of land a kind of *retrait lignager* appears to have operated; as in medieval Europe, kinsmen had the right of first option (Ruth 4:4). Or was it a question of Ruth's dowry in land having to be redeemed at the dissolution of the marriage by death, so that she regained possession?

12 Marriage and property in the Arab world

1 On p. 30 Robertson Smith himself considers an alternative for female eponyms more consistent with recent ethnographic work; it had been previously put forward by J. W. Redhouse (1885:275–92). On the subject of the discussion of the mother's brother, see Radcliffe-Brown (1924), Goody (1959).

2 Unlike some more recent authors Robertson Smith is very clear that it is rights of women, not the women themselves, that are the subject of marital 'purchase' (p. 122).

3 'If you cannot find an equal match', says Cais ibn Zohair, 'the best marriage for them is the grave . . .' (Robertson Smith 1907:97; Cuisenier 1975:38). On the other hand Cuisenier claims that bride-takers are superior to bride-givers (1975:9). We seem to be in the presence once again of the ambiguity over hypergamy encountered in India.

4 Sunni schools allowed a daughter a maximum of half the estate. In Shi'i law a man might bequeath a further third to an entitled heir, bringing the total to five-sixths. If there were no competing heirs, the daughter would be equally entitled to increase her share.

5 A delayed *mahr* is most common in Greater Syria and apparently less so in North Africa and the Yemen (M. Mundy, personal communication).

6 Ernest Gellner points out that central Moroccan Berbers say that a woman only inherits when she dies, at which point her sons can claim her inheritance, although it is nevertheless shameful for them to do so. Until her death her brothers hold her property, justifying themselves on the grounds that they have to look after her if she is repudiated. We have here a fascinating illustration of the alternative possibilities even where a woman's claim is recognised. The retention of her property by her brothers is clearly linked to the fragility of marriage, giving a greater weight to the endowment of the wife (and of the conjugal pair) from the groom's resources, that is, by means of an 'indirect dowry' (or nuptial gifts). Not that retention necessarily led to divorce or vice versa, but the two are closely entailed.

7 In northwest Europe, the late age of marriage is over twenty-six for men and over twenty-three for women (Hajnal 1982:452).

8 Significantly this was not true in the 'African' areas where Arabs reside, namely Mauretania and the northern Sudan where marriage for women is earlier (about fifteen) and polygyny much more frequent (Fargues 1986); these are typically African patterns (Goody 1976).

9 Inheritance is not the only way of acquiring land; for five millennia women as well as men in the Near East have been able to get it by purchase. But purchase was not always free of encumbrance, as in most pre-industrial societies, and to a lesser

extent even in contemporary western Europe. That is to say, individuals did not have an unencumbered right to alienate property which they had acquired by inheritance and which in that sense was allocated not only to an individual but to a line of descent. Individual acquisition was subject to the notion, sometimes explicit, sometimes implicit, that inherited property should not be alienated without due regard to the heirs and to the wider kin group. The existence of land sales in conjunction with family rights is not at all inconsistent. The Norwegian custom of *odelsrett*, of pre-emption (Barnes 1957; Goody 1962), is a well-known example. But the same principle was applied in Highland Yemen of which Mundy writes: 'No individual member . . . had the right to sell any part of the family land to outsiders, and, even when land was divided among the heirs, the local community recognized a right of pre-emption for related family members' (Mundy 1979:164). Sales took place but kin had prior rights.

13 The heiress in ancient Greece

1 In this account of marriage and family among the ancient Greeks I have obviously been highly selective in my sources, as throughout. For a more extensive bibliography see Avezzù (1983:89), Lacey (1968) and the other references.
2 The references are to the English translation, *The Ancient City*, Doubleday Anchor Books, New York, (1955) (originally published in 1864).
3 For references on the subject, see Finley (1955:167) and Köstler (1944).
4 Bremmer (1983) quotes many examples of boys being brought up by their maternal grandfathers and possibly succeeding to their thrones if they were kings without male heirs. In matters of succession to office it is possible to wait longer before selecting a successor than if one requires help on the farm; in the latter case the son-in-law has a more immediate part to play.
5 One has to add that even in Europe there were and are various forms of sale just as there are various forms of ownership. The sale of land is always more problematic than that of movables, especially as even land registered in the name of a single individual may be subject to the claims of others, of a spouse, of descendants, or even of more distant kin under the *retrait lignager*.
6 In the Gortyn code, Cretan women received half a son's portion (the same as in Islamic law) and were permitted to inherit land (Lacey 1968:215).
7 In Athens, in 451, Pericles decreed that both a man's parents had to be citizens if he was to be one. Lacey thinks this restriction on marriage was probably the result of men's desire to get husbands for their daughters and prevent them becoming old maids or harlots (1968:100).
8 Lacey (1968:107–8) sees the dowry arising from the natural imbalance of adult females and adult males. However there are many ways of dealing with this small discrepancy. What greatly aggravated the Greek situation was the difference between the marriage ages of men and women, which inevitably increases the 'old maid' problem. That situation is basically a social one which, as in Ireland, appears to be related to the manner of devolving property.
9 See Plutarch's life of *Alcibiades*, concerning his behaviour towards his wife, Hipparete, who left him because of his continual entertainment of courtesans (*Plutarch's Lives*, book 4, *Alcibiades* VIII).

14 Monogamy in ancient Rome

1 For a criticism of other aspects of this view, see J. A. Crook (1967b).

2 For examples, see Memel-Fote (1988:400).

3 Corbett (1930:152) claims that the dowry was necessary in Greece to establish the validity of the marriage, but see Watson (1967:4).

4 On a similar use of dowry in medieval Europe (Elizabeth of Hungary) for the maintenance of herself and her servants, see Bynum (1987:135) who comments that her refusal to eat any food except that purchased with money from her dowry 'seems to reflect a deep sense that only property from her own paternal line . . . could be trusted as morally untainted' (p. 224). The property of course was parental, not simply paternal.

5 Lewis and Reinhold 1966:485. Braund's translation (1985:268) of the second sentence gives a rather different gloss, and one that does not seem to be borne out by the rest of the eulogy. He writes: 'for you were not interested in acquiring for yourself what you transferred entirely to me'.

6 For Saller, the problem about the function of Roman dowry comes from seeing it as small and therefore as not serving 'the more usual function of an alternative to female inheritance' (1984:103). For the actors it is not so much an alternative as a part of a woman's total endowment, which we see from the fact that under the procedure called *collatio dotis*, the dowry is taken into account in the division of the estate (p. 198).

7 That was the case for testamentary tutelage but not for the agnatic variety which continued until the middle of the first century AD when it was abolished by the Emperor Claudius. On legal drafting, see Watson's comment, 'Unless it was always permitted, a rule certainly developed during the Republic that a husband by will could allow his wife *in many* to choose her *tutor*' (1967:146). Concerning formal changes, in the early Empire women who had several children were freed from *tutela* by the *lex Iulia et Papia Poppaea*.

8 'What poor man hopes the fair one's smile to gain? What poor man counts not on the sire's disdain?' Juvenal, *Satires* 3, pp. 221–2 (trans. C. Bodham, London, 1831).

9 The ages of seven, fourteen, and twenty-one were recognised in law (or perhaps formalised legally) as significant points in the individual life-cycle.

10 Whether the reference is to Greece or Rome does not really matter for our purposes.

11 A facet of the same phenomena is the number of women saints in the Middle Ages 'who were released to follow a religious life by the death of a man' (Bynum 1987:14).

12 In Israel there was a good deal of ambivalence on this subject, except where a dead brother was without a son, that is, except for the levirate itself (Benzinger 1902).

13 Veyne (1978:38) sees it as a 'psychological' rather than a strategic change. Elsewhere he describes the transformation as taking place somewhere in the first two centuries of our era (p. 35).

14 On the objections of medieval historians to the family studies of scholars of modern and early modern Europe, see also Bynum (1987:225ff.).

15 See Hughes (1974:22) and Stone (1977:50) for later Europe.

16 It would appear that in Rome sons almost invariably separated their property during their father's lifetime; *consortia* were always arranged with collaterals.

15 Dowry, continuity and change

1 'No father who knows (the law) must take even the smallest gratuity for his daughter; for a man, who, through avarice, takes a gratuity, is a seller of his offspring' (Manu 3:51).

2 Numbers 24:4; see Goody (1962:319).

3 Paul Sant Cassia suggests to me that there is some evidence of the re-emergence of the direct dowry in the elite urban culture in the contemporary Mediterranean, both in Seville and in Barcelona.

4 Sant Cassia comments that this emphasis on agnation may be the result of the progressive marginalisation of pastoralism in the Mediterranean during the seventeenth and eighteenth centuries due to changes in the international division of labour.

5 Sant Cassia notes that a similar system was found in Athens in the early nineteenth century.

6 I am endebted to Ziba Mir-Hosseini for a discussion of this and other points.

7 It is perhaps significant that it was in a situation of social change, where sons were trying to distance themselves from paternal authority, early female betrothal and late marriage, that Tait noted how the young Konkomba men in northern Ghana became wage-labourers in an attempt to raise the bridewealth they required (1961:95); parallel situations arose in many parts of Africa where parental control was exercised not so much through the endowment of daughters or sons at marriage as through the management of large bridewealth payments.

8 Laslett (1969) gives the figure of 28.5 per cent (overall) as the proportion of households with servants in one hundred English communities between 1574 and 1821. There was a spectacular rise in the use of domestic labour in towns at the end of that period, which began to tail off at the end of the century (Hobsbawm 1968:157; see also Hajnal 1982).

9 It was such children, abandoned in order to avoid the direct responsibility for parenthood or infanticide, who were later to occupy the charitable orphanages of the western world.

10 Sant Cassia points out that this process is facilitated by the similarity of the systems of property transmission among Christians and Muslims.

11 See Sabean (forthcoming) for an excellent analysis of the difference between *Heiratsgut* and *Eigensgut*.

12 On the difference between Eurasia and Africa in this respect, see Goody (1969b).

13 The concentration into larger dwelling units could be mainly a matter of defence as was often the case in northern Ghana. But such collectivities might have relatively little effect upon economic activity and domestic structure (see Goody 1972). Living under one roof did not mean living out of one bowl, although in retrospect the actors often speak as if it did. The existence of large cooperative compounds in the past is sometimes reported by the people themselves, and there seems to be a strong element of nostalgic, golden-age reconstruction in the idea that families were once grander and more united than they are today. To some people a more collective past of this kind is suggested by the existence of a classificatory kinship terminology, which the Albanians possess (Hasluck 1954:30) in contrast to other Europeans, but as we have seen, such a deduction is quite unwarranted for the other societies we have examined. A classificatory terminology is no indicator of the size of domestic groups.

14 Sant Cassia notes that opening a separate entrance is a typical 'North African'

practice which marks the discreteness of the group *vis-à-vis* the outside. In Greece and South Europe it is more usual to have separate cooking areas (which would be implied by the distinct doorways).

15 An 'apartment' is a dwelling unit in a house, a residential unit; the latter is a 'houseful' in Laslett's terminology (1972).

16 Foster brotherhood was widely practised in Greece until the mid nineteenth century, not only among the pastoralists but in the towns. However its role was very different from adoption.

17 It was a failure to appreciate this point that led Maine and others into attempts to saddle archaic Eurasian societies with an ancestry of tight agnatic descent groups holding property in common.

18 Campbell pursues the identification of sheep, quiet, good, with men, and goats, sexy, wild, with women; as is usual with such schema, the identification is more contextual than the table suggests, for the goats are herded by young shepherds.

19 I owe the information in this paragraph to the comments of M. Couroucli. She sees big dowries, which she takes to be recent, as originating in the movements of Aegean migrants to Athens where their seafaring practices became incorporated in national legislation.

20 Couroucli (1987:41) writes of the *pallikaratiko* as 'the gift offered by the widow to her future husband who is marrying for the first time'.

21 Maria Couroucli, personal communication.

22 Maria Couroucli, personal communication.

23 For Finland, see Sweetzer (1964).

24 It is pointed out to me by M. Couroucli that I have taken an individualistic attitude to this mode of accumulating a dowry. While this stance may be more appropriate to the recent situation, it is a fact that siblings in Greece have long helped one another to accumulate an endowment. Brothers have tended to delay their marriage until their sisters have sufficient dowry, a situation that the acquisition of educational qualifications makes more complicated.

25 I am again indebted to Paul Sant Cassia and Maria Couroucli for a discussion of this point.

26 I am indebted to Maria Couroucli for this reference to 'real-estate dowries'.

27 In some cases girls were allotted a major portion of the inheritance, possibly when a widow took over the management of the conjugal estate.

28 The Arabic term *jahāz* or *jihāz* means literally an outfit, but in the larger sense of outfitting a ship. In medieval Cairo the terms *raḥl* and *shuwār*, travel equipment, were also used. The English trousseau, which refers to clothing and apparel, is too limited in meaning, perhaps even to include the jewellery that provided the wife with a kind of reserve fund.

29 In China, this aspect of the association appears to be reversed, possibly because of the nature and distribution of corporation lineages, but in other respects the similarity holds (table 4).

30 Magre is said to constitute an exception, but is this for dowry?

31 In Episkopsi, Corfu, where the basic productive resource consisted of olive trees, a man would divide his holding when he retired from active work (Couroucli 1985a:69). At that time he would call in a professional valuer (p. 77).

32 For an ethnographic account of this 'liberalising' process in China and the increase in production to which it gave rise, see Siu (1989).

33 For Cyprus, see Roussou (1985:296); for Greece, Shapiro (1985:322); for Greeks in Australia, see Bottomley, who notes that in Australia Greek women them-

selves declared that their professional training was considered to be a form of dowry since it made them able to earn an income (1985:161).

16 Asia and Europe

1 It is necessary to insist that the existence of stratification under conditions of shifting or hoe-based agriculture in Africa, especially in states, is not at issue. The question turns on the nature of agricultural production, of craft technology and organisation and of the modes of communication. The presence of a more complex system in Eurasia affects the nature of land tenure, of social hierarchies and of interpersonal relationships more generally.

2 The same may even have been true of the commercial communities in West Africa in the nineteenth century (Memel-Fote 1988), for Africa was not immune to changes in the circulation and accumulation of goods.

3 Did the development of religious trusts invariably proceed family ones? Or is this possibility a function of the fact that in pre-industrial societies, perhaps in all, the family's concern for the welfare of its members takes on a sacred aspect?

References

Abdul-Rauf, M. 1977. *The Islamic View of Women and the Family*. New York
Abrahams, I. 1915. Marriage (Jewish). Article in *Encyclopaedia of Religion and Ethics*, vol. 8. London
Abrahams, R. G. 1986. In-marrying sons-in-law in Finland. MS
Acharya, H. 1974. Some possible variations in family types in Gujarat. In G. Kurian (ed.), *The Family in India – a Regional View*. The Hague
Adam, W. 1865. Consanguinity in marriage. *Fortnightly Review* 2:710–30
Agarwala, S. N. 1966. *Some Problems of India's Population*. Bombay 1967. *Population*. New Delhi
Agathias 1828 Agathiae Myrinaei Historiarum: libra cinque, cum versione latina et annotationibus, B. G. Nierbuhr (ed.), *Corpus Scriptorum Historiae Byzantinae*. Bonn
Ahern, E. 1973. *The Cult of the Dead in a Chinese Village*. Stanford 1981. *Chinese Ritual and Politics*. Cambridge
Ahmad, L. 1986. Women and the advent of Islam. *Signs: Journal of Women in Culture and Society*, 11:665–91
Ahmed, A. 1984. Marriage and status of rural women in Bangladesh. M Phil thesis, Cambridge University
Allen, P. S. 1979. Internal migrations and the changing dowry in modern Greece. *The Indiana Social Studies Quarterly* 32:142–56
Anderson, M. 1971. *Family Structure in Nineteenth-Century Lancashire*. Cambridge
Anon. 1986. *Local Traditional Chinese Wedding* (11th Festival of Asian Arts). Hong Kong Museum of History
Aquinas, St. Thomas 1964. *Summa Theologiae* (60 vols.), T. Gilby (ed.). London
Arensberg, C. and Kimball, S. T. 1940. *Family and Community in Ireland*. Cambridge, Mass.
Ariès, P. 1960. *L'Enfant et la vie familiale sous l'Ancien Bégime*. Paris 1983. *The Hour of Our Death*. Harmondsworth
Aristotle. 1905. *Politics* (trans. B. Jowett). Oxford
Atran, S. 1985a. Démembrement social et remembrement agraire dans un village palestinien. *L'Homme* 25:111–35
1985b. Managing Arab kinship and marriage. *Social Science Information* 24:659–96
1986. *Hamula* organisation and *Masha's* tenure in Palestine. *Man* 21:271–95
Augustine (St.) 1610. *The Citie of God, with the learned Comments of To. Lod. Vives* (trans. J. Healey). London

508

Avezzù, E. 1983. Stilemi associativi et rappresentazioni della parenta nell' Iliade. *Quaderni di Storia* 17:69–97

Baker, H. D. R. 1968. *A Chinese Lineage Village: Sheung Shui*. Stanford

1979. *Chinese Family and Kinship*. London

Balsdon, J. P. V. D. 1963. *Roman Women, their History and Habits* (first pub. 1962). London

Balzac, H. 1897. *Contrat de mariage* (English trans.). London

Banks, M. Y. 1957. The social organisation of the Jaffna Tamils. PhD thesis, University of Cambridge

Barbosa, D. 1866. *A Description of the Coast of East Africa and Malabar in the Beginning of the Sixteenth Century*. London

Barclay, G. W. 1954. *Colonial Development and Population in Taiwan*. Princeton

Barnes, J. A. 1957. Land rights and kinship in two Bremnes hamlets. *J. R. Anthrop. Inst.* 7:31–56

Barth, F. 1987. *Cosmologies in the Making: A Generative Approach to Cultural Variation in Inner New Guinea*. Cambridge

Bateson, P. 1982. Preferences for cousins in Japanese quail. *Nature* 295:236–7

1983a. Genes, environment and the development of behaviour. In T. R. Halliday and P. J. B. Slater (eds.), *Animal Behaviour, Genes, Development and Learning* 3:52–81. Oxford

1983b. Uncritical periods and insensitive sociobiology. *The Behavioral and Brain Sciences* 6:102–3

1983c. The interpretation of sensitive periods. In A. Oliverio and M. Zappella (eds.), *The Behavior of Human Infants*. New York

1983d. Rules for changing the rules. In D. S. Bendall (ed.), *Evolution from Molecules to Men*. Cambridge

Beattie, H. J. 1979. *Land and Lineage in China: A Study of T'ung-Ch'eng County, Anhwei, in the Ming and Ch'ing Dynasties*. Cambridge

Beaucamp, J. 1985. Au XIe siècle, Byzance: le jeu des normes et des comportements. In C. Piault (ed.), *Familles et biens en Grèce et à Chypre*. Paris

Beck, B. E. F. 1972. *Peasant Society in Koṅku: A Study of Right and Left Sub-castes in South India*. Vancouver

Bede 1969. *Ecclesiastical History of the English People*. B. Colgrave and R. A. B. Mynors (eds.). Oxford

Beeston, A. 1957. The position of women in pre-Islamic South Arabia. *Proceedings XXII Congress of Orientalists* vol. 2:101–6. Leiden

Beidelman, T. O. 1959. *A Comparative Analysis of the Jajmani System*. Monographs of the Association of Asian Studies no. 8. New York

Beillevaire, P. 1986. La famille, instrument et modèle de la nation japonaise. In A. Burguière *et al.* (eds.), *Histoire de la famille*, vol. 2. Paris

Bell, H. I. 1949. Brother and sister marriage in Graeco-Roman Egypt. *Mélanges De Visscher. Revue internationale des droits de l'Antiquité* 2:83–92. Brussels

Bellwood, P. 1979. *Man's Conquest of the Pacific: The Prehistory of Southeast Asia and Oceania*. Oxford

Ben-Barak, Z. 1980. Inheritance by daughters in the ancient Near East. *J. Semitic Studies* 25:22–33

Benedict, R. 1936. Marital property rights in bilateral society. *Am. Anthrop.* 38:368–73

Benzinger, I. 1902. Marriage. *Encyclopaedia Biblica* 3:2942–51. London

Berreman, G. D. 1962. Pahari polyandry; a comparison. *Am. Anthrop.* 64:60–75

1972. *Hindus of the Himalayas: Ethnography and Change*. Berkeley

1975. Himalayan polyandry and the domestic cycle. *Am. Ethnol.* 2:127–38

Bertaud, J.-P. 1983. *La Vie quotidienne en France au temps de la Révolution. 1789–95*. Paris

Bianquis, T. 1986. Le famille en Islam arabe. In A. Burguière *et al.* (eds.), *Histoire de la famille*, vol. 1. Paris

Bidez, J. and Cumont, Fr. 1937. *L'Egypte des astrologues*. Brussels

Bogin, M. (1976). *The Women Troubadours*. New York

Bose, N. K. 1975. *The Structure of Hindu Society* (trans. A. Beteille). New Delhi

Bott, E. 1957. *Family and Social Networks: Roles, Norms and External Relationships in Ordinary Urban Families*. London

Bottéro, J. 1982. Le 'code' de Hammu-rabi. *Annali della Scuola Normale Superiore di Pisa* 12:409–44

Bottomley, G. 1985. Perpétuation de la dot chez les Grecs d'Australie: transformations et re-negociation des pratiques traditionnelles. In C. Piault (ed.), *Familles et biens en Grèce et à Chypre*. Paris

Bourdieu, P. 1977. *Outline of a Theory of Practice*. Cambridge

Braund, D. C. 1985. *Augustus to Nero: A Source Book on Roman History 31 BC–AD 68*. London

Breman, J. C. 1974. *Patronage and Exploitation: Changing Agrarian Relations in South Gujarat*. Berkeley

Bremmer, J. 1983. The importance of the maternal uncle and grandfather in Archaic and Classical Greece and early Byzantium. *Zeitschrift für Papyrologie und Epigraphik* 50:173–86

Brough, J. (trans.) 1968. *Love Poems from the Sanskrit*. Harmondsworth

Bryce, J. 1901. *Studies in History and Jurisprudence*. Oxford

Buck, J. L. 1937. *Land Utilization in China*. Nanking

Burguière, A. 1986. Pour une typologie des formes d'organisation domestique de l'Europe moderne (XVIe–XIXe siècles). *Annales ESC* 3:639–55

Burrows, M. 1937. The complaint of Laban's daughters. *J. American Oriental Soc.* 57:259–76

1940. The ancient oriental background of Hebrew levirite laws. *Bull. Am. School Oriental Res.* 77:2–15

Bynum, C. W. 1987. *Holy Feast and Holy Fast: The Religious Significance of Food to Medieval Women*. Berkeley

Cain, M. 1986. The consequence of reproductive failure: dependence, mobility, and mortality among the elderly of rural South Asia. *Population Studies* 40:375–88

Caldwell, P. and Caldwell, J. 1987. The religious and cultural context of high fertility in sub-Saharan Africa. *Pop. Dev. Review* 13:409–37

(n.d.). Lessons on differential health and survival from South India and Sri Lanka. Draft MS

Campbell, J. K. 1964. *Honour, Family and Patronage*. Oxford

Carcopino, J. 1941. *Daily Life in Ancient Rome* (English trans.). London

Carrasco, P. 1959. *Land and Polity in Tibet*. Am. Ethnol. Soc. Seattle

Cartier, M. 1986a. En Chine, la famille, relais du pouvoir. In A. Burguière *et al.* (eds.), *Histoire de la famille*, vol. 1. Paris

1986b. La longue marche de la famille chinoise. In A. Burguière *et al.* (eds.), *Histoire de la famille*, vol. 2. Paris

1988. Dette et propriété en Chine. In C. Malmoud (ed.), *Lien de vie, noed mortel: les représentations de la dette en Chine, au Japon at dans le monde indien*. Paris

Černý, J. 1954. Consanguineous marriages in pharaonic Egypt. *J. Egypt. Arch.* 40:23–9

Chaffee, J. (forthcoming). The marriage of a clanswoman in the Sung imperial clan. In P. Ebrey and R. Watson (eds.), *Marriage and Inequality in Chinese Society.* Berkeley

Chan, W. K. K. 1977. *Merchants, Mandarins and Modern Enterprises in Late Ch'ing China.* Cambridge, Mass.

Chapekar, N. G. 1955. Social change in rural Maharashtra. In K. M. Kapadia (ed.), *Professor Ghurye Felicitation Volume.* Bombay

Chastagnol, A. 1979. Les femmes dans l'ordre sénatorial: titulaire et rang social à Rome. *Revue Historique* 262:3–28

Chattopadhyay, K. P. 1922. Levirate and kinship in India. *Man* 22:36–41

Chen, Chung-min 1985. Dowry and inheritance. In Hsieh Jih-chang and Chuang Ying-chang (eds.), *The Chinese Family and its Ritual Behavior.* Taiwan

Chen, H.-S. 1936. *Landlord and Peasant in China.* New York

1949. *Frontier Land Systems in Southernmost China: A Comparative Study of Agrarian Problems and Social Organization among the Pai Yi People of Yunnan and the Kamba People of Sinkiang.* Inst. of Pacific Relations, New York

Chesneaux, J. 1973. *Peasant Revolts in China 1840–1949.* London

Chrysostom, St. John 1718–38. *Epist. prim. ad Corinth. Opera omn. quae exst.* Paris

Coale, A. J. 1985. Fertility in rural China: a reconfirmation of the Barclay reassessment. In S. B. Hanley and A. P. Wolf (eds.), *Family and Population in East Asian History.* Stanford

Cohen, B. 1967. Regions subjective and objective: their relation to the stage of modern Indian history and society. In R. I. Crane (ed.), *Regions and Regionalism in South Asian Studies: An Exploratory Study.* Durham, N.C.

Cohen, M. L. 1976. *House United, House Divided: The Chinese Family Tradition in Taiwan.* New York

1985. Chinese society on Taiwan under the Ch'ing. MS

Collins, R. 1986. *Weberian Sociological Theory.* Cambridge

Collomp, A. 1983. *La Maison du père: famille et village en Haute-Provence aux XVIIe et XVIIIe siècles.* Paris

Collver, A. 1963. The family cycle in India and the United States. *Am. Sociol. Rev.* 28:86–96

Coquery-Vidrovitch, C. 1969. Recherches sur un mode de production africain. *La Pensée* 144:61–78

1978. Research on an African mode of production. In D. Seddon (ed.), *Relations of Production* (trans. H. Lackner). London

Corbett, P. E. 1930. *The Roman Law of Marriage.* Oxford

Corbier, M. 1985. Idéologie et practique de l'héritage (1er s.av. J.-C–11e s.ap. J.-C). *International Survey of Roman Law* 13. Naples

Coulson, N. 1964. *Introduction to the History of Islamic Law.* Edinburgh

Couroucli, M. 1985a. Lignage, dot et héritage: Episkepsi, Corfu. In C. Piault (ed.), *Familles et biens en Grèce et è Chypre.* Paris

1985b. *Les Oliviers du lignage.* Paris

1987. Dot et société en Grèce moderne. In G. Ravis-Giordani (ed.), *Femmes et patrimoines dans les sociétés rurales de l'Europe méditerranéenne.* CNRS-Sud

Craik, E. M. (ed.) 1984. *Marriage and Property.* Aberdeen

Crane, R. I. (ed.) 1967. *Regions and Regionalism in South Asian Studies: An Exploratory Study*. Durham, N.C.

Croll, E. 1984. The exchange of women and property: marriage in post-Revolutionary China. In R. Hirschon (ed.), *Women and Property–Women as Property*. London

1985. Introduction: fertility norms and family size in China. In E. Cross, D. Davin and P. Kane (eds.), *China's One-child Family Policy*. London

Croll, E., Davin, D. and Kane, P. 1985. *China's One-child Family Policy*. London

Crone, P. 1987. *Roman, Provincial and Islamic Law*. Cambridge

Crook, J. A. 1967a. *Law and Life in Rome*. London

1967b. Patria potestas. *Class. Quarterly* 17:114–22

1986. Women in Roman succession. In B. Rawson (ed.), *The Family in Ancient Rome: Select Studies*. New York

1988. 'His and Hers': what degree of financial responsibility did husband and wife have for the matrimonial home and their life in common, in a Roman marriage? MS

Cuisenier, J. 1975. *Economie et parenté: leurs affinités de structure dans le domaine turc et dans le domaine Arabe*. Paris

Czap, P. 1982. The perennial multiple family household: Mishino, Russia, 1782–1858. *J. Family Hist.* 7:5–26

Das, V. 1976. Masks and faces; an essay on Punjabi kinship. *Contributions to Indian Sociology* 10:1–30

Daube, D. 1969. *Roman Law: Linguistic, Social and Philosophical Aspects*. Edinburgh

Davies, C. 1959. *An Historical Atlas of the Indian Peninsula* (2nd edn). Madras

Davis, K. 1951. *The Population of India and Pakistan*. Princeton

1955. Institutional patterns favoring high fertility in underdeveloped areas. *Eugenics Quarterly* 2:33–9

De, B. 1966. A historical perspective on theories of regionalization in India. In R. I. Crane (ed.), *Regions and Regionalism in South Asian Studies: An Exploratory Study*. Durham, N.C.

de Groot, J. J. M. 1892–1910. *The Religious System of China* (6 vols.). Leyden

Demosthenes 1964. *Demosthenes VI: Private Orations L–LVIII* (trans. A. T. Murray). Loeb Classical Library, Cambridge, Mass.

Dennerline, J. 1986. Marriage, adoption, and charity in the development of lineages in Wu-hsi from Sung to Ch'ing. In P. B. Ebrey and J. L. Watson (eds.), *Kinship and Social Organization in Late Imperial China, 1000–1940*. Stanford

Derrett, J. D. M. 1958. A strange rule of smrti, and a suggested solution. *J. R. Asiatic Soc.* pp. 17–25

De Visscher, F. 1952. 'Conubium' et 'Civitas'. *Rev. int. droits de l'Antiquité* 401–22

de Vos, G. 1984. Religion and family: structural and motivational relationships. In G. de Vos and T. Sofue (eds.), *Religion and Family in East Asia*. Senri Ethnological Studies, no. 11. Osaka

Dien, A. E. 1976. Elite lineages and the T'o-pa accommodation: a study of the edict of 495. *J. of the Econ. and Soc. Hist. of the Orient* 19:61–88

Diodorus Siculus 1933. *Diodorus of Sicily* (trans. C. H. Oldfield), 12 vols. Loeb Classical Library, Cambridge, Mass.

Divale, W. T. and Harris, M. 1976. Population, warfare, and the male supremacist complex. *Am. Anthrop.* 78:521–38

Dixon, S. 1984. Family finances: Tullia and Terentia. *Antichthon* 18:78–101. Reprinted in B. Rawson (ed.), 1986. *The Family in Ancient Rome: Select Studies.* New York

1985a. Polybius on Roman women and property. *Am. J. Philology* 106:147–70

1985b. Breaking the law to do the right thing:the gradual erosion of the Voconian Law in Ancient Rome. *Adelaide Law Review* 9:519–34

1985c. The marriage alliance in the Roman elite. *J. Family Hist.* 10:353–78

1986. Review of J. P. Hallett, *Fathers and Daughters in Roman Society: Women and the Elite Family.* Princeton, 1984. *Am. J. Philology* 107:125–30

Du Boulay, J. 1986. Women – images of their nature and destiny in rural Greece. In J. Dubisch (ed.), *Gender and Power in Rural Greece.* Princeton

Dube, S. C. 1955. *Indian Village.* London

Duby, G. 1977. *The Chivalrous Society* (trans. C. Postan). London

Dumont, L. 1953. The Dravidian kinship terminology as an expression of marriage. *Man* 53:34–9

1957a. Hierarchy and Marriage Alliance in South India. *R. Anthrop. Inst. Occasional paper*, no. 12. London

1957b. *Une Sous-caste de l'Inde du Sud: organisation sociale et religion des Pramalai Kallar.* Paris

1961. Marriage in India, the present state of the question. *Contributions to Indian Sociology* 5:75–95

1964. A note on locality in relation to descent. *Contributions to Indian Sociology* 7:71–6

1966a. A fundamental problem in the sociology of caste. *Contributions to Indian Sociology* 9:17–32

1966b. Marriage in India: the present state of the question – III. North India in relation to South India. *Contributions to Indian Sociology* 9:90–114

1975a. Terminology and prestations revisited. *Contributions to Indian Sociology* 9:197–215

1975b. *Dravidian et Kariera: l'alliance de mariage dans l'Inde du Sud, et en Australie.* Paris

Dumont, L. and D. Pocock, 1957. Kinship (review of Irvati Karve, *Kinship Organization in India*), *Contributions to Indian Sociology* 9:35–60

Duperron, A. 1778. *Legislation Orientale.* Amsterdam

Durkheim, E. 1893. *La Division du Travail* (English trans. 1947). Paris

Dutt, S. 1962. *Buddhist Monks and Monasteries of India: Their History and Their Contribution to Indian Culture.* London

Dyer, C. 1980. *Lords and Peasants in a Changing Society: the Estates of the Bishop of Worcester, 680–1540.* Cambridge

Dyson, T. and Moore, M. 1983. On kinship structure, female autonomy and demographic behavior in India. *Population and Development Review* 9:35–60

Ebrey, P. B. 1981. Women in the kinship system of the Southern Song upper class. *Historical Reflections* 8:113–28

1983. Types of lineages in Ch'ing China: a re-examination of the Chang lineage of T'ung-ch'eng. *Ch'ing-shih wen-t'i* 9:1–20

(forthcoming). Shifts in marriage finance, sixth to thirteenth century. In P. Ebrey and R. Watson (eds.), *Marriage and Inequality in Chinese Society.* Berkeley

Ebrey, P. B. and Watson, J. L. (eds.) 1986. *Kinship Organization in Late Imperial China 1000–1940.* Berkeley

Ebrey, P. B. and Watson, R. (eds.) (forthcoming). *Marriage and Inequality in Chinese Society.* Berkeley

Eglar, Z. 1960. *A Punjabi Village in Pakistan.* New York
Ekvall, R. 1968. *Fields on the Hoof.* New York
Elias, N. 1978. *The Civilizing Process* (English trans.). Oxford
Elvin, M. 1973. *The Pattern of the Chinese Past.* London
Epstein, S. 1962. *Economic Development and Social Change in South India.* Oxford
Erdmann, W. 1934. *Die Ehe im alten Griechenland.* Munich
Euripedes 1978. *Andromache* (trans. A. S. Way). In G. P. Goold (ed.), *Euripedes.* Loeb Classical Library, Cambridge, Mass.
Evans-Pritchard, E. E. 1940. *The Nuer: A Description of the Modes of Livelihood and Political Institutions of a Nilotic People.* Oxford
   1951. *Kinship and Marriage among the Nuer.* Oxford
Evers, H. D. 1967. Kinship and property rights in a Buddhist monastery in Central Ceylon. *Am. Anthrop.* 69:703–10
Fallers, L. A. 1957. Some determinants of marriage instability in Busoga; a reformulation of Gluckman's thesis. *Africa* 27:106–21
Fargues, P. 1986. Le monde arabe: la citadelle domestique. In A. Burguière *et al.* (eds.), *Histoire de la famille*, vol. 2. Paris
Faure, D. 1986. *The Structure of Chinese Rural Society: Lineage and Village in the Eastern New Territories, Hong Kong.* Hong Kong
Fei, Hsiao-tung 1939. *Peasant Life in China.* London
   1946. Peasantry and gentry: an interpretation of Chinese social structure and its changes. *Am. J. Sociology* 52:1–17
Fei, Hsiao-tung and Chang, Chih-I 1948. *Earthbound China: A Study of Rural Economy in Yunnan.* London
Feigin, S. 1931. Some cases of adoption in Israel. *J. of Biblical Literature* 50:186–200
Fêng, H. Y. 1937. The Chinese kinship system. *Harvard J. Asiatic Studies* 2:141–275
Finley, M. I. 1955. Marriage, sale and gift in the Homeric world. *Revue Int. des Droits de l'Antiquité* 3:167–94
   1963. Generalizations in ancient history. In L. Gottschalk (ed.), *Generalization in the Writing of History.* Chicago
Firth, R. 1947. Introduction to Lin Yeuh-hwa, *The Golden Wing.* New York
Forgeau, A. 1986. La mémoire du nom et l'ordre pharaonique. In A. Burguière *et al.* (eds.), *Histoire de la famille.* Paris
Fortes, M. 1945. *The Dynamics of Clanship among the Tallensi.* London
   1949. *The Web of Kinship among the Tallensi.* London
   1950. Kinship and marriage among the Ashanti. In A. R. Radcliffe-Brown and C. D. Forde (eds.), *African Systems of Kinship and Marriage.* London
   1969. *Kinship and the Social Order.* Chicago
   1978. An anthropologist's apprenticeship. *Annual Review of Anthropology.* Palo Alto, Calif.
   1987. *Religion, Morality and the Person.* Cambridge
Fortune, R. 1932. Incest. *Encyclopedia of the Social Sciences* 7:622–5. New York
   1933. A note on some forms of kinship structure. *Oceania* 4:1–10
Foucault, M. 1984. *Histoire de la sexualité.* Paris
Fox, R. G. 1971. *Kin, Class, Raja and Rule.* Berkeley
Frazer, J. G. 1919. *Folklore in the Old Testament* (3 vols.). London
Freedman, M. 1958. *Lineage Organization in Southeastern China.* London
   1962. The family in China: past and present. *Pacific Affairs* 34:323–36
   1963. Chinese domestic family models. *VIe Congrès internationale des sciences anthropologiques et ethnologiques*, vol. 2, part 1. Paris

1966. *Chinese Lineage and Society*. London

Frenzen, P. D. and Miller, B. D. 1988. Domestic organization and fertility in rural India. Paper presented at the fortieth annual meeting of the Association for Asian Studies, San Francisco

Freud, S. 1938. *Totem and Taboo*. London

Fried, M. H. 1953. *Fabric of Chinese Society: A Study of the Social Life of a Chinese County Seat*. New York

Friedl, E. 1959. Dowry and inheritance in modern Greece. *Trans. New York Academy of Sciences* 22:49–54

1962. *Vasilika: A Village in Modern Greece*. New York

1963. Some aspects of dowry and inheritance in Boeotia. In J. Pitt-Rivers (ed.), *Mediterranean Countryman*. Paris

Friedlaender, L. 1913. *Roman Life and Manners Under the Early Empire* (English trans.). London

Friedman, M. A. 1980. *Jewish Marriage in Palestine: A Cairo Geniza Study;* vol. 1, *The Ketubba Traditions of Eretz Israel*. Tel Aviv

Fruzzetti, L. 1982. *The Gift of a Virgin: Women, Marriage and Ritual in a Bengali Society*. New Brunswick, N.J.

Fruzzetti, L. and Östör, A. 1976a. Is there a structure to north Indian kinship terminology? *Contributions to Indian Sociology* 10:63–95

1976b. Seed and earth: a cultural analysis of kinship in a Bengali town. *Contributions to Indian Sociology* 10:96–132

(with S. Barnett) 1976c. The cultural construction of the person in Bengal and Tamil Nadu. *Contributions to Indian Sociology* 10:157–82

Fukutake, T. 1967. *Asian Rural Society: China, India, Japan*. Tokyo

Fustel de Coulanges, N. D. 1864. *La Cité antique*. Paris (English trans. 1873, 1955)

Gallin, B. 1960. Matrilateral and affinal relationships of a Taiwanese village. *Am. Anthrop.* 62:632–42

1966. *Hsin Hsing, Taiwan: A Chinese Village in Change*. Berkeley

Gallin, B. and R. 1982. The Chinese joint family in changing rural Taiwan. In S. L. Greenblatt *et al.* (eds.), *Social Interaction in Chinese Society*. New York

Gardella, R. P. 1982. Commercial bookkeeping in Ch'ing China and the West: a preliminary assessment. *Ch'ing-Shih Wen-t'i* 7:56–72

Gates, H. 1987a. The petty capitalist mode of production. MS

1987b. Sell a daughter, save a farm: on the commoditization of Chinese women. MS

Gaudemet, J. 1961. Aspetti communitari del regime matrimoniale romano. *Jus* 12:450–64

Gaunt, D. 1983. The property and kin relationships of retired farmers in Northern and Central Europe. In R. Wall *et al.* (eds.), *Family Forms in Historic Europe*. Cambridge

Gazetteer of India. Gujarat State. Ahmadabad District 1984. Ahmadabad

Geddes, A. 1947–8. The social and psychological significance of variability in population change. *Human Relations* 1:181–205

Gillion, K. L. 1968. *Ahmedabad: A Study in Indian Urban History*. Berkeley

GJ. Goody, Jack, Fieldwork in Gujarat, India [abbreviated GJ followed by note number]

Glassner, J. J. 1986. Du Sumer à Babylone: familles pour gérer, familles pour régner. In A. Burguière *et al.* (eds.), *Histoire de la Famille*. Paris

Gluckman, M. 1950. Kinship and marriage among the Lozi of Northern Rhodesia and the Zulu of Natal. In A. R. Radcliffe-Brown and D. Forde (eds.), *African Systems of Kinship and Marriage*. London

1956. *Custom and Conflict in Africa*. London

1965. *Politics, Law and Ritual in Tribal Society*. Oxford

Goitein, S. D. 1964. Commercial and family partnerships in the countries of medieval Islam. *Islamic Studies* 3:315–37

1978. *A Mediterranean Society: The Jewish Communities of the Arab World as Portrayed in the Documents of the Cairo Geniza;* vol. 3, *The Family*. Berkeley

Goldstein, M. C. 1971a. Taxation and the structure of a Tibetan village. *Central Asiatic Journal* 15:1–27

1971b. Stratification, polyandry and family structure in Central Tibet. *Southwestern J. Anthrop.* 27:64–74

1976. Fraternal polyandry and fertility in a high Himalayan valley in northwest Nepal. *Human Ecology* 4:423–33

1978. Pahari and Tibetan polyandry revisited. *Ethnology* 17:325–7

Goldthwaite, R. A. 1987. The Medici Bank and the world of Florentine capitalism. *Past and Present* 114:3–31

Goode, W. J. 1959. The theoretical importance of love. *Am. Sociol. Rev.* 24:38–47

1963. *World Revolution and Family Patterns*. Glencoe, Ill.

Goodenough, W. H. 1949. Comments on the question of incestuous marriage in Old Iran. *Am. Anthrop.* 51:326–8

Goody, E. 1973. *Contexts of Kinship*. Cambridge

1982. *Parenthood and Social Reproductions: Fostering and Occupational Roles in West Africa*. Cambridge

Goody, E. and Goody, J. 1966. Cross-cousin marriage in northern Ghana. *Man* 1:343–55

Goody, J. 1956. A comparative approach to incest and adultery. *Brit. J. Soc.* 7:286–305

1958. The fission of domestic groups among the LoDagaba. In J. Goody (ed.), *The Developmental Cycle in Domestic Groups*. Cambridge

1959. The mother's brother and the sister's son in West Africa. *J. R. Anthrop. Inst.* 89:61–88

1961. The classification of double descent systems. *Current Anthropology* 2:3–12

1962. *Death, Property and the Ancestors*. Stanford

1966. Circulating succession among the Gonja, and Introduction. In J. Goody (ed.), *Succession to High Office*. Cambridge

1967. The over-kingdom of Gonja. In D. Forde and P. Kaberry (eds.), *West African Kingdoms*. London

1968. Kinship: descent groups. *Int. Encycl. Soc. Sciences* 8:401–8. New York

1969a. Marriage policy and political incorporation in northern Ghana. In R. Cohen and J. F. Middleton (eds.), *From Tribe to Nation in Africa: Studies in Incorporation Processes*. San Francisco

1969b. Inheritance, property and marriage in Africa and Eurasia. *Sociology* 3:55–76

1969c. *Comparative Studies in Kinship*. Stanford

1969d. Succession in contemporary Africa. *Archiv. Europ. Sociol.* 10:27–40

1970. Sideways or downwards? Lateral and vertical succession, inheritance and descent in Africa and Eurasia. *Man* 5:627–38

1971. *Technology, Tradition and the State in Africa*. London

1972. The evolution of the family. In P. Laslett and R. Wall (eds.), *Household and Family in Past Time*. Cambridge

1973. Bridewealth and dowry in Africa and Eurasia. In J. Goody and S. J. Tambiah, *Bridewealth and Dowry*. Cambridge

1976. *Production and Reproduction*. Cambridge

1979. Slavery in time and space. In J. L. Watson (ed.), *Asian and African Systems of Slavery*. Oxford

1983. *The Development of the Family and Marriage in Europe*. Cambridge

1985. Under the lineage's shadow. *Proc. Brit. Acad.* 70:189–208

1986. *The Logic of Writing and the Organization of Society*. Cambridge

1987a. *The Interface between the Written and the Oral*. Cambridge

1987b. Inheritance. *Palgrave's Encyclopaedia*. London

(forthcoming a). The futures of the family in Africa. In G. McNicoll and M. Cain (eds.)

(forthcoming b). Family, population and development: some remarks. MS.

Goody, J. *et al.* 1981a. Implicit sex preferences; a comparative study. *J. Biosoc. Sci.* 13:455–66

1981b. On the absence of explicit sex differences in Ghana. *J. Biosoc. Sci.* 13:87–96

Goody, J. and Harrison, G. 1973. Appendix, Strategies of heirship. *Comparative Studies in Society and History* 15:3–20

Goody, J. and Tambiah, S. J. 1973. *Bridewealth and Dowry*. Cambridge

Gordon, C. 1937. The story of Jacob and Laban in the light of the Nuzi tablets. *Bull. Am. School Oriental Res.* 66:25–7

Gough, K. 1956. Brahmin kinship in a Tamil village. *Am. Anthrop.* 58:826–53

1961. Nayar: Central Kerala, and Nayar: North Kerala. In D. M. Schneider and K. Gough (eds.), *Matrilineal Kinship*. Berkeley

1968. Implications of literacy in traditional China and India. In J. Goody (ed.), *Literacy in Traditional Societies*. Cambridge

1975. Changing households in Kerala. In D. Narain (ed.), *Explorations in the Family and Other Essays*. Bombay

1978. *Dravidian Kinship and Modes of Production* (The Irawati Karve Memorial Lecture for 1978). Indian Council for Social Science Research. New Delhi

1980. Modes of production in southern India. *Contributions to Indian Sociology* 13:266–91

1981. *Rural Society in Southeast India*. Cambridge

Granet, M. 1920. *La Polygamie sororale et le sororat dans la Chine féodale: études sur les formes anciennes de la polygamie chinoise*. Paris

Granquist, H. 1931. *Marriage Conditions in a Palestine Village*. Helsinki

Gratwick, A. S. 1984. Free or not so free? Wives and daughters in the late Roman Republic. In E. M. Craick (ed.), *Marriage and Property*. Aberdeen

Greenberg, M. 1962. Another look at Rachel's theft of the teraphim. *J. of Biblical Literature* 81:239–48

Greenhalgh, S. 1985. Social causes and consequences on Taiwan's postwar economic development. MS

1990. Land reform and family entrepreneurialism in East Asia. In G. McNicoll and M. Cain (eds.)

Griffith, F. L. 1915. Marriage (Egyptian). *Encyclopaedia of Religion and Ethics*, vol. 8. London

Gronewold, S. 1982. *Beautiful Merchandise: Prostitution in China 1860–1936*. New York

Grosz, K. 1981. Dowry and brideprice in Nuzi. In M. A. Morrison and D. I. Owen (eds.), *Studies on the Civilization and Culture of Nuzi and the Hurrians: In Honour of E. R. Lacheman.* Winona Lake, Ind.

Gunawardana, R. A. L. H. 1979. *Robe and Plough: Monasticism and Economic Interest in Early Medieval Sri Lanka* (Assn for Asian Studies no. 35). Tucson

Gupta, G. R. 1974. *Marriage, Religion and Society: Patterns of Change in an Indian Village.* Delhi

Habbakuk, H. J. 1950. Marriage settlement in the eighteenth century. *Trans. R. Hist. Soc.* 32:15–30

Hajnal, J. 1965. European marriage patterns in perspective. In D. V. Glass and D. E. C. Eversley (eds.), *Population in History.* London
  1982. Two kinds of preindustrial household formation system. *Pop. Dev. Review* 8:449–94

Hallett, J. P. 1984. *Fathers and Daughters in Roman Society.* Princeton

Hamilton, G. G. 1977. Nineteenth century Chinese merchant associations: conspiracy or combination? The case of the Swatow opium guild. *Ch'ing-shih wen-t'i* 3:50–71

Handman, M. 1983. *La Violence et la Ruse: hommes et femmes dans un village Grec.* Aix-en-Provence
  1985. Code civil et droit coutumier: la dot à Pouri (Thessalie). In C. Piault (ed.), *Familles et biens en Grèce et à Chypre.* Paris

Hanley, S. B. 1972. Population trends and economic development in Tokugawa, Japan: the case of Bizen Province in Okayama. In D. V. Glass and R. Revelle (eds.), *Population and Social Change.* London
  1977. The influence of economic and social variables on marriage and fertility in eighteenth and nineteenth century Japanese villages. In R. D. Lee (ed.), *Population Patterns in the Past.* New York

Hanley, S. B. and Wolf, A. P. (eds.) 1985. *Family and Population in East Asian History.* Stanford

Harper, E. B. 1964. Ritual pollution as an integrator of caste and religion. *J. Asian Studies* 2:151–97

Harrell, S. 1985. The rich get children: segmentation, stratification, and population in three Zhejiang lineages, 1550–1850. In S. B. Hanley and A. P. Wolf (eds.), *Family and Population in East Asian History.* Stanford

Harrell, S. and Dickey S. A. 1985. Dowry Systems in Complex Societies. *Ethnology* 24:105–20

Harris. M. 1979. *Cultural Materialism.* New York

Harrison, A. R. W. 1968. *The Law of Athens.* Oxford

Harvey, Y. K. 1979. *Six Korean Women: The Socialization of Shamans.* St Paul, Minn.

Hasluck, M. 1954. *The Unwritten Law in Albania.* Cambridge

Hazleton, K. 1986. Patrilines and the development of localized lineages: the Wu of Hsiu-ning City, Hui-chou, to 1528. In P. B. Ebrey and J. L. Watson (eds.), *Kinship Organization in Late Imperial China, 1000–1940.* Berkeley

Headland, I. T. 1914. *Home Life in China.* New York

Henne, M. 1954. Du mariage entre frères et soeurs dans l'Antiquité. *Revue historique de droit français et étranger* 32:469–70

Heritier, F. 1979. Symbolique de l'inceste et de sa prohibition. In M. Izard and P. Smith (eds.), *La Fonction symbolique: essais d'anthropologie.* Paris
  1981. *L'Exercise de la parenté.* Paris

Herlihy, D. 1974. The generation in medieval history. *Viator* 5:347–64
Herlihy, D. and Klapisch-Zuber, C. 1978. *Les Toscans et leurs familles: une étude du 'castato' florentin de 1427.* Paris
Hershatter, G. (forthcoming). Prostitution and the twentieth-century market in women. In P. B. Ebrey and R. S. Watson (eds.), *Marriage and Inequality in Chinese Society.* Berkeley
Hiatt, L. R. 1965. *Kinship and Conflict: A Study of an Aboriginal Community in Northern Arnhemland.* Canberra
Hindu Marriage Act 1955. *Hindu Marriage Act, 1955.* no. 25 of 1955. New Delhi
Hirschon, R. (ed.), 1984. *Women and Property – Women as Property.* London
Hoang, P. 1915. *Le Mariage chinois au point de vue légal* (2nd edn). Shanghai
Hobhouse, L. T. 1906. *Morals in Evolution: A Study in Comparative Ethics* (3rd edn 1926). London
Hobsbawm, E. J. 1968. *Industry and Empire: An Economic History of Britain since 1750.* Harmondsworth
Hoffmann, G. 1985. Xénophon, la femme et les biens. In C. Piault (ed.), *Familles et biens en Grèce et à Chypre.* Paris
Homans, G. C. 1941. *English Villagers of the Thirteenth Century.* Cambridge, Mass.
Hombert, M. and Préaux, C. 1949. Les mariages consanguins dans l'Egypte romaine. *Hommages à J. Bidez et Fr. Cumont.* Coll.L. 2:135–42. Brussels
Hopkins, A. G. 1973. *An Economic History of West Africa.* New York
Hopkins, K. 1965. The age of Roman girls at marriage. *Population Studies* 18:309–27
  1966. On the probable age structure of the Roman population. *Population Studies* 20:245–64
  1980. Brother–sister marriage in Roman Egypt. *Comparative Studies in Society and History* 22:303–54 (reprinted K. Hopkins, *Sociological Studies in Roman History,* vol. 3. Cambridge, forthcoming)
  1983. *Death and Renewal.* Cambridge
Hsieh, Jih-chang 1982. The impact of urbanization on Chinese family organization in Taiwan. *Bull. Inst. Ethnol. Acad. Sinica* 54:47–69
  1985. Meal rotation. In Hsieh Jih-chang and Chuang Ying-chang (eds.), *The Chinese Family and its Ritual Behavior.* Taiwan
Hsu, F. L. K. 1943. The myth of Chinese family size. *Am. J. Sociology* 48:555–62
  1949. *Under the Ancestors' Shadow: Chinese Culture and Personality.* London
Hughes, D. O. 1974. Urban growth and family structure in medieval Genoa. *Past and Present* 66:3–28
  1978. From brideprice to dowry in Mediterranean Europe. *J. Family Hist.* 3:262–96
Huth, A. H. 1875. *The Marriage of Near Kin.* London
Hutton, J. H. 1946. *Caste in India.* Cambridge
  1972. Foreword. In I. Karve, *Kinship Organization in India* (3rd edn). Bombay
Hymes, R. P. 1986. Marriage, descent groups, and the localist strategy in Sung and Yuan Fu-chou. In P. B. Ebrey and J. L. Watson (eds.), *Kinship Organization in Late Imperial China 1000–1940.* Berkeley
Ibbetson, D. C. J. 1903. Jats. *The Census of India, 1901.* Ethnographic Appendices pp. 74–80. Calcutta
Inden, R. B. and Nicholas, R. W. 1977. *Kinship in Bengali Culture.* Chicago
Ingalls, D. 1959. The Brahman tradition. In M. Singer (ed.), *Traditional India: Structure and Change.* Philadelphia
Issawi, C. 1950. *An Arab Philosophy of History: Selections from the Prolegomena of Ibn Khaldun of Tunis (1332–1406).* London

1982. *An Economic History of the Middle East and North Africa.* New York

Jain, A. K. 1985. Determinants of regional variations in infant mortality in rural India. *Population Studies* 39:407–24

Jamous, R. 1981. *Honneur et 'baraka': les structures sociales traditionelles dans le Rif.* Cambridge

Johns, C. H. W. 1904. *Babylonian and Assyrian Laws, Contracts and Letters.* Edinburgh

Johnston, R. F. 1910. *Lion and Dragon in Northern China.* New York

Jolowicz, H. F. 1932. *Historical Introduction to the Study of Roman Law.* Cambridge

Just, R. 1985. A hommes plus riches, épouses plus jeunes: le cas de Meganisi, île ionienne. In C. Piault (ed.), *Familles et biens en Grèce et à Chypre.* Paris

Juvenal 1831. *Satires* (trans. C. Bodham). London

Kalafati-Papagalani, I. 1985. En feuillant les testaments: la loi et son application à Aghios Petros, île de Leucade, du XIIIe au milleu du XXe siècle. In C. Piault (ed.), *Familles et biens en Grèce et à Chypre.* Paris.

Kapadia, K. M. 1955. *Marriage and Family in India.* Bombay

Karve, I. 1953. *Kinship Organization in India.* Deccan College Monograph Series no. 11. Poona

Kent, F. W. 1977. *Household and Lineage in Renaissance Florence: The Family Life of the Capponi, Ginovi, and Rucellai.* Princeton

Khare, R. S. 1976. *The Hindu Hearth and Home.* Delhi

Kleinman, D. S. 1973. Fertility variation and resources in rural India (1961). *Economic Development and Cultural Change* 21:679–96

Koh, H. C. 1981. Religion and socialization of women in Korea. In G. de Vos and T. Sofue (eds.), *Religion and Family in East Asia.* Senri Ethnological Studies, no. 11. Osaka

Kolenda, P. M. 1963. Towards a model of the Hindu *jajmani* system. *Human Organization* 22:11–31, repr. P. M. Kolenda, 1981, *Caste, Cult and Hierarchy.* Meerut

1967. Regional differences in Indian family structure. In R. I. Crane (ed.), *Regions and Regionalism in South Asian Studies: An Exploratory Study.* Durham, N.C.

1968. Region, caste and family structure: a comparative study of the Indian 'joint' family. In M. Singer and B.S. Cohn (eds.), *Structure and Change in Indian Society.* Chicago

Korson, J. H. 1975. Some aspects of social change in the Muslim family in West Pakistan. In D. Narain (ed.), *Explorations in the Family and Other Essays.* Bombay

Koschaker, P. 1937. Die Eheformen bei den Indogermanen. *Zeitschrift für ausländischer u. int. Privatrecht* 11:86–112

1950. Eheschliessung und Kauf nach alten Rechten. *Archiv. Orientálni* 18:210–96

Köstler, R. 1944. Raub- und Kaufehe bei den Hellenen. *Zeitschrift der Savigny-Stiftung fur Rechtsgeschichte* 64:206–32

Kurian, G. T. 1975. Child marriage – a case study in Kerala. In D. Narain (ed.), *Explorations in the Family and Other Essays.* Bombay

Kwanten, L. 1979. *Imperial Nomads: A History of Central Asia, 500–1500.* Pennsylvania

Labouret, H. 1931. *Les Tribus du Rameau Lobi.* Paris

Lacey, W. K. 1966. Homeric Eana and Penelope's Kypioe. *J. of Hellenic Studies* 86:55–68

1968. *The Family in Classical Greece.* London

Lambiri-Dimaki, J. 1983. Dowry in modern Greece: a traditional institution at the cross-roads between persistence and decline (in the 1960s). In J. Lambiri-Dimaki, *Social Stratification in Greece 1962–1982*. Athens

Lancaster, L. 1984. Buddhism and family in East Asia. In G. de Vos and T. Sofue (eds.), *Religion and Family in East Asia*. Senri Ethnological Studies, no. 11. Osaka

Lancaster, W. 1981. *The Rwala Bedouin Today*. Cambridge

Lane, E. W. 1871. *An Account of the Manners and Customs of the Modern Egyptians Written During the Years 1833–34 and 35* (5th edn). London

Lantz, H. R. 1982. Romantic love in the pre-modern period: a sociological commentary. *J. Social Hist.* 15:349–70

Lardinois, R. 1986a. L'ordre du monde et l'institution familiale en Inde. In A. Burguière *et al.* (eds.), *Histoire de la famille*, vol. 1. Paris
1986b. En Inde, la famille, l'état et la femme. In A. Burguière *et al.* (eds.), *Histoire de la famille*, vol. 2. Paris

Laslett, P. 1969. Size and structure of the household in England over three centuries. *Population Studies* 23:199–223
1972. Mean household size in England since the sixteenth century. In P. Laslett and R. Wall (eds.), *Household and Family in Past Time*. Cambridge
1983. Family and household as work group and kin group: areas of traditional Europe compared. In R. Wall *et al.* (eds.), *Family Forms in Historic Europe*. Cambridge

Last, H. N. 1947. Letter to N. H. Baynes. *J. Roman Studies* 37:152–6

Law Commission of India (1983). *91st. Report on Dowry Deaths and Law Reform: Amending the Hindu Marriage Act, 1955, the Indian Penal Code, 1896 and the Indian Evidence Act, 1872*. New Delhi

Leach, E. R. 1951. The structural implications of matrilateral cross-cousin marriage. *J. R. Anthrop. Inst.* 81:23–53
1954. *Political Systems of Highland Burma*. London
1955. Polyandry, inheritance and the definition of marriage. *Man* 55:182–6
1957. Aspects of bridewealth and marriage stability among the Kachin and Lakher. *Man* 57:50–5
1959. Hydraulic society in Ceylon. *Past and Present* 15:2–25
(ed.) 1960 *Aspects of Caste in South India, Ceylon and North-West Pakistan*. Cambridge
1961 *Pul Eliya, a Village in Ceylon: A Study in Land Tenure and Kinship*. Cambridge
1971. Marriage, primitive. *Encyclopaedia Britannica* 14:938–47

Lee, A. C. 1988. Close kin marriage in Late Roman Mesopotamia. MS

Le Gall, J. 1970. Un critère de differenciation sociale: la situation de la femme. In *Recherches sur les structures sociales dans l'antiquité classique*. Paris.

Legge, J. (trans.) 1885. *Li Chi, Book of Rites*. Oxford

Leong Y. K. and Tao, L. K. 1915. *Village and Town Life in China*. London

Le Roy Ladurie, E. 1972. Système de la coutume; structures familiales et coutumes d'heritage en France au XIVe siècle. *Annales E.S.C.* 27:825–46. English trans.
1976, Family structures and inheritance customs in sixteenth century France. In J. Goody, J. Thirsk and E. P. Thompson (eds.), *Family and Inheritance: Rural Society in Western Europe 1200–1800*. Cambridge
1978. *Montaillou* (trans. B. Bray). London

Levine, B. A. 1968. *Mulūgu/Melūg*: the origins of a Talmudic legal institution. *J. American Orientatal Soc.* 88:271–85

Levine, N. E. 1987. Differential child care in three Tibetan communities: beyond son preference. *Pop. Dev. Review* 13:281–304

1988. *The Dynamics of Polyandry: Kinship, Domesticity, and Population on the Tibetan Border.* Chicago

Levine, N. E. and Sangree, W. H. (eds.) 1980. Women with Many Husbands: Polyandrous Alliance and Marital Flexibility in Africa and Asia. *J. of Comp. Family Studies,* vol. 11, no. 3, special issue

Lévi-Strauss, C. 1949. *Les Structures élementaires de la parenté* (English trans. 1969). Paris

1956. The Family. In H. L. Shapiro (ed.), *Man, Culture and Society.* New York

1966. The future of kinship studies. The Huxley Memorial Lecture 1965. *Proceedings of the R. Anthrop. Inst.* 13–22

1967. *Structural Anthropology.* New York

Levtzion, N. 1965. Early nineteenth century Arabic manuscripts from Kumasi. *Trans. Hist. Soc. Ghana* 8:99–119

Levy, H. L. 1963. Inheritance and dowry in classical Athens. In J. Pitt-Rivers (ed.), *Mediterranean Countrymen.* Paris

Levy, H. S. 1966. *Chinese Footbinding: The History of a Curious Erotic Custom.* Tokyo

Levy, M. J. 1949. *The Family Revolution in Modern China.* Cambridge, Mass.

Lewis, I. M. 1962. *Marriage and the Family in Northern Somaliland.* E. Afr. Studies, 15. Kampala: East African Institute of Social Research

Lewis, N. and Reinhold, M. 1966. *Roman Civilization; Source Book 1: The Republic.* New York

Lewis, O. 1965 [1958]. *Village Life in Northern India.* Urbana

Li, L. M. 1981. *China's Silk Trade: Trade and Industry in the Modern World, 1842–1937.* Cambridge, Mass.

Lightman, M. and Zeisel, W. 1977. Univira: an example of continuity and change in Roman society. *Church History* 46:19–32

Lin, Yueh-hwa 1947. *The Golden Wing: A Sociological Study of Chinese Familism.* New York

Liu Wang, H.-C. 1959. *The Traditional Chinese Clan Rules.* Monographs of the Association for Asian Studies, no. 7. New York

Logan, W. 1887. *Malabar.* 2 vols. Madras

Loizos, P. 1975. *The Greek Gift: Politics in a Cypriot Village.* Oxford

1975a. Changes in property transfer among Greek Cypriot villagers. *Man* 10:503–23

Longo, O. 1984. Su alculni termini di parentela in Pindaro: classificatorio e descrittivo. In *Lirica Greca da Archiloco a Elitis: studdio in Honore di Filippo Maria Pontani.* Padua

Madan, T. N. 1965. *Family and Kinship: A Study of the Pandits of Rural Kashmir.* Bombay

Maher, V. 1974. *Women and Property in Morocco: Their Changing Relation to the Process of Social Stratification in the Middle Atlas.* Cambridge

Maine, H. S. 1861. *Ancient Law* (1955 edn). London

Majumdar, D. N. 1958. *Caste and Communication in an Indian Village.* Bombay

Majumdar, R. C., Raychaudhuri, H. C. and Datta, K. 1953. *An Advanced History of India* (2nd edn). London

Malamat, A. 1971. Mari. *The Biblical Archaeologist* 34:2–22

Male, D. J. 1971. *Russian Peasant Organisation before Collectivisation: A Study of Commune and Gathering, 1925–1930.* Cambridge

Malinowski, B. 1927. *Sex and Repression in Savage Society.* London

Mandelbaum, D. G. 1948. The family in India. *Southwestern J. Anthrop.* 4:123–39

1954. Fertility at early years of marriage in India. In K. N. Kapadia (ed.), *Professor Ghurye Felicitation Volume.* Bombay

1970 *Society in India.* Berkeley

1974 *Human Fertility in India: Social Components and Policy Perspectives.* Berkeley

Mankad, B. L. 1934–35. Genealogical study of some vital problems of population. *J. University of Bombay* 2:280–307, 4:105–29

Mann, S. 1972. Finance in Ningpo: the 'Ch'ien Chuang', 1750–1880. In W. E. Willmott (ed.), *Economic Organization in Chinese Society.* Stanford

1983. What can feminist theory do for the study of Chinese history? MS

forthcoming. Grooming a daughter for marriage: brides and wives in the Mid Qing Period. In R. B. Ebrey and R. S. Watson (eds.), *Marriage and Inequality in Chinese Society.* Berkeley

Maropoulou, M. 1985. Comportements ecclésiastiques et communautaires face à l'augmentation du montant des dots: le cas du Zagori en Epire aux XVIIIe – XIXe siècles. In C. Piault (ed.), *Familles et biens en Grèce et à Chypre.* Paris

Marriott, McK. 1955a. Social structure and change in a U.P. village. In M. N. Srinivas (ed.), *India's Villages.* Bombay

1955b. Little communities in an indigenous civilisation. In McK. Marriott (ed.), *Village India.* Chicago

Maspero, G. 1899. *Histoire ancienne des peuples de l'orient classique: les empires.* Paris

Mateer, S. 1883. *Native Life in Travancore.* London

Mayer, A. C. 1966. *Caste and Kinship in Central India.* London

Mayne, J. D. 1892. *A Treaty on Hindu Law and Usage* (5th edn; 1st edn 1878). London

McAleavy, H. 1955. Certain aspects of Chinese customary law in the light of Japanese scholarship. *Bull. School of Oriental and African Studies* 17:535–47

McCormack, W. 1958. Sister's daughter marriage in a Mysore village. *Man in India* 38:34–48

McLennan, J. F. 1865. *Primitive Marriage.* Edinburgh

McMullen, I. J. 1975. Non-agnatic adoption: a Confucian controversy in 17th and 18th century Japan. *Harvard J. Asiatic Studies* 35:133–89

McNeil, W. H. 1978. *The Metamorphosis of Greece since World War II.* Oxford

McNicoll, G. and Cain, M. (eds.) 1990. *Population and Rural Development: Institutions and Policy.* A supplement to *Population and Development Review*

Meillassoux, C. 1964. *Anthropologie économique des Gouro de la Côte d'Ivoire: de l'economie d'autosubsistance à l'agriculture commerciale.* Paris

1967. Recherche d'un niveau de détermination dans la société cynégétique. *L'Homme et la Société* 6:95–106. Trans. as 'On the mode of production of the hunting band', in P. Alexander (ed.), 1973, *French Perspectives in African Studies*, London

Melis, F. 1974. La società commerciali a Firenze dalla seconda parte del XIV al XVI secolo. *The Third International Conference of Economic History (Munich, 1968).* Paris

Memel-Fote, H. 1988. L'esclavage dans les sociétés lignagères d'Afrique Noire:

exemple de la Côte d'Ivoire precoloniale, 1700–1920. Thèse pour le doctorate d'état. EHESS, Paris

Mencher, J. P. and Goldberg, H. 1967. Kinship and marriage regulations among the Namboodiri Brahmans of Kerala. *Man* 2:87–107

Menefee, S. P. 1981. *Wives for Sale: An Ethnographic Study of British Popular Divorce*. Oxford

Merton, R. K. 1959. *Social Theory and Social Structure* (rev. edn). Glencoe, Ill.

Mielziner, M. 1901. *The Jewish Law of Marriage and Divorce*. New York

Miller, B. D. 1981. *The Endangered Sex: Neglect of Female Children in Rural North India*. Ithaca

1982. Female labor force participation and female seclusion in rural India: a regional view. *Economic Development and Cultural Change* 30:777–94

Minturn, L. and Hitchcock, J. T. 1966. *The Rajputs of Khalapur, India*. New York

Mir-Hosseini, Z. (1989). Some aspects of changing marriage in rural Iran: the case of Kalardasht, a district in the Northern Provinces. *Journal of Comparative Family Studies*

Mitra, A. 1979. *Implications of Declining Sex Ratio for India's Population*. International Council for Social Science Research. Bombay

Monier-Williams, M. 1899. *A Sanskrit–English Dictionary: Etymologically and Philologically Arranged with Special Reference to Cognate Indo-European Languages*. Oxford

Moore, M. P. 1973. Cross-cultural surveys of peasant family structures. *Am. Anthrop.* 75:911–15

Morgan, L. H. 1870. *Systems of Consanguinity and Affinity of the Human Family*. Washington, D.C.

Mossé, C. 1985. De l'inversion de la dot antique. In C. Piault (ed.), *Familles et biens en Grèce et à Chypre*. Paris

Müller, M. 1886. *The Laws of Manu. Sacred Book of the East*, vol. 25. London

Mundy, M. W. 1979. Women's inheritance of land in highland Yemen. *Arabian Studies* 5:161–87

1982. *Land and family in a Yemeni community*. PhD thesis, University of Cambridge

1988. The family, inheritance and Islam: a reexamination of the sociology of *farā'iḍ* law. In A. al-Azmeh (ed.), *Social and Historical Contexts of Islamic Law*. London

Musil, A. 1928. *The Manners and Customs of the Rwala Bedouins*. New York

Myers, R. H. 1970. *The Chinese Peasant Economy: Agricultural Development in Hopei and Shantung, 1890–1949*. Cambridge, Mass.

Nadel, S. F. 1942. *A Black Byzantium*. London

Nair, K. N. 1983. Animal protein consumption and the sacred cow complex in India. Paper given to the Wenner-Gren Symposium, *Food Preferences and Aversions*. Cedar Key, Florida

Nakane, C. 1972. An interpretation of the size and structure of the household in Japan over three centuries. In P. Laslett and R. Wall (eds.), *Household and Family in Past Time*. Cambridge

Naquin, S. 1986. Two descent groups in North China: the Wangs of Yung-p'ing prefecture, 1500–1800. In P. B. Ebrey and J. L. Watson (eds.), *Kinship Organization in Late Imperial China, 1000–1940*. Stanford

(1988). Marriage in North China: the role of ritual. Paper prepared for the Conference on Marriage and Inequality in China, Monterey: January 1988, revised April 1988

Naquin, S. and E. S. Rawski 1987. *Chinese Society in the Eighteenth Century*. New Haven

Nath, V. 1973. Female infanticide and the Lewa Kanbis of Gujerat in the nineteenth century. *Indian Economic and Social History Review* 10:386–404

Neale, W. C. 1957. The market in theory and history. In K. Polanyi, C. M. Arensberg, and H. W. Pearson (eds.), *Trade and Markets in the Early Empires: Economies in History and Theory*. Glencoe, Ill.

Neufeld, E. 1944. *Ancient Hebrew Marriage Laws*. London

Ng, Chin-keong 1983. *Trade and Society in China: The Amoy Network on the China Coast, 1683–1735*. Singapore

Nicholas, D. 1985. *The Domestic Life of a Medieval City: Women, Children, and the Family in Fourteenth-century Ghent*. Nebraska

Nicholas, R. W. 1967. Ritual hierarchy and social relations in rural Bengal. *Contributions to Indian Sociology* 1:56–83

Niebuhr, C. 1792. *Travels through Arabia and other Countries in the East*. Edinburgh

Oppong, C. 1974. *Marriage among a Matrilineal Elite*. Cambridge

Orenstein, H. 1961. The recent history of the extended family in India. *Social Problems* 8:341–50

1965. *Gaon: Conflict and Cohesion in an Indian Village*. Princeton

Paradise, J. 1980. A daughter and her father's property at Nuzi. *J. Cuneiform Studies* 32:189–207

Parish, W. and Whyte, M. 1978. *Village and Family in Contemporary China*. Chicago

Parry, J. P. 1979. *Caste and Kinship in Kangra*. London

Parsons, T. 1937. *The Structure of Social Action*. Glencoe, Ill.

1954. The incest taboo in relation to social structure. *Brit. J. Sociol.* 5:101–17

Pasternak, B. 1972. *Kinship in Two Chinese Villages*. Stanford

1985. On the causes and demographic consequences of uxorilocal marriage in China. In S. B. Hanley and A. P. Wolf (eds.), *Family and Population in East Asian History*. Stanford

Patai, R. 1959. *Sex and Family in the Bible and the Middle East*. New York

Pehrson, R. N. 1954. Bilateral kin groupings as a structural type. *J. East Asiatic Studies* (Manila) 3:199–202

1957. *The Bilateral Network of Social Relations in Konkama Lapp District*. Indiana University Research Centre in Anthropology, Folklore and Linguistics, Publication III. Bloomington, Ind.

Perikhanian, A. 1983. Islamic society and law. In I. Yarshatir (ed.), *Cambridge History of Iran*, vol. 3 (2):627–80. Cambridge.

Peristiany, J. G. (ed.) 1965. *Honour and Shame: The Values of Mediterranean Society*. London

Pestman, P. W. 1961. *Marriage and Matrimonial Property in Ancient Egypt: Contribution to Establishing the Legal Position of the Woman* (Papyrologia Lugduno – Batava 9). Leiden

Peter, Prince of Greece and Denmark 1963. *A Study of Polyandry*. The Hague

Peters, E. L. 1965. Aspects of the family among the Bedouin of Cyrenaica. In M. F. Nimkoff (ed.), *Comparative Family Systems*. Boston

1966. Sex differentiation in two Arab communities. In J. Peristiany (ed.), *Acts of the Mediterranean Conference: Masculine and Feminine in the Mediterranean*. Athens

1978. The status of women in four Middle Eastern communities. In N. Keddie and L. Beck (eds.), *Women in the Muslim World*. Cambridge, Mass.

1980. Aspects of Bedouin bridewealth among camel herders in Cyrenaica. In J. Comaroff (ed.), *The Meaning of Marriage Payments*. London

1990 *The Bedouin of Cyrenaica*. Cambridge

Piault, C. 1985. La gôut de l'aventure. In C. Piault (ed.), *Familles et biens en Grèce et à Chypre*. Paris

Ping-ti Ho, 1954. The salt merchants of Yang-Chou: a study of commercial capitalism in eighteenth-century China. *Harvard J. Asiatic Studies* 17:130–68

Pitt-Rivers, J. 1954. *The People of the Sierra*. London

(forthcoming). *Honor and Grace*. Cambridge

Plautus 1924 *Mostellaria* (trans. P. Nixon). In E. Capps *et al.* (eds.), *Plautus*, vol. 3. Loeb Classical Library, Cambridge, Mass.

Plautus 1938. *Trinummus* (trans. P. Nixon). In T. E. Page *et al.* (eds.), *Plautus*, vol. 5. Loeb Classical Library, Cambridge, Mass.

Pocock, D. 1954. The hypergamy of the Patidars. In K. M. Kapadia (ed.), *Professor Ghurye Felicitation Volume*. Bombay

1972. *Kanbi and Patidar*. Oxford

1973. *Mind, Body and Wealth: A Study of Belief and Practice in an Indian Village*. Oxford

Polo, M. 1958. *The Travels*. Harmondsworth

Pomeroy, S. 1976. The relationship of the married woman to blood relatives in Rome. *Ancient Society* 7:215–27

Potter, J. M. 1968. *Capitalism and the Chinese Peasant: Social and Economic Change in a Hong Kong Village*. Berkeley

1970. Land and lineage in traditional China. In M. Freedman (ed.), *Family and Kinship in Chinese Society*. Stanford

Powers, D. S. 1986. *Studies in Qur'an and Hadith: The Formation of the Islamic Law of Inheritance*. Berkeley

Prasad, B. D. 1987. Dowry practice in the urban setting: a case study. PhD thesis, The Andhra University

Radcliffe-Brown, A. R. 1924. The mother's brother in South Africa. *S. African J. Sc.* 21:542–55

1930–31. The social organisation of Australian tribes. *Oceania* 1:34–63, 206–46, 322–41, 426–56

Ramaswamy, V. 1985. *Textiles and Weavers in Medieval South India*. Delhi

Rattray, R. S. 1923. *Ashanti*. London

Rawski, E. S. 1986. The Ma landlords of Yang-chia-kou in the late Ch'ing and Republican China. In P. B. Ebrey and J. L. Watson (eds.), *Kinship and Social Organization in Late Imperial China, 1000–1940*. Stanford

(forthcoming). Ch'ing imperial marriage: the Emperor as wife-giver and wife-taker. In P. B. Ebrey and R. Watson (eds.), *Marriage and Inequality in Chinese Society*. Berkeley

Rawson, B. 1966. Family life among the lower classes at Rome in the first two centuries of the Empire. *Classical Philology* 61:71–83

1974. Roman concubinage and other *de facto* marriages. *Trans. Am. Philological Assoc.* 104:279–305

(ed.). 1986. *The Family in Ancient Rome: Select Studies*. New York

Reddy, V. E. 1979. A sociological study of the status of women with special reference to their succession rights. *Studies in Social Welfare*. New Delhi. 2:1–11

Redhouse, J. W. 1885. Notes on Professor Tylor's 'Arabian Matriachate' propounded by him as President of the Anthropological section, British Association. *J. R. Asiatic Soc.* 17:275–92

Reich, E. 1864. *Geschichte, Natur- und Gesund des ehelichen Lebens.* Cassel

Renou, V. 1978. *L'Inde fondamentale.* Paris

Rey, P.-Ph. 1971. *Colonialisme, néo-colonialisme et transition au capitalisme.* Paris

Ribeiro, D. 1971. *The Civilizational Process.* New York

Richards, A. I. 1950. Some types of family structure amongst the Central Bantu. In A. R. Radcliffe-Brown and C. D. Forde (eds.), *African Systems of Kinship and Marriage.* London

Rivers, W. H. R. 1914. *Kinship and Social Organization.* London

Robertson, W. 1791. *An Historical Disquisition Concerning Ancient India* (reprinted 1824). London

Robertson Smith, W. 1885. *Kinship and Marriage in Early Arabia* (1907 edn). London

Rocher, L. 1968. The theory of matrimonial causes according to the *Dharmaśāstra.* In J. Anderson (ed.), *Family Law in Asia and Africa.* London

Rose, H. A. 1922. Legitimisation and adoption in Hindu law. *Man* 22:87–96

Rosenfeld, H. 1958. An analysis of marriage statistics for a Moslem and Christian Arab village. *Int. Arch. Ethnology* 48:32–67

Roussou, M. 1985. Système dotal et identité feminine dans la campagne chypriote. In C. Piault (ed.), *Familles et biens en Grèce et à Cypre.* Paris

Ruddle, K. and Akimichi, T. (eds.) 1984. *Maritime Institutions in the Western Pacific.* Senri Ethnological Studies, 17. Osaka

Sa, S. 1985 Marriage among the Taiwanese of pre-1945 Taipei. In S. B. Hanley and A. P. Wolf (eds.), *Family and Population in East Asian History.* Stanford

Sabean, D. (forthcoming), *Kinship and Family in Neckarhausen: Structure and Changes in a Period of Agricultural Intensification and Capitalization, 1700–1870.* Cambridge

Saller, R. 1984. Roman dowry and the devolution of property in the Principate. *Classical Quarterly* 34:195–205

1986. Patria potestas and the stereotype of the Roman family. *Continuity and Change* 1:7–22

1987. Men's age at marriage and its consequences in the Roman family. *Classical Philology* 82:21–34

Saller, R. and Shaw, B. D. 1984. Tombstones and Roman family relations in the Principate: civilians, soldiers and slaves. *J. Roman Studies* 74:124–56

Sangren, P. S. 1985. Ma Tsu, history, and the rhetoric of legitimacy. MS

Sant Cassia, P. 1986. 'Brideprice and bloodmoney have no merit': marriage, manipulation and the transmission of resources in a S. Tunisian village. *Cambridge Anthropology* 11:35–60

Sarkar, L. 1982. Law and population. In *Population of India.* Country Monograph Series no. 10. Economic and Social Commission for Asia and the Pacific. United Nations, New York

Saulnier-Thiercelin, F. 1985. Principes et practiques du partage des biens: l'exemple crétois. In C. Piault (ed.), *Familles et biens en Grèce et à Chypre.* Paris

Schacht, J. 1950. *The Origins of Muhammadan Jurisprudence.* Oxford

Schaps, D. M. 1979. *Economic Rights of Women in Ancient Greece.* Edinburgh

Schneider, D. M. 1967. Kinship and culture: descent and filiation as cultural constructs. *Southwestern J. Anthrop.* 23:65–73

Schneider, J. 1971. Of vigilance and virgins: honor, shame and access to resources in Mediterranean societies. *Ethnology* 10:1–24

Schneider, P. 1969. Honor and conflict in a Sicilian town. *Anthrop. Quarterly* 42:130–55

Schram, L. 1932. *Le Mariage chez les T'ou-jen du Kan-Sou (Chine)*. Shanghai

Segalen, M. 1985. *Quinze Générations de Bas-Bretons: parenté et société dans le pays Bigouden Sud 1720–1980*. Paris

Shah, A. M. 1956. Social change in a multi-caste village. In A. Aiyappan and L. K. Bala Ratnam (eds.), *Society in India*. Madras
   1974. *The Household Dimension of the Family in India*. Berkeley
   1982. Division and hierarchy: an overview of caste in Gujerat. *Contributions to Indian Sociology* 16:1–33

Shah, A. M. and Shroff, R. G. 1958. The Vahivancha Barots of Gujerat: a caste of genealogists and mythographers. *J. Am. Folklore* 71:248–78, reprinted in M. Singer (ed.), 1959, *Traditional India: Structure and Change*. Philadelphia: American Folklore Society

Shapiro, R. 1985. Echange matrimonial et travail féminin: les paradoxes de la modernité. In C. Piault (ed.), *Familles et biens en Grèce et à Chypre*. Paris

Shariff, A. 1985. Socioeconomic and cultural determinants of regional differentials in India's family planning program performance. Seminar on Societal Influences on Family Planning Program Performance, Jamaica. International Union for the Scientific Study of Population

Sharma, U. 1984. Dowry in North India: its consequences for women. In R. Hirschon (ed.), *Women and Property – Women as Property*. London

Shaw, B. D. 1987. The age of Roman girls at marriage: some reconsiderations. *J. Roman Studies* 77:30–46

Shepher, J. 1971. Mate selection among second generation kibbutz adolescents and adults: incest avoidance and negative imprinting. *Archives of Sexual Behaviour* 1:293–307

Simcox. E. 1894. *Primitive Civilizations: Or Outlines of the History of Ownership in Archaic Communities*. London

Singh, K.K. 1957. Intercaste tension in two villages in North India. PhD thesis, Cornell University, Ithaca

Sissa, G. 1986. La famille dans la cité greque, V–IVe siècle avant J.–C. In A. Burguière *et al.* (eds.), *Histoire de la famille*, vol. 1. Paris

Siu, H. F. 1989. *Agents and Victims: Accomplices in Rural Revolution*. New Haven
   1989a. Where are all the women gone? Rethinking marriage and residence in South China. MS
   1989b. Brideprice and dowry: gender and generational roles in a Chinese rural township. MS

Skaist, A. 1975. Inheritance laws and the social background. *J. American Oriental Soc.* 95:242–7

Skinner, G. W. 1964. Marketing and social structure in rural China. *J. Asian Studies* 24:3–43

Slater, M. K. 1959. Ecological factors in the origin of incest. *Am. Anthrop.* 61:1042–60

Slotkin, J. S. 1947. On a possible lack of incest regulations in Old Iran. *Am. Anthrop.* 49:643–7
   1949. Reply to Goodenough. *Am. Anthrop.* 51:531–2

Smith, A. H. 1899. *Village Life in China: A Study in Sociology*. New York

Smith, M. G. 1974. *Corporations and Society*. London

Smith, P. C. 1980. Asian marriage patterns in transition. *J. Family Hist.* 5:58–96

Smith, R. E. F. 1977. *Peasant Farming in Muscovy*. Cambridge

Smith, R. M. 1981. The peoples of Tuscany and their families in the fifteenth century: medieval or Mediterranean? *J. Family Hist.* 6:107–28

Smith, T. 1977. *Nakahara: Family Farms and Population in a Japanese Village. 1717–1830*. Stanford

Smith, T. C. 1959. *The Agrarian Origins of Modern Japan*. Stanford

Sontheimer, G. D. 1977. *The Joint Hindu Family: Its Evolution as a Legal Institution.* New Delhi

Sopher, D. E. 1980. The geographic patterning of culture in India. In D. E. Sopher (ed.), *An Exploration of India*. London

Sotiropoulos, L. and Dimitropoulou, D. 1985. Quelques aspects de la transmission des patrimoines familiaux dans la région de Patras. In C. Piault (ed.), *Familles et biens en Grèce et à Chypre*. Paris

Speiser, E. A. 1964. *The Anchor Bible: Genesis* (2nd edn). New York

Spiro, M. E. 1958. *Children of the Kibbutz*. Cambridge, Mass.

1977. *Kinship and Marriage in Burma: A Cultural and Psychodynamic Analysis*. Berkeley

Srinivas, M. N. 1942. *Marriage and Family in Mysore*. Bombay

1952. *Religion and Society among the Coorgs of South India*. Oxford

1956. A note on Sanscritization and Westernization. *Far Eastern Quarterly* 15:481–96

1962. *Caste in Modern India and Other Essays*. New York

1984. *Some Reflections on Dowry* (J. P. Naik Memorial Lecture, 1983). The Centre for Women's Development Studies. New Delhi

Staal, J. F. 1961. *Nambudiri Veda Recitation* (Disputationes Rheno-Trajectinae 5). Gravenage

Stein, B. 1960. The economic function of a medieval South Indian temple. *J. Asian Studies* 19:163–76

1980. *Peasant State and Society in Medieval South India*. New Delhi

Stenning, D. J. 1958. Household viability among the Pastoral Fulani. In J. Goody (ed.), *The Developmental Cycle in Domestic Groups*. Cambridge

Stern, G. 1939. *Marriage in Early Islam*. London

Stockard, J. 1988. *Daughters of the Canton Delta: Marriage Patterns and Economic Strategies in South China, 1860–1930*. Stanford

Stone, L. 1977. *The Family, Sex and Marriage in England, 1500–1800*. London

Swann, N. L. 1932. *Pan Chao: Foremost Woman Scholar of China*. New York

Sweetser, D. A. 1964. Urbanization and the patrilineal transmission of farms in Finland. *Acta Sociologica* 7:215–24

Taeuber, I. B. 1970. The families of Chinese farmers. In M. Freedman (ed.), *Family and Kinship in Chinese Society*. Stanford

Tait, D. 1961. *The Konkomba of Northern Ghana*. London

Talmon, Y. 1964. Mate selection in collective settlements. *Am. Sociol. Rev.* 29:491–508

Tambiah, S. J. 1958. The structure of kinship and its relationship to land possession and residence in Pata Dumbara, Central Ceylon. *J. R. Anthrop. Inst.* 88:21–44

1966. Polyandry in Ceylon: with special reference to the Laggala region. In C. Fuehrer-Haimendorf (ed.), *Caste and Kin in Nepal, India and Ceylon*. London

1973. Dowry and bridewealth and the property rights of women in South Asia. In J. Goody and S. J. Tambiah, *Bridewealth and Dowry*. Cambridge

Tanizaki, J. 1957. *The Makioka Sisters*. New York

Terray, E. 1972. *Marxism and 'Primitive Societies'*. New York

Thierfelder, H. 1960. *Die Geschwisterehe im hellenistisch-römischen Äegypten.* Munster

Thomas, Y. 1981. Mariages endogamiques à Rome: études d'une mutation. In *Production, pouvoir et parenté dans le monde méditerranéen de Sumer à nos jours.* Actes du Colloque, CNRS–EHESS, 1976. Paris

1986. A Rome, pères citoyens et cité des pères (IIe siècle av. J.–c. – IIe siècle ap. J.-C.). In A. Burguière *et al.* (eds.), *Histoire de la Famille,* vol. 1. Paris

Thomson, G. D. 1949. *Studies in Ancient Greek Society: the prehistoric Aegean.* London

Tillion, G. 1966. *Le Harem et les cousins.* Paris

Tod, J. 1920. *Annals and Antiquities of Rajasthan or the Central and Western Rajput States of India.* Oxford

Topley, M. 1975. Marriage resistance in rural Kwangtung. In M. Wolf and R. Witke (eds.), *Women in Chinese Society.* Stanford

Topley, M. and Hayes, J. 1968. Notes on some Vegetarian Halls in Hong Kong belonging to the sect of Hsien-T'ien Tao: (The Way of Former Heaven). *J. Hong Kong Branch of the R. Asiatic Society* 8:135–48

Trautmann, T. R. 1981. *Dravidian Kinship.* Cambridge

Treggiari, S. 1981. *Contubernales* in CIL 6. *Phoenix* 35:42–69

Turner, J. 1975. A formal semantic analysis of a Hindi kinship terminology. *Contributions to Indian Sociology* 9:263–92

Twitchett, D. C. 1959. The Fan Clan's charitable estate, 1050–1760. In D. S. Nivinson and A. F. Wright (eds.), *Confucianism in Action.* Stanford

1982. Comment on J. L. Watson's article. *The China Quarterly* 92:623–7

Tylor, E. B. 1889. On a method of investigating the development of institutions: applied to laws of marriage and descent. *J. Anthrop. Inst.* 18:245–72

van Seters, J. 1969. Jacob's marriages and ancient Near East customs: a re-examination. *Harvard Theological Rev.* 62:377–95

Van der Valk, M. H. 1956. *Conservatism in Modern Chinese Family Law.* Leiden

van der Veen, K. W. 1972. *I Give Thee my Daughter. Marriage and Hierarchy among the Anavil Brahmans of South Gujerat.* Assen, Netherlands

Vatuk, S. 1969. A structural analysis of the Hindi kinship terminology. *Contributions to Indian Sociology* 3:94–115

1972. *Kinship and Urbanization: white-collar migrants in North India.* Berkeley

1973. Marriage and hierarchy among the Anavil Brahmans of South Gujerat. *Contributions to Indian Sciology* 7:36–52

1975. Gifts and affines in North India. *Contributions to Indian Sociology* 9:155–96

Veyne, P. 1978. La famille et l'amour dans le haut empire romain. *Annales ESC* 33:35–63

Vinogradoff, P. 1920. *Outlines of Historical Jurisprudence.* London

Virdi, P. K. 1972. *The Grounds for Divorce in Hindu and English Law: a Study in Comparative Law.* Delhi

Visaria, P. M. 1967. The sex ratio of the population of India and Pakistan and regional variations during 1901–61. In A. Base (eds.), *Patterns of Population Change in India, 1951–1961.* Bombay

Volterra, E. 1955. La conception du mariage à Rome. *Rev. int. droits de l'Antiquité* 3:365–79

Walther, W. 1981. *Femmes en Islam.* Paris

Waltner, A. 1981. Widows and remarriage in Ming and early Qing China. *Historical Reflections* 8:129–46

Walton, L. 1984. Kinship, marriage and status in Song China: a study of the Lou lineage of Ningbo, c. 1050–1250. *J. Asian Hist.* 18:35–77

Watson, A. 1967. *The Law of Persons in the Later Roman Republic.* Oxford
1975. *Rome of the XII Tables: Persons and Property.* Princeton

Watson, J. L. 1975. *Emigration and the Chinese Lineage: the Mans in Hong Kong and London.* Berkeley
1982. Chinese kinship reconsidered: anthropological perspectives on historical research. *The China Quarterly* 92:589–622

Watson, R. S. 1981. Class differences and affinal relations in South China. *Man* 16:593–615
1984. Women's property in Republican China: rights and practice. *Republican China* 10:1–12
1985. *Inequality among Brothers: Class and Kinship in South China.* Cambridge
(forthcoming). Wives, concubines and maidservants: kinship and servitude in the Hong Kong Region, 1898–1941. In P. B. Ebrey and R. S. Watson (eds.), *Marriage and Inequality in Chinese Society.* Berkeley

Weber, M. 1951 [1916]. *The Religion of China* (trans. H. Gerth and D. Martindale). New York

Westermarck, E. A. 1921. *The History of Human Marriage* (5th edn; 1st edn 1891). New York

Westrup, C. W. 1943. *Recherches sur les formes antiques de mariage dans l'ancien droit romain.* Copenhagen

Wilkinson, G. 1837. *Manners and Customs of the Ancient Egyptians.* London

Wilkinson, H. P. 1926. *The Family in Classical China.* London

Wiser, W. H. 1936. *The Hindu Jajmani System.* Lucknow

Wittfogel, K. A. 1957. *Oriental Despotism: A Comparative Study of Total Power.* New Haven

Wolf, A. P. 1970. Chinese kinship and mourning dress. In M. Freedman (ed.), *Family and Kinship in Chinese Society.* Stanford
1985a. The origins and explanation of variation in the Chinese kinship system. MS
1985b. Fertility in prerevolutionary rural China. In S. B. Hanley and A. P. Wolf (eds.), *Family and Population in East Asian History.* Stanford
1985c. Chinese family size: a myth revitalized. In Hsieh Jeh-shang and Chuang Yin-chuang (eds.), *The Chinese Family and its Ritual Behaviour.* Taipei ·
(forthcoming). *Sexual Attraction, Sibling Incest, and the Incest Taboo: A Defence of Edward Westermarck.* Stanford

Wolf, A. P. and Hanley, S. B. 1985. Introduction to S. B. Hanley and A. P. Wolf (eds.), *Family and Population in East Asian History.* Stanford

Wolf, A. P. and Huang, C.-S. 1980. *Marriage and Adoption in China, 1845–1945.* Stanford

Wolf, E. R. 1982. *Europe and the Peoples without History.* Berkeley

Wolf, M. 1972. *Woman and the Family in Rural Taiwan.* Stanford
1975. Women and suicide in China. In M. Wolf and R. Witke (eds.), *Women in Chinese Society.* Stanford
1985. *Revolution Postponed: Women in Contemporary China.* Stanford

Wolf, M. and Witke, R. 1975. Introduction. In *Women in Chinese Society.* Stanford

Wolff, H. J. 1944. Marriage law and family organisation in ancient Athens. *Traditio* 2:43–95
1952. Die Grundlagen des griechischen Eherechts. *Tijdschrift boor Rechtsgesch.* 20:1–29, 157–81

Woolley, L. 1963. The Beginnings of Civilization. *History of Mankind: cultural and scientific development*, vol. 1, part 2. London

Writing in Ancient Western Asia 1963. London

Wu Ching-Tzu. 1973. *The Scholars* (English trans.). Peking

Xenophon 1923. *Oeconomicus* (trans. E. C. Marchant). In E. Capps *et al.* (eds.). Loeb Classical Library, Cambridge, Mass.

Yalman, N. 1967. *Under the Bo Tree*. Berkeley

Yang, M. 1945. *A Chinese Village: Taitou, Shantung Province*. New York

Yver, J. 1966. *Egalité entre héritiers et exclusion des enfants dotés: essai de géographie coutumière*. Paris

Zborowski, M. 1949. The place of book-learning in traditional Jewish culture. *Harvard Educational Rev.* 19:87–109, adapted in M. Mead and M. Wolfenstein (eds.) 1955, *Childhood in Contemporary Cultures*. Chicago

Zborowski, M. and Herzog. E. 1952. *Life is with People: The Culture of the Shtetl.* New York

Zurndorfer, H. 1981. The *Hsin-an ta-tsu-chih* and the development of Chinese gentry society, 800–1600. *T'oung Pao* 67:154–215

Index

abortion
  in China, 116
  in illegitimate pregnancy, 147
  in Japan, 116
adolescence, 15
adoption, 51, 470, 471, 472, 473
  agnatic link creation, 91
  and care of elderly, 88–9, 277
  and family size, 115, 116
  and lineage strength, 120
  and mourning duties, 120
  and polygyny, 140
  in Ancient Egypt, 341
  in Ancient Israel, 352
  in Arab society, 379
  in China, 49, 105, 109
  in Classical Greece, 391, 393
  in Confucianism, 471, 475
  in Hinduism, 276
  in India, 181
  in Islam, 276, 370
  in Roman Empire, 416
  in Rome pre-Empire, 426, 427
  in Taiwan, 119–20
  in Tibet, 137, 142
  posthumous, 120
  property transmission, 46, 199, 257, 287–8, 370
  replacing levirate, 204, 206–7, 265, 473, 477
  solution to heirlessness, 43–5, 67, 107, 135, 204, 261, 370
adultery
  in Albania, 432
  in Arab society, 376
  in China, 33, 129
  in Homeric Greece, 393, 394
age of Consent Act (1891; India), 273
Amoy, *see* Fukien
apprenticeship, 95

Armana Letters, dowry inventories (Mesopotamia), 315
Asante, 69
autonomy (female)
  definition of, 284
  studies of, 284–7

Babylon, 295
Bagre recitation, 133
Baihu tong (book of ritual), 124
Balzac, H.
  Contrat de mariage, 204–5
Bedouin, 361, 364, 378
Bengalis, 157, 237–9
Ben Zhao (women's textbook), 103
betrothal
  amongst Hakka, 36–7
  and delayed marriage, 58
  binding, 40
  dowry specified at, 389, 390
  early, 208–10, 273–6
  gifts at, 121, 124, 126
  in Albania, 434
  in Ancient Israel, 325, 354
  in Classical Greece, 389
  in Fukien, 36
  in Roman Empire, 417
  in Rome pre-Empire, 426
  in Yunnan, 34
  pre-emptive, 117
  pre-natal, 127
birth, medical attendance at, 278
birth control
  in Ancient Egypt, 341
  in China, 99–100
  in India, 277–9, 311
  in Japan, 115–16
  in Taiwan, 99
black market economy, and dowry, 192
Book of Etiquette and Ceremonial, 124